D1715671

GENDERING
ANTIFASCISM

PITT LATIN AMERICAN SERIES

Catherine M. Conaghan, Editor

GENDERING ANTIFASCISM

Women's Activism in Argentina and the World, 1918-1947

SANDRA MCGEE DEUTSCH

University of Pittsburgh Press

Published by the University of Pittsburgh Press, Pittsburgh, Pa., 15260
Copyright © 2023, University of Pittsburgh Press
Manufactured in the United States of America
Printed on acid-free paper
10 9 8 7 6 5 4 3 2 1

Cataloging-in-Publication data is available from the Library of Congress

ISBN 13: 978-0-8229-4781-3
ISBN 10: 0-8229-4781-1

Cover design: Melissa Dias-Mandoly

In memory of Enrique "Quique" Martínez

CONTENTS

ACKNOWLEDGMENTS

As this project involved exchanges and assistance across borders, I am indebted to many.

Katherine Marino and Rebekah Pite accompanied me throughout the writing process, providing sources, new perspectives, and excellent comments. Richard J. Walter and two anonymous reviewers also read and commented on the entire manuscript. My dialogues with Jorge Nállim and his remarks on two chapters taught me much, as have my exchanges with Aileen El-Kadi, Margaret Power, David Sheinin, and Adriana Valobra. The renowned specialists in Argentine women's history, Donna Guy and Dora Barrancos, supported me, advised me, and supplied contacts. The following persons greatly enriched my work in various sites: Andrés Bisso, Patricia Flier (La Plata); Laura Pasquali (Rosario); Federico Finchelstein (New York); Enrique Martínez and Lila Sintes (Posadas); María Lida Martínez Chas (Oberá); Daniel Campi, María Fernández de Ulivarri, Leandro Lichtmajer, Marcela Vignoli (Tucumán); Mariela Rubinzal (Santa Fe); Alicia Servetto, Adrián Carbonetti, Mónica Gordillo (Córdoba); Noemí Girbal-Blacha, Christine Mathias, María Silvia Leoni de Rosciani (Resistencia). Jonathan Ablard, Marta Bonaudo, Julia Schiavone Camacho, Nina Caputo, Lessie Jo Frazier, Hélène Gutkowski, Misha Klein, Clotilde Lainscek, Laura Liebman, Lowry Martin, Mercedes Martínez, Jadwiga Pieper Mooney, Andrea Orzoff, Corinne Pernet, Marion Rohrleitner, Dora Schwarzstein, Kathleen Staudt, Hilit Surowitz-Israel, Mónica Szurmuk, Liliana Tuccio, Larisa Veloz, Anita Weinstein, José Zanca, and Eduardo Zimmerman helped me conceptualize this book. Sadly, Enrique Martínez, María Fernández de Ulivarri, Marta Bonaudo, and Dora Schwarzstein did not live to see it. I also thank Clara Lida for her encouragement, and Chris Loya, Gabriel Solís, and Jacqueline Lechuga for their aid. I am deeply grateful to Joshua Shanholtzer at the University of Pittsburgh Press for reaching out, listening, assisting, and believing in this project. I also thank Amy Sherman at the press for her generous help.

Many others contributed as well. Marina Becerra, Adriana Brodsky, Gisela Cramer, Lillian Guerra, Marcelo Huernos, Charlotte Ivy, Elizabeth Jelín, Melissa Klapper, Asunción Lavrin, Denise Lynn, Sara Perrig, Alejandra Pita, Ursula Prutsch, Graciela Queirolo, Raanan Rein, Claudia Rojas Mira, and students in my graduate classes offered general and comparative perspectives, sources, and information on research opportunities. The many who enhanced my research and/or my sojourns include Ernesto Bohoslavsky, Hernán Camarero, Irene Cusien, Clara Del Franco, Karina Janello, Mirta Lobato, Daniel Lvovich, Karina Ramacciotti, Leandro Sagastizábal, Horacio Tarcus, María Inés Tato, Nerina Visacovsky (Buenos Aires); Eleonora Ardanaz and Rosario Sagasti (Buenos Aires Province); Alicia Carlino, Emilio Chuaire, Elsa Dellatorre, Mariana Giordano, Nicolás Iñigo Carrera, Lilián Latorre, Oscar Nari, Ester Staroselsky de Jaraz (Chaco); Edda Lía Crespo (Comodoro Rivadavia); Ana Clarisa Agüero, Pedro Sorrentino, César Tcach (Córdoba); Mariana Garzón Rogé (Mendoza); Roberto Carlos Abínzano, Norma Álvarez, María Rosa Fogeler, Alba M. Ibarrola, Gabriela Schiavone, Yolanda Urquiza (Misiones); Elisa Élida Canciani (San Luis); Luciano Alonso, Mariela Coudannes, Sandra Fernández, Claudio Horacio Lizárraga, Susana Piazzesi, Teresa Suárez, Oscar Videla (Santa Fe Province); Elisa Cohen de Chervonagura, Steven Hyland, María Lenis, Rossana Nofal, Elena and Carmen Perrillo (Tucumán). For their valuable help on Uruguay, I thank Alex Borucki, Magdalena Broquetas, Carolina Cerrano, Inés Cuadro, Christine Ehrick, Alicia Fernández, Ana Laura de Giorgi, Gerardo Leibner, Vania Markarian, Ema Massera, Rodolfo Porrini, Graciela Sapriza, Verónica Pamoukaghlian, Lourdes Peruchena, Ariel Silva, and Rita Vinocur. I treasure the friendships made or strengthened during this research.

Several institutions provided financial and administrative backing. I am grateful for the University of Texas at El Paso (UTEP) Arts and Humanities Career Enhancement Award, Dr. and Mrs. W. H. Timmons Professorship, UTEP travel monies, and a National Endowment for the Humanities (NEH) award. I thank John Wiebe, Sam Brunk, Jeff Shepherd, Diana González, and Monica Alvillar for supporting my work and managing the NEH grant and UTEP supplement that accompanied it.

I received much assistance from the directors and personnel of the archives named in the bibliography and many libraries. I especially acknowledge the Centro de Documentación e Investigación de la Cultura de Izquierdas (CeDinCI) and Biblioteca Nacional Mariano Moreno, the places where this book was born, as well as the Biblioteca Nacional de Uruguay and the UTEP Library.

I am grateful to be able to reuse material in this book. Some passages first appeared in "The New School Lecture 'An Army of Women':

Communist-Linked Solidarity Movements, Maternalism, and Political Consciousness in 1930s and 1940s Argentina," *Americas* 75, no. 1 (January 2018): 95–125 (Cambridge University Press, © Academy of American Franciscan History); and in "Argentine Women Against Fascism: The Junta de la Victoria, 1941–1947," *Politics, Religion and Ideology* 3, no. 2 (2012): 221–36, reprinted by permission of the publisher (Taylor & Francis Ltd., http://www.tandfonline.com).

Last but most important, I want to recognize the person who is closest to me. Bill Durrer values and encourages my intellectual pursuits. He solves my computer problems and gives indispensable advice. His patient and loving support helped make this book possible.

LIST OF PERSONS MENTIONED THROUGHOUT THE BOOK

Elena Álvarez	Garment workers union and Victory Board officer.
Dr. Sofía Álvarez Vignoli de Demicheli	Uruguayan senator, member of a conservative sector of the Colorado Party, and Feminine Action member.
Mary Anderson	Director of the US Women's Bureau of the US Department of Labor, 1920–1944.
María Esther Andreau de Billinghurst	President of the Corrientes Victory Board chapter.
Laura Arce	Uruguayan educator, producer of an OIAA-sponsored radio show, and Feminine Action member.
Julia Arévalo	Uruguayan Communist deputy, later senator; Feminine Action member.
Dr. Margarita Argúas	Jurist, university professor, and president of the Victory Board's Once secretariat.
Myra Koudacheff Armour	US ambassador's wife.
Norman Armour	US ambassador to Argentina, 1939–1944.
Antonia Banegas	Textile union militant, Communist, and Victory Board member.
Margarita de Barraza	Criolla cotton farmer in Chaco and Victory Board member.
Dr. Gregorio Bermann	University Reformer, pacifist, and antifascist militant in Córdoba.
Minerva Bernardino	Dominican representative to the IACW and its eventual chair.
Dr. Nina de Borzone	Lawyer, Communist, and member of the Rosario Victory Board chapter.

Heloise Brainerd	WILPF Committee on the Americas chair.
Berta P. de Braslavsky	Communist, pioneer in special education, and Victory Board member.
Dr. Luisa Braverman	First woman medical doctor in Chaco and officer of the Resistencia Victory Board chapter.
Delfina Bunge de Gálvez	Catholic writer married to Nationalist Manuel Gálvez.
Mary Cannon	US government official who visited Argentina.
Lázaro Cárdenas	President of Mexico, 1934–1940, who implemented sweeping reforms and opposed fascism.
Ramón Castillo	Acting Argentine president, 1940–1942; president, 1942–1943.
Luisa Coutouné de Butiérrez	Radical activist, feminist, and member of the La Plata Victory Board chapter.
Clara Drallny	Member of the commercial employees' union, Communist Party, and the Córdoba Victory Board chapter.
Fanny Edelman	Communist, human rights activist, leader of CAMHE and WIDF, UAM and Victory Board member.
Monsignor Gustavo Franceschi	Editor of *Criterio* and an influential cleric.
Manuel Fresco	Nationalist-leaning conservative governor of Buenos Aires Province, 1936–1940.
Angélica Fuselli	Writer, liberal Catholic, and Argentine representative to the IACW.
Carmen Garayalde	Uruguayan Communist, university profesor, education oficial, and Feminine Action leader.
Sofía Goldberg de Molodesky	She and her husband ran a bakery in Resistencia, where she was active in the Communist Party and the Victory Board.
Clara Helman de Oxman	Communist and Victory Board leader.
Juana Juárez	Communist educator and member of the Córdoba Victory Board chapter.
David Kelly	British ambassador to Argentina, 1942–1946.

Lady Marie Noelle Kelly	British ambassador's wife.
Susana Larguía	Socialist and UAM member.
Paulina Luisi	Uruguayan medical doctor, feminist, pacifist, and antifascist connected to transnational networks.
Rebeca de Malajovich	Elderly knitter of the Moisés Ville Victory Board chapter.
Cecilia Marcovich	Artist and member of AIAPE and the Victory Board.
Guillermo Martínez Guerrero	Rancher and UCR leader in Buenos Aires Province; national deputy, 1946–1952.
Angélica Mendoza	Former teacher who joined the Communist and later the Communist Workers Party, first woman nominated as a presidential candidate, IACW secretary in Buenos Aires.
Luciano Molinas	PDP leader and governor of Santa Fe, 1932–1935.
Dr. Alicia Moreau de Justo	Physician, Socialist, feminist, pacifist, and Acción Argentina member.
Silvina Ocampo	Writer, poet, artist, Victoria's sister, and Victory Board member.
Victoria Ocampo	Writer, intellectual, UAM president, Acción Argentina leader.
Gabriel Oddone	Senator and UCR leader, married to president María de la Paz Cremades of the Córdoba Victory Board chapter.
Alcira Olivé de Mollerach	Playwright, provincial government official, president of the Rosario Victory Board chapter.
María Rosa Oliver	Writer, intellectual, active in the AFA and Spanish Republican solidarity, Victory Board vice president, UAM president, worked in the OIAA.
Sir Esmond Ovey	British ambassador to Argentina, 1937–1942.
Lady Marie-Armande Ovey	British ambassador's wife.
Juan Perón	Cabinet secretary, 1943–1945; vice president, 1944–1945; president, 1946–1955, 1973–1974.
Matilde Porta Echagüe de Molinas	President of the Santa Fe Victory Board chapter and wife of PDP leader Luciano Molinas.

Cora Ratto	Mathematician and Victory Board secretary general.
Dr. Elvira Rawson de Dellepiane	Pioneering feminist and medical doctor, UAM and Acción Argentina member.
Teresa Rebasti de Basso	Active in pacifism and the Victory Board.
Telma Reca	Child psychiatrist, university professor, and Victory Board member.
Bernardino Rivadavia	Liberal and first Argentine president, 1926–1927.
Muriel Roberts	A student and office employee who mobilized clerical and sales workers for the Victory Board's Centro secretariat.
Nelson Rockefeller	Coordinator of the OIAA.
Yuquerí Rojas	Communist, pacifist, and Victory Board member.
María Ronconi de Saratino	Entrepreneur, active in Spanish Republican solidarity, and Victory Board member.
Eleanor Roosevelt	First Lady of the United States, 1933–1945; activist; cosponsor of the International Assembly of Women.
Clara Rotman de Baruch	President of the Moisés Ville Victory Board chapter.
Marta Samatán	Educator, lawyer, teacher's union and UAM leader, and Victory Board member in Santa Fe.
José de San Martín	Argentine independence leader who liberated his homeland as well as other South American countries.
Dr. Angela Santa Cruz	Board leader and president of the Asociación Cristiana Femenina and several educational organizations.
Dalila Saslavsky	Human rights activist and Victory Board leader.
Dr. Rosa Scheiner	Dental surgeon; PSO, AFA, and Victory Board member.
Dr. Clara Schliapnik de Filer	Medical doctor and president of the Villa Domínguez, Entre Ríos Victory Board chapter.
Ana Rosa Schlieper de Martínez Guerrero	Philanthropist, Radical, and UAM, IACW, and Victory Board president.
Eugenia Silveyra de Oyuela	Catholic writer who moved from the right to antifascism and collaborated with the Victory Board.

Berta Singerman — Performer and Victory Board sympathizer who recited "La Marseillaise" at a celebration of the liberation of Paris.

Isabel Sors de Santander — President of the Paraná, Entre Ríos Victory Board chapter and wife of Radical congressman Silvano Santander.

Alba Tamargo — Victory Board member and metallurgical union leader.

Dr. Emilio Troise — Distinguished intellectual and antifascist leader linked to the Communist Party

José F. de Uriburu — General who led the overthrow of President Yrigoyen; de facto president, 1930–1932.

Marta Vergara — Chilean writer, feminist, and Communist active in MEMCH and the IACW.

Mary Winslow — US government official and IACW representative.

Polly Yánover de Cutín — Communist and driving force behind the creation of the Victory Board Tucumán chapter.

Hipólito Yrigoyen — Radical president, 1916–1922, 1928–1930.

Julia Zarza de Kanner — Secretary of the Victory Board Oberá chapter, she was a homemaker and helpmate for her husband Marcos Kanner, the labor and Communist leader.

Rosa W. de Ziperovich — Educator, union leader, Communist, and secretary of the Palacios, Santa Fe Victory Board chapter.

María Inés Zoppi del Valle Pardo — President of the Resistencia Victory Board chapter.

ABBREVIATIONS

AASF	Asociación Argentina de Sufragio Femenino
ACA	Acción Católica Argentina
ACF	Asociación Cristiana Femenina
ADECA	Agrupación de Empleadas de Comercio Anti-Nazi
AFA	Agrupación Femenina Antiguerrera
AFP	Acción Femenina Peruana
AIAPE	Agrupación de Intelectuales, Artistas, Periodistas y Escritores
AIB	Açáo Integralista Brasileira
AJN	Alianza de la Juventud Nacionalista
ALN	Alianza Libertadora Nacionalista (continuation of the AJN)
AMA	Agrupación de Mujeres Antifascistas
ANAA	Acción Anti-Nazi de Ayuda a la Unión Soviética y Demás Pueblos en Lucha
APRA	Alianza Popular Revolucionaria Americana
BCC	British Community Council
BWPC	British Women's Patriotic Committee
CAMHE	Comité Argentino de Mujeres Pro Huérfanos Españoles
CDA	Comisión Democrática Argentina (later called Confederación Democrática Argentina)
CNM	Consejo Nacional de Mujeres
CSA	Comisión Sanitaria Argentina
DCF	Defensa Civil Femenina
FACE	Federación de Asociaciones Católicas de Empleadas
FEC	Federación de Empleados de Comercio
FOV	Federación Obrera del Vestido
FPA	Frente Popular Antiimperialista
FRUS	Foreign Relations of the United States
FUA	Federación Universitaria Argentina
FUPDM	Frente Único Pro Derechos de la Mujer (Mexico)
GOU	Grupo Obra de Unificación

IACW	Inter-American Commission of Women
ICANA	Instituto Cultural Argentino Norteamericano
ICUF	Idischer Cultur Farband
JCD	Junta de Coordinación Democrática
LADH	Liga Argentina por los Derechos del Hombre
LCA	Legión Cívica Argentina
LWV	League of Women Voters
MEMCH	Movimiento de Emancipación de las Mujeres de Chile
MNS	Movimiento Nacional Socialista (Chile)
NARA	National Archives and Records Administration (US)
NCWC	National Catholic Welfare Conference
OCD	Office of Civilian Defense
OIAA	Office of Inter-American Affairs
PAWA	Pan American Women's Association
PDN	Partido Demócrata Nacional
PDP	Partido Demócrata Progresista
PPF	Partido Peronista Femenino
PSO	Partido Socialista Obrero
UAM	Unión Argentina de Mujeres
UBA	Universidad de Buenos Aires
UCR	Unión Cívica Radical
UFD	Unión Femenina Democrática
UMA	Unión de Mujeres de la Argentina
UNA	Unión Nacionalista Argentina
UNE	Unión Nacionalista Entrerriana
UNF	Unión Nacional Femenina
UNS	Unión Nacionalista Santafesina
WIDF	Women's International Democratic Federation
WILPF	Women's International League for Peace and Freedom
WIZO	Women's International Zionist Organization

MAPS

N

JUJUY
San Salvador
de Jujuy
Salta
SALTA
FORMOSA
Formosa
MISIONES
San Miguel
de Tucuman
CHACO
Resistencia
Corrientes
Posadas
TUCUMÁN
Santiago del
Estero
CATAMARCA
Catamarca
SANTIAGO
DEL ESTERO
CORRIENTES
La Rioja
LA
RIOJA
SANTA
FÉ
Santa
Fé
CÓRDOBA
Córdoba
Paraná
ENTRE
RÍOS
URUGUAY
SAN JUAN
San Juan
San
Luis
PACIFIC
OCEAN
Mendoza
SAN
LUIS
Buenos Aires
La Plata
Montevideo
MENDOZA
BUENOS
AIRES
Santa Rosa
LA PAMPA
NEUQUÉN
Neuquén
RÍO
NEGRO
Viedma
ATLANTIC
OCEAN
Rawson
CHUBUT
COMODORO RIVADAVIA
SANTA
CRUZ
Río Gallegos
TIERRA DEL
FUEGO
Ushuaia

| 0 | | 300 mi |
| 0 | | 500 km |

Provinces and Territories with
Victory Board Chapters

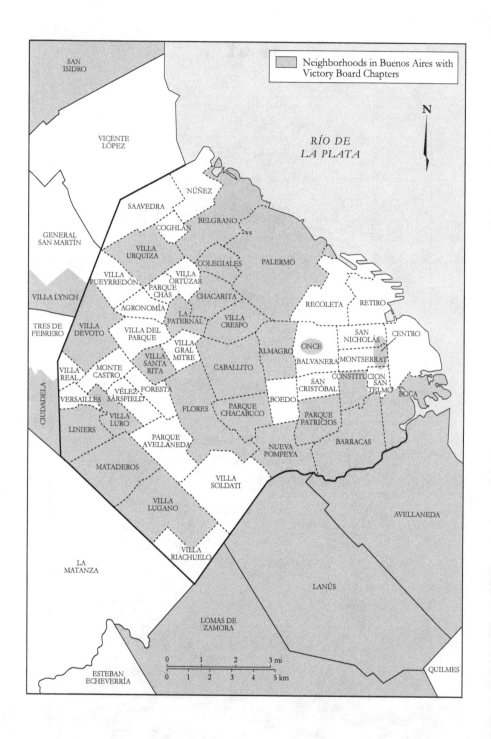

Neighborhoods in Buenos Aires with Victory Board Chapters

N

RÍO DE LA PLATA

SAN ISIDRO

VICENTE LÓPEZ

GENERAL SAN MARTÍN

VILLA LYNCH

TRES DE FEBRERO

CIUDADELA

NÚÑEZ

SAAVEDRA

COGHLÁN

BELGRANO

VILLA URQUIZA

COLEGIALES

PALERMO

VILLA PUEYRREDÓN

VILLA ORTÚZAR

PARQUE CHAS

CHACARITA

AGRONOMÍA

RECOLETA

RETIRO

LA PATERNAL

VILLA CRESPO

VILLA DEVOTO

VILLA DEL PARQUE

SAN NICHOLÁS

CENTRO

VILLA GRAL MITRE

ALMAGRO

ONCE

VILLA SANTA RITA

CABALLITO

BALVANERA

MONTSERRAT

VILLA REAL

MONTE CASTRO

CONSTITUCIÓN

SAN CRISTÓBAL

SAN TELMO

VERSAILLES

VÉLEZ SÁRSFIELD

FORESTA

BOCA

VILLA LURO

FLORES

PARQUE CHACABUCO

BOEDO

LINIERS

PARQUE PATRICIOS

PARQUE AVELLANEDA

NUEVA POMPEYA

BARRACAS

MATADEROS

VILLA SOLDATI

AVELLANEDA

VILLA LUGANO

VILLA RIACHUELO

LANÚS

LA MATANZA

LOMAS DE ZAMORA

QUILMES

ESTEBAN ECHEVERRÍA

0   1   2   3 mi
0 1 2 3 4 5 km

GENDERING ANTIFASCISM

INTRODUCTION

GENDERING ANTIFASCISM

Women's Activism in Argentina and the World, 1918–1947

"I was active in politics . . . in the Junta de la Victoria [Victory Board]," Anita Lang, a former actress, told me proudly.[1] She was one of the persons I interviewed in the early 2000s for a book on the history of Jewish Argentine women.[2] A significant minority of my other elderly interlocutors also highlighted their participation in this group. They said that it was a large organization that spanned the country and sent goods to the Allies during World War II. Although I had researched Argentine history for over twenty years, I had never heard of it.

The Victory Board's mere existence during a time in which Argentine women could not yet vote raised a host of questions. I wondered how these disenfranchised women fought fascism at home and abroad. Who joined the group, and how did it unite and energize people of different backgrounds? What did fascism and antifascism mean to its members, and what were their distinct contributions to antifascism? How did they gender their projects and engage across borders? And how did they and their foes react to each other? These are the questions that inspired this book.

As I investigated this largely forgotten all-woman movement, I found that its antifascism involved much more than dispensing aid. In the 1940s, Argentine women worked to democratize their country—and the world— with knitting needles. If women's gift was to sew and knit, they reasoned, women sewing and knitting together could politicize their labor for a noble cause. The Victory Board defied the neutralist government's reluctance to confront the Axis by making clothing and supplies for Allied soldiers and their families. Rather than a typical woman's philanthropy, the Victory Board was a political organization whose members knit garments as a means of defending what they cherished against fascist onslaught, as if through combat. Its leaders also understood that a true democracy must include women. Without explicitly characterizing itself as feminist, at least initially, the Victory Board promoted women's political rights and visibility more effectively than previous Argentine associations. It attracted as many

3

as forty-five thousand members of varied origins across the nation who contested both local and foreign fascisms. The board's experiences shed light on women's vibrant resistance to fascism, right-wing populism, and misogyny, then and now.

Centering on the Victory Board—and its antifascist precursors—recasts Argentine history. Many Argentines and Argentine specialists have viewed Peronism, which consolidated in 1945, as the first political movement to mobilize diverse women on a massive scale, but antifascism preceded it. The Spanish Republican cause in the mid- to late 1930s, followed by the Victory Board in the early 1940s, rallied thousands of women of different ethnic, class, and political backgrounds. Historians also have credited Peronism for replacing the hegemonic notion of the Argentine melting pot with multiculturalism, yet the Victory Board, with its celebration of ethnic diversity, was its forerunner.

The German invasion of the Soviet Union in June 1941 prompted the creation of the Victory Board, which became *the* pivotal Argentine women's political organization before suffrage in 1947. The Victory Board was the most active, organized, and publicized group to combine women's rights with a concern for a broad conception of democracy. It took its emblem and name from Winston Churchill's "V for Victory" slogan—victory in the global conflict between democracy and fascism that raged on many fronts, including neutral Argentina.

The Victory Board drew upon a rich history of intertwined local, Latin American, and international resistance to militarism, dictatorship, and fascism, beginning with the end of World War I and Benito Mussolini's consolidation of power in Italy. Its precursors and leaders belonged to women's worldwide peace networks, antifascist Popular Front groups, and hemispheric feminist circles. They expressed solidarity with Ethiopia and Republican Spain, victims of fascist bellicosity. Argentine and other Latin American women decried the suppression of women's rights in Germany and Italy and the spread of fascism to their region. Victory Board president Ana Rosa Schlieper de Martínez Guerrero noted that World War II had crossed the ocean,[3] yet the struggle between fascism and democracy had implanted itself on Argentine and Latin American shores years before. The development of women's antifascisms that culminated in the Victory Board is not only an Argentine story—it is a deeply regional, transnational, and global story. This book analyzes Argentine women's activism and their relationships with governments and kindred women in other countries.

Building on these roots, the Victory Board stood out in many respects. It attracted socialites and peasants, professionals and workers, Jews and Catholics, and women of immigrant and Indigenous descent throughout the nation. Argentine women of different classes and backgrounds had interacted largely through unequal exchanges in the marketplace, charitable aid, or domestic service. In contrast, Victory Board members worked together to sew and knit, organize public events, raise money, and resist government and radical rightist attacks. Ushering many women into political involvement, the Victory Board represented an unprecedented local experiment in pluralism, coalition formation, and women's mobilization. The movement emphasized its formal and informal democratic practices. Its mentorship of the Uruguayan antifascist Feminine Action for Victory (Acción Femenina por la Victoria), a sister group that arose in May 1942, also was unique. These and other characteristics made the Victory Board an organization like no other in Argentina, the Americas, or Europe.

This is a pioneering book on a pioneering group. It is the first on Argentine antifascist women, including the Victory Board and its precursors,[4] and the first of its kind in other respects as well. The fine studies of the Mexican Frente Único Pro Derechos de la Mujer (FUPDM), Movimiento de Emancipación de las Mujeres de Chile (MEMCH), and those whom Katherine Marino called Popular Front Pan-American Feminists, concentrate on their women's rights and social justice advocacy rather than on their antifascism.[5] Ariel Lambe's excellent book on Cuban antifascism offers valuable insights on gender but does not analyze feminism.[6] Thus, my study is also the first book-length treatment of a women's movement in Latin America and the Global South to focus both on its feminism and antifascism; indeed, I argue that the two were mutually constitutive. Finally, it is the only monograph to conceptualize antifascist women by dissecting the interplay between the local, national, and transnational.

The Victory Board and Antifascist Studies

Interwar fascism ultimately failed in most Western countries, and antifascism triumphed, as Michael Seidman asserted, noting that antifascism may have been "the most powerful Western ideology of the twentieth century," although Nigel Copsey claimed that its proponents' diverse methods and visions of the ideal society prevented antifascism from being a single ideology.[7] As complex and varied as fascist ones, antifascist movements have received markedly less scholarly attention. The editors of a collection on antifascism published in 1999 described it as "a pan-European phenomenon," and most publications have reflected this mind-set.[8] The literature has focused on European men, their Communist ties, their armed and clandestine resistance to fascist revolts and rule, and a one-way flow of exiles and ideas from this continent. In fact, it has considered other regions marginal and tangential to antifascism. Only one of the seventeen chapters in a foundational compendium on antifascism published in 2016 dealt with a non-European country—significantly, Argentina.[9] Studies examining transnational connections typically have focused on exchanges within Europe or across the North Atlantic. In a journal issue on transnational antifascism that also appeared in 2016, Hugo García observed that antifascism "was to a large extent a 'culture of exile' built in such metropoles as Berlin, Paris, Moscow, Barcelona, London and New York," disregarding Latin American capitals such as Mexico City, Santiago, Buenos Aires, and Montevideo, as well as Latin American exiles. García admitted, however, that "the *peripheral* [my italics] areas of the anti-fascist world system actively adapted concepts and tactics to local cultures and conflicts." Only two of the seven articles in this issue addressed European antifascist contacts with non-Europeans, emphasizing the former's roles in these exchanges. Centering on German-speaking exiles in Argentina, Bolivia, and Mexico, Andrea Acle-Kreysing wrote that "through both exile and contact with a non-European *audience* [my emphasis], anti-fascism became a transatlantic political culture." The use of the word *audience* suggested that Latin Americans passively received the refugees' words, not having already opposed fascism on their own.[10] By concentrating on European voices, these and other authors obscured homegrown activists in other continents, minimized their agency, and ignored their input in transnational exchanges.

Latin Americanists have paid relatively little attention to antifascism, seemingly regarding it as insignificant in this area. Those who have studied it have tended to focus on European sojourners in this region.[11] Perhaps some of them implicitly accepted the notion that antifascism was a largely European phenomenon brought by exiles. This book demonstrates its importance in Argentina and Latin America and emphasizes local actors. Therefore, it is a vital contribution to antifascist studies.

Latin America and other areas outside Europe may be "peripheral" to the literature on antifascism, but not to antifascism itself.[12] Latin America was not marginal to a European antifascist "core," nor did activists in this region simply reproduce European ideas and practices. Reacting to domestic conditions as well as those across the Atlantic, Latin Americans created large movements, such as the Victory Board and its predecessors, and formulated their own antifascisms that differed from European ones. Moreover, by definition, transnational exchanges do not move in a single direction—in this case from Europe—but back and forth in both directions. Along with their peers elsewhere, Argentine and Latin American antifascists engaged in this flow, from the Global South to the Global North, and within the Global South.

Since I started this book, researchers have begun to challenge Eurocentrism. Recent examinations of Global South antifascisms that emphasize their transnational input and local ingredients, including anticolonialism and anticipation and contestation of Comintern policies, are revamping the field.[13] Of particular interest for my work is John Flores's account of the Frente Popular Antiimperialista (FPA), founded by Mexican Communists and allied with the Lázaro Cárdenas government (1936–1940), which opposed the intertwined threats of foreign fascists, local magnates tied to US capital, and opponents of the Mexican Revolution. FPA branches arose in several Mexican diasporic communities in the United States. The Chicago affiliate cultivated bonds with white and Black union organizers and local Cuban and Spanish workers. Its women members taught children using the Mexican educational secretariat's socialist materials. FPA and Mexican labor representatives gave lectures and recruited Mexican Americans to attend the antifascist labor leader Vicente Lombardo Toledano's worker university in the homeland. Such activities tied the FPA and its branches together in a South-North axis that expressed Mexican notions of antifascism.[14] Despite the FPA's male leadership and largely male composition, like this group the Victory Board also conducted South-North exchanges and represented a local style of antifascism.

While works on European men traditionally have dominated antifascist studies, to a lesser degree the literature has addressed European women's involvement in global conferences and networks, support for the French Popular Front government and the Spanish Republic, and clandestine resistance. As mentioned, it also has examined the Mexican FUPDM and the Chilean MEMCH. More current writings on women's antifascisms have explored other countries. Sana Tannoury-Karam found that the vibrant women's section of the League against Nazism and Fascism in Syria and Lebanon added women's rights to Arab antifascism and asserted, like the Victory Board, that a true democracy required women's presence. Caroline Waldron Merithew injected women's mobilization into her account of Ethiopian resistance and attempts to secure transnational support.[15] Recent works on US women have privileged their cultural production, Black women's engagement, and insertion of race and gender issues.[16]

The Victory Board shared several traits of antifascist groups discussed in the older literature. Official persecution also forced it underground between 1943 and 1945. It, too, included political exiles, although these were a minority; absorbed ideas from abroad; and, as a Popular Front group, had Communist links. Nevertheless, this book forms part of the emerging literature. It reveals how the Victory Board, like other movements of the Global South, constructed its own version of antifascism, exercised agency, and engaged in South-North transnational exchanges.

The excellent literature on Argentina's vigorous homegrown antifascist campaigns has focused on men, their ideological discussions, underlying political struggles, and Buenos Aires city and province. The concentration on ideas and competition for power helps account for the absence of women, who were disenfranchised and whose thoughts received less publicity than those of men, although there were exceptions.[17] Just as Argentine antifascism was not peripheral, however, neither were its women activists. With their focus on intellectual and political history, scholars have paid relatively little notice to the sizable groups that sent goods to the Spanish Republic[18] and the Allies, where one was most likely to find women. One of the few scholars to analyze the Victory Board, Adriana Valobra's noteworthy articles highlighted its ties with the Communist Party and with postwar Communist organizations.[19] Rather than focus on the Communist Party and developments after 1945, this book fits the Victory Board into a little-known narrative of intertwined pacifist, antifascist, and women's rights movements dating from World War I that enveloped the nation. It adds cross-border relations into the literature on pre-1945 Argentina. Indeed, transnational connections are largely absent from other works on Latin American antifascisms in this period, except for the handful that treat the FPA, Latin American feminist networks, and solidarity with Republican Spain.[20]

In contrast, cross-border interchanges are at the heart of my book. It traces the conversations among pacifist and feminist women in the Western Hemisphere and the complex debates between progressives and far rightists throughout Latin America that shaped antifascisms in the region. I emphasize the Victory Board's transnational mission of adapting and recirculating imported ideas (while also devising its own), organizing the grassroots by linking the battles against foreign and domestic fascism, forging ties with Uruguayan and Pan-American groups as well as governments in other countries, and sending aid and supportive messages from the Global South to the Global North. The focus on exchanges within the Global South, and with the Global North, sets it apart from most studies on Latin American and women's antifascisms before 1945.[21]

The Victory Board—and my coverage of it—also are unique in other respects. Unlike other southern movements, it did not contest imperialism or capitalism, at least until after 1945, although some of its predecessors had. The Victory Board's accentuation of its democratic alternative to fascism, promotion of multiculturalism, and relationship with Feminine Action for Victory were distinctive. So too were its means of popularizing antifascism. Scholars of Mexican and Chilean feminism discerned antifascist participation in the struggle for women's rights, yet few Argentine specialists have made this connection.[22] I see the board as a missing link in the historiography on Argentine feminism.

I argue that women were vital for mobilizing antifascism, and that antifascism, in turn, was vital for politicizing women in Argentina, Uruguay, and elsewhere in Latin America. Indeed, women activists throughout Spanish- and Portuguese-speaking America had claimed that they deserved the vote to press for amity in a world torn apart by war and fascism. Such reasoning exemplified maternalism, the notion of "gender difference based on motherhood as the foundation for reform and activism."[23] This concept also rests on an exaltation of women's roles in the home and society, conceived as the home writ large. As mothers or potential mothers, women have been seen as compassionate caregivers, helpmates, and disseminators of ethical values. Some feminists contended that women's inherent nature made them uniquely suited for social welfare and peacemaking duties. Their vital reproductive function entitled them to full citizenship, which would enable women to better serve their families and society.

While the literature stresses maternalism as the motive for Latin American women's political involvement,[24] this belief tends to erase women's multiple identities and political experiences. I posit that many joined the Victory Board and its Uruguayan sister not only for maternalistic motives, but to serve in a prestigious global campaign that enabled them to feel useful, fight for rights and recognition, and deepen their militancy.

Just as the stress on maternalism has obfuscated women's activism, so too has the tendency to study antifascism in isolation. Historians have specialized in antifascism or fascism and rarely have analyzed the two together in the same work.[25] However, to understand one it is necessary to understand the other and the interactions between the two. Latin American and Argentine antifascists, including the Victory Board, debated women's roles and related issues with their enemies. Argentine fascists physically attacked board chapters and supported government efforts to repress antifascism. They were known as Nationalists, a coalition of shifting fascist, reactionary, and ultra-conservative groups that shared core beliefs and conducted joint operations. Other fascist movements and regimes, such as the Italian variant, also represented coalitions of this type. In times of crisis the ideological distinctions between these sectors tend to fade, as they did in Argentina in the 1930s–1940s.[26] Rather than define *fascism* and *antifascism* in detail, I prefer to let my protagonists and their opponents explain their own perceptions of these two amorphous concepts throughout the following chapters.[27]

The relationship between the Communist Party and the Victory Board also deserves examination. When studying Communist-influenced movements, scholars often have exaggerated the degree of party control. Two Communists, the writer María Rosa Oliver and mathematician Cora Ratto, set the Victory Board into motion, and the male-dominated Communist Party may have asked them to do so. It instructed Fanny Edelman and probably other militants to join.[28] However, this Popular Front movement contained many women in the leadership and ranks who were nonpartisan or loyal to other parties. While the Victory Board endorsed Soviet wartime policies and sent the bulk of its aid to the Soviet Union, non-Communists inside and outside the group agreed with these stances, reasoning that this country was the main battlefield and its needs were desperate. One must recognize that the board had agency, as Francisca de Haan and Jadwiga Pieper Mooney have argued for the Communist-linked Women's International Democratic Federation (WIDF).[29] For these reasons I describe this women's movement as relatively independent of men. The Communist impact on the Victory Board, however, became clearer after the end of World War II.

A Sinuous Path

When I began this study, the Victory Board was largely absent from historical memory, a point I will address in the conclusion. I started on a lengthy research trail and could not predict where it headed. When my interviewees told me about the board, I noticed information on it in the Communist publication *La Hora*. This and other Buenos Aires newspapers held in the Biblioteca Nacional contained Victory Board members' names and a wealth of data on the group's quotidian activities. I continued with the autobiographies of cofounder María Rosa Oliver, who described its beginnings, and Fanny Edelman.[30] Multiple sojourns in the Biblioteca Nacional, Centro de Documentación e Investigación de la Cultura de Izquierdas (CeDInCI), and Archivo del Partido Comunista in Buenos Aires uncovered a few Victory Board documents and publications, as well as leftist, pacifist, and feminist periodicals of the 1920s–1940s. The Biblioteca Nacional and Biblioteca Tornquist offered scattered information on a few board members. I did not want to simply examine Buenos Aires. After all, the area outside this city and province accounted for over half of the population in the 1940s.[31] In the Archivo Intermedio of the Archivo General de la Nación, I found official accounts of the repressive national context of the 1930s and 1940s. I followed the trail to provincial collections, where I read local periodicals, government documents, municipal guides, and personal papers. Donated by a US visitor to Argentina, the single most valuable document I discovered was in the Harvard Widener Library: the proceedings of the Victory Board's first national convention, with national and local leaders' speeches and reports. Often ignored, abridged, or filtered by the press, these accounts in the women's own words of the obstacles the movement faced, its inner workings, and its successes and failures were a gold mine.

Still, something was missing. I wanted to recover the lives of women who had made history but were forgotten. Although several prominent figures—such as Oliver, Ratto, and Schlieper—tie the book together, this is primarily a study of ordinary women. Biographical dictionaries and other printed sources focusing on notable, let alone undistinguished, Argentine women are scarce.[32] Even the aristocrats and professionals who joined the Victory Board are largely unknown. How can one learn about the occupations, activism, political affiliations, and friendship networks of women who rarely left papers? The board's size and scope mandated limiting myself to a few locations and samples of members. I picked Buenos Aires, the federal capital at that time, and municipalities in three provinces and two territories. Since no membership lists have survived, I drew names from newspapers. Most Victory Board adherents passed away by the time my research intensified, so after my initial interviews I turned to their descendants. Some had no idea that their mothers or grandmothers had been involved in such an organization, but many knew about their social networks, pursuits outside the board, and political inclinations. Local historians and longtime residents supplied further information on these women.

The federal capital's numerous barrios and huge population also complicated researching members' identities.[33] In smaller provincial locations, where many people are acquainted with or have heard of each other, it was easier to find descendants to interview as well as informed observers who could identify the rank and file than in a metropolis like Buenos Aires. In Santa Fe I met with a focus group composed of journalists, people of various sectors, and elderly inhabitants. I read aloud my list of names, one by one, and the persons in attendance opined on each woman's identity, relatives, and friends, sometimes disagreeing with each other but usually reaching a consensus.[34] In such places, newspaper social pages, which did not only report on the elite; archives and city guides; social registers; and published reminiscences also were useful.[35] Understanding the makeup of local chapters helped me paint a fuller portrait of the Victory Board's overall composition.

Nevertheless, gathering information on commoners in any setting was challenging. I could not find data on a sizeable percentage of the women surveyed. This likely means that they were housewives, workers, or both, which in itself is noteworthy. It also proved extremely difficult to identify women of color, perhaps because many Argentines thought it disrespectful to refer to one's race or preferred to see their compatriots as part of a white society.[36] I present what I have because it is critical to study the ordinary women who have filled the ranks of many movements and enabled them to succeed. We know little about them, and we need to know more. Furthermore, my data demonstrates patterns, especially when combined with qualitative material.

Early in my research I spotted hints that the Victory Board's transnationalism exceeded its exchanges with the Allies. Coverage of its national conventions alerted me to the presence of Uruguayan women. Believing they might have represented an antifascist group, I embarked for Montevideo, where my hunch paid off. Periodicals and several Feminine Action for Victory publications stored in the Biblioteca Nacional attested to this movement's existence, significance, and contacts with the Victory Board. The Archivo General de la Nación and Fondo Centro Republicano Español de la Facultad de Humanidades y Ciencias de la Educación, Universidad de la República, furnished documents on the Uruguayan antifascist context.

I had an inkling that the Victory Board's and its predecessors' cross-border contacts stretched to other places, and again found proof in many collections. The US National Archives, Schlesinger Library on the History of Women in America, Swarthmore College Peace Collection, Franklin D. Roosevelt Library, and Library of Congress provided crucial data on the Victory Board's precursors, deliberations, connections to women's groups in the Americas and Europe, and relations with US government officials and the First Lady. Oliver's papers, held at the Princeton University Special Collections and Rockefeller Archives Center, discussed her ties with US functionaries and service at Nelson Rockefeller's Office for Inter-American Affairs. British Foreign Office records shed light on the Victory Board's contacts with British officials and Anglo-Argentine associations.

My search for data led me along a winding route with local, national, and transnational side streets. Detecting local variations is crucial to avoid homogenizing countries and groups, a tendency sometimes found in comparative and transnational studies.[37] I studied chapters throughout the country not just to explain the Victory Board's composition, but to gauge these regional differences and the entanglement of antifascism with local histories. Often perceived as a conservative backwater, save for a few cities, the "interior" defied this stereotypical notion. It contained hotbeds of political mobilization, even in tiny remote settings. Victory Board leaders were aware of these struggles and tried to unite "the city and the nation" in a progressive campaign and promote dialogue among the metropole and other internal spaces.[38] As was true for members' identities, understanding the local can alter our vision of the national:[39] in this case, by demonstrating that antifascism, leftism, and Nationalism had followers throughout the country. And understanding the transnational can alter our visions of Argentina: cross-border exchanges of ideas and goods influenced the Victory Board at its local and national levels. Melding the local, national, and transnational is crucial for comprehending the Victory Board and antifascists worldwide and merits attention.[40]

Overview of the Book

This book is organized chronologically and thematically, with most chapters treating the intersection of the local, national, and transnational. Chapter 1 traces the development of women's antifascist consciousness, strategies, and links with hemispheric and international activism from 1918 on that peaked in the Victory Board. The rise of fascism in Europe, the Italian invasion of Ethiopia, and the Chaco War prompted Latin American women to collaborate with the Women's International League for Peace and Freedom. They closely followed the women's sector of the antifascist Amsterdam-Pleyel movement, which led to the Communist International's sponsorship of broad-based antifascist coalitions known as the Popular Front. As in Europe and elsewhere in the Americas, Argentine women's Popular Front associations combined pacifism, feminism, and antifascism. They protested official efforts to curtail women's rights, so evocative of Germany and Italy; organized peace conferences in Buenos Aires; and participated in the feminist Inter-American Commission of Women. Progressive women throughout Argentina and the region engaged in South-North solidarity with the Spanish Republic. Many of these women had initially condemned warfare in all instances, but they reluctantly conceded that only arms could defeat fascism. The Victory Board inherited this legacy.

To comprehend antifascists, one must grasp their interactions with their opponents. Chapter 2 continues to examine what fascism and antifascism meant to progressive women by analyzing their South-South debates with radical rightist men and women across the region. In the 1930s, feminist and leftist women in Argentina and Latin America refined their identities against internal and European fascisms. Most fascists believed that "liberating" women meant sending them home, while feminists disputed this notion. Each side accused each other of destroying women's mission. Surprisingly, some extreme rightists outside Argentina seemingly agreed with progressives on the need for women's suffrage, education, and equal opportunities and salaries. Fascists and antifascists—who soon would include Victory Board members—saw each other as a challenge, a menace, and a force they could not afford to ignore.

Building on its precursors and on diverse struggles throughout Argentina, the Victory Board and its brand of antifascism are the topics of chapter 3. Born in 1941, this Popular Front group expanded across Argentina and engaged in South-North solidarity by sending encouragement and handmade goods to the Allies. Participating in a distinguished global campaign to promote democracy overseas and linking it to efforts to strengthen it at home energized Victory Board adherents and popularized antifascism in their communities, as did displaying and dispatching their tangible products. The board distinguished itself from the fraudulently elected civilian governments of the 1930s and 1940s and the Nationalists by presenting itself as a model of genuine democracy. Its support for women's rights was another contribution to Argentine antifascism.

The Victory Board's members and how it united them are the themes of chapter 4. Through its fostering of mutual respect, humanitarianism, and common goals, the Victory Board attracted women of different class, ethnic, religious, and partisan backgrounds. It drew upon the many Spanish Republican sympathizers and the smaller numbers of feminists. Contesting the reactionary church hierarchy, Victory Board orators beseeched Catholics to oppose Nazi persecution of their brethren overseas by joining the organization. Nazi antisemitism and brutality led Jewish and other women with roots in occupied Europe to affiliate, as did the Victory Board's oft-expressed pride in its diversity, which helped spread acceptance of Argentina as a multicultural society. The board weakened the regional divide between Buenos Aires and the rest of the country. Nevertheless, it could not completely close the ideological gap between social classes.

Chapter 5 focuses on the Victory Board's manner of gendering antifascism. The only major Argentine antifascist association composed entirely of women, it carried out tasks typically coded as female. The Victory Board bolstered yet contested these customary roles. Through hand work antifascism became part of women's daily lives, and the board blended private and public by making these domestic labors visible. Reproducing antifascism in their homes also melded public and private. Antifascist couples shared political commitments that buoyed comradeship and sometimes alleviated women's household duties, but could cause friction. While the Victory Board prepared women for citizenship, and its leaders backed women's suffrage, its male allies had little interest in women's rights. Men dominated other antifascist organizations, which often differed from the board's feminized antifascism by concentrating on speechmaking, issuing antifascist tracts, and maneuvering for political gain.

As discussed in chapter 6, the Victory Board's transnational partners ranged from reluctant to enthusiastic. As head of the Inter-American Commission of Women, Victory Board president Ana Rosa Schlieper de Martínez Guerrero forged ties with delegates across the Americas, and the board's cofounder, María Rosa Oliver, served in Washington, DC, as a cultural liaison between the United States and Latin America. Although the Victory Board received US and British government support, the FBI and some embassy officials from these countries tended to disparage it as Communist. Lower-ranking US diplomats in Buenos Aires also made belittling sexist remarks about the board president. The relationship with Feminine Action for Victory was far more positive. Like the Victory Board, this Popular Front association supplied the Allies, defended democratic ideals, and promoted women's citizenship. At first, the Victory Board served as Feminine Action for Victory's mentor, but the relationship shifted into a deeper, more reciprocal alliance that endured during the Argentine military dictatorship (1943–1946), when the board went underground. The intertwined histories of the Victory Board and Feminine Action for Victory offer an extraordinary example of antifascist women's South-South and South-North solidarity.

The next chapter treats the interactions between the Victory Board and the Nationalists. Both were preoccupied with women's roles in a changing world, peace and war, and social justice, but formulated different solutions. Nationalists labeled the Victory Board as oligarchical, imperialistic, and "Jewish" for provisioning foreigners while many Argentines went hungry. That it ignored the plight of needy locals was the Nationalists' most compelling critique of this group. The Victory Board responded that charity would not cure inequality; only government action after the war's end could usher in a more equitable society. At times Nationalists agreed, yet their favored social, gender, and political order and opinion of the Axis clashed with the Victory Board's views. They attacked the board physically as well as verbally.

The final chapter examines the Victory Board's fate as World War II ended and the Cold War began. The military government allowed it to re-emerge from the shadows, yet still repressed it. Feminine Action for Victory delegates arrived to demonstrate their solidarity. The two groups affiliated with WIDF and adjusted their programs to fit its agenda. The Victory Board still sent aid to Europe but also turned to domestic issues, such as women's suffrage and, tardily, inequality. Rather than receive the vote from Juan Perón, whom they regarded as a fascist, Victory Board members and other women pressed for an elected Congress to pass a suffrage law and collaborated with the anti-Peronist Democratic Union (Unión Democrática). Perón's electoral victory in 1946 and shifting Communist strategies in the new Cold War context precipitated the Victory Board's decline. Abandoning the Popular Front, like Communists elsewhere, the Communist Party now regarded the Victory Board as a liability because of its association with the elite and US and British imperialism. It created a new organization to replace the Victory Board, some of whose members joined this group, while others dispersed in varied political directions.

The conclusion assesses the group's significance and considers its relevance for today. The movement contributed to the Allied triumph, fostered women's public roles, politicized women throughout Argentina, and promoted suffrage. Limited by the conflicting interests of its multiclass coalition, wartime alliances, and international Communist strategy, it did not effectively combine antifascism with social justice. This failure, its anti-Peronism, and the mistaken perception of the Victory Board as upper class helped bury it into oblivion, even as many former adherents continued their activism. Yet its distinctiveness is memorable. Differing from its counterparts, the Victory Board tutored and partnered with a similar group in another southern country, sent aid from the Global South to the Global North, and cultivated and underlined its democratic alternative to fascism. It propelled feminism in postwar Argentina and presaged the feminist groups that followed. The Victory Board demonstrates the heterogeneous, contingent, and complex nature of antifascism. Some of its strengths can help inform women's and other democratic resistance movements today. So, too, can knowledge of its pitfalls.

The time has come for a book on women's antifascism in the Global South. We need historical context to help us comprehend the resurgence of right-wing populism and neofascism—in Brazil and Latin America as in other places—as well as the challenges of creating democratic resistance groups that cross ethnic, religious, class, regional, and national borders. The questions posed at the beginning of this introduction are as relevant to the study of current mobilizations as they are to an understanding of the past. Women have always been at the forefront of struggles against authoritarianism in Latin America—and perhaps the globe. We have much to learn from the successes and failures of the Argentine women who took up knitting for the Allies eighty years ago and forged links throughout the world.

CHAPTER 1

A HERITAGE OF TRANSNATIONAL DEMOCRATIC STRUGGLES IN ARGENTINA AND THE WORLD, 1914–1941

María Ronconi de Saratino, the co-owner of a family textile firm in Buenos Aires, first became conscious of the horrors of combat, as well as her love of freedom, during World War I. These feelings led her to participate in what she called "democratic struggles." In the 1930s Ronconi and her workers darned old stockings and sent them to needy children in the beleaguered Spanish Republic. Her personnel also signed the feminist and pacifist Declaration of the Argentine Woman of December 1936, surely with her endorsement. World War II had barely started when she began to collaborate with British friends to send supplies to Great Britain. In 1941 Ronconi quickly perceived the significance of the Victory Board (Junta de la Victoria). She joined the chapter of Parque Chacabuco, where one of her factories was located, and convinced its 150 women laborers to do the same. Whether they felt pressured is unclear, but many other women of their class also affiliated. Ronconi's workers paid what little dues they could—twenty or fifty cents a month—and set up a commission in the plant to make goods to dispatch overseas.[1]

Ronconi's testimony provides insight into the evolution of Argentine women's antifascisms, leading up to the Victory Board. Beginning in 1914, these women faced a convergence of domestic and international crises that prompted activism within their country and across borders. The Chaco War (1932–1935) led them to participate in peace movements, which intertwined with feminism and antifascism. Some of these associations were influenced by and contributed to a burgeoning transatlantic antiwar and antifascist surge. From the Global South, Argentine women engaged in exchanges with international women's networks and solidarity efforts in the Global North. Feminists resisted efforts to curtail their rights and tried to expand them.

Upper-, middle-, and lower-class women like Ronconi's workers participated to varying degrees in these efforts, which evinced yet also contested
maternalism. These local, national, and transnational democratic struggles
illustrated how women fought fascism and authoritarianism at home and
abroad, involved themselves in international affairs, defined *fascism* and
antifascism in their own terms, and gendered their projects.[2] Directly and
indirectly, their ideas and activism culminated in the Victory Board.

This chapter focuses on women's groups, goals, and intersections, as
well as the main figures, many of whom would join the Victory Board. It
treats their views on peace, democracy, and, to a certain degree, women's
rights. Chapter 2 extends the discussion of women's rights and roles by
probing fascist-antifascist debates on these issues.

World War I and the Rise of Local Fascism

Many Argentines mobilized for the Allies or neutrality. They included
women, who engaged in demonstrations and solidarity with combatants.
Nourished by ties to the military, the Catholic Church, and conservatives,
homegrown fascism emerged in the late 1920s, as did opposition to it.

When World War I broke out in 1914, it roused a massive display of
sentiment. Huge numbers of men and women marched through the streets
of Buenos Aires, favoring neutrality or the Allies. The immigrant roots of
many Argentines prompted some of these feelings. Cultural affinity with
France, long-standing economic and political ties to Great Britain, and anger over the German sinking of several Argentine ships led many to back the
Allies; nationalist desire for autonomy from Britain and the United States
galvanized the neutralists. The women's presence was especially marked in
public celebrations of the Allied victory in 1918 in the federal capital and
Córdoba. Perhaps including Ronconi, women also participated in groups
sponsored by foreign communities and local philanthropists that sent aid
abroad, mostly to the Allies.[3] This activism manifested their growing engagement with foreign affairs and solidarity with foreign causes.

As they would during World War II, supporters praised the Allies as the
standard-bearers of democracy and civilization against German militarism
and barbarism. For their part, neutralists criticized British imperialism and
tied government policy to traditional Argentine diplomacy. They represented a wide political spectrum, much of which was neither pro-German nor
right-wing, including President Hipólito Yrigoyen (1916–1922, 1928–1930)
and other members of the centrist democratic Radical Civic Union (Unión
Cívica Radical, UCR) Party. Such notions and the composition of the non-
interventionists characterized most protagonists in the 1940s as well.

The neutralist camp in World War II, however, also contained radical rightists who backed the Axis. Beginning in 1919, by the late 1920s, they created what became a coherent but disunited movement that turned in a fascist direction from 1930 on.[4] A German sympathizer during World War I, General José Félix Uriburu led the coup d'etat that overthrew President Yrigoyen, thus ending Argentina's short-lived electoral democracy and inaugurating the thirteen-year rule of a conservative alliance, known as the Concordancia, through fraudulent elections. Boosting his fascist Nationalist followers, Uriburu (1930–1932) appointed them to office and officially sponsored a Nationalist paramilitary organization, the Legión Cívica Argentina (LCA). His administration employed censorship, torture, and deportations to repress laborers, leftists, and Radicals. Succeeding governments also clamped down on unions and "subversives."[5]

While they differed in many respects, the boundary between Nationalism and the conservative parties was permeable. Nationalists sometimes allied with provincial conservative factions, who used them for partisan advantage. They also overlapped—and practically became identical with—the rightist hegemonic sector in the Catholic Church during the 1930s and 1940s.

Nationalists frequently attacked workers, leftists, and Jews throughout Argentina. In several cities they tossed tear gas and bombs into synagogues and theaters presenting films and plays they deemed anti-Nazi or pro-Jewish. They killed laborers in Buenos Aires and Santa Fe, and the Socialist provincial deputy José Guevara in Córdoba. While Tucumán's Radical government prosecuted some Nationalist terrorists, and Córdoba's conservative administration took steps against Guevara's murderer, conservative national and provincial authorities often failed to charge Nationalists for their violence. Antifascists also attacked their opponents, yet they rarely escaped arrest.[6]

Not surprisingly, many Argentines overlooked the theoretical distinctions between conservatism, Catholicism, and Nationalism and tended to conflate them under the vague category of *fascism*, as did numerous antifascists outside Argentina.[7] They perceived such disparate phenomena as electoral fraud, clientelism, militarism, social inequality, official collusion with imperialism, and religious education in public schools as parts of a package. A transnational understanding of fascism helped inform their definitions of this phenomenon. Italian immigrants and others had begun to raise awareness of the Benito Mussolini regime in the 1920s. Whether women participated in such efforts is unclear.[8] Cognizant of European fascist tactics and policies, union, leftist, and democratic militants knew what to expect under such a regime and resisted any possible move in that direction.[9] As the anarchist publication *La Protesta* warned, the fascist threat in Argentina was no "empty phrase."[10]

Popular Resistance

Women throughout Argentina mobilized against homegrown and foreign fascism. They engaged in leftist groups, solidarity with political prisoners, and activism against war and imperialism, which they linked to fascism. Warfare in the early 1930s reinforced these linkages and stimulated Argentine ties to global pacifist movements.

Women's resistance took on many shapes, ranging from small to large movements. Among them were anarchist women's associations that attempted to translate their "sentiments of liberty, of justice, of solidarity" into "tangible reality."[11] One of these was the Agrupación Femenina Antifascista of San Fernando, a Buenos Aires suburb. It humbly characterized itself as a "nucleus of proletarian women," a mere "grain of sand" that would do its part to halt fascist infiltration of all sectors.[12] Other anarchist women took to the streets to counter what they considered fascist oppression. Beginning shortly after Uriburu seized power, they publicly defied the dictatorship's assault on political expression and human rights. Describing themselves as mothers, comrades, girlfriends, and daughters of political prisoners and deportees, the self-styled Mujeres del Pueblo met at the Plaza del Congreso on October 18, 1930. Some of them lectured the crowd on the regime's harsh policies, which the establishment press did not report. Then they took their stories to the major newspapers, resisting the police along the way. The next day, a multitude congregated at the Avenida de Mayo, where an anarchist gave a speech. Women and men surrounded the orator, keeping the police from arresting her.[13]

Anarchist and other leftist men and women founded groups in solidarity with political prisoners, but women tended to be the most active in the day-to-day tasks of helping the jailed and their families. Preeminent was the Communist-linked International Red Aid, whose Argentine branch expanded into what became known as the Liga Argentina por los Derechos del Hombre (LADH). Its public layer defended the basic liberal freedoms and gave prisoners legal support. Operating in the shadows, working-class women supplied prisoners with food and other necessities and informed relatives, neighbors, and coworkers of their incarceration. These semiclandestine activists were especially prey to official harassment. Future Victory Board members Fanny Edelman, a Communist, and Dalila Saslavsky, who became close to the Communist Party, were involved in the unconcealed efforts; proletarian Jewish and Italian women, some of whom also joined the Victory Board, stood out among the aid givers.[14] Tinier in scope were associations such as the Comité de Ayuda Popular of Moisés Ville, which supported those victimized for political or antisemititc reasons.

The presence of armed Nationalist militias in the streets and fascist sympathizers in corridors of power alarmed Dr. Rosa Scheiner, a Socialist dental surgeon who would join the LADH, Socialist Worker Party (Partido Socialista Obrero, PSO), which allied with the Communist Party (Partido Comunista), and the Victory Board. Sharing her apprehensions, women joined myriad organizations and protests against fascist violence and racism during the 1930s. In 1933 Socialists in Buenos Aires held a rally to denounce the murder of José Guevara. Among the participants were Dr. Alicia Moreau de Justo, a physician, feminist, and widow of the Socialist party leader Juan B. Justo, and the Alianza Femenina Antifascista Nacional. Following a Nationalist attack on a labor demonstration in Santa Fe in 1935, centrist and leftist politicians, students, workers, and intellectuals, including Dr. Marta Samatán, an educator, teacher's union militant, and lawyer, formed the local Comité Popular Antifascista. It demanded that the Argentine government close Nationalist offices and disband the LCA. Communists organized larger national-level associations, such as the Comité Contra el Racismo y el Antisemitismo, in 1937.[15] An aristocratic Communist writer and Victory Board cofounder, María Rosa Oliver served as the lone woman in the comité's leadership circle in 1940.[16]

Another future Victory Board member, Dr. Clara Schliapnik de Filer, a leftist physician in Villa Domínguez, Entre Ríos, feared it was just one step from fascism to war.[17] In fact, women had been working for peace even before the rise of fascism. One such initiative sprang out of the Consejo Nacional de Mujeres (CNM), an aristocratic-led federation of women's associations and charities that advocated mild social reform and education for women. Responding to requests from foreign organizations, including the International Council of Women, with which it was affiliated, to help them end World War I, a member blamed general unruliness and class conflict for destroying order and inciting strife. To address these problems, she advised women to promote family, education, and prudence. In accordance with these beliefs, in the 1930s the CNM established an internal peace committee that collaborated with Latin American affiliates to promote harmony within and between their nations.[18] Another conservative group, the Argentine branch of the Confederación Femenina de la Paz Americana was established in 1926.[19]

Leftist pacifists were more important for this study. In 1931 Socialist women formed the Comité Pro Paz, headed by Moreau. It advocated dismantling war-related industries and military forces and fostering amity among nations through economic cooperation, the free movement of peoples and goods, and cultural, intellectual, and laborers' exchanges. Glorifying peace rather than war in the schools would reduce bellicosity, as would arbitration and an end to secret diplomacy.[20]

Samatán addressed this theme more radically. She was the secretary

of the Unión de Escritores Proletarios of Santa Fe, probably linked to the
International Union of Revolutionary Writers, founded in Moscow in 1927.
In the unión's magazine in 1932 she discerned that capitalism and the desire for profit lurked behind war. It was insufficient to denounce war; one
had to fight imperialism and exploitation. "The struggle against war forms
part of this enormous battle sculpted to forge the humanity of tomorrow,"
the future Victory Board member declared.[21] Despite the periodical's likely
ties to Communism, Samatán's political affiliation, if she had one, is unclear, and her radicalism mellowed somewhat over time.

Samatán's article coincided with the beginning of the Chaco War in
1932, which women along the political spectrum opposed. The Liga Femenina Pro Paz del Chaco, for example, circulated petitions for peace. Calling
itself "a magazine of feminine thought and connection in Ibero-American
countries," the Buenos Aires–based *Mujeres de América* promoted wom-
en's emancipation, social reform, and peace between Bolivia and Paraguay. Women throughout Argentina celebrated the treaty that ended the
fighting.[22]

This activism was tied to Europe, where pacifism, anti-imperialism, and
antifascism entwined. The Japanese invasion of Manchuria (1931–1932) led
European pacifists and leftists to hold an antiwar conference in Amsterdam
in 1932, which identified bloodshed with imperialism and capitalism. The
Amsterdam contingent congregated anew in Pleyel Hall in Paris in 1933,
after Adolf Hitler assumed power in Germany. These meetings precipitated
the founding of the World Committee against War and Fascism. The Nazi
threat led Communists to cooperate with other antifascists in these gatherings and, by 1935, in broad antifascist coalitions known as the Popular
Front, endorsed by the Communist International, or Comintern. Mobilizing women became an explicit Popular Front strategy.[23]

By this point French leftist pacifist women had realized that negotiations with fascist regimes would not temper their militarism or repres-
siveness. They shifted from total adherence to nonviolence to antagonism
toward fascism, which they regarded as the greatest impediment to peace.
Moreover, they believed that peace was tied to social justice and women's
rights; in France as in Argentina, women had not yet attained the vote.
French and other women active in the World Committee against War
and Fascism, also known as the Amsterdam-Pleyel movement, organized
a global congress in Paris in 1934 that denounced war, fascism, and the
suppression of women, which they saw as interconnected. The World Committee of Women against War and Fascism emerged from this meeting.[24]

While only one Argentine, Angélica Mendoza, may have participated
directly in the Amsterdam-Pleyel movement, many heard of it. One of the
organizers of the Paris conference was the Uruguayan feminist and physi-

cian Dr. Paulina Luisi, who frequently addressed audiences in Argentina. In 1934 Dr. Nydia Lamarque, a Communist lawyer and International Red Aid activist, spoke in Rosario on the Paris assembly and the unity of French women against war and fascism. More importantly, the Amsterdam-Pleyel movement created a transnational ideological context that considered resisting fascism and protecting the Soviet Union as essential to peace—not only had this country overthrown capitalism, but it presumably had liberated women, who were the peacemakers. A flurry of leftist peace mobilization occurred in Latin America, leading up to a congress in Montevideo in 1933 and the creation of the Communist-backed Comité Latinoamericano Contra la Guerra. Representing the comité, Lamarque visited France the following year and informed a Communist journal that politically diverse Argentine women had founded a provisional group against fascism and war.[25]

Meanwhile, the Agrupación de Intelectuales, Artistas, Periodistas y Escritores (AIAPE), an Argentine Popular Front movement that spanned national borders, was organizing. Founded in 1935, AIAPE built upon the example of a French antifascist intellectuals' association, which in turn grew out of the climate fostered by the Amsterdam-Pleyel movement. In its view, Argentina and Europe witnessed the same economic crisis that had weakened ruling-class hegemony and prompted the rise of militarized fascist groups. AIAPE battled this counterrevolutionary tide by defending liberal rights, denouncing the persecution of intellectuals, and sponsoring cultural activities. Its members claimed that so-called Nationalists imitated European fascism and subverted local interests, yet AIAPE also melded nationalism with internationalism, as well as liberalism with revolution. The organization created branches in Argentine cities and Montevideo. Artists Cecilia Marcovich and Norah Borges, human rights activist Dalila Saslavsky, and Beatriz Ludmer of Rosario joined AIAPE and eventually the Victory Board.[26]

The Popular Front had arrived in Latin America, and it incorporated women. The feminist and antifascist Movimiento de Emancipación de las Mujeres de Chile (MEMCH) and Frente Único Pro Derechos de la Mujer (FUPDM) of Mexico arose during this juncture, in 1935.[27] So did another Communist-backed movement, the Argentine Agrupación Femenina Antiguerrera (AFA). Perhaps this was the incipient group to which Lamarque referred. The AFA was a women's peace network with centers in Buenos Aires, Córdoba, Mendoza, and Miramar, Buenos Aires. Among its three thousand to four thousand members were workers, employees, housewives, students, teachers and other professionals, and intellectuals of varied political persuasions, including Socialists and anarchists. The AFA argued for a ceasefire in the Chaco, disarmament, reduced military service, slashing military budgets in favor of cultural and social projects, an end to militaristic education in the schools, freedom for imprisoned antiwar protesters, and women's rights.[28]

According to the AFA, imperialism was largely responsible for many evils. Like other leftist groups, it accused US and British firms of using the Chaco War to gain control of the region's oil.[29] British and US political, economic, and cultural domination prevented Argentina from freely developing itself and leaving its colonial heritage behind. Intimately connected to imperialism, fascism terrorized its own people and provoked war by fueling national rivalries. To halt this bellicose movement in Argentina, the AFA demanded the suppression of local fascist militias.

The AFA believed that if women understood how war affected their everyday lives, they would become ardent pacifists. Women worked in factories that made the arms that killed their loved ones. Replacing men who were at the front, they left their homes to labor for low wages. War resulted in hunger, the rising cost of living, unemployment, the spread of disease, and family disintegration. As givers of life, women should not allow it to be destroyed, the AFA declared.

Such ideas resonated because they accorded with widely accepted views of "a woman's place." Many embraced maternalism, but not all militants in the AFA or other movements saw themselves this way.[30] Nevertheless, it was a superb tactic for unifying women and justifying their entry into the polity.

The AFA was significant for several reasons. It drew in a cross-section of women who might not have responded to feminist appeals. The AFA's distaste for capitalism made its pacifism far more radical than that of the CNM. For the AFA, as for Samatán, working for peace meant preparing for revolution. It related war and international affairs to the concerns of ordinary women, often in the face of police harassment. It also served as a training ground for future Victory Board members, including Scheiner, Oliver, and Teresa Satriano, a Communist biochemist and professor. In AFA meetings and publications, Oliver accused imperialist forces of brainwashing civilians with war propaganda.[31]

Increasingly attuned to fascist militarism abroad, Argentine women denounced the Italian invasion of Ethiopia (1935–1936). The AFA beseeched women to send medical aid there. Speaking for the group Mujeres Contra la Guerra in Rosario, Yuquerí Rojas, a Communist and future Victory Board member, urged fellow pacifists in Córdoba to campaign against Italian domination of the African nation. She recommended using Argentine foreign minister Carlos Saavedra Lamas's argument against recognizing land seized through armed conquest. Rojas thought this would undermine local movements that favored Italian fascism and the support she believed they derived from the Argentine government.[32]

Córdoba was fertile ground for activists of all stripes. As the author José Aricó pointed out, it was a border zone between traditional and modern, clerical and secular, ultra-revolutionary and ultra-reactionary. Founded in Córdoba in 1918, the University Reform campaign fought for the modernization, secularization, and democratization of higher learning, first in this province and then in Argentina and Latin America. It sparked a large progressive movement that stretched in many directions, including pacifist antifascism. Yet Córdoba also was a strong Nationalist and rightist Catholic base. Each side gathered steam as it confronted the other. It was no coincidence that the AFA and kindred groups were vigorous in this city and province, organizing chapters, cultural events, and lectures. The antiwar publication *Flecha* reported that women's activity in Córdoba was "singularly interesting" and more enthusiastic than that of men.[33]

Argentine women directly engaged with another transnational peace movement besides the Amsterdam-Pleyel movement. The Women's International League for Peace and Freedom (WILPF) arose in 1915 in opposition to World War I. Founded by suffragists, WILPF saw liberty, democracy, and women's rights as the mainstays of peace. Its French and German members leaned to the left, and the organization affiliated with the Paris conference of 1934. That year the more centrist US contingent became responsible for outreach to Latin America, and its members began to visit this area to publicize the organization and establish chapters. WILPF Committee on the Americas chair, Heloise Brainerd, observed that the "primitive Indian population" and climate of Latin America had limited its progress. Nevertheless, she believed the United States needed to abandon its superiority complex and imperialist policies toward the region and embrace a Pan-Americanism respectful of other nations. The Committee on the Americas shared Latin American suspicions of US corporate influence in the Chaco War and agreed that inequality and capitalism impeded peace, although the economic remedies it proposed were timid.[34]

WILPF inaugurated the People's Mandate campaign in 1935 to convince national leaders to utilize peaceful means of settling disputes. It sought millions of signatures worldwide for a petition demanding that governments abide by their adherence to the Kellogg-Briand Pact of 1928, which renounced war as an instrument of national policy, and to forge agreements for economic cooperation and arms reduction. The People's Mandate committee distributed the petition to the CNM, the Confederación Femenina de la Paz Americana, the Asociación Argentina de Sufragio Femenino (AASF), the AFA, and other groups. Their combined labors netted approximately eighty thousand signatures by August 1936.[35]

Women of the Argentine peace movement did not passively comply with the People's Mandate's request, as the petition contained ideas they had supported for years. The letters back and forth between South and North exchanged opinions and requested favors. The Confederación Femenina de la Paz Americana, for example, won WILPF's active backing for its cherished goal of a league to set national boundaries in South America.[36] Thus Argentine pacifist women laid the groundwork for Pan-American cooperation.

While the People's Mandate committee did not publicly address fascism at this time, Moreau did. In a radio address in mid-1936, she highlighted the significance of European events for her country. Political and economic trends connected all global inhabitants; if war broke out in Europe, it inevitably would touch Argentina. Yet the world was divided between those who favored peace, freedom, and justice as the bulwarks of democracy, and those who advocated dogmatism, authoritarianism, and a coercive social hierarchy. Eventually the democracies would need arms and popular support to defend themselves against the dictatorships. On the side of peace and democracy were women, whose reproductive roles made them pacifists by nature, although Moreau admitted that some betrayed it.[37] As had French women, Moreau reluctantly inched her way toward a new understanding of peace that included armed resistance to fascism.

Peace Conferences of 1936

Three significant peace conferences occurred in Buenos Aires in 1936. Governments of the Americas sent delegates to the official meeting. Argentine Socialists invited diverse men and women throughout South America to their "Popular Conference." Still another consisted exclusively of women. Women played roles in all of these.

Preoccupied with fascism in Europe, President Franklin Delano Roosevelt (1933–1945) called for representatives of the American nations to discuss peace in the hemisphere. The Inter-American Conference for the Maintenance of Peace took place in Buenos Aires in December 1936. With over two hundred women from the Americas observing from the galleries, several People's Mandate delegates from the United States and one from Brazil presented the petition with over a million signatures, with no concrete result.[38]

The upcoming Inter-American Conference gave the Argentine peace movement the opportunity to gather under conditions of relative freedom. Sponsored by the AFA, the AASF, Asociación Cristiana Femenina, the Unión Argentina de Mujeres (UAM), Mujeres Contra la Guerra in Rosario, and other groups, the Argentine Conference of Women for Peace met in early November. The AFA and its members Scheiner and Satriano were the key organizers. A critic dismissed it as a tiny fractious leftist gathering;

indeed, one conference officer asked the police to close it because of the Communist presence, but another convinced the authorities to reopen it. It recommended the reallocation of funds from the military budget; support for the League of Nations; the free flow of ideas, goods, and persons across borders; peace curricula in the schools; the unification of pacifist women's groups, and collaboration with like-minded women in other countries. On a more radical note, the conference called for nationalizing weapons industries to undermine international arms monopolies, as well as nationalizing natural resources to prevent the imperialist competition that participants saw as the main cause of war. Peace, it claimed, was only possible under a democratic government that respected constitutional freedoms—a jab not only at Germany and Italy but also the Argentine administration. The conference advocated the enforcement of women's labor laws, salaries equal to those of men, and women's full political and civil rights, which would enable them to promote peace.[39]

Two new associations emerged from the Argentine Conference of Women for Peace. One was the Federación Argentina de Mujeres por la Paz, representing the more leftist-tinged peace groups, the PSO, and the Communist-influenced garment workers' union. Several women associated with the conference and the federación, along with Marta Vergara of MEMCH and Frances Stewart of WILPF, discussed creating a Latin American organization that would advance Popular Front notions of women's rights, peace, antifascism, and anti-imperialism. Vergara was a Chilean journalist, feminist, and Communist; more radical than other WILPF members, Stewart had befriended Scheiner. These and other individuals founded the second association, the Confederación Continental de Mujeres por la Paz, and the Federación Argentina de Mujeres por la Paz became its local affiliate. A federación and confederación representative aligned with the Communist Party, Dr. Susana G. de Lapacó, sought contacts at the Second World Youth Congress, held at Vassar College in 1938. She then journeyed to France to confer with members of the World Committee of Women Against War and Fascism. The confederación delayed several proposed reunions, which eventually fell prey to the German-Soviet Nonaggression Pact of 1939 (more commonly known as the Molotov–Ribbentrop Pact).[40] With this agreement, the Soviet Union temporarily abandoned the Popular Front strategy.

Yet another important pacifist meeting occurred in November 1936. Socialists invited a wide array of men and women from across Latin America to a gathering in Buenos Aires that counterposed the official conference and intended to influence it. Members of Argentine women's associations led the planning commission, headed by Moreau, which used the Comité Pro Paz's points as a basis for discussion. In the end, about three hundred

Argentine groups, including those that had sponsored the Argentine Conference of Women for Peace, and citizens of other nations adhered to the Popular Conference for Peace in America. Fending off threats by the police, who claimed its organizers were Communists, Moreau and several other Socialists negotiated with the authorities, who allowed the Popular Conference for Peace in America to proceed.[41]

Moreau, the president of the Popular Conference for Peace in America, declared in her speech that "pacifism takes refuge in democracy, as war incubates in fascism," a phrase that delegates repeated among themselves. Honorary president Víctor Raúl Haya de la Torre, the imprisoned Peruvian founder of the Alianza Popular Revolucionaria Americana (APRA), blamed war on imperialism, noting that Latin American oligarchs, as its agents, used armed conflicts to distract people from internal problems. He supported the Popular Conference's call for Indo-American economic unity as a means of uplifting the nations and reducing the gap between them and industrial powers, such as the United States.[42]

While men dominated the proceedings, they reiterated numerous planks of the women's Comité Pro Paz. They urged the official Inter-American Conference for the Maintenance of Peace to broaden labor legislation to cover all rural and urban workers in the hemisphere. They also recommended equal civil, political, and economic rights for men and women, measures inserted into the agenda by Doris Stevens and Marta Vergara, members of the Inter-American Commission of Women (IACW), an intergovernmental agency discussed in the next section. The Popular Conference favored integrating women—as mothers, wives, teachers, citizens, and voters—into peace efforts. While it saw motherhood as women's primary role, as did many Latin American feminists, and ignored their participation in the labor force except as educators, it regarded them as members of civil society.[43]

Feminism and the IACW

Pacifism and the three conferences intersected with Argentine feminism.[44] The lines between women's peace and feminist groups were blurred; the former tended to advocate conceptions of women's rights, while the latter championed peace and democracy. The most important feminist groups of this period were the AASF and the UAM. Both interacted extensively with the IACW.

Affiliated with the London-based suffragist International Alliance of Women, the AASF was founded in 1931. The largest Argentine feminist movement as of the mid-1930s, it focused on voting and citizenship rights. It also was heavily involved in collecting signatures for the People's Mandate campaign and sending information on Argentine women's status to the IACW. The AASF's ties to clerics and right-wing politicians, opposition to divorce, and desire to limit suffrage to native-born literate women and naturalized women of long residence in Argentina indicated its conservatism. Despite its extensive lobbying with politicians, the vote stalled in Congress.[45]

An assault on gains already won prompted the formation of another feminist organization that embraced antifascism. In 1935–1936 Congress considered a bill that threatened to overturn married women's rights specified in the 1926 Civil Code. This proposal shocked a small circle of women into establishing the UAM in 1936. Victoria Ocampo served as president, followed in this role by Ana Rosa Schlieper de Martínez Guerrero and María Rosa Oliver. Their political differences notwithstanding—Ocampo was nonpartisan and Oliver was a Communist—these upper-class authors were close friends and collaborators in *Sur*, an antifascist literary magazine. Another blue blood, Schlieper was a Radical philanthropist. These and other members used their elite credentials to lobby public officials and recruit prominent feminists to their cause, such as Moreau; Carolina Horne de Burmeister, the aristocratic AASF head; and Dr. Elvira Rawson de Dellepiane, a physician and veteran feminist leader loosely tied to the UCR. Socialists, Communists, Radicals, the left-of-center Progressive Democrats (Partido Demócrata Progresista, PDP), and unaffiliated women joined the UAM's chapters, located in Buenos Aires, Santa Fe, and Rosario. Like the AFA, it was a Popular Front group "oriented, controlled or influenced by the Communist Party," as a party document stated. Despite its militancy, the UAM received subsidies from the national government and the federal capital's legislative council.[46]

Safeguarding married women's freedoms was not the UAM's only mission. It was dedicated to uplifting women's consciousness of their problems and those of the broader society. Elevating women culturally and spiritually, helping them develop their abilities, improving their working conditions and wages, and seeking their equality with men were among its goals. The UAM hoped to protect children from premature entry into the labor force and promote their health and education. Finally, it would foment peace and solidarity among nations.[47]

The UAM was active on many fronts. Its members investigated relevant labor laws and conditions for working women by interviewing legal experts, teachers, legislators, laborers, and union members, the first time many of them crossed class boundaries for purposes other than charity. The UAM negotiated with officials and politicians and sponsored publications and lectures on women's rights. Its chapters hosted renowned intellectuals, including Luisi and other women. The newspaper *El Mundo* published articles authored by UAM members and their international contacts on such issues as feminism, peace, social legislation, and poverty. The UAM brought together thirty-five women's groups in the Junta Pro Derechos Políticos de la Mujer, and it asked political parties to nominate women candidates and include women's rights and social welfare provisions in their platforms.[48]

Years later, Dr. Ángela Romera Vera, a lawyer and former UAM member in Santa Fe, jokingly critiqued the UAM's national officers. These *porteñas* (inhabitants of the federal capital) discussed equally meticulously whether one should first pour the milk or the tea into a cup and whether the government should legitimize children born out of wedlock. Romera admired their rejection of oligarchical norms with their dedication to social justice. "Yet when the show ended everything returned to the way it had been before."[49]

The UAM, however, did not simply consist of aristocrats, and it reached out to laborers. Romera, Samatán, who presided over the Santa Fe chapter, and other middle-class educators and professionals widened its ranks. So, too, did Socialists and Communists, and at least one well-known anarchist, Ana Piacenza, a member of Mujeres Contra la Guerra in Rosario who taught in the UAM's social work school in that city. Born into a proletarian Jewish immigrant family, Edelman belonged to the UAM. Assisted by Edelman and fellow Communist Party members, the UAM drew women workers into political debates. It distributed twenty thousand copies of a flyer titled "The Woman Who Works Demands," at the May Day 1938 labor demonstration in Buenos Aires. Denouncing the proposed change in the Civil Code as a threat to women's "honest work" and peace within the family, the flyer asked bitterly, "Do we deserve this insult?," adding that women's economic and social contributions justified the bestowal of equal rights. The UAM sponsored lectures on politics and civic culture courses taught by Dr. Dolores Madanes, a lawyer, advocate for women's prison reform, AFA member, and secretary general of the Federación Argentina de Mujeres por la Paz. It planned a women's rally in a working-class porteño neighborhood, with speakers from the PSO, the Communist-led textile union, with which the UAM had a close relationship, and other groups. The UAM's Junta Pro Derechos Políticos de la Mujer held activities for a popular audience; at one such event, the orator explained to women laborers that suffrage was needed to attain childcare facilities, better housing, school meal programs, reductions in the cost of living, and salaries equal to those of men. In this manner the UAM tried to show plebian women how legal and political issues affected their lives, although its Socialist secretary, Susana Larguía, complained of their apathy.[50]

The UAM further demonstrated its interest in workers and teachers. In 1941 the Buenos Aires center commended the Chamber of Deputies for considering a bill regulating work conducted in the home, as requested by seamstress unions, and it asked an official agency to include daycare centers, parks, and kindergartens in its plans for working-class neighborhoods. The Santa Fe chapter sponsored cultural events for educators and hospitalized women, films for children, home economics classes, and a women's legal clinic. Resembling upper-class charities, this affiliate distributed milk and clothing to needy children, whereas the Rosario branch handed out toys and candies at Christmastime.[51]

The UAM's leftist, pacifist, and antifascist allegiances were clear. The Santa Fe chapter met at the Sociedad Cosmopolita, one of this city's few progressive forums. The UAM participated in the leftist Argentine Conference of Women for Peace; supported its offshoot, the Federación Argentina de Mujeres por la Paz; and sympathized with Republican Spain. The Chilean poet Gabriela Mistral, hosted by the Santa Fe affiliate in 1938, urged women to send aid to the hard-pressed Republic. After the Spanish Civil War (1936–1939), the UAM wrote the French ambassador in 1941, urging his government not to hand Federica Montseny, a controversial anarchist and the first woman cabinet minister in Spain, now exiled in France, to the Francisco Franco regime. Accompanied by women textile workers, UAM delegates attended the antifascist Congress of Democracies in Montevideo in 1939.[52]

The UAM cultivated ties with women's groups in other countries. Samatán established relations with MEMCH leaders in Chile in 1938. The UAM sent the fruits of its research to the IACW and corresponded with its leader, Doris Stevens, and Heloise Brainerd of WILPF. The Argentine group's ideas and priorities did not always mesh with Stevens's, but, as Larguía told her, at least they could agree on the need to expand women's rights.[53]

By 1940–1941, the UAM seemed to lose impetus. Now under Oliver's direction, the Buenos Aires chapter, consisting of about one hundred members, focused on planning an exhibition called *The Woman in National Life*. It sent questionnaires to women throughout Argentina and requested materials on women's participation in multiple aspects of society. This endeavor was supposed to publicize women's achievements and win support for their aspirations, but it never took place. In 1943 the military imposed a Nationalist-influenced dictatorship, which in the following year dissolved the group.[54]

All along the UAM had faced indifference and even persecution, according to Larguía. Oliver observed that women of her class saw UAM members as "crazies" involved with matters that did not concern them, since many were well-off. Judges, policemen, and conservative politicians reproached and insulted them, and authorities arrested women for supposedly causing a public disturbance by distributing one of Ocampo's feminist writings in the streets. A well-known priest claimed the organization's desire to help unmarried mothers stimulated immorality, while religious puritans censured its subdued approval of divorce. The Jews, anarchists, and supposed traitors among the UAM's followers in Rosario aroused Nationalist enmity. Larguía complained that the UAM confronted an archconservative atmosphere. The mere utterance of the word *Communism*, she claimed, frightened women so much that they timidly accepted being little more than baby-makers.[55]

Still, the UAM did not leave everything as it had been before, as Romera contended. It helped defeat the proposed reform of the Civil Code, partly thanks to the IACW's support. UAM leaders worked with the IACW to convince the Inter-American Conference for the Maintenance of Peace in Buenos Aires in 1936 and the Eighth International Conference of American States in Lima in 1938 to recognize women's rights, with some success. A number of UAM members extended their activism through solidarity with Republican Spain and later through the Victory Board. Oliver and Schlieper became the board's vice president and president, respectively, and other UAM adherents joined its ranks. At least six Santa Fe chapter leaders formed part of the Victory Board, as did nine of the founding members of the Rosario affiliate. They contributed ideas and strategies to the board, such as cultivating ties to the lower class and kindred women outside Argentina and melding aspirations of social justice, antifascism, and women's political inclusion.[56]

The IACW converged with the UAM and other women's associations, eventually including the Victory Board. Women across the Americas, including members of WILPF and the US National Woman's Party, which advocated equal rights for women, had convinced the Sixth International Conference of American States, held in Havana in 1928, to create this official organization. It studied the legal status of women throughout the hemisphere, transmitted this information to the Pan-American Union's international conferences, and advised them on women's issues. The IACW also promoted women's rights, the first such intergovernmental agency in the world to do so. The US representative, Doris Stevens, a member of the National Woman's Party, served as IACW chair from 1928 to 1939, when it pursued peace and equal rights.[57] Stevens sought out, corresponded with, and invited Latin American feminists to join national liaison committees that supported the IACW's goals. In frequent touch with the AASF, the UAM, Confederación Femenina de la Paz Americana, Federación Argentina de Mujeres por la Paz, and Socialists, she attempted to harmonize them by placing them in such a committee.[58]

The influences went both ways. Stevens had not considered attending the Inter-American Conference for the Maintenance of Peace of 1936, which did not plan to discuss women's issues and only included a few women representatives. Nevertheless, her Argentine contacts convinced her of its importance as a space to lobby for women's rights.[59] Invited by Moreau, Stevens arrived early in Buenos Aires to attend the Popular Conference for Peace in America, which struck her as the most stirring public display of people's desire for freedom she had ever witnessed. The Popular Conference and her conversations with activist women taught Stevens that Latin Americans were struggling against authoritarianism to attain their full rights. Inspired by them, Stevens decided to press for an equal rights resolution instead of simply lobbying for the vote, as she had intended.[60]

Stevens's most productive and insightful relations with Latin Americans were with Vergara and UAM leaders. They discussed the proposed resolution, formulated strategy, coordinated lobbying efforts, and reported on their dialogues with US and Latin American officials. These exchanges helped convince Stevens of the tactical significance of mentioning social welfare and antifascism, issues that concerned her Latin American colleagues but did not interest her or People's Mandate visitors to the region. Therefore, they presented the resolution to diplomats as a means of attaining social justice and peace in the face of fascism. Supported by Stevens, the UAM's maternalist "Declaration of the Argentine Woman" beseeched the conference to pass a resolution favoring equal rights and citizenship duties for women in order to assure peace. Argentine feminist, pacifist, and Spanish Republican solidarity groups signed this document, as did a women's union in Las Breñas, Chaco, site of a future Victory Board chapter, and the Ronconi factory personnel, as already noted.[61]

In the end, the conference served as a focal point for debates on women's issues. Its delegates passed a milder resolution stating that governments should promulgate laws necessary to assure women's rights and citizenship duties. The exchanges among Argentine and other women contributed to what Marino called a "Popular Front Pan-American feminism" dedicated to women's rights, social justice, democracy, and antifascism.[62]

Future Victory Board President Ana Rosa Schlieper de Martínez Guerrero

As the 1938 Eighth International Conference of American States approached, the Argentine government selected a new IACW representative to replace the one who had resigned. When UAM president Victoria Ocampo decided she did not want the post, the UAM helped convince the administration to choose Ana Rosa Schlieper de Martínez Guerrero. Her appointment was an opportunity to expand the UAM's women's rights efforts to the international arena and learn about women's actions elsewhere. The UAM may also have thought that Schlieper's rising prestige could help push women's rights bills through congress, but it did not.[63]

Who was Schlieper, and how had she reached this post? Born in 1898, she completed her education at an aristocratic Catholic secondary school. Inspired by a priest to help others, as a teenager she set up a workshop in her home that made clothing for flood victims. Like other upper-class women, Schlieper attained stature through philanthropy rather than a profession. She and her husband, Guillermo Martínez Guerrero, a wealthy rancher and Radical leader, lived part of the year at his estate in General Madariaga, Buenos Aires province. There she bore three children, and in the 1920s established a charity that funded hospital beds and a facility for orphans and schoolgirls. Schlieper became the president of the local chapters of the Catholic philanthropy, the Conference of Ladies of St. Vincent de Paul, and of the Liga de Protección a las Jóvenes, the Argentine affiliate of an international organization that probably monitored trafficking in women. In 1933 she participated in the First Congress of Social Assistance in Buenos Aires. Schlieper's activism in Catholic and charitable circles taught her that effective social legislation required women's input, and this, she said, gave rise to her feminism. Women, she believed, could devise practical solutions to social problems, but only if they had equal rights and opportunities. The drastic global situation required women to move beyond quiescence and submissiveness. While Schlieper claimed to oppose "a grotesque struggle" with men, she served in the AASF's leadership, helped direct the UAM, and lobbied congressmen for women's suffrage.[64]

Journalists and officials tended to perceive Schlieper as an embodiment of upper-class allure and customary gender roles. Observers and photographs in the Argentine and US press highlighted her beauty, blonde hair, and whiteness. A newspaperwoman noted approvingly how she combined motherhood with feminism; a male reporter praised her as "elegant, refined, smooth, with a clear gaze and sweet visage," insisting that her soft manner of speaking differed from the aggressive tone adopted by other politically active women.[65] Schlieper's charm, elite background, and Radical connections helped her circulate easily among diplomats, businessmen, and government personnel, and negotiate with them. She was not, however, the typical socialite. Elise Musser, a US Democratic Party politician and delegate to the Inter-American Conference for the Maintenance of Peace of 1936, perceived Schlieper's efficiency and dedication to women's issues as well as her attractiveness. Unusual for women at this time, Schlieper was an experienced pilot who flew regularly from her ranch to Buenos Aires.[66] Her involvement with Popular Front Pan-American feminism and collaboration with Socialists and Communists in the UAM expanded her horizons. Schlieper's openness and fortitude belied the stereotypical images of her.

Sometimes Schlieper utilized maternalist appeals. In a radio broadcast on Pan American Day in April 1938, she observed that women in Latin America favored peace and fraternity among its peoples. A "suffering humanity" cried out for aid, and women wanted to provide it, but to do so they needed political and civil rights. Traditions and prejudice impeded many Latin American women from attaining them. They did not want to abandon their homes, but to work alongside men to help others. Indeed, motherhood had facilitated her own humanitarian efforts.[67]

As UAM president and IACW member, Schlieper addressed the Eighth International Conference of American States, held in Lima in December 1938, more forcefully. She implored delegates to forego "nice words," acknowledge women's abilities, and issue a "formal" and "transcendental" pledge that women would obtain their rights. The feminist leader dismissed the old canard that political rights would remove women from their homes; the need to support the family had already done so. Women would be better wives and mothers if they could vote and serve as legislators, for they would influence laws to aid the family and help prevent wars that would kill their children. No longer "impassive witness[es]," women should be able to use their "moral sense" and understanding to save humanity. Schlieper predicted that the Argentine woman would soon exercise her full rights; as a "rational, conscious and cultured being," she deserved them.[68] Her speech combined maternalist and nonmaternalist arguments.

Conflict surrounded the Eighth International Conference of American States. The Roosevelt administration wanted to remove Stevens from the IACW because of her equal rights stance and conservatism on other issues. Regarding the embattled chair as domineering, imperialistic, and insufficiently antifascist, Schlieper and other Latin Americans did not back her. The US government maneuvered Stevens into resigning in 1939 and named Mary Winslow, a Women's Trade Union League activist, functionary in the US Department of Labor Women's Bureau, and strong opponent of equal rights, to take her place. Schlieper, Larguía, and the MEMCH representative Graciela Mandujano spurned housing offered by the Peruvian dictatorship, which they considered fascist. Furthermore, Schlieper faced opposition in the Argentine delegation. It abstained from voting on the Lima Declaration in Favor of Women's Rights, which stated that women merited political and civil equality and full protection in their work. The Argentines justified their abstention on the grounds that these issues were local rather than international.[69]

Previously, the IACW enjoyed independence within the Pan American Union (PAU), and its members owed allegiance to the women's groups to which they belonged within their countries. The Lima assembly recognized the IACW as a permanent organization to advise PAU conferences on measures to improve women's status, with each commissioner appointed by her government. As the IACW became a subsidiary of the PAU, and the members were responsible to the governments that appointed them, the IACW lost autonomy, although it gained stability and some official financing and support.

The Eighth International Conference of American States solidified Popular Front Pan-American feminism. Its proponents, including Schlieper, came together at the meeting and substituted a Latin American movement for Stevens's colonialist rule. The Conference's antifascist and anti-imperialist statements satisfied them. One was the Declaration of the Principles of American Solidarity, which included democracy, peace, humanitarianism, racial and religious tolerance, and the determination to resist foreign interference. The Declaration of American Principles called for nonintervention in the hemisphere and opposition to force.[70]

After the Eighth International Conference of American States, in 1939, Schlieper became the new IACW head. The US Department of State had picked her, partly because it perceived her as a beautiful philanthropist unlikely to cause political dissension.[71] She soon defied this impression. Insisting she could not move to Washington, DC, she set up headquarters in Buenos Aires, although the executive secretary remained in the United States. Other IACW members who lived in or near Washington opposed this change, but it nevertheless took place. Vergara supported it because she thought it would boost Latin American feminism. One wonders if Schlieper made this decision simply because she lived far from the United States, or if she thought that it would signal that Latin American women were setting the IACW's agenda. To justify her action, she wrote Nelson Rockefeller of the Office of Inter-American Affairs, which had strong ties with the IACW. Congratulating him on his agency's defense of democracy in the Americas, Schlieper claimed she was following its lead by making the Buenos Aires office a space of guidance for US visitors and conciliation. Backing Schlieper's decision, Winslow described her as an extremely capable and charming woman who had secured Argentine government funding for the IACW office and expenses. The two women became friends during Winslow's visit to Buenos Aires in 1940.[72]

Mary Cannon of the Women's Bureau also spent considerable time with Schlieper in 1941 when she was touring South America, investigating conditions for women workers and meeting with groups interested in their welfare. The IACW president invited Cannon to use the organization's facilities and helped her make contacts. Cannon had a very favorable impression of Schlieper and the local IACW secretary, Angélica Mendoza, who was knowledgeable on unions and other organizations relevant to Cannon's research.[73] Schlieper reinforced ties with these and other US government officials when she traveled to the United States each year to preside over annual IACW conferences and address women's associations.

In a speech delivered to a Catholic women's gathering in Detroit in 1940, and in the presence of the prominent reformist Archbishop Edward Mooney, Schlieper explained that she had aimed to unite Argentine women to consolidate their social labors. But she came to realize that given the critical world situation, working within one's nation's boundaries was insufficient. More than ever, women in the Americas had to base their efforts on cooperation and understanding among all its inhabitants, regardless of race, creed, or sex. Identifying herself as a Catholic, Schlieper reminded her listeners that God had said we must love one another.[74] Her acceptance of diversity was also evident in her support for bringing child war refugees, including Jews, to the Americas and Palestine.[75]

Her IACW duties and Mendoza's presence also reveal much about the Victory Board's future president. A former teacher, Mendoza had been jailed for participating in union struggles. She joined the Communist Party and later the Trotskyist Communist Workers Party, which chose her as its candidate in the presidential elections of 1928, the first Argentine woman to be nominated for this position. She may have attended the antiwar conference of 1932 in Amsterdam. Leaving partisan politics, Mendoza published leftist writings, including a book describing her prison experiences, earned a degree at the University of Buenos Aires, and in 1948 a doctorate in philosophy at Columbia University.[76] Cannon and Schlieper drew upon her firsthand knowledge of the labor movement. Since the IACW president probably knew of Mendoza's radical past, the fact that she hired her further demonstrates her willingness to collaborate with people of varied political persuasions. Equally noteworthy is the fact that as a philanthropist, UAM leader, and IACW president charged with collecting data on women's work and status, Schlieper was knowledgeable about Argentine social conditions.

Solidarity with the Spanish Republic

By the time of the three conferences of 1936, the Spanish Civil War had broken out. This conflict evoked strong emotions in Argentina, as it did throughout Europe and the Americas. The tragedy of a motherland that had finally established a progressive republic and now fought for its life against a counterrevolutionary insurgency won tremendous sympathy from Argentines of many backgrounds.[77] It reminded them of their own country's plight since 1930, when the military allied with rightists overturned its short-lived democracy. Italian and German backing for the rebels underlined the threat of fascist aggression and convinced a broad spectrum to join the pro-Republican cause. Giving further impetus to local antifascists—and fascists—was the notion that a Republican victory would strengthen democratic forces in Argentina, whereas a rightist victory would benefit the Nationalists, conservatives, and clericalists, who supported Francisco Franco and his forces. In her words, Edelman and her husband "tilted passionately toward the movement of solidarity with Spain, which stirred up the massive adhesion of our people."[78] They were among the Argentine women and men who joined the Republicans in Spain.

Oliver's testimony illustrates the significance of this transnational struggle for many Argentine antifascist women. Argentine liberals and leftists had denigrated Spain as reactionary and backward. As a student, Oliver had identified with Indigenous and independence struggles against the Spanish empire. Gradually she comprehended that these revolutions represented progressive forces—including in Spain—warring against regressive ones. When the Republic arose in 1931, her generation began to look to Spain for new ideas. Oliver and others believed that the Republic was fighting for everything they valued, and their future depended on its destiny. Fearing that defeat could hinder revolutionary change throughout the world, Oliver and her peers ardently backed the Republicans.[79]

These ideals prompted Oliver to join other intellectuals, including Spanish exiles, in organizing benefits and gathering supplies. Government repression made the members of her circle double their efforts and sing while they worked; Oliver never heard so much singing, nor did she ever sing as much or as enthusiastically. Anthems from the Spanish front assuaged political disagreements, tightened their solidarity, and helped them cope with fear and frustration.[80]

The passions aroused by the Spanish conflagration reinforced the pacifist shift to antifascism. Did peace activists genuinely oppose war if they supported Republican combat against the rebels? In their minds they did by equating war with fascist bloodshed in Ethiopia and Spain and fascist destruction of hard-won rights, as was evident in the Asociación Femenina Antiguerrera's letter to León Blum in 1937. This women's group in Mendoza, probably the AFA affiliate, urged the French president to take steps to prevent Italian and German troops from entering Spain and converting a civil war into a "fascist invasion." Democratic passivity was allowing fascist countries to destroy the legacy of the French Revolution, they claimed. A rebel triumph would incite these powers to carry out a larger war, and France and the rest of the democratic world would directly "suffer the consequences." Peacemaking meant preventing further killing and strengthening democracy, which the Asociación Femenina Antiguerrera saw as the "synonym" of peace. President Clementina R. de García and interim secretary Teresa Rebasti de Basso, future Victory Board members, signed the prophetic letter.[81]

The AFA, Socialists, anarchists, and small nonpartisan groups such as Ronconi and her factory workers were among the many women who sent goods to the Spanish Republic.[82] Of all the women's organizations, the Comité Argentino de Mujeres Pro Huérfanos Españoles (CAMHE) was the most significant, although we know little about it. A founder and leader of this Communist-aligned Popular Front organization, Edelman described it as the first mass political movement of women in Argentina. Its links to Communism were loose in some areas outside Buenos Aires, where Socialists and other political groups were stronger. CAMHE's 150 branches sent their handmade clothing and other items to the children of slain Republican soldiers and sponsored childcare facilities for them. Answering the plea of the renowned Spanish Communist "La Pasionaria" (Isidora Dolores Ibárruri Gómez), CAMHE members prepared five thousand sets of baby garments and dispatched them to Barcelona.[83] These aid givers practiced a motherly, hands-on style of transnational solidarity that invested them in the cause and helped them feel close to the orphans they clothed and sheltered.

Although CAMHE recruited and worked in a maternalistic fashion, its goals were unconventional. Its activities supported a revolutionary Spanish government that, albeit briefly, instituted democracy, curbed the Catholic Church, initiated land reform, and incorporated women, workers, and peasants into the political system, with attendant changes in women's roles. While maternalism may have attracted numerous women, once they entered CAMHE, many acquired political convictions that transcended this belief. They contested fascism, capitalism, and inequality and promoted women's citizenship in Argentina as well as Spain. Numerous women involved in pro-Republican solidarity would enter the Victory Board and other progressive groups.

Scheiner argued that one must apply "the drama of Spain to our own drama," for events at home were evolving in that direction. She urged Argentines to imitate the Spanish example and create a Popular Front. Whereas male efforts to establish a Popular Front alliance of political parties faltered, many women took matters into their own hands by forming CAMHE, the UAM, the AFA, and other Popular Front groups, eventually including the Victory Board.[84]

Reactions to World War II

The outbreak of World War II in September 1939 split antifascists. Communists in particular received much criticism for deserting the ranks. A variety of anti-Axis groups arose, some of which sent aid to the Allies, whereas others, like Acción Argentina, concentrated on strengthening democratic beliefs and denouncing pro-Axis activities. Women were vocal Acción Argentina members.

Preoccupied with defending the Soviet Union and its Nonaggression Pact with Germany, Communists abruptly shifted from advocating the Popular Front to emphasizing class struggle, neutrality, and anti-imperialist nationalism. While dampening their invectives against fascism, they claimed that they still opposed it but also opposed the war, which represented a clash between rival imperialisms. Communists charged the colonialist powers Great Britain and France with hypocrisy for claiming to fight for democracy while having allowed the destruction of Republican Spain. Bitterly decrying the abandonment of Spain, anarchists shared some of these beliefs. In their view, capitalists were behind the conflict and laborers would be the victims. More resolutely anti-Nazi than the Soviet Union at this moment, however, anarchists believed in combating fascism to gain a victory for workers, not for the bourgeoisie.[85]

Contesting anarchist and Communist depictions of strife between competing imperialisms, Moreau defended the British Empire as one that generally treated its subject peoples peacefully and accorded them relative autonomy. It represented the "grand expansionism of the white man," who had brought advanced technology and ideas to less civilized areas. In contrast, Germans were taking over nations that were equally advanced; its imperialism and that of Italy were based on fanatical totalitarianism and militarism. Moreau hoped for the victory of Great Britain, the birthplace of democracy and freedom.[86]

Unlike her colleague, Socialist Josefina Marpons defended the Allies without resorting to racism or lauding British imperialism. "Argentinism" and "Americanism" ordinarily justified anti-imperialism, but at this critical time an anti-imperialist stance meant siding with fascists who were fighting the democracies. Whatever their sins, Britain and France formed a dike against the Axis, and for this reason alone one should support them. Pacifism, which she embraced, did not mean "Buddhist contemplation." Helping the Allies, voicing Argentine ideals, and guarding against "those who sow confusion and intrigues," meaning Communists and Nationalists, strengthened the country and did not affect Argentine neutrality.[87]

Socialist women issued a statement denouncing fascists for invading peaceful countries, justifying war as a means of acquiring raw materials, persecuting their own populations, and attacking the "free human person." As inheritors of European culture, the authors proclaimed they would defend it. While praising Argentine neutrality they called for support of local "anti-totalitarian" forces. Socialist women forwarded this declaration to WILPF, which replied that the war illustrated the failure of male-dominated rule, grounded in killing, and the need for women's political participation to create genuine fellowship among peoples. It hoped that Argentine women would soon acquire the political equality they deserved to help attain this goal.[88]

The fall of France to German forces in May-June 1940 traumatized many Argentines, who revered its culture and revolutionary legacy. In her "Letter to France," a heartbroken Ocampo lamented that she could not help this cherished nation despite her desperate wish to return a little of what it had given her. Yet Argentines believed in France and knew it too well to doubt its eventual victory.[89]

Ocampo and other Francophiles founded a new antifascist group, Acción Argentina, in May 1940. Acción Argentina included Socialists, Radicals, Progressive Democrats, and conservatives, and excluded Communists. For the first time since independence, it declared, Argentina was in danger; those who failed to understand this (namely, Communists) could fall prey to those who sought to undermine national unity and foment weakness (Nationalists). Rather than view the war as a struggle between two imperialisms, it was vital to recognize that one side threatened the world and opposed the principles that had long guided the Argentine nation. Acción Argentina did not want to suffer the fate of Czechoslovakia and Poland; instead, it wanted to protect and reinforce the country's freedoms.[90]

Like other antifascists, Acción Argentina saw the internal and external contexts as entwined. Argentina's destiny rested on democracy in Europe, which was under siege, and in turn Europe's fate depended in part on strengthening Argentine democracy. Argentina should cooperate with hemispheric efforts to resist German aggression from the outside and "fifth column" (pro-Axis) threats from within.[91]

While affirming support for Argentine neutrality, Acción Argentina spokespersons questioned it. Moreau, for example, wondered whether this policy meant anything after the German conquest of nonaligned Denmark, Norway, and the Netherlands. Furthermore, in the name of neutrality, the government permitted the circulation of fascist propaganda, yet confiscated leftist publications. She concluded that rightists used neutrality to achieve their own ends.[92]

As Acción Argentina grew, it offered solutions to internal problems. Opening markets in the Americas, developing industry and mining, distributing lands and decreasing rents, reducing the cost of living, building modestly priced housing, and equalizing men's and women's wages were among its proposals to meet wartime economic challenges, lower inequality, and thus strengthen democracy. To augment local freedoms and constitutional rule, Acción Argentina men examined Argentine traditions, pointed out electoral fraud and government abuses, and denounced fascist sympathizers. They publicized these issues in speeches, the press, publications, meetings with teachers, rallies, and conferences called *cabildos abiertos*, which evoked the reunions that played crucial roles in Argentine independence. They also lobbied with authorities. Acción Argentina leaders tended to be prominent businessmen, professionals, and politicians. The group's prestige along with its message influenced many to join. Thousands of men and women flocked to what became the largest Argentine antifascist organization.[93]

Ocampo was the only woman in Acción Argentina's central leadership between 1940 and 1942; after that date, there were none. Schlieper, however, belonged to the first executive committee in the capital, and she attended the *cabildo abierto* of 1941. Other women participated through the Acción Argentina Central Feminine Commission in Buenos Aires and local commissions attached to Acción Argentina male chapters throughout the country. Cristina Correa Morales de Aparicio, a feminist intellectual and translator, was the commission secretary general, and Moreau, Rawson, and the writer Adriana Piquet de Leumann were among its main activists. The Central Feminine Commission tended to follow its male colleagues' lead, distributing pro-democracy flyers with gender-neutral slogans, yet sometimes tailoring its messages and activities for a female constituency. The commission wooed working-class families with free parties and films and sent delegates throughout Argentina to establish affiliates and give speeches, sharing podiums with men. Its orators addressed totalitarianism, fifth column threats, women and democracy, and Pan-Americanism and entreated audiences to struggle for a free society. In late 1940, the Central Feminine Commission requested signatures for a petition stating that "Argentine women, mothers and teachers, workers and university personnel, united by . . . love of the fatherland," wanted to safeguard homes, schools, and democracy. It asked the administration to assure respect for Argentine laws, sovereignty, and history, and prevent military, civilian, and educational authorities from supporting totalitarianism. Its missive to Congress in May 1941 pointed out that while women lacked formal political roles, they were concerned with problems such as unemployment and the vociferous opponents of democracy, and this body's apparent indifference to these matters was unpatriotic. While they asserted themselves in the political sphere, however, Acción Argentina women exercised little power in the organization.[94]

Although Acción Argentina endorsed sending aid to the Allies, initially its followers did not engage in this form of solidarity. Women connected to combatant and occupied nations stepped into the breach. The British Women's Patriotic Committee, a federation of 145 groups across Argentina, arose with the onset of war. The committee made garments and raised money for British soldiers. The Unión Femenina de Francia Libre, the women's section of the Comité de Gaulle, formed in April 1941 and spread throughout the nation. Its thirty constituent groups knitted and sewed for French soldiers and refugees in Britain and hired others to do so as well. To raise funds, its members sold flowers and homemade French confections in the Free France store and solicited contributions in their celebrations of French patriotic holidays. Polish, Dutch, Norwegian, Belgian, Greek, Yugoslavian, and Jewish groups and eventually US residents also engaged in solidarity.[95] Women of other origins collaborated with these foreign and immigrant communities. Some solidarity was spiritual. Over two hundred society women invited people of varied faiths, Argentine officials, and diplomats and citizens of the Allied and occupied countries to a mass honoring civilian hostages executed by Nazis in the lands they dominated.[96]

Even the Communist Party participated in aid efforts. Despite its support for the German-Soviet Nonaggression Pact and silence on the German and Soviet division of Poland, it was not indifferent to the suffering created by these events. Probably responding to the wishes of the party's large Eastern European Jewish contingent, the Communist-aligned Organismo de Ayuda Directa a las Víctimas Judías de la Guerra en Polonia arose in February 1940. The organismo sent money and goods to Polish Jews through the American Jewish Joint Distribution Committee; both were anti-Zionist, in contrast to the main communal organizations. It established chapters and women's committees in cities, small towns, and Jewish agricultural settlements. Dr. León Lapacó was its president, and his wife, Susana, an officer of the Federación Argentina de Mujeres por la Paz, also participated.[97] This was yet another sign of the intersections between women's pacifism, feminism, and antifascism.

In 1933 future Victory Board member Yuquerí Rojas wrote that something very different and consequential was happening for the first time: women now were playing important roles in the struggle to create a better world.[98] Beginning in 1914, Argentine women participated in interwoven movements. From the Global South, they sent aid to the Global North: to combatants in World War I, Spanish Republicans, and the Allies in World War II. Through these efforts, as well as their support for political prisoners, solidarity became a tool of ideological struggle. Many regarded World War II as a continuation of the conflict between democracy and tyranny that had begun in Spain. Opposition to militarism and dictatorship motivated this activism, which took place at the local, national, and transnational levels.

Transnational exchanges were critical for Argentine women's groups. The CNM and the AASF were affiliates of global organizations. These and other international women's associations sought Latin American collaborators. Pan-Americanism offered a space for sharing and refining ideas and uniting the hemisphere behind antifascism and women's rights. Argentine associations exchanged perspectives, tactics, and support with the IACW, WILPF, and People's Mandate. The Communist-aligned Amsterdam-Pleyel movement and related groups in Latin America and Argentina engaged in cross-border discussions of anti-imperialism, antifascism, and pacifism. Furthermore, as a response to fascism in Europe, Argentine antifascism inherently formed part of a transnational exchange.

Women of varied political persuasions mobilized for peace; in fact, they led the peace movement. In the wake of the Chaco War and a history of US interventions in Latin America, they called for greater comprehension among the American nations and signed petitions to outlaw war. For Socialists and Communists, pacifism entailed analyzing the economic roots of conflict; for Socialists, it also meant advancing toward a free union of peoples and, for Communists, advancing toward revolution. Over time, progressives realized that complete pacifism was suicidal given fascist expansionism. Peace signified freedom and liberation from exploitation, whereas fascism signified repression, militarism, and imperialist domination. Fascist warfare meant the sacrifice of husbands and sons. Since amity was only possible under democracy, a nebulous concept, a pacifist movement had to be antifascist.

Women's peace organizations were feminist to varying degrees, and the feminist ones were pacifist. Feminists struggled to awaken women's consciousness, protect the rights of married women and extend those of working women, and secure equality with men in all arenas. The ability to vote and hold office, they argued, would enhance women's ability to promote peace. This justification demonstrated the confluence between the feminist and pacifist movements. Moreover, as fascists opposed these goals, feminists were antifascists; the two were mutually constitutive.

Gender notions permeated women's activism. Preoccupied with their children's future, women supposedly felt a deeper desire for peace than men. Many Argentines believed that these sentiments and women's inculcation of harmony in the home and classroom made them natural peacemakers and antifascists. They also thought that these qualities enabled women of different backgrounds to work together. Feminists, pacifists, and antifascists used maternalism and the gendered connotations of peace to claim roles in politics and foreign affairs. Furthermore, by caring for Argentine political prisoners, Spanish Republican children, and Allied soldiers, they practiced a motherly type of solidarity. Yet they also desired rights as citizens, not only as mothers.

Except at the provincial level in San Juan (1927–) and the municipal level in Santa Fe (1927–1943, under varying rules),[99] Argentine women could not vote. Even without the franchise, activists aimed at integrating women into politics. In doing so, the Popular Front groups crossed class, ethnic, religious, political, and regional lines to appeal to a broad spectrum. To recruit women who had never been politically active, the AFA and the UAM related abstract diplomatic and ideological issues to women's daily lives. Spain's dramatic plight sparked the largest political mobilization of women in Argentina until this point.

Women of different political backgrounds joined these movements, yet Socialists and Communists were the most influential in laying the groundwork for the Victory Board. Socialists such as Moreau and contributors to the Socialist publication *Vida Femenina* developed pacifist, feminist, and antifascist thinking. Women of this party mobilized the Popular Conference for Peace in America and nourished Acción Argentina's female sector. Communist women helped shape the LADH, the AFA, AIAPE, the UAM, the Federación, CAMHE, and techniques of solidarity.

The Victory Board inherited much from these democratic struggles. It built upon its precursors' innumerable transnational exchanges. Adapting European antifascism and Popular Front Pan-American feminism, its opposition to fascism was linked to peace, democracy, women's rights, and the hope of a better world. The Victory Board justified its aid to combatants by arguing that fulfilment of these issues only was possible under democracy, which the Allies epitomized. As a Popular Front movement, the Victory Board sought to integrate women into the political arena, make broader issues relevant to women's quotidian existence, attract diverse adherents, and spread outside Buenos Aires. Like other groups, it thought that women had a "natural" interest in opposing fascism derived from their sex, but the board expressed a mixture of maternalist and non-maternalist attitudes. Both CAMHE and the Victory Board followed customary practices by making garments, but with a political twist. The Victory Board shared a nuanced and critical view of neutrality and a belief in a rigid democratic/antidemocratic binary with Moreau, Acción Argentina, and others. Finally, it too faced hostility from extreme rightists and the authorities.

The Victory Board did not arise in a vacuum. The rich experiences of women like María Ronconi de Saratino in a multitude of political causes informed its views and activities. Yet while it drew from and expanded its predecessors' efforts, it differed from them in some important respects. Before examining the board, however, one must understand another aspect of the context in which it arose—namely, the rivalry between Latin American antifascists and fascists and how this manifested itself in "conversations" on women's issues. This is the topic of the next chapter.

CHAPTER 2

DEFINING WOMEN'S ROLES IN THE ERA OF FASCISM

Transnational "Conversations" between Latin American Fascists and Antifascists, 1930–1941

In 1935 Cecy Tolentino de Souza, a Brazilian, expressed pride in the fact that she studied, worked, voted, and claimed rights equal to those of men.[1] A year later the Chilean Dr. Badilla Urrutia called for "the liberation of the woman."[2] Surprisingly, these individuals were not among the Latin American feminists and progressives who were mobilizing for women's equality. Both belonged to fascist groups: Badilla Urrutia to the Movimiento Nacional Socialista (MNS), and Souza to Ação Integralista Brasileira (AIB). One wonders why extreme rightists seemingly favored the expansion of opportunities for women or even entertained the notion of "freeing" women, which seemed antithetical to their desire for a stratified gender and class system that stressed duties rather than rights.

The previous chapter treated the evolution of Argentine women's antifascisms, explaining how they addressed fascist violence, dictatorship, militarism and, briefly, the suppression of women. I now turn to a detailed transnational analysis of women's roles and prerogatives, as Latin American progressives and radical rightists saw them, and how these notions intertwined with questions of social order. Julie Gottlieb has argued, "Before we can understand the contemporary antifascist explications and apprehensions . . . we must examine closely what they were reacting against."[3] Only then is women's antifascist militancy intelligible. For our purposes, this entails an examination of how each side—and particularly its women participants—viewed and responded to the other.

The relationship between the opinions expressed at both ends of the ideological spectrum throughout Latin America was more complicated than one might expect. Fascists and leftists/feminists not only opposed and disagreed with each other. Their debates reveal parallels and intersections as well as discord and misrepresentations. One might characterize these dialogues as a discursive formation, which Peter Ullrich and Reiner Keller defined as "social arenas, constituting themselves around contested issues, controversies, problematizations, and truth claims in which discourses compete with each other."[4] The degree to which these competitors communicated directly with each other is debatable. Nevertheless, these transnational "conversations" helped shape radical rightist and progressive identities and programs throughout the region and antifascist women's interpretations of fascism and antifascism. They explain why numerous women felt the need to fight for their rights against fascists. This, then, was the setting in which Argentine antifascist women mobilized.

This chapter juxtaposes radical rightist and leftist/feminist statements and some practices regarding women between 1930 and 1941.[5] The homegrown rightist movements and individuals under study usually were the most extreme members of what Arno Mayer called the "antirevolutionary triad" of conservatives, reactionaries, and counterrevolutionaries: they were the counterrevolutionaries, and, by the 1930s, one can consider most, if not all of them, fascists.[6] The progressives discussed here included feminists, pacifists, Socialists, Communists, and Communist sympathizers, all of whom held at least some views that many contemporaries considered radical.[7] Most of the voices are women's, but I incorporate some of men on the far right, as their pronouncements often outnumbered those of women.

Many specialists agree that one cannot comprehend rightists or leftists, counterrevolution or revolution, in isolation from each other; they are interwoven. Verónica Valdivia called attention to the "interdependence" between leftists and rightists, which she did not see as a relationship of cause and effect, or "action and reaction," but rather "as part of a same process."[8] They share the same context but address its predicaments in distinct ways. As Enzo Traverso put it, "The extremes do not meet, but their opposition may proceed from the same starting point."[9] For Latin American fascists and antifascists, the starting point was the spread of capitalism and attendant inequalities, the rise of mass politics, the Bolshevik Revolution and its program for women, and the entry of women into the urban labor force, higher education, and the professions—in other words, modernization.

In contrast to Valdivia's notion of interdependence, numerous scholars have claimed that since the French Revolution, rightists and leftists have developed precisely in relationship to each other.[10] One especially sees this operating by the mid-1930s, when what Eric Hobsbawm called an "international ideological civil war" broke out.[11] In this juncture, María Rosa Oliver and many other political activists passionately believed that one had to choose between fascism or antifascism; neutrality was impossible.[12] Fascists and antifascists were sharply setting themselves apart from the detested Other. Focusing on women's roles and rights, I trace this process of self-definition, identity formation, and mutual exclusion in Latin America that led up to the Victory Board (Junta de la Victoria).

The Context: Rightists versus Leftists

A combination of external and internal forces set off an international leftist and radical rightist surge in the 1930s. The rise of Nazi Germany catalyzed the two sides to an arguably greater degree than had the Bolshevik Revolution and Italian fascism.[13] Fascist advances in Europe and the Great Depression stimulated the transnational development of related and contrary movements in Latin America and drove their exponents to clarify their identities and strategies.

The German threat to European culture and political mores spurred antifascists into action, while at the same time the spread of fascism from Italy to Germany galvanized its sympathizers, who were convinced that it was the wave of the future. As we have seen, the Comintern responded to Adolf Hitler's assumption of power by promoting the Popular Front, which mobilized women in Latin America. The Popular Front, in turn, prompted a National Front in some locations. The Spanish Civil War fanned the flames of antifascism and fascism, drawing support and recruits from both groupings in Latin America and other places.[14]

Argentines attempted to create Popular Front and National Front party alliances. Radicals, Progressive Democrats, Communists, Socialists, and labor unions considered forming the Popular Front, whereas the proposed National Front drew upon the ruling Concordancia alliance. While Popular Front aspirants backed egalitarian political and economic goals, those of the National Front opposed Communism and what they saw as the corrupt, incompetent, and demagogic Radicals who used the Popular Front as a vehicle for regaining power. They claimed to support a moderate democracy ruled by selfless men who would curb the "capricious decisions of the obfuscated masses."[15] Similar to Nationalist beliefs, this "democracy" did not include universal male suffrage. Partisan divisions, however, prevented the consolidation of either front.

Both sides pressed to define themselves and the Other. Opponents of fascism saw it as a counterrevolution to shore up capitalism in insecure times at the expense of workers, women, and progressive forces. Antifascism signified defending democracy and securing as well as broadening gains already won by laborers and women. It stood for a better world with social justice and rights for all. A movement that upheld family, fatherland, and tradition, fascism was a counterrevolution against leftism, liberalism, democracy, and feminism. Yet its proponents also saw it as a revolutionary alternative to socialism, a nationalized version that sought social justice within a country, a people unified under a dynamic corporatist regime, change within order, and women in the home. Fascism opposed the trappings of capitalism and the bourgeois "spirit," if not bourgeois control of property. In place of struggle between classes, fascists perceived a struggle between proletarian and capitalist nations, and between those who belonged to the nation versus Jews and others who in their view did not. In these ways, as well as their penchant for violence, youth, and masculinity, fascists seemed revolutionary; indeed, Hobsbawm called them the "revolutionaries of counter-revolution." Whether they truly were revolutionary is another matter. Revolutions overturn property and power relations, but fascists gained control through alliances with conservative power holders in the antirevolutionary triad, and once in charge of government they retained capitalism, albeit a heavily regulated version thereof.[16]

Argentine leftists and rightists did not swell within a vacuum. In Latin America, widespread inequality and the authorities' inability to address the Great Depression challenged liberalism and induced changes of government, some of which opened new spaces for political participation. On the far right, women joined the Integralistas (male Camisas Verdes, female Blusas Verdes), the Chilean MNS (Nacistas), and Argentine Nationalism. Mexican president Lázaro Cárdenas's (1934–1940) sweeping reforms and sympathy for the Spanish Republic incited support and dissension. Numerous Mexican women congregated in the leftist Frente Único Pro Derechos de la Mujer (FUPDM) and counterrevolutionary Unión Nacional Sinarquista.[17] The Chilean Movimiento de Emancipación de las Mujeres de Chile (MEMCH) was another Popular Front group, as was the Argentine Comité Argentino de Mujeres Pro Huérfanos Españoles (CAMHE). Debates over women's rights and roles ensued as leftists and rightists radicalized in this decade.

Women's Emancipation, Left and Right

Antifascist and fascist women advanced disparate views on peace and women's rights, both claiming to oppose war and imperialism. Popular Front movements tied women's emancipation, social justice, and pacifism to antifascism. Fascist women did not match the transnational efforts of their rivals. Leftists blamed fascism and capitalism for suppressing women; fascists blamed liberalism, Communism, and modernity. Men on opposing sides tended to ignore women's participation in their groups.

Fascist women related their mission of class conciliation and nationalism to women's liberation. According to Blusa Verde Nilza Perez, a global war between Communists and nationalists had begun. Writing in 1937, she denounced the Comintern for attempting to destroy the family by taking women out of the home and fostering feminism. Separating people by sex when they were already divided by politics would further weaken Brazil and hand it over to Communism. It was absurd for women to issue demands while humanity was fighting for its very existence against this evil force. She and her comrades were not interested in feminist rights when those of the fatherland and Christianity were threatened. Once this struggle ended and their country was free, Brazilian women would be content and their rights—which Perez did not enumerate—assured.[18]

Counterrevolutionary women saw progressives as warlike; tranquility and their "emancipation" from Communism rested upon vanquishing the other side. The Legión Cívica Argentina's (LCA) women's branch believed that women should cultivate love and respect for the military; spread ideas of order, hierarchy, and nationalism in and outside the home; and defend the (male-headed) family. Through charity they would further contribute to social harmony.[19] LCA women and the Asociación de Damas Argentinas, with its slogan "Fatherland and Home," also kept memory of General José Félix Uriburu and his coup d'etat alive by celebrating his birthdate and congregating at his tomb.[20]

In contrast, for feminist and leftist women, implementing peace meant countering militarism, preventing armed conflicts—and more. Women at the 1934 World Congress of Women Against War and Fascism affirmed that these goals were tied to women's "total emancipation." Defying fascist regimes that had stripped women of their rights, they demanded the full gamut of civil and political freedoms, measures enabling women to combine domestic and workplace duties, equal access to education and professional and government employment, and the right of "conscious maternity"—that is, birth control.[21]

Influenced by this congress and the World Committee of Women Against War and Fascism, the Communist-linked AFA connected imperialism and fascism to the oppression of women. US and British control kept Argentina in a dependent status, which hurt women by reinforcing their subordination to men. While they had to work outside the home to support their families, economic underdevelopment limited their opportunities and increased their reliance on men's salaries. Fascism expelled women from professional, government, and industrial jobs, imprisoned them in the home, and transformed them into bearers of future soldiers.[22] Clearly, the AFA defined itself in reaction against such movements.

Perhaps because antipathy for capitalism meshed with its anti-imperialism, the AFA did not regard Latin American fascists as genuinely hostile to foreign control. Nevertheless, fascists insisted that they were. The most radical Argentine counterrevolutionaries of the 1930s–1940s, the Alianza de la Juventud Nacionalista (AJN) lambasted the domination of Yankees, foreign capital, and Jews as part of its campaign to "liberate the working masses" and create a "free, powerful and just" nation. It also demanded the return of the Malvinas/Falklands from Great Britain. Yet it did not analyze imperialism through a gendered lens. Nor did the AJN include women in its plans for "liberation" and social reform, beyond vaguely supporting motherhood and the "Christian family."[23]

Unlike the AJN, the AFA offered specific proposals to liberate women. It favored an eight-hour workday, enforcement and expansion of labor and maternity legislation, higher wages, childcare facilities, the expansion of education, and the prevention of sexual abuse. It decried male domination inside and outside the home. Since their status would only deteriorate further under fascism, to emancipate themselves women would have to struggle against its local and international manifestations.[24] Antifascism and feminism were interdependent.

The First National Congress of Women in Uruguay, held in Montevideo in April 1936, upheld such stances. Urban and rural workers, Afro-Uruguayans, Communists, feminists, and Argentine and Cuban delegates attended the conference. Like the AFA, they alternated their demands for women's rights and the alleviation of poverty with condemnations of fascism and war. AFA representative Marta Pastoriza called for the repression of armed fascists in Argentina. Negotiations with fascists were useless, argued Sofía Arzarello, a Uruguayan Communist-aligned poet, since they did not honor agreements. One could not defeat fascism through Christian love; women would have to fight this threat combatively and tenaciously.[25]

While the AFA supported women's emancipation, it did not explicitly mobilize women to achieve it. This implied that contesting and eventually quelling warfare, imperialism, and fascism would automatically liberate women. Communist leaders directed the AFA and its spin-offs to focus on concerns directly related to the struggle for peace, advising them that "the woman's political and social rights should be treated . . . as aspects of issues derived from" this larger cause.[26] Peace and protection of the Soviet Union were the priorities, not women's rights.

The Communist Party, however, also backed the Unión Argentina de Mujeres (UAM), another Popular Front women's movement, which, as noted, arose in reaction against a proposal to nullify married women's rights specified in the civil code. Reminiscent of German and Italian measures, it declared that a married woman could no longer work outside the home, join a commercial or civic group, or give or receive donations without the permission of her husband, who also could challenge her management of her income and property. Aside from seeking to defeat this bill, the UAM planned to change laws that limited women's activities, campaign for new measures to improve women's working conditions and wages, and seek compliance of existing ones. The UAM expressed concern for housewives, who labored without pay, and impoverished women who sold their bodies. It dared to encourage respect and protection for wed and unwed mothers, thus subverting the category of deserving mothers to include the unmarried. Furthermore, while UAM did not explicitly argue for divorce, it hinted that it was opportune.[27]

Perhaps Communist leaders reasoned that dividing responsibilities between the UAM and the AFA would promote efficacy. Yet this strategy hurt the cause of women's rights, since the AFA was larger than the UAM and more popular in composition. Even though the AFA had agency, it faced male restraints that seemed counterproductive.

So did another movement that combined antifascism, pacifism, and a forceful advocacy of women's issues and social justice. A massive Popular Front federation of groups throughout Mexico that arose in 1935, FUPDM drew upon perhaps fifty thousand women of varied political stripes and degrees of radicalism, with Communists figuring prominently at the top. Its slogan, "For the liberation of the woman," summed up its many concerns.[28] Its diverse members and dynamic organizers pressed for improved economic, educational, and health conditions for women and families, land reform, social security, suffrage, and various community issues. Some members boldly compared unequal gender relations to unequal class relations. Nourished by connections with other progressive women of the region, FUPDM exemplified Popular Front Pan-American feminism. Over time, its fervent mobilization for the vote overshadowed other, perhaps more far-reaching, demands, yet FUPDM could not secure this goal. Communist leaders decided to curtail FUPDM's independence by incorporating it into the official Partido de la Revolución Mexicana, thus reinforcing their partnership with the ruling party in the Popular Front. This action subdued FUPDM's militancy and prevented it from negotiating effectively with the government. This was another instance of women on the left—and, as we will see, on the right—falling victim to what men considered more important.

What hampered women's liberation, according to fascists? Dr. Badilla Urrutia, a Chilean Nacista, believed liberalism was largely responsible for masculinizing women and hence curbing their true nature. The privations imposed by the liberal economic system forced women to "enter the arena of combat" and compete with men in the struggle to earn a living. Assuming men's professions and tasks caused them to neglect their training in the responsibilities of their sex. Liberalism sought to superimpose "men's heads on women's faces and bodies," which would prevent men from becoming husbands and women from becoming mothers. By differentiating between the two sexes, Nacism would "liberate" women from this "semi-slavery." Countering the leftist argument that capitalism enslaved women, radical rightists preferred to admonish liberalism and Marxism for removing women from the home, although some attributed this problem to "speculative" or "international" capitalism, usually characterized as Jewish.[29] Badilla

Urrutia attributed this subjugation to the burden of freedoms that they supposedly enjoyed under liberal regimes. These illusory liberties elevated decadent individualism above collective interests, thus fragmenting the nation and creating a spiritual wasteland that drained men and women alike. While the MNS did not seek to free women from male domination, it recognized that some men were irresponsible. Nacistas would emancipate women by replacing exploitation with cooperation among rich and poor and instructing men to fulfill their obligations. This would eliminate penury and tensions between social classes and between husbands and wives, and it would allow women to perform their domestic duties.[30] Liberating women meant sending them home.

It also meant respecting the feminine honor and decorum so integral to the radical rightist conception of women's roles. In their early years, the Chilean Nacista and Mexican Sinarquista presses rarely identified the women who gave speeches, wrote articles, or appeared in demonstrations. To do so would have offended this prized sense of modesty. Yet the main reason for downplaying women's participation was the fascist emphasis on masculinity and virility. However, leftist publications also tended to overlook women's names and presence. To obtain recognition and voice their thoughts freely, progressive women in several countries founded their own periodicals. Although the Brazilian AIB vaunted its masculinity and sometimes urged women to return home, women's names and signed articles frequently appeared in its press, which included a women's magazine. That the AIB began to recruit women early on to create a truly popular movement influenced this practice. Nevertheless, when congresses of Blusas Verdes and Camisas Verdes took place simultaneously in 1936, the leading Integralista newspaper covered the men's meeting more extensively.[31]

Integralistas shared Nacista views on liberalism's nefarious effect on women, yet they also blamed other forces for holding women in bondage. Obeying Communist orders, feminists masculinized women by encouraging them to fight against men, wear men's clothing, and enter unsuitable occupations. Manipulated by "international Jewry," the dictates of fashion further subjected women. Women married men for money to satisfy their desire for goods, rather than out of love and moral responsibility. False scientific theories that reduced everything to sex converted them into libertines and instruments of pleasure for men. Immoral films and literature further subordinated women to the reign of the flesh. Thus Integralistas not only set themselves apart from their enemies, but repudiated modernity in the form of conspicuous consumption, advertising, Freudianism, and sexual openness. According to the AIB, cultivating their feminine and spiritual qualities rather than satisfying material and sensual appetites would help women attain true freedom. At least Integralistas allotted women some agency.[32]

Integralistas partly held Communists responsible for women's subjection to vile sensual instincts. Nilza Perez argued that by destroying private property, Communists also destroyed families (at least the bourgeois version), forcing huge numbers of them to cohabit in mammoth buildings in "the most repugnant and hateful of promiscuities." These and other practices undermined marriage. Since the Soviet Union permitted divorce, marriage under these circumstances amounted to "officialized prostitution" that left women without protection. Communists saw women as sexualized bodies and reproductive animals. As shared living spaces and divorce also existed in non-Communist societies, this passage again reflected fear of modernity as well as Bolshevism.[33]

Other radical rightists entertained similar thoughts. As governor of Buenos Aires Province in the late 1930s, the Nationalist-inclined Manuel Fresco denounced institutions sheltering children as rife with immorality and free love.[34] In his view and Perez's, shared abodes inherently undermined propriety and family, as well as motherhood and homemaking. The confluence of opinions reminds us that they were part of a transnational discursive formation.

Yet unlike the Popular Front and pacifist networks that stretched across the Americas and Europe, cross-border contacts between counterrevolutionary women were scarce. The former secretary of the LCA's women's sector, Carmen Padilla Ibáñez, journeyed to Rio de Janeiro in 1936 to forge such ties. Visiting the AIB men's offices and women's branches, she pointed out similarities between the LCA and the AIB and suggested cultivating relations among kindred South American movements, with no concrete results. Brazilian and Southern Cone fascist periodicals covered movements in neighboring countries, and some male militants developed cordial relations and attended events across borders. Although ideological influences crossed boundaries, rivalries and ideological differences beset efforts to form alliances or fascist internationals. Moreover, perhaps the organizations were too preoccupied with national politics to create such links or saw little benefit in doing so. Subordinated in these movements and perhaps in their homes, women lacked the autonomy and resources to sustain such relations on their own.[35]

Homemaking and Motherhood

Unlike fascists, some leftist feminists regarded homemakers as slaves in need of liberation,[36] although they recognized that involvement in extradomestic labor had not always benefitted women. Some also insisted that women should be able to prevent pregnancy, which fascists denounced. The latter thought fascism would enable women to be genuine mothers, based on their perceptions of Italian and German policies. Feminists and fascists blamed each other for destroying women's maternal mission; each side reproduced its beliefs in the home.

Future Victory Board member Dr. Rosa Scheiner argued that women's biological role had given men a pretext for confining them to the household and controlling them financially. By pushing many women into the labor force and collective life, capitalism had liberated them somewhat from domestic servitude and economic dependence. Yet poverty and numerous obligations still shackled them. They needed full political rights to build a socialist system that would truly liberate humankind. The Catholic Church and the elite resurrected the old unjustified argument of women's maternal mission to deny them the vote, although many women had no children, those who did spent only a portion of their lives raising them, and privileged women handed their children over to servants.[37] Extending this argument, some Panamanian feminists derided the aggrandizement of motherhood as fascist.[38]

MEMCH concluded that fascist policies promoting women's "wondrous" return to the home would mean starving children, women leaving university to become unpaid domestics, and only one miserable male salary to support the family. It admitted, however, that women's incorporation into the labor force in Chile had not necessarily uplifted them. They suffered from a double day, lack of government regulation and aid, and wages unequal to those of men. They were not allowed to decide on issues that affected them, nor could they choose whether to have children or not. Given this situation, women laborers were justified to free themselves from the burden of bearing infants they could not feed or keep alive. MEMCH argued for emancipating women by allowing "conscious maternity," echoing the 1934 World Congress of Women Against War and Fascism. It supported the dissemination of contraceptives and legalization of abortion, although it hoped that the latter practice would diminish with the availability of birth control. All in all, MEMCH fought to solve these problems through "an integral liberation" that included women's biological, economic, legal, and social rights.[39]

MEMCH was not the only progressive forum to face right-wing condemnations for discussing birth control; for example, so too did the National Congress of 1936 in Uruguay.[40] Fascists strongly objected to preventing reproduction, which they regarded as women's hallowed duty and fundamental service to the nation. They also blamed the Soviet Union for robbing parents of their right to provide and care for their offspring, thus stripping marriage of its higher meaning and attacking women's mission. Integralista Belisário Penna claimed that under Communism, women were nothing more than cows providing milk for children, who belonged to the state. *A Offensiva* alleged that the Soviet government removed children from their mothers, whom it forced to leave milk each day for babies who were not theirs. This Integralista newspaper published explicit photographs of Italian women breastfeeding babies alongside images of Russian women giving babies bottles. It contended that these pictures proved that Communism converted women into "machines to manufacture slaves for the Soviet,"[41] which they differentiated from women's revered motherly roles. *A Offensiva* asserted that parents outside the Soviet Union, who "owned" their children, would raise them to be "free" men.[42] How "owners" would rear "free" children under this hierarchical familial arrangement was unclear.

The newspaper's assertions were inaccurate. It did not mention that some Soviet women volunteered to donate breast milk for needy infants, and that many working mothers nursed their children in factory crèches during working hours. Perhaps giving babies bottles struck Integralistas as dehumanizing; it might have surprised them to know that in fact the Soviet Union encouraged women to breastfeed. Nor did the Integralista press inform its readers that the Italian National Agency for Maternity and Infancy promoted the use of infant formula as well as breastfeeding. Furthermore, the photographs and descriptions seemed to contradict Integralista assurances that Benito Mussolini's Italy gave mothers respectful individual attention. Instead, they suggested that both the fascist and Soviet regimes engineered motherhood and child-rearing in assembly-line fashion.[43] Evidence to the contrary notwithstanding, Integralistas and like-minded Latin Americans claimed that fascism would liberate women from government-regimented motherhood.

In fact, many leftists also embraced women's maternal roles and denounced the other side for crippling them. AFA members and other progressives similarly criticized the German and Italian regimes, claiming that they subordinated women by converting them into baby-making machines that produced cannon fodder. Dr. Paulina Luisi pointed out that these dictatorships took over young children and indoctrinated them in militarism. Thus fascism abolished women's mission by obstructing their ability to raise their offspring, inculcate them with their values, and keep them alive.[44] The Argentine Popular Conference in 1936 countered the fascist notion of increasing the birth rate to produce soldiers with that of a maternal culture. In this environment, women would learn to be conscientious mothers, and schools would promote cooperation, peace studies, democratic values, and children's self-governance.[45]

Valuing women's engagement in social and political reproduction, Argentines of varied persuasions tore down the barriers between public and private by politicizing their homes. For rightists, motherhood involved instilling children with piety, obedience to the established order, and nationalism, whereas for feminists it meant motivating youth to challenge entrenched class and gender barriers and work for social justice. Antifascist and fascist mothers remodeled their households to represent their political beliefs. During the Spanish Civil War, CAMHE members made clothing for Spanish children at their kitchen tables, often enlisting their daughters in this task. Sewing and knitting for the progressive Spanish republic, these mothers exemplified emancipatory ideas and leftist solidarity for their families. Leftist politics and class consciousness entered their minds and homes, in many cases never to depart.[46] Politics of a very different kind entered the brains and hearths of local women who backed Francisco Franco's rebel army, much fewer in number and of more exalted status than Republican sympathizers. Some of them also made garments for Spanish orphans, whom they feared would be sent to other countries, including the Soviet Union.[47] Like CAMHE, they appealed to maternalism, but in support of Catholic counterrevolutionaries who sought to "free" Spanish men and women from leftism, democracy, anticlericalism, and feminism. Just as *franquista* women converted their households into Catholic fascist centers, CAMHE members transformed theirs into antifascist centers, and, as we will see, Blusas Verdes into AIB electoral centers. All politicized motherhood in favor of what they saw as a liberating revolution, although the leftist versions varied markedly from radical rightist ones.[48]

Feminism and Femininity, Rightist-Style

Latin American fascists agreed on "liberating" women from impediments to gender mandates, along presumed German and Italian lines. Some, like the AIB, recognized that until they assumed power and implemented new policies, they needed to accept women's work outside the home. This movement went further and appropriated the feminist label. Fascists outside Brazil were not as forward-looking or opportunistic, nor did all of their women comrades agree with them.

Latin American fascists endorsed Italian and German policies to foster large families, decrease women's enrollment in universities, remove women from the labor force, and give their jobs to unemployed men.[49] Nevertheless, neither regime managed to increase family size to its satisfaction. As the German economy recovered from the Great Depression in the mid-1930s, women reentered the labor force, generally assuming low-wage jobs coded as female. Doris Dauber, a German journalist exiled in Argentina, noted that the demand for women's labor in arms industries overshadowed Hitler's belief in women's domesticity.[50] Yet many on both ends of the political spectrum did not seem to grasp these developments.

Nacistas and Integralistas reluctantly accepted that until they controlled government and could implement a "family salary" for men that would allow women to be full-time homemakers, many women would have to earn wages. In the meantime, the AIB favored equal salaries for equal work for men and women.[51] Yet it did not rule out the possibility of women entering diverse occupations under an Integralista regime, assuming they could fulfill their domestic duties.[52] Although it still privileged mother-hood, this was a more positive view of women professionals than that of other Latin American fascist movements. In contrast, Argentine National-ists saw them as "'masculinized' women, 'inverted men,' monstruous crea-tures that defied the natural order of things."[53]

Not all Nationalist or Nationalist-leaning women, however, may have agreed. In 1941 a white-collar worker and attentive reader of the National-ist newspaper *Crisol* challenged its reporter for insisting that women were inferior to men and could not adequately perform extra-domestic labor. Moreover, she disproved the notion that women's participation in the labor force caused men to lose their jobs. "'Work was not a privilege created ex-clusively for men, but simply the means of ensuring life,'" the author con-tended, asserting that women had as much right to life as men. She might have agreed with the Cuban feminist Pilar Jorge de Tella, who in 1939 had argued for "women's right to work as a 'human and essential right.'" Letters that contested men's pronouncements, however, were rare. Nationalist jour-nalists described poor working conditions in factories, especially those that were Jewish-owned; sympathized with women laborers; and occasionally supported non-leftist union struggles.[54] They attributed working women's problems to democracy, liberalism, Communism, and Jews. Denouncing these forces and thereby promoting Nationalism rather than analyzing women's issues was the priority.

Before the 1930s, some right-wing Argentine Catholic women defend-ed the notion of women working outside the home to fulfill themselves.[55] It also occurred to some Integralistas that women might want to engage in paid labor for reasons other than need. Progressive feminists, however, endorsed this option more enthusiastically and without necessarily insist-ing on a double day, unlike rightist women. Dr. Telma Reca, a pioneering juvenile psychiatrist and future Victory Board member, wrote that she had sought a career that would allow her to explore her intellectual curiosity, think and act on her own, help others, and be self-sufficient. Her autonomy might not have pleased Integralistas. Reca's concern for her patients and frustration with the poverty that limited their ability to follow her treat-ment plans revealed a deep engagement with her profession that also may have transcended what Integralistas had in mind for women.[56]

Radical rightists insisted that the Catholic Church elevated women's status, for it regarded men and women as equals with a common spiritual end. As Blusa Verde Margarida Corbisier observed, however, they had different attributes, psychologies, and functions. She opposed "masculinist" theories that denigrated women and the "equal falsehood and abuse of 'feminist' concepts" that denied the differences between men and women. Corbisier believed that their cooperation was necessary to assure a harmonious and productive society.[57] While she distinguished herself from feminism, there was no indication that she had read feminist writings, some of which, in fact, accepted gender difference. This presumed equality notwithstanding, another AIB spokeswoman, herself a professional, approved of the fact that married women had fewer civil rights than single women and widows because this insured order in the family. Moreover, husbands deserved more rights than wives since they had more obligations.[58] She agreed implicitly with Nacistas that women need not be liberated from male domination in the household.

Despite these contradictions and disagreements, Integralistas stood out among Latin American fascists for their advanced statements on women's roles. Blusas Verdes who worked outside the home appeared in the AIB press, such as Rosa Malta Lins Albuquerque, an officer of the women's and youth branch and telephone company employee. She proclaimed that women should end their submissiveness and acquire a sense of their own self-worth and autonomy. By seeking their collaboration in instituting charitable projects in a spiritual context, Integralism, she claimed, gave women genuine aspirations.[59] Albuquerque did not say that women developed their own aspirations, but still her words imparted a sense of liberation.

Indeed, some Brazilians thought the AIB was dangerously feminist, or so Nilza Perez alleged. Inhabitants of the interior feared that the movement stood for Yankee- and Soviet-style "dissolvent and corrupting feminism." Yet upper-class women in large cities denounced Integralism for seeking to return to the past and abolish their rights. Neither was true, she insisted. The AIB taught women never to forget their roles as "mother, wife, daughter." It intended to preserve the Brazilian family and its Christian underpinnings. Integralistas wanted a "feminine" woman, one who always smiles at her husband but also a "superior" woman who will enter the university. "Integralism will make our woman—a Sèvres doll"—one who is "learned, intelligent, useful to society."[60]

One can understand why some Brazilians might have seen Blusas Verdes as feminist, despite such denials. In fact, some spokespersons described the AIB's views as "a rational feminism" and "a true, Christian and Brazilian feminism." Integralism skillfully appropriated and adapted feminist lingo to suit its purposes, while at the same time assuaging traditionalist concerns.[61] Having won the vote for literate women, feminists arguably had made greater advances in Brazil than in other Latin American countries with prominent fascist movements.[62] With its claim of being modern and revolutionary, and its desire for women's votes, Integralism needed to acknowledge feminism. While fascists theoretically opposed elections, and the Integralista leader Plínio Salgado explicitly warned Blusas Verdes that voting was passé, the AIB and the MNS ran candidates to spread their message and gain followers, given the space available for new political contenders. AIB leaders even thought it might be possible to reach power through electoral politics. The fact that literate women could vote at all levels—unlike in Argentina, Mexico, and Chile—made them a more important constituency for Integralistas than they were for groups in the other countries.[63]

Perhaps for this reason, Argentine Nationalist opinions differed markedly from those of their Brazilian peers. Whereas Nilza Perez spoke of a feminine woman who pursued higher education, Nationalists, according to Salvador Ferla, envisioned one who was "delicate, conciliatory—woman!" Her place was in the home, not in the public arena, which was the province of the "strong, audacious man." The distinction Ferla drew between "¡mujer!" and "¡hombre!" echoed the British fascist leader Oswald Mosley, who declared that "'we want men who are men, and women who are women.'" Ferla added that the United States exported feminism to foment passivity in other nations and keep them from combatting its imperialism.[64] Hardly passive, the AFA better fit Nationalist Juan Carulla's characterization of feminism as a belief that provoked revolution. In fact, an article in the Nationalist publication *Bandera Argentina* tied feminism to Moscow.[65]

Far more than Nationalism, Integralism inserted women into new roles. Tutored in ideology, public speaking, and other fields, women spread AIB doctrine in literacy courses and gave speeches to men and women. Integralistas were the first among their Latin American peers to hold women's congresses. They offered athletic training to improve women's health and strengthen them for childbearing, yet this physical activity also may have given them confidence. Blusas Verdes, some of whom had already run for and won office, were critical to the AIB's efforts to create a mass party during the campaign for the national elections scheduled for January 1938. It exhorted them to sign up to vote and required them to teach and register at least one man or woman. If necessary, Integralista women were to instruct illiterates—perhaps their domestic servants—in their homes, which would become electoral centers. Whether leaders would have pushed women into public view without the exigencies of political strategy is unclear. This may be a case of a male priority that happened to benefit women. However, AIB member or sympathizer Rosalina Coelho Lisboa, a diplomat and intermediary between President Getúlio Vargas and Plínio Salgado, favored women's political and civil rights and lobbied for them at the 1936 and 1938 Pan-American conferences. Through Integralism, women found new ways of engaging in the community and in tasks once reserved for men. In this manner, they may have experienced the self-worth and autonomy that Albuquerque encouraged.[66]

Rightist and Leftist Dissidents

Like the disgruntled Argentine office worker, some rightist—and leftist—women held more expansive notions of their rights and roles than their male comrades. Fascist men both criticized and lauded them. Equally contradictory depictions of fascist women as soldiers suggested that they deserved full citizenship. Women on either side also confronted opposition from authorities and the Other.

Blusa Verde Cecy Tolentino de Souza claimed that she and her peers were "modern" women who studied, worked, and went to the streets to defend "with manly valor" their innermost selves and beliefs. They marched alongside men to the polls, where they cast their votes "with the same freedom of thought." Integralista men and women, she contended, shared equal rights and possibilities.[67] This differed little from the Argentine Socialist leader Dr. Alicia Moreau's observation that "modern girls" were emancipating themselves through education and work, and their thoughts centered on attaining equal rights and opportunities. However, the Blusa Verde might have found fault with the low importance these young women placed on looking for husbands, at least according to Moreau.[68]

Several counterrevolutionary women outside Brazil approved of voting, despite opposition within the ranks. Nacista Isabel Carrera hailed Chilean women's attainment of municipal suffrage and their first opportunity to cast ballots in April 1935. Thus, "the brave, educated, and conscientious woman, man's true friend and cooperator" had replaced the "useless doll." She justified this new task by claiming that the city was the extension of the home. Distancing herself from feminism, Carrera contended that Nacista women could never accept a political role beyond the vote, as their duty was to care for the family and the poor. Despite her conservative maternalism, Carrera's viewpoint contrasted with that of the MNS newspaper *Trabajo*, which denounced female suffrage.[69]

In a radio address in 1932, Nationalist Isabel Giménez Bustamante happily predicted that women would soon have suffrage. Even without it, the woman had always engaged with public affairs, "serene and valiant, in her place, with true spirit of sacrifice, impelled by her great love for the fatherland." Women studied, worked, and involved themselves in many pursuits, but they were mothers above all, said the bachelorette. Accusing foreigners of undermining patriotism, and in particular immigrant Communist mothers of teaching their offspring to despise the nation, Giménez Bustamante wanted to restrict voting rights to native-born literate women, who would protect their homes, Catholic faith, and the country's social stability. The conservative feminist Asociación Argentina de Sufragio Femenino (AASF) also opposed suffrage for naturalized women, but it made an exception for those who had resided in Argentina for many years.[70] In contrast, progressive feminists wanted the vote for all women.

Giménez Bustamante's position was intolerant, but it was still more liberating for Argentine-born women than other Nationalist viewpoints. The Asociación de Damas Argentinas announced its opposition to women's suffrage a year after her remarks.[71] In 1938 *Bandera Argentina* claimed that giving women the vote was "insane." Another writer for this newspaper declared that granting political power to women would lead to social dissolution.[72]

Several radical rightist women pursued a degree of license and agency that contradicted gender norms extolled by their movements. Maria José Nunes, a single woman from Amazonas, worked as a typist in Bauru, São Paulo. Regarded as a "macho woman," she smoked, wore trousers, and proudly donned the Blusa Verde (which she revealingly called the Camisa Verde) in public. Taking part in an Integralista parade in 1934, she exchanged insults with workers, who threw stones and cigarettes at Nunes and other demonstrators. The ensuing violence left a male Integralista dead.[73]

The Brazilian Communist writer Patrícia Galvão (Pagu) may have outmatched Nunes. Her novel *Parque Industrial* (1933) attacked women's domestic and motherly roles, and her sexual freedom ridiculed the institution of marriage. Pagu hired a nurse to care for her infant son and devoted less attention to him than to her militancy and writing. Her brazenness alienated the party, which rebuked her for her bold feminism and explicit descriptions of the sexual abuse of women workers.[74] Pagu's notions of liberation far exceeded what her male comrades found permissible.

Another woman who challenged her male peers' gender notions was Teresa Bustos, a Sinarquista textile worker. Carrying its flag, she headed a procession to the burial of six slain comrades in Celaya, Guanajuato, in 1939. The police killed her and several other marchers. Ironically, she became a symbol of courage for a movement that implored women to follow her example, yet simultaneously told them to remain in the home and the rearguard.[75] Argentine Nationalist men similarly tried to restrict the women in the movement yet praised them for defying leftist aggression at a May Day rally by lifting "a threatening raised fist in the noble and significant Roman salute."[76]

Women on the left and right required fortitude to handle the animosity hurled at them.[77] The conservative Argentine newspaper *La Prensa*, for example, repudiated the militarized LCA as unsuitable territory for women.[78] Sometimes authorities targeted progressive movements, such as the AFA, whereas fascists like Nunes faced hostility from their opponents. In 1934 leftists, Integralistas, and the forces of order fired at each other during an Integralista rally in São Paulo. Shooting surrounded the Blusas Verdes. Resembling the Nationalist women at the May Day gathering, they raised their arms in the fascist salute and sang the national anthem.[79] Their fearlessness won Corbisier's admiration and helped convince her and other women to become Integralistas.[80] Maybe the AIB "liberated" them from the social prejudices that silenced and deterred them from activism, as Perez declared was one of its aims.[81] Indeed, Souza remarked on the determination and sense of autonomy that she and other Blusas Verdes shared.[82] Still, the gender notions of most Latin American fascist movements may have discouraged their women followers from being as rebellious as leftist women.

Unwilling to seek refuge in the domestic sphere, Nunes, Bustos, and women who braved leftist onslaughts were soldiers for the cause. Some rightist movements described their women followers using martial-sounding language. Iveta Ribeiro, editor of the AIB women's magazine, *Brasil Feminino*, advised the Integralista woman to "honor and dignify your Blusa Verde in the hours of moral combat for the victory of Integralism, with the same ardor and the same enthusiasm with which soldiers honor and dignify the uniform during rough fights to defend the Fatherland."[83] More explicitly, Nacistas organized women into "feminine brigades."[84] Portraying women as or comparing them to soldiers, however, threatened to undermine maternalist constructs. Circumventing the contradiction between domesticity and the military, Nacistas lauded their women comrades as "phalanxes of future mothers of the Naci State."[85] At least in part these women's childbearing destiny distinguished them from what the MNS considered the distasteful army of "red women."[86] Employing martial terms also ran the risk of suggesting that women were citizens and hence deserved the vote, as citizenship and suffrage often rested upon military service.[87] As we will see, the Victory Board adapted this notion. One could interpret the Nacistas' and Integralistas' words as liberating messages, albeit perhaps unintentional ones, consistent with the contradictory nature of counterrevolution.

Progressives and counterrevolutionaries obviously disagreed on numerous points. They held markedly different visions of the ideal society, as the former supported private ownership of the means of production, and progressives, except for moderate feminists, opposed it. Since feminists tended to link their liberation to the welfare of the entire society, and in many cases to its conversion to Socialism, this distinction was crucial. Leftists regarded class conflict as an inevitable and positive motor of change; their rivals sought to repress it. Believing in gender as well as class hierarchy, extreme rightists—and especially the men—usually saw the emancipation of women as a top-down process. Most progressives thought women should emancipate themselves.

Engaging in a discursive field, at times extreme rightists used the same terms or discussed the same problems as progressives but interpreted them differently. In the 1930s, for most fascists, liberating women meant sending them home, while feminists disputed this notion. They advocated a thorough-going liberation that would permit women to enjoy the same rights and opportunities as men. Counterrevolutionaries generally opposed such equality or obfuscated the issue. For the rightist spectrum, peace meant a disciplined, stratified society; only gradual change managed from above, if any, was acceptable. For leftist and feminist women, it signified an end to militarism, class and gender oppression, and the regimes that fostered them. They usually approved of married women who earned their own income, laying the groundwork for more egalitarian relations between husbands and wives. Most radical rightists decried this growing parity, seeing in it the seeds of family disorder, which in turn they linked to national fragmentation and decline.[88] While leftist feminists would alleviate tensions between spouses in impoverished households by directly curtailing male domination and capitalist exploitation, fascists would instruct men to fulfill their duties and urge cooperation among classes. Radical rightists like Badilla Urrutia usually preferred to remove women from the labor force and institute a family salary for men, whereas leftists favored organizing women workers to claim their rights. Both were inclined to link women's liberation to a broader vision of social change, but the rightist type was limited.

Progressives and counterrevolutionaries paralleled each other in some respects. Each thought that peace and women's liberation depended on defeating the other side; each accused the other of destroying women's mission and converting women into baby-making machines. Both politicized the home. Men on the left and right often saw women's issues as lower priorities. They dominated leftist and counterrevolutionary movements, and the latter and sometimes the former placed women members into subordinate branches. Leftist and extreme rightist men omitted women's names from publications and ignored or downplayed women's participation. Progressive and feminist women at least established their own periodicals; on the far right, only Blusas Verdes appeared to have one. While some progressive and radical rightist women alike created their own organizations, women across the ideological panorama, and especially those on the far right, found it difficult to set their own course. According to scholars Victoria González and Karen Kampwirth, this still was the case in Latin America at the end of the twentieth century.[89] Indeed, many of the rightist gender views analyzed in this chapter are apparent throughout the world today.

Another parallel was the diverse views on women's roles and rights within progressive and rightist ranks. Unsurprisingly, men of various political stripes, and particularly the counterrevolutionaries, held more restrictive notions than their women comrades, some of whom challenged them. Yet some fascist women also disagreed with each other. Furthermore, the extreme rightist movements differed among themselves, with Integralistas proposing a more robust emancipation than Nacistas, Sinarquistas, and Nationalists. In general, progressives were more consistent than their foes. However, this difference also points to a larger tendency of counterrevolutionaries—then as well as now, their ambiguous, shifting style enables them to appear backward-looking at certain moments and forward-looking at others, thus heightening their appeal. Their craftiness and deviousness must have struck feminists as menacing.

Sometimes the views of the opposing sides overlapped. Counterrevolutionaries emphasized and applauded maternalism and gender difference, as did many feminists and leftists. Progressive women and a number of extreme rightists, particularly in Brazil, apparently could agree on the need for suffrage, education, paid labor, and equal opportunities and salaries. Both sides recognized economic injustice, and UAM members and Nacistas alike favored responsible paternity. The AIB seemingly endorsed a Catholic and nationalized version of feminism. González and Kampwirth noted that, at times, rightist and progressive women have concurred on certain issues.[90] Nevertheless, as when they borrowed far-reaching phrases such as *women's liberation*, the far right's radicalism often appeared more rhetorical than substantive.[91]

Fascists did not give the impression of reading feminist or progressive statements, much less contacting their authors. Progressives seemed to have more accurate information about counterrevolutionaries than vice versa, although sometimes it lacked nuance or was outdated. Enzo Traverso discerned the "impossibility of a dialogue" between leftist and rightist extremes in this period, claiming they lacked the "common public space" and mutual respect required for such efforts. He found that a few Europeans on opposing sides tried to exchange ideas, but were unable to breach the gap. Similarly, when the Argentine Socialist Victoria Gucovsky addressed Nationalists at one of their rallies, her party expelled her.[92] Instead of mentioning specific leftists or feminists, fascists referred to amorphous forces, which, in their view, had allied to destroy bourgeois notions of femininity, family, property, and the *patria*. According to Arno Mayer, they combined "the glorification of traditional attitudes and behavior patterns with the charge these are being corrupted, subverted and defiled by conspiratorial agents and influences. . . . [a] charge [that] includes a clarion call for ritualistic purification."[93] Counterrevolutionaries demonized progressives and twisted their ideas, even as they adapted some of these notions and phrases. Progressives also defined themselves in relation to their enemies, but without appropriating their positions. All of this resembles current political practices.

But the two sides also arose out of the same process and thus were interdependent. They were reacting in different ways to modernization. Perez's denunciation of Soviet-style marriage, divorce, and living arrangements strikingly illustrated rightist fears that modernity would cause social dissolution. Yet in some respects and at different moments, she and other Blusas Verdes accepted aspects of modernity.

So why did extreme rightists seemingly favor the expansion of women's roles or even entertain the notion of "freeing" women? Their interpretations of women's emancipation did not necessarily contradict their goal of gender and class hierarchy. Even when they did, they served to demonstrate how modern and forward-looking counterrevolutionaries could be, at least in style and rhetoric. Theoretically, this trait could serve to attract popular support in the dawn of mass politics in Latin America. Without the backing of the armed forces, Catholic Church, and moderate rightists, however, such support proved insufficient to bring them to power. Precisely because of support from these sectors, only the Nationalists succeeded at times in obtaining influential government positions in the 1930s and 1940s and were constantly present until the 1990s.

Gender was—and still is—fundamental for rightists and leftists. Counterrevolutionaries saw feminism alternately as a challenge, a threat, and, especially in Brazil, a force they could not afford to ignore. Their viewpoints orbited progressive notions of women's liberation, occasionally approaching them in complicated ways. Radical rightist women intermittently combined fervent anti-leftism with a modicum of interest in political and civil rights. In turn, progressives and feminists also regarded fascism as a challenge, a threat, and a movement they could not afford to ignore. This was especially true for the Argentines, who faced long-lasting foes less willing to accommodate feminism than Integralistas or even Nacistas and had powerful allies who thought similarly on women's issues. Although the Victory Board would draw upon the ways progressives and feminists had framed their responses to fascism, it would proceed cautiously on women's rights, given rightist strength. The next chapter turns to the rise of the Victory Board, its collision with these and other obstacles, and its ideas and practices.

CHAPTER 3

KNITTING TOGETHER THE LOCAL, NATIONAL, AND TRANSNATIONAL

The Rise of the Victory Board, 1941–1943

Axis prowess on the battlefields of Europe and Asia, and their Nationalist sympathizers' visibility and impunity at home, drove many Argentines to support the Allies, despite their country's official neutrality during most of World War II. With the German invasion of the Soviet Union in June 1941, the Communist Party (Partido Comunista) veered abruptly from backing neutrality to defending the beleaguered motherland and put aside its enmity toward British and US imperialism. This shift prodded two Communists into action—the mathematician Cora Ratto, and María Rosa Oliver, writer and Unión Argentina de Mujeres (UAM) cofounder. Their goals were to furnish aid to the Allies and preserve socialism in the shape of the Soviet Union. First they recruited among fellow activists in the UAM and Spanish Republican solidarity movements. Recognizing that success depended on attracting conservative and politically disengaged women as well, they began to mobilize a broad spectrum of women along the lines of the Popular Front. Since a wide array of Argentines, including leftists, admired the Conservative British prime minister for his eloquent resistance to Nazism, the new group drew upon his aura and words. It adopted as its emblem Winston Churchill's "V for Victory," hence the name the Victory Board (Junta de la Victoria).[1] As Oliver told guests at a celebration of Churchill's birthday, it would help the warriors in the frozen Russian steppes, African deserts, and Chinese valleys; it would not stop until victory.[2]

In this chapter I examine the Victory Board and its organizational structure, democratic mission, and cultivation of self-worth and enthusiasm among its followers and their communities. I describe its resistance to fascism at home and abroad and some of its contributions to Argentine antifascism. This account treats aspects of the group's transnational, national, and regional levels from 1941 to 1943, until the eve of a mili-

tary coup d'etat that forced the Victory Board underground. The founders pieced together a sizable and complex organization, mobilized diverse
women across the country, and established campaigns that sent supplies
from the Global South to the Allies in the Global North. They drew upon
a rich history of collaboration with the transnational women's peace movement, the Inter-American Commission of Women (IACW), Popular Front
Pan-American feminism, and Spanish Republican cause. Their declarations
and actions reflected the ardent Latin American critiques of European fascism and debates with its local manifestations. These and other cross-border
connections continued throughout the Victory Board's life-span. Yet the
board also grounded itself in the national context. It represented a reaction
against Nationalism, coercive governments, and inequities, which it tied
to events sweeping the world. Local histories of resistance to exploitation
and authoritarianism helped fuel affiliates outside Buenos Aires and their
antifascist fervor, further heightened by their involvement in the Victory
Board's global campaign.

Federico Finchelstein implied that Argentine antifascists did not construct "an explicit viable alternative to fascism,"[3] yet the Victory Board did.
Its alternative was democracy, as it defined and practiced it in an increasingly harsh atmosphere. Interwoven with solidarity, inclusiveness, women's
rights, and formal and informal practices, the board's unique interpretation
of democracy underlay its words and deeds. It stood out as the Argentine
women's political group that combined size with democratic praxis and the
highest visibility and level of organization.

National and Transnational Beginnings

The Victory Board already hummed with activity before its inaugural ceremony, which linked the national and transnational. It joined the European women's "army of liberty" and US-promoted hemispheric unity against
foreign and domestic fascism. Other local threats to democracy included
government authoritarianism and possible German interventions.

In early September 1941, the Victory Board opened its headquarters on
the second floor of an old building in downtown Buenos Aires and started
to receive visitors throughout day and night. Oliver spotted "a continuous
procession of women" of different origins who climbed the worn wooden
staircase to inquire about the movement, pay membership dues, and knit
for Allied soldiers or pick up wool to knit at home. The minimum membership fee was twenty cents a month for individuals—affordable even for
workers—and ten pesos a month for groups. It announced that its collective workshops would operate daily from 9:00 a.m. to noon and 2:00
to 9:00 p.m. Young working women, professionals, socialites, writers, and

artists began knitting together, while other volunteers were telephoning, typing, organizing benefits, and welcoming guests. Amidst a cacophony of languages, informal translators circulated among the immigrants to facilitate communication. Letters and contributions from all over Argentina streamed into the bustling office.[4] Oliver helped inform diplomats and their spouses of the new organization and greeted them when they visited.[5]

The founders elected officers from among their small circle: Ratto as secretary general, Oliver as vice president, and Ana Rosa Schlieper as president. Since Ratto and Oliver had set the group into motion, it was logical to pick them for high-ranking posts. A well-known intellectual, activist, and intermediary between people of different political postures and nations, Oliver was an obvious choice for vice president. In 1942, however, she left to work for the US government (see chapter 6). While she continued to fight fascism and retained interest in the Victory Board, she no longer was intimately involved in it.[6] Ratto had been active in the Federación Universitaria Argentina (FUA), the campaign against the Chaco War, and solidarity with the Spanish Republic, through which she joined the Communist Party. German persecution of Jewish scientists disturbed this budding mathematician and influenced her antifascism.[7] A talented organizer and thinker, Ratto may have been the brain behind what became a vibrant and coordinated movement and supervisor of its operations. Schlieper also possessed excellent credentials. An Acción Argentina member, former UAM head, and IACW chair, she interacted smoothly with persons of varied political persuasions, Argentine officials, and foreign diplomats, and enjoyed extensive contacts in the Western Hemisphere. Ana Berry, a UAM colleague, thought she was facing much anguish and incomprehension in Acción Argentina.[8] Perhaps Schlieper conflicted with Acción Argentina's male domination. This may have led her to help create a new all-woman antifascist organization.

On September 13, the twenty-nine founders officially inaugurated the Victory Board's administrative center. They sold badges bearing the "V for Victory" to the distinguished audience, which included Argentine congressmen; local antifascist figures; the British ambassador's wife, Lady Marie-Armande Ovey; and Mexican, Norwegian, Danish, and Czech diplomats.[9] Starting with this ceremony, Victory Board leaders demonstrated how they combined their understandings of the national and international contexts. Schlieper told the guests that the war had crossed the ocean, alluding to fascist and authoritarian inroads in Argentina. She saw Russian and British resistance to German attacks and local struggles for liberty and democracy as intertwined.[10]

Continuing with this theme, at the Victory Board's first convention in April 1942, Ratto characterized the fledgling organization as a "national movement to help those who fought to defend the possibilities of human progress, creating at the same time the consciousness that through helping the democracies we could best defend the integrity and sovereignty of our fatherland." These statements illustrate the board's belief that World War II represented a global conflict between democracy and fascism that raged on many fronts, including neutral Argentina. Unspoken was the opinion that neutrality meant complicity with tyranny, which Schlieper only verbalized explicitly after the war. She stated that board members would contribute to the democratic cause overseas by sending clothing and supplies to the Allies, and at home they would reinforce the sense of determination and unity that the country needed to defend its independence and free institutions.[11]

World War II represented a continuation of another transnational conflict that, in their view, pitted democracy against fascism—the Spanish Civil War—and the Victory Board built upon the solidarity with Republican Spain.[12] Founders such as Dalila Saslavsky, daughter of a wealthy family of Jewish origins, Oliver's close friend, and Liga Argentina por los Derechos del Hombre (LADH) activist, had sent relief to the Spanish Republicans. She spoke at the LADH's event honoring martyrs of liberty at home and abroad on Bastille Day 1942, which again tied together Argentine and European despotism. Saslavsky recalled her despair when Western powers refused to support the hard-pressed Spanish government, thus permitting a fascist takeover. The Munich Agreement (1938) and the outbreak of war deepened her anguish, as Germans erased the universal principles of liberty, equality, and fraternity in France and other occupied countries. English, Russian, and US resistance, however, renewed her sense of hope. Saslavsky insisted that Argentina's tradition of freedom dictated helping the Allies.[13]

At the Victory Board's opening festivities, it sent a solidarity message to British and Russian women, informing them that Argentine women had founded the organization to assemble moral and material aid for "you who fight against Nazism." By defeating the common enemy, it would "push away from our fatherland and our homes the horror that today hovers over yours." The Victory Board expressed its strong support for the victory of Great Britain and the Soviet Union, which were defending the cause of free people everywhere. Loyal to Argentina's historic principle of freedom, the Victory Board saluted these women overseas and joined the "army of liberty" to which they heroically belonged.[14]

Later that month Schlieper carried another message overseas, to the United States, where she presided over the annual IACW meeting. Schlieper presented First Lady Eleanor Roosevelt, whom she knew through IACW and diplomatic circles, with a formal greeting personally signed by Victory Board members in Buenos Aires. They and many other Argentine women admired the First Lady for her public advocacy of social justice.

Mrs. Roosevelt thanked the Victory Board and wished it success, adding that at this juncture it was vital for all believers in democracy and freedom to close ranks.[15] Sharing this aim, Schlieper sought to connect Argentina and the United States, and especially the women of these two countries.[16]

Victory Board members agreed with Mrs. Roosevelt on the need to unite against threats to democracy at home as well as abroad. The Nationalists posed one of these threats. From 1930 to the early 1940s, this homegrown far-right coalition had attracted followers throughout much of Argentina. Of the kindred South American movements, it seemed the least willing to compromise with the political system or alter social and gender norms. Nationalists' support for the government's neutrality policy won adherents. The main reason for their stance was their view that Argentina's traditional neutrality in world conflicts accorded with national interests, such as trading with both sides. However, they also sympathized with Germany and Italy on ideological grounds. That Axis attacks weakened Great Britain, which had dominated Argentina, further gratified Nationalists.

Government authoritarianism also imperiled democracy. Administrations of the 1930s and early 1940s ruled through electoral fraud and persecuted leftists and other dissidents. Authorities within and outside the capital frequently repressed peaceful antifascist demonstrations, yet often seemed to tolerate Nationalist provocations and violence. In December 1941, after the creation of the Victory Board and US entry into the war, the conservative acting president, Ramón Castillo (1940–1942, president 1942–1943) obtained state of siege powers, which he used to limit freedom of assembly and the press and suspend habeas corpus. The purpose was to prevent open disagreement with official neutrality. While he cozied up to some Nationalists, Castillo did not favor the Axis. His dictatorial measures, wartime policies, and ties with civilian and military Nationalists helped him maintain power.[17]

The state of siege plagued the Victory Board and other antifascist groups. The authorities prohibited a rally supporting the American nations at war planned by Acción Argentina women. Nor did they allow the display of Allied flags at the Victory Board's first giant fundraiser, or any speeches, not even the message Eleanor Roosevelt had given Schlieper to read to Argentine women. From this point on, the Victory Board sought official guarantees of security and permission to hold events, which the government did not always keep.[18] It repressed these antifascist women in other ways as well, as discussed in the next section. This climate helps explain why the Victory Board and other progressives tended to lump Nationalists and conservative administrations together under the rubric of fascism and insist that it threatened Argentina.

The widely perceived danger of German incursions and espionage added to such fears. In 1939 British warships chased the German cruiser *Admiral Graf Spee* into the Río de la Plata. The damaged ship docked in Montevideo, where the captain scuttled it. Although the British won the Battle of the River Plate, it brought the war close to Argentina. Eventually, the Argentines interned many crew members, about a third of whom managed to escape. Some returned to their country, while rumors spread that a number remained in and spied on Argentina. Reports of Nazi espionage and infiltration in local German communities proliferated. While the Argentine government clamped down on German and other foreign-language schools, organizations, and periodicals, anxiety over possible Axis activities persisted in pro-Allied sectors (and the United States).[19] These concerns again highlighted the linkage between presumed fascist threats at home and abroad.

Initial Mobilization

Women quickly learned of the Victory Board, which was visible and outspoken from the start, unlike far rightist women's organizations. It disseminated publicity through the press, its publications, and word of mouth. Not without challenges, organizers constructed chapters by drawing upon friendships, sociability, and cultural interests. Other factors also facilitated women's participation.

To keep the Victory Board in the public eye, its press commission furnished information on meetings and fundraisers to newspapers and placed ads in them, and its propaganda commission published flyers and pamphlets.[20] Board chapters outside the federal capital also established publicity committees. Major newspapers across Argentina reported on its birth, goals, activities, national conventions of April 1942 and May 1943, and the Buenos Aires provincial convention of October 1942. In Buenos Aires, such notices appeared in newspapers ranging from the liberal-conservative *La Prensa* to the Communist *La Hora*. Perhaps because of the Victory Board's Communist ties, the Socialist *La Vanguardia* gave it less notice, preferring instead to publicize Acción Argentina, in which Socialists featured prominently. The novelty of a massive women's group untethered to the Catholic Church or a male association and headed by distinguished personalities caught the press's attention. Yet the familiarity of a movement whose members knitted and sewed for others, apparently conforming to standard gender roles, seemed appealingly nonthreatening. One should recall that journalists had complimented Schlieper for being softly feminine rather than aggressively feminist.

Members also publicized the group. Communist and pro-Spanish Republican leader Fanny Edelman, and Elida Gerbino and Elena Álvarez of the food industry and garment worker unions, respectively, who belonged to the Victory Board's national directive commission, were among the militants who spread the word among women laborers.[21] Feminists, solidarity advocates, and progressive writers and artists did the same within their organizations. Ratto and other former student activists probably contacted the FUA and its branches. Influential in small towns, teachers articulated the Victory Board's mission outside their classrooms. Once they heard of the board through these means, interested women convinced friends, relatives, and coworkers to join.

Additional factors facilitated women's activism in the Victory Board. Dues were low, and if women could not pay them, they could donate their labor. Men's participation in union, leftist, and pro-Allied groups sometimes facilitated their wives' involvement. Family support was critical; a member in a working-class suburb of Buenos Aires could dedicate time to solidarity because her husband and children performed household chores that ordinarily would have fallen to her.[22] The Victory Board offices' extended hours of operation also enabled some women to combine volunteerism with a job or family. The absence of political partisanship and male domination may have attracted many.[23] Emphasizing knitting and sewing tempered the opposition of husbands and parents and convinced homemakers that it was safe to join this presumably nonpolitical organization. Indeed, at times, the Victory Board deliberately presented itself as nonpolitical to avoid government harassment—usually in vain.[24] Exceptional circumstances—such as World War I, the Spanish Civil War, and now World War II—seemingly legitimized women's public engagement. So did the opportunity to associate with a prestigious global cause—and with prestigious socialites.

Ratto identified another circumstance that encouraged women's engagement. Whatever their class or background, they all had something that Nazism wanted to take away. This sinister force denied them their condition as thinking human beings. Each woman had a child whom she wanted to raise free of racism and hatred. Maybe she had a desire to work or study, or a belief or religious faith that she did not want to see "profaned." This speech harked back to antifascist women's embrace of both enlightened motherhood and the right to fulfill themselves through pursuits outside the home, which fascism denied. Thus, as Ratto concluded, every woman had a reason to participate in the Victory Board.[25]

And many did participate. Small groups of women began to establish chapters in neighborhoods of varied class character in the federal capital and suburbs. The Victory Board estimated it had 8,124 members in Greater Buenos Aires by April 1942.[26] Affiliates sprang up in outlying areas between the federal capital and the provincial capital of La Plata, which became the third largest hub of board activity, after Buenos Aires and Rosario. Not all who wrote, knitted, or congregated in the Victory Board's central office, however, could consistently devote time to it or afford to become dues-paying members. Because of these limitations, women slid in and out of the organization, and there were numerous sympathizers on its edges who pitched in from time to time.[27]

How did women—many of whom lacked organizing experience, according to Ratto—build these chapters? The following account of this process draws heavily from the Communist publication *La Hora*, which followed it closely, interviewed members, and promoted the fledgling movement, and especially the proceedings of the Victory Board's first national convention in April 1942, a unique and vibrant source offering the participants' words.[28] Women in Buenos Aires formed aid groups when Germany invaded the Soviet Union, and the Victory Board amalgamated them. Some women affiliated spontaneously and recruited others by knocking on doors, contacting former schoolmates, and calling on coworkers, which was the case for the Centro (downtown) "secretariat," as the *porteño* chapters were called. Twenty-one-year-old Muriel Roberts was its secretary. The granddaughter of Welsh immigrants to Patagonia, she moved to Buenos Aires to study mathematics and supported herself by working in an office. Outraged over the German occupation and treatment of Europe, Roberts joined the Victory Board because she judged women's united action to be the best means of helping democratic countries defeat Nazi "barbarism." She convinced her twenty-four officemates to affiliate, then thirty-six fellow boarders at the ACF. The recruitment drive spread to Gath y Chaves, where 250 employees joined, and then to other department stores, Casa Tow and Harrods. In April 1942 the Centro secretariat contained eight hundred members, largely from the staffs of commercial offices and retail firms. Roberts aimed to channel antifascist feelings into efficient work, and indeed hers became the most effective secretariat in Buenos Aires by this date, attracting the largest number of adherents and raising the largest sum of money.[29]

Some branches attracted women through sociability. The secretariat of Belgrano, a largely middle- to-upper middle-class barrio with numerous German-speaking Christians and Jews, initially drew upon a circle of friends who knit together. The congenial atmosphere in the house that members rented, and the lectures and concerts it accommodated, lured homemakers with leisure time who sought fellowship and cultural stimulation. There they knitted and sewed, discussed issues, attended events, and studied civic democracy. The Victory Board leadership followed a similar strategy by holding expositions and recitals at its downtown headquarters. The central offices also became a space of conviviality, with frequent afternoon receptions to honor volunteers and esteemed guests, such as Lady

Ovey. Like Unión Femenina de Francia Libre, secretariats held "teas of camaraderie."[30]

Other porteño branches struggled to overcome hurdles. The secretariat in Once, a neighborhood that included Jewish immigrants and their businesses and institutions, began shakily but settled into steady activity. Located in a working-class suburb, the Liniers secretariat could afford only a tiny office, but it utilized it to the fullest, becoming the highest producer in the first knitting campaign, described in the next section. By April 1942, relatively few had joined the secretariat of middle-class Caballito, nor had it received many donations. However, it recruited all the women workers in a neighborhood factory.[31]

The *filial* (chapter) of the Buenos Aires industrial suburb of Berazátegui confessed a different problem: skepticism and discouragement. Residents had backed the Spanish Republicans wholeheartedly, and Francisco Franco's victory disillusioned them. With some effort, Victory Board members managed to revive enthusiasm for the Republic and convince people to transfer it to the Allied cause. Now their challenge was to persuade women to support their suffering peers in Allied and fascist-occupied countries.[32] That the Victory Board supported the Spanish Republican exiles, denounced the Franco regime, and enjoyed strong ties with pro-Republican Spanish immigrants aided its cause.

Organizing Aid

The Victory Board managed to acquire materials, donations, and quarters throughout Argentina. Celebrities collaborated with its innovative fundraising. Unlike some groups, the board chose to make garments and supplies rather than hire others to do so. Administering campaigns and dispatching goods to the Allies were massive feats.

Even before the Victory Board's formal inauguration, when its central office still lacked furniture, a "mountain of wool" had accumulated there.[33] Through their previous social, charitable, and solidarity efforts, Victory Board leaders had developed contacts with entrepreneurs. It is likely that some of these wealthy friends paid for rent and installation costs, as they did when the Victory Board moved to a larger space in 1942.[34] The Nilsen Olsen and Malinski Brothers companies donated much of the first raw wool received by the board, which Ezra Teubal's firm dyed and spun into yarn. A notable Sephardi industrialist, Teubal was known for his philanthropy. Women in the barrios also utilized their own networks and familiarity with neighborhood businesses to reinforce such relationships. The Constitución secretariat obtained its headquarters from the Salmúns, a Sephardi family that sold fabrics in this district. The visibility of Jews among the donors reflected their tradition of charity and prominence in the textile and garment industries. They and non-Jewish business collaborators with the Victory Board opposed fascism for political, humanitarian, or personal reasons, such as friendships with Anglo-Argentines, as in Ronconi's case, and kinship or ethnic solidarity with inhabitants of combatant or occupied countries, as was true for Jews.[35]

The Victory Board acquired additional donations, monies, and assistance. Two porteño firms loaned trucks twice a week to collect aluminum foil and other recyclables, which the board then sold. Individuals and enterprises provided refreshments, pro-Allied films, items to raffle, equipment, and entertainment locales for the benefits the central Victory Board and its chapters held, including teas, cocktail receptions, banquets, picnics, bazaars (kermesses), soccer tournaments, lectures, dances, concerts, and movie showings. The US government expedited loans or rentals of movies and newsreels, and the British embassy sponsored a film festival organized by several secretariats. Groups of immigrant women from occupied countries contributed funds and garments. Ordinary people donated wool, used clothing, and money, sometimes solicited by board members going from door to door, or deposited in collection containers placed in businesses and homes. The Victory Board encouraged supporters to ask their guests at private parties and gatherings for contributions. It also collected funds through membership dues and sales of its magazine, *Mujeres en la Ayuda*, pamphlets, badges, "V for Victory" insignias, and coupons for specific campaigns. During "days of sacrifice," women would forego a cup of coffee, a pack of cigarettes, or an outing, and instead contribute the money to the movement. This may have represented a small sacrifice for its privileged adherents, but a sizable one for its working-class and rural ones. Following the Comité de Gaulle's initiative, the Victory Board sold flowers in the streets one day each month to wear in honor of France and of Paul Colette, a young Resistance member who shot and wounded two prominent Vichy collaborators, Pierre Laval and Marcel Déat. Colette was condemned to death, but his sentence was commuted.[36]

Entertainers and speakers contributed their services to help the Victory Board raise money. The singer Paloma Efrón ("Blackie"), film stars María Duval and Libertad Lamarque, and the reciter Berta Singerman and her sister Paulina, a comedic actress, were among the performers featured in the giant benefit shows the Victory Board staged in Luna Park and other large venues. Blanca Irurzún, a Socialist writer and educator of Santiago del Estero, was the most poetic orator who appeared at board fundraisers outside the capital. As she remarked in Santa Fe, the Victory Board knitted with wool for the wounded, while she "knit with words" a message for women on its behalf.[37]

Through such appeals the Victory Board gathered funds to purchase materials for members and supporters to make goods in the organization's offices, at home, or in cooperating factories after hours. The chapters remitted the finished products to the central Victory Board offices in Buenos Aires. The organization could have purchased garments and bandages or hired people to fabricate them, as did various groups. Unión Femenina de Francia Libre made some garments for the Allies, but it also hired women who worked in clothing industries. Men's groups that sent goods typically paid others to produce them.[38] But the Victory Board chose not to do so for several reasons. It built on a long tradition of women sewing and knitting for the needy, and for soldiers and refugees during independence and civil wars,[39] World War I, and the Spanish Civil War. In this manner the Victory Board could fit its actions within customary gender roles and simple humanitarianism, thus strengthening its appeal to ordinary homemakers and appearing nonpolitical. Perhaps most important, board leaders understood that the act of making something with their hands invested women in the project, as discussed below.

The Victory Board's aid was concrete and continuous. First was the campaign of twenty thousand sweaters, announced on August 22, 1941. As it did in all subsequent drives and fundraising, the Victory Board asked members and sympathizers to choose the destination of the item they made or the one to be made from the money donated, thus further investing them in the Allied cause. The knitters sewed a blue *V* on the sweaters earmarked for British soldiers and red on those for the Soviet; future campaigns would use white for Free (de Gaulle) France, yellow for China (an odd choice for an antiracist organization), and, after Pearl Harbor, green for the United States. It did not attach *V*s to the items it gave the International Red Cross to distribute in occupied countries.[40] No sooner did one campaign end than the next one began. Following the one for twenty thousand sweaters were the drives to produce ten thousand coats for children and infants in Allied countries and stockings for Norwegian sailors. Next came the "sanitary" campaign to prepare medical and hospital supplies, and then the one to raise money to buy materials. The climax was the huge campaign, beginning in October 1942, honoring the heroes of the Battle of Stalingrad, the enormous nearly six-month battle on the Eastern Front.[41] The Soviet defeat of Germany shifted the war to the Allies' favor. Behind the scenes of these and other special efforts, Victory Board members continued to sew, knit, and collect nonperishable food, medicine, used clothing, and recyclables. Its adherents expressed their solidarity not just through democratic verbiage and supportive messages, but through tangible results, which they displayed in expositions of the garments and other goods they made.

How did the Victory Board's aid reach the Allies? The national head-quarters handed over goods to the wives of the two British ambassadors who served during these years, first Lady Ovey and then Lady Marie Noelle Kelly; the US ambassador's spouse, Myra Armour; the British Women's Patriotic Committee; and the International Red Cross and the British Red Cross. Occasionally, individual chapters sent goods directly to the Red Cross. From time to time the Victory Board entrusted goods to particular groups, such as the four hundred pairs of knitted socks it sent to Norwegian sailors through a local committee of Norwegian women. In addition, it assembled its finished products for the *embarques*, the periodic large pooled shipments dispatched by Argentine and Uruguayan antifascist groups to the Soviet Union. The brutal Japanese occupation of China and the meager attention this received in Argentina led one member to attach yellow *V*s to the sweaters she knit during the first campaign, the only person in her chapter to do so. The war in the Pacific made it difficult to send goods there, despite the assistance of contacts in the Chinese community.[42]

Each campaign required considerable organization at the local and national levels. The central board obtained and distributed materials, sent information on how to make the items, and recorded the components it handed out and finished products it received. Fundraising for and promoting the effort were essential, as was ensuring that there would be enough women in each chapter to work on it. During the first week of every month, the Belgrano secretariat sent out groups to spread the word in the barrio and recruit volunteers. Then it established teams of fifteen to twenty women who attended the workshop regularly. The workshop was open Monday through Saturday from 2:00 to 7:30 p.m. While women could knit apparel individually, the sanitary campaign depended on coordination, since it took several women working together to assemble the more elaborate braces and bandages.[43]

Popularizing Antifascism

Meeting production quotas and deadlines, celebrating these achievements, and receiving Allied gratitude roused Victory Board members and their communities. The tangible nature of the board's project, tied to women's roles, further popularized antifascism, as did its use of the "V for Victory." The movement's appropriation of this international symbol distinguished it from Acción Argentina and the Nationalists.

The Stalingrad campaign displayed this enthusiasm. Saslavsky thought constantly of this huge battle and its drastic toll on Russian lives. Even the many non-Communists in the movement understood that these events would determine the future of the war. Thus, Victory Board members

poured their energies into what became the most significant and complicated of their campaigns. The Victory Board coordinated with other antifascist groups to set a joint goal of goods worth five million pesos and
inaugurated its drive with a Russian music concert in the Rex cinema in
Buenos Aires. Then it spread to neighborhoods and localities, where members held smaller fundraisers and solicited donations from residents, businesses, restaurants, and theaters, selling badges with small red hearts. To
garner support, the Victory Board issued a flyer, "For the Heroes of Stalingrad!," that quoted Wendell Willkie, the 1940 US Republican presidential
candidate: "It is evident that to win this war we must make it *our war*, the
war of all of us." Framing this message in maternalist terms, the flyer asked
"the woman who loves peace" if she had sewed bandages for the wounded,
knit garments for children, and in other ways helped and honored the soldiers who defended her.[44] Through these hands-on tasks, women made it
their war, as Wilkie urged. This was one of their contributions to Argentine
antifascism.

Such practices electrified Board offices and chapters, neighborhoods,
and communities. The public viewings of hand-made or assembled items
instilled pride in the women who had labored over them. Meeting deadlines for the campaigns and *embarques* incited last-minute frenzies in the
Victory Board's national headquarters and local branches. In August 1942,
when the board gathered items worth 275,800 pesos for the fourth *em-
barque*, the Spanish Republican musician Elisa Aguilar and others worked
day and night, remaining in the central workshop until 2:00 or 3:00 a.m.,
drinking coffee with milk on the run.[45] Excitement mounted in neighborhoods and towns as members raced to fulfill their production quotas on
time for the ship's departure. One of them was a Communist seamstress in
the working-class porteño barrio of Barracas who labored for two days and
nights straight to finish making clothes and jackets for the board's Stalingrad campaign. The task completed, she and her neighbors of varied political persuasions went to Luna Park for a festival bidding farewell to the ship.
The giant auditorium was so jammed with well-wishers that not even a pin
could have fit, she claimed.[46] When vessels like this one were about to sail,
all those present at the national headquarters pitched in to pack crates with
clothes, hammer them shut, and place them in piles that stretched from
the floor to the ceiling.[47] Dispatching their handmade goods and words
of solidarity overseas galvanized members, as did the countries' acknowl-
edgements of the aid they had received, duly reported in newspapers. These
statements of appreciation from the Allies—one of them authored by First
Lady Eleanor Roosevelt—and their representatives in Argentina made Victory Board members even in remote areas feel they were part of an esteemed
global cause.[48]

Furthermore, the clear and concrete nature of this project served as a rallying force, and not only within the Victory Board. Its members' steadfast sewing, knitting, and gathering of materials; dedication to their tasks; and exhibitions of their products earned widespread admiration. No doubt the conventional gendered overtones of their labors and their associations with philanthropy enhanced this reputation. Board members, along with their communities, especially working-class neighborhoods and small towns, felt invested in furnishing aid. With huge crowds attending its rallies, Acción Argentina, the largest Argentine antifascist group, also amassed support. It had 235 chapters, many more than the Victory Board, including in areas where the latter had no presence. Nevertheless, I argue that the Victory Board's emphasis on personal engagement—on making World War II *their war*—popularized antifascism around the country to a greater degree than Acción Argentina's abstract speeches, passive attendance at its public reunions, and sociability. The Victory Board also promoted sociability, but much of it centered around tables where women knitted and sewed. Significantly, a year after the Victory Board was established, Acción Argentina's Feminine Commission created the Knitters of Liberty, which donated its goods to volunteers from neutralist and subjugated countries who served in Charles de Gaulle's forces, through Unión Femenina de Francia Libre as an intermediary. Adorned with the blue and white of the Argentine flag and Acción Argentina's emblem, the garments highlighted Acción Argentina women's nationalism as well as their desire to compete with the Victory Board and capitalize on the popularity of its *ayudismo* (aid giving). Nevertheless, making clothes was not their priority.[49]

The Victory Board's symbol also popularized antifascism. In the opening ceremony Schlieper had declared that the "V for Victory" slogan did not belong to any particular country, but to all who wanted liberty. It stood for "the triumph of the spirit over matter, of civilization over barbarism, of reason over brute force, and freedom over slavery." Contesting Acción Argentina's nationalism and Nationalist extremism, this powerful international mark graced the items it made. The Victory Board's insignia featured its name atop a big *V* filled with the words ARGENTINE WOMEN'S AID TO THE COUNTRIES THAT FIGHT AGAINST NAZISM. The group's title and emblem festooned its publications, flyers, office walls, and events, cementing its association with the "V for Victory" campaign. Newspapers in Tucumán referred fondly to the Victory Board as "the entity of the V" or simply as "the V," and others may have used similar names. Many years later, the son of a member in Santa Fe called it "the V of Victory."[50] Most Argentine antifascists, and the numerous less politicized persons who simply favored an Allied victory, identified with Churchill's "V for Victory" campaign, but the Victory Board seemed to have appropriated this term. Its popularization of the symbol and what it represented was another contribution to Argentine antifascism.

Across the Nation

Women across the nation made it "their war" through the Victory Board. Spurred by board leaders' regional tours, chapters arose—but also faded. Chapter sites tended to have experienced immigration, economic growth, and labor and leftist mobilization, and the movement built upon this activism. Branches throughout Argentina confronted repression and other obstacles, yet many were hardy.

Erroneously attributing the Victory Board's creation to Eleanor Roosevelt, the newspaper *El Territorio* of Resistencia insisted that *chaqueñas* could not fail to answer the call that she and distinguished *porteñas* had issued. President María Inés Zoppi del Valle Pardo claimed that women of this city had founded the chapter she headed to highlight the budding freedom, solidarity, and idealism that had accompanied the territory's economic progress. This signaled that Chaco had "arrived," unlike the stagnant neighboring province of Corrientes,[51] which would have only two Victory Board branches in contrast to Chaco's six.

Beyond this competition for distinction, the Victory Board was spreading outside greater Buenos Aires even before its inauguration ceremony. In early September 1941, as a Moisés Ville affiliate recalled, women throughout Argentina heard that efforts were underway in the federal capital to organize "the first and largest Argentine feminine aid movement." Señoritas in the Acción Argentina chapter of nearby San Cristóbal, Santa Fe, were among those who read this news in the press and decided to form a filial. (Indeed, Acción Argentina and Victory Board members in this town continued to collaborate.) In Comodoro Rivadavia, Oberá, Mar del Plata, and other places, women were already gathering and knitting goods. These became cores of Victory Board chapters. After some negotiation, several women's circles fused to create the Rosario and Córdoba *filiales*. In Jujuy a broad aid committee asked women to help collect goods and money; when the committee realized the extent of interest, it established a Victory Board chapter. Young women and students of La Plata formulated a list of one hundred names, headed by the British vice consul's wife, whom they invited to their first Victory Board meeting in the Club Español. This Spanish organization, along with the Comité de Gaulle and Sociedad Francesa, offered the new Victory Board chapter the use of their facilities; such associations throughout the nation worked with this organization. Sometimes individuals took the initiative; in other instances chapter leaders encouraged women in neighboring communities to form their own branches. This was the case for Rosa W. de Ziperovich, the Communist educator and union militant, who, along with other members of the Palacios, Santa Fe, affiliate, helped organize one in Las Palmeras, a nearby hamlet.[52] National Victory Board figures also tapped acquaintances outside the capital to establish filiales, such as Matilda Porta Echagüe de Molinas, the philanthropist and wife of the former Santa Fe governor, Luciano Molinas, a leader of the center-left Progressive Democrats (Partido Demócrata Progresista, PDP). She presided over the Santa Fe chapter.

Victory Board dignitaries toured regions by train to raise interest, advise incipient chapters, and officiate at their opening ceremonies.[53] When their contacts met them at the train stations, for Oliver the pleasure of seeing them was "mixed with the dispiriting proof that we always were the same . . . minority." Yet the rallies organized by these tiny contingents showed that "many thought and felt like us, they shared our fervor" and lit the flame among "the indifferent, lukewarm, apathetic," even in what appeared to be unlikely locations.[54]

By April 1942, the Victory Board claimed to have about 16,000 members nationwide, with approximately 42–45 affiliates in the interior and 20 secretariats.[55] By 1943, the respective tallies had grown to 45,000 members, 113 chapters outside Buenos Aires, and 22 secretariats.[56] The actual number of members probably waxed and waned as some chapters fluctuated between periods of lethargy and activism; the Victory Board's figures may have reflected memberships at their peak or overestimations.[57] Argentine voluntary associations commonly exaggerated their sizes. The Asociación Argentina de Sufragio Femenino (AASF) had boasted of 80,000 or even 100,000 members in the 1930s, when it claimed to have sent pleas to Congress with as many or more signatures. According to Dora Barrancos, the fact that the AASF never revealed the actual signatures casts doubt on its numbers. Possibly more women were involved in the Comité Argentino de Mujeres Pro Huérfanos Españoles (CAMHE), which Edelman maintained had 150 units—more than the Victory Board's 135—but no membership statistics are available. The three groups may have been comparable in their magnitude and political engagement, but only the Victory Board coupled women's rights with a tight organization and an explicit fixation on democracy.[58]

The largest number of Victory Board affiliates were in the federal capital and provinces of Buenos Aires, Santa Fe, and Entre Ríos; followed by Córdoba, Mendoza, and Chaco Territory; then Tucumán, San Luis, Corrientes, and Misiones Territory, with two affiliates each; and one affiliate each in Santiago del Estero and Jujuy Provinces and Comodoro Rivadavia and Río Negro Territories. Acción Argentina chapters also were located in many of these sites (see table 1), suggesting the popularity of different antifascisms and the room for cooperation—or competition—among them. Except for Tucumán and Jujuy, the Victory Board was absent from the mountainous northwest, and its only Patagonian outposts were Comodoro Rivadavia; General Roca, Río Negro; and Patagones, at the southern boundary of Buenos Aires Province.

The chapter locations generally shared certain characteristics. With several exceptions, host provinces and territories had experienced significant immigration and economic growth.[59] Although the number of foreigners who settled in Tucumán was relatively small, these Spaniards, Czech and Arabic speakers, Jews, and Italians played important roles in economic development, accelerated by the construction of sugar mills and the railroad. Most of the Chaco affiliates were located in the cotton-growing zone, which had received newcomers from Eastern and southeastern Europe, Spain, and Italy. Immigrant agricultural settlements, including Italians, German speakers, and Ashkenazi Jews, abounded in Santa Fe and Entre Rios. The city of Rosario was second only to Buenos Aires in terms of its Victory Board contingent, population, immigrant presence, working-class communities, and industrial and commercial upswing. Serving as a nexus of exchange between the interior and the littoral regions, it had the largest river port in Argentina. Poles, Ukrainians, Germans, and Swedes were among the cultivators of yerba mate and tobacco in the rainforest surrounding Oberá and Picada Sueca in Misiones. A hub of oil production, Comodoro Rivadavia housed diverse inhabitants. The development of the wine industry and fruit cultivation in Mendoza also attracted immigrants, particularly from Italy, Spain, and France. Southern and Eastern Europeans migrated to the city of Córdoba, where military and raw-material processing industries had prospered since the early 1900s.[60]

The inequality that accompanied economic expansion prompted labor and leftist contention in some of these locations. The Victory Board built upon this resistance in places like Oberá. The police had long surveilled Marcos Kanner, the most important Communist and union militant in northeastern Argentina. He participated in an abortive revolution in Encarnación, Paraguay, in 1931, and numerous strikes, which frequently landed him in local and *porteña* prisons. In 1940 Kanner made Oberá his base, establishing a leftist bookstore and a branch of the Communist Party, which he had cofounded in Misiones. He directed his efforts toward yerba mate cultivators, mostly Poles and Ukrainians, and impoverished harvest workers. In 1936 the authorities had brutally repressed farmers who protested the exploitation of intermediary associations controlled by large producers, low prices, and legal disputes over the public lands they occupied. Kanner organized these small producers into a cooperative and the laborers into a union. Even the police admitted that he was a bold and gifted intellectual who helped workers win benefits. He also collected aid for the Soviet Union during World War II and exchanged blows with pro-Nazi German settlers. Scholars have debated Nazi strength in Misiones; nevertheless, many locals believed this movement was powerful and threatening. This perception, along with the social struggles, strongly influenced the Victory Board chapter in Oberá. Kanner's wife and helpmate Julia Zarza was its secretary, and other members also were married to Communist activists.[61]

La Forestal, a huge British-dominated quebracho enterprise encompassing northern Santa Fe Province and reaching into Chaco, was another scene of worker strife and Victory Board mobilization. Employer suppression and murder of strikers between 1919 and 1922 left unions in shambles and inhabitants in poverty. When labor protests resumed, Victory Board filiales arose in the company towns of Villa Ana and Villa Guillermina with worker support. Ironically, impoverishment and perhaps the need to dispel government suspicions led the two chapters to depend heavily on La Forestal management for transportation, meeting spaces, and contacts with potential donors.[62] Opposition to Nazism may have been the only opinion the unions and firm shared.

A similar pattern characterized the Comodoro Rivadavia chapter. It arose in March 1942, when authorities were stamping out the remnants of a labor conflict in the oil industry with mass arrests. Women in this city had long engaged in solidarity with male strikers, and according to Ratto, most of the filial members were married to railroad and oil laborers. A prominent adherent actively supported the Spanish Republic, and the women's committee of a group aiding Spanish Republican refugees formed the original core of this branch. The chapter's president, however, was the wife or daughter of a high-level manager of the British oil firm, and the secretary was principal of a school located on company grounds. As in the La Forestal case, perhaps the more radical members elected prestigious officers to negotiate with businesses and government.[63]

The background in Chaco resembled that of Misiones. Small farmers and laborers affiliated with the Junta de Defensa de la Producción y de la Tierra, headquartered in Rosario, in the mid-1930s. Socialists and Communists collaborated in this organization, which established branches in Las Breñas, Villa Angela, Charata, and Presidente Roque Sáenz Peña, among other places. Demanding higher prices from the foreign companies that purchased their cotton, its members refused to deliver crops in 1936 and blocked access to towns and cotton gins. Sympathetic workers in Machagai and Resistencia struck for higher wages and threatened to prevent the shipment of cotton downriver. These were the Chaco municipalities that would host Victory Board chapters. Authorities spied on, maltreated, and arrested activists and Spanish Republican sympathizers. They jailed

Junta leaders, most of whom were Eastern European Communists, and sent five of them to prison in Buenos Aires. Their wives launched a national campaign to free their husbands and went to the capital to plead with the government, which nevertheless deported the prisoners. To escape persecution, some Communist Party militants fled the countryside for the relative safety of Resistencia, including at least one future Victory Board member, Sofía Goldberg de Molodesky.[64]

Police vigilance reached another height in 1942. The authorities found a new target: the embryonic Victory Board chapter of Resistencia. They arrested its accountant and, according to some reports, its treasurer, Dr. Luisa Braverman, the first woman doctor in the territory. Married to a Radical, Braverman denied that she had been detained and that the Victory Board had any partisan (i.e., Communist) ties. President Zoppi del Valle Pardo, also wed to a Radical, insisted that the movement was democratic rather than Communist. When she inaugurated the filial's headquarters, she pointed to the windows, exclaiming that all passersby could look inside, for members had nothing to hide.[65]

Even before these accusations, Braverman complained about official harassment at the Victory Board's first convention. She blamed the Chaco government for creating the impression that the board was subversive, thereby scaring away potential members. A delegate from Presidente Roque Sáenz Peña told the first national convention that the forces of "reaction" refused to authorize her incipient filial, claiming the state of siege did not permit new organizations, despite the creation of board chapters in other places. She urged her listeners to write the governor in protest.[66] The peasant and labor struggles had cast a long shadow.

These were among the numerous resistance movements throughout the nation that fed the Victory Board. The University Reform movement had set off intellectual and political ferment in Córdoba and beyond. Leftists fought Nationalists in Tucumán and elsewhere. Excluded from power through the Concordancia's electoral manipulation, Progressive Democrats in Santa Fe and Radicals in Tucumán and other provinces belonged to the antifascist opposition. The Victory Board affiliate in Cosquín, Córdoba, included women who had begun to fight "for the noble cause of liberty" before the Spanish Civil War.[67] Frequently participating in rallies and benefits with students, laborers, Spanish Republicans, and embattled political parties, the Victory Board allied with them and extended their activism.

Partly because most provincial and territorial chapters organized after the declaration of the state of siege, governments stymied their efforts from the onset. Policemen regularly disrupted Victory Board members' marches, such as those held by the Córdoba chapter, and burst into the Mendoza filial's first fundraiser and ordered people to leave. Some branches reported difficulties obtaining official permits for their events. When a British manager in Mendoza forbade the chapter from distributing flyers to his factory's women workers, law enforcement officers stood at the door, seemingly backing his false claim that they had forbidden such practices. The inauguration ceremony for the Rosario chapter consisted of lines of sympathizers quietly filing through its office, as authorities insisted that the state of siege prohibited speeches and concentrations of people.[68] Only one delegate from the interior to the first convention claimed her chapter, in Basavilbaso, Entre Ríos, enjoyed good relations with authorities.[69]

Some officials thought the Victory Board went too far in attributing Argentine freedoms to the Allies. Linked to the Concordancia, the Santa Fe provincial government prohibited the board from posting signs thanking Allied soldiers for enabling Argentines to celebrate the May 25th independence holiday as a "free people." Argentine sovereignty did not depend on foreign countries, nor did it stem from wars which did not involve the country, this administration retorted. Had Argentines forgotten their patriotic duties and national heroes?[70]

Repression also occurred in the capital. Police arbitrarily interrupted the Victory Board's public events, cutting off songs and speeches, especially those of Communists, and closing them down, and broke into its centers and arrested members. When women in the porteño working-class neighborhood of Villa Lugano refused to close their chapter in February 1943, the officials who issued this demand carted them to the grim anti-leftist Special Section. On another occasion, policemen broke into the central board's officially authorized kermesse and declared they were halting it. Anita Lang, an actress, screamed at their leader, "*Nazi de porquería* [Nazi garbage]!" She shed her distinctive green hat and hid in a closet, while officers searched for her, calling out, "Where is the one with the green hat?" Lang loosened her hair, donned her eyeglasses, and reentered the room. Luckily, the lawmen did not recognize her. In yet another incident, police jailed members of the Centro secretariat and looted their homes.[71] The Victory Board offered the option of contributing to any of the major Allied nations; some who picked the Soviet Union encountered baffling legal issues.[72]

Other difficulties also plagued various filiales, as recounted at the Victory Board's first convention. Some residents did not accept the vital need for women's defense of freedom and democracy, complained the representative of the Jewish agrarian colony of Gilbert-Escriña. Even more than in Buenos Aires, many in rural Argentina saw women's political participation as an unseemly distraction from their household duties, which were particularly onerous in the countryside. Aggravating the poor roads and communication in these areas, heavy rains created huge gullies filled with water and mud in Entre Ríos. To mail clothing to the federal capital, members had to ford rivers whose waters reached waist-high. Lacking electricity, peasant women knit by candlelight or kerosene lamps. In 1943 the loss of the cotton harvest in Chaco made it hard for members and sympathizers to feed their families, let alone contribute to the organization.[73]

Nevertheless, areas outside greater Buenos Aires boasted dynamic branches. They held activities similar to those of the porteño secretariats, adding others that fit their settings. For example, rural members gave some of the proceeds of their crop and egg sales to the Victory Board, while others donated wool from their sheep. During warm weather, filiales charged entry to barbeques and picnics they offered in parks and private estates. The La Plata chapter hosted receptions for British and US sailors stationed on ships docked nearby. Maybe partly to dispel concerns about Communism, the Resistencia chapter honored those who died in service to the fatherland and replaced the city's battered flag.[74]

Determining the chapters' level of engagement is not easy. Presence at conventions is a possible measure (see table 1), but sources on the second national meeting are incomplete. Furthermore, lack of money and time rather than interest may have kept provincials from attending. Levels of fundraising and production of aid are better indicators, although this information is scattered. According to Victory Board records, Liniers was the highest producer in the early campaign of twenty thousand sweaters. As of the end of its first year, Centro, Once, and Belgrano had gathered the most money in the federal capital. Moisés Ville raised the highest sum for the heroes celebrated in the Stalingrad campaign, followed by, in descending order, Mar del Plata, Tres Arroyos, Patagones, Berisso, and Oberá. Of the agricultural areas, the Victory Board singled out the colonies in Entre Rios and villages in Misiones for their general contributions; among cities and towns, it commended Villa Ana and Villa Guillermina, Mar del Plata, Tucumán, Moisés Ville, Bahía Blanca, Tandil, Necochea, Comodoro Rivadavia, and the outskirts of Buenos Aires. Except for Centro, these were not among the largest Victory Board chapters, and some were located in poor communities.[75] The ever-changing rankings indicated the dedication of many filiales throughout Argentina.

A Democratic Mission

Raising money and making goods were only part of the Victory Board's antifascist mission of fostering democracy, a word it defined broadly. Cooperation among a wide spectrum of women and an emphasis on the board's internal practices of clean representative governance formed part of its democratic alternative to the Nationalists and the Concordancia. Some hierarchy and continuity of leadership, however, may have impeded its democracy to a certain degree. Aside from these formal aspects, the Victory Board also engaged in "everyday democracy."[76] Infused with solidarity, these informal practices included listening to and learning from other members, expressing democracy in their own terms, working together with their hands, and empowering each other. The Victory Board's concept of democracy also entailed promoting a nonracialized sense of civilization.

To understand what democracy—and therefore antifascism—meant to the organization, one should examine several definitions of the former term. Researchers usually have regarded majority rule with minority rights; the rule of law; regular, open, and honest elections; and civil liberties as its elements. Some scholars, however, have added reducing poverty and increasing opportunities for all to these traits. They also consider it crucial to insert men and women of different classes, faiths, ethnicities, and regions into the polity, so that they can participate as "free and equal citizens."[77] The Victory Board addressed these criteria and added more.

The Victory Board's predecessors had searched for democratic models abroad—in Spain, the United States, Great Britain, France, and the Soviet Union, which Communists saw as the epitome of a classless egalitarian society. They had discussed how to strengthen democratic ideals with the Women's International League for Peace and Freedom (WILPF), the IACW, Popular Front Pan-American feminists, and participants in the 1936 popular peace conferences. The Victory Board drew upon these cross-border conversations in its words and procedures. In her inaugural speech, Schlieper mentioned how members were of all origins, classes, and ideologies. Often repeated by other speakers, this statement not only highlighted the group's wide support but implied that its heterogeneous adherents had put aside their differences to work together. It indicated that pluralism, mutual respect, and cooperation were hallmarks of democracy. Schlieper explained that the movement would work with the government to promote social justice, national unity, ties with other countries, and regard for the constitution, laws, and populace. She implied not only that these duties were inherently democratic, but that the administration had neglected them. Her remarks underscored all aspects of the definitions of democracy offered earlier.[78]

As the Victory Board grew, it emphasized that each chapter drew up its work plans and governed itself democratically.[79] While other Argentine women's groups followed representative norms, as did antifascist women's associations elsewhere, they did not call particular attention to them. That the board did so indicated the importance it placed on women's democratic roles in the antifascist struggle. It showed that women were prepared to vote outside as well as inside the organization. It also was a means of educating people on the nature of democracy and indicting official and Nationalist authoritarianism. Only rarely did the Victory Board specifically mention the shortcomings of Argentine "democracy." Instead, by highlighting its own internal democratic practices, the Victory Board subtly criticized the Argentine government's use of electoral fraud, censorship, and coercion. Competing with Nationalist utterances and practices, which usually included opposition to electoral politics, the Victory Board cast itself as a model of a genuine and peaceful democracy based on pluralism, equality, and freedom. Distinguishing itself from both Nationalism and officialdom, the movement favored integrating women into the polity, as discussed further in chapter 5.

The Victory Board's statutes laid out the framework for its internal governance. Its Directive Commission (Comisión Directiva) was composed of twenty members from throughout the country, whereas the twenty-six members of its Executive Board (Junta Ejecutiva) resided in Buenos Aires. Each body had its own elected officers. The Directive Commission met twice a year to set guidelines for the Victory Board's aid work, and its president and secretary handled relations with the government. The Executive Board met fortnightly, and its president publicly represented the organization, which seemed to overlap with the Directive Commission officers' duties. If important decisions needed to be made between the Directive Commission's two meetings, the Executive Board consulted it. The Executive Board president supervised the internal commissions, charged with such matters as finance, organization, publicity, and the making of goods. The central office in Buenos Aires served as the meeting place for these commissions. It also disseminated written documents and flyers, wool and other materials, and some funding to the chapters. The vice president's sole duty was to substitute for the Executive Board president in her absence. Victory Board members gathered in assemblies each year to elect the Executive Board, whereas balloting for the Directive Commission took place annually at the national convention; both Directive Commission and Executive Board members could be reelected.[80]

Conventions and other gatherings displayed the formal democracy the Victory Board considered vital. As mandated in the statutes, balloting for the Directive Commission took place at the second national convention in May 1943 and for the Executive Board shortly thereafter.[81] Notices of chapter elections and meetings filled the press throughout Argentina. Before each national convention, leaders toured the country, meeting with filiales to inspire them, encourage their participation, and acquaint them with the agenda, which generally concentrated on the Victory Board's principles, the tasks at hand, and a review of its labors, including chapter reports. Branches elected their envoys to the conferences, approved the reports to be presented there, and listened to and discussed the delegates' reactions upon their return.[82] They also offered nominations for the Executive Board and the Directive Commission.

At the first national meeting, Executive Board officers chose a panel that approved the delegates, who voted on the convention's officers and three commissions to set the Victory Board's priorities. To achieve balance, these leaders and commissions included persons from much of the nation. The president of the convention was Schlieper; Porta Echagüe of Santa Fe and Isabel Sors de Santander of Paraná, wife of the outspoken antifascist Radical deputy Silvano Santander, were the vice presidents. Ratto and Dr. Margarita Argúas, a prominent jurist and an Acción Argentina as well as a Victory Board member, served as secretaries, and Braverman of Resistencia and Aguilar as recording secretaries. Convention delegates ratified the composition of the Executive Board and nominated persons for the Directive Commission, but as some of them were not present, its composition was sealed later. Proposals to change the statutes arose from the floor. After the commissions modified their reports, as requested by several delegates, the convention approved them by acclamation, as it did the future work plan and resolutions.[83]

Many resolutions offered in 1942 and 1943 had democratic connotations. At the first convention, the Victory Board agreed to send messages of solidarity to Allied women, President Roosevelt, the congressional commission investigating the "fifth column,"[84] and the former Spanish ambassador under the Republic. In 1942 it pledged to draft a manifesto urging compliance with the resolutions of the conference of Latin American foreign ministers, regarding hemispheric unity against Nazism, and to ask women to sign it. It also resolved that chapters should notify the central headquarters if fascists impeded their functioning. When the government prevented filiales from holding events, the second convention urged them to push for their constitutional rights. It prodded the Chaco delegation to demand that authorities legalize their activities.[85]

Andrés Bisso argued that hierarchy and continuity of leadership kept Acción Argentina from being truly democratic,[86] and similar problems may have afflicted the Victory Board. Regarding hierarchy, members spoke up at chapter and national meetings and gave reports at the conventions. The Communist periodical *Orientación* claimed that delegates from the interior at the second national gathering did not necessarily accept what others said; they discussed everything and made their wishes known.[87] Still, the degree to which they and their peers from the federal capital actually formulated policies was unclear. The fact that Schlieper headed both the Executive Board and the Directive Commission in 1941–1942, and then shared the post of Directive Commission president in 1943 with Porta Echagüe, eliminated a potential conflict over who served as the Victory Board's public face.[88] Although this could have concentrated more power in her hands, Schlieper seemed to work closely with Ratto and other founders, making the leadership more collegial than singular. Some filiales duplicated this pattern. The officers in Oberá knew each other well and labored collectively, and this probably was true for other chapters as well, particularly the smaller ones.[89] Furthermore, Schlieper's leadership style as IACW chair rested upon courtesy, subtle persuasion, and a spirit of collaboration rather than command, and it is likely that she employed similar techniques as the Victory Board's head.[90]

There also was the issue of regional hierarchy. One might question why a movement that wished to include the interior rather than subordinate it gave more power to the Executive Board, consisting solely of porteñas, than to the Directive Commission, which contained provincial and territorial voices, or even why it divided the leadership into two. Given the expensive and time-consuming nature of travel, poor road conditions in many places, and women's household duties, however, it would have been impossible for members in outlying areas to travel to Buenos Aires every two weeks.

Like Acción Argentina, Argentine women's groups exhibited continuity of leadership, which may have reflected larger antidemocratic tendencies in the society. Yet the Victory Board's national- and local-level officers changed somewhat over time. For example, Sors was a member of the Directive Commission in 1942, but in 1943 she became vice president. In 1943 María Elena Mitre de Noble, the aristocratic wife of an Acción Argentina leader, joined Schlieper as copresident of the Executive Board.[91] Still, the Victory Board's most dynamic phase lasted less than two years, from September 1941 to June 1943, too brief to expect a massive turnover or more than one election of the Executive Board and the Directive Commission.

Despite these complexities and other potential flaws discussed in chapter 4, the Victory Board expanded democracy in crucial ways that transcended formal procedures. To comprehend this accomplishment, one must probe how the board conceptualized its relationship with its aid recipients. Some Christian members considered it one of religious charity or duty.[92] Did the Victory Board offer philanthropic largesse or gifts to the Allies? Anthropologist Marcel Mauss has pointed out that "giving" is a complex exchange involving "freedom and obligation" and "generosity and self-interest," accompanied by an expectation of gratitude and reciprocation.[93] Perhaps for the Victory Board, the recipients' thankfulness, the prestige it earned, and the satisfaction of helping defeat fascism constituted appreciation. Another possible recompense was a future victory for women; as Dr. Argúas argued, their service to the Allies could win them civil and political rights after the war.[94]

Alternatively, Moreau had insisted in 1938 that aiding the Spanish Republic was not an act of generosity, but rather an obligation to repay what was owed to those who endangered their lives fighting fascism.[95] Some Victory Board adherents might have viewed their pro-Allied efforts similarly. In effect, this meant that the Allies, and especially Europeans, were the givers. If one accepted the Europeans' gifts of cultural transmission and antifascism without paying them back, one acknowledged subservience to a foreign master. A bountiful repayment, however, could lift the Argentines to an equal or higher status. This would further suggest that Europe was no longer the model for Latin Americans—including its women activists—to follow, but rather the other way around.[96]

These notions provide insight into the Victory Board, but it is vital to recognize that it consistently framed its mission as one of solidarity, a word whose meaning differs from paying back what is owed or bestowing a present. Influenced by women's activism in the LADH and especially CAMHE and other Spanish Republican support groups, solidarity was a key ingredient of the Victory Board's democratic alternative. Officers and members frequently declared that theirs was a transnational solidarity movement and related even their most prosaic functions to this practice, as when a member of the Once secretariat claimed that its fundraising fashion show and dance expressed "the profound significance of . . . solidarity with the cause being defended in the Old World."[97] According to Catherine Sameh, solidarity is a "bridge that enables people to connect to or meet each other across significant divides," and a concept that "emphasizes trust, justice, equity, democracy, mutuality, and love in the building of movements, ties, and relationships."[98] Bridging divides was precisely one of the Victory Board's main goals (see chapter 4). Love for those fighting for democracy, the hope for victory over the Axis and the creation of a more equitable postwar world, and a mutual relationship with the Allies characterized the Victory Board. Mutuality also suggests reciprocity, but the emphasis on equality and love sets solidarity apart from merely giving to others and meeting obligations, even when these actions are based on respect. Solidarity means fraternity, or in this case sisterhood, whereas charity and settling debts imply hierarchy.

Sameh added that solidarity "attempts to build ethical relationships based on equity while acknowledging and challenging the economic and political structures that create inequality between people."[99] This relates to the broader definition of democracy offered earlier in the chapter. Although Schlieper explicitly mentioned social justice in her inaugural speech, whether the Victory Board challenged socioeconomic inequality was questionable, as chapter 4 explains. Nonetheless, the Victory Board complied with the first part of Sameh's sentence: it addressed beneficiaries and fellow members alike as equals. It regarded its aid recipients as partners in the struggle for democracy. The Victory Board's workshops and other collective endeavors promoted equitable face-to-face relations among the heterogeneous women in the ranks, as part of its everyday democracy. Eating and drinking together at teas and banquets fostered sharing and bonding among members, and among them and kindred spirits. A prime example was the massive farewell dinner honoring the delegates from the interior and Pan American Day that closed the first national convention. A US diplomat estimated that there were 1,000–1,200 guests of various political sectors and social classes.[100] On such occasions, "food provides a common voice for diverse people," according to Carole Counihan and Rebekah Pite.[101]

This sharing and bonding may have been particularly intense at large meetings. The president of the Bahía Blanca chapter valued "tightening the ties of friendship with democratic women" throughout the nation during the first convention. The representative from Oberá delighted in the cordial atmosphere and lessons learned from the other delegates' reports. After hearing rural members recount their taxing days of agricultural work, domestic chores, and knitting for the Allies, Schlieper declared that "rarely have we lived moments of such intense emotion. . . . Our friends from the countryside, from the far-off farm, from the remote corner of our fatherland" inspired members in Buenos Aires to redouble their efforts. "We [porteñas] have learned much from your will, determination, and sacrifice."[102] This praise for women in poor communities and outlying regions undercut the common impression of porteño arrogance and demonstrated the Victory Board's intent to equalize the relationship between the capital and the rest of the country. Returning to Sameh's definition of solidarity, here was an example of how it challenged political structures that created regional inequality.

Offering previously excluded women the opportunity to speak freely and equally in public settings met one of the broader democratic criteria offered earlier. So too did listening respectfully to ordinary people, many of whom were not well-educated. Knowing that others are paying attention to one's words can generate creativity, initiative, and "excitement and enthusiasm through democratic participation," labor organizers have observed.[103] By taking their words to heart, the listeners made these speakers feel that what they said carried weight and fomented a sense of trust, so essential in collaborative efforts.[104] Such practices of everyday democracy energized the Victory Board's ranks.

In these and other ways, the Victory Board was innovative. Argentina had never had a large independent women's movement like this one, Ratto insisted. Even the massive Spanish Republican aid effort had not served as the basis for such an association. Many women were isolated from each other and had little experience working together beyond occasional efforts to address specific philanthropic and cultural goals. Lacking political rights and precedents that could guide women to organize themselves, the Victory Board was a pioneer, she claimed. Its campaigns were not only transnational responses to the fascist threat in Europe; they also mobilized and trained women to partake in determining the future. Acquiring knowledge and skills from each other, they would model an inclusive and therefore "true democracy."[105]

Spokeswomen expressed their own sentiments of democracy and mutuality in terms that resonated among audiences. Sometimes they appealed to local pride. An officer claimed that her chapter had initiated pro-Allied aid in Tucumán, thus honoring this city's tradition of liberty as the cradle of Argentine independence. There was no question that Rosario, the "city of workers," would strongly support the heroes of the Battle of Stalingrad, the president of this branch boasted.[106] Others resorted to essentialism. According to the Córdoba delegation at the first convention, "the sense of understanding, of humanity, and of solidarity is greatly developed in the heart and mind of every woman," and the *cordobesa* would apply these qualities to "the noblest cause . . . : *peace, based on a true democracy* [emphasis in original]."[107] Speaking at the Buenos Aires provincial convention in October 1942, María M. de Kruuse, the elderly "dean" of delegates, urged her listeners to obey Christ's admonition to love one's neighbor as oneself. But religion was not her only theme. Just as the soldiers overseas were helping us, she said, so were we helping them. Would we want someone to send our children to concentration camps, destroy our homes, and enslave our men? She answered with a thundering "No!" If we had to fight to defend ourselves, would we want assistance? "Yes!" We must support those who keep our homes afloat and provide our children and grandchildren with the possibility of a happy future, she concluded.[108] For Kruuse, transnational solidarity, reciprocity between partners, free and contented families, and Christian love formed the basis of the Victory Board's democratic mission. By incorporating their own ideas, these and other speakers adapted, recirculated, and popularized imported antifascist messages.

Women's voices like Kruuse's cemented "the emotional cohesion between the members" and "the mutual support they . . . [gave] each other in their battle for common goals," which Kurt Bayertz saw as essential characteristics of solidarity.[109] This emotional cohesion and mutual support empowered humble and politically inexperienced Board adherents. A *criolla* (generally meaning "mestiza") peasant of the Las Breñas, Chaco, chapter, Margarita de Barraza exclaimed that through the Victory Board she experienced a sense of solidarity that made her feel useful for the first time in her life.[110] This encouragement of self-worth and personal liberation was an additional ingredient of everyday democracy, which contested Nationalist men's authoritarianism and misogyny.

Official repression and Nationalist opposition created fear, but solidarity among members helped them convert their anxiety into resistance and productivity.[111] The delegate from Cosquín to the first convention declared that now that they knew each other and had seen how so many women had sacrificed for the cause, "We feel strong, eager to work, closer than ever to Victory."[112] Their triumph over multiple dilemmas instilled a sense of accomplishment; in fact, the Victory Board's mere existence enhanced self-esteem. As the Moisés Ville delegate put it, the "yearning to aid those who suffer permitted the unification of . . . women," which roused "the respect and attention of which we are worthy."[113]

Making goods by hand deepened the solidarity among members and between them and the Allies. Sewing and knitting garments helped women care for, envision, and put human faces on the beneficiaries. Sitting around tables to make clothing connected a range of women, "from barely adolescent girls to old ladies of all conditions, of all origins, of all creeds," in a partnership, as in the La Plata chapter.[114] Ceremonies honoring the most productive knitters heightened their sense of achievement and eagerness to participate.[115] Working together may have united members more than did the Victory Board's high-sounding principles but also may have clarified and materialized these abstractions.[116]

Hand labor was a public political act, despite some board leaders' disclaimers. The Córdoba filial would be a center of work to implement its precepts of freedom, democracy, justice, and law, declared its president.[117] As Ratto asserted, unlike the typical women's charities that merely collected money and goods, the Victory Board was "an organization of work and struggle" whose members regarded their stitches and words as means of defending their treasured rights and duties. By helping the Allies defeat fascism, they sought to continue engaging in dignified labor and "studying and researching and believing and praying according to the free dictates of . . . [their] consciences."[118] Perhaps Argentine women could not fight with bullets, but as the Tucumán chapter observed, making a sweater or a bandage was as valuable as wielding a gun.[119]

The Victory Board's democratic mission was connected to its views of civilization. It and like-minded Argentine groups consistently placed themselves on the side of civilization against fascism, which they considered barbaric for its glorification of war, ruthless violence and murders, racism, misogyny, and destruction of liberty and democracy. The board's membership card stated, "To save the world from barbarism. / For the future of your children and your home. / For your rights as a civilized woman. / In defense of your human dignity. / For the Fatherland."[120] Following President Domingo Faustino Sarmiento (1868–1874), who distinguished between the "barbaric" gauchos, usually people of color, and the "civilized" inhabitants of European descent, many Argentines had identified "civilized" behavior as white and "barbaric" behavior as nonwhite.[121] The Victory Board rejected the racist elements of this trope by referring to white European fascists as barbaric and local antifascists—among them, criolla and Jewish members—as civilized. Its concept of civilization fit the pluralistic notion of democracy in that it embraced freedom lovers of racialized groups, at least before 1945.[122]

The Victory Board's cultural programs formed part of its democratic project. Claiming that they stood for civilization against fascist barbarism, board members upheld culture against those whom they thought destroyed it, as had the Agrupación de Intelectuales, Artistas, Periodistas y Escritores. The secretary of the Resistencia chapter explained that there were two competing concepts at play, one standing for culture, the foundation of civilization, and the other for tyranny and domination, which sought to extirpate "the very human nature . . . that unravels the mysteries of the Universe" and creates art and science.[123] In reality, rather than demolish culture, fascists devised their own variants of it. Nevertheless, the Victory Board made visual art, classical music, films, and literary and political forums accessible to ordinary people, thus expanding their knowledge and moving toward a more egalitarian society.[124] Board offices displayed women's artistic works and hosted performers who belonged to or sympathized with the organization. Its headquarters exhibited painter Raquel Forner's heartrending *Exodo*, evoking the fall of Paris to the Germans through women's bodies and offering a feminized awareness of the horror of this war. While the depiction may have traumatized viewers, it likely stimulated resistance as well.[125] Believing that a strong culture helped guarantee peace within democracy, a Victory Board member in Córdoba recommended connecting chapters to artistic and intellectual institutions.[126]

Cultural programs and other public occasions served purposes beyond forging solidarity and democracy. They spread information about the group within and outside it. Discussions at conventions on increasing efficiency, recruiting members, coordinating with other aid organizations, and creating new initiatives oriented the branches. The ability to orchestrate such events and attract participants and guests from afar, including distinguished Argentine political and intellectual figures and foreign diplomats, won the Victory Board admiration and prestige. These august persons' attendance also assured it a measure of security. So too did the presence of Governor Rodolfo Moreno and Minister of Government Vicente Solano López, both of the National Democratic Party (Partido Demócrata Nacional, PDN) contingent of the ruling Concordancia, on the Buenos Aires

Provincial Convention's Honor Commission, as well as President Roberto Ortiz's expressions of support at the first national convention.[127] Persecution of the Victory Board and its democratic mission, however, increased over time.

In the meanwhile, Ratto and Oliver must have been pleased with what they set into motion. Despite the hindrances, soon after its birth the Victory Board was providing substantial amounts of aid to the Allies and especially to the Soviet Union. It was growing in numbers and importance. Oliver observed that at its headquarters one could meet "the most dynamic men and women in the anti-Nazi struggle," including foreign luminaries, such as the Brazilian novelist Jorge Amado. "In intimate touch with the sorrow of the world," she continued, volunteers working in this office nevertheless manifested "cordiality, gayety, and even optimism over the cups of tea."[128] Solidarity among members helped convert their initial pessimism into a fragile hopefulness.

Just as they knitted sweaters for the Allies, board members knitted together their understandings of the global, national, and local. Linking Argentine political and social conditions to the worldwide conflagration, they believed that supporting democracies overseas by sending aid from the Global South to the Global North would strengthen democracy at home. Local histories of resistance, women's prior experiences with transnational movements, and cross-border debates with extreme rightists guided the Victory Board as it constructed its democratic alternative to fascism and proclaimed its solidarity with the Allies. More broadly based than most Argentine female groups, it acquainted women throughout Argentina with each other.

The Victory Board's democratic alternative made it unique. Its emphasis on its internal democratic processes, which it touted to demonstrate women's political capabilities and contrast itself with the Concordancia and Nationalists, distinguished it from other movements in Argentina and elsewhere—or at least the literature on them. Solidarity and its tenets of equity, mutual support, and community were integral to the board's everyday democracy, which involved welcoming, boosting, sharing with, listening to, and learning from women of different backgrounds. The Victory Board's discourses, consisting of words and quotidian practices, contested and competed with those of fascists. Its measures to balance the federal capital and the rest of the nation also set it apart.

The Victory Board energized people in many ways. Through cultural outreach, it uplifted ordinary citizens. It addressed women as mothers and housekeepers but also as citizens in the making. Its orators adapted and crafted antifascist messages in terms that resonated with and animated locals. Notices of aid received reminded women of their part in an honorable global campaign. Women's investment in making goods, the exhibitions of their output, and the frenetic activity to meet quotas incited enthusiasm in chapters and communities. Forming ties with women across the nation who "thought and felt like us," as Oliver put it, fomented camaraderie and excitement. The concrete nature of their aid and the appropriation of the "V for Victory" slogan helped make World War II "their war." The creation of a sophisticated central organization, circumvention of obstacles, and efficient organizing of conventions promoted members' confidence in their abilities. Support from fellow members led women to believe that they had something to offer. These and other elements of solidarity, including encouraging the ranks to express themselves, empowered them and promoted democratic engagement.

One of the goals of solidarity is to connect people. The Victory Board sought not only to bridge divides between Argentines and the Allies, but those among its members and their communities. Aside from the leaders, who were these members? To what extent did this movement bring together classes, ethnic/racialized groups, religions, political parties, and regions? Did such efforts fulfill its democratic promise? The next chapter will address these queries.

CHAPTER 4

BRIDGING DIVIDES

Born in 1917 in an industrial suburb of Buenos Aires, Clara Drallny was the daughter of impoverished Eastern European Jewish immigrants. Her father, a match factory laborer, and her mother died when she was fourteen. She and a brother moved to Córdoba to live with their aunt and uncle. For economic reasons, Drallny could not finish secondary school, but she read on her own and studied languages. She worked in a clothing store and joined a left-wing Yiddish cultural organization. Drallny probably made her way into the Communist Party (Partido Comunista) through her activism in the commercial employees' union. In her mid-twenties she joined the Victory Board (Junta de la Victoria) and served as a delegate to its first national convention. At this time she met her future husband, a law student, who also was involved in the Communist Party and an antifascist group.[1]

One of her fellow Córdoba chapter members could not have been more different. A pioneering woman in university circles, Dr. María Luisa Aguirre was born into a distinguished upper-class family linked to the conservative Democratic Party, a component of the national ruling Concordancia. After earning her medical degree in 1928, she started her private practice and eventually rose to the position of chief of services in the pediatric clinic of the Hospital de Niños. She also served as director of a public milk dispensary and played an active role in the local pediatric society. Tied to US culture, Aguirre won a scholarship from the Instituto Cultural Argentino Norteamericano (ICANA) to spend a summer at Columbia University in 1942. She reported approvingly that North Americans trusted in an Allied victory, and that women were very much involved in the war effort.[2]

Drallny and Aguirre seemed an unlikely fit for the same organization. Yet such contrasts in the Victory Board were not unusual. A newspaper observed that at the first national convention, "Women factory workers alternated with lawyers, teachers with mothers of families, artists with peasants. All social classes, all religions."[3] A few accounts showed it also drew upon women of different ages, including youngsters.[4] Who belonged to the Victory Board? Who were the women who met board leaders at distant train stations and, in Oliver's words, "thought and felt like us?"[5]

This chapter describes the backgrounds of members in selected branches, offers portraits of some, and explains how the Victory Board attracted and brought them together. It examines the class, ethnic/racial, religious, political, and regional divisions among members and the extent to which the Victory Board surmounted them. It also analyzes the organization's embrace of the "liberal" minority of an otherwise ultra-rightist Catholic Church, a sector with transnational Pan-American ties. While I discuss national-level figures, I focus largely on the rank and file, particularly outside of Buenos Aires. It is important to study the provinces and territories, and not only because they contained over half of the population, as already noted.[6] Knowing the local alters our understanding of the national, in this case by providing insight into the individuals and networks that gave rise to the Victory Board. Exploring the composition of the movement outside Buenos Aires is also critical for the methodological issues discussed in the introduction. We must harness the information we can find—notwithstanding its paucity—to study politically active women, especially the non-elite ones.

The Victory Board's diversity enriched the movement, facilitated its work, and fostered some aspects of democracy while impeding others. It could not, however, completely bridge all the divides. To varying degrees, the social and ideological gaps between the lower and more privileged classes persisted.

Class

The Victory Board arose when certain subjective class barriers in Argentina were fading while others remained rigid. Still, its class mixture was unusual for the early 1940s. In the interwar period, the social and cultural influence of the largely immigrant-descended and heterogeneous middle class was gradually eclipsing that of the landowning upper class. This nebulous middle saw itself as the group fostering progress and civilization in Argentina. Its values and tastes were spreading to the upper class, but could not match the latter's consumption levels. While the middle sector was intruding into social spaces once regarded as elite territory, this did not necessarily promote direct interaction, much less intermarriage, between the two classes. The few historical studies on Argentine class identities, however, barely consider women's specific experiences.[7]

Arguably the least permeable barrier was between the privileged and laborers, whom the former often regarded as uncultured, rebellious, and dark-skinned. Upper- and middle-class hostility to the suburban workers who "invaded" the capital in support of Juan Perón on October 17, 1945, manifested these opinions.[8] Yet many workers absorbed—or already possessed—middle-class values, tastes, and the desire to consume and to improve their status. Thanks to economic growth, public education, and their own efforts, some entered the middle class. Numerous others could not escape extreme poverty.[9] Radio programs, films, and other elements of popular culture strengthened labor identities and set rich against poor.[10] The question is to what extent the Victory Board crossed the divide between the well-off and the poor.

The presence of laborers like Drallny conflicted with a widely held image of the Victory Board as aristocratic, a perception the group often seemed to cultivate. Ana Rosa Schlieper de Martínez Guerrero and María Rosa Oliver pertained to the elite, as did some other founders and officers. The Victory Board's upper-class members included Anglo-Argentines, landowners, and scions of traditional families such as Aguirre. Responding to allegations that the "chic ladies" who created the Victory Board were Communists, a US reporter quipped that "Communism in Argentina seems to have first taken a turn through the Rue de la Paix,"[11] a Parisian street lined with exclusive shops. Perhaps it did, for a few. Even the Communist newspaper *La Hora* called attention to the group's illustrious character. The group courted good relations with Allied ambassadors and their wives, wealthy businessmen, and political leaders, including Concordancia adherents. They and other distinguished persons attended the Victory Board's benefit teas, banquets, cocktail parties, and other events. The Victory Board and *La Hora* probably accentuated the movement's aristocratic appearance and links to foreign embassies to help it recruit, obtain prestige and support, and operate safely.[12] Yet this impression obscured much of the group's composition.

The Victory Board also prided itself on its diversity. Two union militants and a Communist leader of proletarian background served in the original Directive Commission (Comisión Directiva). A journalist detected women of all social classes and pursuits—professionals, intellectuals, artists, feminists, political and labor activists, and workers—at the Victory Board's central office. Missing from her list, housewives and socialites were very much present. She spotted these distinct women sitting closely together at tables, almost touching each other, concentrating on their knitting without speaking.[13] Many chapters in greater Buenos Aires drew in women of varied class backgrounds—for example, middle-class Caballito and well-off Belgrano enlisted factory laborers.[14] Working-class women congregated with wealthy Anglo-Argentines and Argentine wives of Englishmen at the Victory Board office in the suburb of San Fernando, where they knitted and held teas and raffles. A middle-class French-Polish Jewish woman and her friends went to the homes of fellow board members of Catholic high society to make bandages together. Unlike the silent knitters the reporter observed, these members spoke with each other cordially, but did not seem to form genuine friendships.[15]

Still, at this time such relationships in Buenos Aires may have been rare. A Spanish visitor described well-dressed women walking alongside modestly yet tastefully clad women workers and servants on fashionable Florida Street in the city center. Only the better-off, however, could afford to buy the elegant items displayed in store windows. Moreover, one wonders how often even this limited intersection occurred. Countless young women who lived and labored in the outskirts of the city rarely if ever went downtown. Education also separated women. If they studied outside their homes, upper-class women went to elite Catholic schools, whereas other women attended public institutions. Middle- and lower-class students intermingled in public *colegios*— including prestigious ones—but often the latter had to drop out to work. Charity, commercial transactions, and domestic service brought together women of different classes, yet the distinctions among them were clear. Nor did charity mean heartfelt solidarity with the poor. According to Donna Guy, photographs of Catholic upper-class philanthropists revealed their coldness toward the recipients of their largess. Through the Victory Board, diverse groups of women became acquainted and collaborated in pursuit of a shared goal. Their cooperation and mutual respect served as models for the nation, according to *La Hora*.[16] The Victory Board's mixing of classes also may have set it apart from male antifascist groups.

Some members worked long days in factories, workshops, and modest households, while others employed servants.[17] In the Victory Board, however, they knitted, sewed, and assembled medical supplies in common; in this sense they occupied the same level. Somewhat speciously, Schlieper claimed that all board members were workers; all "are making clothing and first aid articles."[18] For wealthy women, laboring with their hands may have been novel; for working-class women, it was customary. However, even if the latter engaged in activities that resembled their usual tasks, the conditions differed greatly from those in the workplace. As Elena Álvarez, a Victory Board officer and union leader, put it, "With how much love these garment workers will knit these sweaters . . . without foremen or daily wages!"[19] No boss stood over them while they knitted, and they, like the more privileged women, had volunteered for this unpaid activity. This was not alienated labor in the Marxist sense, because they organized it themselves, saw their completed product, and used it to help humanity rather than put money in capitalist pockets. Furthermore, performing these tasks beside well-off women accorded them respectability and a sense of importance.[20] Photos of board women knitting, sewing, and making other items often depicted them in smocks, which further smoothed over class differences and symbolized this unity.[21] The depth of this unity was questionable. Ironically, one could argue that the Victory Board was engaging in class conciliation, much as Nationalist women did, for they, too, wore smocks.[22] Yet in some respects the Victory Board inverted class hierarchy. Textile and garment workers tutored upper-class socialites on the fine points of sewing and knitting after their workday. Even the most capable had something to learn from those who toiled alongside them, Cora Ratto declared.[23] Through such words and quotidian practices of everyday democracy, the Victory Board reached across classes. Working together created a sense of community, with solidarity as the bridge.

The Victory Board attracted distinguished middle- and upper-class career women. Eminent in the arts and literature were the writers Oliver and Silvina Ocampo; sculptor and painter Cecilia Marcovich; and the Portela sisters, María Carmen, an engraver and sculptor, and Margot, an author and painter. The president of the Rosario chapter, Alcira Olivé de Mollerach, a prize-winning playwright, and the *porteña* publisher Sara Maglione de Jaime enjoyed important careers in letters and culture, as did Rosa Diner de Babini of Santa Fe. A history teacher who lectured on varied topics, Diner was the founder and guiding spirit of La Peña, an intellectual salon of the 1930s.

Cora Ratto, a mathematician, was one of the Victory Board's professionals and researchers. So too was Dr. Telma Reca, a well-known psychiatrist who was dedicated to her pursuit of knowledge and to the children and juvenile delinquents she studied and treated. She served as a public health official and professor at the University of Buenos Aires. Other medical personnel included dentist Dr. Rosa Scheiner of Buenos Aires and pediatrician Dr. María Luisa Aguirre of Córdoba. The Resistencia chapter included two pioneers: Dr. Luisa Braverman, the first woman medical doctor in Chaco, and Dr. Rita Waisman, its first woman biochemist. Dr. Margarita Argúas of Buenos Aires and Dr. Nina de Borzone of Santa Fe were legal experts.

Sugar-mill owner Amalia Minetti of Tucumán was among the loftiest entrepreneurs in the Victory Board, along with María Ronconi of Buenos Aires. Businesswomen members more commonly were modest shopkeepers and participants in family enterprises. One was Sofía Goldberg de Molodesky, who, as noted, fled oppression by moving to Resistencia. There this former factory worker ran a bakery with her husband.

Pedagogues abounded in the Victory Board. Among the school principals were Irene de Nadal Gahn, who headed the most important public school in Resistencia; Inés García de Marqués, founder of an Indigenous school and museum there; and María Elena Saleme, a respected French teacher and luminary in Tucumán. A devotee of Sarmiento, Saleme fittingly headed the school that bore his name. Other prominent educators included Samatán of Santa Fe, the local Unión Argentina de Mujeres (UAM) president; Dr. Angela Santa Cruz, head of the Asociación Cristiana Femenina (ACF) and several educational organizations, and Berta P. de Braslavsky, who pioneered special education in Argentina, both of Buenos Aires; Rosa W. de Ziperovich, of Palacios, Santa Fe; and the *rosarina* Bernardina Dabat de López Elitcherry, a national educational inspector.[24]

Yet the majority of Victory Board members were middle- and lower-class homemakers. One was Rosa de Cusien, who lived in the comfortable Buenos Aires suburb of Martínez with her physician husband and infant daughter. Recruited for her typing skills, Cusien had the means and the time to participate, except when her child was ill. In contrast, proletarian housewives like Rebeca Bzostek could barely afford to pay dues. After quitting her job in a meat-packing plant in Berisso because its cold temperature impaired her health, she prepared meals for other laborers. When she moved to Buenos Aires and married a textile worker, she concentrated on her home, the Victory Board, and other political involvements.[25]

My study of Victory Board members in the federal capital and six other localities confirms their varied class affiliations and occupations. As complete membership lists have not survived, I culled their names from newspapers and board publications. They tended to be officers, convention delegates, and the most active participants. The women of Buenos Aires belonged to the central leadership and secretariats, the others to chapters bearing the name of the locality. I chose the cities of Buenos Aires, Córdoba, Resistencia, Santa Fe, and San Miguel de Tucumán (hereafter Tucumán), and the towns of Oberá and Tafí Viejo because of their varying characteristics. These were municipalities of different sizes located in territories and provinces, some with many chapters and others with few. Greater Buenos Aires contained many factories, a politicized and unionized working class, a large percentage of immigrants, and important Communist and Socialist contingents. Unlike industrialized and centrally located Córdoba were the littoral agricultural centers of Oberá, Santa Fe, and Resistencia. Near the Andes, Tucumán was less literate, prosperous, and immigrant in composition than Córdoba and Santa Fe. Its suburb, Tafí Viejo, was an industrial, working-class community. Socialists and Radicals competed in municipal elections in Chaco, but Communists were active among laborers and farmers there and in Oberá. Radicals were strong in Córdoba and Tucumán Provinces, as were Progressive Democrats in Santa Fe. I could not find data on a sizeable percentage of the women surveyed, who probably were housewives, workers, or both, which in itself is significant. Despite the gaps, these statistics, along with the qualitative examples in the text, suggest patterns.

Table 2 reveals class affiliation. As indicated, the Argentine middle was less distinct than the upper and lower classes, and the literature on class formation focuses on social, cultural, and political factors. I rely on social indicators and livelihood. Informants alternately characterized some women as upper- or upper-middle class, so I combined these categories.[26] Nineteen percent of Victory Board members overall were upper or upper-middle class; the percentage was higher in Córdoba (42 percent) and Tucumán (44 percent). The middle class formed the majority in most locations and a plurality (38 percent) overall, whereas the working-class component was 13 percent, although significantly higher in Buenos Aires (31 percent) and the labor bastion of Tafí Viejo (80 percent).[27]

Unsurprisingly, Victory Board members in Buenos Aires—the industrial, intellectual, and population hub (table 3)—engaged in a much wider array of occupations than did their colleagues in the interior. Eighteen percent of those on whom I found data had careers related to the arts and letters, and 14 percent had doctoral degrees. Yet the most substantial category was laborers (31 percent), followed by teachers (17 percent). Outside Buenos Aires (table 4), teachers constituted by far the largest contingent (54 percent), followed by women who either owned a business or worked in a family enterprise (22 percent). Except for Rosario and Córdoba, few factories in the provinces and territories employed women, and commerce was a more likely pursuit.

Working-class involvement in the Victory Board probably was much higher than these various statistics indicate. Surely such women figured among the 30 percent in table 2 for whom data is lacking. Many chapters were located in proletarian neighborhoods. In the federal capital, this included the secretariats of Constitución, Almagro, Barracas, La Paternal, Liniers, Mataderos, Villa Lugano, Parque Patricios, and Parque Chacabuco (with its laborers from the Ronconi factory), and branches in such surrounding communities as Villa Sarmiento, Avellaneda, Berazátegui, Berisso, Ramos Mejía, and Villa Lynch. The pattern in larger municipalities elsewhere was to create neighborhood *sub-filiales* or *seccionales*, separate from the main urban chapters, and some were located in working-class areas within or just outside cities. Fitting into this category were Villa Luján in Tucumán; Barranqueras in Resistencia; Barrios Inglés and Observatorio in Córdoba; Saladillo and Arroyito in Rosario, and Villa Diego on its outskirts; and perhaps Oeste in Santa Fe. One should also consider the Victory Board chapters in neighborhoods encompassing the meat-packing plants on the edge of Buenos Aires, oil installations of Comodoro Rivadavia, quebracho processing establishments of northern Santa Fe Province, and cotton mills of Chaco Territory. According to a union militant, the Victory Board mostly consisted of commoners, including workers. A member's daughter described the board as "popular and pluralist." Edelman agreed, observing that the Communist Party played a critical role in mobilizing these women.[28]

The creation of secretariats in Buenos Aires and sub-filiales elsewhere may have reduced mixing between proletarian and bourgeois members, but it seemed necessary. Lacking money and laboring double or triple days, working-class women would have found it difficult to regularly attend meetings in downtown locations. Yet certain members of the neighborhood subsidiaries, which sometimes included various classes, visited the central headquarters, where they turned in the items they had made and the money they had collected. They attended the discussions preceding and following the national conventions and the receptions for visiting porteña leaders in the main *filial*, as well as the inexpensive fundraisers.

The Victory Board found means of persuading women workers to collaborate, if not join. One was to encourage the establishment of female factory commissions. Commissions in textile plants in Barracas contributed to the corresponding board secretariat, as did similar groups in the Colón and Durán factories in Rosario. Employers in Almagro, Parque Patricios, Chacarita-Colegiales, Boca, and Valentín Alsina allowed the Victory Board to disseminate flyers and sometimes collect money in their factories and workshops. Seeking greater cooperation, the first national convention resolved to ask the US and British ambassadors to speak with owners and managers of factories owned by citizens of their countries to allow the organization to spread its propaganda in these premises.[29] National Board leaders visiting Resistencia met with factory managers, urging them to open their doors to the local chapter. Having received management authorization, board members in Santa Fe dropped into businesses, industrial enterprises, and public offices, coaxing women to join.[30] Unions with strong ties to the Victory Board, largely thanks to its Communist backing, aided these efforts. The board invited women in low-income neighborhoods to free or inexpensive film festivals.[31] Many filiales asked women laborers to attend their ceremonies and meetings; Avellaneda, for example, invited women from two meat-packing plants and not long thereafter threw a party in their honor.[32]

Such efforts extended to white-collar and sales personnel, who straddled the lower and middle classes. Using the language of the time, Graciela Queirolo considered clerical women as "workers" or "women who work." That they labored for wages yet possessed educational and feminine-coded skills, plus opportunities for upward mobility, complicated their class affiliation.[33] Board authorities hailed the Centro secretariat for its numerous productive members recruited from shops and offices. To honor and recruit Gath y Chaves department store employees, this secretariat and the national board held teas for them. The Rosario chapter formed a saleswomen's committee that invited fellow employees to benefits and enlisted them, while the Tucumán branch honored such women at a special fiesta. Probably encouraged by its president and Victory Board member Clara Drallny, the Group of Anti-Nazi Women Commercial Employees (Agrupación de Empleadas de Comercio Anti-Nazi, ADECA) of Córdoba contributed its knitted goods to the local filial.[34]

The Victory Board attracted many small farmers in Chaco, Misiones, Santa Fe, and Entre Ríos. One was *chaqueña* Margarita de Barraza, whose self-esteem the board had lifted. Originally of poverty-stricken Santiago del Estero, this criolla delegate to the second national meeting had six children. Her household raised cotton, yet aphids and excessive rain had ruined the harvest that year. How well she could feed her own brood or read is unclear; we know only that she spoke in simple words and that the Victory Board taught her and her daughter to knit.[35]

Ratto perceived that some delegates at the first convention were illiterate.[36] One suspects that many of these were rural cultivators, who were among the neediest members. Table 5 shows that 5 percent of members overall had little to no education, 13 percent had finished primary school; 43 percent had spent some time in secondary school, and 39 percent in a tertiary institution. The percentage of unschooled members may have been much higher, given the lack of information for 69 percent of those studied.

Social Justice

Victory Board leaders reached out to the rural and urban poor and wanted to end destitution. Its educators, professionals, feminists, labor militants, and leftists had advocated social causes under other auspices. Dr. Aguirre touted the government and union social assistance that enabled the United States to avoid the severe malnourishment common in Argentina.[37] Board member and metallurgical union leader Alba Tamargo demanded that women laboring in this dangerous sector receive wages equal to those of men and higher remuneration for both.[38] Tamargo, Schlieper, and Santa Cruz served on a commission that pushed for changing the existing maternity law to expand benefits. It was unjust that women—rather than both sexes—contributed to maternity pensions, Schlieper argued, and that some mothers, especially outside the capital, did not receive the payments they deserved. One wonders why, then, board meetings and speeches rarely touched upon such topics, which lay at the heart of Popular Pan-American feminism.[39]

At the Victory Board's inauguration in September 1941, Schlieper said that promoting social justice was one of the organization's aims. Later, how-

ever, while admitting there were grave local problems, she insisted there
was no point in creating yet another group to transitorily reduce distress
in a world moving toward totalitarianism. Only the government could end
social injustice—and only after a democratic conclusion to the war. Then,
with their wartime experience in working together, board women could
turn to studying social problems and offer their findings to political leaders.[40] Ziperovich, the secretary of the Palacios, Santa Fe, filial, agreed that
this was not the time to address social issues: "My contact with the people
of the countryside, the knowledge of their . . . wretchedness, unemployment, and abandonment, made me understand that this situation would
aggravate considerably with a despotic regime like the Nazi one. Instead,
with the triumph of democracy . . . the force and capacity for progress,
which are latent in the peasant people, will be able to flourish."[41] For these
and other spokeswomen, the priority was defeating the Axis, which would
usher in a postwar utopia that would promote freedom, prosperity, and
equality for all.

These attitudes were common among antifascists on both sides of the
Río de la Plata.[42] Yet not all agreed. Alicia Moreau endorsed a report presented at Acción Argentina's Cabildo Abierto meeting of 1941, which stated that economic and social reforms were needed to sustain democracy.
When urging people to defend democracy, she argued, one had to explain
to them exactly what they were defending.[43] Even within Argentina, there
were competing women's antifascisms.

Soviet policies dating back to the Spanish Civil War influenced the
Victory Board's priorities. Most Spanish Republicans, including the Communist Party, had set political democracy as their immediate goal, as they
reckoned it would permit the creation of a more egalitarian society. In line
with the Comintern, the party did not press for a social revolution, unlike
anarchists. Yet social revolution remained its long-term goal, and its grassroots militants participated in the collectivization of farms and factories.[44]
Communist Popular Front and wartime strategies that favored class unity
in the struggle against fascism also helped determine the Victory Board's
position. Nor could it afford to alienate privileged and conservative members and supporters by advocating sweeping change. Generally, Argentine
antifascists avoided acrimony over divisive social and economic issues.[45]
Maintaining a multiclass coalition ultimately meant emphasizing political
freedoms over the social justice desired by poor Argentines, which proved
to be a fateful decision.

The failure to address local socioeconomic problems triggered opposition. Writing for an opinion column in a Tucumán newspaper, a university
student proudly asserted his "Argentinism," which he detached from antidemocratic "Nazifascism" and Communism. Collecting funds for Europe

while so many Argentines faced penury infuriated him.[46] Whereas statements published in this column that favored helping the Allies greatly outnumbered those opposed to it, many people throughout the country may
have quietly agreed with this student. Quick to embrace this competing
discourse, Nationalists contested antifascist calls for helping the Allies with
appeals for helping the Argentine rural poor, especially the children.[47] Their
hostile remarks and the perception of public disapproval of, or indifference
to, its aid campaign put the Victory Board on the defensive.

Engaging in this discursive field, the Victory Board attempted to
block the Nationalists' argument by asserting its devotion to Argentine
welfare and prosperity. The first convention agreed to publish a pamphlet
explaining that supplying the Allies was the best means of helping impoverished Argentine youngsters. The second convention proposed elucidating
to women's groups how aiding the warring democracies boosted national
well-being and helped "the children of the north so often mentioned in
Nationalist propaganda."[48] Whether the Victory Board implemented these
plans is unclear. More concrete was its creation of a dining hall in downtown Buenos Aires, where office and sales workers could lunch at reasonable
prices.[49] Resistencia, which donated money to a Catholic orphanage, was
among the branches that worked for local causes. The Tafí Viejo chapter
gathered pharmaceuticals and money for a campaign to help municipal
hospitals; some of the contributors were themselves board members. The
leaders of this filial explained that the collection drive, like Allied combat,
signified a struggle for victory over injustice. "The Victory Board will always give its support and its determined aid to whomever justly needs it."[50]

The Victory Board also supported national industry. The first convention's work plan included a plea to housewives to substitute Argentine-made
products for foreign manufactures. Having gathered and sold portions of
its members' cotton crops to raise money, the Resistencia filial advised other chapters to do the same with goods produced in their areas, to spur
the national economy.[51] Nationalists issued similar proposals. Schlieper
claimed that the Victory Board invested money in Argentina by purchasing
local products and materials for its shipments.[52] Yet it is doubtful that these
board statements convinced Nationalists and other skeptics that it was suf-
ficiently concerned with domestic economic conditions.

Two other Argentine women's antifascist groups nodded to Nationalist
sympathies. Unión Femenina de Francia Libre made some clothes for the
Allies, but its members also paid a small monthly fee to hire women factory laborers, as they could produce large quantities of apparel much more
efficiently than the volunteers. It claimed that in this manner it employed
Argentine women and paid them higher than average wages.[53] The Acción
Argentina Feminine Commission prepared clothing for Charles de Gaulle's

forces, but it also called for donations of ten thousand sweaters for impoverished children throughout the country. Some distributions took place at
least in the federal capital, but Acción Argentina actions were no more effective than the Victory Board's in curtailing complaints.[54]

The Victory Board faced a quandary. Directing more resources to domestic concerns would have collided with its transnational mission. Hiring
laborers to sew and knit would have threatened its members' personal investment in its solidarity project. Giving more to the poor would have belied its identity as an organization of political struggle rather than a philanthropy. This would have weakened the Victory Board's outreach to women
of all classes, since such endeavors usually were identified with the privileged. Furthermore, calls for altering class relations or passing costly social
welfare legislation probably would have splintered its multiclass coalition.
Yet neglecting the issue of socioeconomic rights contradicted an aim of
solidarity—the critique of economic structures that promote inequality[55]—
and undermined the board's democratic aims. Thus the movement could
not completely close the ideological fissure between the rich and poor in
its ranks or in society. The Victory Board's leftist contingent seems to have
reasoned that unifying and training women for civic endeavors and removing them from the home at least prepared them for future social struggles.[56]

Ethnicity and Nationality

The Victory Board, however, bridged another divide by attracting women
of different national and ethnic origins. The strength of these barriers varied from one group to another, depending on their arrival date, class status,
attachment to their language and customs, and the perceived difference between them and the dominant culture. Even so, Buenos Aires, "compared
to other multi-ethnic cities . . . [had] one of the lowest average indexes
of segregation in the world."[57] People of different backgrounds interacted
in their neighborhoods. Here it was not hard to cross the ethnic/national
divide, at least superficially, which may not have been true elsewhere, especially in rural areas.

The information I gathered reveals more on some groups than others. While in most municipalities surveyed the majority or plurality of
members' surnames were Spanish and Italian, it was difficult to determine
whether these persons had long roots in Argentina, or if they were first-
or second-generation immigrants who closely identified with their own or
their parents' original homelands and cultures. The backgrounds and allegiances of inhabitants in small, tightly knit communities were much clearer
(table 6). Eight of the thirteen Victory Board members in proletarian Tafí
Viejo for whom data is available were of Czech origin, and four came from

Spanish families who had arrived relatively recently. All of the former were related to skilled workers from this country employed in the railroad factory, and all of the latter were involved in Spanish cultural associations. Of the twelve known Oberá adherents, eight were Christian Eastern Europeans, two were Paraguayan, and two were Swedish, reflecting the composition of the population, save for German settlers, suspected of Nazi sympathies. It also was relatively simple to identify Eastern and Central European Jews through their distinctive last names and, in some cases, participation in communal organizations. In most branches studied, Jews formed a significant component (table 8). I also found a few women of English, French, and other backgrounds in some of these places.

Qualitative evidence and other scholars' findings substantiate the variety of nationalities and ethnicities. Dora Schwartzstein concluded that exiled Spanish Republican women's participation in the Victory Board represented their most significant involvement in any Argentine political group. A former board member recalled the Spanish mothers and daughters who formed the majority in the Constitución secretariat, along with Irish, Russians, and Hungarians.[58] Chapters and subchapters in rural settlements teemed with immigrants and their offspring. According to Ernesto Maeder, foreign newcomers in the *chaqueña* countryside, especially from Central Europe, retained a keen interest in their ancestral homelands, which helped account for the Victory Board's popularity among them.[59] The filial of Las Breñas had five subchapters in agricultural colonies: two Czech, one Bulgarian, one Ukrainian, and one criollo.[60] These and other rural members organized separately by farming community and language.

Many women of foreign roots who preferred to speak their native tongue formed their own antifascist aid associations. The Victory Board's magazine described these organizations, which often supported its activities. French, German, Austrian, Italian, Jewish, US, Hungarian, Spanish Republican, Ukrainian, and Armenian antifascist groups adhered to the Victory Board's "Fiesta for Liberty," which took place in the Luna Park stadium in December 1941. Jewish and Lithuanian (presumably Christian) organizations contributed significantly to the Rosario chapter. In turn, the Victory Board participated in events sponsored by such associations, such as a fundraiser for Jewish war victims in Córdoba in December 1942. Persons of varied origins regularly turned up at each other's functions.[61] They crossed ethnic/national/linguistic divides through antifascism.

Criollas and Jews

Criollas and Jews were the quintessential outsiders in Argentina. They were racialized and many were poor, although Jews were moving out of the working class. A religious/ethnic minority, Jews were influential in the Victory Board.[62] It celebrated both groups, even though they were not welcomed in many other circles.

During the Nazi era, Argentine denunciations of racism almost always equated it with antisemitism, whose advocates usually considered Jews to be a nonwhite race. Groups such as the Comité Contra el Racismo y el Antisemitismo rarely if ever discussed prejudice against dark-complexioned people.[63] Seldom did people mention skin color, perhaps to avoid undermining the national myth of Argentina as a white European country, or to ensure they fit into this myth. Hence the neutral term *criollo*, with its pliable and shifting meanings. It referred both to the colonial Spaniards' descendants born in the Americas and the generally impoverished people of mixed European, Indigenous, and/or African ancestry. Furthermore, the term denoted Indigenous who were losing their culture and moving toward Europeanness, thus joining the nation—as lesser citizens, poor, rural, and uneducated.[64] Even when seen as lowly, however, criollas shared Catholicism, an important component of identity, with most Victory Board members, including those of higher status.

Victory Board publications and press notices scarcely broached skin color, but the few such references were revealing. Two upper-class women in the national headquarters who coordinated knitting efforts told a reporter that a criolla cook brought them a sweater she had made. The Victory Board asked women to sew a *V* for victory on each sweater, but she had not done so because she could not read or write.[65] Aside from the overlap between race, class, and illiteracy, what stood out was that the aristocrats called attention to the Allied sympathies of a humble woman of color. Barraza, the *chaqueña* delegate to the second national convention, also received notice. *La Hora* described her "very black hair, face burned" by the Chaco sun; her body and face, it reported, seemed "taken out of an engraving that define[d] . . . what was purely Argentine." Her appearance, "weathered hands of an authentic worker of the Argentine countryside," and involvement in the Victory Board made her a "symbol," the newspaper declared. At this convention, Schlieper asked the audience to applaud the Chaco representatives for their hard work under grim conditions, and two of them went up to the stage. In laudatory tones, *La Hora* characterized one (probably Barraza) as "a genuinely Argentine woman, dark and typical" of the northern part of the country, and the other as a pale blonde from the Bulgarian colony.[66] The Victory Board and its ally *La Hora* saluted brown-hued members as integral parts of the antifascist cause and of a multiracial, multicultural nation, contrasting with Nazi white supremacy.

The cook and Barraza could not have been the only criolla members and collaborators. In the 1930s and 1940s, provincials migrated in droves to greater Buenos Aires and other cities, searching for employment. The Victory Board had chapters in impoverished hinterlands and suburban neighborhoods, and there must have been criollas in many of them. They were subsumed under the lower-class mantle.

In terms of religion, even urban, middle-class Jews were more distant than criollas from other board members. How strong was the Jewish-Catholic divide? Jewish porteños were not as segregated as in the United States, but they still more segregated than other immigrant groups.[67] Some officials and other influential figures considered Jews white; others saw them as racially unfit, antinational, unruly, greedy, and therefore nonwhite. "Despite some ambivalence and hostility, the government and society generally consented to the Jewish presence," I concluded elsewhere.[68] Even as immigration restrictions, Nationalist actions, and discrimination in some professions made antisemitism more evident in the 1930s–1940s, Jewish women were inserting themselves into society. Still, the degree of Jewish rural and urban participation in the Victory Board and its reception of these members were striking.

In 1930 about 230,000 Jews lived in the capital, other cities, and agricultural settlements.[69] The vibrant Jewish farming communities were shriveling by the 1940s, but they still fostered networks of women who encouraged each other to join various causes. In 1942 seventeen of the Victory Board's approximately forty-five chapters in the interior were located in Jewish colony zones sponsored by the Jewish Colonization Association or in areas populated by Jewish and other farmers (table 7).[70] A plurality or majority of the seventeen branches consisted of Jews, mostly Ashkenazim, along with some German speakers, reflecting the local Jewish populations.[71]

In a number of Jewish agricultural colonies, almost all adult women joined the Victory Board.[72] Some of these chapters were surprisingly large, given their locations in hamlets. By 1942 Basavilbaso (Entre Ríos) had 426 members, Moisés Ville had 400, and Rivera (Buenos Aires) had 208. This compared favorably with the figures for the much larger cities of Córdoba (500) and Bahía Blanca (270). Jewish women headed the filiales in six Jewish colonies and two agricultural centers. Three rural branches had Jewish vice presidents, and many had other Jewish officers as well.[73]

The Jewish presence was considerable in urban chapters (table 8), ranging from 16 percent in the federal capital to 40 percent in Resistencia. The Oberá branch, however, had no identifiable Jews, and Tafí Viejo appeared to have only one. Nevertheless, in the municipalities studied overall, Jews amounted to 23 percent of the core activists, at a time when they composed 2.56 percent of the national population.[74] Eastern and Central European and at least a few Sephardi and Italian Jews joined non-Jewish women in urban chapters; as many Sephardim had Spanish last names, they can be difficult to identify, so there may have been more.[75]

Jews were key players in urban filiales. In 1942 sixteen of the approximately twenty secretariats in Buenos Aires had Jewish officers. Jews served as presidents of Palermo and Liniers and vice presidents of four secretariats, including those of Almagro, La Paternal, and Villa Crespo, neighborhoods that had appreciable Jewish minorities.[76] So did Versalles, Once, Belgrano, and Caballito, which also hosted secretariats, and the industrial suburbs of Villa Lynch and San Martín, which housed chapters as well as Jewish-owned textile factories and Jews who labored in this sector.[77] Jewish women presided over the branches of Concordia, Entre Ríos, and Laguna Paiva, Santa Fe. Those of Bahía Blanca, Concordia, Resistencia, and Tucumán had Jewish vice presidents. The chapters of La Plata, Rosario, Santa Fe, Córdoba, Mendoza, and probably other cities also had Jewish participants.[78]

Women of Jewish origins were among the Victory Board's authorities and highest aid contributors. The artist Cecilia Marcovich pertained to its initial Executive Board (Junta Ejecutiva), which eventually would include Clara Helman de Oxman, Scheiner, Dalila Saslavsky, and Fanny Edelman, all of them Communists or sympathizers. Jews belonged to five of the Victory Board's early national-level committees. As of 1942, Clara Rotman de Baruch, president of the Moisés Ville chapter, served in the Victory Board's Directive Commission.[79] Moreover, Jewish delegates from rural and urban chapters attended the national conventions, which offered visibility and an entrée into the board's leadership. Since Argentine Jewish women did not affiliate en masse, it is somewhat difficult to measure their contributions to the Victory Board, but one example is illustrative. In the 1940s, the agricultural center of Moisés Ville contained between five thousand and seven thousand inhabitants, mostly Jews. Its chapter donated more to the board's Stalingrad campaign than any other, including those located in the largest cities.[80] The Victory Board recognized this filial, whose largely Jewish identity was apparent, for its achievements, and applauded its ninety-five-year-old member, Rebeca de Malajovich, the oldest woman in the entire organization and one of its most prolific knitters.[81]

Spokeswomen highlighted the Victory Board's ethnic and religious pluralism, sometimes referring specifically to Jews. Ratto observed that the organization contained a tremendous variety of women. It was easier for people of the same beliefs and origins to collaborate than for those of such distinct backgrounds, she acknowledged, but learning from each other was necessary to create a truly democratic society, in which "all have acquired the right to not be left excluded."[82] Thus Ratto signaled and lauded the inclusion of women, workers, and minorities, among them Jews, in the polity and the movement, another aspect of the latter's everyday democracy. At the first national convention, Schlieper asserted that the Victory Board brought together women of different "creeds" and ideologies, which Drallny and another Jewish delegate of Córdoba confirmed.[83] When Ratto described the occupations of members to the convention, she highlighted the first Jewish teacher educated in Argentina.[84] After a US tour, Schlieper reflected on how its military provided for the spiritual needs of soldiers of different faiths, suggesting endorsement of its religious pluralism.[85] Such pronouncements must have heartened Jewish Argentines.

Jewish members and sympathizers made their presence known. Saslavsky, Oxman, Scheiner, Ziperovich, and other members of Jewish origin often spoke for the Victory Board. The well-known Singerman sisters— Berta the reciter and Paulina the comedic actress—performed in its benefits and wrote in its magazine. Rosa Vainberg, a member and former teacher in a Jewish agricultural colony, contended in its pages that as a woman and "as a Jew, I suffer doubly a vile injustice."[86] Their activism and words showed that the Victory Board welcomed Jews and their frank remarks.

Furthermore, Christian members displayed concern about the Holocaust. The Argentine branch of the Women's International Zionist Organization (WIZO) collected money for Jewish refugee children in Palestine in 1943, and Schlieper gave a speech at one of its fundraisers. She and the president of the Córdoba chapter also spoke on behalf of WIZO's fruitless efforts to bring thousands of Jewish children from Europe to Argentina.[87] Conversing with Jewish and other factory workers in Almagro, the Christian president of this secretariat declared that the crimes against Jews, among other German atrocities, fed her determination to demolish Nazism.[88]

Women of Jewish origins were found throughout the Victory Board, working alongside those of other backgrounds. At this time Jews interacted with non-Jews in public education, intellectual and cultural life, the Communist and Socialist Parties, unions, and several antifascist groups, but few, if any, participated in other important nonpartisan secular women's organizations, such as the Consejo Nacional de Mujeres.[89] The Victory Board may not have explicitly recruited them, but its positive references to Jews and ethnic/religious diversity, its steadfast opposition to Nationalism, and Jewish visibility in its ranks and leadership served as magnets. The critical need to defeat fascist antisemitism at home and abroad, as well as Jewish women's engagement with leftism, especially the Communist Party, also propelled them into the Victory Board.

Bridging Divides to and among Catholics

The Victory Board did not target Jews in its recruitment campaigns, but it singled out Catholics for special appeals. It was vital to obtain support from this majority component of the population, but the board faced a formidable enemy in the local church's leading sector. Nevertheless, it had Catholic allies at home and abroad.

Many clerics and lay Catholics "flirted" with Nationalism, in Miranda Lida's words; one could even say that Catholicism and Nationalism overlapped.[90] These "clericofascists," as Federico Finchelstein called them, supported the rebel side in the Spanish Civil War, Francisco Franco's dictatorship (1939–1973), and, to varying degrees, the Italian and German fascist regimes.[91] Yet growing understanding of Nazi subordination of the Catholic Church and defiance of its teachings, according to Communist intellectual Rodolfo Puiggrós, was transforming some Catholics into antifascists.[92] The Victory Board tried to increase these numbers and convert them into members.[93]

The Victory Board called attention to its devout adherents and, in contrast to Nazism, its harmony with church doctrine. It issued a pamphlet on Nazi treatment of Catholics that contained photos of cities and churches destroyed by German attacks. "Love your neighbor as yourself" appeared underneath a snapshot of German soldiers aiming their rifles. Eugenia Silveyra de Oyuela, a Catholic writer and activist, wrote in this publication that unlike the Axis, the Victory Board envisioned a peaceful world in which all could serve Jesus Christ.[94] Underlining this distinction, the organization placed a huge Christmas tree in the center of Luna Park for its December 1941 fundraiser, to remind the audience of people who could not peacefully and freely celebrate this holiday. Various filiales urged Catholic women to support defenders of their faith by joining the Victory Board, for it and the Allies advocated religious freedom and helped the victims of Nazism. They noted that concentration camps contained Catholics and church officials had denounced Nazi atrocities. Christ's mandate to love one another convinced the head of a Catholic relief organization to join the Victory Board and become a chapter president. In her view, helping those fighting for freedom also meant fighting for the freedom to practice her religion. The Victory Board pointed out that a leader of Acción Católica Argentina (ACA), the mass organization of antiliberal Catholics, presided over the Lanús chapter and spoke at the Buenos Aires provincial convention, and ACA members attended the first national convention.[95]

The Victory Board publicized its ties with Catholic groups and placed Catholic figures in conspicuous positions. The chapter of Villa Mitre, just outside Bahía Blanca, gave materials to the Sisters of Charity, who used them to knit clothes for babies and soldiers. The nuns handed them over to the filial, saying that they could be given to the United States, Great Britain, China, or, significantly, the Soviet Union.[96] Santa Cruz of the Asociación Cristiana Femenina was elected to the Directive Commission in 1943.

The Victory Board attracted members of this group and the Federación de Asociaciones Católicas de Empleadas (FACE), headed by Elisa Espósito, who served in the Directive Commission from 1941 to 1943. Some FACE adherents joined the Centro secretariat, as did women who belonged to the commercial employees union Federación de Empleados de Comercio (FEC).[97]

As FACE president, Espósito was closely tied to Monseñor Miguel de Andrea, the founder and director of this organization and the unofficial leader of the Catholic Church's "liberal" minority, which also included Silveyra and other vocal Catholic antifascists. Considering his influence on FACE and other Catholic Victory Board members and sympathizers, it is critical to understand his thoughts and actions. The bishop of Telmos had long sought to create harmony between classes, political groups, and nations. Throughout his career he was conservative and anti-leftist, but by the 1930s his positions were more nuanced and judicious than those of Nationalists within and outside the clergy. Andrea's parish church was located near downtown department stores, where the FEC was organizing. First led by syndicalists and then by Communists, this union formed in 1919; it is no coincidence that FACE arose three years later. His opposition to Communism and militant unions like FEC partly explains Andrea's outreach to women in this sector. Saleswomen, clerical workers, government and bank employees, seamstresses, and some teachers and professionals joined FACE. Its main purpose was to offer members religious, cultural, educational, recreational, and medical services, along with affordable meals and vacations. Promoting respectability, social peace, and maternalism, FACE did not push for better wages or working conditions until the mid-1930s, when it began petitioning Congress and the national labor department to enforce and extend legislation on maternity benefits, piece work, and paid annual vacations, as well as to pass new labor laws. To achieve these goals, Andrea and FACE worked together with unions such as the Communist-led garment workers' federation (Federación Obrera del Vestido, FOV), in Popular Front style.[98]

This cooperation helps explain FACE members' involvement in the Centro secretariat, Andrea's appearance at the Victory Board's Buenos Aires provincial convention, and Espósito's presence in the board's leadership, alongside Elena Álvarez of the FOV. Yet at the same time, the bishop of Telmos associated with the anti-leftist Liga Patriótica Argentina, as he had since its founding in 1919. He continued to support the private ownership of property even as he pressed for worker benefits.[99]

Andrea was linked to transnational Pan-American antifascist currents in the Catholic Church, as was Schlieper, more loosely, when she spoke to a Catholic audience that included reformist Archbishop Edward

Mooney in Detroit in 1940 (see chapter 1).[100] Like Mooney, Andrea combined concerns for social justice and democracy. While he opposed liberal free-market economics, unrestrained individualism, and secularism, he favored personal liberty and mass participation in governance, which meant that he and FACE supported women's suffrage. Andrea accepted the Argentine Church's neutral stance during World War II, but approximated pro-Allied sentiments. The bishop cultivated contacts with US clerics, and President Franklin D. Roosevelt publicly complimented him as part of the wartime Good Neighbor policy. He was one of a few Latin American Catholics invited by the National Catholic Welfare Conference (NCWC), the voice of the US hierarchy, to the first meeting of Catholic leaders from across the Americas. Underwritten by the Office of Inter-American Affairs (OIAA), which endorsed the Catholic initiative for hemispheric unity, this Inter-American Seminar, "The Americas and the Crisis of Civilization," took place over three weeks in several cities in 1942. Mooney, the NCWC chair, declared in his keynote address that "statesmen of the Americas have already gone far towards setting up in this hemisphere a policy which, if broadened and deepened, may yet be the working model for a much more satisfactory world order than any we have recently known. By emulating in our own field of religion their inspiring example, we as Catholics can not only more effectively develop our spiritual heritage but we can also make it fruitful of great good for human society in this hemisphere and in the world."[101]

Andrea added his own thoughts to this notion of "Pan-American Catholicism," as *Time* magazine called it. Congruent with the Victory Board's views, in his speech for the seminar, Andrea said that the postwar world must be based on democracy, social and political justice, and freedom of individuals and nations. Without freedom, "life is not worth living," he insisted, tying this and other principles to God and Christianity. Goods needed to be better distributed among populations, for "the living space of families within nations" was more vital than "the living space of nations," a critique of a Nazi concept. Andrea hailed President Roosevelt's pledge that the United States would not seek vengeance and instead would implant a new international order. To the Argentine priest this meant a Christian and human peace untied to any particular country. He urged Catholics to engage with this upcoming era of accord and social justice for all.[102] Andrea's participation in the seminar and his speech further explain his and FACE's rapprochement with the Victory Board.

Well-received in Washington, DC, this speech was broadcast throughout Latin America and widely reproduced in Argentine newspapers.[103] Roosevelt, who met privately with Andrea, and US ambassador to Argentina Norman Armour were impressed with him, and US officials thought that

Andrea had helped alleviate suspicions of Argentine alignment with the Axis. Since Andrea did not disavow neutrality, his remarks did not necessarily offend the church hierarchy or the Argentine government, although Nationalists found fault with them.[104] Espósito, by now a member of the Victory Board's Directive Commission, sent a similarly ambiguous message to Mary Cannon of the US Women's Bureau. FACE identified with the pain of women throughout the Americas whose countries were at war, she wrote, adding that she and Cannon were among the women who struggled for peace throughout the globe.[105]

Andrea's positions on freedom and democracy resembled those of the antifascist magazine *Orden Cristiano*, which often printed his speeches and sermons.[106] Eugenia Silveyra de Oyuela, the Victory Board's premier Catholic spokeswoman, was among its contributors. One could not have predicted her journey toward antifascism. In the 1930s, this ACA activist wrote for *El Pueblo*, the archbishopric's mouthpiece, and the Nationalist *Clarinada*, a magazine edited by her brother Carlos that spun vicious conspiracy theories about Jews, Communists, and other presumed enemies of the fatherland. In these and other publications she praised Franco for defending the church and suppressing Communism, called for importing his anti-leftist crusade, and claimed that (far rightist) totalitarianism was compatible with Catholicism. Yet José Zanca observed that Silveyra did not transfer her support for Franco to fascism, which she came to regard as a form of paganism that had elevated race, state, and leader above God.[107]

This awareness led Silveyra to rethink her *franquismo* and other notions, as she spelled out in *Orden Cristiano*, which the church hierarchy did not view kindly, and another antifascist periodical, *Argentina Libre*. In September 1941 Silveyra still decried Communist influence in Republican Spain and Republican attacks on the Catholic Church during the Spanish Civil War, tepidly crediting Franco with reviving Catholicism. Yet while she denounced Communist atheism and its "unnatural" political order, Silveyra began to appreciate its concern for the poor. She also turned against rightist authoritarianism. After the Victory Board's creation, she observed that some identified democracy with liberalism, secularism, and atheism, which were anti-Catholic, and thought that totalitarianism could purify society of these traits. The nineteenth-century dictator Juan Manuel de Rosas (1829–1852), a precursor of such beliefs and Nationalist hero, had also claimed that he would purify Argentina, but instead he perpetrated bloodshed and arbitrariness. Nazi-style totalitarianism could not help people fulfill divine law, since it did not permit freedom, but democracy did. The Catholic Church did not reject all democracies—it supported those with God. Silveyra approvingly discerned Christian characteristics and priestly influence on Argentine democracy during the independence era. In her view, Rosas's liberal Unitarian opponents were more genuinely Catholic than the dictator, since they favored the Christian principles of morality, freedom of conscience and education, self-governance, and private property. In contrast, Rosas exploited religious sentiments to bolster his rule.

Realizing that Franco's totalitarianism had violated Catholic precepts, by 1945 Silveyra repudiated him. She also chided Franco's ambassadors for disseminating racism in Argentina under the guise of Hispanism, a fascist policy of tying the Iberian nation to its former colonies. God's grace, not a supposedly superior Spanish race, was responsible for the conquest of Muslim Spain and Latin America. Indeed, Argentines belonged to only one race—the human race. Silveyra condemned "Catholics without Christianity" (Nationalists) who defended dictators like Franco and Rosas, denigrated Rosas's opponents, and indulged in "Hispanic racism," "'religious' anti-Semitism," and "megalomaniac nationalism," all of which the Catholic Church had rejected.[108] These views fit well with the Victory Board's.

Silveyra's opinions on Jews, however, were equivocal, notwithstanding her speeches at communal events. In 1942 she noted that the blood of Israel was soaking an "apostate Europe" that had abandoned the Christian doctrine of "fraternal love." She insisted that the Catholic Church had condemned antisemitism and defended Jews against German savagery, although the degree to which it did so was questionable. Among Jews there were many innocents, especially children, but sinners as well, Silveyra claimed; however, all of humanity had sinned by forgetting God. God would judge Jews as individuals, not as a group. They had fulfilled their mission of transmitting God's word and bringing forth the Messiah, and they continued to nourish Christianity by offering the faithful opportunities to sacrifice their freedom and lives to save Jews and thus perform charity, justice, and brotherhood. All blameless victims of this war, Jewish and Christian, would receive just recompense from heaven. Silveyra hinted that Jews existed to serve Christianity and had "rejected" Christ. Her inability to acknowledge their beliefs conflicted with the Victory Board's practices of mutual acceptance, respect, and understanding. Still, Silveyra's statements were more tolerant than those of *Orden Cristiano*'s editors, who accepted notions of Jewish treachery even as they denounced antisemitism. The magazine reproduced an article printed in the archbishopric's official mouthpiece, which argued that Jews were deceitful and untrustworthy and lacked concern for members of other faiths. It added that Catholics needed to guard against dangers presented by certain individuals and peoples, implying Jews, but this did not justify Nazi extremism; converting Jews was a better solution.[109] It was difficult for ardent Catholics, no matter how "liberal," to escape the church's traditional antisemitism.[110]

The Victory Board invited Silveyra to speak at its functions, starting with the banquet at the first national convention. Nazism threatened freedom and Christianity, she declared, so Catholics must resist it. One form of resistance was to help Russia, which did not mean one agreed with Communism. Those who considered this disgraceful overlooked the Christian doctrine of love and justice.[111]

News of Silveyra's upcoming appearance at the opening ceremony of the Córdoba chapter awakened interest among Catholics in this city, prompting local supporters of *Orden Cristiano* to meet privately with her and attend the inauguration. She may have convinced some to join. In her speech at the larger ceremony, Silveyra insisted that Catholics who did not support justice and charity by aiding the Allies were untrue to their faith. Furthermore, Nationalists were spreading racist Hispanism to divide the Americas, breaking the ties of freedom and democracy that joined its inhabitants together. "As Argentines we cannot be anything other than Americans. We Americans should be united in liberty."[112]

Silveyra gave a longer address at the Córdoba chapter's festival the next day. By liberating Argentina from the Spanish yoke, the founding fathers had won freedom of thought and conscience, which Argentine Catholics had to defend at any cost. The pope had prohibited collaboration with atheist Communism, but he in fact opposed all atheism, and he loved the Russian people. Straining credulity, Silveyra insisted that Nazism was Communist in its policies and atheist in its religious aspect, so the papal ban applied to it as well. In fact, Bolshevism originated in the desire for social justice and equality, although it negated God's law. In contrast, German National Socialism imposed social injustice, the belief in racial inequality, and power over others. Christianity, therefore, could spring from Bolshevism, but not from Nazism.[113]

It was unclear whether Silveyra formally joined the Victory Board. Several newspapers reported that she had been elected to the Directive Commission at the first convention, but the board's magazine did not mention her as such.[114] Nor did she ever appear in any list of national officers. Still, she was closely associated with the organization and heavily influenced its leaders who identified themselves as Catholics. One was the president of the chapter of Cañada de Gómez, Santa Fe, who affirmed that she followed Silveyra's lead. Like Silveyra, she attributed her antifascism to her love for others, her belief that Nazi barbarism did not permit the free practice of her religion, and her desire to keep Argentina safe from foreign aggression. Another was the vice president of the Córdoba filial, who declared that Christianity, the Argentine independence struggle, and the overthrow of Rosas inspired the Victory Board's principles and solidarity with the Allies.[115]

How many ardent Catholics Silveyra, FACE, and their antifascist coreligionists might have attracted to the movement is unknown, but most of the Victory Board's adherents were at least nominally Catholic. They participated alongside Protestants, Jews, Spiritists, and the nonobservant.[116] Through FACE and Andrea the Victory Board was tied to transnational Catholic antifascism. Its support for religious freedom and its pluralism bridged divides among and within faiths and helped forge an unusual movement for this pre-ecumenical era.

Political Divisions

Perhaps more than one might expect, the Victory Board's political composition also was diverse. It was a national political alliance that stretched across partisan and regional lines. The board forded more political divides outside Buenos Aires than within it. Not all its members, however, fully embraced broad notions of democracy.

The political sympathies of 67 percent of the women surveyed are unknown, yet the patterns for the rest are striking (table 9). At least some of the 67 percent probably had no partisan ties. Among the known cases, Communists accounted for 50 percent overall, ranging from 78 percent in Buenos Aires to 25 percent in Tucumán. All members of Oberá for whom information is available were linked to the Communist Party, as was a plurality in Santa Fe. Radicals and Socialists were associated with Acción Argentina, and some had reservations about the Victory Board's Communist connections. Yet many Radicals joined the Victory Board in the interior. They came in second place overall (29 percent), with a high of 58 percent in Tucumán, a plurality of 48 percent in Córdoba, and a low of 1 percent in the capital, where President Schlieper was the sole person identified as Radical. Socialists occupied third place, with 10 percent overall, 11 percent in the capital (their stronghold), and 25 percent in Resistencia. The Radical and Socialist presence shows how studying areas outside the federal capital complicates our understanding of the Victory Board. My data accords with Edelman's testimony that members were mostly Communist-aligned or nonpartisan, but they were more politically diverse in the provinces and territories.[117]

These affiliations outside Buenos Aires largely reflected local particularities. In my survey, Progressive Democrats (Partido Demócrata Progresista, PDP) only appeared in the Santa Fe chapter (29 percent of those with known partisan ties), which was plausible since this province was the party's center of operations. This chapter's president was married to the popular PDP ex-governor, and his party was strongly antifascist. Led by Marcos Kanner, Communists were very active in Oberá, and his wife was the secretary of the local Victory Board filial. I found no information on members' political ties in Tafí Viejo, but eight of them were daughters of skilled Czech workers, and Socialists and Communists had strong support among them. Socialists (25 percent) and Radicals (42 percent), the major competitors in local elections, were well represented in the Resistencia filial, and its first president was a Radical. In 1934 Radicals in Tucumán broke with the party over its abstention from electoral politics, and from then until a national intervention in 1943, they ruled this province. The majority of women surveyed in Tucumán had ties to Radicals. When Radicals abandoned the abstention policy in 1935, they won elections in Córdoba, where they retained power until the 1943 coup d'etat. The wife of Senator Gabriel Oddone, a national Radical leader, presided over the chapter in Córdoba city. A Radical activist in her own right, Isabel Sors, married to Radical congressman Silvano Santander, presided over the chapter of Paraná, Entre Ríos, a province in which Radicals were the majority party.[118] The leftist sympathies of some Radicals, and intermittent Socialist collaboration with Communists outside Buenos Aires, as in the agrarian struggles in Chaco in the 1930s, helped explain their involvement with the Communist-influenced board.[119] Partisan loyalties and anger incited by the Concordancia's attacks on electoral democracy also aided the Victory Board outside the national capital.

Moreover, feminist concerns led some Radicals to the Victory Board. A homemaker, María Luisa Coutouné de Butiérrez spent much time reading on her own and discussing politics with her husband, a Radical militant. In 1932 she founded a Unión Cívica Radical women's committee in La Plata. Such groups, however, were not formally integrated into the party's structures or leadership and had no voice in its deliberations. Facing hostility from the police and the party, the committee fought for women's suffrage, its autonomy, and its existence. Coutouné's advocacy of women's rights and democracy prompted her and like-minded cohorts to join the Victory Board.[120]

A pioneering feminist connected to the Radical party, Dr. Elvira Rawson de Dellepiane hovered around the Victory Board. She met in October 1941 with the Juana Manso Committee, a Radical women's group which she served as honorary president, to discuss whether to become a board chapter. This did not happen, but rumors persisted that she belonged to the Victory Board's ruling circle. In December 1941 she spoke on Argentine women's fifty-year struggle to obtain their rights at the opening of the Centro secretariat. In 1942 she participated in the board's effort to coordinate the various organizations sending aid to the Allies. The following year Rawson headed a group of women eager to create a movement opposing the wartime killing of Jews, hostages, and other defenseless people. They invited many women's associations, including the Victory Board, to a meeting, but it seems nothing came of it. Rawson never joined the Victory Board, instead affiliating with Acción Argentina and the Comisión Sanitaria Argentina (CSA), a group of health professionals who sent hospital supplies to the Allies.[121]

Some Socialists collaborated with the Victory Board. In early 1942, this party's branch in Resistencia recommended teaming up with any group seeking to protect democracy, freedom, and countries fighting for these principles. Responding to this call, the women's youth affiliate decided to work with the Victory Board. "Those who pass by the Casa del Pueblo [Socialist headquarters] will see thirty young Socialist girls" working to aid the "soldiers of liberty" and their families, its secretary declared.[122] Socialists in other areas may have done the same.

Table 9 shows a few board members with Concordancia connections, in Córdoba, Santa Fe, and the capital. They included the lawyer Argúas and physician Aguirre. Yet others linked to conservatism also joined the Victory Board. The National Democratic Party (Partido Demócrata Nacional, PDN), a linchpin of the Concordancia, had its "liberal" antifascist sectors, particularly in Córdoba, Mendoza, and Buenos Aires Province. The president of the Mendoza chapter, Nelly Ávila de Romero Day, was connected by marriage to this liberal PDN segment. In 1942 the *mendocino* branch of this party began to court women's participation, although seemingly in the traditional manner of supporting their menfolk. Perhaps its female sympathizers responded to the appeal by working for the Victory Board as well as the PDN.[123]

The Victory Board had male Socialist, Radical, and Concordancia backers. Dignitaries of the first two parties appeared at the inauguration of the La Plata chapter. Socialists and PDN members were present at the opening of the board's national headquarters, and Radical officeholders, including Senator Oddone and Vice Governor (and future president) Arturo Illía, attended that of the Córdoba filial. Two Socialist congressmen turned up at the Victory Board's fundraiser at Luna Park in December 1941, and the venerable party leader Nicolás Repetto praised the group and gave it a donation. A prominent Independent Socialist, a component of the ruling coalition, and minister of finance from 1933 to 1935 and 1940, Federico Pinedo spoke at the banquet during the first national convention and graced other board functions. The liberal PDN governor Rodolfo Moreno and conservative PDN caudillo Alberto Barceló, both of Buenos Aires Province, declared their support for the organization. A PDN liberal of Mendoza, Emilio Descotte addressed a meeting there of Allied aid givers convoked by the Victory Board; later he headed a committee coordinating their *ayudismo*.[124] The Victory Board garnered support across political lines.

Were its politically diverse adherents fully committed to the Victory Board's democratic mission? Aside from the board's internal democratic practices, maybe only a narrow focus on political democracy in the nation, rather than an expansive view that embraced social justice, could have knit together women of varied classes and beliefs. Some members' allegiance to even this limited version of democracy, however, was suspect. Democracy is a slippery concept susceptible to varying interpretations. Some Catholic members once may have supported Franco, as had Silveyra. Women tied to the Concordancia at least implicitly assented to its election rigging. They probably shared Silveyra's respect for the founding fathers, contempt for Rosas, and Christian principles. They may have defined democracy as loyalty to traditional governing institutions, classical liberalism, and England and France, nations admired by María Ronconi, Victoria Ocampo, and many other antifascists.[125]

More progressive members may have had questionable notions as well. Socialists also were complicit in the electoral practices of the 1930s. Radical party abstention from elections had allowed Socialists to win offices that otherwise the former would have obtained. The former did not protest national interventions in opposition-ruled provinces and other democratic failings under President Hipólito Yrigoyen (1916–1922, 1928–1930). Communists and their Socialist Worker Party (Partido Socialista Obrero, PSO) allies supported democratic rights, at least temporarily. Yet as Scheiner once had noted, a capitalist democracy was incomplete. Activists needed to spread their ideas and attract support through electoral politics, but this was insufficient to construct socialism. She and other Marxists believed that a true democracy meant a classless society rather than a bourgeois electoral system. Some European antifascists also interpreted democracy equivocally.[126] By discouraging partisan debates the Victory Board seems to have surmounted these divides and prevented these inconsistencies from damaging its internal democratic practices.

The Victory Board bridged yet another divide that was political yet also regional and historical: the split between Buenos Aires and the rest of the country. As already seen, its national leaders treated members from the interior equitably and learned from them. The first national convention demonstrated these practices, which also contested the Nationalists' suggestion that the board slighted this broad region. The meeting lasted about two full days and an evening, and the reports from provincial and territorial chapters took up an entire afternoon. They occupied twenty-four of the sixty-seven pages of proceedings, in contrast to a mere two-page description of selected porteña secretariats. The assembly spent additional time discussing the accounts from these areas. More delegates from outside than inside the federal capital attended the second national convention, where, as in the earlier conference, they and porteñas alike offered remarks on the floor. *Orientación* observed that one of "the most notable . . . characteristics of the Junta de la Victoria is the way the delegates of the interior . . . were integrated."[127]

Unity through Pluralism, Networks, and Culture

The Victory Board engaged with diverse people and bridged divides through respect. It united women by building on social networks and interest in culture. Through these means it promoted a new sense of *argentinidad*.

Integrating heterogeneous women did not mean erasing difference. During the Victory Board's early days a Señora Arkhariguelsky numbered among the intermediaries and translators who assisted immigrants who flocked to the national headquarters. She tended to the Russians, Ukrainians, Poles, Czechs, and French. A sense of common purpose promoted cordiality among the different peoples, she observed.[128] The Victory Board called attention to and respected their distinctive roots, rather than blotting them out, while at the same time uniting women for political engagement. One could argue that women of varied ethnic and national groups "became Argentine" through the Victory Board, while maintaining their identities. In the process they helped change what it meant to be Argentine—from an ingredient dissolved into a melting pot to a component of a pluralistic society.[129] Its words and actions foreshadowed Audre Lorde's compelling reflections: "Difference must not merely be tolerated, but seen as a fund of necessary polarities between which our creativity can spark like a dialectic. Only then does the necessity for interdependency become unthreatening. Only within that interdependency of different strengths, acknowledged and equal, can the power to seek new ways of being in the world generate, as well as the courage and sustenance to act where there are no charters. . . . In a world of possibility for us all, our personal visions help lay the groundwork for political action."[130] Board leaders observed that each person had something to contribute to the organization, and the members' variegated backgrounds enriched this potential. Solidarity rests upon embracing difference; without it, one cannot connect people "across significant divides," as Sameh put it, much less build a movement based on equality and mutual esteem.

A gathering in Chaco illustrated Victory Board attitudes toward persons of different backgrounds. A porteña delegation toured this territory in April 1943 to stimulate its chapters, prepare them for the upcoming convention, and strengthen ties between them and national leaders. Members of the Las Breñas filial and sympathizers from the vicinity took the guests to a farm for a meal and party. Over five hundred people—mostly immigrants and criollos—awaited them. Featuring European and criollo dancers dressed in their respective national costumes and a Bulgarian orchestra, the festivities lasted until the early morning. The porteñas questioned settlers on rural matters and practiced pronouncing words in the latter's native tongues. Everyone would long remember "the cordial friendliness and informality with which the delegates fraternized," a reporter observed. Despite their "education and customs"—code words for class—in keeping with their democratic beliefs, these women got along well with the other guests, no matter their rank, he wrote; the wealthiest to the poorest felt their camaraderie. Known for his critical mind-set, this journalist was credible. In this manner, he claimed, the visitors reinforced local sympathy for the Allies and the global movement toward "true social justice."[131] These board leaders and their hosts forded boundaries among ethnicities, classes, and rural and urban dwellers.

Julia Zarza de Kanner of Oberá echoed the reporter's sentiments. Based on her experience at the second national convention, she described board dignitaries to her family as affable and approachable. This was a telling remark from a seamstress of humble Paraguayan origins known for her sincerity.[132] Again, it demonstrated the Victory Board's ability to bring together women of varied nationalities and stations in life.

Sandra Fernández asserted that one must study the social ties among members that enable groups to function.[133] The Victory Board built on and united preexisting networks. Its founders tapped contacts in the interior, probably forged through political work, to create chapters. Either singly or consolidating with similar entities, preexisting aid circles formed the core of some filiales. These groups likely were based on social and family ties, as were the resulting board chapters. As noted, a circle of friends who knit together founded the Belgrano secretariat. Twenty-seven members out of fifty-eight in Santa Fe were close to at least one other woman in that sizeable chapter; thirteen out of fifteen members in Tafí Viejo had at least one friend in the small filial. A number of adherents met each other in schools, such as a contingent of the Tucumán chapter educated at the Escuela Sarmiento, whose principal, Señorita Saleme, was a board member. Some attended the same balls, charitable functions, athletic clubs, weddings, and birthday parties. Regarding kinship, four interrelated women belonged to the tiny Oberá chapter (out of fourteen members surveyed). In the much larger Córdoba filial (forty-five), kinship was entwined with politics. It featured two sets of relatives: in one set, four had Radical connections, and the other had three Communist-aligned women. The Santa Fe chapter contained three pairs of family members, one of which was loyal to the Progressive Democrats. In some other cases, political ties alone likely created bonds that led women into the Victory Board. Various chapters drew upon coworkers, such as the factory laborers who joined the Caballito secretariat and officemates who joined the Centro one.[134]

The Tucumán chapter contained a seemingly improbable friendship. Often appearing in the social pages, Amalia Minetti came from a wealthy entrepreneurial family and owned a sugar mill. Her husband, Dr. Miguel Figueroa Román, was a prominent judge, university professor, and leftist Radical leader who had visited the Soviet Union. Polly Yánover de Cutín was born in Ukraine to a poor Jewish family. She had sold lottery tickets and may have attended secondary school. Polly was a Communist, as was her husband, Adolfo Cutín, a dentist. Minetti met Cutín when he began to work in the clinic at her sugar mill; through this relationship and a shared interest in solidarity the upper-class businesswoman and the former prole- tarian became close. Attractive and outgoing, Yánover seems to have orga- nized the filial by drawing upon her wide and varied circle of friends.[135] In this and other cases, friendships straddled ethnic, class, and political lines. These women had already crossed boundaries before joining the Victory Board.

Other board members besides Yánover possessed social capital. One was Muriel Roberts, who mobilized clerical and sales workers, FACE Cath- olics and FEC union militants alike, for the Centro secretariat. Drallny probably incorporated her Group of Anti-Nazi Women Commercial Em- ployees into the Córdoba chapter. Through her work in the family book- store, Zarza had contacts to draw upon for the Oberá branch. Matilde Porta Echagüe de Molinas, whom the national leadership had asked to organize the Santa Fe filial, possessed contacts galore. Her unpretentiousness and involvement in social life and philanthropy gained her many friends. The cordial relations with the Jewish community—uncommon in Santa Fe at that time, according to her granddaughter—and extensive political ties that she and her husband had cultivated also facilitated recruitment. Porta Echagüe knew women connected to the Universidad Nacional del Litoral, such as Marta Samatán and Matilde Trucco, the rector's wife, who, in turn, probably helped usher their intellectual friends and Samatán's fellow UAM members into the Victory Board.[136]

Another agglutinating factor was interest in culture, a broad and vague category that resists measurement but nonetheless was a critical ingredient of the Victory Board's antifascism. Numerous members manifested this interest in different ways. The many adherents who were teachers served as intellectual leaders in small communities, and the smaller numbers of uni- versity professors did the same throughout Argentina. A progressive theater in Tucumán drew upon this filial for its casts and crew. Five of the fifty women surveyed in Resistencia were active in the Ateneo del Chaco, which hosted lectures, concerts, and readings of theatrical scripts. Encouraging ar- tistic creation and irreverence, the Fogón de los Arrieros of that city offered a library, gallery, plays, and speeches, some given by board members from other municipalities. Nine cultural enthusiasts of the local chapter gathered at the vibrant Fogón. In the mid-1930s, their counterparts in Santa Fe had frequented Diner's La Peña, which invited speakers from Buenos Aires and held a film festival.[137] Other board adherents were involved in US, Spanish Republican, and French cultural groups. Aguirre, for example, participated in the Instituto Cultural Argentino Norteamericano. Reverence for French culture crossed class lines, prompting teachers of this language, devotees of French literature, and daughters of French immigrants to join the Victory Board.[138]

These were not the only board members considered *cultas* (cultured). Descendants, relatives, and friends of Victory Board members also used this term to describe some with little formal schooling or cultural activism. The key was their love of books, art, and music, through which they filled gaps in their education. An interviewee noted that her mother, a member in Córdoba, had been a musician and avid reader, adding that most in the chapter resembled her. These devotees bonded—and others wanted to learn from them and share their cultured status. The Victory Board's regard for culture and its programs attracted such women. In fact, one filial originated in a library. The Israelite Association had the only public book collection in Villa Ángela, Chaco, and Jews and non-Jews met each other here as they returned and borrowed volumes. According to a longtime resident, the local board chapter stemmed from these interactions.[139]

Looking over my list of names for Resistencia, Cristina de Pompert de Valenzuela concluded that the majority and/or their husbands formed part of a preexisting social and cultural web.[140] This was not necessarily true of all chapters, some of which were more heterogeneous and consisted of several networks joined together. Still, women's cultural proclivities and the Victory Board's promotion of them unified many chapters.

World War II was a time of crisis when women around the world stepped out of their usual spaces. Nevertheless, the Victory Board's heterogeneity was unusual for these years in Argentina, as several keen observers confirmed. André Gattegno was born in 1940 to Sephardi Jewish parents involved in the textile business. They fled Nazi-dominated France and reached Buenos Aires in 1943. He returned to France for several postwar sojourns, settling permanently in Argentina in 1957. Having experienced persecution in different settings over many generations, Gattegno's cosmopolitan family had honed acute understandings of their surroundings in order to survive. When I described the Victory Board to Gattegno, he claimed that its diversity was exceptional, indeed inconceivable, even for years after its demise in 1947. Dr. Jorge Mosset Iturraspe, the son of a deceased member of the Santa Fe chapter, added that my list of names demonstrated that the Victory Board overcame the extreme divisions in that city to unite communities, classes, and religions.[141] It did so throughout the nation, utilizing sundry verbal appeals, allies, and practices of everyday democracy. Spokeswomen continually expressed pride in the diverse ranks, praised Jews and criollas, and made them visible. Their condemnation of Nazi assaults on Catholic teachings and figures impelled many of this faith, led by the "liberals" among them, to affiliate. Thus leaders visualized Argentina as a multicultural pluralistic nation, breaking with the hegemonic view of a melting pot. Raanan Rein attributed the acceptance of multiculturalism to Peronism, but the Victory Board preceded it.[142] The movement reached out to workers and small farmers and inverted the class hierarchy in some respects. An interest in culture, which the board reinforced through its artistic exhibitions, recitals, and other events, brought women together. Astute organizers with social capital recruited from their wide circles of acquaintances and linked established networks. Even if some already knew each other as friends, the Victory Board ushered many into a different kind of relationship in which they worked together politically, which created a new bond.[143] The national meetings congregated women of different backgrounds, rural and urban dwellers, porteñas and provincial and territorial residents in a respectful atmosphere.

As a nonpartisan movement that stretched across regions, the Victory Board could appeal to persons of varied political allegiances, and to those who had none, throughout the nation. The backing it received from politicians of distinct stripes reinforced this image. Yet some politicized members' adherence to democracy in the broader polity seemed dubious. Evidently, the Victory Board crossed more partisan divides outside the federal capital than within it.

Perhaps not all, however, affiliated of their own choosing. A number of laborers may have felt pressured by their pro-Allied employers. Antifascists like Marcos Kanner convinced their wives that the cause was vital, although others did not need convincing. Some male professionals may have wanted their wives to be recognized as board members to elevate the couples' standing.[144]

To evaluate the breadth and diversity of this movement, it is useful to compare it to another large, voluntary, nonpartisan women's organization, the Consejo Nacional de Mujeres (CNM), created in 1900.[145] The Argentine branch of the International Council of Women, it had transnational ties and affiliates throughout the country, like the Victory Board. As had the Victory Board's precursors, it worked for peace, although it was not explicitly antifascist. While feminist university graduates left the group in 1910, the aristocratic-led CNM slowly evolved and by 1932 favored women's political rights to a certain degree.[146] The group discussed issues related to women and offered them cultural programs and services. Composed largely of middle- and upper-class philanthropists, teachers, and writers, the council's membership was narrower than the Victory Board's. While lower-class women benefited from some of its activities, they did not belong to the group, nor did its magazine mention Jewish adherents. Moreover, the council was a federation of independent women's societies, not a consolidated nationwide movement. Most of these societies were beneficent; others were patriotic, cultural, educational, and professional; and some represented immigrant communities. Breaking the conservative mold were two new affiliates in the 1930s: Unión y Labor, a Socialist-linked educational group, and the Clorinda Matto de Turner association of feminist intellectuals. By 1938 the CNM had eighty-eight adhering groups, but only eight outside Buenos Aires sent delegates to its assembly of 1942, and six did so in 1944.[147] No evidence suggests that the CNM tried to recruit laborers or stimulate greater involvement from affiliates outside the capital. Nor is it clear whether it engaged as extensively across national borders in its later years as the Victory Board. Compared to the CNM, the Victory Board was unique.

Clara Drallny and Dr. María Luisa Aguirre of Córdoba may not have become friends. Perhaps they had little in common other than antifascism, but that meant a great deal. The Victory Board fostered an antifascism that stressed acceptance, comprehension, and even celebration of difference. Under these conditions, the two women and many others could bridge divides that separated them to collaborate in a compelling cause.

Nevertheless, the Victory Board could not surmount all divides. Its neglect of socioeconomic issues left a fissure between it and the underprivileged.[148] The board's emphasis on aiding the Allies eventually lost out to the competing Nationalist position on aiding locals, which Juan Perón inherited. Some might argue, however, that gender was another commonality that tied the all-woman board together, as discussed in the next chapter.

CHAPTER 5

GENDERING ANTIFASCISM IN A PATRIARCHAL SOCIETY

When the Victory Board (Junta de la Victoria) chapter of Resistencia arose in October 1941, its president, María Inés Zoppi del Valle Pardo, appealed to "all the mothers and women" of Chaco to join. Nine months later she proudly inaugurated its headquarters. Here, Zoppi declared, members knew about mothers because there were mothers among them, they thought of children because they loved them, and understood pain and tried to alleviate it. Within these walls they showed their love for freedom by helping its defenders, who were suffering and needy.[1] The nonprofessional wife of a prominent Radical businessman, Zoppi probably was one of these mothers.

Unlike Zoppi, Victory Board cofounder María Rosa Oliver rarely glorified women's usual roles or regarded motherhood as the basis for activism. After contracting polio at the age of ten, she was confined to a wheelchair. Her mother did not consider her disabled daughter a potential bride and hence excluded her from discussions of courtship, marriage, and motherhood. A doctor informed Oliver that she could have children, but she did not want them. As a girl she began to create a feminine identity detached from maternity and the expectations imposed on upper-class women. Conservative yet open-minded, her father encouraged her to develop her own ideas and rebel against social dictates. In the 1930s Oliver learned about Marxism and the importance of the Russian Revolution, and she believed that the fate of the Spanish Civil War would determine the future of revolution worldwide. By 1937 she became a Communist. As a participant in Agrupación Femenina Antiguerrera (AFA) and Unión Argentina de Mujeres (UAM), she decried attempts to confine women to childbearing and the household as fascist. Oliver's antifascism was tied to leftist and feminist politics, literature, and the friendships she formed in these transnational circles.[2]

While all Victory Board members were women, these examples show that no single notion of womanhood bound them together. Myriad variables—among them, class, politics, ethnicity, and socialization patterns—shaped each of their individual female identities. Whether they embraced maternalism, political ideals divorced from it, or both, prevailing gender constructs and the experiences and exigencies of living in a patriarchal society strongly affected the adherents and the organization in complex ways. In this restrictive context, even spokeswomen who did not believe in maternalism sometimes found it useful. As I stated elsewhere, "Maternalism was a heartfelt sentiment for many, but it was also the most durable and versatile sword in women's arsenal, honed by decades of use."[3] It assuaged uneasiness about women's assertiveness, united heterogeneous women, and justified their entry into the political arena. Nevertheless, it was not the Victory Board's only sword; increasingly, nonmaternalistic political aims entered women's arsenals.

All politics is gendered, but the Victory Board gendered its activities along women's lines. The only leading Argentine antifascist association led by and composed entirely of women, the Victory Board's ideas and practices differed from those of antifascist men. It believed it had a unique antifascist mission that only women, with their presumed attributes, could fulfill. It supported women's political rights and participation in civil defense, thus asserting citizenship and preparing them for political duties in the broader society. In South-North collaboration with the Inter-American Commission of Women (IACW) and the US government, board leaders helped foster civil defense projects as well as other novel forms of women's mobilization and activism, while adapting older forms. Although the movement often extolled women's homemaking roles, it also wanted to take women out of their households. Its sewing and knitting activities conformed to customary gendered practices, yet transcended them. The Victory Board had to negotiate with men as husbands and as fellow antifascists, who tended to respect this movement while stereotyping it in customary gendered terms. Despite its relationship with the Communist Party (Partido Comunista), this women's group exercised agency.

A Unique Mission

The Victory Board's unique mission consisted partly of unifying women and aid givers and heartening the democratic masses. In its view, this task was earmarked for women. It drew largely upon maternalistic notions.

At a banquet honoring Prime Minister Winston Churchill on his birthday, Oliver praised him for his eloquent calls for unity against Nazism. Following his lead, she said, the Victory Board also stood for unity, having brought together diverse women to work as one.[4] While many pro-Allied Argentines recognized that all democratic forces had to pull together, Ana

Rosa Schlieper de Martínez Guerrero insisted that women were the first to grasp that unity across ideological and religious lines was possible. This insight, she claimed, propelled them to launch the Victory Board.[5] Commonly identified with promoting harmony in the household, evidently women alone could implement this fusion, pluralism, and camaraderie. The belief that women were "natural" conciliators underlaid this conviction.

To complete this part of its mission, a board flyer stated that it hoped to "congregate all antifascist women" in the country, adding that every woman who favored the defeat of Nazism "could and should" participate. Theoretically this meant *all* women, for, Cora Ratto believed, each had a reason to oppose fascism.[6] Local branches issued their own versions of these calls—for example, the Berazátegui chapter urged mothers, wives, and prospective brides to come together through the Victory Board to support their anguished counterparts in war-torn nations. Adding to this maternalistic outreach, it defined the board's mission as lifting Argentine women's "consciousness of antitotalitarian unity and solidarity" and of the threat that indifference posed to their homes.[7] The Victory Board's magazine epitomized the desired unification by covering all the major women's aid groups.[8]

Although the Victory Board made a determined effort, it could not attract all democratically minded women, much less all women. Yet it had its eyes on another broad mission. In some locations, antifascist men were trying to harmonize pro-Allied aid. In Córdoba, for example, several male-led organizations formed a coordinating committee in September 1941, which enveloped the British Red Cross and neighborhood, ethnic, and women's groups, including the local Victory Board chapter. Yet this committee and another umbrella association faded from the press.[9] Given these apparent failures, the board assumed the role that it thought only women could accomplish: to unify *ayudistas*, as they unified their families.

The Victory Board's first national convention resolved to coordinate all aid groups in the republic. A month later the organization held a meeting in Buenos Aires, which appointed Radical senator Gabriel Oddone, Progressive Democratic Party (Partido Demócrata Progresista, PDP) leader Luciano Molinas, Dr. Alicia Moreau de Justo, Dr. Elvira Rawson de Dellepiane, and others to a national aid commission. Later that year, following board directives, chapters in several cities tried to synchronize the ayudistas' activities at the local level. An assembly in Mendoza, for example, convoked representatives from the Victory Board, Acción Argentina, Comisión Sanitaria Argentina (CSA), Comisión Democrática Argentina (CDA), and other groups, as well as important political figures and the British vice consul. Former peace activist and president of the Mendoza chapter, Teresa Rebasti de Basso, opened the assembly, which chose a board officer and two others to write a manifesto. What became of this and other undertakings was unclear; perhaps neither women nor men could bring antifascists together. However, the Victory Board had more success with its initiative to coordinate the Stalingrad campaign. Its efforts led to the creation of a committee that drafted a plan for collecting five million pesos worth of goods for the Soviet Union, which ayudistas seemed to follow.[10] Women had at least united antifascists for this vital crusade.

Beyond forging unity, women's unique mission included injecting antifascism with determination and spirit. When the Victory Board arose, its ally publication *La Hora* observed that "women were the ones who were called to restore the faith, the will and the union that were indispensable for the country to defend its liberty and independence." Schlieper remarked "that during these trying times women must be responsible for maintaining morale in the face of danger, by creating a firm faith in a noble cause."[11] Apparently they were the only ones who could do this—and not only within Argentina. Schlieper extended this task across national borders, telling IACW representatives meeting in Washington, DC, that "Nazi poison has infiltrated this hemisphere and weakened it. Now it is up to women to work a miracle: they must rekindle in the people and institutions of this hemisphere that sacred fire that keeps alive the democratic spirit that is our ancestors' legacy to us."[12] This gendered duty related to women's usual tasks of inspiring and supporting their menfolk and children in their endeavors. Perhaps it was not just the clear and concrete nature of their solidarity, their personal investment in making goods, and their appropriation of the "V for Victory" slogan that popularized antifascism and stimulated hope but also the Victory Board members' displays of optimism and backbone in the face of adversity.

Autonomy from Men

Politicizing women and advocating their rights also formed part of the Victory Board's unique mission. Its all-woman composition facilitated its ability to assert female citizenship. While the group faced constraints, it had considerable autonomy.

Although a few antifascist spokesmen wrote in favor of the women's vote,[13] male-led groups lagged behind. Feminists had joined Acción Argentina's Central Feminine Commission, which included Victory Board members Schlieper and Dr. Angela Santa Cruz. They enjoyed a degree of independence in expressing opinions that differed from those of Acción Argentina dignitaries, all of whom were men except for Victoria Ocampo, during her two years in its board. Yet women's local commissions, which did not have the status of *filiales*, were subject to the latter's supervision. The extreme preponderance of men in Acción Argentina's governing circle and the fact that it did not endorse women's suffrage until 1943 further demonstrated that women had little input into its policies. They gave speeches with feminist messages and engaged in democratic practices, but the organization as a whole did not focus on women's concerns.[14]

These issues help explain why the Victory Board solely consisted of women. Organizing by themselves promoted women's ease, self-confidence, leadership, and freedom of action. The Victory Board also drew upon the rich global heritage of the World Committee of Women Against War and Fascism, as well as the Agrupación Femenina Antiguerrera (AFA), Comité Argentino de Mujeres Pro Huérfanos Españoles (CAMHE), and the UAM. Backed by the Communist Party, all these groups explicitly supported women's rights, save for CAMHE, which implicitly favored them by backing a Spanish government that had incorporated women into the polity.

Communist advocacy of women's rights and mobilization of women separately from men continued with the Victory Board. Two Communists, Ratto and Oliver, had set the board into motion, perhaps at the party's behest. Samuel Kaufman, a Communist leader in Tucumán whose wife was a member, recalled that the party "was pushing hard" for it; "it was a watchword to participate." The Communist Party lay at the center of the movement, he judged, adding, however, that many others also were involved. A renowned educator and Communist activist, Berta P. de Braslavsky thought the Communist Party, among other democratic organizations, "encouraged" the Victory Board. "We were linked through the Party," she said, describing herself, Ratto, and other Communist adherents, suggesting they formed a contingent within the group. They deeply understood the need for the Popular Front and antifascist unity. Regarding solidarity with the Soviet Union as "fundamental," the Communist Party assigned Fanny Edelman to serve in the Victory Board. Edelman insisted that while board members gave themselves completely to this endeavor, for Communists it was essential to do so. She claimed that the Communist Party stimulated the establishment of chapters throughout Argentina and convinced "*mujeres del pueblo*" to join.[15] Nevertheless, to camouflage its presence the party usually did not insert its main figures in Communist-aligned groups like the Victory Board, or in their leadership.[16]

The Communist Party, then, was instrumental in initiating the Victory Board, stoking and even delegating some militants to participate, organizing working-class women, publicizing the movement (through *La Hora* and *Orientación*), and emphasizing its importance. Communists and sympathizers had a notable presence (table 9), numbered among the most dedicated members, and may have seen themselves as a distinct cohort within it. The Communist Party gave the organization more support than other political parties did. Yet did this mean that it exercised substantial control over the Victory Board? After all, the Communist Party had limited the AFA to treating only aspects of women's rights that related to peace issues. Perhaps, however, there was little need to direct the Victory Board since its diverse adherents agreed with Communists on the most pressing matter: it was imperative to aid the Allies, and particularly the Soviet Union. Significantly, Kaufman noted that the Victory Board varied from one place to another, implying the degree of Communist influence also differed.[17] Furthermore, any obvious attempt to dominate the organization would have undermined its Popular Front character and alienated its many non-Communist members.

The literature on other Popular Front women's groups provides further insight into this query. Communists also were influential in the antifascist Movimiento de Emancipación de las Mujeres de Chile (MEMCH) and Frente Único Pro Derechos de la Mujer (FUPDM), but they shared power with other women. Nevertheless, the Communist Party dominated the former for a few years and eventually oversaw the latter.[18] The Women's International Democratic Federation (WIDF, 1945–) arose in Europe and quickly attracted affiliates across the world, including the Victory Board (see chapter 8). According to Francisca de Haan, it was "strongly associated with the Communist world," but non-Communists as well as Communists participated in it at all levels. Cognizant of the war that had just ended, the organization pushed for peace and antifascism as well as women's and children's welfare and women's rights. Partly because WIDF contested US foreign interventions, US officials denounced it as Communist, claiming it was not genuinely engaged with feminism, but rather deferred to Soviet interests. This "continuing Cold War paradigm," as Haan called it, also has affected scholars, some of whom have slighted or ignored WIDF, despite its enormous size, political diversity, and dedication to women's issues. Haan, Yulia Gradskova, Jadwiga Pieper-Mooney, and other scholars have shown that Soviet policies triggered contention, and representatives of the Global South pressed for the insertion of their own non-Communist goals into WIDF's program. One should not assume that WIDF was a monolithic Soviet Bloc tool, or that liberal Western women's groups have been more independent of men than Communist-backed ones.[19]

Similarly, one should not surmise that the Victory Board lacked agency or was necessarily subservient to the Communist Party.[20] Its non-Communist and even its Communist members may have had aims that differed from those of party leaders. Indeed, the party favored the movement's political consciousness-raising and training of women, practices that encouraged their independent thinking. Communist sway, however, became more apparent after World War II.

Another Communist-influenced women's aid association, the Comisión Central Femenina Israelita de Solidaridad (CCFIS), began as a male commission's auxiliary but broke away from it, perhaps because it sought autonomy. As Ratto said of the Victory Board, this Yiddish-speaking group claimed to be an "organization of struggle and work" rather than a beneficent society.[21] Unlike the Victory Board, it boldly declared itself free of "romantic" or "motherly" sentiments. Its members recognized that the fight against "Nazifascism" also was a fight for women's "liberation" and social justice for all. CCFIS celebrated the fact that women were freeing themselves from the isolation, tedium, and subjugation of domestic tasks and laying the groundwork for future engagement in democracy—and revolution—alongside men.[22] This rhetoric was more bluntly militant than the Victory Board's, demonstrating the variation even among Communist-linked women's organizations. The board's milder promotion of women's rights and entry into public life among a broad swath of the population, along with its focus on modeling democracy, distinguished it from CCFIS and male brands of antifascism.[23] Still, both women's groups had agency.

Feminism

Victory Board spokeswomen decried their exclusion from the polity. Feminists joined the movement, some grounding their support for women's rights on motherhood and some on citizenship. Through their participation other women probably adopted feminist views. Not all members did, however, and before 1945 the board's feminism usually was cautious.

The Victory Board began advocating women's rights early on, without necessarily characterizing itself as "feminist." This word might have repelled not only conservative women, but Communists who, throughout the world, sometimes opposed what they called "bourgeois feminism" for halfway measures that in their view slowed women's emancipation.[24] Schlieper had pushed for women's suffrage and other demands through the UAM and the IACW. Shortly after the Victory Board's inauguration she observed approvingly that US women had voted for decades, implicitly calling attention to Argentine women's inability to do so. Soon thereafter, the board's representative at an antifascist rally in Córdoba declared that without women there was no democracy. The group's membership card stated, in part, "For your rights as a civilized woman." The Victory Board did not clearly define these rights, but evidently these were ones that "barbaric" fascism denied her.[25]

Long before fascism, governments and men had denied women their full citizenship, thus precluding genuine democracy, according to Schlieper. She quoted Argentine president Bernardino Rivadavia's 1823 speech marking his creation of the Sociedad de Beneficencia, the semiofficial women's charitable organization: "Civil and political inequality between the woman and the man has given the world more calamities than wars and revolutions." Schlieper deemed his statement prophetic, now that the ugliest conflict in history was raging in a world almost exclusively governed by men, their mistakes had victimized women and children, and barbarism and coercion threatened to destroy liberty and justice. The Victory Board president suggested that the exclusion of half of the population from political life had prompted these disasters. As the cornerstones of family and nation, women deserved full civil and political rights. One could measure a country's level of advancement by looking at women's status, but Argentina contradicted this notion. Here Schlieper implied that true modernization and national pride dictated lifting their standing. Yet she was hopeful. Just as World War I had provided the conditions for US women to secure the vote, so would World War II enable Latin American women to demonstrate their abilities and convince governments to grant them their rights. Indeed, Argentine women were eager to show their worthiness. And Schlieper insisted that only those countries where men and women were equal resisted aggressors effectively, which was essential in this moment.[26]

An educator and Victory Board spokeswoman, Santa Cruz also strongly supported women's suffrage. Denying it reduced women to a status lower than that of the least qualified male voters. A positive element in Argentine institutional life, women were capable of making electoral choices with good judgment.[27] It is noteworthy that Santa Cruz and, to some extent, Schlieper, justified the vote for reasons other than motherhood.

These two women were board leaders in Buenos Aires. Did the ranks, especially outside the capital, share their sentiments? UAM leaders who joined the Rosario and Santa Fe branches—nine in the former city and six in the latter—did.[28] President Alcira Olivé de Mollerach of the Rosario filial, a cultural figure and former educational official during Molinas's governorship, and other UAM members may have spread feminism in their chapters. One of these was Marta Samatán of Santa Fe, who in 1942 wrote that no woman with any awareness could oppose suffrage. To do so meant doubting women's ability to participate in public life and accepting the fascist "invitation" to imprison oneself in the kitchen.[29]

Other supporters of women's rights joined the Victory Board. Among them were María Luisa Coutouné de Butiérrez, the militant Radical of La Plata, and Dr. Sara Fradkin. Fradkin, a dentist and Spanish solidarity activist, became the vice president of the Bahía Blanca chapter. She respected the organization not only for its aid-giving, but for its promotion of women's political and civil rights in a municipality where few women had assumed active public roles. A Communist, teacher, and member of the Córdoba chapter, Juana Juárez also strongly backed women's rights.[30] Other professionals, educators, intellectuals, and workers, including those who had responded to the UAM's campaigns, may have joined the Victory Board because they already espoused such ideas or were receptive to them. Or, as Michelle Chase depicted Cuban women who opposed Fulgencio Batista's dictatorship in the 1950s, their mobilization pushed them in a feminist direction, although they did not necessarily call themselves such.[31]

Dr. Nina de Borzone, a lawyer in Rosario who soon became a Communist, was a Victory Board member whose robust advocacy of women's rights led her to admonish fellow antifascists for not doing enough to raise women's status. In 1943 she wrote several trenchant articles on incorporating women into democracy. A common belief, she noted, was that women were content only if they stayed at home, and this was true for some. Nevertheless, this argument disturbingly resembled the insistence that slaves had been satisfied with their lives. In reality, their relegation to isolation and ignorance, and exclusion from socially useful work and political discussion, dissatisfied many women. Society devalued women because they lacked rights. Moreover, a closed-off home under one person's authority was a "school of arbitrariness and submission," a microcosm of despotism. It was no coincidence that those who advocated dictatorship saw the traditional family, with a repressed wife imprisoned in an indissoluble marriage, as the base of society. In addition, such notions ignored the fact that numerous women did not live in an idealized home because they had to earn wages, could not find husbands, and/or were unwed mothers. Nor could one analyze women's conditions apart from the broader context of the persecution of labor, unemployment, low earnings, the high cost of living, illiteracy, and electoral fraud. While they understood these issues, many women activists were so preoccupied with helping the democracies fight fascism that they forgot their own banishment from Argentine democracy. Lamenting the dearth of strong local movements pushing for women's rights, Borzone urged women to demand a role in governance.[32] This was part of the Victory Board's mission, but her comments suggested that there were members who overlooked it.

Indeed, some board members did not speak of women's rights. This was true of President Matilde Porta Echagüe de Molinas of Santa Fe and her friend Genoveva Yofre de Simián, the treasurer and a homemaker.[33] Nor is it likely that Julia Zarza de Kanner of Oberá, who deferred to her husband, did.[34] Succeeding chapters discuss the military dictatorship's (1943–1946) closure of the Victory Board for almost two years. When it reopened, some chapters revived or morphed into new groups which supported women's suffrage much more actively than before. Perhaps uncomfortable with this stance, a number of members left the Victory Board, including Porta Echagüe and Yofre.

At least one woman who may not have subscribed to feminism never-theless approvingly described the Victory Board as such. President Zoppi of Resistencia declared that its rootedness in people's souls, strong actions, di-versity, and patriotic and humanitarian core beliefs distinguished the Vic-tory Board from other local women's groups and made it "a feminist current of new physiognomy."[35] It was unclear whether she included women's rights among the Victory Board's convictions or if she called all women's associa-tions feminist. Yet it was significant that she used this word positively in a small remote city.

The Victory Board's feminism had its limits. Contrasting with kindred groups such as MEMCH, it did not uphold reproductive rights. There were several reasons for this omission. It prioritized assembling aid for the Allies and, through this task, training women for political roles. Even without raising controversial issues, such as birth control, the Victory Board faced hostility and persecution. It also sought a broad base, which meant attract-ing devout Catholics. Advocating conscious maternity would have roused further enmity from a patriarchal right-wing clerical hierarchy and alien-ated the pious.[36]

Yet the Victory Board encouraged women's self-expression and learn-ing. Dr. Margarita Argúas, a jurist, lectured the Once secretariat, which she headed, on women's civil rights. This was one of her filial's regular gather-ings in which women listened to presentations and debated issues while pre-paring aid.[37] Whether other chapters commonly addressed women's legal status before 1945 is uncertain. However, some members discussed family problems as they sewed and knitted. These conversations may have raised their consciousness of the predicaments they faced as women living in a male-dominated society.[38] Moreover, events held in chapter and national headquarters tended to feature women artists, performers, and thinkers. In this manner the Victory Board not only gave members opportunities to exchange ideas and expand their outlook but also contested fascist aims to remove women from public arenas and curtail their education.

Mobilizing and Training Women for Political Duties

Even if they were not explicitly feminist, members accepted the Victory Board's insertion of women into the public sphere and initiation of their political involvement. It fostered their managerial skills and mobilized them in new ways. The board provided spaces for women's activism in areas outside the capital where, as Fradkin discerned in Bahía Blanca, few had existed. And it took women out of the house.

One of these was Adelina Cornejo de Elkin of Córdoba. Of a modest background, she finished secondary school and married soon thereafter.

Cornejo was devoted to playing the piano and attending to her household; health problems also may have kept her mostly in the domestic sphere. While not a devout Catholic, she attended church for consolation over the death of two children. Yet she also was close to the Communist Party, where she probably heard of the Victory Board. Home, church, the cemetery, and the Victory Board were the places Cornejo frequented. Through the filial she learned of world affairs and met other women. Participating in it was a means of liberation, of extending her horizons beyond her residence, according to her son.[39]

This was a first step toward training members for future service to the nation. The Victory Board was a political organization, and not only because it fought fascism. Members followed parliamentary procedures, elected officers, gave speeches, and worked in committees. The chapters compiled reports on their activities, which they presented at the conventions, where delegates discussed and voted on plans, resolutions, and policies. Schlieper observed that the Victory Board instructed women in manual labors, discipline, fraternal "norms of collective coexistence and . . . tasks useful for the State and its defense."[40] They managed budgets and organized fundraisers, national conventions, and the distribution of materials from Buenos Aires to filiales, and from there to homes, farms, and factories. Members wrote flyers and pamphlets, disseminated news of their activities to the press, and interceded with authorities. Thus, as Ratto affirmed, they received a practical education "in the exercise of democracy and acquire[d] consciousness of their force and effectiveness."[41]

President Olivé of Rosario claimed that the first convention demonstrated Argentine women's administrative skills. She commended Schlieper for giving the Victory Board the type of organization found in the United States, one that had set up a conference that displayed "speed, concrete and clear exposition of aspirations, categorical resolution."[42] The Victory Board president also credited the delegates for their dedication, enthusiasm, and ability, which showed how Argentine women were advancing and soon would share leadership with men.[43]

The second convention showed that some had, at least in a neighboring country. Two Uruguayan women parliamentarians attended this conference: Julia Arévalo, the first Communist congressional representative in the Western Hemisphere, and Dr. Sofía Alvarez Vignoli de Demicheli, of a conservative faction of the Colorado Party, the first woman senator in South America.[44] Both belonged to Feminine Action for Victory (Acción Femenina por la Victoria), the Victory Board's sister group (see chapter 6). As we will see, the Victory Board had several reasons for hosting Feminine Action delegates. One was to inspire its members by spotlighting women voting, holding public office, and participating in policymaking across the

River Plate. The implication was that Argentine women should aspire to such roles and were preparing to do so through the Victory Board.

Among Argentine women's associations, perhaps only the Sociedad de Beneficencia, which administered various welfare institutions, and CAMHE, which handled huge quantities of aid from across the country for shipment to Spain, came close to equaling the Victory Board's organizational feats. The Sociedad de Beneficencia and the CNM did not have chapters outside Buenos Aires, although preexisting groups affiliated with the latter. While CAMHE and Acción Argentina's Central Feminine Commission had branches throughout the country, neither held national meetings. As Acción Argentina's central ruling body authorized the creation of women's commissions, and they operated under the control of the local male chapters, it is unclear to what extent the Central Feminine Commission coordinated or financed them. The CNM did not supervise large amounts of funds or exercise much oversight over its few affiliates, and only a handful of delegates from them attended its conventions.

In contrast to these groups, the Victory Board established new national patterns of women's mobilization. It was keenly interested in its chapters, frequently sending them directives, propaganda, materials for workshops, and requests for statistics, particularly on membership, fundraising, and the production of goods. *Porteña* representatives toured the provinces and territories to meet, inform, and energize members. At the conventions board members listened to their colleagues and established cordial ties with them. Leaders in Buenos Aires broke down regional lines to construct a national network that trained women for political involvement.

A practice that was not new but was unusual, at least for bourgeois women, was participation in marches. The Victory Board took part in them, such as one sponsored by the Federación Universitaria Argentina commemorating Argentine independence in May 1942, in which Schlieper headed a column of members and gave a speech. Yet authorities frequently repressed demonstrations. Chapters such as the one in Córdoba braved the police as they marched.[45] In this manner the Victory Board maintained a public presence in defiance of Nationalists and conservatives who wanted to confine women to homes, churches, and charities. Its visibility and militancy suited its role in the "army of liberty."

Civil Defense

The Victory Board had declared its allegiance to the Allied women's "army of liberty" at its inaugural ceremony (see chapter 3). In line with such views, it sought to train women in civil defense to enhance national security, assert citizenship, and elevate domestic roles. This campaign was part of an initiative that stretched across the Americas. Despite a lack of government support, the Victory Board promoted civil defense widely.

When war was declared in 1939, the IACW, heavily influenced by US representative Mary Winslow, shifted its focus away from women's rights to defending the Americas. While this change disgruntled prominent feminists like Paulina Luisi, Schlieper and other Latin American delegates saw hemispheric defense as a means of safeguarding and even extending women's gains. They linked the war against fascism with women's rights, which Germany and Italy had overturned. And they continued to press for their rights, which they believed could only thrive under democracy. Such efforts gathered steam with President Roosevelt's advocacy of human rights in the 1941 "Four Freedoms" and Atlantic Charter, which Pan-American Popular Front feminists wanted to broaden to include women.[46]

Thus the Victory Board's involvement in defense efforts was connected to its feminist agenda. Since men's privileges as citizens rested partly on their military duties, women claimed that they, too, were soldiers, albeit on the home front.[47] The Victory Board frequently related women's service to men's combat duties. "The point of a needle is worth as much as a rifle shot," the Ensenada, Buenos Aires, chapter insisted.[48] National leader Clara Helman de Oxman compared the Allied men of all social classes, who were fighting and perishing for a common ideal, to the Victory Board members of all backgrounds who had united to defeat "Nazifascism."[49] When the board informed women overseas that it was joining their "army of liberty," it was claiming full citizenship. Working in civilian defense seemed logical for this women's "army."[50]

Winslow was not the only IACW activist to push for civilian defense programs and for women's involvement in them. This was also a South-North initiative. Before the attack on Pearl Harbor, the Mexican feminist and IACW representative Amalia de Castillo Ledón began organizing such projects in her country. At the November 1941 IACW meeting, delegates approved her resolution calling for preparing women to engage with civil defense in each nation and coordinating these endeavors throughout the Americas.[51]

The IACW sought the cooperation of the US Office of Civilian Defense (OCD) to disseminate information and institute programs in the Western Hemisphere. Working with the OCD, and through her duties at the Office of Inter-American Affairs (OIAA), Winslow planned to comply. She proposed to bring Latin American women and men to the United States to study such matters and provide consultants to implement relevant projects in the Americas. She also wished to produce informational materials on civilian protection, organization of volunteers, first aid, child welfare, nutrition, community education, and preparing women for industrial jobs. The breadth of coverage reflected the belief of First Lady Eleanor Roosevelt, who had served as the OCD's assistant director for volunteer coordination, that medical care, childcare, diet, and women's involvement were vital for national defense. The completed materials, however, omitted women's training.[52]

Having studied civilian defense, viewed some of its US manifestations, and discussed it with Winslow and other IACW delegates, Schlieper was well acquainted with this issue. In early 1942 she presented to the Argentine War Ministry a broad project on organizing and instructing women for civilian defense, presumably through the Victory Board. She failed to gain its support.[53]

Despite this setback, the Victory Board started to implement this new form of women's mobilization. During the first national convention, Ratto discussed the need for civilian defense courses. The board planned to sponsor instruction on first aid, meal preparation, childcare, public health, communications systems, driving, and foreign languages. The first three topics demonstrated the importance of domestic duties for civic needs. Starting in September 1942, the Victory Board offered free first aid courses to members in several cities, generally staffed by CSA members. Prestigious doctors taught classes on treating wounds, burns, and the effects of poison gas for the Córdoba chapter. Its president, María de la Paz Cremades de Oddone, described the aim as training women for the passive defense of the nation, as opposed to the active defense of combat, again a reference to women's quasi-military service. Such courses potentially could empower women by enabling them to promote the health of the community as well as the family and entrusting them with "scientific" health practices that opposed folk medicine. Other filiales also hosted series on these issues, and the Buenos Aires Provincial Convention pledged to establish blood donation programs. Despite these auspicious beginnings, however, this civilian defense program stalled. The Stalingrad campaign, which began in early October 1942, became the Victory Board's overarching priority and eclipsed other goals.[54]

Meanwhile, other groups took up this mission. The stated goal of the Comité Femenino de Afirmación Democrática y Defensa Argentina was to train women to work alongside men in such tasks. In July 1940 it advertised courses on aviation, the Argentine road system, driving, parachuting, telegraph usage, and first aid and physical exercise. It also offered a civics class, accompanied by remarks on the constitution given by feminist Adelia di Carlo, who had helped organize the Argentine Conference of Women for Peace in 1936.[55]

More important was the creation in June 1942 of Defensa Civil Femenina (DCF), a group of mostly young women who asked Schlieper to
serve as their advisor. Stung by the government's rejection of her plan, she
wrote Mary Cannon that the new organization would challenge official
apathy based on the naïve view of the war as a faraway shadow.[56] It is noteworthy that three of the five women on the DCF's advisory board were
Victory Board members—Schlieper, Santa Cruz, and Alba Tamargo—and
a fourth, Eugenia Silveyra de Oyuela, was a close collaborator.[57]

The DCF declared that the ideals of liberty upheld by the independence
leader José de San Martín and other patriotic heroes inspired its members to
support men in defending their homes, national sovereignty, and the constitution. The fact that their peers in combatant nations had replaced men
in many occupations vital to the war effort also influenced them. Of varied
religions, political persuasions, and "races," DCF women prepared to re-
spond to any emergency, not just war. Despite local conservatism and their
alleged "timidity," provincial women also formed DCF chapters. Adherents
learned to serve as nurses, telegraph and Morse code operators, automobile
mechanics, and drivers. The Argentine Automobile Club offered driving
classes, and the Red Cross provided first aid instruction to DCF members,
who also studied nutrition, hygiene, and other matters related to the home.
The domestic nature of some of its programs   notwithstanding, the DCF
truly mobilized women for new tasks.[58]

Compared to the DCF's women mechanics, the Victory Board's seamstresses and knitters seemed mired in old-fashioned female-coded roles.
While young unmarried women predominated in the DCF leadership and
probably the ranks, the Victory Board encompassed women of all ages,
although its Centro secretariat, Tafí Viejo filial, and perhaps other chapters had numerous young members. It may have created a youth branch.[59]
Still, there were many similarities between the two associations, starting
with their shared democratic mission. Like the Victory Board, the DCF
sought members throughout society and the nation. Both had male collaborators of varied political backgrounds; the DCF's, however, included
several military officers but no Communists. The two movements formed
part of transnational Latin American currents: the Victory Board joined
women's antifascisms in the region, and the DCF figured among its wom-
en's civilian defense groups, which arose in Cuba, Uruguay, Brazil, Mexico,
and Panama.[60] The most important resemblance was the underlying notion
that women were capable of performing a full range of jobs and organizational duties, which surely led many in the two associations to believe that
they were qualified to participate in political affairs. That both were "good
soldiers" of a "true army of civilian aid," according to a journalist describing
the DCF, justified roles in the polity.[61]

Sewing and Knitting

Was it indeed accurate that the Victory Board's seamstresses and knitters conformed to old-fashioned women's roles? In some ways they did, and in other ways not. These practices had complex meanings, implications, and significance and enabled them to create new identities.

Sewing and knitting symbolized customary notions of femininity, domesticity, and respectability. They also were associated with livelihood, as working-class women often labored in tailoring and textile enterprises and engaged in piecework and garment-making at home. Working for pay within rather than outside the household helped ensure wives' honor and placate chauvinistic husbands. The main Jewish women's charity in Buenos Aires donated sewing machines to impoverished women; other beneficent societies trained orphans to use them and procured needlework jobs for indigents. Under Peronist rule, the Eva Perón Foundation gave these machines away, and government credit facilitated private purchases of them. Many lower- and even middle-class girls took sewing lessons to learn to make affordable and attractive clothes for themselves and their future families, which would reinforce their identities as reputable women and loving mothers.[62]

Yet the practices that surrounded the Victory Board's sewing and knitting challenged some of these roles and class connotations. Natalia Milanesio argued that sewing per se extended networks, since women who sewed for their families sometimes helped those neighbors who sewed for pay meet their quotas. The Victory Board's workshops further broadened social networks by removing women of diverse backgrounds from their homes and banding them together. Through their customary hand labors, women created an extraordinary cross-class space where they could speak with one another. Their conversations may have eased not only concerns about their family problems in Argentina, but despair over the fate of their European relatives and the world. As Bruce Scates found for Australian aid givers during World War I, Victory Board offices fostered women's companionship and "solace amidst the anguish of war," even if this lasted only for a few hours of sewing. Unlike some aid groups in other countries, board members were not divided by race or even class; although a number of chapters were neighborhood-based, the composition of these barrios was not necessarily homogeneous.[63] Working-class board adherents could teach their social "betters" about their craft, whereas laborers in segregated groups elsewhere could not. Moreover, while many Argentines regarded women laborers as potential prostitutes, Victory Board members' involvement in a prestigious cause made them respectable. The organization's mission was political rather than economic; sewing and knitting needles were its weapons against fascism and its tools for creating a more egalitarian society, rather than a means of earning a living. Through knitting and sewing, antifascism became a tangible part of ordinary women's daily lives. According to Lynn Dumenil, the bandages and apparel they made for armies "brought women symbolically close to men on the field of battle." Such activities enabled them to form new identities as democrats, antifascists, citizens and even soldiers that overlapped their old identities as mothers, housewives, and workers.[64]

No matter how much the Victory Board supervised production, the scarves, stockings, and the like that its members knit for combatants may not have met military specifications. Small variations in design and technique probably distinguished one woman's output from another's. Dumenil suggested that one could interpret these distinctions as a means of countering the "depersonalizing qualities of modern armies and modern warfare." This evidence of concern and caring for the individual soldier fit within what Scates called the "emotional labour" of women's war work. It was emotional but not necessarily maternalistic, unlike the Paraguayan upper-class "godmothers of war" described by Bridget María Chesterton, who corresponded with and aided impoverished rural soldiers during the Chaco War.[65] With their knitted goods, board members may have tried to keep the recipients warm, as if they were their sons, but they also regarded them as valuable comrades in the struggle.

The Victory Board's needlework was acceptable in part because it represented the extension of domestic tasks and conventional female virtues outside the home. But as Linda Colley observed of English women's sewing circles during the Napoleonic Wars, this activity was more far-reaching. Like their British precursors, the Victory Board members carried out solidarity with unrelated men in distant armies, demonstrating that their noble qualities "possessed a public as well as a private relevance." They engaged in political discourse with their needles and thread and thus spanned private and public, as did the Platine women during the early 1800s analyzed by William Acree, who sewed emblems and uniforms that symbolized political identities. Their expositions of their products further highlighted the public character of their efforts. Even when ayudistas sewed or knitted in their abodes, these spaces were hardly isolated or marginalized. They converted their homes into sites of political agency that were integrated into the antifascist resistance.[66] Its blurring of lines between public and private set the Victory Board apart from men's antifascist groups, which operated exclusively in the public sphere. Pro-Franco and Nationalist women, however, also broke down these borders.[67]

This analysis brings to mind what Dr. Clara Schliapnik de Filer said about fellow adherents in Villa Domínguez, Entre Ríos, the seat of a Jewish agricultural colony. A leftist medical doctor, outspoken critic of fascism and antisemitism, and contributor to the Socialist publication *Vida Femenina*, she presided over the local Victory Board chapter. When the military assumed power in 1943 and repressed the Victory Board, Schliapnik disbanded the filial. She refused to divulge members' names to the police, merely replying that they were simple women who wanted to sew for Allied soldiers.[68] Yet the connotations of sewing and knitting were anything but simple.

Maternalism

Sewing and knitting were related partly to maternalism. So too was the emphasis on childcare and food preparation in the Victory Board's civil defense program and articles on these topics that appeared in its magazine. Similarly, the so-called sacrifice campaigns, also held by other antifascist groups, in which women donated to the cause what they ordinarily spent on cigarettes and other indulgences, resonated with the values of abnegation and martyrdom customarily ascribed to mothers. Adriana Valobra argued that with its appeals to motherhood and domesticity, the Victory Board attracted many more women than did strictly feminist organizations with their slogans of women's rights. Yet the board was not uniformly maternalistic—unlike Nationalist women. Following in the footsteps of the AFA and other precursors, it sometimes addressed women as mothers, sometimes as citizens, democrats, patriots, or workers, and sometimes as a mixture of these categories.[69]

Zoppi was one of the spokespersons who primarily regarded women as mothers and Victory Board tasks as domestic. As cited earlier, she emphasized the presence of mothers in her chapter. Utilizing the image of a lioness protecting her cubs, Zoppi insisted that Argentine women were lions ready to defend the democratic system that they had inherited from their parents and wanted to pass onto their children. This desire represented an extension of women's typical roles. All board activities should display the characteristics of "home life, eminently sentimental and sympathetic," President Cremades de Oddone of Córdoba advised.[70]

Caring for those who were distressed or infirm was also associated with motherhood. The Berazátegui branch called for mothers, wives, and prospective brides to unite behind their suffering counterparts in occupied and combatant countries. According to Zoppi, the Victory Board was supplying the Allies because Argentine women could not be indifferent to the sorrow of so many mothers, wives, fiancés, sisters, and daughters across the ocean. Even though the battlefields were far from Argentina, a delegate told the first national convention that "the woman felt within herself the pain of her sisters." The Victory Board expressed love and solidarity with those in despair, said the president of the Avellaneda chapter, adding that despite their seemingly safe households, members regarded the tragedy of destroyed homes elsewhere as their own. Making bandages and other medical supplies especially touched women's hearts, observed the head of the Belgrano secretariat, since it meant helping the wounded.[71]

The belief that their progeny's future depended on the war's outcome reinforced women's antifascism. Nazi indoctrination of children horrified Victory Board activists, as it had AFA and UAM members. Whereas Germany had been a country of "fairy tales," according to Saslavsky, an "ogre" appeared in 1933. Formerly an enchanted city of honey cakes and toys, Nuremberg had become a center of the arms industry. Women who had sung Mozart melodies to their sons were crying over their deaths in combat, while their sons who had listened to these tunes had turned into "monsters of killing." The Nazi ogre had transformed the nation and undermined women's mission of spreading peaceful and ethical values; its penchant for violence and war endangered children everywhere. As long as fascism existed, women would worry about their offspring, Helman added.[72]

Even women who did not uphold these customary views may have expressed them to avoid censure for contesting gender roles or harming the family. Moreover, the leftists among them may have deployed such rhetoric to hide their militancy for security or tactical reasons. Maternalism served as a unifying force superseding political differences, for all women were mothers or potential mothers. As Chase argued for Cuban women activists in the 1950s, maternalism enabled Victory Board members to claim "moral authority, righteousness, and a shared grief"[73]—in the Argentine case, grief over the fate of European relatives and the possible fate of their own children—in their struggle against local and foreign authoritarianism.

Nevertheless, Oliver and Ratto rarely referred to motherhood. The desire to save socialism and the Soviet Union, create a free and just postwar world, and foster equal rights for women drove Oliver's wartime antifascism. Adolf Hitler's racist imperialism and disdain for Latin Americans as "monkeys" also repelled her.[74] According to Ratto, the Victory Board fought for a genuine era of peace and liberty in which women could work, study, research, think, and pray freely. All but the last were critical for this budding mathematician. Also, the Nazi ill-treatment of Jewish scientists troubled her.[75]

These two figures were not alone in downplaying or lacking maternalist sentiments. One must recall the Victory Board spokespersons' constant references to the workers, professionals, intellectuals, writers, and artists who, along with homemakers, made up their movement. Political concerns prompted many to affiliate besides Ratto and Oliver. Inspired by Argentine women's historic solidarity with freedom and democracy, members of a chapter in greater Buenos Aires felt compelled to join the struggle against the Axis aggressors; to do otherwise signified "cowardice . . . cruelty . . . treason." The delegates of Cañada de Gómez, Santa Fe, declared at the first convention that their filial revered democratic freedoms. They belonged to the Victory Board because it stood for liberty, independence, and a great and prosperous Argentina. Working for the "final triumph of justice against oppression, light against darkness, life against death" propelled the Mendoza branch.[76]

Other board members combined maternalism with political ideals. The Santa Fe chapter wrote Eleanor Roosevelt after Pearl Harbor, stating that the time had come for American countries to fight. This included "women who prefer liberty and justice to life; the mothers who do not want criminal forces to continue bombarding children."[77] Schlieper had long fit in this category. She declared her wish for a "democratic, human, and just" postwar order that would rest upon equal rights and duties for all men and women, of all races and religions. If women still lacked the right to participate on an equal footing with men, they would be at the same level as minors, excluded from forging a better world. Women were responsible for imparting to children their first lessons of democracy, freedom, and conscientious citizenship. Yet one could not teach what one did not feel or possess.[78] Belittling women contradicted democratic ideals and imperiled the postwar utopia of which so many dreamed.

Maternalism suffused the Victory Board, but it also issued other overtures. This belief influenced solidarity, yet it was absent from the training of women for political involvement. Borrowing from the board's predecessors, Schlieper, and others at times, used women's motherly, humanitarian, and peacemaking "nature" to justify citizenship, whereas Oliver and Ratto used political aspirations. Women wore different hats on different occasions,[79] or always wore the same hat, or wore two at the same time. Which appeals proved more compelling is unclear.

The Victory Board and Antifascist Men

Antifascist men collaborated with and lauded the Victory Board, although their maternalistic rhetoric constricted it. They overlooked board activities apart from aiding the Allies. Perhaps the lack of competition among antifascist organizations, which functioned along professional and gendered lines, promoted their approval of the board.

Shortly after its founding, an article on the Victory Board appeared in the women's column of *La Hora*, edited by Hilda Schiller, a Communist educator and officer of the La Plata chapter. It reflected the largely male-led

Communist Party's viewpoint, as well as that of some women, perhaps including Schiller. It declared that the group embodied the sentiments of the mothers, wives, fiancés, and sisters of the nation, who were applying their "impassioned capacity for emotion and tenderness" to the task of defeating those who threatened the home, popular well-being, and women's emancipation. Members realized that their campaigns for women's economic, political, and social rights could only be fulfilled with the defeat of "Nazifascism." The Victory Board was an extension of these campaigns; it stood for "a humanitarian militancy, a democratic militancy, and a militancy of generosity and tenderness."[80] Evidently the author did not perceive women as workers, professionals, or students, or believe it was possible for women to attain rights until after victory. The article acknowledged the Victory Board's desire to improve women's status, yet affirmed that its priority was an Allied victory. Schlieper and other board leaders agreed with this priority, but they did not simply identify women with emotions, motherly qualities, and familial roles.

Antifascist men respected the Victory Board, generally praising it in terms that were even more maternalistic than La Hora's. In September 1941 a democratic newspaper reported on its nascent headquarters. The women's "smile of peace for the men at war" permeated the space, as did piles of wool. The journalist observed that the knitted goods the Victory Board would make for Allied soldiers represented the double warmth of this wool and women's smiles.[81] This and other writings extolled women as loving helpmates.

Another common means of applauding the Victory Board was to compare it to the women of Cuyo (later known as Mendoza) who had donated their jewels to San Martín's independence army. The Centro Republicano Hispano Americano in Santa Fe made this connection. Having supported the Spanish Republic, the centro renewed its commitment to democracy by sponsoring the Victory Board's fundraising banquet in March 1942. It valued this collaboration with board members who, "with their patriotism, courage, generosity, and noble presence" were the "worthy heirs and continuators" of the women who had contributed to the Liberator's struggle for freedom and sovereignty.[82] Thus the centro linked the Victory Board to a cherished historic movement and to the founding mothers of the nation and their womanly sacrifices. Yet it and others who made this identification, including some board members, overlooked women's more active roles in the independence war, such as hosting salons, engaging in revolutionary plots, sewing military uniforms, and fighting in battles.[83] In this manner, they reduced their agency.

The Centro Republicano Hispano Americano and the journalists who published such descriptions of the Victory Board saw them as commendatory, and numerous women would have appreciated them. Yet maternalism also limited women to the domestic sphere and activities associated with it and obscured their militancy and independent thought. Men tended to extoll board members for their motherly "abnegation" and ayudismo,[84] but not for their other contributions to antifascism, such as modeling democracy, training women for civic engagement, and promoting unity.

Across the River Plate, however, a distinguished Argentine antifascist man and a Communist Party–linked newspaper praised the Victory Board in nonmaternalistic terms. The former president of Agrupación de Intelectuales, Artistas, Periodistas y Escritores and the Committee against Racism and Anti-Semitism, CDA officer, and Communist sympathizer, Dr. Emilio Troise continued his activism in exile in Uruguay during the military dictatorship (1943–1946). Speaking at an event in Montevideo in 1944, he paid tribute to the Victory Board, which *Diario Popular* hailed as the largest group aiding the Allies in the Americas. Troise declared that he had seen its members work and organize this movement "with enthusiasm and the noblest passion."[85]

Men less eminent than Troise thought highly enough of the Victory Board to work with it. As mentioned, some took on domestic chores, enabling their wives to dedicate themselves to board activities. The Berisso delegate at the first convention praised the partnership among working-class adherents and male supporters, who sacrificed their brief hours of rest: "The women knitting, circulating lists, helping in the organization of a festival, the men handing over up to their last coin in the festivals we carried out, and also offering themselves" for various chores. And, she added, humble men and women sold their "radios, bicycles, sets of tableware" to contribute money.[86] Male laborers donated to its campaigns,[87] and businessmen bequeathed materials, funds, publicity, and spaces for activities.

Antifascist organizations led by and composed completely or largely of men asked the Victory Board to participate in many joint ventures and meetings. For example, board representatives attended the CDA's national conference in 1942. Acción Argentina invited a board delegate to participate in a committee organizing a ceremony honoring President Roque Sáenz Peña (1910–1914), whose support for the secret ballot was reflected in the law that bore his name. Board leaders spoke at men's gatherings, such as Schlieper's address at a democratic journalists' farewell dinner for Alberto Gerchunoff, who was leaving to visit the United States. A distinguished audience of intellectuals, foreign diplomats, and members of the press heard her speech.[88] Such groups paid attention to the Victory Board, included it in their activities, and accorded it more visibility than Nationalists did for their women's affiliates, but ignored its feminist aspirations.

Men accepted the Victory Board because they perceived an urgent need for ayudismo, and it abided by the gendered division of responsibilities among antifascist movements. In fact, antifascist groups did not seem to regard each other as competitors or oppose each other, except for Acción Argentina's antagonism toward the CDA for its Communist links. Indeed, the former expelled some men who also belonged to this association.[89] However, its anti-Communism did not prevent Acción Argentina from inviting board representatives to events. Acción Argentina was mostly devoted to formulating ideas, lecturing, issuing propaganda, holding rallies, and agitating for political power. The CDA's main tasks were collecting and purchasing materials and mobilizing worker volunteers who used them to make shoes and other items for the Allies. It also shipped preserved foodstuffs to the Allied nations. A few women doctors, such as Dr. Telma Reca and Rawson, lent their efforts to the largely male CSA, which sent medical supplies to the Allies, established a registry of potential blood donors, and offered courses on surgery for war-related injuries to medical personnel and on first aid to the Victory Board, Acción Argentina, and other groups. It seems that the CSA prepared the medicines and equipment it dispatched.[90] The Victory Board also made bandages and other hospital goods and received donations of clothing from other women's associations. Nevertheless, the board was the only major antifascist organization whose members were dedicated to sewing and knitting large quantities of items to be sent overseas. This was among its uniquely gendered activities.

Antifascist Couples

The Victory Board's ties with most antifascist men's organizations seem relatively straightforward. The personal relationships that many members formed with antifascist men, however, were far more complex. To understand how women *lived* antifascism, one cannot neglect their quotidian experiences with their husbands and partners. María Eugenia Bordagaray observed that shared political commitments and daily conversations shed light on women's and men's contributions to the cause.[91] Yet it is difficult to document intimacies in the home. The intermingling of the personal and the political followed no single pattern, for the tenor of these relationships varied. Nonetheless, a few cases revealed a degree of gender equality.

To grasp these dynamics, it is useful to examine the case of the Chileans Marta Vergara, Popular Front Pan-American feminist and IACW representative, and Marcos Chamudes. Vergara's autobiography offers a much more detailed account of an antifascist couple than any Argentine writing for this period and suggests questions to ask of one's material. When she met her future husband in the early 1930s, he was a Communist militant and journalist, and she was a newspaper correspondent and feminist activist who had participated in international conferences and organizations, at times as an official Chilean delegate. Vergara believed that women's issues transcended the class struggle, and that the Communist Party should encourage feminist collaboration against imperialism, whereas Chamudes and the party opposed such alliances and overlooked women's concerns. Nevertheless, Vergara sympathized with Communism, seeing it as a means of contesting poverty, colonialism, militarism, and Nazism. Women, she believed, had to oppose fascism because it demeaned them, and Communists were practically the only ones combatting it. Once women attained the right to vote and be elected to posts at the municipal level in 1934—which she had fought for—Vergara ran for office on the Communist ticket. As the decade wore on, she grew to admire Chamudes for his oratory, engagement with antiwar and antifascist groups, and successful campaign for a congressional seat. The rise of the Popular Front and the creation of MEMCH alleviated some of Vergara's concerns about the party, which she joined in 1936. Around the same time, she became a MEMCH leader and married Chamudes.[92]

Tensions beset the relationship from the beginning. Vergara wanted to attend the 1933 Pan American Union conference in Montevideo, which would discuss critical women's issues, but Chamudes and the Communist Party did not want her to dally with bourgeois feminists and imperialists and forbade her from going. She felt conflicted about getting married because she was nine years older than her lover, and the party had forced Chamudes to choose between her and another woman, a militant. Her liaison with a Jew also struck some as scandalous, although that did not seem to bother her. After the rise of the Popular Front, Vergara was able to attend the Buenos Aires Peace Conference of 1936, where she was in touch with Schlieper and other UAM members. Communist policies abruptly changed with the German-Soviet Nonaggression Pact of 1939 and accompanying suspension of the Popular Front. The party's attempt to control MEMCH and limit its membership to Communists and workers rankled Vergara, who separated herself from this women's group, although she continued her feminist activism. The party's shifts resulted in its expulsion of the couple. Vergara followed her husband to the United States, where he became a photographer and she worked for the IACW and taught Spanish. They lived apart, which she admitted improved their relationship.

This account points to several matters for analysis. Did antifascist couples exhibit the gender equality that Victory Board leaders envisioned for society? How did these relationships affect their militancy and vice versa? How did they negotiate power with each other? Did they occupy gender-differentiated roles in their political struggles? In response to the last question, Vergara and Chamudes did not—both were activists, journalists, and public officials, although her primary allegiance was to feminism and his to Communism, at least until his expulsion from the party. Vergara continually asserted her equality in the relationship, although initially Chamudes obstructed her engagement with women's rights. They had strong personalities and frequently clashed on political and other issues; their negotiations were rancorous, although they may have been more amicable during the Popular Front period. His subservience to the Communist Party, its interference with their relationship, and the effect of its tactical fluctuations on the couple were striking.[93]

According to Ariel Lambe, a power differential characterized a non-Communist Cuban couple. Pablo de la Torriente Brau had courted Teresa Casuso since she was a young girl and he was a teenager, and he helped form her identity. From childhood on she became the "reliable follower" and he the "heroic leader." Married as adults, they worked together to protest Cuban dictators, US imperialism, and fascism. Their activism continued in exile in New York and, for Torriente Brau, in the Spanish Civil War. He wanted to experience the Republic's revolutionary resistance and "'to be seen as a man.'" Moreover, he feared that a *franquista* victory in Spain would strengthen fascism in Cuba and the region. Although Casuso had participated fully in the same political struggles, Torriente Brau did not want her to accompany him, and she accepted this. He died in combat, and Casuso returned to Cuba and organized a group that helped Spanish children.[94]

Communist leader Marcos Kanner's influence on his wife was even stronger than Torriente Brau's on Casuso. He helped convince her to join the Victory Board, yet he sought to limit her involvement. Victoria Wickstrom, a Swedish immigrant who by 1943 presided over the Oberá chapter, spoke Spanish poorly and therefore wanted Julia Zarza to accompany her to the second national convention. Wickstrom asked Kanner to permit his spouse to go, which he refused, but upon her insistence he finally gave in. Then he wrote a speech for Zarza, who had only a primary school education, to deliver at the convention, which she duly practiced. He did so to assist her and make her shine; she thought it natural and acceptable that the man of the house would do this for her. Attending the meeting only because Wickstrom intervened, Zarza barely negotiated with Kanner over this or other matters, simply following his lead. The relationship between husband and wife was decidedly unequal.

Kanner wanted Zarza at home, where she cared for him and their children and provided a secure foundation for his militancy. Her presence facilitated his activism, and his presence helped stimulate hers. She handled domestic and business matters during his frequent imprisonments; took in sewing to keep the family afloat; welcomed his guests, who often were clandestine organizers; and kept their secrets. Aware of injustice, Zarza valued and supported her husband's efforts to end exploitation. She was a *luchadora* (fighter) who protected her loved ones from many threats. Both husband and wife belonged to antifascist groups, but their roles differed in gendered ways. Zarza the homemaker made sandwiches to sell at Victory Board fundraisers and sewed garments alongside her friends; Kanner the intellectual addressed antifascist gatherings. Far less visible than he, she was a Communist antifascist militant in her household and community, whereas his public prominence stretched beyond Oberá to the Argentine Northeast and the entire country.[95]

Other Victory Board members, like Vergara, did not defer to their spouses. Polly Yánover de Cutín and Dr. Adolfo Cutín in Tucumán were Communists who hosted party meetings, visiting militants, and political debates in their home. Perhaps to mask Communist influence in the Victory Board chapter or escape persecution, she was not an officer until 1945, when she became secretary, but behind the scenes she recruited and participated actively. As cofounder of an agency promoting Soviet-Argentine cultural relations and head of the local CDA branch, her husband was more in the public eye than she, at least before 1945, obeying a gendered pattern that characterized most of the couples portrayed here. When I asked their son if his mother absorbed her ideas from his father, he replied that there was an affinity between their ideas, adding that Yánover was independent and did not take orders from anyone! Their own negotiations were among the debates that occurred in their household. Nonetheless, their shared views and militancy probably smoothed their antifascist activism and reinforced their egalitarian relationship. After the Victory Board's decline, Yánover's public role seemed to outstrip Cutín's, as she became a Communist Party leader, took part in Communist-linked groups, and campaigned for municipal and provincial offices on the Communist ticket.[96]

In other cases, the man remained more prominent than the woman. Clara Drallny of the Córdoba filial met her future husband, Oscar Eugenio Reati, a law student, in Communist or antifascist circles. A well-known militant, he was the secretary general of the local coordinating committee of pro-Allied aid, a Communist youth leader, and candidate for provincial senator in 1946. Not having completed high school, Drallny respected Reati's intellect. Only later did she earn a secondary school degree, study languages, and take university courses. She had less formal education than her husband, which was common among women at this time, but she too was an organizer and orator. Probably the Victory Board was her principal arena of activism, whereas her husband stood out in the local Communist Party as well as in antifascism. In subsequent years Drallny showed a photograph of herself giving a speech at a Victory Board event to prove that she, too, had engaged with an important cause. In this manner she competed with Reati, but they admired each other as *luchadores* and supported each other's struggles. The grim revelations about Stalinism in the 1950s prompted both to leave the party, although they did not always agree about politics.[97]

Numerous non-Communist Victory Board members also were married to antifascists. One was President Matilde Porta Echagüe de Molinas of the Santa Fe branch and a national board dignitary. Removed from his governorship by a federal intervention, her husband, Luciano Molinas, opposed the Concordancia's fraudulent practices. The couple backed the Spanish Republic, detested Nazism, and admired Joseph Stalin for halting the German advance and the Roosevelt administration for modeling democracy. They had cordial relations with Communists, whom Molinas defended against repression, and Jewish communities. He also belonged to the antifascist CDA and Frente de la Libertad y la Democracia.[98]

On the surface, Porta Echagüe appeared to be a traditional wife who supported her husband's political career. She accompanied Molinas in his campaigns and shared his views; the respect she earned as a hospital volunteer and as the former head of the local beneficent society enhanced his prestige. Her granddaughter recalled that she served dinner to her spouse and children before she sat down to eat. Born into a wealthy landowning family, her lifestyle in downtown Santa Fe resembled that of a lady in her manor. Dedicated to cooking, gardening, and sewing, Porta Echagüe made vinegar and perfume, cultivated fruit, and raised chickens. Yet she was more than an upper-class homemaker and helpmate, and her public roles were not exclusively female-coded. Her contacts extended beyond high society, which helped her recruit for and lead the local Victory Board. Porta Echagüe participated more than other women of her class in political gatherings at her home, and these discussions kept her well-informed. She considered her board activism vitally important because of her eagerness to defeat Nazism. Accustomed to speaking in public, the Santa Fe president, unlike Zarza, did not need her husband's coaching. Hardly a figurehead, she was proud of the intellectuals in her filial and of knitting socks for Russian soldiers.[99] Porta Echagüe did not challenge her husband, who supported her ayudismo, much less push for equality within the household, although she was a strong figure. The life she shared with Molinas harmoniously blended politics and old-fashioned domesticity.

Schlieper and her husband, the wealthy rancher Guillermo Martínez Guerrero, supported each other through difficult times. Until the late 1930s, their principal residence was their estate near General Juan Madariaga, southeast of Buenos Aires, where she began her public philanthropic service. As a UCR leader and president of the city council in 1916, Martínez

Guerrero clashed with local PDN officials. He served as a provincial senator from 1922 to 1928 and represented Buenos Aires Province at the UCR national convention in 1931 in the capital and perhaps the one in 1933 in Santa Fe. During the convention in Santa Fe, a rebellion broke out in that city, which President Agustín P. Justo's administration (1932–1938) blamed on the Radical Party. Soon thereafter, the government jailed Martínez Guerrero and other distinguished Radicals and then sent them to Ushuaia, Tierra del Fuego, where they had to pay for their own lodging and present themselves daily to the police. Winning widespread admiration, Schlieper and two other women journeyed to this remote and primitive city to share their spouses' exile and lift the prisoners' spirits. She arranged musical recitals and radio transmission of family members' greetings to their persecuted menfolk. Unmentioned in Schlieper's writings or interviews, this experience nevertheless must have been crucial. It likely strengthened the couple's relationship and their opposition to authoritarianism.[100]

Near the end of the decade, the couple moved to the capital, where Schlieper engaged in charitable endeavors, feminism, and antifascism. When she joined the IACW, she traveled to the United States each year, and her spouse apparently accepted her absences and activism. By 1943, Martínez Guerrero pertained to a staunchly Yrigoyenist faction that opposed the faulty elections within the provincial Radical Party structure. He and others in this movement initially approved of the 1943 coup d'etat for its proclaimed desire to cleanse politics, but surely changed their minds when the dictatorship turned repressive. After the war, Martínez Guerrero was elected national deputy on the UCR ticket.[101] As we will see, both suffered under Peronist rule. This sketch of the couple suggests mutual understanding of each other's political commitments. Schlieper's, Yánover's, and, to a lesser degree, Porta Echagüe's, marriages reflected the gender balance in society that Victory Board leaders favored.

The Antifascist Household

Victory Board members created or reinforced antifascist households in respects beyond their marriages. Resembling CAMHE members—and Nationalist and *franquista* women—they politicized their homes, shaping them into "ideological battlegrounds."[102] As women knitted, sewed, and made bandages in their households—some alongside their daughters— they probably explained to their offspring and spouses how this aid could help defeat fascism and construct a better world. These women modeled democracy, militancy, and, in many cases, leftist solidarity and the belief in a more equitable social order for their loved ones. They enlisted family members to assume some of their domestic tasks so that they could work for the Victory Board. Or, like Zarza, they assumed their husbands' duties to keep their families safe and fed when the men were imprisoned or focused on their activism.

And they reproduced antifascism and leftism in their households. Adelina Cornejo de Elkin of Córdoba sent her children to collect aluminum foil for the Allies. Named the Victory Board's most productive knitter in 1943, the venerable Rebeca de Malajovich of Moisés Ville and her grown daughter Sara, also a member, donated their jewelry to a board fundraising raffle. In this small tight-knit community, where many women belonged to the Victory Board, running in and out of neighbors' houses probably reinforced the political ideas children imbibed at home. Margarita de Barraza, the *criolla* farmer of Las Breñas, Chaco, learned to knit alongside her daughter when they joined the movement. At the behest of his mother, Polly Yánover de Cutín, the youngster Luis Cutín rode his bicycle around Tucumán distributing a Communist periodical, discretely hidden in envelopes, and made posters for the Victory Board, whose pennant graced his bedroom wall. He may have listened to board members, such as Fanny Edelman, who visited his house. Involved in the local affiliate of Idischer Cultur Farband (ICUF), the Soviet-sponsored transnational Yiddish leftist cultural movement, the Cutíns sent Luis to its summer camp, Zumerland.[103]

Other Victory Board members also helped set the younger generation on a militant path. Rosa Faingold of the Tucumán chapter was married to fellow Socialist Felipe Villagra, a lawyer and politician. Three of their four daughters were active in leftist movements and went into exile in the troubled 1970s. Sofía Goldberg de Molodesky was active in the Resistencia chapter and in Communist groups. During the military dictatorship of 1976–1983, she and another former board member braved threats and bombings to protect their leftist children. Her daughter-in-law stated that she learned from this tenacious *luchadora* how to fight for a socialist society.[104]

Not surprisingly, the all-woman Victory Board contrasted with local male antifascist organizations. Its leaders believed that antifascist women had a unique mission that only they could perform. Part of this mission consisted of unifying such women in this group, and all antifascists in coordinating committees, neither of which they achieved, except for the Stalingrad campaign. In addition, the Victory Board aimed to boost optimism for the cause, and here it seemed more successful. Both efforts rested upon gendered notions of women as natural mediators and morale-boosters. Another aspect of the mission was politicizing women and supporting their rights. In contrast, antifascist men showed little interest in building a true democracy by including the other half of the population.

Nevertheless, they respected and collaborated with the Victory Board. Businessmen, laborers, neighbors, and loyal husbands contributed to the organization and attended its functions. Male or largely male antifascist groups held benefits and rallies with the board, but they usually described it in ways that circumscribed its field of action.

Given these attitudes, the Victory Board understandably organized separately from men. But how independent was it, given its relationship with the Communist Party? The party encouraged if not ordered militants to join, and significant numbers did, although the size of their presence varied by location. The male-dominated Communist Party influenced this Popular Front movement, but did not necessarily control it. The Victory Board had agency, at least until its final days.

And it practiced feminism, whether it used the word or not. Up to 1943, the Victory Board's feminist practices consisted largely of training women to exercise democracy in quotidian ways. By modeling democracy, it helped political neophytes understand this form of governance and gave them opportunities to engage in it. The male-led antifascist groups also followed parliamentary procedures, but this had a different meaning because men had long been political actors. Publicizing this function demonstrated women's political readiness. The Victory Board provided spaces for discussing personal and political issues and listening to women intellectuals and Uruguayan women politicians. Members participated in meetings, committees, and conventions and conducted numerous managerial duties. Civil defense, with its citizenship connotations, formed part of this training and was a new form of women's mobilization that the board helped establish. Another was the construction of a national women's network through close supervision and contact with chapters. Thus the Victory Board prepared women for political involvement. Its version of feminism, however, did not include reproductive rights.

The Victory Board both encouraged and contested customary and ethnic/class-bound notions of womanhood. Its spokespersons envisaged women as mothers, workers, professionals, and citizens. This was evident in speeches and workshops, which removed women from their usual spaces to interact with colleagues of different backgrounds. They sewed and knitted to oppose fascism and inequality, rather than for their families, charity, or pay. Through hand work, politics became part of their daily lives, and the board made these domestic labors visible, thus blending the private and the public.

Antifascist households and marriages further blurred boundaries between private and public. These stories reveal how board members *lived* antifascism within and outside the domestic sphere. Women reproduced antifascism and, in many cases, leftism in their homes, converting them into centers of resistance. Sympathetic spouses and children shouldered domestic tasks, allowing women to work for the Victory Board. Antifascist couples were not free of conflicts, competition, or inequality, yet these shared political commitments often facilitated mutual comprehension and activism. Nonetheless, their means of exercising politics sometimes differed along gender lines.

María Inés Zoppi del Valle Pardo espoused maternalism, and María Rosa Oliver challenged it. No single pattern emerged regarding such gendered issues as relations with antifascist husbands and partners, the formation of antifascist homes, or maternalism, although board orators frequently used such rhetoric and some members participated in nonmaternalistic activism. The Victory Board's antifascism encompassed many strains. Even so, in this patriarchal society, all members had to negotiate with men and grapple with long-standing notions that limited women's roles.

Hemispheric conversations on women's roles in civil defense and lifting morale gendered antifascism from the Global South to the Global North, and, with the Uruguayan presence at a board convention, in a South-South circuit. The next chapter extends this transnational dimension by further examining the Victory Board's ties with women in Uruguay, the United States, and the IACW. It also analyzes the board's negotiations with US and British male diplomats, who were not as accepting as one might expect. Patriarchy and anti-leftism were hardly exclusive to Argentina.

CHAPTER 6

THE CLOTH THAT BINDS

Transnational Relationships with the United States, Great Britain, and Uruguay, 1941–1944

In 1942 María Rosa Oliver traveled to Washington, DC, to work in the Office of Inter-American Affairs (OIAA), the cultural wing of US hemispheric diplomacy. Shortly before leaving Buenos Aires, Oliver offered a metaphor for inter-American pro-Allied action: "Now they arrive, now they depart—men and women bearing from one nation to another their spirit and their faith. The silver-winged planes come and go from one end of the Americas to the other, and like the shuttles of a spindle they weave a fabric close knit, durable, yet many-colored. . . . We are waiting to see of what stuff that fabric will be made."[1] The Victory Board (Junta de la Victoria) wanted to be as closely knit to its partners as the sweaters it made. It entwined with its sister group in Uruguay, Feminine Action for Victory (Acción Femenina por la Victoria). Some British and US officials preferred a sturdy cloth, while others wanted to unravel it.

In this chapter I examine the Victory Board's associations with Great Britain, the United States, and Uruguay as Argentina moved from civilian autocracy to military dictatorship. These three transnational relationships differed in tenor, breadth, and allegiance. The Victory Board supported US policy in the Western Hemisphere and welcomed President Franklin Delano Roosevelt's and Prime Minister Winston Churchill's wartime statements and leadership. By producing and dispatching concrete aid and supportive messages to these and other Allied nations, the group demonstrated fealty to the global struggle and engaged in South-North solidarity. Whether US and British personnel were as loyal to their Argentine partner is another issue. The Victory Board's survival methods in a hostile climate and its president's actions and personality annoyed some embassy officers from these countries. The US ambassador, officials in Washington, and distinguished women and women's organizations in the United States, however, regarded the board more favorably.

In contrast, the Victory Board cultivated a uniformly close association with kindred women across the River Plate. In May 1942 Feminine Action

arose in Montevideo, explicitly imitating the Argentine model. It, too, became a Popular Front movement, with thousands of diverse members who
produced clothing and supplies for Allied soldiers and defended democratic ideals. Sharing its organizational experience, at first the Victory Board
mentored Feminine Action, yet as a member later noted, the relationship
evolved into a partnership that was "more lively and profound,"[2] one that
epitomized South-South as well as South-North solidarity. This intimate
cross-border bond among antifascist women's groups was unprecedented
in the world.

Relations with the British

The Victory Board developed good relations with members of the British
community and consulates, but cooler ones with the embassy. Its ties to the
ambassadors' wives were equivocal. Moreover, the Argentine government
subtly warned British diplomats to stay away from this group.

Many board members admired Churchill—or praised him for tactical
reasons. Portraits of the three major Allied leaders festooned the walls of
board offices. As Oliver remarked at a banquet celebrating his birthday,
Churchill's face smiled down at board members sewing and repeating his
words among themselves. His speeches evoked a powerful sense of unity
against Nazism, with its slogan of "divide and conquer." Oliver commended Churchill for emphasizing this togetherness, for some people did not
understand that helping the Soviet Union, an Allied power, did not mean
one was a Communist, just as those who helped Britain were not necessarily
conservative.[3] Ambassador Sir Esmond Ovey and Lady Ovey were in the
audience listening to her speech.

The Victory Board pursued connections with the British, and particularly their consulates, for several reasons. One was to publicize fulfillment
of its mission. Another was that these entities could facilitate the transmission of aid, cooperation from British-owned enterprises, and relations with
kindred British organizations. The board wanted to demonstrate British
support and, by linking itself to British prestige, secure more followers and
protection from official harassment. Since consuls and vice-consuls generally served long terms and had closer ties with locals in outlying communities
than did their superiors in Buenos Aires, they may have developed affinity
with the group. Some were married to board members. It is unclear whether
the embassy wanted consuls and vice-consuls to attend board functions, or
if they did so on their own initiative. It might have sent these lower-ranking
officials in place of the ambassador, to avoid slighting the Victory Board
while granting it little recognition. Whatever the motives, these officials
frequently appeared at board gatherings. The British consul was present at

the Mendoza chapter's opening ceremony and its reception for Ana Rosa Schlieper de Martínez Guerrero and other *porteña* delegates. The consul in Córdoba toured the local chapter's exposition of goods to be sent to injured children overseas. His counterpart in Rosario attended the *filial's* banquet for Schlieper as well as its reception honoring British women for their sacrifices and heroism.[4]

Women of British descent and British officials' wives had contact with the Victory Board. The wife of the consul of La Plata, who served as president of a local British women's group, addressed the board's Buenos Aires Provincial Convention. The spouse of the vice-consul in Santa Fe and three other board members participated in British Red Cross and British community functions. An Anglo-Argentine member of the Tucumán filial was also involved in the British Red Cross and the local Anglo-Argentine Club. Other Anglo-Argentine Victory Board activists most likely followed a similar pattern.[5]

The British Women's Patriotic Committee (BWPC), described in chapter 1, operated nationwide under the British Community Council (BCC). The wives of the two British ambassadors during World War II served as its honorary presidents. Lady Ovey attended the Victory Board's inauguration and several receptions, the BWPC sent flowers to the board's first national convention, and Lady Marie Noelle Kelly greeted delegates to the second national convention who visited the BWPC office. Lady Ovey, Lady Kelly, and BWPC representatives appeared at public ceremonies in which they received the Victory Board's donations of goods.[6]

Given these connections, it is not surprising that two very different individuals—a board member's daughter and FBI director J. Edgar Hoover—believed the British were partly responsible for creating the Victory Board. The former, a university professor closely tied to local antifascists and leftists, offered as proof that the Córdoba chapter sometimes met in the British consulate, where the workshop was located. I cannot substantiate these claims, but at least one other branch arose in a British setting. An Englishman's Argentine wife convoked a meeting at the English Club of Lomas de Zamora, just outside the federal capital, which resulted in the creation of the local filial.[7]

British embassy officials, however, distanced themselves from the Victory Board. In 1942 Minister of the Interior Miguel J. Culaciati told the British press attaché S. R. Robertson that his wife, Hortensia Spinetto, had attended some board functions at Lady Ovey's insistence. Disavowing alleged board statements that Spinetto was a leader of the organization, the minister said he had forbidden her participation in it, presumably because he considered it Communist-influenced. He claimed that Lady Ovey refused to be identified with the Victory Board and hoped that Lady Kelly would adopt the same attitude. Culaciati asked Robertson to relay this information to Ambassador Ovey.[8] The embassy appeared to heed this apparent warning, seemingly abstaining from direct involvement with the Victory Board.[9] Perhaps because of their aloofness, Schlieper criticized Ovey and other British diplomats.[10]

Culaciati's remarks seemed questionable. Spinetto indeed accompanied Lady Ovey to a Victory Board–sponsored tea in the latter's honor. That her husband felt compelled to prohibit her involvement hinted that she might have been genuinely interested in the board. Perhaps he presented her as merely complying with a friend's wishes in order to absolve her—and himself—of any accusations of Communist links.[11] One also wonders why, if the British ambassador's wife was anxious to avoid the Victory Board, she attended its events. Possibly she disengaged herself over time or felt obliged to go.

The Victory Board's handling of its banquet honoring Pan American Day, the closing event of the first national convention in April 1942, raised further suspicions. Communicating with each other, the British and US embassies realized that to obtain permission for the occasion, board representatives told the police that the two ambassadors would be there, without asking them beforehand. Not wishing to offend these countries, the police chief was afraid to refuse. To entice Ovey and US Ambassador Norman Armour to the banquet, Schlieper said that government dignitaries would attend, without having secured their commitments. Another troublesome aspect of the banquet was that the initial publicity and invitations indicated the Inter-American Commission of Women (IACW), an official entity, was sponsoring it, without mentioning that it would be the finale of the Victory Board's first national convention. Following Culaciati's advice, neither Ovey nor Armour attended the dinner.[12]

Understandably, this episode led some British and US officials to consider Schlieper and the Victory Board duplicitous. Yet it is important to recognize that antifascist Argentines were operating in a repressive context. Under the state of siege, the Castillo administration had curtailed board activities, jailed some members, and interrupted or shut down its events. Board leaders searched for any means of securing permission for their functions, which they knew could easily be denied or taken away once ceded. In their view, struggling for democracy in the face of fascist-like restrictions—and male chauvinism—justified sneaky tactics. Women in a patriarchal society that denied them the vote often had to resort to circuitous ways of convincing men to grant their requests. Sometimes equally chauvinistic British and US male diplomats did not take into account the limitations the Victory Board faced or its efforts to circumvent them.

The United States

The Victory Board had distinct interactions with various US-related interest groups and government agencies in the United States and Argentina. These included Schlieper's involvement with the IACW, which intertwined with her activity as board president; Oliver's engagement with the cultural Good Neighbor policy; and board contacts with the embassy, US Women's Bureau, and the OIAA. The Victory Board sought most of these connections to implement its mission and acquire security and prestige, as in its British ties, and to improve Argentine relations with the United States, tighten Pan-Americanism, and work for democracy and women's rights at home. US officials responded in different ways. Unwanted by the Victory Board, the FBI monitored it.

As the IACW head, and before the Victory Board's formal inauguration, Schlieper had welcomed Mary Cannon of the US Women's Bureau and the US IACW representative Mary Winslow to Buenos Aires. During Cannon's three-month stay, she and Schlieper became good friends. In a letter to Mary Anderson, the director of the Women's Bureau, the IACW president praised Cannon for her perceptiveness, congeniality, good command of Spanish, and the detailed information she shared on US women laborers. Schlieper requested an exchange with Washington, in which more women like Cannon would visit Argentina and knowledgeable Argentine women would study women's work, mobility, and participation in organizational life in the United States. Upon their return to Buenos Aires, they would apply their experience to improving conditions for local women. She implied that such exchanges would also promote US understanding of Latin America.[13]

Seeking to dispel fascist influence and unite the Americas behind the war through cultural means, the OIAA shared Schlieper's interest in hemispheric exchanges.[14] Its coordinator, Nelson Rockefeller, asked US women's organizations to join a campaign to inform the country about Latin America. Winslow, now serving as his advisor on women's projects, became his intermediary in arranging inter-American initiatives through the League of Women Voters (LWV) and other groups.[15] One series of events involved Schlieper.

Schlieper cultivated ties with the United States, and her US acquaintances cultivated her. After becoming Victory Board president, she continued to travel to the United States to preside over the annual IACW meetings and toured the country from the fall of 1941 to early 1942, and again in the fall of 1942. Winslow recommended to the LWV that it sponsor her visit of 1941–1942 as part of an effort to encourage face-to-face contact between distinguished Latin American women and their US counterparts and advise the former on creating hemispheric cooperation programs in their nations. Impressed with Schlieper's charm, beauty, and understanding of hemispheric relations, the LWV president agreed. Regarding her as an asset in fostering Pan-American unity and knowledge of Latin America, Rockefeller financed Schlieper's trip through the OIAA. Cannon asked Anderson to enable her to observe LWV and Women's Trade Union League board meetings, which she thought would enhance Schlieper's management of the groups she headed. Aside from conversing with LWV chapters in the Midwest and on the East Coast, Schlieper lunched with First Lady Eleanor Roosevelt at the White House and with the Women's National Press Club, where she discussed bills on the women's vote pending in the Argentine Congress. Schlieper participated in a panel of Latin American women on inter-American understanding in Troy, New York, moderated by the First Lady. Here she received an honorary degree from Russell Sage College, and an award from Barry College in Miami for her inter-Americanism.[16] Katherine M. Marino observed that US officials were grooming Schlieper as the suitably white face of Pan-American feminism.[17]

While Winslow and the US government downplayed feminism in favor of wartime hemispheric bonds, Schlieper and other Latin Americans in the commission moved it from the back to the front burner.[18] At the IACW meeting in November 1941 she proposed resolutions advocating women's right to vote, hold office, preside over juvenile courts, and be appointed to government educational agencies and diplomatic and consular services. Another favored sending representatives of women's organizations to attend legislative sessions. All passed. At the opening of the 1942 meeting, Assistant Director Pedro Alba of the Pan American Union noted that the US vice president Henry Wallace, in a famous speech, paraphrased President Abraham Lincoln's famous words that a government (i.e., nation) could not be half slave and half free to say that the globe could not be half slave. Schlieper retorted that in Latin America the slaves were women. She hoped their contributions to the war effort would finally lead to the recognition of all their rights.[19]

Some of Schlieper's pronouncements on Pan-Americanism at forums with US women may have been bland and general. Indeed, her erstwhile friend and Unión Argentina de Mujeres (UAM) colleague, Susana Larguía, a Socialist, observed sardonically that she handled such shallow activities very well.[20] Nevertheless, these encounters and especially the substantive IACW assemblies emphasized the promotion of democracy and inter-American solidarity against fascism, as well as women's rights and roles in these efforts, and as such conformed to the Victory Board's stances and actions. In fact, her IACW and Victory Board activities reinforced each other. When Schlieper returned to Argentina from these trips, she reported to the Victory Board on what she had done and learned, and IACW periodicals disseminated information on the board.[21] She also persisted in contacting US women by inviting Winslow and representatives of the National Women's Trade Union League to the second national convention, although they did not attend.[22]

Women in the US government continued to champion the Victory Board and its president. In 1942 Schlieper asked Winslow to suggest a US organization to which the board could send goods. Ready to oblige, she approached several agencies, informing them that while the amount would not be sizeable, an expression of interest was vital. An officer of the Navy Relief Society agreed, recommending other possible groups because its storage spaces were full. As the contribution would reinforce the Good Neighbor policy, he emphasized that the offer had to be accepted. Not long thereafter Winslow praised the Victory Board to Rockefeller and forwarded Red Cross supplies to Schlieper for civil defense purposes.[23]

Winslow took Schlieper's side in a disturbing altercation. As the November 1942 IACW meeting was taking place, the United States was implementing an economic boycott and arms embargo against Argentina over its position on the war.[24] Minerva Bernardino, the Dominican representative and IACW vice chair, proposed a resolution urging Chilean and Argentine women to lobby their governments to break relations with the Axis. Schlieper argued that such issues were outside the IACW's purview, which was to study women and relevant legislation in the Americas, and other delegates backed her. The IACW asked Bernardino to withdraw her resolution, and it passed an alternative one that simply entreated all Latin American nations to support the Allies. In a message to Under Secretary of State Sumner Welles, Winslow supported Schlieper and her explanation. According to Marino, however, Schlieper had deeper reasons for opposing Bernardino's resolution. To remain in the IACW (and, I would add, to keep the Victory Board alive), she could not afford to publicly oppose the Argentine government and its foreign policy. Bernardino also had other motives. She wanted to become IACW chair and was jealous of Schlieper for having attained this post. Winslow and Schlieper complained that Bernardino engaged in hostility, lies, and scheming, and the US commissioner believed that the Dominican wanted to undermine both of them.[25]

The UAM, however, backed Bernardino, and Ana Berry, who had sympathized with Schlieper's frustrations with Acción Argentina (see chapter 3), voiced its concerns. She wrote President Rowe of the Pan American Union that the UAM disagreed with the withdrawal of Bernardino's resolution and would ask the Argentine government to break relations with the Axis. She enclosed a copy of this letter in a missive to Schlieper, in which she wondered why her chum had chosen a vague and meaningless resolution that retained the status quo. Schlieper's good relations with the US government and poor ones with the Argentine, which wanted to end the IACW and the subsidy it paid to it, made her decision even less comprehensible. Berry regretted this for her dear friend's sake, just as she had regretted Schlieper's involvement in the Victory Board. Seemingly linking Schlieper's action to Communist influence in the board, Berry, a Chilean believer in reformist socialism, wondered if Communists were as opportunistic as they had been in the past. It remained to be seen, she noted, whether the Victory Board would cause Schlieper harm.[26] That the US Office of Censorship intercepted this letter suggested that this government was monitoring Schlieper, and its relations with her were not always as cordial as Berry thought. Nor is there evidence that Communists affected the board president's decision. Argentine antifascist women were divided; not even the UAM, in which Schlieper still participated, necessarily supported the Victory Board.

Nevertheless, Winslow backed Schlieper. She asked Cannon to contribute an article to the IACW bulletin, which Schlieper was publishing in Buenos Aires. The periodical looked good, and Winslow wanted her Argentine colleague to acquire good pieces for it. Agreeing to do so, Cannon followed up with an affectionate note to the Victory Board president. By this time, however, the new military regime (1943–1946) had closed the board and expelled Schlieper from the IACW.[27]

Cannon had witnessed the Victory Board's tribulations under President Ramón Castillo's state of siege. She noted approvingly to Anderson that despite this repression, as of April 1943 it had moved into larger offices and was moving forward. Yet concerns over Communist members had surfaced. Undeniably the movement had some, she judged, but it also had many other women. One noticed the Soviet flag throughout the headquarters, and Cannon found it startling to see it hanging above the US flag in one room, but there was no reason why, in Argentina, it should not, she reasoned.[28]

Other US officials were not as open-minded or sanguine. This concern mounted during discussions of the problematic Pan American Day celebration in April 1942. An embassy functionary told Schlieper that it would be inconvenient for the US ambassador to attend and thus be identified with her organization. He referred gingerly to the controversies surrounding the Victory Board, including the purported Communist presence. Schlieper responded that the government had never supplied concrete evidence to back up the rumors of Communism. When she insisted that she had received the police chief's permission for the event without giving Armour's or Ovey's name, the skeptical diplomat hinted she was lying.[29] Nevertheless, another member of the embassy staff, writing for Armour, told Secretary of State

Cordell Hull that its huge and diverse audience, speeches across the political spectrum, and extensive press attention made the Victory Board's Pan American Day banquet the most important of the commemorations held in Buenos Aires.[30] Over 1,500 people attended it.[31]

The Communist issue intermingled with some embassy officers' gender-inflected dislike of Schlieper. One of them claimed that she knew that the Communist Party (Partido Comunista) supported the Victory Board, but said nothing about it because her leadership of the group put her in the limelight. He went on to accuse her of voracious ambition.[32] Whether he would have made these judgments about a man is doubtful; certainly US women officials did not perceive her this way.

By 1943, J. Edgar Hoover also had his eye on the Victory Board. He thought that it was organized with British monies but then evolved into a front organization headed by a woman of leftist leanings, which made it easier for Communists to dominate her. Schlieper was merely a figurehead attracted by the attention she received, he insisted, echoing several members of the embassy staff. The real power was Cora Ratto, whom he claimed the Communist Party had earmarked for this purpose. Hoover cited the Communists and sympathizers in the leadership; the support the Victory Board received from Communist figures, unions, and publications; and the board's shipment of most of its aid to the Soviet Union as evidence of party control. He ignored the importance of the Eastern Front and the fact that the Soviet Union was a US ally, as well as the heterogeneity in the Victory Board's national ruling circle and the entire organization. Hoover further claimed that the Victory Board had not publicly accounted for its funds other than general reports on some of the goods it sent overseas. The board, however, provided a detailed accounting in its convention proceedings, and a US journalist noted that "one of the most reputable firms of chartered accountants" supervised its records. Ironically, Hoover praised the La Plata branch for its excellent (presumably non-Communist) leaders and entertainment of British and US sailors whose ships docked at the local port. That the national board asked La Plata (and other) members to write the military government, urging it to free board adherents it had jailed, however, was enough to convince Hoover that the Victory Board's pro-Allied stance only thinly disguised its Communism.[33] Apparently, US authorities were willing to work with the Soviet Union, but not with Latin American leftists. Nor was this the only case of FBI surveillance of leftist feminist and antifascist forces in the region.[34]

Schlieper was aware of Communists in the movement; after all, she had collaborated with some of them in the UAM. She understood that their presence provoked Argentine and US opposition, and that is why she denied it, but it did not trouble her. Perhaps influenced by the government's repression of dissidents like her husband, she was willing to work with people of all political backgrounds, which her choice of Angélica Mendoza as IACW secretary and her board activities and statements on diversity indicated. Furthermore, the official persecution she would suffer shows that her motives ran deeper than publicity and ambition.

Schlieper peppered local OIAA representatives with suggestions for smoothing relations between Argentina and the United States, spreading antifascism, and changing Castillo's neutral stance. She proposed several times that large foreign-owned businesses hire young professionals, instead of older insiders whom she named and characterized as Nazis, designations which a US diplomat denied. Lacking opportunities, the younger generation was likely to turn against foreign capitalists or become Nationalists. Schlieper's desire to recommend other more democratic lawyers struck a US official as cronyism. The Victory Board president declared that if the lawyers for these firms pressured President Castillo to alter his foreign policy, he would comply. Schlieper also urged US funding for a democratic educational journal edited by a well-qualified woman and read by teachers in the interior. But an OIAA officer demurred, noting that US firms were not interested in paying for ads in this publication, given its tiny circulation, and to subsidize it would violate the OIAA Coordination Committee's policy. Her insistence that the Washington office had said the Buenos Aires branch could finance this periodical did not produce results. The committee ignored her idea of advising US firms to pay their employees overtime if they had to work more than eight hours a day. During her visit to the United States in late 1942, Schlieper broached these and other matters with Rockefeller, who listened to her respectfully. Complying with the Buenos Aires OIAA branch's request, however, he made no commitments.[35] Yet the OIAA coordinator told this office that he hoped it could help this important ally.[36]

Schlieper's opinions had a legitimate basis. The lawyers she criticized were on the far right, and local antifascists commonly labeled such persons as Nazis, even if they technically were not. It was and still is standard practice in Argentina (and elsewhere) to endorse friends for positions in a politically fractured society with many candidates chasing after few jobs. Teachers strongly influenced their communities and could awaken antifascist sentiments there, like the numerous educators in the Victory Board were doing. Improving US businesses' labor practices could decrease anti-US feelings.

Local OIAA representatives also asked Rockefeller not to commit himself to an enterprise that involved Schlieper. In 1942 she and several others founded the Pan-American Distributor, to produce antifascist films and distribute them in Latin America and the United States. The company planned to make movies that would reaffirm Argentine democratic traditions and American unity and to employ actors, screenwriters, and other personnel from throughout the Western Hemisphere. The purported goal was not so much to earn money, but to build inter-American understanding. Although Rockefeller was interested in such ventures, the Buenos Aires branch distrusted this one. It questioned whether the fledgling company was as well-organized and funded as Schlieper claimed; it also had little faith in the proposed film director. Possibly the Victory Board president would try to make arrangements with US film distributors, but such efforts had usually floundered due to the limited market. Another concern was whether the firm's purpose was really a commercial one with a pro-Allied veneer.[37]

Schlieper persisted in asking questions, offering advice, requesting support, and keeping the Victory Board alive through deceptive maneuvers if necessary. She played the Washington OIAA office against the OIAA Coordination Committee in Buenos Aires, and figured out the latter's workings, which it tried to keep secret.[38] Embassy and OIAA officers agreed that Schlieper tried to bamboozle them. One admitted her charm, but saw her as a nuisance who demanded treatment befitting a queen. Schlieper's supposed lust for publicity and power struck them as unsavory for a woman. The contrast between her refinement and beauty and what some men perceived as nonfeminine behavior, along with her acuity, jarred them. According to Robert Wells, chairman of the Coordination Committee, Schlieper had to be managed diplomatically, but steadfastly—akin to an errant wife.[39]

Nevertheless, local OIAA representatives recognized the Victory Board's achievements and helped it a bit. A member of the Motion Picture Sub-Committee lauded the board's Victory Review, held at the Cine Gran Rex, the biggest film theater in Buenos Aires, in December 1942. The most sizeable Argentine women's pro-Allied group, he reported, had pulled off the first massive pro-Allied fundraiser, featuring radio, theater, and film stars, and reconstructions of scenes from recent Argentine movies, as if they were being shot then and there. Priced reasonably, all the tickets sold. Even studios not on the Allied side cooperated, and most important performers, including some suspected Axis sympathizers, took part or allowed the use of their names. According to the OIAA functionary, the police threatened to cancel the event, claiming that the organizers had not secured the proper permit, but after a long delay finally allowed it to take place. A Victory Board member, however, reported that the authorities cut it short, insisting that it exceeded the length allowed under a municipal ordinance. Still, the OIAA observer judged the Victory Review a great success, albeit a bit disorganized. He remarked that the Motion Picture Sub-Committee had supported this totally national effort in only a small unofficial way.[40]

The OIAA interceded with companies to obtain films and tickets for the Victory Board and other antifascist groups. The Motion Picture Sub-Committee helped the board acquire sixty movie tickets during the first national convention. Board chapters in Rosario, Bahía Blanca, and elsewhere solicited films to show at their benefits, initially receiving some without paying rental fees. Although the sub-committee approved of the Victory Board, it eventually agreed that the movie companies could charge small fees. Rumors that members of certain filiales had dipped into benefit proceeds may have alienated some on the Coordination Committee. It did, however, loan the Victory Board two instructional films. Ursula Prutsch concluded that OIAA funding was limited and largely symbolic.[41]

There were other contacts between the Victory Board and US Americans. Members of the North American Women's Club attended a board reception in 1941. After the attack on Pearl Harbor, the ambassador's wife, Myra Koudacheff Armour, attended its assembly that year, as did the president of the US Auxiliary Red Cross. Separately from the national board, the Rosario chapter also wrote Armour and Mrs. Roosevelt of its support.[42]

The US ambassador generally supported the Victory Board. Schlieper and Ratto relayed to Armour the first convention's message of solidarity with US women, which he forwarded to Washington, requesting that a women's organization publicize it. He did not attend the controversial Pan American Day banquet, but he telegrammed his congratulations to Schlieper for her work as IACW president—although not as Victory Board president—in furthering inter-American understanding and cooperation. The ambassador sent the consul general in his stead.[43] Oliver considered Armour an exemplary diplomat who respected the country to which he was assigned and the locals with whom he conversed.[44] These attitudes seemed to guide his relations with the Victory Board.

María Rosa Oliver and the OIAA

María Rosa Oliver was another Victory Board interlocutor who had significant ties with the United States and the Americas. When Oliver was UAM president, Cannon wrote to the US Women's Bureau, commending Oliver for her abilities, perfect command of English, and good relations with US visitors.[45] Oliver's opinions of the United States were complicated. In her view, it was a model of technological and women's progress for her country. While she opposed US capitalism, she thought that President Roosevelt and New Deal programs such as the Tennessee Valley Authority could move the United States toward public enterprises. Oliver's readings of works by John Dos Passos, John Steinbeck, and Ernest Hemingway, and their criticism of the United States, further convinced her that it was receptive to change.

She lectured on these authors and became friends with Armour and several others in the embassy who had sympathized with the Spanish Republic. Myra Koudacheff Armour, a member of the former Russian nobility, won Oliver's heart by embracing the Victory Board and its desire to help her country of origin, unlike some other diplomats' spouses. Oliver also grew to admire Henry Wallace through his writings and information gleaned from her friend, the US writer Waldo Frank.[46]

Enrique Sánchez de Lozada, a former Bolivian diplomat and one of Wallace's advisors, invited her to join the North Americans and Latin Americans working together against Nazism in the OIAA. Inspired by this project that seemed to embody a true Pan-American spirit, and compelled to fight alongside opponents of fascism, even the British and US empires, Oliver accepted the post. Later she realized the irony of fighting Adolf Hitler while based in a racist country, the fallacy of US gender equality, and the temporary and hierarchical character of US wartime relations with Latin America.[47]

As she had in the Victory Board, as a Latin American advisor in the OIAA (1942–1944), Oliver engaged with its mission of promoting mutual understanding in the Americas. She believed that people could comprehend other nations by reading their books and meeting their inhabitants. To this end she worked on translation projects and exchanges of authors, teachers, and laborers. One of the antifascist cultural figures she convinced the OIAA to invite to the United States was the Argentine writer Alberto Gerchunoff, not only to encourage the circulation of ideas but to support democratic forces in her country. Pointing out that Latin American pupils commonly studied English, Oliver argued for compulsory Spanish or Portuguese classes in US schools. She strongly advocated the use of geography and history textbooks covering the entire hemisphere so Latin American and US children alike could grasp its unity. Oliver lectured on Latin American literature, geography, and social problems at the Claremont Graduate School and other US institutions. Speaking at a conference on interracial understanding sponsored by the Pan American Women's Association in 1943, Oliver downplayed racism in Latin America while condemning its prevalence in the United States, adding that US racial prejudice obstructed continental unity. At the end of her Washington sojourn, Oliver set off on a speaking tour in Mexico, Colombia, Ecuador, Peru, and Chile that centered on bringing together the two Americas. Countering ardent anti-imperialists, especially in the first two countries, she asserted that a unified Latin America could deal with the United States as an equal.

Offering advice and insight to the OIAA on many matters, Oliver criticized the deficiencies of US films on Latin America, helped plan Wallace's successful trip to Latin America in 1943, and informed Rockefeller and, through him, the State Department, on Argentine politics and Latin American reactions to the United States. She noted that young Latin Americans along the political spectrum thought that politicians had sold out their countries to foreign imperialistic businessmen. She urged the United States to conduct transparent and equitable economic policies. If the youth saw that US businesses conducted themselves forthrightly, they would view that country more favorably. Oliver beseeched the US government to give moral support to popular democratic movements and cooperate with the inevitable shift toward a South America unified economically and culturally. This union would be a much better partner than the various, compact, and insecure nations, but it would have to be democratic, for authoritarian rulers would split the region for their own profit and against the United States. Do not make deals with them, she implored.[48] These were prescient words.

And they were striking ones uttered by a complex person who was both a Communist and, at this moment, a conciliator between the United States and Latin America. Anderson considered Oliver a liberal and superb orator and writer.[49] Rockefeller agreed that Oliver was a remarkable author and woman leader.[50] Oliver's admirers in Washington seemed unaware of or undisturbed by her Communist allegiance, at least until the Cold War.

Uruguay and Latin America

Meanwhile, antifascist women formed groups in other Latin American countries, including Uruguay. The Argentine and Uruguayan circumstances that catalyzed women's antifascist mobilization resembled, yet also differed from, each other. The ties between activists in these two countries strengthened as they forged a unique partnership.

The Lima Conference of 1938 had tasked the IACW with defending democracy, and it in turn encouraged the creation of "feminine action" organizations to implement this goal. The Victory Board was one of them. Another was Acción Femenina Peruana (AFP). Originally founded in 1937 to help prepare for this conference, it renewed its activity during World War II, when it sought to unite women around democracy and antifascism. Made up of teachers, professionals, writers, employees, laborers, and housewives, the AFP linked its program of women's political and labor rights to Roosevelt's Four Freedoms and the Atlantic Charter. It offered services for impoverished women and established a subsidiary that made clothing for children in Allied countries. While the AFP paralleled the Victory Board in some respects, its political partisanship and more outspoken feminist and labor activism set it off from the Argentine group. Yet another feminine action movement was the Comité Coordinador Femenino por la Defensa de la Patria, founded in Mexico after it entered the war in 1942. Drawing upon former Frente Único Pro Derechos de la Mujer activists, this committee promoted civil defense and suffrage. I found no evidence of contact between it, the Victory Board, and the AFP. Still, the existence of such groups points to the larger context of Latin American women's antifascism in which the Victory Board operated.[51]

Yet the Victory Board was intimately connected to Feminine Action. To understand Feminine Action and this relationship, one must review Uruguayan history.[52] This country experienced far-reaching reforms under José Batlle y Ordóñez (1903–1907, 1911–1915) and his wing of the Colorado Party. The Constitution of 1918 provided for universal male suffrage, six years after its neighbor across the River Plate, but women obtained suffrage in 1932, fifteen years before their Argentine peers. Rightist economic and political forces, including the ultra-conservative sector of the National (Blanco) Party, backed a coup d'etat in 1933 by the sitting Colorado president, Gabriel Terra. The Montevideo police, headed by Terra's brother-in-law Alfredo Baldomir, and the armed forces also supported these actions, although the latter did not play a major role. The regime quickly dissolved Parliament and jailed and deported political dissidents, killing a few of them; some opponents also went into exile. Although the government censured the press, restricted labor and rival partisan activities, and often suppressed hostile demonstrations, it did not prohibit any political party. Instead, it tried to legitimize itself through several elections and a plebiscite over a new constitution. While Terra's policies generally benefited the economic interests behind the coup d'etat, the need to address the Great Depression resulted in the retention of Batllista projects and its tradition of strong government involvement, much to the business sector's dismay. Nor did Terra create a corporatist state or promote radical rightists. His authoritarian regime was not as brutal, fascist-inspired, or as much of a departure from the past as José Félix Uriburu's dictatorship (1930–1932) in Argentina.[53] There, the Nationalist-influenced military remained the power behind the throne.[54]

Terra's successor, Baldomir (1938–1943), renounced his Terrista and rightist links. Heeding public opinion and US pressure, Baldomir invalidated some of his predecessor's antidemocratic measures by carrying out his own coup d'etat—albeit one respectful of individual freedoms and supported by the Communist Party. Further contrasting with Argentina, the small yet vehement far-right contingent faded as Uruguay adopted a nonbelligerent wartime stance that favored the United States. The Catholic Church, which had gained some stature under Terra,[55] tended to support Franco, but the hierarchy shifted toward the Allies during World War II, unlike its Argentine counterpart. Supported by Baldomiristas and Batllistas, President Juan José de Amézaga (1943–1947) completed the transition to democracy and antifascism.

Although Terra's government may not have been fascist, strictly speaking, many saw it as such. Mobilization against this oppressive regime with fascist leanings, which is how Dr. Paulina Luisi characterized it,[56] took various forms. A Communist-backed rebellion in 1935 failed and attempts to create a Popular Front ultimately proved no more successful in Uruguay than in Argentina.[57]

Uruguayan women had won the vote, but the Terra dictatorship had restricted freedom of expression, and many women protested by abstaining from elections. Even so, they participated in solidarity with the Spanish Republic, protests against deportations, and other democratic struggles. Intellectual women (and men) affiliated with the Uruguayan branch of Agrupación de Intelectuales, Artistas, Periodistas y Escritores (AIAPE), the Argentine Popular Front association that defended culture against fascism. Women formed many peace groups in the mid-1930s, including the local branch of the World Committee of Women Against War and Fascism. Luisi figured prominently in this organization, as did future Feminine Action members. It and like-minded associations around the country, Communists, and workers affiliated with the Unión Femenina Contra la Guerra. Under the auspices of this Popular Front organization, women marched against Italian aggression in Ethiopia in 1935. This and other demonstrations contested not only fascism overseas but Terra's rule at home. The Unión Femenina Contra la Guerra also convened the First National Congress of Women in April 1936 (see chapter 2). Numerous women were among the marchers in July 1938 who pushed the newly inaugurated President Baldomir toward democracy.[58] While these activities resembled those of the AFA and other Argentine peace movements, they were bolder, in part because they faced less official intimidation.

Despite the differences, Uruguay and Argentina shared episodes of repression, resistance, and solidarity that would expedite collaboration between Feminine Action and the Victory Board. Inhabitants of both countries were knowledgeable about conditions across the estuary. A Uruguayan flyer of the mid-1930s denounced the Argentine Nationalists who assassinated laborers and politicians such as Socialist José Guevara (see chapter 1). In a speech delivered to the UAM, Luisi summarized the plight of Argentine feminist campaigns, declaring it beyond belief that women in this culturally advanced nation could not vote.[59] In 1942 *Argentina Libre* described the Uruguayan women running for parliament and interviewed one of them, Laura Cortinas, future president of Feminine Action.[60]

These two groups also would draw upon a heritage of political exchanges between their respective countries.[61] Argentine and Uruguayan politicians had long escaped domestic turmoil in each other's nation. Activist women crisscrossed the Río de la Plata: the Uruguayan freethinker María Abella de Ramírez spent much of her feminist career in Argentina, and the Argentine-born Dr. Paulina Luisi was mostly active in Uruguay, yet often returned to her birthplace to lecture and attend forums. According to Francesca Miller, "The transnational arena held a particular appeal for Latin American feminists," since they usually were excluded from their countries' formal political systems and could express themselves and work for change through international meetings.[62] Antifascism reinforced these transborder contacts. For example, Marta Pastoriza of the AFA was among several Argentine speakers at the First National Congress of Women in Montevideo. Luisi was in frequent touch with the UAM and established ties with Acción Argentina and between it and Uruguay.[63] AIAPE was present in both countries. Argentine delegates also attended the Congress of Democracies held in Montevideo in 1939, which sought to unite the Western Hemisphere against fascism, racism, and war.[64] These encounters and mutual understandings would bolster the ties between Feminine Action and the Victory Board.

Feminine Action for Victory and the Victory Board

What eventually became known as Feminine Action arose with the German invasion of the Soviet Union, as had the Victory Board. Unlike the latter, however, it originated as the women's committee of the largely male-led Acción Anti-Nazi de Ayuda a la Unión Soviética y Demás Pueblos en Lucha (ANAA). ANAA and its Ladies Commission were more clearly tied to the Communist Party than the Victory Board, since they arose from attempts to aid the Soviet Union, and their leaders were Communists or sympathizers. As the Ladies Commission grew, it contacted the Victory Board and became the independent Feminine Action. The Victory Board's relationship with it evolved from mentorship to partnership. The distinctions between them notwithstanding, both promoted women's citizenship.

Hearing that Argentine women were amassing goods to ship to the Soviet Union, the Ladies Commission followed their example. It also started to recruit broadly throughout the country, calling upon women of the democratic parties—Batllistas, Baldomiristas, Independent Nationalists, Communists, and Socialists—to its first assembly on August 30, 1941. Included in the invitation were Catholics and Protestants (Jews were not mentioned), and Uruguayans and foreigners, along with workers, students, professionals, housewives, and mothers. To fit accepted gender roles, the commission declared that since the meeting was not political in nature, attending it would not hurt women's respectability. Uruguayan women could vote, but many had not yet done so, and the Ladies Commission, like the Victory Board, sought to overcome their potential fear of political activism and calm male apprehensions. Nevertheless, it managed to convoke thousands of women for a march through Montevideo to publicize their campaign for democracy at home and elsewhere and attachment to hard-won rights. Two months later, the commission claimed to have twenty-five committees throughout the nation.[65]

In December 1941 the Ladies Commission and the Victory Board came into contact. Commission president Amalia Polleri, a Communist teacher and artist, and secretary Sylvia Mainero, a Communist militant, pertained to the ANAA delegation that delivered the Uruguayan contribution to a Soviet ship in Buenos Aires harbor. While in Buenos Aires, Polleri discussed with board dignitaries how to expand women's *ayudismo*. Back in Montevideo, she described how the Victory Board operated and ensured accountability and efficiency. Imitating the board's practices, the Ladies Commission advised its committees that were making sets of clothing for Soviet infants to report how many they had started, how much material they needed or could return to the central office, how they were raising money for this campaign, and how they would meet their stated goals. The commission then cosponsored a visit by Victory Board officer Scheiner to further discuss aid. Mainero and another commission member, along with the ANAA president and secretary, attended the Victory Board's first national convention in April 1942 and listened to the board officers' presentations on organizational and fundraising matters and reports by provincial delegates.[66] These experiences enabled the Ladies Commission to learn from its Argentine cohort.

Transcending its connection with the Communist Party, in May 1942 the Ladies Commission remodeled itself as Feminine Action. Elia Rodríguez Belo de Artucio, a well-regarded intellectual, high school history professor, and officer of the new group, declared that the Victory Board served as a model for Uruguayans, who wanted to unite women of different social sectors to help the Allies, protect Uruguay, and defeat Nazism. Feminine Action's initial campaign was to make blankets for Allied soldiers, and it opened its first workshop.[67]

According to its initial manifesto, Feminine Action's aim was to clarify Uruguayan women's democratic consciousness, reducing their isolation in their homes or workplaces so they could understand the need to defend national independence, culture, and well-being against the fifth column and possible foreign aggression. It was women's duty to defend the nation, since this task was an extension of defending the home. The group would make and dispatch aid overseas, while within the country it would mobilize democratic women and work with the Ministry of National Defense.

This collaboration included training auxiliary nurses in public schools and stocking official emergency posts with medical supplies.[68] Feminine Action proceeded to organize activities like those of its Argentine mentor.

Feminine Action grew throughout the republic. Branches sprang up and withered, but as of September 1944, it claimed seventeen chapters outside Montevideo, twelve neighborhood and seven affiliated committees in the capital, and a total membership of 6,400. Each affiliated committee consisted of a particular labor sector or immigrant community. Jews, Hungarians, and Yugoslavs formed the immigrant committees, and national meatpacking plant personnel, along with commercial, telephone, and municipal employees, made up the worker ones. Like the Victory Board, Feminine Action aimed recruitment efforts at industrial laborers; at least some joined neighborhood committees in Montevideo, and textile workers at one time formed an affiliated committee.[69] The neighborhood chapters were situated in middle-, working-, and mixed lower- and middle-class barrios.[70] Although membership lists are lacking, most members in the capital probably were lower- to middle-sector housewives, matching the Victory Board's profile. The filiales outside the capital included women of varied classes, most of whom worked in some capacity in or outside their abodes, as homemakers, members of landowning families, teachers, employees in small businesses and family enterprises, and telephone workers.[71]

Some leaders were of distinguished origins, such as the first two presidents, María Emilia Mendívil, scion of a wealthy and highly placed Colorado family, and Laura Cortinas. A writer and feminist, Cortinas was the sister of a high-ranking Independent Nationalist. Eventually, she became a diplomat.[72] Other prominent members such as Julia Arévalo, a party founder and organizer, *luchadora*, and congresswoman, and Bernarda Martínez, a union leader, were working-class Communists. Among numerous intellectuals was Laura Arce, recipient of an American Association of University Women's fellowship to study in the United States, secondary school professor, and producer of an OIAA-sponsored radio show on women in history. Of those officers who were professionals, largest number consisted of educators, with lawyers in second place. They were loyal to the Communist, Colorado, Independent Nationalist, Socialist, and the pro-Terra Blanco-Acedevista Parties, in declining order. The social and political diversity and members of cultural, activist, and friendship networks resembled the Victory Board.[73]

Feminine Action generally replicated the Victory Board's position that reforms would have to await the war's end. Somewhat more than its Argentine counterpart, however, Feminine Action wove social concerns into its antifascist statements. Its initial manifesto stressed the need to decrease the cost of living because poverty led desperate people to extreme ideologies, like fascism. Other spokeswomen claimed that if Nazis won the war or took over Uruguay, they would suspend its incipient industrialization as well as its democracy. The country would sink back into a mere ranch, supplying food for the "superior race" (notwithstanding Uruguay's continued dependence on agrarian exports). Nazism would force women to work at low pay under poor conditions. Working for an Allied victory would help Uruguay determine its own socioeconomic future and safeguard women laborers' rights.[74]

There were other differences between the two groups. The most critical was that the pro-Allied Baldomir and Amézaga administrations and the armed forces supported Feminine Action and permitted it to operate freely. The president's wife, Sofía Terra de Baldomir, and a representative from the Ministry of National Defense attended Feminine Action's opening ceremony, and some of the group's workshops in Montevideo were housed in public schools.[75] There were extreme rightist violent acts and provocations, including harassment of at least one Feminine Action event,[76] but such instances were more frequent in Argentina. Jews strongly engaged with both movements yet followed distinct organizational patterns. The Comité Central Femenino Israelita in Montevideo, encompassing the entire spectrum of the Jewish population, formed an affiliated committee, and its leader eventually sat on the organization's board. The main activists in this Jewish committee, however, were Ashkenazim.[77] In contrast, Eastern and Central European Jews joined women of other backgrounds in Victory Board chapters and had a higher profile within the group. Feminine Action also had fewer transnational relationships than the Victory Board, although the wife of the former British ambassador spoke at its opening ceremony.[78] Nonetheless, Ratto and other board leaders often visited.[79]

The two groups had several reasons for interaction. Seeking to cooperate with democratic women elsewhere, the Victory Board wished to help a kindred group organize effectively, and Feminine Action embraced its advice. Each desired to meet the other and promote good relations and future coordination. The two movements could use these encounters, which demonstrated that antifascist aid drives were gaining momentum and spreading over national boundaries, to raise publicity and encourage bystanders to join. Finally, the relationship seemed a logical continuation of the ties between Uruguayan and Argentine political figures, reinforced by antifascist exchanges in the preceding decade.

By November 1942, the Uruguayan and Argentine women were forming a more collaborative relationship. Feminine Action hosted a fundraising exhibition and sale of artistic works donated by Argentines and Uruguayans. The Argentines Antonio Berni, Lino Spilimbergo, Victory Board sympathizer Raquel Forner, and board members María Carmen de Portela, Norah

Borges, and Cecilia Marcovich contributed their artistic compositions, as did Feminine Action leaders Carmen Garayalde and Amalia Polleri. A lecture series accompanied this event, in which Feminine Action officers and other intellectuals spoke on war-related cultural production and women's roles in the antifascist struggle. The exposition also featured Uruguayan poets, who extolled Russian resistance, as well as a book sale and display of Feminine Action's handmade goods for Allied armies.[80] The exhibition not only raised money, but cultural awareness as well. Like the Victory Board, Feminine Action considered it fundamental to move art into spaces accessible to ordinary people to help create a more just society. Holding cultural events—including ones featuring women cultural producers—was part of their alternative to fascism.[81]

The Christmas Bags campaign of 1943–1944 also was innovative. Feminine Action distributed empty bags decorated with symbols of the designated countries, to be filled with practical gifts for Allied children. It asked supporters to bring or purchase items from the organization to fill them. Leaders praised members for making this effort successful and for their "faith and anti-Nazi hatred." The word *hatred* did not conform to maternalistic views of women's emotions or the bags campaign's maternalistic connotations.[82]

The Christmas Bags campaign was not the only time Feminine Action assigned women duties that resembled their usual roles. Yet like the Victory Board it, too, departed from these roles. Feminine Action trained them for political activism within and outside the organization in much the same manner as the Victory Board. However, unlike the latter, it did not call attention to these activities, perhaps because Uruguayan women already could vote. Arévalo and Cortinas were among the movement's leaders who strongly supported women's rights. Feminine Action as well as Victory Board spokeswomen insisted that the goods they supplied to the Allies did not constitute a woman's charity, but rather a political struggle. Engaging in civil defense and calling themselves anti-Nazi "combatants," who wielded sewing needles instead of rifles, enabled the Uruguayans to claim citizenship. Feminine Action educated members through lectures on international issues, mobilized women for marches, and urged them to work for an Allied victory, which would usher in democracy, peace, and equality between the sexes and classes. Garayalde, a Communist university professor and education official, stated, "The woman enslaved by prejudices [today] tomorrow will be the conscious builder alongside man of a happier and more just life."[83]

Its membership, collection of funds, and production of materials steadily increased by early 1943, yet Feminine Action faced financial problems and recruitment challenges, especially among workers. The Communist-aligned *Diario Popular* called upon all *ayudistas* to increase their efforts in view of the growing authoritarianism across the estuary. Uruguayans needed to take full advantage of their freedom and the fact that their government opposed fascism and favored the Allies.[84]

The Victory Board's second annual convention of May 1943, which *Diario Popular* called a "meeting of Río de la Plata and anti-Nazi solidarity," manifested a more equal relationship between Feminine Action and its much larger ally.[85] Feminine Action had the honor of sending adherents who were parliamentarians: Deputy Julia Arévalo and Senator Sofía Álvarez Vignoli de Demicheli. This time the Uruguayans gave speeches rather than simply listen to board members. Raquel Berro de Fierro, a pro-Spanish Republican member of a traditional Blanco family, and fellow officer Dinorah de Echaniz, a secondary school French professor and Socialist intellectual, detailed Feminine Action activities. In addition, Echaniz accentuated the solidarity among women of the two nations and the rest of the world. Álvarez Vignoli affirmed her devotion to Catholicism and democracy and exhorted women of the Americas to maintain their sisterly ties. Adding to the transnational theme, Arévalo electrified the crowd by proclaiming that they represented two peoples linked through histories of liberation who, once again, were united in the pursuit for freedom. Stirred by Arévalo and the thunderous applause she received, President María Esther Andreau de Billinghurst of the Corrientes chapter grabbed the microphone and urged Argentine mothers like herself to defend democracy by imitating their Uruguayan sisters.[86] This reversed the previous pattern, in which Feminine Action imitated the Victory Board.

This meeting underscored the cross-border solidarity that supplied inspiration, ideas, and publicity to the two groups. Feminine Action's congresswomen heightened its stature and fortified its and the Victory Board's advocacy of women's rights. The senator's Catholic allegiance reinforced the board's campaign to recruit pious Catholic women. The convention approved the Uruguayan delegates' proposal to conduct a joint ten-day pro-Allied campaign in July.[87] Now the Victory Board and Feminine Action were partners.

The Argentine Dictatorship

The Argentine military coup d'etat of June 1943, which overthrew President Ramón Castillo, however, forestalled this plan. Influenced by Nationalists, these officers established a severe dictatorship that jailed and tortured leftists and union militants, closed Congress, fired democratic teachers, imposed strict censorship, and installed Catholic education in public schools. Swayed by economic and strategic motives, like Castillo, and to a lesser degree by some pro-Axis officers, the regime embraced neutrality.[88] It quickly shut down the Victory Board and other ayudista groups in the federal capital. The authorities confiscated the Victory Board's goods and persecuted its members. Soon it also harassed British organizations.

Schlieper wrote President General Pedro Pablo Ramírez, describing the effects of the closure, the Victory Board's purpose and achievements, its honest handling of funds, and its Argentine and Allied support. She sent financial records, an issue of its magazine, lists of national and local officers, and other documents. While the closure technically only applied to the federal capital, authorities throughout Argentina could do as they wished with local chapters, which the defunct central office could no longer coordinate. Thus, Schlieper noted, the entire Victory Board was paralyzed. The national government had authorized the creation of this organization, yet now had suspended its labor for unknown reasons, she claimed. Schlieper denied that the Victory Board's work undermined Argentine neutrality, as Nationalists insisted. She demanded a meeting with the president and Minister of the Interior Colonel Alberto Gilbert, who instead closed all aid entities, accusing them of Communist influence, although the order also applied to the anti-Communist Acción Argentina. The government claimed that even if these groups' stated purposes were not Communist, they could serve as instruments for developing such views.[89]

The authorities did not only suppress Argentine antifascists. While not banned, nonpartisan Free France women faced official hostility.[90] More importantly, the police applied the same decree that closed the Victory Board to the Victory Shop, located in a Buenos Aires suburb. The British embassy declared that this aid entity had no connection to the board; rather, it was under the BCC.[91] British "stitchers" for the Allies felt threatened; one woman called her husband each time she went to her sewing circle to assure him she had not been imprisoned. When police intimidation of British associations, including the BCC, persisted, Ambassador David Kelly told Minister of Foreign Relations Rear Admiral Segundo Storni that he, as honorary president of the BCC, and his wife, who occupied the same position at the BWPC, had always avoided identification with the Victory Board.[92] This was not true of British consulates and groups, whose contacts with the board continued under the military government, when board members in several places offered to donate their remaining stock to the BCC and the BWPC.[93] Kelly worked behind the scenes to protect British organizations and insure the flow of supplies to his beleaguered country. Nevertheless, the regime obstructed British aid providers for several months, at times insisting that they donate half of the funds and materials they collected to Argentine charities.[94]

US Ambassador Norman Armour also worked behind the scenes, but to help antifascist Argentines. In mid-July he told Storni that the government seemed more interested in repressing pro-democratic groups like the Victory Board, alleging Communism, than in repressing the Nationalists who had assaulted the ardent antifascist Waldo Frank, Oliver's friend and a US Jewish intellectual. When Schlieper and Ratto asked Armour to intercede, Armour replied that he already had told Ramírez that the closing of the Victory Board and other pro-Allied groups had created a bad impression in the United States. He spoke with Storni again, and with Minister of Finance Jorge Santamarina, but to no avail. While Armour thought these two men might have sympathized with such groups, as Storni was Schlieper's friend and favored the Allies, and Santamarina was an economic liberal, they either perceived Communist sway over the Victory Board or succumbed to pressure from Nationalist military factions. Even FBI director J. Edgar Hoover now viewed the crippled Victory Board more favorably, admitting that it had done critical work, while adding that the Argentine government considered it a Communist front group.[95]

Schlieper contacted US diplomats once more when her IACW post seemed imperiled. In early August 1943 she told an embassy official that after the coup d'etat, she had offered her resignation to Storni, assuming the new government might prefer someone else. Recognizing her utility in promoting hemispheric cooperation, he encouraged her to stay on. Then another Ministry of Foreign Relations official told her that one of the president's aides requested her resignation, since she had headed a Communist organization. This same aide wanted to withdraw the nation from the IACW but relented when the ministry pointed out that Argentina had committed itself to participate in the program at the Pan American Conference of 1928. Now Schlieper informed Storni that she refused to step down because that would seem to acknowledge that the Victory Board was Communist and deserved to be closed as such. When Storni told her that therefore the government would remove her, Schlieper asked Armour for his support. Secretary of State Cordell Hull advised Armour to tell Storni informally that Schlieper's departure would foster a negative image among her many US friends and admirers. It would strengthen the belief here that the Argentine government was opposed to the institutions valued by US inhabitants. The conversation between Armour and Storni was fruitless, and Schlieper eventually relinquished her position as Argentine representative, which also meant giving up her presidency of the IACW.[96]

The government appointed Angélica Fuselli, a devoutly Catholic writer, to take Schlieper's place. Noting that Fuselli had published several books, Schlieper judged her capable of editing the *IACW Bulletin*. Were her beliefs in line with the regime's? In a talk she gave in the United States in April 1944, Fuselli conveyed Argentine women's admiration for the Roosevelts, calling Franklin a champion of democracy. She described the women of her country as democratic and opposed to leftist and rightist totalitarianisms. They supported the type of feminism found in Pope Leo XIII's encyclical *Rerum Novarum*, she declared, which advocated the roles of wife, mother, and social worker. These views were closer to the dictatorship's than Schlieper's were.[97] Yet while Fuselli wrote for *Criterio* and had longstanding ties with Franceschi, she also numbered among Monseñor Miguel de Andrea's followers. She would form part of the Catholic antifascist minority and espouse positions opposed to those of the military government.[98]

In November 1943 Schlieper told Cannon that Argentine women were facing hard times. The government had disbanded the Victory Board and the UAM and taken over women's charitable organizations, a step that represented a long overdue national consolidation and reform of the social welfare system.[99] Having founded and officiated over several philanthropies, Schlieper probably opposed this measure because it reduced women's authority and put more power in the dictatorship's hands.

Two US journalists quipped that the persecution "reached the point where a woman felt positively subversive to be caught with a pair of knitting needles in her hands."[100] Although they may have exaggerated, the military government treated the Victory Board harshly. Policemen throughout the country demanded the organization's records, materials, and monies, sometimes forcing chapter leaders, such as Moisés Ville president Clara Rotman de Baruch, to show them where these items were stored so they could confiscate them. Those who refused faced jail. Some, however, managed to keep goods hidden in their homes. The authorities mined the documents for names to add to their files. Various board members who were educators lost their jobs, while other colleagues were imprisoned; Marta Samatán of Santa Fe suffered both these fates.[101]

The night that authorities closed the central office in Buenos Aires, they loaded everything they found into trucks and drove away. Warned of this incursion by a phone call, Victory Board leaders sped to the scene, but could not stop it. The one thing they salvaged was their financial records. When the police demanded these papers, the organization gave them up only after photographing them and inserting a final entry for this expense, thus cautioning officers not to falsify or add to the ledgers.[102]

Solidarity across the River Plate

The repression did not wipe out the Victory Board. It went underground and collaborated with Feminine Action on a joint campaign that helped both groups fulfill their aims. Solidarity across the Río de la Plata insured continued solidarity with the Allies.

The Victory Board notified Feminine Action that police had taken money, clothing, sanitary materials, and other supplies worth about three hundred thousand pesos (approximately seventy-five thousand dollars). "It makes one despair to think about it," Berro de Fierro bemoaned, adding that her organization had to gird itself to demand redress from the Argentine dictatorship. If this achieved no results, then it would have to convert Uruguay into the center of ayudismo. Feminine Action telegrammed President Ramírez, imploring him to allow the Victory Board to reopen. Instead, in January 1944 a government decree confirmed the prohibition of all pro-Allied activities.[103]

Yet Argentines' solidarity with the Allies continued. Argentine tourists vacationing in Uruguay contributed to local ayudistas. Some aid groups moved to this neighboring country, along with politicians who sought refuge there. Others operated secretly under pseudonyms; the Victory Board's was Colmena. When police closed its offices, some members met privately, even in leaders' elegant homes; Schlieper herself attended several covert gatherings. Board members sewed, knitted, and solicited goods unobtrusively. One teenager gathered clothing, sheets, pillowcases, and bandages, and sewed as well. Her cousins and friends did the same, but for security reasons all worked individually. After ensuring the materials were clean and in good shape, the adolescent put them in a well-washed potato sack, sewed the top together, and dropped off the package. She left each package in a different location. Sometimes her father, who secretly was active in a pro-French aid group, took her to these places, usually situated in nonelite neighborhoods.[104]

Aside from these clandestine pursuits, the Victory Board transferred to its partner money it had concealed from the authorities. Feminine Action used some of these $17,355.78 Uruguayan pesos to buy materials to assemble 25,586 bandages and the rest to make winter garments, dispatching these products to the Victory Board's specified recipients. Their Argentine colleagues' contribution and ongoing struggle for freedom under dire circumstances inspired the Uruguayans to work even harder, a chapter officer remarked. Now both antifascism and a bond with the indomitable women across the estuary motivated them.[105]

Feminine Action presented numerous homages to the Victory Board. It exhibited the bandages on the anniversary of Argentine independence, May 25, 1944, as a mark of respect for the Argentine group. Another function that year celebrated July 9, 1816, when Argentine patriots swore their allegiance to liberty and self-rule, an event that symbolized their current struggle. On this occasion, antifascists underlined the discrepancy between this patriotic date and the Argentine prisons crammed with democratic citizens. Feminine Action president Cortinas opened this ceremony in the prestigious Ateneo de Montevideo. Four fellow members—Álvarez Vignoli, Arévalo, Batllista deputy Magdalena Antonelli Moreno, and Batllista senator Isabel Pinto de Vidal—extolled the Victory Board. Dr. Emilio Troise thanked the Victory Board's Uruguayan "sisters and comrades" for their solidarity, which he predicted would reinvigorate the Argentine group.[106]

Now this transnational relationship was crucial for both organizations. According to *Diario Popular*, through its partnership with the Victory Board, Feminine Action's fame transcended national boundaries.[107] The July 1944 ceremony provided the latter another opportunity to spotlight Uruguayan women politicians. The collaboration enabled the crippled Victory Board to keep its mission alive, and Feminine Action to finance aid. Perhaps most importantly, the joint campaign amplified the cross-border sisterhood so meaningful to the two movements. The ayudistas may have imagined the faces of distant soldiers and families who wore the garments they shipped from South to North. It was easier to picture their coworkers across the Río de la Plata, some of whom they had met, and the deeply personalized South-South solidarity between them.[108]

The fabric that bound together the Victory Board and Feminine Action was tightly woven. Several different materials linked US Americans with the Victory Board, some more durable than others. And while up to 1943 Great Britain's embassy preferred a tattered cloth, its consulates and community groups favored an undamaged one.

One might think that US and British figures would have praised Schlieper and hailed the Victory Board's pro-Allied solidarity. But some did not. While Eleanor Roosevelt, women officials in Washington, high-ranking diplomats like Rockefeller and Hull, and Ambassador and Mrs. Armour respected the Victory Board and its president, Hoover and some US embassy officers and local OIAA representatives suspected them. British consulates and groups such as the British Red Cross collaborated with this organization, but Ambassadors Ovey and Kelly and other members of the embassy staff treated it circumspectly. They were reluctant to partner openly with a movement the Argentine government considered subversive and with its controversial president. The British and US governments were not monolithic in their dealings with these Argentine antifascist women.

Aside from the South-North material backing it offered the Allies, what did the Victory Board give Great Britain and the United States, and what did it receive or hope to receive from them? It furnished moral support, anti-Axis propaganda, and reinforcement of local British (and, to a lesser degree, US) efforts to supply their troops. Oliver and Schlieper offered advice to US officials, who did not necessarily follow it. For their part, the

British and US Americans provided a modicum of safety, status, and appreciation for the Victory Board's South-North mission.

The Victory Board was much more important for US than for British interests. Rockefeller, Hull, Winslow, Cannon, Eleanor Roosevelt, and the League of Women Voters saw it as an ally of US hemispheric policy against fascism, and Armour's actions reflected these attitudes. Rockefeller and other functionaries valued Schlieper and Oliver for improving US understanding of Latin America and Argentina, and vice versa, and smoothing relations with these areas. These board leaders urged exchanges of persons, knowledge, and culture between the United States and Latin America, which dovetailed with the OIAA's purposes. By funding Schlieper's trip to the United States in 1941–1942 and facilitating her contacts with women's groups, Rockefeller and Winslow enhanced her ability to manage the IACW and Victory Board and represent Pan-Americanism.

The relationships between the Victory Board, the United States, and Great Britain changed somewhat over time. With Armour's defense of the movement in 1943, the US government seemed to become more uniformly supportive of it. The British later shifted toward a more positive view of this organization.

The intertwined histories of the Victory Board and Feminine Action offer an unusual, more intimate example of cross-border antifascist collaboration. This South-South relationship drew upon a decades-long circulation of ideas and activists and some political commonalities. Leaders of both movements combined antifascism with feminism. The Victory Board served as an organizational model and teacher for Feminine Action, and as the mentorship faded their cooperation and mutual support facilitated their ability to meet their goals. Joint appearances raised favorable publicity for both groups and may have attracted new members. In addition, Álvarez Vignoli reinforced the board's campaign to recruit devout Catholics. The Victory Board furnished the monies that Feminine Action needed to make goods for the Allies; in turn, this financial assistance enabled the board to continue its efforts despite persecution and clandestinity. They kept each other alive.

The contacts between the Victory Board and Feminine Action also influenced their respective nations. Through their joint appearances leaders of the two groups pointed to their diverse membership, thereby promoting respect for ethnic, religious, and class pluralism, which is fundamental for democracy. Furthermore, speakers at these events advocated women's citizenship and accustomed the populace to women occupying public and political roles. The cross-border presence of distinguished figures such as Arévalo and Álvarez Vignoli demonstrated to Argentine women that they could aspire to high-ranking positions within political parties and the polity, and it may have helped fuel local campaigns for women's suffrage. These ideas and practices were anathema to Argentine Nationalists, which I discuss in the following chapter. Nevertheless, the Victory Board's relationship with Feminine Action continued to influence their movements and countries.

CHAPTER 7

"V FOR VICTORY" OR VENDEPATRIA?

Nationalists versus the Victory Board, 1941–1944

The Victory Board's (Junta de la Victoria) initial solidarity message to British and Russian women of September 1941 (see chapter 3) rankled María Teresa Rodríguez Dondis, the head of the women's section of the Unión Nacionalista Santafesina (UNS).[1] Speaking for her group, she denounced the Victory Board, founded and led by *porteñas*, for claiming it represented Argentine women. Most Argentine women did not share the board's views, she argued. Those outside the federal capital were far less concerned with Communist and British women's "heroic and bellicose acts" than with local "heroic acts" against the hunger and poverty that afflicted mothers, sisters, and wives of laborers and *campesinos*. True Argentine women upheld Catholic beliefs, peace, and social harmony, never war. Their "feminine spirit" demanded that they join together to pray for continued neutrality and to free the country from imperialism.[2]

Her colleague, María Esther Méndez, further contrasted the UNS with the Victory Board. She praised UNS girls, pious and nationalistic, who distributed clothing and goods to underprivileged Argentines and collaborated with Nationalist men to forge "a free fatherland" purged of Jews, politicians, Yankee ideas, and foreign exploitation. Contesting depictions of them and their menfolk as antipatriotic Nazis, Méndez declared that Nationalist women stood for criolla traditions, religion, home, motherhood, and womanly love—all opposed by Communists. Indeed, Communist women lacked feminine instincts and virtues. The humble young UNS women inspired their male comrades and fought Communism alongside them. The aristocrats of the Victory Board, on the other hand, deserved nothing better than sneers. These "old grotesque figures, Jews, Communists" only abandoned their habitual "unhealthy idleness for a 'cocktail' or 'bridge game'" to raise money for the Russians. Unlike Nationalist women, the Victory Board had fame and money, which it collected from prominent businessmen who ignored UNS entreaties for goods to help the Argentine poor. Yet the UNS members' faith in God and Nationalism made up for their lack of resources.[3]

These two Nationalists introduced many themes of this chapter.[4] Their words illustrate how Nationalist women defined themselves and the Victory Board, and why they fought each other. Chapter 2 analyzed Latin American fascist-antifascist debates in the 1930s, centering on women's rights and roles and their relation to the social order. Picking up from this discussion, here I examine in detail Nationalists' thoughts on overlapping issues that intersected with the Victory Board's principles and practices. I explore how they and their allies, who did not always speak with one voice,[5] reacted to the board and local antifascisms and how this affected their identities. Since the intervening chapters have shown to a certain degree how the Victory Board contested Nationalists, here I concentrate on how Nationalists contested the board. These rivals continued to present competing discourses on topics introduced previously—women's roles, mass politics, inequality, Communism, and modernity, and now I add the war, imperialism, the ideal society, charity, and Jews. Extreme rightists also physically attacked the Victory Board and collaborated with government efforts to suppress it. Disagreements and distortion still characterized the verbal exchanges, as did some parallels and intersections. Although fascists and antifascists "conversed" more directly than before, their mutual animosity was as deep as ever. At least one leading Nationalist appeared to consider the Victory Board the greatest leftist threat to social peace.

Preserving Gender and Class Hierarchy

The divisions among them notwithstanding, during these years, Nationalists and right-wing Catholics tended to concur on desirable female roles and attributes, with a few exceptions.[6] Their press referred to women as mothers, wives, daughters, sisters, and girlfriends. It ridiculed and denigrated those who sought citizenship, professional status, or work outside the domestic sphere. Strict adherence to customary gender notions was necessary to uphold order within and outside the household. Nationalists also claimed to speak for the nonelite.

For *Crisol*, representing the extreme Nationalist flank, everyone had a place in society, and the woman's place was in an honorable home. This implied that social and gender hierarchies were static. The Argentine woman was dedicated to homemaking: a life of love, domesticity, simplicity, and sacrifice. Hers was a Christian family based on order, respect, and affection. Proper womanly behavior meant modesty and shunning the limelight, and Nationalists criticized Victory Board president Ana Rosa Schlieper de Martínez Guerrero for not abiding by these norms. Like some US diplo-

mats, Nationalists lambasted what they saw as Schlieper's indecorous ambition and desire for attention. They derided her for basking in the free
publicity she garnered through her radio broadcasts in the United States,
which were heard throughout the world. *Crisol* also poked fun at Schlieper
and the Victory Board for attempting to train women to defend the Western Hemisphere by laboring in factories, ships, and trains while men went
to war. Instead of fussing over hypothetical totalitarian incursions, they
should be comparing food prices and doing laundry and cooking, duties
that seemed prosaic but were vital. The "viragos and androgynous" women
without marriage prospects who frequented such discussions and sought
civil defense duties should instead learn to prepare delicious meals to find
husbands.[7]

Evidently, antifascism only attracted desexed or masculinized women
and old maids. They were elderly "monstrosities," exhausted and decadent,
whereas Nationalist women were young and vigorous, according to Méndez. The contrast she drew typified local and foreign fascist rhetoric. The
pro-Nazi publication *Clarinada* noted that Nationalism rebelled against
"the old, obsolete, worn-out, and useless."[8] In fact, board members ranged
from adolescents to the aged, some married, others not.

Echoing Chilean Nacista Dr. Badilla Urrutia (see chapter 2), a writer
for *Crisol* claimed that performing the same hard labor as men "virilized
women," converting them into "neutral beings" who could not become
healthy mothers. Until a Nationalist state could restore their dignity by
instituting family salaries for men and sending women home, the bourgeois matrons who entertained themselves by sewing the "V for Victory"
onto garments instead could help these impoverished women.[9] Apparently
the Victory Board should redirect its aid to dispelling women's financial
exigencies.

Méndez, *Crisol*, and other Nationalist voices insisted that board members—whether they considered them patricians or Communists—were
wealthy. To a certain extent, this mimicked the Victory Board's own publicity, which sometimes emphasized the prestigious socialites in the movement.
Yet it also publicized its robust working-class component, which Nationalists strategically ignored. Instead, the Alianza de la Juventud Nacionalista
(AJN), the most dynamic Nationalist group of the early 1940s; the UNS;
and kindred organizations highlighted their inclusion of workers and asserted that they were the genuine standard-bearers of the downtrodden. Competing with Victory Board and leftist discourses, however, theirs insisted on
class conciliation and acceptance of one's position within the social order.[10]
Transgressing gender as well as class boundaries undermined this order.

Occasionally, Nationalist newspapers pointed out that women who labored in factories, workshops, and stores, or as street vendors, did so out

of need. The plight of seamstresses, who earned little and sewed in dirty cramped spaces rife with tuberculosis, stirred *Crisol* to recommend congressional action on their behalf. Such instances were rare, however. *Bandera Argentina* vilified women in public administration, insisting, without evidence, that 70 percent of them simply wanted to use their earnings to be modern, purchase elegant garb, go to theaters, and sip cocktails. It applauded Italy and Germany for removing women from the sexual license and frivolity rampant in government bureaucracy and permitting men to recover these spaces. This Nationalist daily was pleased to report that Vichy France and the Argentine military dictatorship were considering doing the same. Such measures would strengthen families and increase the birth rate.[11] With its members in the labor force, support for women's rights, and training of women for greater participation in society, the Victory Board embraced modernity and opposed European fascist restrictions on women.

While concerned about working women neglecting their families, a few Catholic voices were more temperate. Monsignor Gustavo Franceschi, editor of the influential *Criterio*, agreed that women and girls belonged in the home, but this was impossible under the existing economic order. Unlike some Nationalists and antifascists, he realized that not even Germany and Italy had been able to keep them there. A number worked to indulge in pleasures, which he deplored. Yet the Catholic Church should encourage and offer Christian guidance to those who needed to support themselves and their families, and others who planned to study, have a career, and sustain themselves honorably.[12] For her part, Delfina Bunge de Gálvez, a Catholic writer married to the Nationalist Manuel Gálvez, had long favored women seeking employment for income or professional satisfaction. But she also advised a Christian sense of balance between one's occupation and one's home. This came closer to the Victory Board's orientation, although many members might have disagreed with her belief in male authority over the family.[13]

Evidently, *Crisol* recognized that women had reentered the German labor force, for paradoxically it approved of women in its defense plants. Women's intelligence, dexterity, and adaptability made them suitable for these jobs, particularly ones that required much accuracy. It justified their involvement in a male occupation by claiming that they were helping their nation at war and not competing with men.[14] Still, this was a notable departure from the newspaper's customary hostility toward women's activities outside the household and association of femininity with tenderness and peace. Only support for Nazism can explain it. And while Schlieper and other Victory Board leaders regarded women's involvement in US defense industries as an advance toward equality, members with pacifist backgrounds may have lamented it.

Peace and Neutrality

Both Nationalists and Victory Board members claimed to support peace. The Victory Board equivocated on neutrality, asserting its stance did not contradict this policy, but clearly supporting the Allies. Nationalists criticized antifascist elevation of abstract principles over the national interest, which they insisted formed the basis for their neutral position. Their neutrality, however, leaned toward the Axis. Rightists' denunciations of Allied imperialism and flawed democracy often rang true, but they ignored Axis depredations.

Nationalists often charged that antifascists had belligerent aims. Esther Dumrauf of the feminine section of the Unión Nacionalista Argentina (UNA) in Tornquist, Buenos Aires, advised her comrades not to be fooled by *vendepatrias* (those who sell out their country) who sought to drag the country into a disastrous conflict. The Victory Board must have been among those she saw as sellouts. *Bandera Argentina* charged it specifically with the crime of pushing Argentina toward abandoning neutrality.[15]

The Victory Board's position was nuanced. At the Victory Board's opening ceremony on September 13, 1941, Schlieper said that the war had crossed the Atlantic. Then, at the first national convention, she noted that as women and mothers board members wanted peace, but public indifference would not help Argentina avoid entry into the war.[16] She seemed to regard this prospect as inevitable. The first convention resolved to petition the government to comply with the resolution of the hemispheric conference in Rio de Janeiro in January 1942 to break diplomatic and economic ties with the Axis countries.[17] Considering its decision and pro-Allied solidarity, the Victory Board was decidedly not neutral, but it never advocated engaging in combat. However, as noted, at times it described its work in martial terms.

According to Rodríguez Dondis, genuine Argentine women favored peace, and a writer for *Crisol* noted that they were struggling for it. Women participated in the Peace Plebiscite, a petition endorsing President Ramón Castillo's support for neutrality, Argentine sovereignty, and the national interest. The Nationalist organization Defensa Social Argentina initiated this venture, and many Nationalists were among the men in its commission of honor. Its commission of ladies, mostly aristocrats and probably Nationalist or Nationalist-leaning, exhorted women to sign the petition, and women helped gather signatures in a campaign that swept the nation. At its conclusion in September 1942, the leaders handed President Castillo a list that they claimed contained over a million adherents.[18] As before, women on both sides cloaked themselves with the mantle of peace: the Nationalists with the Peace Plebiscite and the Victory Board with its belief that defeating the Axis would establish global concord.

In January 1942, some Nationalist men created another neutralist vehicle, the Patriotic Front. It stated that groups connected to both sides in the
war for international hegemony were trying to enlist Argentina. The 1,500
signatories of this declaration opposed locals who were agitating to enter
the war–implying on the Allied side—arguing it was not in the national interest to do so, and only the national interest, not abstract principles, should
guide the country. Patriotic Front adherents were willing to fight, but solely
to defend what was Argentine.[19] In its solidarity with the Allies, however,
the Victory Board insisted precisely on following the "abstract principles"
of freedom, democracy, pluralism, and equality.

While seemingly regarding the Allies and the Axis as equally objection-
able, Delfina Bunge de Gálvez delighted in pointing out what she regarded
as pro-Allied Catholics' contradictory stances. Some Catholics castigated
Nazism for its measures against the church, but the Communists, liberals,
Protestants, and Masons—all anti-Catholic—among the Allies, and Soviet
persecution of the church, did not bother them. Those who favored the Allies denounced German racism against Jews but did not address US racism
against Blacks or Europeans' racism against their colonial subjects. Racism
was not new nor unique to Germany, and it often permeated conquerors'
treatment of the conquered, as in Jewish conduct toward the Canaanites
in biblical times. Only Christian charity, which was not evident on either
side of the war, could heal these wounds. Eugenia Silveyra de Oyuela and
other devoutly Catholic board sympathizers and members, however, often
described their aid to the Russians as Christian charity, although Bunge
surely disapproved of these actions and justifications. In her view, Axis and
Allied supporters were serving foreign interests rather than tackling growing local threats to Christianity: secular education, Communism, social injustice, and the decline of morality, due partly to Jews and the film industry
they controlled. Communists, for example, were more visible than before,
as witnessed in their improbable alliance with aristocrats in *"ayudismo."*
Bunge, then, would have considered the Victory Board dangerous. She also
criticized those who believed that admirers of Germany wanted it to take
over Argentina or to adopt its form of government. Bunge considered this
fear unjustified, as was the congressional committee scrutinizing alleged
Nazi infiltration.[20] This comment as well as her antisemitism evinced a Nationalist tilt.

The Nationalist periodical *El Fortín* denied that it was neutral; rather, it
opposed everyone. In an issue published before the attack on Pearl Harbor,
it saw little difference between those who thought Argentines owed much
to the British and those who predicted Argentines could gain much from
Germany. *El Fortín* disdained Anglophiles and Germanophiles who lauded
the foreign and were consumed with the struggle raging abroad. Not strict-

ly in-between, however, *El Fortín* asserted that at least those who favored Germany were against the British and Jews who suffocated Argentina.[21]

The Nationalist Rodolfo Irazusta believed that Argentina was not truly neutral. While it exchanged ambassadors with the British and dealt regularly with their diplomats, it had no diplomatic mission in Berlin, and mere "doormen" staffed the German embassy in Buenos Aires. Both claims were inaccurate. There was an Argentine mission in Berlin, led by Chargé d'Affaires Luis Luti, and Chargé d'Affaires Erich Otto Meynen headed the German embassy in Argentina. Although they lacked ambassadorial rank, they were seasoned diplomats, and neither was unimportant. Irazusta may have ignored the Argentine legation because Luti was antifascist and disparaged the German embassy because Meynen joined the Nazi Party late and opportunistically. His argument that locals gave much larger donations to the British war effort than to the German more persuasively demonstrated Argentine partiality toward Britain. In Irazusta's opinion, this false neutrality obscured continued British sway over Argentina. However, he downplayed German influence and espionage, which the Victory Board probably exaggerated.[22]

El Fortín and perhaps Irazusta betrayed sympathy for Germany, as did other Nationalists. Applying Catholic principles, *Crisol* described the Axis countries' initiation of combat as a just war. Their legitimate authorities had taken this step only after long and fruitless negotiations over the vindictive Treaty of Versailles. Furthermore, the avowedly secular democracies had allowed purported Jewish reprisals against Christians and Masonic hatred against God, crimes largely avoided by Germany and Italy. According to *Bandera Argentina*, the "plutocracies" had imposed the war to halt the German regime's revival of prosperity, respect for laborers, and programs on their behalf, fearing that this "social wisdom" was garnering proletarian backing around the world.[23] For their part, the Victory Board and other antifascists denounced the Nazi and the Italian Fascist destruction of labor rights and unions, as well as German antisemitism and hunger for war.

Writing in August 1941, the Nationalist Alberto Ezcurra Medrano denied that England protected Christian civilization, the free peoples of the world, and the dignity of the human person, as antifascists contended. This was a Protestant country tied to Jews, Masons, the profit motive, and international capital. Its economic system treated human beings as cogs in a machine, and its imperialism was brutal and exploitative. By opposing liberalism, democracy, and capitalism,[24] he claimed, the "New Order" opened a path toward a Christian order. Admittedly, this path could be problematic, but that did not call for Argentine intervention. Employing the same term as his ideological rivals, Ezcurra Medrano regarded the internal enemy that served foreign causes—namely, the Allies, as the genuine "fifth column."[25] The Victory Board formed part of this alternative fifth column that he reviled. Carlos Silveyra, the editor of *Clarinada*, added that Great Britain was fighting to maintain its interests, threatened by the resurgence of the German and Italian economies.[26]

Nor was the United States altruistic. The Nationalist author Manuel Gálvez claimed that this country was not fighting for liberty, as it funded Latin American dictators. He added US blacklists of supposed Axis sympathizers, "invention" of the fifth column, and pressure on Argentina to align itself with US foreign policy to the long history of US imperialism in the region. Ironically, he condemned US alliances with brutal leaders yet supported the repressive Argentine military dictatorship, albeit largely because of its social programs.[27] No doubt leftist board members also disapproved of US neocolonialism, yet they, like María Rosa Oliver, believed it necessary to ally with the United States to defeat the greater threat from Germany.

Unlike the Allies, Germany and its European partners resisted Communism, strengthened the family, and supported Christian socialism and morality, *Crisol* averred. Communists did not defend democracy (nor did *Crisol*) and human dignity. Did Señora Martínez Guerrero understand that Communism was immoral and therefore no Catholic could possibly desire a Soviet victory?[28] In contrast, the Victory Board and other antifascists believed that one could not remain neutral in the struggle between life and death, civilization and barbarism, and for them the choice was equally clear.

Eugenia Silveyra de Oyuela was a Catholic who supported aid to the Soviet Union, which Nationalists considered unpardonable. She did not want to destroy the Communist regime, because this contradicted Christian respect for human beings and love for one's enemies. Far from opposing the Russian people, *Crisol* claimed, Catholics hoped to save their souls by obliterating Communism. They only fought the Soviet government, which had persecuted Christianity, stripped people of property, and undermined marriage and the family, measures that Silveyra evidently had forgotten. And yet she blamed Germany for being anti-Christian! Even if she had reason to criticize some aspects of Nazism, how could Silveyra "prefer the red annihilating barbarism to the salvational movement of German rehabilitation and grandeur?" Her pro-British and anti-German sentiments aside, if she truly sought what was good for humanity, she would favor demolishing the Soviet regime, which was what Catholics had sought since the Bolshevik Revolution and what Adolf Hitler's "providential armies" were achieving.[29] Considering her attitudes toward a system condemned by popes, *Clarinada* urged church authorities to deny that she was the voice of Argentine Catholic women, as the Victory Board claimed. Although Silveyra characterized herself as a leader of the militant Acción Católica Argentina (ACA), this magazine insisted that it had expelled her, although whether that was true is unclear.[30]

Communism and Jews

Nationalists associated antifascism with Communism, which they saw as inherently Jewish, and Jews with capitalism, money, and corruption.[31] In their eyes, Communists, Jews, and dishonest wealth—one and the same—controlled the Victory Board. Although this and other Nationalist observations on the board's makeup and policies strained credulity, a few were incisive.

María Elena Huergo, a self-described pious anti-liberal adolescent, attributed the Victory Board's ayudismo to its Jewish nature. She observed that members of the "deicidal" race had transformed themselves into patrician leaders of this Communist group that masqueraded as criollo. Jews duped Catholic adherents into soliciting contributions outside churches. Thus they endeavored to wither Argentine unity, religion, family, and pocketbooks.[32]

To the French saying "Look for the woman," *Crisol* retorted, "Look for the Jew."[33] The Jewish presence in the Victory Board did not surprise Nationalists. That its president appeared at some Jewish community events further contaminated this organization in Nationalist eyes. In their usual manner of identifying what they disliked with this stigmatized group, Nationalists typecast Schlieper and other Christian adherents as Jews. The unusual multiclass, multiethnic, and multiparty composition of this pro-Allied movement seemingly confirmed their belief in a Jewish-capitalist-Communist conspiracy tied to foreign imperialism. To "prove" this theory, *Crisol* published a diagram showing how the British purportedly had created the "V for Victory" symbol by lifting it out of the Star of David.[34]

A peddler of such conspiracies, as well as of the notion that the Victory Board was a "movement of social disintegration,"[35] *Clarinada* followed it closely. It regarded Cora Ratto as the brain behind the organization, which seemed credible. Less likely was its claim that she had ordered a purge of anti-Communists from this group, waiting until "the Jewess Schliepper [sic]" departed for "Yankee-land" to carry it out in late 1942. Judicious and placatory, Schlieper had opposed Ratto's tactic, yet the combination of the two personalities suited Stalinist Popular Front policy. Schlieper had become so useful for the Communist Party (Partido Comunista) that she and José Peter, the Communist leader of the meatpacking workers' union, jointly issued a call for the meeting to inaugurate the Stalingrad aid campaign. Demonstrating typical Communist deceit, in *Clarinada's* view, the press release of the event did not mention the Communist Party members who attended.[36] These articles were perceptive in discerning that Ratto and Schlieper balanced each other, although I found no evidence of any such purge in this period of organizational growth. *Clarinada* did not consider that the illegal Communist Party had to disguise its involvement because publicity could result in jail and torture, which, at any rate, the periodical would have applauded.

According to this magazine (and J. Edgar Hoover), Communists dominated the Victory Board and assured its compliance with this party's directives. It is more precise to say that the Victory Board was diverse politically, although its objectives tended to mesh with Communist wartime interests, and some Communists were prominent in it. Schlieper was a devoted Radical, but *Clarinada* saw her as a "Communist lying in ambush." However, it correctly identified seven other leaders aligned with the party. Also accurate were its assertions that immigrant wives of Communists composed and led the Victory Board chapter of Oberá, and that it and other Communist-linked groups there had prospered thanks to Marcos Kanner.[37]

Crisol dismissed the notion, spread by Ratto and several other Victory Board adherents, that women were equal in the Soviet Union; since men had no rights, women had none, either—not that this newspaper advocated them. It added that Russian women's involvement in dangerous and heavy physical labor, combined with childbearing and homemaking, overwhelmed them.[38] The Victory Board pointed out that Argentine rural women, including some of its members, shouldered similar burdens.

Nor was the fundraising for the Soviet Union clean and transparent, partly due to Jewish involvement, according to *Crisol*. One of the Santa Fe chapter's raffles raised money for the Russians—and supposedly its members' pockets. It took place in a Jewish home, and most of the attendees were Jews. Only a few "Argentines" were there—but they were Argentine in name only. For *Crisol*, neither Jews nor Christians who associated with them could be truly Argentine. Chapter president Matilde Porta Echagüe de Molinas wore a new hat to this event, which *Crisol* hinted that she had purchased using funds siphoned off from a previous benefit. A Jewish businessman supposedly known for fraudulent practices bought a painting being raffled, which he returned to Porta Echagüe so guests could bid on it again. Jews had never lost the custom of selling used goods, the Nationalist mouthpiece joked.[39]

In keeping with its belief in Jewish corruption, Nationalists accused the Victory Board and other antifascists of deliberately keeping poor records and swindling innocent contributors. Without evidence, *Crisol* claimed that *ayudistas* sent only half the aid they collected to the Allies and kept the rest for themselves, consoling itself that at least this half remained in

Argentina. The Victory Board also stole in another manner: its "campaigns of sacrifice" squeezed money out of Argentines to send to other countries. This was indeed a sacrifice for our hard-pressed people, *Crisol* observed bitterly. Another Victory Board fundraising technique stoked further anger. It charged ten cents to guess the number of chickpeas in a glass jar, with a dessert as the prize. The newspaper condemned this means of taking pennies from poor children. *Bandera Argentina* welcomed the military regime's closure of the Victory Board, the Comisión Sanitaria Argentina (CSA), and the Comisión Democrática Argentina (CDA), describing them as "caves of con men and Communists." Warning this measure might not prove sufficient, it urged the regime to jail Schlieper and other ayudistas to halt their wrongdoing.[40]

Nationalists insisted that Schlieper benefitted personally from corruption. She felt like such an important person, *Clarinada* mocked, in her travels through the United States in late 1942, paid for by the Victory Board.[41] The suggestion was that Schlieper used the board's funds to boost her vanity. As noted, however, the US government funded this trip.

Contradicting its own notion that the Victory Board served Soviet defense interests, *Crisol* claimed that its motive was to create "a reserve fund" for Jews. As the New Order was making it difficult for Jews to stay in Europe, under the pretext of raising funds for the Allies "Sadowsky" (Ratto), "Schliperosky" (Schlieper), and their colleagues were collecting money to bring them to Argentina. These donations acquired from democratic Christians would help support Jews fleeing places where they could no longer "harm others." The Nationalist paper insinuated that these funds could also sustain Jews in the future, when righteous Christian Argentines would force them into ghettos or concentration camps.[42]

Nationalists saw Jews in the Victory Board and elsewhere as malevolent forces. Sometimes they betrayed ignorance of Jewish Argentines as flesh-and-blood human beings. Eva Katz de Leiserson of the Delfín Huergo board chapter, on the border between Buenos Aires and La Pampa Provinces, told *La Hora* that the wives of all seventy families in the local agricultural colony belonged to it. She added that the owner of the only large estate in the vicinity, Elisa R. Uribe de Echeverría, headed the group.[43] A month later, *Clarinada* offered its interpretation of this article. It claimed that Uribe, a "fervent Communistoid Allied-lover," had recruited the adult women in the neighboring agricultural settlement, which the magazine assumed was her domain. She picked up and drove the *filial* leaders to meetings; none would "dare to snub her boss." This leader of a branch of a "democratic" movement must have pushed her impoverished tenants into joining. The anti-Nationalist press, however, insisted they joined the chapter freely because of their political views. This is how "'democratic history' is written,"

Clarinada quipped.[44] Ironically, *Clarinada* seemed to sympathize with the members; despite Katz's name, it did not seem to realize they were Jewish. Nor did it understand that the president was not their "boss" and could not have pressured them, since they lived in an independent Jewish Colonization Association settlement.[45] In fact, the Jewish colonists may have asked her to be the president so that she could intercede with authorities and they could use her car, which she placed at their disposal. So much for the accuracy of Nationalist history.

Nationalists criticized Jews for supposedly separating themselves from others, yet it wanted to keep Catholics separate from them. *Clarinada* decried the presence of Catholics alongside Communists (innately Jewish, in its view) at Victory Board events and what it considered Jewish Communist penetration in the ACA, referring to this purported influence on Silveyra and devout Catholic board members. It thought that contact with Jews would invariably infect and Judaize Catholics. Illustrating this effect, the magazine published a cartoon of Silveyra reading a speech to Zionist women from a Torah-like scroll, lamenting Nazi oppression of Jews. Her face was grotesquely distorted with a hooked "Jewish" nose.[46] Contesting such notions, the Victory Board lauded and encouraged interaction among different groups, thus promoting a modern pluralistic Argentina.

The Ideal Society

Both sides stood for certain principles. Nationalists sought a male-ruled hierarchical society united around Spanish Catholic roots and customs. In contrast, Victory Board leaders envisioned a modern cosmopolitan nation united around democracy, in which women played roles equal to those of men. Each considered the Other divisive and threatening.

Unity was important yet elusive for both fascists and antifascists. The Victory Board could not bring together all democratic Argentines, or even all democratic women, as it had hoped, beyond coordinating the massive Stalingrad campaign and collaborating with other aid ventures. Neither were Nationalists able to consolidate their factions under a single leader, although they sometimes mounted joint attacks on leftist and Jewish targets. Nazi Germany offered a compelling model of unification that Nationalists could not match.[47] Nor could the Victory Board duplicate Allied unity. The Peace Plebiscite, Patriotic Front, and appeals to Catholicism and tradition were means of Nationalist bonding, just as knitting and sewing around the same table were for the Victory Board. Calls to fight the Other may have been the most effective glue for each side.

Yet neither side presented itself as merely opposing the Other. *Bandera Argentina* wanted to unify the nation to protect *argentinidad* and establish

a Catholic order that would assure morality and a modest living standard
for all. It distinguished this "sacred union" of national dignity from what
it considered the other side's simple desire to unite in combat against the
Axis.[48] Rather than merely advocating a united front *against* fascism, however, the Victory Board also stood *for* national, religious, and ethical values, albeit liberal democratic ones that advocated cross-border solidarity. As
stated on its membership card, it defended women's dignity and rights.[49]
Moreover, it favored a more equitable postwar society.

Nationalists saw antifascists as divisive. *Bandera Argentina* charged that
Acción Argentina had infiltrated homes and threatened to split the "Argentine family." Equally menacing in its opinion was the Victory Board,
with its "foreign and ridiculous insignia."[50] "The tip of the V of victory"
had driven a "wedge into the heart of our people," setting brothers against
brothers, sons against fathers, and wives against husbands. Implicit was
the fear that friction among spouses and among progeny and fathers could
undermine male rule in the household, which in turn could set off anarchy
in the nation. Antifascism stimulated "passionate ideological antagonisms"
and foreign "super capitalist" pressures that incited civil war. The newspaper applauded President Castillo's imposition of a state of siege in late 1941,
seeing it as a measure to halt this strife.[51]

Manuel Fresco, the former National Democratic Party (Partido
Demócrata Nacional) governor of Buenos Aires (1936–1940), now the
head of the UNA, denounced these antagonisms. His rhetoric and guber-
natorial policies were Nationalist, although some Nationalists distrusted
him.[52] Fresco perceived a conspiracy of Communists, liberal democrats,
the press, economically insecure intellectuals, and the "bellicose financial
international" that fomented chaos and division among Argentines. The
social rift between rich and poor also facilitated Marxist-impelled class
conflict. Heading his list of pro-Stalinist groups sowing discord was the
Victory Board. Perhaps his conservative gender views led him to regard
this women's movement as particularly subversive.[53] This underscores the
Victory Board's visibility and influence. At any rate, board members also
viewed Nationalism as divisive, pitting its authoritarianism and xenophobia
against those like themselves who embraced the pluralistic and democratic
country in the making.

Furthermore, Nationalists exacerbated the imagined cultural and
political rift between the federal capital and the rest of the nation. They
identified with the latter for its supposed adherence to conservative values
implanted by the Spanish conquerors. Rural criollos, *Crisol* argued, were
the genuine nationalists, while it and other radical rightist publications
disparaged the modern, outward-looking, and ethnically diverse character of Buenos Aires.[54] Rodríguez Dondis insisted that provincial women

were concerned with more significant issues than the porteña-led Victory Board's goals. For its part, however, the board sought to unite the federal capital and the country through its national structure and conventions. Moreover, the provinces and territories were hardly monolithic or static—immigration, modernization, and social conflicts had affected many areas, including the countryside, and influenced the Victory Board. These factors belied Nationalists' facile distinctions.

By this time, some descendants of immigrants were becoming Nationalists, and perhaps for this reason the latter reluctantly began to accept at least those of Latin backgrounds as part of the nation. Persons of these origins had contributed to Argentine progress and established Argentine homes and families, the AJN admitted. Despite the immigrants' materialistic motives that undermined the idealistic nation *Crisol* wished to mold, it conceded that Latins shared culture, spirit, and blood with Argentines, providing the essential unity for the *patria*.[55] Other newcomers apparently did not belong. According to *Clarinada*, the Popular Front elements who claimed to represent the "authentic Argentine people" instead stood for the "cosmopolitan people." This "scum" consisted of malcontents who brought their "ancestral hatreds," hinting they were Jews and revolutionaries.[56]

As if responding directly to the Victory Board's embrace of women of varied backgrounds, *Crisol* announced, "We do not want to be an aggregate of diverse peoples." Rather, Nationalists wanted a fatherland with a consolidated history and a soul and culture inspired by Catholic Spain. Culture, according to *Clarinada*, was nation-bound. It served the ideals of "the fatherland, people, race, and God," not abstract notions, internationalisms, or individualism. Nationalists sought to outlaw "licentious liberties" and would not permit cultural research to attack "Faith and Truth." Argentines, not foreigners or Jews, should construct their own culture.[57] With its defense of democracy, individual freedoms, pluralism, and values that knew no national borders, the Victory Board defied this obscurantist view.

Vendepatria

Nationalists regarded their Popular Front opponents as not only polarizing, but foreign. In their view, local antifascist periodicals could just as easily have appeared in London, Moscow, or New York; there was nothing national about them. The Victory Board was sensitive to the needs of foreigners whom Argentines did not know and with whom they had little in common. Yet Jewish-British-US imperialism, which generated hunger and poverty throughout the country, did not perturb this group. The "V for Victory" actually stood for "international vampirism," tied to Marxism and plutocracy, and its standard-bearers were traitors, *Crisol* asserted.[58] They were vendepatrias and *cipayos* (sepoys), the word that originally described Indian soldiers in the British army. Both terms denoted sellouts to foreign interests. The Victory Board, however, regarded Nationalists as the genuine sellouts.

Such terms abounded in *El Aguijón*, a Nationalist mouthpiece of Rosario. It reported that "cipayos" in this city welcomed Schlieper at a banquet attended by her "satellites" and local "reds" and liberals. All kneeled before this "*cipaya*," who, in turn, kneeled before the United States. It did not surprise this rag that in her speech Schlieper praised Bernardino Rivadavia, the nineteenth-century liberal Anglophile whom it regarded as the premier vendepatria. These women thought that by "smoking . . . cigarettes and crossing their legs"—in other words, performing as sophisticated modern women—they could fix a world consumed in an all-out war between "a new order and a defunct exploitative regime." The moment was coming soon when Argentines would use "a red-hot iron" to brand such women with the *V* for vendepatria. In preparation, the newspaper staff was compiling data on antifascists and feminists for its "red list," countering US blacklists of alleged pro-Axis companies and activists.[59]

Bandera Argentina exposed the Victory Board president's concrete ties to US interests, citing Schlieper's negotiations with the US film industry and Nelson Rockefeller to produce and distribute "democratic" Argentine movies in late 1942 (see chapter 6). The films' viewpoints would please the Yankee paymasters, and Schlieper would be satisfied with her earnings. "The trip has been happy and the business successful," the Nationalist daily taunted.[60] It was unlikely, however, that Schlieper received a contract.

Conforming to Argentina's liberal traditions and identity as an immigrant haven, the Victory Board contended that it was truly national, in contrast to Nationalists' imported fascist doctrines, which violated the country's political and social norms. These extreme rightists were the ones who had sold out the nation. This was the board's most effective argument against the Nationalists.

Charity Begins at Home

Both Nationalism and the Victory Board addressed the issue of inequality. Although Nationalists and board leaders agreed that this problem required government action rather than additional charities, the former denounced the latter for sending goods overseas when the poor needed them at home. Nationalists extolled their female adherents for dedicating themselves to helping the needy, which accorded with women's customary duties. This discourse, then, was partly a reaction against women's new roles.

Was it proper to send aid to foreigners? Luis Barrantes Molina, an editorialist for *El Pueblo*, the most important Argentine Catholic newspaper, noted that Christians were supposed to love their neighbors, which he interpreted as meaning the persons closest to them, such as family members and brothers in the faith. Russians, however, were not our coreligionists or relatives, he wrote, although this Costa Rican native admitted they were related to some immigrants in Argentina. Argentines were not indebted to them as they were to the Spanish for their religion and civilization, he claimed. It would have aided humanity to have defended Christian Nationalist Spain against barbaric Soviet Communism during the 1930s, but it would not serve this purpose to defend the anti-Christian Soviet Union against Germany.[61]

Were the Allied children for whom the Victory Board was making winter clothes the "neighbors" whom Argentines should love? The board wanted to keep some youngsters warm while those on the other side froze, *Crisol* decried, suggesting that both groups were the neighbors to help. But the newspaper mainly believed that charity began at home, which became a Nationalist and right-wing Catholic refrain. Since board members lived in Argentina, they had a duty to help its people, implying the former were immigrants. *Crisol* assured Argentines that infants would receive warm garments once Nationalists liberated the country and eliminated the Victory Board.[62]

According to Huergo, board members clad in revealing clothing and speaking foreign languages claimed that their bridge games, "garden parties," and kermesses exemplified loving one's neighbor. These "Catholics of modern Judaic cut" and Jews who led them loved only their "neighbors" in other nations, ignoring the native Argentines who were starving, sickly, and shivering. They did not spare a thought for this country, which had enabled the Saslavskys (Dalila Saslavsky) and Sadoskys (Cora Ratto de Sadosky) to prosper.[63]

In November 1942, Schlieper announced that the thirty-two thousand board members were sewing garments for Russia and China. If each of these women made one outfit a month for Argentina, this would amount to almost four hundred thousand per year, *Crisol* estimated, enough to clothe all underprivileged children in impoverished northwestern provinces. The money that families normally spent on such items could be used to purchase food, which would improve youngsters' health and performance in school. Girls could grow up to be mothers and boys to be soldiers— even to defend Schlieper's vaunted "democracy." Thus these thirty-two thousand women could perform a great service for Argentines rather than foreigners.[64]

Nationalists doubted that the mighty British Empire or the Colossus of the North required the Victory Board's ayudismo. They wished that Argentines had the same living standards that the British and US Americans enjoyed even in wartime. Not only the board's handmade garments, but the CSA's medicines and the CDA's preserved foods would benefit locals far more than the Allies.[65]

Nationalists' critiques of the Victory Board and ayudismo extended to their supporters. Wealthy ranchers were pleased to help people in far-off places, but not malnourished Argentine youths, they argued. A businessman donated an attractive vase to a Victory Board chapter in Rosario for its raffle to raise funds for a local hospital. The sole bid it received was for two pesos. *Crisol* acerbically commented that it attracted only this tiny amount because it was to help Argentina, not another land.[66] Adulation of the foreign exemplified the internalized colonialism that Nationalists deplored.

These fascists thought that the military coup d'etat of 1943 would implement charity at home. *Crisol* reported gleefully that the Paraná police confiscated the Victory Board's supply of winter clothes destined for Europe and planned to distribute them to Argentine children.[67] Whether this happened is unclear.

Nationalists often framed their campaigns to help locals, particularly the rural poor, as "gaucho aid." Apparently they had just realized that *campesinos* suffered privation, *La Hora* sneered. When a smallpox epidemic broke out in Salta, home of the prominent Nationalist Carlos Ibarguren, *La Hora* did not notice any "gaucho aid" distributions there. The real "gaucho aid," it claimed, stemmed from the nation's historic solidarity with freedom fighters, beginning with the local armies that helped South Americans liberate themselves from Spain.[68] Indeed, Schlieper remarked that Nationalists would have considered San Martín's assistance to Chile and Peru unpatriotic.[69] For her and the Victory Board, solidarity with principled causes elsewhere was a proud Argentine custom.

"Goodness has no borders, nor economic or social positions," asserted President Porta Echagüe of the Santa Fe chapter, adding that certain persons did not understand this. Despite their reproofs, the Victory Board would continue to provide succor to others, imbued with "human and fraternal meaning," and without provoking hatred or divisions. Thus it would comply with Jesus's commandment to love one another.[70] Her powerful advocacy of transnational solidarity set the Victory Board apart from Nationalists in this debate and underlined the Catholic rightists' hypocrisy in touting their faith. Concerned about Argentine poverty, Porta Echagüe and her fellow antifascists nevertheless felt obliged to involve themselves at this critical moment in the struggle for freedom against "despotism and the craving for conquest."[71]

The use of the term *gaucho aid* suggests a hypermasculine view of the countryside,[72] yet Nationalists handed this duty to women. Distributing goods to those overlooked by democratic governments and the powerful was the Nationalist women's main task, according to *Crisol*. It reported that with much sacrifice and few resources, UNS women distributed food and clothing to the poor once a year. During the Christmas season of 1941, it helped over one hundred criollo families in Rosario. UNA women in Tornquist handed out provisions and garments on the patriotic holiday of July 9, 1943. In August 1944 university student Elda Domínguez of the Unión Nacionalista Entrerriana (UNE) spoke at the inauguration of its women's center in a working-class barrio in Paraná on Nationalist patriotism and humanism and the need to assist poverty-stricken criollos. Afterward, she and a male comrade visited families in this neighborhood, giving each a little money, and pledged to ask the government to help them. Domínguez was but one of "the Christian ambassadors of Nationalist charity," according to the Nationalist publication *El Federal*.[73]

Nationalists believed that it was proper for women to help needy Argentines. They did not regard these efforts as political, which they considered unseemly for women. Yet these labors were deeply political because they allayed dissatisfaction with the existing socioeconomic system. In contrast, board leaders declared that they were engaged in political struggle rather than charity. Nationalists perceived this group as triply transgressive: not only did it oppose neutrality and tilt toward leftism and feminism, but it participated in an activity they deemed masculine.

Significantly, however, Nationalists and the Victory Board acknowledged the same problem—namely, inequality—and agreed that charity could not solve it. Schlieper insisted that only the government could end social injustice—and only after an Allied victory. According to *Crisol*, UNS women understood that their meager assistance could not eradicate poverty, but hoped that others throughout the nation would follow their example. Another Nationalist organization, the Unión Nacionalista Patagónica, recognized that its help for poor criollos and Indigenous people could not truly liberate them—only a Nationalist administration could. "What Nationalism wants for Argentines is not alms but justice," *Crisol*'s editor Enrique Osés declared.[74] Board leaders would have concurred with this statement as well as with their rivals' belief that the government would have to step in. But they disagreed with Nationalist concepts of justice and governance.

Victory and Utopia

Both sides hoped that the war's end would lead to beneficial changes. Nationalists wanted to see an emphasis on hierarchy and unity, small property ownership, and an end to poverty and foreign control. The Victory Board supported an inclusive political democracy, but its socioeconomic goals were hazier than those of its rivals.

Crisol insisted that a German victory would inaugurate a "New Order" favorable for have-not countries like Argentina. As in Occupied France, it would pacify and purify the population and replace partisan fissures and absolute equality with "national discipline" and hierarchy. The New Order would end British and US imperialism, along with Jewish usury and speculation, and provide benefits for the needy.[75] Other Nationalists agreed with elements of this "utopia," but did not tie it as explicitly to a German triumph.

In late 1943, the Alianza Libertadora Nacionalista (ALN), the newly renamed AJN, described its notion of rule. A truly sovereign nation would keep land and production in Argentine hands for the benefit of Argentines and exclude foreign beliefs. Neither liberal nor socialist, the new economic system would oppose capitalist and Communist exploitation and treat laborers as human beings rather than commodities. Latinity, nationalism, and Catholicism would permeate public education. Free of divisive parties that permitted foreign domination, citizens would unify through faith in the nation. Unstated was the fact that this meant a corporatist dictatorship. By forging social programs and a common ideal that overrode class divisions, the government would reinforce unity. Ending poverty, stimulating the development of private wealth, and encouraging large families by providing them with houses and other assistance would promote justice.[76]

Crisol agreed with these goals and added others. A Nationalist state would promote women's domesticity and prepare them for motherhood. It would provide family salaries, aid to widows and families headed by men unable to work, and suitable jobs for their wives. This newspaper hoped the military regime (1943–1946) would nationalize energy and transportation companies, subsoil rights, public riches, and the press, so they would fulfill Argentine rather than foreign interests. It urged wage increases and the cleansing and control of all cultural activities.[77]

Indeed, some of these ideas overlapped those of the Nationalist-influenced government. Dr. David Uriburu, former president José Félix Uriburu's nephew and interventor in Corrientes Province, declared in August 1944 that the government was trying to create a sovereign and just fatherland under God, where a "single and superior Christian and criollo fellowship" linked the boss and peon while maintaining the hierarchy between them. It was implanting an economy of producers, in which a human being was no longer a piece of "merchandise" who could be bought or sold. Argentines who worked the land would own their labor and lives.[78] *El Federal* rejoiced that the military leaders were ending the liberal regime of "freedom" that enslaved many.[79] The official largely responsible for increased wages, Christmas bonuses, frozen rural rents, construction of homes for workers, and other social measures was Vice President and Minister of Labor Colonel Juan Perón.

The ACA claimed that both sides in the war had their own "New Order."[80] This was as true for the Victory Board as it was for its rivals. The board thought that an Allied triumph would bring about genuine peace and social change. Within its ranks, teachers and other adherents advocated secular education, and feminists like Schlieper wanted women to exercise suffrage, participate in governance, and aspire to a range of occupations. The Victory Board championed a political democracy that protected liberal freedoms and could legislate social reforms. While many spokeswomen probably favored an economic democracy, largely to retain a multiclass coalition, they did not explain what social reforms they supported. Schlieper declared that the board backed a country and a world in which respect for institutions and personal dignity would guarantee collective well-being; as they were intimately connected, it was not possible to have such a nation without this type of global order.[81] The dictatorship silenced the movement, along with its leftist and reformist allies who might have proposed more specific changes for the postwar era. Even before this suppression, the Victory Board's vagueness contrasted with the Nationalists' explicit social goals. Nor could it possibly match Perón's concrete achievements.

"To hate is a macho thing/ because it is only the men/ . . . who can make the gauchos' knives speak," *Crisol* declared.[82] Yet Nationalist women's antisemitism and critiques of the Victory Board often were as crude as the men's. By voicing these sentiments, Méndez, the UNS feminine section, and Huergo seemed to defy their assigned characteristics of peace and love. Perhaps they justified these transgressions as vital to safeguard their homes and Christian society.

Nationalist men took part in more destructive activities. Unsatisfied with denouncing and threatening the Victory Board, they lobbied local governments to cancel its events, not always successfully. For example, they urged provincial authorities in Jujuy to prevent a board fundraiser, condemning the organization as Communist. Board members, however, convinced officials to allow the event. Nationalists attacked at least three chapters, two of them, Ramos Mejía and Ciudadela, located in working-class suburbs adjoining the federal capital. The action against the Ciudadela headquarters took place at night, when men hurled containers of tar at the building's façade. Young Nationalists screaming, "Viva Franco!" assaulted the Centro filial in Buenos Aires after Perón became president, likely in retaliation for the Victory Board's outspoken opposition to him. Coordinating with police, Nationalists assaulted board member Marta Samatán's home in Santa Fe and handed her over for imprisonment.[83]

Yet Nationalists expressed most of their antagonism through verbal discourses competing with those of the Victory Board. Their most persuasive argument was that charity began at home. A letter signed by "an Argentine" and published in *Crisol* advised the La Plata chapter president to travel through the country and see its poverty. Be patriotic by helping these destitute people, he wrote, and Argentines with a profound sense of nationality will respect you.[84] Many Argentines probably shared this opinion, even those who were not on the far right. In contrast, the Victory Board encouraged love for one's neighbor through transnational solidarity; according to Porta Echagüe, "Goodness has no borders." Nationalists, however, did not regard the Allies as neighbors.

Calls to fight the Other helped consolidate the Victory Board and the Nationalists, although neither could unite all like-minded persons under its umbrella. In this manner each group forged and continually reinforced its identity, as seen in the lead-up to May Day 1942. Trying to nationalize and appropriate this worker celebration,[85] the AJN planned a march for neutrality on this date. The other mass May Day demonstration, according to Ratto, would champion a very different cause: solidarity with those fighting for liberty and democratic institutions.[86] Naturally, the Victory Board adhered to this rally.

Axis-leaning neutrality was one of many positions that set Nationalists against the Victory Board: their notion of women's roles was another. With a few exceptions, Nationalists and right-wing Catholics believed that women belonged in the home, not in the labor force, lecture halls, or political arena. Their only legitimate spaces outside the domestic sphere were philanthropy and the Catholic Church. Male authority over the household symbolized the desired class hierarchy and authoritarian rule. Women who assumed "masculine" qualities and tasks subverted male domination inside and outside the home. In contrast, the Victory Board promoted women's activities in the larger society and emphasized equality and representative governance. This conduct probably led Fresco and some other Nationalists to find these women particularly threatening—a measure of their significance.

Each blamed the other side for the same misdeeds. They accused each other of forming part of the fifth column, which they defined differently. Each regarded the other as divisive: the Victory Board fomented discord within families and society, while Nationalists provoked opposition to the country's liberal democratic institutions. Rodríguez Dondis blamed the Victory Board for upholding porteño views against those of provincial women, but the board claimed it united women across the nation. Each charged that the other was foreign and betrayed the fatherland; each asserted its nationalist credentials. The Victory Board's most powerful argument against Nationalism was that its imported fascist doctrine was un-Argentine.

Nationalists and the Victory Board insisted they stood for something beyond opposing their rivals. In their distinct ways they claimed to support human dignity, culture, and the national character. The Nationalist versions of these terms emphasized Catholic values and a Spanish and Latin heritage, cleansed of Jewish and other foreign elements. The Victory Board stressed secular liberties, religious freedom, women's rights, and multiculturalism.

As in the previous decade, there were parallels between fascism and antifascism. One was the level of importance that men assigned to women's participation. Recruiting women was a low priority for the hypermasculine Nationalists. While many women joined Acción Argentina, they exercised relatively little influence over the predominantly male leadership. Men on both sides tended to appreciate their female comrades but deployed maternalism, which limited their agency, although many women also espoused it. Yet the democratic press gave far more attention to the Victory Board than the Nationalist press did to its women followers.

Nationalists thought the Victory Board undermined neutrality, Catholicism, Latinity, and an arcane gender and social order. The board thought Nationalists undermined democracy, pluralism, and modernity. Thus the two sides defined themselves in reaction to each other, but they also arose out of the same context and were interdependent. Both addressed the war, poverty, ethnic diversity, freedom, and workers' and women's increasing visibility. Like the Victory Board president, many Nationalists admitted that ending inequality required official action, although they disagreed on the desired shape of postwar society. They concurred on the need for national liberation but envisioned it distinctly: liberation from repressive governance and exclusion of women, in the Victory Board's case, or from liberal economics, foreign control, and anticlericalism, for Nationalists.

The Nationalist press only occasionally mentioned María Teresa Rodríguez Dondis and María Esther Méndez, the former fading from view after 1941 and the latter after 1944.[87] Their ideals, however, lived on. So too did those of the Victory Board, which emerged from clandestinity in April 1945. As I discuss in the next chapter, the two sides would continue to clash. They also would have to adjust to complex transformations in the international and local contexts that dissatisfied both.

CHAPTER 8

TRANSNATIONAL CITIZENS

Women's Resistance and Foreign Collaborators, 1945–1947

On April 7, 1945, the Victory Board (Junta de la Victoria) triumphantly emerged after nearly two years of operating in the shadows. Cora Ratto was among the speakers at the assembly that marked its reopening, attended by delegates from Buenos Aires and other cities. She claimed that in its first twenty-two months of existence, the board's membership grew from twenty-odd to forty-eight thousand. In this process, the board grasped the people's fortitude, the importance of those who contributed the little they had, and the significance of its mission of solidarity rather than charity. During the subsequent twenty-two months, from July 1943 to March 1945, members withdrew into themselves. One could not say anything that others could hear, help hard-pressed mothers overseas, or assist Argentina when it finally broke relations with and declared war on the Axis. Only the liberation of Paris gave members a moment of satisfaction. Ratto stirred the audience by declaring that this reunion celebrated not just the Victory Board, but its actual *victory*.[1]

In this chapter I examine the heady moments of renewed Victory Board activity in the context of the approaching Axis defeat and the rocky transition from military to civilian governance. The liberation of Paris underscored the sense of transnational citizenship that bound antifascist Argentines to Allied forces and French civilians. By April 1945, the regime began to allow the Victory Board and other democratic groups to function while repeatedly limiting their right to do so, reinforced by Nationalist attacks, both physical and verbal. Masses mobilized for and against military rule and Juan Perón's presidential aspirations. In addition, women organized for the vote, now one of the board's oft-repeated goals.

Perhaps to avoid government oversight or emphasize the drama of persecution, Ratto did not mention the Victory Board's underground collaboration with its Uruguayan partner. Yet the board continued to engage in South-South and South-North relationships as World War II neared its end and the Cold War began. Uruguayan solidarity with Argentine student activists strengthened the ties between the Victory Board and Feminine Action for Victory, as did their affiliation with the Women's International Democratic Federation (WIDF). At the same time, however, both the Victory Board and Feminine Action for Victory began to give way to new movements. Some board figures interacted with US organizations and the United Nations. Nevertheless, its shipments overseas declined, as did its ties to US and British diplomats.

The Victory Board still contributed to the antifascist struggle, contested its fascist enemies, united diverse women, and engaged across borders. Yet times had changed, and the board could not keep up. The Allied victory and Perón's benefits for workers led it to add internal social programs to its mission, but it was too little, too late. Perón won the 1946 presidential elections. Furthermore, the Communist Party (Partido Comunista) shifted to a policy of hostility against the upper class and the United States and Great Britain, as was true elsewhere, and competed with Perón for labor allegiance. These changes prompted divisions within the Victory Board and its loss of Communist Party support. Although the party had not necessarily controlled this politically multifarious group, it was a serious blow. The Victory Board fell victim to Perón's victory and the fractured Popular Front and Allied alliances.

Breaking with the Axis and the Liberation of Paris

After the regime that assumed control in 1943 severed relations with the Axis in January 1944, a military faction that included Perón forced President Pedro Pablo Ramírez to resign. The United States refused to recognize the new government. The liberation of Paris prompted massive antifascist demonstrations throughout Argentina and official repression. Nationalists turned from condemning the regime for ending neutrality to supporting its measures against the antifascist resistance.

The dictatorship faced challenges by early 1944. The Soviets were on the offensive against the German invaders. The United States relentlessly pressured Argentina to abandon neutrality, and US arms deliveries to Brazil, which had joined the Allies, preoccupied the military. To tighten its control, in the first half of January, the Ramírez government dissolved all political parties, Nationalist groups, and pro-Allied organizations. It curbed its Nationalist sympathizers to preclude a violent response when it broke relations with Germany and Japan later that month. [2]

The government, however, could not completely silence the Nationalists. Some bitterly condemned the regime and its foreign policy shift, while a number resigned from public posts. [3] The Nationalist intervenor in Tucumán's capital lowered flags to half-mast throughout the city as an act of mourning, and the like-minded intervertor at the Universidad Nacional de Tucumán did the same. Cheered by Nationalists, the two men were jailed briefly.[4] The authorities closed the pro-Nazi Nationalist newspaper, *El Pampero*, which promptly reopened under another name, *El Federal*.

A series of complex events followed. The Nationalist-leaning Grupo Obra de Unificación (GOU) of military officers who had carried out the June 1943 revolt pushed Ramírez into resigning in late February.[5] They contested the rupture of diplomatic ties with the Axis and believed he was preparing to declare war on it. Vice President General Edelmiro Julián Farrell took over the presidency, and Perón, a leading member of the GOU, secretary of labor, now also minister of war and soon to be vice president, became the dominant figure within the government. The United States regarded the Farrell regime as fascist and pro-Axis. Ironically, Perón, whom many Nationalists blamed for breaking with Germany and Japan, sought to reduce Nationalist influence in governing circles.[6] Disturbed by the ouster of Ramírez and determined to impel Argentina into declaring war, the United States did not recognize the new government and withdrew Ambassador Norman Armour in June. Reluctantly, Ambassador David Kelly, whose views of the Argentine government were considerably more nuanced, also departed for Britain, in early July.[7]

Despite cutting relations with the Axis, the government did not allow antifascists to renew their activities, but the Allied advance toward Paris in late August 1944 gave them opportunities to express their pent-up democratic sentiments. Various groups in Buenos Aires requested permission to celebrate the highly anticipated liberation of Paris, but the police decided that one *acto* alone could be held in the Plaza Francia, to place a wreath and observe a moment of silence. The public outpouring, however, exceeded these limits. "Even before Paris was officially liberated the rejoicing began," two US visitors noted. As the Allies entered the French capital, *porteños* congregated in the streets and around newspaper offices, avidly following the unfolding events, singing "La Marseillaise," and shouting praise for France and liberty. Defying the state-of-siege decree that forbade the display of foreign flags without official permission, businesses posted the French flag alongside the Argentine and sold tiny versions of both. Women donned red, white, and blue corsages, and men pinned ribbons of the same colors to their lapels. They headed to the Plaza San Martín and bedecked the independence hero's statue with flowers, honoring the liberation of Argentina from Spanish rule, and of France, which had sheltered José de San Martín in exile, from German and Vichy domination. These spontaneous acts symbolized the desire for freedom at home.[8]

Many people prepared for the evening event at the Plaza Francia, a site that the authorities may have picked because it was difficult to reach by public transportation. Mothers and children arrived early with their lunches, and students played truant. Men and women of all income levels and pursuits gathered, although observers judged that the majority were middle-class. Representatives of British, French, and US associations; clergy; Acción Argentina members; Spanish Republican sympathizers; politicians; and even four generals, including Ramírez and Rawson, were there. Secretly convoked by their leaders, numerous Victory Board members were among the huge crowd. Adding to the many wreaths at the monument donated by France to honor the 1910 centenary of Argentine independence, the Victory Board placed a V-shaped bouquet of flowers boldly festooned with its name. Listeners applauded the famous performer and board ally Berta Singerman for her recital of "La Marseillaise" in Spanish. Onlookers sang the French and Argentine anthems, yelled pro-democratic and pro-French slogans, and demanded speeches. The venerable Socialist Alfredo Palacios obliged them, declaring the liberation of Paris marked the "sunset of all the dictatorships," "Long live France, free and eternal!" and "Long live free Argentina, sacred ground!" His remarks received a strong ovation.[9] What was supposed to have been a silent homage to France turned into a massive protest against fascism abroad and authoritarianism at home.

Backed by Nationalists, the administration reacted harshly to this demonstration. When the multitude at the Plaza Francia clamored for freedom, armored vehicles sped to the scene. Police threw tear gas, arrested many, and struck resisters with clubs and guns. Mounted police rode into the throng, wielding their sabers at men, women, and children fleeing the plaza. The establishment newspapers *La Nación* and *La Prensa* observed that police treated women with marked brutality. The police chief retorted that they were "extremists," suggesting that they deserved it.[10] Evidently they were not "real" women, but unnatural creatures, as Nationalists had long asserted. The Alianza Libertadora Nacionalista (ALN) held a counterdemonstration, and its members, along with other Nationalists, joined in the melee, fighting democrats in the streets and yelling "Long live Perón!," "Long live Farrell!," "Sovereignty or death!" Notwithstanding their disillusionment over the end of neutrality, Nationalists detested antifascists more than they did the government, and they were inching toward supporting it.

Outside Buenos Aires, the authorities generally allowed the French community to celebrate indoors but prohibited or limited public functions. Braving Nationalists and police, some antifascists in Santa Fe demonstrated outdoors nonetheless, and Rosario and La Plata followed a similar pattern. In Tucumán pedestrians spontaneously sang "La Marseillaise" in the streets, claiming bonds of citizenship with "the cradle of Western freedom," demonstrating once more that antifascism was transnational.[11] There the government originally permitted a group, including past and future Victory

Board members, to hold a march and ceremony. After the violence in Buenos Aires, however, it reversed itself, allowing only an outdoor lunch minus speeches. Following the meal, the assemblage sang the Argentine and French national anthems and called for democracy and an Allied victory. Male university students on the sidelines led chants against the dictatorship and for elections. Women students and homemakers—among them at least one future Victory Board adherent—sometimes initiated the rallying cries. When the young men ignored police warnings to stop, lawmen beat and arrested them, while women bolted from the scene.[12] Resistencia was one of the rare larger cities where police did not disrupt a public ceremony.[13]

The enormous popular response to the liberation of Paris surprised the Argentine government. The British embassy conjectured that it mishandled the situation by not embracing the French cause, which Perón may have wanted to do, but his military colleagues overruled him. By employing excessive violence to quell innocuous throngs, the regime angered many Argentines and galvanized the centrist press.[14]

One means of appeasing the opposition was to send aid to France. During the Paris celebrations, the government declared it was making one hundred thousand tons of wheat and five thousand tons of meat available to French authorities to relieve hunger there. This offer was a means of convincing the Allies and their Argentine supporters that it truly was helping their cause, as officials claimed. However, it also was part of a broader policy directed toward several countries. Even before the promise of food for France, as Allied troops marched toward Rome, the regime pledged fifty thousand tons of wheat to the once-fascist Italy. It also sent grain to liberated Greece; Finland, a latecomer to the Allied side; and neutral albeit *franquista* Spain. Amidst news of citizens gathering supplies for France, the Nationalist publication *Bandera Argentina* insisted that the government effort eliminated the need for private initiatives.[15] It hoped to forestall the resurgence of antifascist aid groups, as did the dictatorship, which seemed to be coopting their project. Ironically, Nationalists and rightist Catholics who had denounced the *ayudistas* for shipping goods abroad now praised the authorities' generosity.[16]

Many Nationalists regarded the "liberation" of Paris as a sham. The armies that had "freed" Italy only to reduce it to poverty now had opened France to Communism. Those who sought to dominate nations like Italy—and Argentina—were not liberators. Nationalists blamed the demonstrators in the Plaza Francia for advocating the democracy of immorality, Jews, and Popular Fronts that had drained France of its energy and handed it over to an invader.[17]

Despite officials' and Nationalists' wishes, democratic figures, including Victory Board members, were resurfacing. Ana Rosa Schlieper de

Martínez Guerrero and Berta Singerman appeared at the Argentine Automobile Club's banquet celebrating the liberation of Paris, featuring over a thousand guests who, according to *El Federal*, sang "La Marseillaise" twice as many times as the Argentine national anthem. The newspaper ridiculed "the thriving Amazons" of the "extinct" Victory Board, old worn-out Radicals, and "Jewish" leftists who sang the French anthem, contending that they were not really honoring France, but preparing the climate for renewed electioneering. They could not attack the government directly because the pueblo would fight in the streets for the lower rents, higher wages, and other reforms it had provided. So the *antipatria* diverted people's attention by singing "La Marseillaise" and harping on freedom, antifascism, and democracy—drugs used to maintain the country's subjugation.[18]

A columnist in *El Pueblo* insisted he, like Alfredo Palacios, favored an end to dictatorships, but this meant the overthrow of Joseph Stalin as well as Adolf Hitler. He and the current government wanted a free Argentina: free of foreign companies, foreign-imposed puppet rulers, and fraudulent politicians. They desired the freedom to worship in the founding fathers' churches, hang the blue-and-white flag rather than the red flag, control Argentine land and resources, pay impoverished criollos more than a pittance, and fulfill the constitutional mandate for a republic rather than a democracy, which stood for demagoguery or Communism.[19]

Yet the liberation of Paris touched the hearts of many Argentines for whom France had tremendous symbolic value. This triumph in a place they venerated instilled hope in the men and women who opposed the dictatorship and inspired them to rally and defy repression. The celebrations revealed glimmers of the Victory Board but also of decreasing lower-class support for antifascism. They highlighted the stark cleavages between Nationalists and antifascists, yet demonstrated that rightists reworked antifascist terms like *freedom* even as they attacked their rivals.

The Declaration of War and the Victory Board's Return

As the military regime moved slowly toward its end, it legalized the Victory Board. Its supporters, now including British diplomats, welcomed its reappearance. Nevertheless, the Argentine government imposed obstructions resembling those the group had experienced prior to the coup d'etat. Board members also feared violence and the prolongation of dictatorship. Once again facing off against police and Nationalists, they and other antifascists celebrated the victories over Germany and Japan.

From late 1944 through August 1945, Argentina witnessed an uneven evolution toward constitutional rule. Perón reduced the Nationalist presence and influence within governing circles. Responding to internal challenges from within and outside the military, and external events, the authorities stepped forward and backward on reestablishing university autonomy; loosening restrictions on political activity, the press, and speech; and ending the state of siege. It claimed to have freed political prisoners but did not necessarily release them, or simply re-imprisoned them. This pattern stoked further resistance, particularly in the universities. With the Allied victory in sight, Argentina declared war on the Axis on March 27, 1945, and signed the Act of Chapultepec on April 4, enabling it to rejoin the international community. Among other matters, this accord established commitments to economic and social justice and women's political and civil rights, favored the continuation of the Inter-American Commission of Women (IACW), and called for including women in the national delegations to the San Francisco meeting that would create the United Nations.[20] A few days later the United States resumed normal relations with Argentina, near the end of the month Ambassador Kelly returned to Buenos Aires, and in May the new US ambassador, Spruille Braden, arrived. There he began his infamous counterproductive campaign against Perón, whom he denounced as a fascist.

After Argentina declared war, the Victory Board asked permission to convoke its Directive Commission (Comisión Directiva); whether the government granted it or not, the meeting took place. The Directive Commission created a committee to negotiate with officials to end the closure and return the confiscated aid materials or pay the organization for them. It asked the Treasury Ministry to reopen its bank accounts and called for an assembly of delegates from around the country. The Interior Ministry allowed the Victory Board to reopen throughout the republic, and it did so on April 2. It declared it would help the victims of Nazism overseas and the Argentine people in their struggle against enemies at home.[21]

The Victory Board hosted an improvised assembly on April 7, giving its branches only two days' notice. The representative from Presidente Roque Sáenz Peña, Chaco, reported that her chapter received the telegram at 2:00 p.m., hastily summoned a meeting at 3:00 p.m. to decide what to do, and in less than forty-eight hours she was en route to Buenos Aires. Barely arriving on time, the Moisés Ville president Rotman de Baruch gleefully related that the police chief who in 1943 had forced her to lead him to the chapter's funds, materials, and records so he could seize them was jailed for robbery. Delegates came from Greater Buenos Aires, La Plata, Chaco, and Santiago del Estero, Corrientes, Córdoba, and Santa Fe Provinces; others found out too late. The Victory Board's assistant secretary, María Isabel Villamil de Marcó, announced that the central office would open soon and advised leaders to reconstitute their chapters. Some representatives disclosed that their *filiales* already had received contributions; in fact, the indefatigable elderly Rebeca de Malajovich of Moisés Ville knitted clothing for the Allies even after the government closed the Victory Board.[22]

Several speakers evoked the Victory Board's emphasis on democracy within and outside the group, adapted to the new context. Villamil stressed the importance of creating a truly democratic organization in which all members could participate in leadership and gain the civic awareness needed to be free citizens in a democratic country. Schlieper advised the board to push for constitutional governance in the country, to which Corrientes president Andreau de Billinghurst added it should ensure the regime's compliance with its treaty obligations. Dalila Saslavsky underlined the need to make Argentina a genuine democracy by incorporating women, restoring Sarmiento-style education, and eliminating extreme nationalism, racism, and antisemitism.

The reunion was jubilant. At one point, attendees stood up and heavily applauded the ceremony; at another they acclaimed Ratto for her aforementioned rousing speech. Father Pierre Charles, a French priest associated with *Orden Cristiano*, pleased the women by thanking them for helping his and other nations. Six members who were teachers fired under the dictatorship rose to their feet for a moment of silence, followed by an ovation. Board adherents enthusiastically resumed their tasks.

Previously skeptical about the movement, British diplomats welcomed its reappearance. The Victory Board's communique in the April 12 issue of *Antinazi* won their strong praise. They particularly commended its stated commitment to feeding people and aiding reconstruction in Allied countries. The British did not comment on other significant parts of this declaration, such as how board spokespersons continued to distinguish their political motive from Christian charity. Nor did they mention the eloquent preamble, which pointed out that the June 1943 decree that "dissolved" the organization should have said "'closed' the premises in which it functioned," for an official order could not dissolve the "spiritual ties" that bound its members. One could not destroy solidarity so easily. The Victory Board also affirmed that it would educate women on their civic rights and duties, especially the duty to combat Nazism in all its explicit or disguised forms. In doing so it would prepare mothers to raise patriotic children.[23] As in the past, the board combined maternalistic with nonmaternalistic political appeals.

Seemingly, the dictatorship allowed the Victory Board to reopen as part of the postwar democratic opening leading to the 1946 election. Yet when the Uruguayan Acción Anti-Nazi de Ayuda a la Unión Soviética y Demás Pueblos en Lucha congratulated its reemergence after a period of "painful, arduous, and selfless illegal labor," the Victory Board confessed it faced difficulties. Two days after its statement in *Antinazi*, the police revoked authorization for the board's first fundraiser. In early May it denied permission to hold another event; later that month the authorities imprisoned Schlieper for eight hours. On June 1, the Interior Ministry ordered the Victory Board to halt activities until it issued a formal decree to reopen it.[24]

Remarkably, the Victory Board was the only major antifascist organization to receive official authorization, although the Argentine government fitfully rescinded what it had granted. Did the board fight more persistently for the right to exist than the antifascist movements led by and composed mostly of men, who had other political outlets? Did the regime see this group as less threatening than Acción Argentina, which did not receive clearance though it operated somewhat?[25] Did the Victory Board have more international sympathizers, who could further damage the government's reputation and interests? Perhaps it was a combination of these factors.

Despite the prohibition, chapters outside the federal capital were functioning. The filiales of Tucumán, Resistencia, Córdoba, and Mendoza reactivated in April, La Plata in early November. Having provided aid covertly since the coup d'etat, the Córdoba chapter simply shifted toward operating openly. The Mendoza chapter, however, struggled in vain to obtain official permission and faded away in late September.[26]

The government declared a holiday marking the liberation of Berlin and the German surrender in May 1945, allowing the display of flags but little more. As one observer remarked, Buenos Aires on V-E (Victory in Europe) Day resembled Paris during the German occupation. A British diplomat thought that authorities went to ridiculous extremes to prevent demonstrations in the federal capital, to the point of dispatching trucks filled with soldiers through the streets and searching men and women pedestrians for arms. It even prohibited the singing of the national anthem in public.[27] As in August 1944, the usual pattern was to restrict festivities to closed settings. Board members and fellow antifascists hosted a "Cocktail of Victory" in the Confitería París in La Plata, and the Córdoba chapter organized a similar event. Board adherents and other women in various cities defied regulations by congregating at monuments honoring democratic figures such as San Martín, although the police did not always allow them to reach or remain at their destinations.[28]

With the (temporary) lifting of the state of siege in early August, political parties, including the now legalized Communists, could operate freely. The Victory Board assumed it could as well and openly renewed its activities.[29] The government declared a two-day holiday and allowed celebrations when the Japanese surrendered, ending the war. The opposition, including the Victory Board, took advantage of this opening to rally for the Allies and against the regime. Spurred on by junior army officers, Nationalists attacked several demonstrations, and police and Nationalists fought student protesters. The violence gave police an excuse for clamping down on subsequent public meetings, which sparked further protests across the country.[30]

Celebrations were less restricted outside Buenos Aires, however, and board members participated in many of them. The new president of Resistencia, Ivonne Pradier de Kedinger, a Socialist, school official, and French professor, helped organize a broad-based gathering. The Victory Board's column of marchers joined others in shouting, "Constitution!," "Freedom!," and "Out with Farrell and Perón!" In her address Pradier noted that by contributing to the Allied victory, women around the globe had expanded their roles irrevocably.[31] The Tucumán chapter posted flyers around the city, inviting nurses, seamstresses, saleswomen, "women who work and study, who think and feel" to a demonstration. Two women, probably filial members, led the throng, carrying a V-shaped wreath, which they deposited at the foot of a statue honoring liberty. Speaking for the Victory Board, Polly Yánover de Cutín declared that its struggle for democracy had not ended; now it fought for a return to legal rule. That one day the dictatorship offered civil war and the next day offered women the vote showed the need for stability and consistency. Women should attain suffrage, but through constitutional norms. Their votes would help strengthen and democratize Argentina, enabling it to join the free nations of the world.[32]

Yánover alluded to three intertwined issues that had emerged in the preceding months. One was government and Nationalist violence against the opposition.[33] Perón aggravated concerns about bloodshed by declaring that he, as a military officer, did not fear a civil war. Decrying his words, numerous *cordobesas*, including Victory Board members, counterposed their Christian spirit with the vice president's apparent belligerence and assigned the task of promoting peace to women. In addition, they asked leaders to reflect on the horrors of the recent war and avert a conflagration by reestablishing democratic governance. Many women throughout Argentina endorsed this statement.[34] Demanded repeatedly by the opposition, the restoration of constitutional rule was the second issue. Intertwined with the second, the third issue was women's suffrage.

Women's Suffrage and Resistance

Having signed the Act of Chapultepec, the Argentine government needed to comply with its stipulations on women's political rights. Furthermore, as Schlieper had pointed out and Pradier had hinted, women's wartime efforts and changing roles signaled it was time to confer their political rights. This opinion won a wide consensus among women of different ideological standpoints, including Victory Board members, and galvanized their activism. Some men agreed as well. The question was who would grant these rights.

Perón had begun to demonstrate interest in women's concerns a year before, when he founded the Division (later renamed Directorate) of Women's Labor and Assistance within the Labor Secretariat. The directorate created a women's suffrage commission, including some veteran feminists, which sponsored an event in the Chamber of Deputies in late July 1945, which Perón attended. He promised to bring the women's vote to fruition. Historians differ as to whether he stated that the government would issue a decree to this effect. Whether or not Perón intended a decree, many believed he did.[35]

The government's statute on political parties, issued in early July, seemed to contradict Perón's presumed backing for suffrage. Schlieper observed that it ignored women, who apparently could not even join political parties, much less vote. In the countries that had won the war women had the same political rights as men, whereas the defeated nations had forbidden their political participation and relegated them to the home, she declared, implicitly placing Argentina in the same category as the former Axis.[36]

Women in the opposition insisted they did not want a dictatorship to hand them the vote, which would taint it.[37] Nor did they want the government's charity. An elected Congress should pass this measure as a law, which hinged on a return to constitutional rule. Women's political participation would strengthen democracy, but first Argentina had to restore democratic institutions. This became the Victory Board's position.

Some prominent Catholics favored this stance. One was Angélica Fuselli, who had replaced Schlieper as IACW representative.[38] Franceschi reminded readers that years before, he had announced his support for women's suffrage. Citing Fuselli, he observed that women voted in most countries, and as a signatory of international agreements providing for the equality of men and women, Argentina was obliged to implement it. Franceschi insisted that the women's vote was consistent with Catholic teachings and practices. He, too, believed that a restored Congress should reform the electoral law. Skirting the question of the regime's legitimacy, he emphasized that putting suffrage into effect was a complicated process, involving the creation of new identity cards for women and other bureaucratic changes that required legislative action.[39]

Liberal Catholic journalist Mila Forn recalled that over twenty-five years before, the Centro de Estudios Blanca de Castilla, directed by Franceschi, had educated young Catholic women on political and social matters. Its members discussed feminism and considered the vote "an indisputable right." (In fact, the centro's survey of its adherents revealed some ambivalence.) Such opinions were controversial at that moment, but now only "retrograde mentalities" opposed women's suffrage. Nevertheless, an elected Congress should approve it, and an elected president should sign it.

The Argentine woman should enter her rightful space "through the door of legality and not through the window. Above all else she is a *lady* [italics in original], and as a lady she deserves all the honors."[40]

Many Catholics, however, voiced reservations about women's suffrage, and Nationalists opposed or ignored it. After Pope Pius XII issued his qualified approval for women organizing as Catholics who supported female rights, *El Pueblo* supported it reluctantly as a means of protecting the home, social welfare, and peace against Communism.[41] *La Fronda* claimed that women should not spurn political rights granted by decree, since the future elected Congress could ratify them, as had happened in France. The only reason Argentine feminists were not imitating the French, as they usually did, was to oppose the government. The newspaper's editors believed that suffrage was coming, one way or another, and would reveal the folly of women's involvement in matters of state. The sooner this happened, the better, for then women could be excluded once more.[42]

Why did the Victory Board and its offshoots insist that a duly elected Congress legislate women's suffrage? Did this position contradict their feminism? The board's primary mission had always been to strengthen democracy, partly by inserting half of the population. As Yánover suggested, Argentina lived under an arbitrary and repressive dictatorship that could eliminate women's rights as quickly as it granted them, resembling its pattern of releasing political prisoners only to imprison them again and lifting the state of siege only to restore it. Incorporating women under these circumstances would not serve democratic goals and might not last.[43] Moreover, women added to the electorate by decree might vote for Perón out of gratitude.

The debates over the interwoven issues of violence, constitutional rule, and suffrage affected the Victory Board and helped kindle a new militant spirit among antigovernment women. Their altered mood was evident not only in their defiant manifestos and demonstrations, but in the board's changing composition. More vocal women joined the movement in some locations, displacing former leaders. Their boldness and unvarnished feminism may have led officers like Matilde Porta Echagüe de Molinas to drop out.[44] New Victory Board filiales arose in a few provinces, such as San Luis. The Tucumán, La Plata, Resistencia, and Córdoba chapters shouldered on, although some of the latter's most dynamic members moved into a new organization, the significantly named Junta Feminista, and eventually into the Radical women's branch.[45]

As in Córdoba, much of the feminist initiative was shifting toward recently founded groups. The Junta Femenina de Cultura Cívica, headed by Alcira Olivé de Mollerach, the former local Victory Board president, replaced the Rosario board chapter, and the Agrupación Democrática Femenina succeeded the Santa Fe branch. Both contained previous Victory Board members. Catholic women formed associations to train women for political engagement along church lines, of which the most prominent was the Centro Femenino de Cultura Cívica y Política, which included Fuselli and Forn. Socialist women established the Liga de Educación Política.[46]

The Victory Board, Feminine Action for Victory, and Protest

Unlike Argentines, Uruguayans freely celebrated the liberation of Paris, the German surrender, and the end of the war. While the two countries' situations differed markedly, the leaders of the Victory Board and its Uruguayan partner, Feminine Action for Victory, faced a similar juncture in 1945: both hoped to feed and clothe Europeans and contribute to reconstruction, yet they also recognized the need to tackle domestic conditions. New groups and campaigns focused on these issues. Feminine Action continued its solidarity with its cohort during Argentina's tumultuous passage to civilian democracy.

Feminine Action deliberated its future tasks at its second annual convention in early October 1944 and invited Schlieper to attend.[47] At the same time, Communists and others were organizing a rally in Montevideo for democracy, hemispheric solidarity, and uninterrupted aid to the Allies. These efforts gave birth to Unión Nacional Femenina (UNF), which sought to coordinate women's institutions' implementation of these three aims and fight for better conditions for women and society as a whole. Diverse associations in Uruguay and other countries sent delegates to the UNF's first conference. Headed by the Uruguayan president's wife, Celia Alvárez Mouliá de Amézaga, who became the UNF president, the congress pressed for equal pay for equal work, enforcement and extension of existing labor laws, married women's rights, greater recognition of labor unions, a minimum rural salary, agrarian reform, economic diversification, health programs for women workers, aid to the Allied countries, and solidarity with the Argentine people and its political prisoners.[48]

Feminine Action participated in the assembly and other UNF endeavors. Lifting Uruguayans out of poverty required laws and government action, and the movement cooperated with the UNF to obtain them. While aid for Europe remained its priority, increasingly it too emphasized the consolidation of democracy and social justice. Feminine Action wrote the United Nations, at its inaugural meeting in San Francisco in April 1945, urging elimination of "the invisible armies of Nazism" that had fostered the class domination, racism, capitalist imperialism, and enmities among nations that led to World War II. Demanding equality of women and men in all spheres, it affirmed that women were eager to collaborate with men in the construction of a free and equitable world—but as equals. Meanwhile, senator and Feminine Action member Isabel Pinto de Vidal was a delegate in San Francisco, fighting for women's rights and equal participation in all UN organs.[49]

Pent-up hopes for postwar reforms and the Communist Party's evolving strategies led women in the two countries to follow analogous trajectories. Uruguayan and Argentine Communists turned to mobilizing popular sectors for social change and upcoming elections, which the Argentine government pledged to hold. A further motivation for the Argentines was addressing the Peronist challenge.

The Victory Board had largely limited its action to helping the Allies, Ratto observed, but now it could set new priorities and duties. It summoned women around the country for a National Assembly of Women in early September 1945 to update its agenda. Preparing for the meeting, which resembled the UNF's congress, board chapters and other women's organizations discussed issues to raise and chose delegates. National assembly branches sprang up in various cities for this purpose, some containing Victory Board officers, illustrating the carry-over between the two. The Mendoza board chapter gave way to such a branch. Women in several porteño neighborhoods declared that aside from political rights, they wanted higher wages and standards of living, and improved maternity legislation, childcare, and kindergartens. Jewish leftist women's foremost demand was a law against racism and antisemitism.[50]

Members of the Victory Board and the aforementioned groups, plus white- and blue-collar workers, community activists, students, educators, and other professionals from throughout Argentina were among the over four hundred participants in the National Assembly of Women. Schlieper, Dr. Margarita Argúas, Dr. Angela Santa Cruz, and Communist labor activist Antonia Banegas of the Victory Board, plus former board leader Olivé, gave speeches, along with Victoria Ocampo and other non–Victory Board members. A UNF officer and two Feminine Action delegates attended the assembly. One of the latter, Ángela Mures, chronicled the Uruguayan group's activities and urged the Victory Board to continue aiding Europe. The assembly advocated higher wages for rural and urban working women, enforcement of the maternity law, assistance for single mothers and their children, reduction of the cost of living, free medical clinics and childcare, democratic secular public education, and an end to racism, antisemitism, and repression. Nevertheless, the main topic was the reestablishment of formal democracy and its connection to the vote. The former treasurer of the Córdoba chapter, now president of the local Junta Feminista, proclaimed the rebirth of Argentine feminism amidst a tortuous struggle for freedom. To fulfill their aspirations, she declared, feminists had to oppose the rule of force and promote the rebuilding of democratic institutions. Accordingly, the assembly insisted on a return to constitutional rule and the vote through a law passed by an elected Congress.[51]

During the rest of 1945 and 1946, the Victory Board implemented some of the National Assembly of Women's resolutions. Its chapters studied women laborers and poverty in the provinces; established kindergartens, daycare, clinics, and other projects aimed at working women and their families; and protested antisemitism, the high cost of living, and intermittent impositions of the state of siege. Several filiales offered classes in first aid, sewing, and dressmaking; the one in Resistencia donated toys and candies to a school at Christmastime and collected funds for flood victims in Chaco. The central Victory Board established an economical dining hall for women wage earners and a library in Buenos Aires. The assembly gave rise to the women's branch of the Junta de Coordinación Democrática (JCD), which evolved into the Democratic Union (Unión Democrática), the alliance of the Radical, Progressive Democratic Party (Partido Demócrata Progresista), Socialist, and Communist parties against Perón.[52]

Nor did the Victory Board neglect Europe. It made clothing for Hungarians and for Spanish refugees, on whose behalf it conducted numerous fundraisers. Board members demonstrated against the Franco regime and bombarded Argentine officials with requests to help save Spanish political prisoners from execution. Allied with Spain, the unsympathetic Argentine government instead clamped down on the Victory Board's anti-Franco activities. Of equal if not greater concern was the plight of child war victims, for whom the board mounted a giant campaign to send warm clothing. Yet some fundraisers had a novel feature: donors could choose to help children overseas or board chapters' social projects for the local poor, demonstrating the organization's shift.

The opposition clamored for constitutional liberties, the transfer of power to the Supreme Court, and early elections in the largest demonstration ever seen in Argentina up to this point. Defying bureaucratic obstacles, the disappearance of public transportation, and Perón's warnings of violence, over two hundred thousand took part in the March for the Constitution and Liberty on September 19, 1945, organized by the JCD. Numerous women and men climbed into taxis, independently owned buses, and private cars and trucks displaying special signs that took them to Congress, from which people walked to the Plaza Francia. One woman cried out, "Juancito [Perón] ya te decía—que sin tranvías igual se hacía!," telling Perón that the lack of trams had not deterred them, which many applauded and repeated as they marched. They sang the national anthem and chanted the usual slogans against the dictatorship, as well as brief and often vulgar verses about Perón and his mistress, Evita. Schlieper headed a massive column of board members. Contesting Perón's insistence that only the rich opposed him, several observers, including British diplomats, spotted modestly dressed laborers as well as chic aristocrats; others, however, discerned a mostly middle- and upper-class presence. Despite Perón's admonitions, the march was peaceful, with few policemen or Nationalists at the scene. This enormous display of democratic sentiments exhilarated the anti-Peronist forces and convinced them of their mass support.[53]

La Fronda insisted that the March disproved the opposition's assertion that Argentines lacked freedom. In fact, it showed an unbraked liberty that extended to unruliness. In the name of freedom and the constitution, the march fomented discord, political ambitions, and tyrannical foreign interests. No such march could take place in the Soviet Union, even if a US ambassador like Braden served there. To further disparage the march, it pointed out the many women participants and dearth of authentic laborers.[54]

After the march, Ambassador Braden returned to the United States to become assistant secretary of state for Western Hemisphere affairs. From this position he continued his campaign against Perón. Schlieper figured among those who bade him farewell at the airport. Whether she and the Victory Board had had direct contact with him is unclear.[55]

Collaborating with some opposition figures, General Arturo Rawson planned a coup d'etat. The government halted it on September 24, reimposed the state of siege and censorship, and arrested the plotters, JCD leaders, university officials in several provinces, and even some Nationalists. Although most were freed a few days later, and Farrell insisted that elections would take place, this backsliding from the transition to democracy angered many. Students around the country conducted strikes and occupied universities. In response, authorities imprisoned students, faculty, and administrators and closed the universities in La Plata, Buenos Aires, and Santa Fe.[56]

When policemen stormed the University of Buenos Aires on October 4, they slashed at the male and female students who had barricaded themselves and arrested them. The next day mounted police attacked several demonstrations, wielding the flat of their swords, tear gas, and water hoses against men and women alike. A separate women's protest took place at the Plaza de Mayo, headed by mothers of the detained students and probably including Victory Board members. The mounted police also charged into this multitude, striking women to the ground.[57]

From across the River Plate, Feminine Action pledged solidarity with Argentina, and especially with its women. Uruguayan women professors and students, including Feminine Action adherents, sent representatives to Buenos Aires to deliver a supportive letter to the imprisoned women students and a note to the minister of the interior insisting on their release.

Carmen Garayalde and another Feminine Action member led the delegation. Schlieper, Ratto, other board members, and students greeted them at
the port on October 12 and took them to the Plaza San Martín, occupied
by protesters. A few days before, Perón's military rivals had forced him to
resign. Discussions about Perón and the future of the regime were taking
place in the Círculo Militar, across the street from the plaza. As Garayalde
and an Uruguayan student walked to the podium to address the throng,
Argentine women hugged and kissed them in gratitude for their presence.
The police fired on demonstrators and killed a male student and a doctor
who was treating the wounded. The Uruguayan witnesses to this bloodshed
accompanied the funeral cortege to the cemetery. They handed the newly
freed prisoners the letter in a ceremony at the Victory Board headquarters.
They also interviewed professors and students in Buenos Aires and La Plata,
as well as board member Argúas, who had negotiated with the police to free
the young women. When they returned to Montevideo, they related what
they had seen to faculty and student groups, who demonstrated in favor of
severing diplomatic relations with Argentina.[58]

Sympathy for the women, students, and the Victory Board motivat-
ed Feminine Action's involvement. It also had another compelling reason
for its outreach. Now that the Allies had defeated fascism in most of the
world, Southern Cone antifascists wanted to do the same in their region.
As they saw it, the last remaining fascist stronghold, outside of Spain, was
Argentina, although some Latin Americans also considered the Trujillo and
Vargas regimes as fascist.[59] Sharing this goal, the Victory Board welcomed
Feminine Action's solidarity and used the resulting publicity in Uruguay as
a means of evading local censorship.

October 17 and Its Aftermath

Meanwhile, on October 17, 1945, working-class people streamed in from
the industrial suburbs ringing Buenos Aires to the Plaza de Mayo, demanding Perón's release from confinement and his return to power. Peronists
and anti-Peronists disputed the nature of this mobilization. In the ensuing
presidential campaign, Nationalists increasingly jumped on Perón's band-
wagon. They backed the socioeconomic and religious measures in Perón's
platform, whereas antifascists emphasized political issues.

If the March for the Constitution and Liberty had been the largest
demonstration in Argentine history until then, *La Fronda* estimated that
one hundred thousand more people gathered in front of the presidential
palace, the Casa Rosada, on October 17.[60] Luis Alberto Romero, however,
observed that there may have been fewer persons than on September 19,
but many more were laborers.[61] At any rate, Perón appeared on the Casa

Rosada's balcony and spoke to great acclaim, initiating his presidential campaign.

On this and the following day, working-class demonstrators in greater Buenos Aires and other parts of the country engaged in verbal abuse and violence against universities, students, elite social clubs, and the liberal press, all of which opposed Perón. But this was not the only reason for these attacks, or for the lack of the usual decorum that characterized labor marches. The drumming, singing of popular tunes, dancing, wearing of flamboyant or work clothing, and more brazen behavior contested established codes and symbols of social hierarchy. So, too, did the "intrusion" of workers from the periphery into the center of Buenos Aires, seen as a middle- and upper-class space. The assaults on newspapers, students, and centers of learning asserted the value of their labor experience against the "unequal distribution of cultural power," Daniel James stated.[62]

Now leading the conservative feminist Unión Femenina Democrática (UFD), Eugenia Silveyra de Oyuela compared the two huge rallies of September and October. She contrasted the well-mannered, disciplined march of September 19 with the "disorderly and aggressive mobs" of October 17. The uncouth masses used public fountains as bathtubs and sources of drinking water, she wrote. Silveyra decried their slogan, "*Alpargatas* [a low-cost espadrille] yes, books no!"[63] She and other middle- and upper-class listeners considered such sayings barbaric and anti-intellectual. Shared by many privileged porteños, these stereotypes of workers as uncivilized suggested they were nonwhite. For Peronists, however, this rallying cry had another meaning. Alpargatas symbolized the workers' poverty, class identity, support for Perón, and resistance to inequality.[64]

The Victory Board activist of Mendoza and now the secretary of its local successor group, Teresa Rebasti de Basso believed that support for demagogues demonstrated the vital need for popular education. The cry for alpargatas divided the country and impeded its development; Argentina would become one when all its inhabitants could afford to buy better shoes.[65] Unlike Silveyra, she recognized inequality.

Sharing the anti-Peronist discourse, Victory Board members reflected on the recent turbulence. Silvina Ocampo described it in a poem titled "This Spring of 1945, in Buenos Aires":

I have heard as in dreams a tyrant
with a whining exaltation
interrupt the night, in a balcony . . .
I have seen blind horses shoot, and the sables rise like lightning
punishing women in the plazas.
I watched students die sadly,

assassinated by the police;
and in the blue profundity of the day
cowardice, abject, unrepentant.
I saw a hysterical, uncivil mob
that was approaching the Casa Rosada." [66]

Alluding to Perón, Clara Drallny of Córdoba spoke of a man who used Benito Mussolini–like phrases and incited street violence to serve his totalitarian and electoral ambitions. The "vandal masses" he set loose, she insisted, did not represent Argentine ideals.[67]

Delfina Bunge de Gálvez contested such views, characterizing the demonstrators as peaceful and respectful, hoping to rescue a benefactor. She compared them to the impoverished multitudes who had followed Jesus. Her husband, Manuel Gálvez, hastened to explain that Bunge was not comparing Perón to Christ. They were among the Nationalists and right-wing Catholics who applauded Perón's outreach to workers.[68]

Alienated by the official turn against the Axis and Perón's removal of several Nationalist officers from the government, others did not. Some Nationalists considered him a dangerous demagogue. Perón's promise of retaining religious education in the public schools, however, mollified many on the far right, as did his denunciations of foreign capital and the upper class. The ALN issued a carefully worded statement on October 18, declaring that it was with the pueblo that defended the national interest and opposed Communism, regardless of its partisan sympathies. Not long thereafter this group and other Nationalists decided to back Perón's presidential candidacy. At least Perón shared some of their views, and supporting the liberal Democratic Union, which included Communists, was unthinkable. Ambassador Braden's blatant opposition to Perón also swayed them.[69]

The ALN and like-minded Nationalists attacked Perón's opponents and Jews. The Sociedad Hebraica Argentina protested the many anti-Jewish incidents in Buenos Aires as well as police involvement in an assault on this cultural institution. With its concentration of Jewish organizations, businesses, and population, Once was the most heavily targeted neighborhood. Its Victory Board secretariat held an event that denounced this antisemitic wave.[70] Perón also condemned the Nationalist attacks.[71]

Peronists and their Nationalist supporters regarded the opposition as elitist. Nevertheless, Democratic Union's program included agrarian reform, the nationalization of public utilities, retirement pensions, and the defense and expansion of benefits laborers had received, presumably from Perón. The Democratic Union's women's branch, including the Victory Board, sought a lower cost of living, strict compliance with labor and maternity legislation, equal pay for equal work, and improved working conditions for servants and rural women, along with more far-reaching social reforms after democracy was restored. On such issues there was little disagreement between antifascists and Peronists. Yet the opposition saw the dictatorship's socioeconomic policies as designed to reinforce fascist rule. Moreover, it mostly campaigned on democratic political goals, such as adherence to the constitution; ending the state of siege and the police's Special Section, which persecuted and tortured leftists; and eliminating totalitarianism and antisemitism rather than its socially conscious platform.[72] Still, its key problem was that it had been out of power and was unable to provide gains for the poor, unlike Perón and the military regime.

Transnational Relationships and the Victory Board's Final Years

Antifascist entreaties to international organizations proved unsuccessful in pressuring the Argentine dictatorship. Furthermore, the war's end, Perón's electoral victory, and new Communist strategies crippled the Victory Board. It and Feminine Action developed ties with the Communist-influenced WIDF. New organizations replaced these Argentine and Uruguayan groups and continued their South-South and South-North exchanges, largely through WIDF. In the Victory Board's final moments, Schlieper participated in a very different global assemblage of women.

Activists such as Dr. Gregorio Bermann of Córdoba regularly informed US antifascist and women's groups of human rights abuses in Argentina. Their aim was to encourage foreign pressure against the Argentine administration and petition the nascent United Nations to act against it, for example, by excluding Argentina from its first assembly. The Pan American Women's Association (PAWA); associate members of the New School, which had sheltered European scholars fleeing Nazism; and the International League for the Rights of Man held a public meeting on Argentina at the New School in mid-December 1945. Bermann spoke at this gathering, as did Frances Grant, PAWA president, chair of the International League's Latin American committee, and a frequent visitor to Latin America. She praised Argentine women as "second to none in their courage and sacrifices in the face of imprisonment and even armed assaults." Grant asked women of the Americas to urge their governments to intercede with Argentine officials,[73] as Uruguayans had done.

Heloise Brainerd wrote Schlieper, expressing WILPF's admiration for her and her colleagues who braved the police in their defense of freedom. In February 1946, perhaps in response to Grant's appeal, WILPF convened women from North America and twelve Latin American countries, most of the latter residing in the United States, to meet in solidarity with democratic forces in the hemisphere opposing fascist reemergence. WILPF particularly singled out Argentine "Nazi-Peronism" as a threat.[74] By the following year, however, Brainerd became suspicious of Schlieper and Communist influence over the Victory Board.[75]

Board members endorsed the effort to lobby the United Nations. Schlieper, Ratto, Oliver, and three other board figures, along with Silveyra, signed a manifesto on the eve of the United Nations General Assembly's first meeting in early 1946 in London. It urged the UN to ensure its effectiveness and win the peace by destroying Nazifascism everywhere. It should not let any legal measure, such as the principle of nonintervention, obstruct this task. The authors opposed the US imperialistic interventions carried out before President Franklin D. Roosevelt, but favored UN intercessions that protected human rights and the sovereignty of peoples. The assembly had already accepted the Argentine delegates' credentials, however, and took no action.[76] This manifesto and Grant's and WILPF's appeals were fruitless.

Meanwhile, the Victory Board was developing a more significant transnational connection. Women survivors of the French Resistance, along with British activists, envisioned a new organization that built upon the legacy of the World Committee of Women Against War and Fascism of the 1930s while incorporating masses of women around the globe. Dolores Ibárruri, "La Pasionaria," the famous Spanish Communist now in exile, notified Feminine Action member Julia Arévalo of the group's foundational meeting. Arévalo passed the word to Garayalde, who informed Schlieper. She and Ratto, representing the Victory Board, and Banegas, representing women workers, were among the over eight hundred delegates from forty countries—five of them Latin American—and five continents at the World Congress of Women in Paris in late November 1945. Board offshoots and other organizations asked the delegation to carry their messages to this momentous event. The coordinating board of democratic women's groups of Rosario, for example, wanted the congress to know that it pledged to uphold the fight against racism and fascism, provide aid for war victims, support governments and socioeconomic systems that promoted liberation, and offer "unconditional adhesion in the struggle for the woman's social and political independence."[77]

The World Congress of Women marked the birth of WIDF, which has promoted peace, antifascism, women's and children's welfare, and women's rights to the present. The proceedings taught Ratto that Argentine democratic women should coordinate their activities and encourage their largely unorganized women compatriots to press for their rights. They needed to focus on how voting and other forms of activism would enable them to accomplish concrete goals, such as acquiring food for their children, strategies that harked back to the UAM in the 1930s. The Argentine delegates also contributed to the congress. Aside from participating in discussions, Ratto and Schlieper gained posts in the WIDF council and were the only Latin Americans named to the WIDF Executive Committee.

The Victory Board held a second National Assembly in mid-December 1945, this one directed exclusively toward its members. The delegates from ten localities—a shrinking number—brought up women's political rights, deepening violence and repression, and enforcement of women's labor laws. The greater focus on ordinary homemakers and their needs than in previous board meetings may have reflected what Ratto learned in Paris. The Victory Board proposed organizing them to protest the long lines at stores, shortages of items of prime necessity, and high cost of living. It resolved to raise awareness of the impoverished provinces, which Nationalists had accused the board of ignoring.[78]

The Democratic Union paralleled the Victory Board's weakness. Disunited until shortly before the February 1946 election, and then merely papering over the cracks, the Democratic Union chose the Radical José Tamborini as its presidential candidate. He could not match Perón's charisma, vigor, or record on social welfare. A British diplomat observed that the Radicals' fifteen years of exclusion, persecution, and electoral abstention had impeded the rise of youthful talent from the ranks. Church backing, his manipulation of resentment toward Braden, and his head start over the divided opposition also boosted Perón. Still, his victory stunned the Democratic Union. In the end, a majority of the (male) electorate chose his populist notions of economic democracy rather than the antifascist emphasis on political democracy. The fact that he won only 54 percent of the vote did not console his defeated rivals.[79]

Some antifascists quietly may have favored Peron's victory. Perhaps they wondered why it had taken so long to implement social programs. El Pueblo pointed out that politicians and theorists had spent decades studying and debating such ideas to no useful end. The revolution of 1943 had halted these pointless discussions and taken action.[80] Any number of antifascist men and women, including Victory Board members, and especially those from the working class, might have concluded that these measures—and possible future ones—outweighed Perón's authoritarianism.

The end of the war, Perón's election, and the women's suffrage law in 1947 removed the Victory Board's main purposes. Building on the dictatorship's efforts, the new administration further coopted the board's program by organizing its own aid campaign. In November 1947 Eva Perón began sending goods to Europe, and her foundation continued these efforts. Now that the Victory Board's work accorded with the government's policy, it was legalized. According to Ratto, in July 1946 policemen returned the goods they had confiscated three years before; she did not mention the looted funds or the goods taken from chapters.[81] Nevertheless, the group experienced sporadic repression.[82]

Meanwhile, the Victory Board carried on. It revised its statutes, which differed from the previous ones in several crucial respects. Whereas the old version simply declared that the board would send aid to countries that fought Nazism, the new one stated the board would ally with any attempt to exterminate fascism, implying within as well as outside Argentina. It would work to establish peace, defend women's rights, and promote children's health and education, goals missing from the earlier statutes. And it adhered to WIDF,[83] as its activities demonstrated. While nothing new, its aid for children of former occupied European countries and of Spanish Republican families, and its protests against the torture of Spanish political prisoners, partly responded to WIDF campaigns. Board leaders at the national and chapter levels read aloud WIDF's commemorative message at their celebrations of the first anniversary of the Allied victory. The Victory Board still exercised local initiative, however. For example, during the drive for European children, the Córdoba filial gave donors the option of contributing clothing to Argentine youth.[84]

The Victory Board held its third national convention in June 1946, preceded by its leaders' customary regional tours to drum up interest and introduce its principal topics for consideration: aid for the victims of fascism, support for Spanish Republicans, and the creation of a lasting peace. These themes aligned with WIDF directives, yet also typified the Victory Board's previous goals. Over one hundred delegates from Greater Buenos Aires and thirty-five other branches attended (see table 1). The largest cities represented were Buenos Aires, Córdoba, Tucumán, and Resistencia. Two new filiales from San Luis Province and two more from Buenos Aires Province sent delegates, as did the Uruguayan UNF. The attendees elected the Directive Commission, with Schlieper as president, Ratto as secretary general, and two new vice presidents, and approved the four WIDF presidents as honorary heads of the convention. WIDF sent its greetings and congratulations to the Victory Board for its aid to Spanish Republicans and children. The guests at the convention banquet included local Spanish, Slavic, Italian, and Chinese ayudistas, as well as a representative of the Soviet news agency Tass. The absence of US and British diplomats was noteworthy.[85]

The Victory Board always had reflected Soviet wartime policies, along with other interests, while exercising agency. The Cold War had begun, and the third convention's resolutions demonstrated the shifting Soviet strategies (and WIDF influence). The movement now opposed reactionary British and US warmongers. It criticized what became the Inter-American Treaty of Reciprocal Assistance of 1947, a collective security pact under which the United States furnished military aid to Latin America to guard against Communism, as an imperialistic plan that inhibited peace.[86] The Victory Board applauded the Perón administration's establishment of diplomatic relations with the Soviet Unión, but urged it to break ties with Franco's Spain, push to free its political prisoners, and recognize the Spanish government in exile. It asked the government to admit immigrants, especially children, victimized by fascism. The Victory Board reaffirmed its adherence to WIDF and women's rights and resistance to racism, antisemitism, and anything that smacked of fascism. Once more it emphasized its diversity and nonpartisanship, signaling it accepted Peronists; indeed, it had Peronist members.[87] As it pointed out, since Argentines now agreed on assistance for war-torn countries, Peronists and non-Peronists could come together, at least on this issue.

No longer requiring a Popular Front to assure its security, the Soviet Union returned to its old tactics of class struggle and hostility toward its wartime allies. Moreover, the Democratic Union's defeat demonstrated to the Argentine Communist Party the limits of joining with bourgeois elements and other political forces against what it regarded as fascism. Such alliances had sidelined the party's anti-imperialist and proletarian allegiances and alienated the Peronist masses. Communist leaders decided to compete with Peronists for worker support and reclaim the discourses of social justice, anticolonialism, and class conflict. As part of this effort, Victorio Codovilla and Fanny Edelman advocated recruiting more women laborers for the Communist Party. Their aims were to unite women in a large movement centering on concrete socioeconomic issues that they would connect to the broader struggle against the oligarchy, latifundia, and imperialism, thus moving Argentina toward socialism. Reflecting these plans, in a speech in January 1946 Ratto explained that the Victory Board delegates to the World Congress of Women considered themselves representatives of all Argentine women and especially of "the great Union of Argentine women that should be created."[88]

Communist Party heads concluded that the Victory Board could not convert itself into such a movement, and not only because the war that had united these diverse women had ended. Although the agenda formulated at the board's national assemblies accorded with the Communists' new goals for women's mobilization, and the third national convention solidly backed WIDF, the party decided to create a new organization, less identified with the upper class, British and US foreign policy, and anti-Peronism. Francisca de Haan suggested that deliberations at the World Congress of Women may have influenced this decision. Ironically, prominent Communists now seemed to believe their own publicity that had magnified the Victory Board's patrician membership. Divisions within the board were another reason for starting anew. Adriana Valobra found a letter written by Edelman in 1946, noting that she and other Communists wanted to continue exercising leading roles in the Victory Board, but some Directive Commission members questioned Communist influence and affiliation with WIDF. The party sanctioned Ratto for apparently encouraging this dissension.[89]

The Communist-backed Unión de Mujeres de la Argentina (UMA) arose in July 1947. A month later the Victory Board dispatched its final shipment to Europe, consisting of clothing and shoes for WIDF distribution to orphans.[90] While the two Argentine groups coexisted for a time, the Communist withdrawal of support damaged the board. As it faded away throughout the year, the UMA absorbed many of its chapters and laborer participants, proving that the Victory Board had not been as oligarchical as the party now claimed. Working-class and peasant organizations also affiliated with the UMA, which included some Peronists.[91] In effect, the more proletarian UMA replaced the Victory Board.

This resembled the trajectory of Feminine Action and the UNF, despite contextual differences. The 1946 elections sent Arévalo to the senate, and five other Communists became deputies. By 1948, however, Cold War tensions pushed the Communist Party away from the Uruguayan government in a narrow orthodox direction that estranged many supporters. Meanwhile, Communists, workers, and other groups began to assign more importance to internal conditions than external assistance, and the UNF emerged as the umbrella organization of women dedicated largely to local issues.[92] Feminine Action collaborated with it, continued to support the Victory Board, and conducted activities resembling those of its Argentine partner.[93] It affiliated with WIDF, as did the UMA and the UNF. Paralleling the Victory Board's experience with the UMA, as Feminine Action waned, the UNF waxed.[94]

The contact between Uruguayan and Argentine antifascist women was increasingly subsumed under their involvement in WIDF. Feminine Action and Victory Board members embarked on the same ships to several WIDF congresses, witnessed the devastation in Europe, and promised to help alleviate it. Having largely displaced Feminine Action, the UNF collaborated with the Victory Board to plan Marie-Claude Vaillant Couturier's visit in August-September 1946. As WIDF secretary general, Vaillant Couturier wanted to strengthen her organization's ties with Uruguayan and Argentine women's groups. Her trip built upon the Victory Board's celebration of International Women's Day the previous March, which was dedicated to women who had fought fascism. A Communist deputy, member of the French Resistance, survivor of Auschwitz and Ravensbrück concentration camps, and witness at the Nuremberg trials, Vaillant Couturier was an outstanding example of such women.[95]

The French deputy spoke in both countries about WIDF, her wartime experiences, women in the postwar era, and Europe's need for aid. She thanked Victory Board members for their help but asked them to continue to send clothing and struggle for peace and their children's future. Vaillant Couturier discussed WIDF with Victory Board leaders and chapters in greater Buenos Aires and nearby municipalities and lectured to broader audiences in the federal capital and Mendoza. Peronists and Radicals in the Chamber of Deputies, including Schlieper's husband, Guillermo Martínez Guerrero, received and honored the French deputy. Schlieper and Ratto attended some of Vaillant Couturier's engagements in Montevideo.

Vaillant Couturier's courage, political prominence, and three years spent in concentration camps moved her listeners. Her talk at a chapter in an industrial suburb of Buenos Aires stirred great enthusiasm and emotion, an officer recalled. So many people arrived, they could not fit in the salon. The marks of torture on the Resistance fighter's thin body grieved the audience. Fearing that the cold winter would cause the French visitor further suffering, Victory Board filiales chipped in and bought her a fur coat.[96]

A UNF member best expressed what the South Americans and Vaillant Couturier offered each other. The Frenchwoman's call for freedom, peace, and redistribution of wealth exhilarated her and fellow activists. Their faith in humanity and Vaillant Couturier's heroism gave them the will to address this daunting agenda. In return they offered their solidarity efforts, self-sacrifice, dedication to peace, and experience in artistic creation, factories, and schools. They wanted the WIDF secretary general to tell antifascist women around the globe that their Uruguayan sisters also struggled for liberty, amity, and socioeconomic change.[97] The Victory Board and the UMA surely desired the same publicity for Argentines.

This was the Victory Board's final transnational project with Uruguay, but it was not the end of Argentine relations with WIDF. In upcoming years, Argentines would strengthen their share of this transnational exchange. UMA president Margarita de Ponce sat on the organizing committee of the WIDF Congress of 1948 in Budapest, where Edelman, now an UMA leader, spoke on Argentine and Latin American women. Edelman would serve as WIDF secretary general from 1972 to 1978 and vice president from 1981 to at least 1989.[98] These trajectories stretched beyond the boundaries of this study.

A very different cross-border exchange took place a month after Vaillant Couturier's tour. Sponsored by Eleanor Roosevelt and Alice McClean, the head of the American Women's Voluntary Services, which had carried out rear guard duties supporting the war effort, the International Assembly of Women met at McClean's farm in New York State. Taking part were 150 women from fifty-three countries, along with fifty from the United States. The assembly's theme was "The World We Live In—The World We Want."

Rather than relying on governments or men to select delegates, a committee of female organizers chose women they considered important. One was Schlieper, who along with her old rival Minerva Bernardino and Laura Arce of Feminine Action for Victory numbered among twenty Latin Americans. The participants included government and international agency officials, professionals, writers, radio personalities, social service and women's organization activists, and former Resistance members. Three labor leaders were in the US contingent. Of varied religious, racial, and political backgrounds, attendees ranged from pious conservative Colombians to Madeleine Braun, the Communist vice president of the French Constituent Assembly. Since they had to pay for their trips to the United States, their economic backgrounds probably were not as heterogeneous.[99]

Surrounded by autumnal beauty and rural tranquility, McClean's farm was a congenial spot for representatives to become acquainted. Experts explained the conference's political, economic, social, and spiritual themes, but the major portion of the International Assembly of Women consisted of small group discussions, allowing participants to learn from each other and dismantle prejudice and other barriers. In this manner women prepared to reinforce the United Nations' work and address the common problems facing humanity. They did not, however, vote or draw conclusions.

The Latin American delegates feared that the organizers hoped to establish a US-dominated group to compete with WIDF. Even the non-Communists among them opposed this possibility. One of them, the Chilean feminist Amanda Labarca, praised WIDF while wishing it had a more politically diverse leadership. She saw no need to duplicate this and other international women's organizations. The North Americans denied wanting to create a permanent group, but McClean proposed a new bureau to spread news on women's international activism. There was sharp disagreement over this project. Braun pointed out that WIDF's existing facilities could disseminate information. Nevertheless, McClean and others announced an information service unconnected to the International Assembly of Women that would operate until the United Nations Educational, Scientific, and Cultural Organization (UNESCO) could take over this function.[100]

At a minimum, the International Assembly of Women projected a Cold War–style moderation. Offering a more progressive statement than many others, Dr. Vera Micheles Dean, a foreign policy specialist, advised the United States to accept the Socialist countries and help them rebuild economically. Although Labarca characterized most attendees, especially the non-US ones, as leftist, the written summaries of sessions were liberal reformist and did not mention suggestions of radical economic measures. According to historian Leila Rupp, the US organizers did not want any statements that approximated Communism. While some Soviet-dominated Eastern European countries sent representatives, no Russians attended; when asked why, the coordinators claimed they had invited some but received no answers. Braun was only able to enter the United States because of her parliamentary status, whereas Eugénie Cotton, a French physicist, Communist, and WIDF president, said the United States denied her a visa to attend, which US officials disputed.[101]

Nor did the meeting emphasize feminism. In fact, the summary of one session declared that "human rights rather than women's rights should be emphasized," adding that more women should fill government positions, "not as women but as qualified citizens." This coincided with Eleanor Roosevelt's views. The participants supported equal pay for equal work, benefits for homemakers and domestic workers, and women's suffrage, although the English speakers thought that the last issue was resolved. The Latin American representatives criticized this disregard of the countries that still excluded women from voting, including eleven in their region. Speaking for the delegation, Arce urged setting a five- to ten-year limit for nations to comply with the UN charter, whose preamble specified equal rights for men and women. If they did not meet this deadline, they should be expelled from the UN. What role Schlieper played in these deliberations is unclear, since she did not want her political utterances to be published, probably fearing Peronist retribution.[102] Behind the scenes she likely pushed for compliance.

As was true for WIDF, antifascism loomed large in the conference. Several women, including former Resistance fighters and the first German woman civilian allowed to visit the United States after the war, recounted their dire experiences under fascist rule. A French delegate sang a song written in a concentration camp: "The shots that ceased . . . [neither] night nor day / The bloody wounds, the cries, the bitter tears." A Czech woman jailed by Nazis who now was vice mayor of Prague warned that "'there are still little Hitlers and Himmlers everywhere.'" Thirty women from former occupied countries in Europe and Asia demanded the annihilation of fascist remnants, such as the Franco regime.[103]

Schlieper felt impelled to address the continuing fascist threat. She participated in a panel on spiritual and moral aspects of society during the last day of the conference, which took place in New York. Breaking her silence on politics and scrapping her prepared remarks, she exclaimed, "'No spiritual or moral force can live in a country where people are dominated by dictators like,'" paused briefly, perhaps restraining herself from naming Perón, and then added "'Hitler and Mussolini.'" She entreated women living in democracies to think of other places where freedom was absent. To create genuine peace, women would have to unite to fight Nazis defeated on battlefields, yet still active throughout the world. When asked why she had changed her topic, Schlieper answered, "'There is nothing else if dictatorships exist.'"[104]

The International Assembly of Women was connected to the Victory Board's mission. Both focused on solidarity, diversity, mutual respect, and listening to others. The gathering resembled Schlieper's plan for the board: it would prepare women to forge their vision of the desired postwar order and lobby government to create it. Transferring these duties to the transnational level, the assembly was a training ground for women's participation in the UN. How the conversations and contacts it promoted might have affected the Victory Board is unknown, since the Argentine movement petered out. However, her attendance showed its president's openness to varied ideological perspectives.

When Ratto gave her speech at the Victory Board's reopening in April 1945, she could not have predicted its future. Little did members realize that their exultance would be short-lived. They would face obstacle after obstacle, police brutality, and a military regime that granted freedoms only to rescind them. After the election, the official legitimization of the board offered it a bit more liberty. Still, the relatively low attendance at the reopening—a vivid contrast with the board's huge events years ago in Luna Park—was a harbinger of things to come.

The Victory Board fell prey to several intertwined issues and events. One was Perón's election. Another was the Communist Party's changing strategy in the face of the Peronist triumph and the new global context. The Communist-influenced WIDF may have promoted the creation of the UMA, which replaced the Victory Board. Set into motion by the board, the explosion of women's activism for political rights, along with expanded opportunities for women to mobilize through political parties and the Catholic Church, eclipsed the veteran organization.

Seemingly indicating that feminism was not their top priority, the Victory Board and its allies pushed for democratic rule to be followed by acquiring the vote through legislative procedure. Yet these women understood that nothing could be certain under a fickle dictatorship, not even a decree granting this right. Borrowing from Popular Front Pan-American feminism, the Victory Board connected women's rights to broader political and social issues, including democracy in its many connotations. Eventually, they achieved their goal of suffrage through congressional action in 1947, albeit under a president many members regarded as fascist.

Unsurprisingly, the antagonism between Nationalists and the Victory Board continued. The former praised the dictatorship until it shifted toward the Allies. Embittered by the liberation of Paris and Berlin, rupture of ties with the Axis, and declaration of war against it, Nationalists thought these occurrences opened the gates to Communism and diminished Argentine autonomy. Obviously, board members viewed these events very differently. Nevertheless, some Nationalists reconciled with the Peronist government over its social welfare programs, relations with the church, and anti-US stance. Internationalism, Jews, feminists, and Communists—all associated with the Victory Board—were the Nationalists' targets; violent rhetoric and acts were their practices.

The Victory Board continued its South-North solidarity of shipping goods to Europe and engaged extensively with like-minded women in other countries. It received solidarity from fellow Southerners in Uruguay, as well as from the Northern WILPF, US women's and human rights groups, and, subtly, the International Assembly of Women. Feminine Action and UNF members who accompanied board adherents to antigovernment protests in Buenos Aires reinforced the close ties between Argentine and Uruguayan antifascist women. As Feminine Action declined, the UNF took up these exchanges, a pattern replicated in Argentina as the Victory Board gave way to the UMA.

Contacts between the Victory Board and the two Uruguayan groups influenced their respective nations. The Uruguayans helped their Argentine sisters resist Peronism and military authoritarianism. These Uruguayans and Argentines assisted each other in promoting women's citizenship and antifascist consciousness, most notably by organizing Vaillant Couturier's visit. The French deputy had a powerful impact on both nations. Her involvement with the Resistance and the political arena, and her reception in the Argentine Chamber of Deputies, gave women's struggles visibility and legitimacy. Vaillant Couturier's witnessing of Nazi genocide heightened public awareness of antisemitism and intolerance, thus underlining the vital democratic trait of pluralism.

The Victory Board's relationship with WIDF was significant for several reasons. It demonstrated the group's alignment with Communist Cold War strategy. Never before had the board affiliated with a particular global women's organization. WIDF inspired the Victory Board, tutored it in organizational techniques, sent it directives, and offered it a global stage. In turn the board provided it with officers, and the Argentines and Uruguayans offered it aid for war victims and an understanding of Latin American women and their struggles. One wonders how WIDF's liberal alternative, the International Assembly of Women, might have influenced the Victory Board had the latter survived.

From their beginnings, board members had felt overseas events as their own. The celebrations marking the liberation of Paris, in which they and other antifascists asserted ties of citizenship with the birthplace of liberty, made this clear. This allegiance stretched across national boundaries, uniting them with other advocates of freedom. The sense of transnational citizenship was one of the Victory Board's most striking characteristics. Despite its distinctive traits, few Argentines today know of this group. The reasons why are among the topics addressed in the conclusion.

CONCLUSION

One day in 2013 while I was perusing sources in the Instituto de Investigaciones Geohistóricas in Resistencia, Dr. Ernesto Maeder, a prominent specialist in Chaco history, came by to ask me about my research. He thanked me at the end of our conversation for teaching him something new. He was not the only scholar who was unfamiliar with the Victory Board (Junta de la Victoria). As I stated in the introduction, I had never heard of the Victory Board until the early 2000s, nor had other historians with whom I spoke before that time. There were few references in the existing literature.[1] The most important Argentine women's political movement before 1946 seemed largely consigned to oblivion.

What accounted for this historical amnesia? What happened to Board figures? Ultimately, what was the Victory Board's relation to Peronism? The Peronist legacy, political shifts, and the belief that the Victory Board was subversive helped blot its memory and determine the fate of its leaders. This conclusion also answers the questions posed at the beginning of this book and specifies the Victory Board's unique contributions to antifascism, including its South-South partnership with Feminine Action for Victory and democratic alternative. In addition, I demonstrate how the Victory Board fits within the history of feminism and of women's long struggles against different forms of authoritarianism in Argentina, which few have recognized. Centering on this group and its precursors, then, transforms the study of antifascism in Argentina, Latin America, and the world, and of Argentine women's activism. It teaches us about fascism as well as its opponents. Furthermore, the Victory Board's achievements and failures—such as inadequately addressing poverty—provide lessons for activists today.

Peronism

That the Victory Board differed from Peronism should not astonish readers, nor should the Peronist authorities' fitful repression of it. Yet the relationship between the two was more complex than polarity and persecution. Indeed, the resemblances between the Victory Board and Peronism may surprise many.

The Victory Board and Peronism were not always far apart. Both movements stood for solidarity by supporting social justice (at least in the future, in the board's case), encouraging mutual respect and emotional cohesion among their followers, and empowering them. The Victory Board sought to diminish inequality by surmounting class barriers among its members; Peronism subverted these boundaries symbolically, as on October 17–18, 1945, and literally through socioeconomic programs. Many antifascists may have favored these programs, although leaders tended to label them as demagogic. The Victory Board aimed at incorporating women into the polity through its internal democratic practices and feminist advocacy, and Peronism through the vote, the Partido Peronista Femenino (PPF), and Eva Perón's compelling example as a strong woman, a leader, and an advocate of women's political participation, despite her seeming acceptance of customary gender roles. The two movements mobilized a wide spectrum of women, including workers and *campesinas*. Peronism eventually embraced humanitarian aid to Europe, the Victory Board's original raison d'être. The Victory Board and Peronism even had sewing and knitting in common, although the latter valued these practices as means of enabling housewives to provide for their families.

President Juan Perón recognized and appreciated ethnic diversity, including the Jewish presence, another characteristic he shared with the Victory Board. He largely fulfilled Jewish women's demands communicated to the National Assembly of Women in September 1945, by inserting in the 1949 Constitution an amplified version of the 1853 Constitution's ban of religious and racial discrimination. The Organización Israelita Argentina, considered the Jewish section of the Peronist Party, helped integrate Jews politically and socially. Perón appointed Jews to high offices, supported Zionism, eased Catholic education in public schools and eventually eliminated it. In addition, he legalized the status of the many Jews who entered Argentina illegally in the 1930s–1940s, although his administration restricted further Jewish immigration.[2]

The differences between Peronism and the Victory Board, however, were sharp. Board leaders equated Peronism with fascism; for his part, Perón was hostile to this organization's liberal and Communist influences and to the elite, including some board adherents. In contrast, the Victory Board did not criticize the upper class. It pressed for political democracy and aid for suffering people overseas; Perón advocated economic democracy and prioritized helping poor Argentines. Nor did Perón take kindly to the opposition, which under his rule suffered antagonism, imprisonment, and torture.[3] This included former Victory Board members.

What Happened to Victory Board Figures?

Argentine and even US governments oppressed former Victory Board adherents, particularly leftists, Radicals, and intellectuals. Nevertheless, many remained active in public affairs, such as Fanny Edelman and others who joined the Unión de Mujeres de la Argentina (UMA). Their partisan allegiances and beliefs varied, as was true for members during the Victory Board's existence.

The most poignant case of such persecution was Ana Rosa Schlieper de Martínez Guerrero, who was imprisoned four times between 1946 and 1953. Her outspoken remarks at the International Assembly of Women in 1946 possibly fueled her victimization, as well as her Radical activism. In the late 1940s, she was involved in this party's mobilization of women and served as first vice president of its initial women's congress. The incarceration of her husband, Radical deputy Guillermo Martínez Guerrero, may also have precipitated her confinement. Both suffered ill treatment in detention. Her spouse died two months after his release in 1953. Schlieper's 1953 imprisonment lasted three months, forty days of which she spent in solitary confinement. She lost twenty pounds and suffered a heart attack afterward.[4] The couple had shared his internment in Patagonia in the early 1930s and now shared harrowing detention, albeit in different prisons. In their own ways, both resisted arbitrary rule.

Schlieper rebounded after Perón's overthrow. She worked for Arturo Frondizi's successful presidential campaign in 1958. He appointed her to head a women's committee on cultural exchanges; in this capacity and as his unofficial envoy, she traveled once more to the United States. There she exclaimed, "We have fought and won our revolution, we have re-established our democratic government, and now we welcome with open arms the help of North Americans to stay democratic."[5] Many Argentines would have strongly disagreed with her claim that their country was democratic, given the military's ouster of Perón in 1955 and proscription of the Peronist Party. Nor would they have welcomed US involvement. Perhaps Schlieper did not realize that the United States of the New Deal, Good Neighbor policy, and Four Freedoms was not the same as the United States of the Cold War. Her views on this nation distinguished her from her former Communist colleagues. Moreover, Schlieper saw the suppression of Peronism as vital to democracy, even if this entailed martial intervention. She died in 1964, before the military dictatorships of 1966–1973 and 1976–1983 fully revealed the brutal consequences of this belief.

The Peronist government also repressed other Victory Board members and sympathizers. The former closed Lautaro, the progressive press run by Sara Maglione de Jorge, a national board officer, and confiscated its books,

papers, and furniture. Lautaro reopened only after Perón's fall.[6] President
Ivonne Pradier de Kedinger of the Resistencia *filial* and her husband dedicated themselves to the Socialist Party and anti-Peronism after 1945. Their
political activities made it difficult for them to obtain passports during
Perón's administration, as was the case for the entertainer Berta Singerman, the Victory Board's collaborator. Outspoken opponents of fascism
and Francisco Franco, Berta and her sister Paulina, a comedic actress, could
not perform onstage during these years.[7] Following the 1943 coup d'etat,
President Dr. Clara Schliapnik de Filer of Villa Domínguez refused to give
members' names to policemen, who harassed her for years. After moving to
Buenos Aires in 1945, Schliapnik had to clean her police file, which dated
back to her student radicalism in the 1920s, to obtain a position in a municipal hospital. Peronist contacts helped her do so, but not all copies of the file
were destroyed, and police raided her home. For years she could not leave
the country without an official certificate of good conduct.[8]

Teacher, union militant, Communist, Victory Board spokeswoman,
and former secretary of the Palacios, Santa Fe, chapter, Rosa W. de Ziperovich lost her job as school principal in Rosario in 1950. At the same
time authorities also shut the provincial teacher's federation in which she
was active, although she continued to work in it clandestinely.[9] Ziperovich,
Schliapnik, and other colleagues had been involved in leftist politics. To
what extent their board involvement induced their persecution is unclear;
the police probably saw it as part of a subversive—and in some cases, Jewish—package. Perón's acceptance of Jews did not necessarily trickle down
to these officials.

Victory Board adherents' political histories followed them. Although
Clara Drallny of the Córdoba chapter and her husband, Oscar Eugenio
Reati, left the Communist Party in the 1950s, after these years, policemen
still treated them as if they were members. When they arrested Drallny
in 1966, during the military dictatorship, they demeaned her, saying she
would always be a Communist, Jew, and marginal person—in other words,
a pariah. She felt she was the victim of a pogrom. During the next military regime (1976–1983) they imprisoned Drallny again, along with her
husband and two sons. Her interrogators scolded her for belonging to the
Victory Board over three decades before, adding that they would turn her
Jewish body into soap, referring to the Holocaust.[10]

The Buenos Aires provincial police intelligence division kept files in
the late 1940s–1970s that traced individuals' political activism. At least
five mentioned women's Victory Board affiliations. One described this
movement as biased, another as leftist. Documents with updates for 1949,
1952, 1956, 1962, and 1963 noted these women's membership, in one case
inaccurately. This police unit drew upon these records when it executed

terror between 1976 and 1983.[11] Unlike many other Argentines, it had not forgotten this antifascist organization.

Cora Ratto experienced exclusion from several quarters. In early 1947, the Communist Party expelled her, her husband Manuel Sadosky, and others for their nuanced view of Peronism. These dissenters eventually formed a splinter group, the Movimiento Obrero Comunista, which regarded Peronism as a mass movement that favored national emancipation and anti-imperialism and thus could encourage a proletarian revolution.[12] Ratto and Sadosky left to study in Europe and returned to Argentina in 1950. Experiencing political difficulties at the Universidad de Buenos Aires (UBA), they taught classes on their own and accepted journalistic assignments. After Perón's removal and the restoration of university autonomy and self-governance, they reentered the UBA and Ratto attained her doctorate. The military's stripping away of these university prerogatives in 1966, followed by a police assault on UBA personnel, including Sadosky, precipitated their resignations from the university. Still considering herself leftist, Ratto engaged in politics once again, denouncing local human rights abuses and the Vietnam War. Under threat, the couple escaped into exile in 1974.[13]

US policy harmed María Rosa Oliver more than Peronism and official persecution. Her disillusionment with the United States grew with the Cold War, prompting her involvement in the Communist-linked Movimiento por la Paz en la Argentina, founded in 1949; regional peace conferences; and the Soviet-sponsored World Peace Council, created in 1950. These groups opposed US imperialism and warmongering, starting with the Korean conflict.[14] This activism reprised the Communist-influenced peace campaigns in the 1930s that identified militarism with fascism, in which Oliver had also partaken. The difference was that now the United States took the place of Nazi Germany and Fascist Italy, seemingly representing a new version of fascism.

Oliver justified her political position to her US acquaintances. She told Mary Cannon that if the Latin American masses rebelled, it was to improve their desperate living conditions. She insisted that they had nothing to defend in Korea, nor did they have reason to obstruct the liberation of colonialized peoples in Indochina or elsewhere.[15] In a letter to Women's International League for Peace and Freedom (WILPF) leader Heloise Brainerd, Oliver observed that her movement sought to prohibit the use of weapons of mass extermination and institute a peace agreement between the five major world powers. Surely the pacifist WILPF also favored such steps.[16] Oliver confided to her friend and former boss Nelson Rockefeller that she had believed that once they achieved victory, the Allies would continue to work together to construct a peaceful and better world. With this end in mind, she had worked for the US government. Her views had not changed, she declared, but those of the United States had. Oliver informed Rockefeller that the FBI considered her a menace because she actively opposed US Cold War policies, and she could no longer enter the United States.[17] Whether these individuals answered the letters is uncertain. Perhaps they thought that ongoing contact could compromise them, or that Oliver had placed herself on the other side of an unbreachable barricade. Rockefeller might have feared that it could jeopardize his political future.

Moreover, Oliver's involvement with Communist organizations and her acceptance of the Lenin Peace Prize in 1958 created a rift between her and her old friend Victoria Ocampo. As a result, Oliver left the magazine *Sur,* in which she had collaborated with Ocampo for many years. Yet they remained in touch, although often disagreeing with each other.[18] Friendships could soften political differences to a degree, as they had in the Victory Board.[19]

Fear, Silence, and Forgetting

After its demise, the Victory Board largely disappeared from public memory. Fear and regrets about its policies kept some former adherents silent, and Peronist achievements drowned out earlier activism. Sexism and inadequate access to sources impeded research until recently.

Many were scared to discuss the Victory Board after 1947. Its association with the upper class and anti-Peronism, its leftist connections, and police files on its members made it dangerous to speak of the movement, especially in areas long rife with repression, such as Chaco and Misiones. Said a political activist and librarian in Resistencia: "Who wouldn't be afraid?"[20] Despite the fact that Victoria Wickstrom had presided over the Oberá chapter, in later years her family and local residents hardly mentioned the Victory Board, according to her grandson. Nor did Wickstrom's son, a newspaper publisher and author, refer to it in his many writings on the region.[21] Perhaps they wanted to distance themselves from any hint of Communism or anti-Peronism.

Over time, the memory of the Victory Board receded among the populace. Some of the board members' children and relatives I met knew little or nothing about the organization or their kin's participation in it. A daughter was surprised to hear that her "timorous" mother, as a señorita, had belonged to the Victory Board's Tafí Viejo chapter and served as its secretary. And yet as we discussed her mother's life, her path to the Victory Board seemed clear: a daughter of anti-Franco Spanish immigrants, she was a member of the local Sociedad Española; after marriage she largely supported her family with her earnings as a piano teacher; and she gave benefit concerts for worthy causes. She had preexisting connections to antifascism, initiative, and concern for her community.[22] Perhaps she and other former adherents did not tell their children about the Victory Board to shield them, or they put their activism behind when they married. Their husbands also might not have wanted them to speak of these matters.[23]

In Misiones, I learned of additional reasons for silence. One was the perception of a local Nazi threat and the alarm this induced (see chapter 3). Historian Yolanda Urquiza added that patriarchalism and Nationalist activism also may have quelled discussion of women's involvement in the Victory Board. Moreover, according to anthropologist María Rosa Fogeler, the pressure to assimilate and anxiety over acquiring titles for their land may have gagged Eastern European immigrants in this territory.[24]

A Communist primary school teacher when she belonged to the Victory Board, Juana Juárez of Córdoba had a different motive for reticence about her past involvement. She eventually concluded that the Communist Party's (and the Victory Board's) opposition to Perón and participation in the Democratic Union (Unión Democrática), tied to the oligarchy and US imperialism, were serious mistakes. Failing to address this contradiction, the Communist Party lost popular support and never recovered. Juárez left the party in the 1940s and became a sociology professor. A strong supporter of women's rights, she grasped Eva Perón's importance. Juárez worked with Peronists in some women's groups, but never became one. While Juárez did not discuss her antifascist activism, her daughter thought she probably did not regret it, but rued the anti-Peronism that separated the Victory Board from the masses.[25] Her trajectory and views resembled Ratto's, and other former members may have felt similarly.

The Peronist victory in 1946 set into motion a process that helped expunge the historiographical memory of the Victory Board, its antifascist allies, and other progressive groups until the twenty-first century. Peronist hegemony swept these competing movements into the dustbin of history, implying they were ineffectual, obsolete, or mere "prologues" to Peronism, unimportant in their own right.[26] Many Peronists regarded antifascism as a sinister alliance of defunct political parties, the oligarchy, and imperialism that favored an unjust status quo and opposed the national interest.[27] In contrast, the administrations of 1946–1955 fulfilled sweeping goals that activists long had dreamed of but could not achieve. For example, women attained the vote, for which Evita Perón and Peronism received credit, and Evita organized women politically in the PPF, whose membership outstripped the Victory Board's. Forgotten, overlooked, or denigrated were the feminists who had fought for suffrage and antifascist women who opposed the new power holders.

Borrowing ironically from Milan Kundera's powerful description of

Communist takeovers in postwar Eastern Europe, one might say that Perón sought to create "an idyll of justice for all." Those who, like the Victory Board, challenged this idyll "implicitly den[ied] its validity" and hence became "invisible and forgotten," leaving "a single unblemished age of unblemished idyll."[28] Even as Argentine politics twisted and turned after 1955, with Peronists often persecuted, their triumphalist narrative persisted, though it was not necessarily imposed from above.

Peronists may not have achieved an idyll or remained perpetually in control, but the persistence of their narrative somewhat resembled what befell a number of Cuban antifascists after 1959. According to Ariel Lambe, it became crucial for the Cuban Revolution to demonstrate its continuity with the past, showing that then as now, Cubans participated in struggles around the world for freedom and radical transformation. The official narrative has celebrated Communists and adherents of the revolution who fought for or worked in solidarity with Republican Spain in the 1930s, while erasing or minimizing the activists who did not fit in these categories.[29]

Writing in 1997, Jorge Cernadas, Roberto Pittaluga, and Horacio Tarcus agreed that the rise of Peronism had curtailed interest in studying Argentine leftism—which in my view, essentially included the Victory Board. Leftist inability to reach power even before 1945 also helped explain this inattention. Yet the most important factor, aside from apathy, was the lack of access to sources. Official indifference toward creating or maintaining libraries and archives with relevant materials combined with leftist parties' monopoly over their records to stymie investigation. The latter vigilantly guarded their collections, preventing researchers outside their groups from consulting them and discouraging probing reflection within their own ranks.[30]

Furthermore, as various administrations repressed leftist movements, the latter's archives often disintegrated. In some cases, as with the central Victory Board offices, the authorities carted them away and they never reappeared. Militants also hid, destroyed, and scattered documents. Only after the last military dictatorship ended in 1983 was it truly possible to research leftist and resistance groups more thoroughly and analytically. Searching for greater understanding, and daring to topple former icons, many Argentines raised critical questions about the national past. They began to find answers in painstakingly constructed or reconstructed leftist archives.[31] All sorts of collections have blossomed in Argentina since the 1990s. Now the forgetting of leftist groups could diminish and the remembering of them flourish—although Lewis Hyde noted that "every act of memory is also an act of forgetting."[32]

As Yolanda Urquiza observed, silence and forgetting encircled women's contributions even more profoundly. Onlookers and scholars—women and men alike—assigned little importance to women's organizations like the Victory Board, although its male collaborators had valued it. However, the broad political and scholarly opening that began in 1983 extended to women's studies. National and international currents of feminism and feminist scholarship, social history, and postmodernism nourished work on women and gender. Research centers, scholarly meetings, journal issues, university professorships, and graduate degrees related to these topics have proliferated in Argentina from the 1990s on.[33] This also facilitated memories of the Victory Board, as well as my project.

Within Communist circles (and the police), however, the memory of the Victory Board never completely died. The offspring of Communist Victory Board members were more likely to know of their mothers' involvement than the children of other adherents. The UMA claimed it was following in the Victory Board's footsteps, as well as in those of such Board precursors as Agrupación Femenina Antiguerrera (AFA), Comité Argentino de Mujeres Pro Huérfanos Españoles (CAMHE), and Liga Argentina por los Derechos del Hombre (LADH). It aligned itself with the Victory Board's antifascism, solidarity, and participation in the Women's International Democratic Federation (WIDF).[34]

The Questions That Inspired This Book

I started this book with questions I sought to answer. One was what fascism and antifascism meant to the women I studied. Fascism meant a halt to democratization and the inclusion of laborers and women, for which many had fought so hard. Despite its aim of returning women to the home, it undermined women's maternal and pacifist mission. Leftists feared fascism would delay the revolutions that would overthrow capitalism and create just societies. To antifascist women it signified war, misogyny, racism and antisemitism, authoritarianism, inhumanity—in a word, barbarism. They saw fascists not as cardboard characters, but real persons who assaulted workers, leftists, and Jews in Argentina and elsewhere. In contrast, antifascism embodied multiculturalism and the tenets of Popular Front Pan-American feminism: peace, women's rights, egalitarianism, and democracy, which the Victory Board hoped would be implemented after the war. Antifascism also stood for culture, as well as solidarity in words and deeds, which some advocates identified with a true Christianity.

Another initial question was how the Victory Board—and Feminine Action for Victory—fought fascism at home and abroad. Drawing upon the heritage of women's activism, the Victory Board presented itself as a microcosm of a true democracy. Promoting women's entry into the polity, it encouraged their public roles, sense of self-worth, and personal liberation. It emphasized its modeling of formal democratic procedures and informal quotidian practices, such as society ladies listening to and learning from laborers, welcoming a wide array of participants, and working together to produce handmade goods for the Allies. Each aspect of its democratic alternative challenged fascist precepts and the 1941–1943 Argentine government's fraudulent rule.

The Victory Board sought to rid the globe of fascism through its South-North solidarity with the Allies, and it spread this mission to Uruguay, where it tutored Feminine Action for Victory. Feminine Action for Victory sent aid to Europe and organized women's marches to help set the country on a firm democratic footing in the ongoing transition from the dictatorship of 1933–1938. Influenced by discussions within the Inter-American Commission of Women (IACW), the Victory Board and Feminine Action for Victory tried to implement civil defense measures to protect against Axis attacks. As World War II ended the Victory Board demonstrated against the military dictatorship (1943–1946), demanded elections, and advocated women's suffrage and, belatedly, social reforms. However, Perón's notions of economic democracy defeated the antifascists' brand of political democracy.

Another question I posed addressed how antifascist women and their foes reacted to each other. Throughout Latin America from 1930 to 1941, they engaged in a discursive field, offering competing responses to modernization. Usually discordant and antagonistic, their "dialogues" and practices also revealed parallels and overlap. Some counterrevolutionaries appropriated their rivals' terms but defined them differently. For example, both sought to "liberate" women: feminists from obligatory domesticity, extreme rightists from the labor force. The Brazilian Integralistas' self-styled feminism was Catholic, nationalized, and distant from the other strain. This and other borrowings revealed a desire to appear as forward-looking as their opponents. Both sides politicized the home and placed women's liberation within broader—and disparate—transformational projects. Each blamed the other for perverting women's mission. Leftist and especially rightist men assigned less importance to women's issues and held more restrictive notions of women's roles than their women comrades, a few of whom defied them. Yet fascist women and movements differed among themselves, with Integralistas welcoming women's public roles more than others. Many progressives and fascists alike believed in maternalism and gender difference and decried poverty.

In Argentina, unlike in Chile and Brazil, local fascists (Nationalists) remained a significant force in the 1940s and beyond. Their debates with the Victory Board not only revolved around women's roles and modernity, but the war, solidarity, impoverishment, and pluralism. Nationalists and the Victory Board fought over many issues. They charged each other with promoting divisiveness and foreign doctrines. The board's most powerful accusation against Nationalists was that their imported fascist creed betrayed Argentine traditions. The latter insisted on the need to provision the local poor rather than the Allies, who were fighting a war that did not involve Argentina. Many Argentines probably agreed with this argument, which was the most effective in the Nationalists' arsenal. The Victory Board embraced transnational solidarity and claimed that setting up another charity would not mitigate poverty, which Nationalists sometimes admitted was true. Nor did the Victory Board accept the latter's neutrality, which often only thinly disguised pro-Axis sentiment. The Victory Board's belief in democracy and equality conflicted with Nationalist backing of class and gender hierarchy, women's confinement in the home, and authoritarian rule. Nationalists praised the country's Spanish, Latin, and Catholic heritage, which it wanted to purify of Jewish and other "foreign" elements. The Victory Board lauded secular freedoms and multiculturalism and included proud Jewish members.

Nationalists thought the Victory Board endangered neutrality and the religious, gender, and social order. The board believed Nationalists endangered a modern, pluralistic, and democratic society. They agreed on the need for national liberation, but their definitions of this phrase varied markedly. Nationalists sought liberation from foreign imperialism, anticlericalism, and liberal economics, whereas the Victory Board desired liberation from fascist interlopers, repressive governance, and suppression of women.

How the Victory Board attracted, united, and energized people of different classes, ethnic and national origins, and regions for its cause was another research question. It reached out to women in their neighborhoods, communities, unions, and workplaces, convincing them that their backgrounds and beliefs dictated opposition to fascism. Leftist militants, Jews, and immigrants from occupied Europe needed little convincing. Leaders welcomed diverse members, celebrated multiculturalism, and created spaces for ordinary women to be heard in an atmosphere of respect and attentive listening. Building upon local struggles and women's networks, organizers forged vibrant chapters, which board leaders pieced together into a national movement. National board officers coordinated the branches by touring provinces and territories, naming their inhabitants to national posts, and including them in national conventions. By doing so, they sought to transcend the long-standing rivalry between Buenos Aires and the nation.

Fostering unity as well as everyday democracy, textile and garment workers taught socialites to sew and knit as they labored side by side. Yet the Victory Board did not fully bridge the ideological fissure between social classes. The desire to close its diverse ranks against the Axis led it to prioritize an Allied victory, which the board claimed would lay the groundwork for an egalitarian order. In its view, one could not work simultaneously for social change and the war effort. Maintaining a multiclass following meant emphasizing liberal freedoms over discussions about reducing poverty.

Nevertheless, the Victory Board members' core activity stimulated enthusiasm. By investing themselves in sewing and knitting for the Allies, they made it "their war." They expressed their antifascism not just in abstract words, but in mounds of tangible products that people could see and whose impact they could imagine. Working around the clock to meet deadlines and displaying their handmade goods, dispatching them overseas, and receiving acknowledgement of their receipt galvanized Victory Board and Feminine Action for Victory members and popularized antifascism in their communities.

The South-South and South-North character of their solidarity also was instrumental in energizing the two groups. Feminine Action for Victory and Victory Board leaders combined forces at key moments, creating a spirit of South-South collaboration across the River Plate that vitalized both movements. The Victory Board's appropriation of the "V for Victory" and exchanges with groups and governments in the United States and Europe made even its most remote chapters perceive and take pride in their global impact, partly because they overturned the usual hierarchy between South and North. Furthermore, linking their participation in a distinguished worldwide campaign with the encouragement of democracy at home resonated among many Argentines and Uruguayans.

A key question was how the Victory Board—and Feminine Action for Victory—gendered antifascist politics. Politics inevitably is gendered, but the Victory Board gendered it in ways unlike those of men. It assumed the tasks of bringing together diverse constituencies and lifting morale, which it regarded as missions that only women could perform. Inspiring, unifying, and quelling differences were maternalistic skills attributed to women as "natural" peacemakers. Making garments also resembled domestic duties. Sewing and knitting needles were the weapons it and its Uruguayan partner used to fight the Axis. Through handwork antifascism became part of women's daily lives, and the Victory Board made these domestic labors visible, thus blending the private and the public. Adherents brought antifascism into their homes, handing it down to their children and negotiating with husbands who may have shared their beliefs. One also perceives the blending of public and private in the intimate lives and activism of antifascist couples. Often these shared political commitments promoted understanding and lightened women's chores, but they were not free of conflicts or competition. At least a few relationships seemed relatively equal.

Even as the Victory Board fostered homemaking roles, it took women out of the household. Its spokespersons envisioned women not only as mothers, but as workers, professionals, and citizens. Claiming that democracy was incomplete without women, board leaders prepared members for citizenship by stimulating involvement in the group's internal governance and interest in politics and foreign affairs. Antifascist men also conducted their meetings in parliamentary fashion, but these practices had a more radical meaning for women, who were excluded from the polity. The Victory Board constructed an unprecedented tight-knit women's political network that stretched across much of Argentina and held massive campaigns that trained adherents in organizational techniques. Feminine Action for Victory and the Victory Board provided spaces for women's self-expression through speeches, discussions, and the arts. Their involvement with civil defense and references to women as combatants evoked citizenship, as did the Victory Board's endorsement of suffrage, which became more overt by 1945. Unlike their Argentine neighbors, Uruguayan women had won the vote, and Feminine Action for Victory urged them to use it. Schlieper's participation in the IACW reinforced the Victory Board's feminist leanings.

Another gendered aspect concerns the Victory Board's relations with male political movements. The fact that it consisted solely of women distinguished it from the other major Argentine antifascist groups. If not completely autonomous from men, it exercised agency, at least until after the war. There was a division of labor between the Victory Board and some antifascist organizations mainly composed of and led by men, particularly Acción Argentina. Whereas the Victory Board made goods for the Allies, Acción Argentina focused on speechmaking, holding events, and struggling for power. Other antifascist men respected and collaborated with the Victory Board, but generally characterized it in maternalistic terms that limited its scope. Nor did they show much interest in women's rights.

In myriad ways, then, gender was fundamental for the Victory Board and its precursors, because of their desire to expand women's roles and rights and the fact that they operated in a patriarchal context. It also was central for Latin American fascists, especially the Argentines, who defined women's and men's roles rigidly and saw the male-dominated home as the model for society. The Victory Board's style of gendering antifascism, which entailed more than simply inserting women, was part of its unique contribution to this phenomenon in Argentina.

The question of how the Victory Board and its predecessors engaged across borders extends the literature on Argentine antifascism, which usually has concentrated on its local practices and ramifications. During World War I, Argentine women's groups began to embrace pacifism. This preoccupation intensified with the Chaco War and the rise of fascist re-

gimes, leading to collaboration with the Swiss-based WILPF. The World
Committee against War and Fascism, its women's branch, and the Comintern stimulated coordination and conversation among many antifascists
around the world, including in Argentina. Argentines and other Latin
Americans protested the Italian invasion of Ethiopia, and huge numbers
sent aid in a South-North direction to Republican Spain. Slowly, many
pacifists realized that fascism, the greatest threat to world peace, could only
be defeated through armed combat. The formation of the Popular Front
echoed throughout the region, where men and women founded a host of
broad-based, Communist-influenced antifascist movements. Argentine
women formed Popular Front associations such as the AFA, CAMHE,
and Unión Argentina de Mujeres (UAM). The AFA and other antifascist
women's groups organized Latin American and women's peace conferences
in Buenos Aires in 1936 and spurred the creation of a regional confeder-
ation of pacifist women. The UAM and other progressive Latin American
women worked with the IACW to promote women's rights, in the process constructing Popular Front Pan-American feminism. Following up on
these efforts, in which future members had participated, the Victory Board
engaged with the IACW and conducted South-North solidarity with the
Allies. Its aid promoted goodwill among prominent women and some diplomats of those nations. The Victory Board mentored and then partnered
with Feminine Action of Uruguay. Board members experienced the liberation of Paris as if it were their own. After the war, both movements joined a
new global antifascist and women's rights initiative, the Communist-linked
WIDF. The protagonists of my study were transnational citizens.

Reshaping the History of Antifascism

Until recently, specialists on antifascism focused on Europe and described
groups outside this continent as peripheral. Along with the emerging literature, this book decenters Europe by demonstrating the Victory Board was
not peripheral to a European antifascist core, nor did it merely imitate or
recast European notions and praxis. In effect, the Victory Board and Feminine Action for Victory presented themselves as new models of civilization,
which was decaying if not dying in an "old world" beset by two catastrophic
wars and fascist onslaughts. Various characteristics set the Victory Board
apart from other female and male antifascist movements worldwide, or at
least from the literature that describes them. It constructed its own democratic alternative to fascism, consisting of formal representative and informal egalitarian practices that stimulated inclusion, pluralism, and solidarity in the ranks. The Victory Board highlighted its "everyday democracy"
to contest authoritarian governance and homegrown and foreign fascisms.

Its promotion of multiculturalism facilitated a shift in Argentine society away from the ideal of a melting pot to one of ethnic diversity. Its methods of popularizing antifascism and mentoring and partnering with a group in another country also were unique. Not quite as rare but still distinctive, the Victory Board and Feminine Action for Victory participated in South-North exchanges of goods and encouragement.[35]

Antifascism was important in Latin America, and women played crucial roles in it. In this regard, Argentina was especially significant among Latin American countries. Its prolonged rivalry with the United States for hemispheric leadership set it apart from other Latin American nations, and its unwillingness to support the Allies ignited antifascist opposition. Its antifascists contested the most enduring and arguably most influential fascist movement in the area. Argentina's lengthy saga of women's grassroots movements for peace, social justice, and rights evolved into antifascist activism. Victory Board members publicly engaged with Argentine politics and international diplomacy, thus subverting customary gender roles. This was Nationalist Manuel Fresco's likely reason for considering the board so threatening (see chapter 7).

The Victory Board and Argentine Feminism

It is vital to show not only how the Victory Board fits into the history of antifascism, but how it fits into the history of Argentine feminism, which has played a critical role in the region to this day.[36] Indeed, the Victory Board's feminism and antifascism were interdependent. It followed in the UAM's footsteps and was connected to the IACW and Popular Front Pan-American feminism. Its leaders saw the group as a vehicle for obtaining suffrage and training women for public engagement. By 1945, the Victory Board and its successors, like other feminists, clamored for the vote, albeit through congressional action. This occurred in 1947, with Evita's prodding, the year that the Victory Board crumbled.

The context for women changed radically under Peronism (1946–1955), the alternation of military-civilian governance (1955–1983), the rocky transition to democracy, and political and economic crises ever since. Former board members dispersed among Communist, Radical, and other political formations. Now that they could vote, women pushed for new rights and power within their parties. They fought for equal pay for equal work, legalization of contraception and abortion, women's equal representation in office, laws to curtail domestic violence, and other measures the Victory Board never envisaged. Most activists were unaware of this precursor. Yet while the details differed, the key general concerns for feminists remained the same as the Victory Board's: democracy, empowerment, and emancipation. Both engaged in solidarity, consciousness-raising, and transnational ties, and faced autonomy and diversity issues.

The Victory Board regarded the observance of democratic norms as intrinsically good for its own sake, adding, however, that achieving women's rights and social justice was only possible under this form of government. Succeeding events confirmed these opinions' veracity. Women obtained the vote and won office under Peronist populist democracy, which also provided economic benefits for the majority. Periods of military rule thereafter hurt women's causes, whereas under democracy feminism revived. But these revivals were limited in scope, for the persistent threat of coups d'etat, along with leftist calls for social and national liberation, often led feminists to minimize their demands.[37] The dictatorship of 1976–1983 was the harshest. For this reason, according to sociologist María del Carmen Feijoó, the transition from it to civilian governance was the first in which social movements prioritized formal democracy as positive in itself, without serving as a stepping stone to socialism or another end.[38] This had been the Victory Board's position all along. What was new was the widespread acceptance of this notion and reflection on the roots of authoritarianism, which led many women to analyze male domination.

The Victory Board sought to empower women politically and include them in the public sphere. After its demise, there still was a long way to go. Eva Perón modeled how to engage in politics by gaining power in public spaces and contesting male strictures. In 1947 she mobilized thousands of women to stand outside Congress to pressure legislators on the women's vote, leading hundreds into the balcony of the lower house. The formation of the PPF increased participants' confidence and consciousness, as had the creation of the all-woman Victory Board. Evita even fought husbands' and fiancés' control over PPF women. Under her leadership, the PPF imparted Peronist doctrine to its members and trained them to recruit for their neighborhood sections and provide services to their communities. They acquired experience traveling and making contacts. Through this party, women won the highest number of congressional seats they held before the 1990s. In these and other ways Evita empowered women, despite her antifeminist rhetoric and exaltation of customary gender roles. During Radical Raúl Alfonsín's presidency (1983–1989), women secured laws permitting divorce and equal parental rights, as well as compliance with the UN Convention on the Elimination of All Forms of Discrimination Against Women. Feminists drew up a bill that evolved into the 1991 Quota Law, mandating that women compose at least 30 percent of each party's candidates for national office. Women's participation in the drafting of the new constitution of 1994 insured the inclusion of affirmative action in the electoral system, among other clauses.[39] Enforcement problems notwithstanding, it seemed that Schlieper's vision of women taking their rightful places in government alongside men would be fulfilled. Massive women's involvement in protests during the severe economic crisis of 2002–2003 prompted further questioning of gender norms and new legislation.[40]

Victory Board members listened to each other, learned about the dilemmas faced by fellow adherents in rural and poor communities, and validated their colleagues. Subsequent movements took this consciousness-raising in a different direction. Fortified by readings of Simone de Beauvoir and radical British and US activists, a new wave of feminism began in Argentina around 1970 and moved underground during the military dictatorship of 1976–1983. These middle-class activists formed small groups in which they reflected on gender oppression, women's liberation, and intimate relations with men. They realized that others shared their problems. Issues such as contraception, abortion, and violence against women surfaced in these dialogues, although lesbianism remained a "silenced experience," in Marcela Nari's words. The topic of lesbianism, however, left the closet in the 1980s.[41] Board members divulged family concerns as they knitted, but probably not such explicit sexual matters.

Women sought sexual and reproductive emancipation, as well as liberation from physical abuse. They lobbied for what became a presidential decree in 1986 that ended restrictions on the distribution and use of contraceptives. After a long struggle for what advocates significantly called "reproductive democracy,"[42] in December 2020, Congress passed a law legalizing abortion. Another protracted battle culminated with the legalization of same-sex marriage in 2010, followed by additional pro-LGBTQ+ laws. Activists achieved legislation against domestic violence in the 1990s and created groups to assist victims.[43] These notions of emancipation far eclipsed the Victory Board's.

The Victory Board issued feminist appeals based on the notions of women as citizens and mothers. Well into the 2000s, popular women's movements still identified themselves with motherhood but not feminism, most notably the Mothers of the Plaza de Mayo. Yet their feminist consciousness grew over time. In the economic crisis of 2002–2003, women who protested the lack of food for their loved ones also denounced sexism. Women caring for their families and communities during the COVID-19 pandemic, organizing soup kitchens, providing health services, and agitating for access to water and sanitation, call themselves *feministas villeras* (shantytown feminists). They attach #NiUnaMenos (Not One Woman Less) signs decrying femicide below their violet-hued (the feminist color) soup pots. One woman stated, "'In reality we have always been feminists . . . we just did not see ourselves as such.'" Theirs is a "territorial" feminism that represents the women and LGBTQ+ inhabitants of the impoverished communities that ring Buenos Aires and other large cities, who face hunger, unemployment, poor health, domestic violence, and racial, class, and gender discrimination.[44] In its broad sweep it is reminiscent of Popular Front Pan-American feminism, although lower-class rather than privileged women initiated it. Argentina's recurring economic problems and the pandemic have stimulated a feminism tinged with maternalism, as was the Victory Board's, but in more radical intersectional ways.

The Victory Board's history indicates that during emergencies, such as World War II, relations of solidarity can cross class divides. This was also true for women in 2002–2003. As Elizabeth Borland and Barbara Sutton noted, "The crisis brought people with diverse agendas and backgrounds together and meant that activists had to handle tensions and negotiate their visions, political histories and social locations." Building coalitions entails painful compromises, but it can yield results, such as the Victory Board's aid to the Allies and recent protesters' attainment of household subsidies and legalization of abortion, among other measures.[45]

Feminists have continued the Victory Board's pattern of engagement in national assemblies and international networks. Having absorbed feminist ideas in exile, women returning to Argentina and the region joined these nonofficial encounters. "Of all classes, ethnic groups, sexual orientations," members of feminist movements, political parties, and grassroots organizations have met annually since 1986 in the Encuentros Nacionales de Mujeres, held throughout Argentina. These very diverse women have discussed a wide range of problems and possible solutions. Some Encuentros have occurred in conservative locations, where they have spread understanding of sexual and reproductive rights. Similarly, starting in 1981, a broad spectrum of women has gathered in the Encuentros Feministas Latinoamericanos y del Caribe to discuss the region's multifarious feminisms and LGBTQ+ issues, contest norms constructed by men, learn from each other's struggles, and form networks and common agendas. The debates at both sets of gatherings have often been contentious yet fruitful. Edelman particularly commended the Encuentros Feministas Latinoamericanos y del Caribe for bridging class, ethnic, racial, and urban/rural divides, which the Victory Board, to which she had belonged, had attempted. She also praised these forums for constructing feminisms that explicitly addressed classism, racism (based on skin color), and imperialism.[46] This the Victory Board did not do, unlike its Panamanian contemporaries.[47]

The board and later groups faced the challenge of autonomy. Evita's control over the PPF deprived members of independence, but in return they joined a powerful political coalition, accessed educational and social services, and some were elected to office. The main issue for other women, however, was the knotty relationship with male-ruled political formations.

For the Victory Board, this meant the Communist Party connection. As women increasingly joined political groups after 1947, and especially leftist ones, concerns over double militancy grew. Feminists believed that leftist parties and movements assigned much greater importance to class struggle than to the women's struggle. Those who belonged to leftist organizations faced rejection from other feminists and male comrades alike.[48] The Encuentros Feministas Latinoamericanos y del Caribe frequently discussed such difficulties. Years before, Ratto's expulsion from the Communist Party already indicated this predicament.

Feijoó and Nari declared that "the struggles of women against the dictatorship [1976–1983] have been understood as a novel phenomenon, but they are part of a historical tradition of women's struggles that can be traced back to the later part of the nineteenth century."[49] The Victory Board's battle against despotism and women's exclusion fits into this tradition. Argentina has served and continues to serve in the forefront of feminist organizing in the Americas,[50] and the Victory Board is part of that history. It foreshadowed the dynamic movements that to this day have advocated and practiced democracy, pluralism, transnational connections, human rights, consciousness-raising, and women's emancipation and empowerment, often mixing maternalism and citizenship claims in the process. Then as now, feminism has combined with broader efforts for change.

Lessons for Today

Theodor Adorno claimed that fascism still lurked in liberal democracies after 1945; until these societies achieved equality, they could once again generate such movements.[51] Indeed, we are living in a moment when rightist white-supremacist populisms that approximate fascism are sweeping the globe.[52] As during the Victory Board's lifetime, gender has been fundamental for extreme rightists, most of whom still extol the heterosexual male-headed household as a microcosm of the ideal hierarchical society and expect women to abide by it.[53] The Victory Board's focus on democracy, women's rights, multiculturalism, and resistance seems as vital as in the 1940s, despite changes in the broader context.

Therefore, it is fitting to end this study by reflecting on the relevance of its experience for antifascist women today. A contemporary US activist urged constructing "'democratic space[s] where people can get involved for the first time . . . [to] create a culture of solidarity and respect.'"[54] By adopting these practices, the Victory Board ushered political newcomers into its ranks and formed a massive movement.

The Victory Board praised and courted women of many different backgrounds, which exemplified its democratic pluralist vision. Diversity and inclusiveness were among its strengths, yet they could produce dilemmas. Then and now, unifying a broad base involves grueling negotiation and accommodation. The board's most significant accommodation was to prioritize winning the war overseas over addressing poverty at home. Instead of emphasizing its political version of democracy, which lost out to Perón's economic version, it would have been better to hitch the two together effectively. This teaches us that movements that downplay inequality do so at their peril. They must push for economic betterment and a broad notion of democracy, even if they lack the power to implement them. Unwittingly echoing Alicia Moreau (see chapter 4), an antifascist activist recently exclaimed, "'Don't lose track of what we're fighting *for*!'"[55] One also must try to understand the people on the other side—in the Victory Board's case, Peronist workers; in the current US case, disinherited whites—rather than simply denigrate them.[56]

Despite these liabilities, the Victory Board's clear project served as a rallying force. This trait has facilitated the success of current women's movements, like the US #MeToo and the Argentine #NiUnaMenos. It helped enable the first to spread throughout the world and the second throughout Latin America. Hopefully, the Victory Board's experience will help inform the rise of democratic, popular, innovative, and feminist antifascisms. In this manner, people will once more remember this pathbreaking Argentine women's organization.

APPENDIX

Table 1. Victory Board Branches[a]

	Local Acción Argentina Chapter[b]	1st Convention[c]	Provincial[d]	2nd Convention[e]	3rd Convention[f]
I. Federal Capital Secretariats					
Almagro	—	✓	—	✓	—
Barracas	—	—	—	✓	—
Belgrano	✓	✓	—	✓	✓
Boca	—	✓	—	—	—
Caballito	✓	✓	—	—	—
Cangallo (Centro)	✓	✓	—	—	✓
Constitucion	—	✓	—	—	—
Chacarita-Colegiales	—	✓	—	—	—
Flores	—	✓	—	—	—
La Paternal	✓	✓	—	—	—
Liniers	—	✓	—	—	—
Mataderos (1945–)	—	—	—	—	—
Nueva Pompeya	—	✓	—	—	✓[g]
Once	—	✓	—	—	✓
Palermo	✓	✓	—	—	✓
Parque Patricios	✓	✓	—	—	✓[g]
Parque Chacabuco	—	✓	—	—	—
Villa Crespo	✓	✓	—	—	—
Villa Devoto	✓	—	—	—	✓
Villa Lugano	✓	—	—	—	—
Villa Luro	✓	—	—	—	—
Villa Urquiza	✓	✓	—	—	—

II. Buenos Aires Province					
Adrogue (1945–)	✓	—	—	—	✓
Avellaneda	✓	—	✓	—	—
Bahia Blanca	✓	✓	✓	—	—
Banfield	✓	✓	✓ [h]	—	—
Berazátegui	—	✓	✓	—	—
Berisso	✓	✓	✓	✓	—
Bernal	✓	—	—	—	—
Boulogne (1945–)	—	—	—	—	—
Bragado	✓	—	✓	—	—
Chacabuco (1945–)	—	—	—	—	✓
Ciudadela	—	—	—	—	—
Coronel Pringles	—	—	—	—	—
Delfín Huergo [i]	—	—	—	✓	—
Dock Sud	—	—	—	—	—
Ensenada	✓	—	✓	—	—
Haedo (1946–)	—	—	—	—	—
Ing. White	—	✓	✓	—	—
La Florida	—	—	✓	—	—
La Plata	✓	✓	✓	✓	—
Lanús	✓	✓	✓	—	—
Lobería	✓	—	✓	—	—
Lomas de Zamora	✓	—	—	✓ [h]	✓
Mar del Plata	✓	✓	✓	—	—
Mechita	✓	—	✓	—	—
Miramar	✓	—	—	—	—
Morón	—	—	✓	—	—
Munro	—	—	—	—	—
Necochea	✓	✓	✓	—	—
Palermo	—	—	✓	—	—
Pasteur	—	Adhered	—	—	—
Patagones	—	—	✓	—	—
Punta Alta	—	✓	✓	—	—
Ramos Mejía	✓	✓	✓	—	✓
Rivera, BA	—	—	✓	—	—
San Fernando	✓	—	—	✓	—

San Isidro (1945–)	—	—	—	—	—
San Martin	✓	—	—	—	—
Sarandí	—	—	✓	—	—
6 del Septiembre, BA	✓	—	✓	—	—
Tandil	✓	✓	✓	—	✓
Trenque Lauquen	✓	—	—	—	—
Tolosa	✓	—	—	—	—
Tres Arroyos	✓	✓	✓	—	—
Valentín Alsina	—	—	—	—	—
25 de Mayo	—	—	✓	—	—
Villa Ballester	—	✓	✓	—	—
Villa Lynch	—	—	—	—	—
Villa Mitre	—	—	—	—	—
Villa Sarmiento	—	—	—	—	—
III. Other Provinces and Territories					
Chaco Territory					
Charata	✓	—	—	—	—
Las Breñas	✓	—	—	✓	—
Machagai	✓	Adhered	—	—	—
Presidente Roque Sáenz Peña	✓	✓	—	—	—
Resistencia	—	✓	—	✓	✓
Villa Angela	—	—	—	—	—
Comodoro Rivadavia Territory					
C. Rivadavia[j]	✓	✓	—	✓	✓
Córdoba Province					
Córdoba	✓	✓	—	✓	✓
Cosquín	—	✓	—	—	—
Río Cuarto	✓	✓	—	✓	✓
San Francisco	✓	✓	—	—	—
Corrientes Province					
Corrientes	✓	—	—	✓	✓
Goya	—	Adhered	—	—	—
Entre Ríos Province					
Basavilbaso	✓	✓	—	—	—

Concepción del Uruguay	✓	—	—	—	✓
Concordia	—	—	—	—	—
Diamante	—	—	—	—	✓
Galarza	—	—	—	—	—
Gilbert-Escrina	✓	—	—	✓	—
Gualeguay	—	—	—	—	—
Gualeguaychú	—	—	—	—	—
La Capilla	—	—	—	—	—
Paraná	✓	✓	—	—	✓
Villa Clara	—	Adhered	—	—	—
Villa Domínguez	—	—	—	—	—
Jujuy Province					
Jujuy	—	✓	—	—	—
Mendoza Province					
General Alvear	—	—	—	—	—
Maipú	—	—	—	—	—
Mendoza	✓	✓	—	—	—
San Rafael	✓	—	—	—	✓
Misiones Territory					
Oberá	✓	✓	—	✓	—
Picada Sueca	—	—	—	—	—
Río Negro Territory					
(Fuerte) General Roca	✓	✓	—	—	—
Santa Fe Province					
Cañada de Gómez	✓	✓	—	—	—
Casilda	✓	—	—	—	—
Gálvez	—	—	—	—	—
Laguna Paiva	—	✓	—	—	—
Las Palmeras	—	✓	—	—	—
Moisés Ville	—	✓	—	✓	—
Palacios	—	✓	—	—	—
Rosario	✓	✓	—	—	—
San Cristóbal	✓	✓	—	—	—
Santa Fe	✓	✓	—	✓	—
Villa Ana	✓	✓	—	—	—
Villa Constitución	—	—	—	—	—

Villa Diego	—	—	—	—	—
Villa Guillermina	✓	✓	—	—	—
San Luis Province					
Mercedes (1945–)	—	—	—	—	✓
San Luis (1945–)	—	—	—	—	✓
Santiago del Estero Province					
Santiago del Estero	—	—	—	—	—
Tucumán Province					
Tucumán	✓	—	—	✓	✓
Tafí Viejo	—	—	—	—	—

Notes: [a] The neighborhood subcommittees for Córdoba (3), La Plata (2), Resistencia (4), Rosario (6), Santa Fe (2), and Tucumán (1) are not included. Sources for this table include Bisso, *Acción Argentina*, 351–58; Junta, *Primera convención*; *Mujeres en la ayuda*; *La Hora*; and other newspapers. Blank spaces/dashes indicate that the Acción Argentina had no chapter in this location (column 1), and/or the chapter did not attend this convention.

[b] A check mark indicates if there was an Acción Argentina chapter in this locality, according to Bisso, *Acción Argentina*, 351–58.

[c] A check mark indicates it sent delegates to first national convention of 1942 or stated it could not do so (adhered). This is the most accurate list of all the board's conventions, because the attending chapters were mentioned in the proceedings (Junta, *Primera convención nacional*, 5–8).

[d] A check mark indicates it sent delegates to the Buenos Aires provincial convention of 1942.

[e] A check mark indicates it sent delegates to the second national convention of 1943.

[f] A check mark indicates it sent delegates to the third national convention of 1946. The Victory Board claimed that representatives from Greater Buenos Aires and thirty-five chapters in the interior attended, but the press mentioned only a small number.

[g] As Patricios-Pompeya chapter.

[h] As Banfield-Lomas chapter.

[i] This chapter eventually may have melded into the Rivera one.

[j] Until 1943 it formed part of Chubut; from 1943 to 1955 it pertained to the Comodoro Rivadavia territory.

Table 2. Class Composition of Core Activists, by Locality[a]

Locality	Upper/Upper Middle[b]		Middle[c]		Working[d]		Total Known[e]	Total Surveyed[f]
	No.	%	No.	%	No.	%		
Buenos Aires	19	27	29	41	22	31	70	99
Córdoba	13	42	16	52	2	6	31	45
Oberá	2	18	6[g]	55	3	27	11	14
Resistencia	4	12	25	76	4	12	33	50
Santa Fe	12	28	30	70	1	2	43	58
Tafí Viejo	0	0	2	20	8	80	10	15
Tucumán	8	44	9	50	1	6	18	27
Totals	58	19	117	38	41	13	216	308

Notes: Percentages may not add up to 100 because of rounding.

[a] Information in this and tables 3–6 and 8–9 comes from the interviews, consultations, and biographical sections in the bibliography, as well as newspapers and their social pages.

[b] Upper/upper middle class means belonging to a distinguished family, as indicated by their inclusion in a social register or prestigious social club, their husbands' high professional ranking, and/or the judgment of local informants. Informants alternately characterized some women as upper- or upper-middle class, so I combine these categories.

[c] This category stretches from lower middle to middle class, and it depended on ownership or family ownership of a small business, professional status, and/or the husbands' professional status.

[d] I included laborers, wives of laborers, a few who had only recently moved up to middle-class status, and employees as members of the working class. There were four employees from the federal capital and two from Córdoba. On their vague class status, see text.

[e] Number of those for whom information is available. The percentages in this table refer to the proportion of women for whom there is data.

[f] Total number of persons surveyed.

[g] The husbands or families of some of these women had plots of land, which at times only allowed a precarious existence. Nevertheless, they do not fit in the worker category.

Table 3. Occupations[a] of Core Activists in the Federal Capital

Occupation	No.	% of Total for Whom There Is Information
Artist	2	3
Business[b]	2	3
Employee	4	6
Lawyer/Jurist	1	2
Government Official	1	2
Laborer[c]	22	35
Medical Doctor/Professor of Medicine	4	6
Midwife	1	2
Musician	2	3
Nurse	1	2
Photographer	1	2
Publisher	1	2
Teacher[d]	11	17
University Student	1	2
Unspecified "Doctor"[e]	4	6
Writer[f]	5	8
Total	63	
Total Unknown[g]	36	
Total Surveyed	99	

Notes: Percentages may not add up to 100 because of rounding.

[a] In some cases, the person did not derive an income from this activity.

[b] Women who owned a business or worked in a family enterprise.

[c] Includes a dressmaker, seamstress, and four employees.

[d] Includes primary (*maestra*) and secondary school (*profesora*) teachers.

[e] Persons who held unspecified doctorates.

[f] Includes two writers who also were artists as well as a writer who was also a lecturer.

[g] Number of those for whom no information is available. Often this indicates they were homemakers, laborers, or both.

Table 4. Occupations of Core Activists[a] outside Buenos Aires, by Locality

Occupations	Córdoba		Oberá		Resistencia		Santa Fe		Tafí Viejo		Tucumán		Total	
	No.	%[b]	No.	%	No.	%	No.	%	No.	%	No.	%	No.	%
Biochemist	—	—	—	—	1	5	—	—	—	—	—	—	1	2
Business[c]	—	—	7	77	5	23	—	—	1	33	1	20	14	22
Employee	2	14	—	—	—	—	—	—	—	—	—	—	2	3
Farmer	—	—	2	22	—	—	—	—	—	—	—	—	2	3
Laborer[d]	—	—	—	—	—	—	—	—	1	33	—	—	1	2
Lawyer	—	—	—	—	1	5	1	8	—	—	—	—	2	3
Medical Doctor/ Dentist	2	14	—	—	2	22	1	8	—	—	—	—	5	8
Pharmacist	—	—	—	—	—	—	—	—	—	—	1	20	1	2
Teacher[e]	8	57	—	—	13	59	10	83	1	33	3	60	35	54
Univ. Student	2	14	—	—	—	—	—	—	—	—	—	—	2	2
Total[f]	14		9		22		12		3		5		65	
Unknown[g]	31		5		28		46		12		22		144	
Total Surveyed	45		14		50		58		15		27		209	

Notes: Percentages may not add up to 100 because of rounding. Dashes on the table indicate that none of the people, for whom there is information, specified having one of those occupations.

[a] In some cases, the person did not derive an income from this activity.

[b] The percentages in this table refer to the proportion of women for whom there is data.

[c] Women who owned a business or worked in a family enterprise.

[d] A dressmaker.

[e] Includes two women who gave private lessons, in language and music, respectively.

[f] Total number of persons for whom there is information.

[g] Number of those for whom no information is available.

Table 5. Extent of Formal Education, by Locality

Locality	0-Little		Completed 1°[a]		Some 2°		Some 3°		Total Known[b]	Unknown[c]
	No.	%[d]	No.	%	No.	%	No.	%	No.	No.
Buenos Aires	3	11	—	—	7	26	17	63	27	72
Córdoba	—	—	1[e]	7	7	50	6	43	14	31
Oberá	1	50	2[f]	50	—	—	—	—	4	10
Resistencia	—	—	1	6	9	53	7	41	17	33
Santa Fe	—	—	3	15	14	70[g]	3	15	20	38
Tafí Viejo	—	—	2	100	—	—	—	—	2	13
Tucumán	—	—	3	27	4	36	4	36	11	16
Total	5	5	12	13	41	43	37	39	95	213

Notes: Percentages may not add up to 100 because of rounding.

Blank spaces indicate that I found no persons in these categories.

[a] 1° refers to primary, 2° to secondary, and 3° to tertiary (university or *profesorados*, which prepare persons to teach secondary school in a particular subject).

[b] Total number of persons for whom there is information.

[c] Number of those for whom no information is available.

[d] The percentages in this table refer to the proportion of the women on whom there is data.

[e] Later on this woman completed secondary school and attended a university.

[f] Later on one of these women took university art courses.

[g] One of these persons passed a university entrance exam (*bachillerato*).

Table 6. Ethnic/National Origins in Two Towns

Origins	Oberá		Tafí Viejo	
	No.	% [a]	No.	%
Czech	—	—	8	62
Eastern Europe[b]	8	67	—	—
Paraguayan	2	17	—	—
Spanish	—	—	4	31
Swedish	2	17	—	—
Total	12		13	
Unknown[c]	2		2	
Total in Survey	14		15	

Notes: Percentages may not add up to 100 because of rounding.

Blank spaces indicate that I found no persons in these categories.

[a] Percentages in this table refer to the proportion of women for whom information is available.

[b] Eastern European (Russian, Ukrainian, Polish) Christian (Orthodox or Catholic).

[c] Number of persons for whom no information is available.

Table 7. Victory Board Chapters Located in or Near Jewish Agricultural Zones

Buenos Aires Province

Delfín Huergo[a]
Rivera

Chaco Territory

Charata
Las Breñas
Machagai
Presidente Roque Sáenz Peña

Entre Ríos Province

Basavilbaso
Concordia
Galarza
Gilbert-Escriña
La Capilla
Villa Clara
Villa Domínguez

Santa Fe Province

Las Palmeras
Moisés Ville
Palacios
San Cristóbal

Notes: [a] This chapter may have combined eventually with the one in Rivera.

The information in this table comes from Junta de la Victoria, *Primera convención*; *Mujeres en la Ayuda*; *La Hora*; and other newspapers.

Table 8. Core Activists of Jewish Origins

	Number of Jews	Total Members Surveyed	Jews as % of Total Surveyed
Buenos Aires	16	99	16
Córdoba	11	45	24
Oberá	0	14	0
Resistencia	20	50	40
Santa Fe	17	58	29
Tafí Viejo	1	15	6
Tucumán	5	27	19
Total	70	308	23

Table 9. Political Ties[a] of Core Activists, by Locality

Party	Buenos Aires		Córdoba		Oberá		Resistencia		Santa Fe		Tafí Viejo[b]		Tucumán		Total	
	No.	%[c]	No.	%	No.	%	No.	%	No.	%	No.	%	No.	%	No.	%
Communist[d]	21	78	12	41	5	100	4	33	6	35	—	—	3	25	51	50
Concordancia[e]	1	4	3	10	—	—	—	—	1	6	—	—	—	—	5	5
Progressive Democrat (PDP)	—	—	—	—	—	—	—	—	5	29	—	—	—	—	5	5
Socialist Worker (PSO)	1	4	—	—	—	—	—	—	—	—	—	—	—	—	1	1
Socialist	3	11	—	—	—	—	3	25	2	12	—	—	2	17	10	10
Radical Civic Union (UCR)	1	4	14	48	—	—	5	42	3	18	—	—	7	58	30	29
Total	27		29		5		12		17		—		12		102	
Unknown[f]	72		16		9		38		41		15		15		206	
Total in Survey	99		45		14		50		58		15		27		308	

Notes: Percentages may not add up to 100 because of rounding.

[a] This category includes women who affiliated with a particular party, publicly expressed support for a particular party or belonged to a women's group that did so, and those whose families and/or husbands pertained to a party.

[b] No information is available for this Victory Board chapter. However, eight women were daughters of skilled Czech workers, among whom Socialists and Communists were very active.

[c] The percentages in this table refer to the proportion of women in that chapter for whom information is available.

[d] Party member or sympathizer.

[e] Conservative parties that formed part of the ruling Concordancia alliance, including the National Democrats and Radical Civic Union Anti-Personalists.

[f] Number of persons for whom no information is available, some of whom may have been nonpartisan.

NOTES

Introduction: Gendering Antifascism

1. Lang, interview, 2000. Lang and Braslavsky supplied written consent for their interviews; all others I interviewed gave oral consent.

2. Deutsch, *Crossing Borders*.

3. *La Hora*, September 14, 1941, 5.

4. On the Victory Board, see Deutsch, *Crossing Borders*, 185–89, and "Argentine Women against Fascism"; Valobra, "Las comunistas argentinas," 74–75; "Formación de cuadros," 142–46, 148; "La UMA en marcha," 160–62, passim; and "Partidos, tradiciones y estrategias," 68–73. See also Prutsch, *Creating Good Neighbors?*, 428–30; Barrancos, *Mujeres en la sociedad*, 176–78; Del Franco, *Mujeres, ese fuego, esas luchas*, 26–32; Carlson, *¡Feminismo!*, 180, 184–86; Rein, *Franco-Perón Alliance*, 150–52, 286n39. Bisso, ed., *El antifascismo argentino*, contains Victory Board documents on 148–52, 162–68, 218–24, 228–29, 366. On Feminine Action for Victory, see Deutsch, "Hands across the Río de la Plata"; De Giorgi, "Entre la lucha," 218–19.

5. Marino, *Feminism for the Americas*; Antezana-Pernet, "Mobilizing Women in the Popular Front Era," later published as *El MEMCH*; Gaviola Artigas et al., *Queremos votar en las próximas elecciones*, 68–72, 81–83, 88–93; Rojas Mira and Jiles Moreno, *Epistolario emancipador del MEMCH*, and "La extraordinaria"; Montero Miranda and Rubio Soto, "El Movimiento pro-Emancipación"; Rosemblatt, *Gendered Compromises*; Esperanza Tuñón Pablos, *Mujeres que se organizan*; Oikión Solano, "Mujeres en el Partido Comunista Mexicano," 154–63; Olcott, "Center Cannot Hold," and *Revolutionary Women*. One exception is Marino, "Anti-Fascist Feminismo."

6. Lambe, *No Barrier Can Contain It*.

7. Seidman, *Transatlantic Antifascisms*, 1; Copsey, "Preface," xx.

8. Kirk and McElligott, "Introduction," 2.

9. García et al., ed., *Rethinking Antifascism*.

10. García, "Transnational History," 566, 569. Elsewhere in this issue, see

Acle-Kreysing, "Shattered Dreams," 668; she belied this notion in "Antifascismo." With one exception, the papers presented at "Anti-Fascism as a Transnational Phenomenon: New Perspectives of Research," Saarbrücken, October 2014, focused on connections within Europe. Seidman, *Transatlantic Antifascisms*, discussed contacts and comparisons between Europe and the United States.

11. Among other works, see Fernández Aceves, "Belén Sárraga Hernández"; Domínguez Prats, "La actividad de las mujeres republicanas"; Lida, "Redes atlánticas de solidaridad"; Von Mentz and Radkau, "Notas torno al exilio"; Newton, "Indifferent Sanctuary"; Pasolini, "Antifascist Climate." Sometimes it is difficult to distinguish between exiles escaping fascism and immigrants who came earlier or for nonpolitical reasons. Works that may combine the two include Newton, *"Ducini, Prominenti, Antifascisti"*; Huernos, "Las redes americanas"; Bertonha, "Anarquistas italianos nas Américas"; Fanesi, "Italian Antifascism and the Garibaldine Tradition." That Argentina and southern Brazil were immigrant societies in which European newcomers mingled with native-born inhabitants is a further complication.

12. Braskén et al., "Introduction," 1.

13. See Braskén et al., eds, *Anti-Fascism in a Global Perspective*, and, among other works, Louro, *Comrades against Imperialism*; Framke, "Political Humanitarianism in the 1930s"; Ortiz, "Spain! Why?"; Fronczak, "Local People's Global Politics"; Robinson, *On Racial Capital.*

14. Flores, *Mexican Revolution in Chicago*, 93–116.

15. Tannoury-Karam, "No Place for Neutrality"; Braskén, ed., *Antifascism in a Global Perspective*; Merithew, "'O Mother Race,'" 9–10, 13–14.

16. Lynn, "Women on the March," "Antifascism and the Fear of Pronatalism," "Fascism and the Family," and "Socialist Feminism and Triple Oppression." See also Bergin, "African American Internationalists and Anti-Fascism"; Vials, *Haunted by Hitler*, and "Red Feminists and Methodist Missionaries"; Weigand, *Red Feminism*; McDuffie, *Sojourning for Freedom.*

17. Nállim, "Del antifascismo al antiperonismo," and *Transformations and Crisis of Liberalism in Argentina*; Bisso, *Acción Argentina*; García Sebastiani, ed., *Fascismo y antifascismo*; Pasolini, *Los marxistas*; Zanca, *Cristianos antifascistas*. Nállim, Bisso, and Zanca discussed several women; the following concentrated on them: Sitman, *Victoria Ocampo y Sur*; Valobra, "El particular ideario"; Clementi, *María Rosa Oliver*; Becerra, "Maternidad y ciudadanía en la Argentina"; Zanca, "Dios y libertad"; Bordegaray, "Antifascismo, género e historia," and "Luchas antifascistas y trayectorias generizadas."

18. Aside from Casas, "La guerra civil española"; Ardanaz, "Pelando papas," and "Maternalismo y política en el antifascismo argentino"; Rein, "Trans-National Struggle."

19. See note 4.

20. Regarding Argentine aid to Spain, see note 18; on the rest, see Lambe,

No Barrier Can Contain It; Marino, *Feminism for the Americas*, and "Anti-Fascist Feminismo"; Flores, *Mexican Revolution in Chicago*, 93–116; Zubillaga, *Niños de la guerra*. See also Pasolini, *Los marxistas*; Celentano, "Ideas e intelectuales."

21. On South-North exchanges, see Hatsky and Mor, "Latin American Transnational Solidarities"; Marino, *Feminism for the Americas*; Lambe, *No Barrier Can Contain It*.

22. Barrancos, *Mujeres en la sociedad*, 176–78; Valobra, "Formación de cuadros." Marino, *Feminism for the Americas*, mentioned the Victory Board, 173–74, but focused on antifascist feminists in other Latin American countries.

23. Klapper, "Those by Whose Side," 640.

24. Among numerous works on Argentina and the Southern Cone, see Lavrin, *Women, Feminism, and Social Change*; Nari, *Políticas de maternidad*, and "Maternidad política y feminismo"; Bouvard, *Revolutionizing Motherhood*; Guy, *White Slavery and Mothers Alive and Dead*; Sapriza, "Historia reciente de un sujeto"; Mooney, *Politics of Motherhood*. See also Barrancos, "Maternalismo"; Di Marco, "Maternidad social"; Deutsch, "A Labor Filled with Love."

The nuanced approaches offered by Chase, *Revolution within the Revolution*, and Marino, "Transnational Pan-American Feminism," have informed my views, as have my conversations with these authors. Also see Rosemblatt, *Gendered Compromises*, and Olcott, *Revolutionary Women in Postrevolutionary Mexico*. I contested maternalism in "New School Lecture."

25. Lambe, *No Barrier Can Contain It*, 3–7, passim; Valdivia Ortiz de Zárate et al., *Su revolución contra nuestra revolución*; and Traverso, *Fire and Blood*, are exceptions.

26. Deutsch, *Las derechas*, 207, 245–46; Finchelstein, *Ideological Origins of the Dirty War*. On such fascist coalitions, see Blinkhorn, ed., *Fascists and Conservatives*, and Mayer's *Dynamics of Counterrevolution*. Spektorowski, *Origins of Argentina's Revolution of the Right*, 7, 9, and passim; and Buchrucker, *Nacionalismo y peronismo*, 230–34, concluded that the Nationalists were fascists. Finchelstein described them as "clericofascists" in *Transatlantic Fascism*, and as fascists, plain and simple, in *Ideological Origins*. Navarro Gerassi, *Los nacionalistas*; Rock, *Authoritarian Argentina*; and Newton, *'Nazi Menace' in Argentina*, did not regard them as fascists.

27. Copsey, "Preface," xiv, xv, regarded antifascism as more nebulous than fascism.

28. Edelman, interview, 2009.

29. De Haan, "La Federación Democrática Internacional de Mujeres," and Mooney, "Fighting Fascism and Forging New Political Activism," 54. See also chapter 5 of this volume.

30. Oliver, *Mi fe es el hombre*; Edelman, *Banderas, pasiones, camaradas*.

31. Mathias, "Long-Distance Charisma."

32. Sosa de Newton, *Diccionario biográfico de mujeres argentinas*, and De Berte-

ro, *Quién es ella*, are the only biographical dictionaries of women I have found. See note 35.

33. Del Franco, *Mujeres, ese fuego, esas luchas*, 26–32, handled these problems by focusing on a few working-class neighborhoods where she had long-standing contacts.

34. I thank Graciela and Héctor Busaniche for generously organizing this collective meeting, and sociologist Hélène Gutkowski, whose skillful use of focus groups served as a model.

35. Such sources plus biographical dictionaries and women's biographies are found in the biographical section of the bibliography. Also see the interviews and consultations sections.

36. Alberto and Elena, eds., *Rethinking Race*.

37. Cohen and O'Connor, eds., *Comparison and History*; Seigel, "Beyond Compare."

38. The quote borrows from the title of Scobie's classic book, *Argentina: A City and a Nation*. See also Sandra Fernández, "Olga Cossettini," 135–36.

39. Ardanaz, "Con el puño en alto," 122, and the panel on "Interior History: Rethinking Brazil from the Inside," American Historical Association meeting, New York, NY, January 5, 2020, helped me conceptualize this point.

40. García et al., "Beyond Revisionism," 5–6; Olcott, *Revolutionary Women in Postrevolutionary Mexico*, 6 and passim.

Chapter 1: A Heritage of Transnational Democratic Struggles in Argentina and the World, 1914–1941

1. *La Hora*, May 22, 1942, 8. The Declaration is discussed below. In 1914 newspapers cost ten cents and film tickets between twenty and fifty cents; see Rubinzal, "El caso."

2. Fronczak, "Local People's Global Politics"; and Gottlieb, "'Broken Friendships and Vanished Loyalties,'" highlight antifascist involvement in foreign affairs.

3. For this and the following paragraph, see Tato, "La contienda," and "La movilización"; and email communication, March 9, 2021. See also *La Voz del Interior*, November 6, 1918.

4. Deutsch, *Counterrevolution in Argentina*. I describe fascism in chapter 2.

5. For this and the following paragraph, see Deutsch, *Las derechas*, chap. 10; Finchelstein, *Fascismo, liturgia e imaginario*, and *Transatlantic Fascism*; Camarero, *A la conquista*, xxix, 157, 161–72; López Cantera, "Criminalizar al rojo."

6. Fernández de Ulivarri, "Trabajadores, sindicatos y política," chap. 8; *El Alba*, February 26, 1935, 1, September 10, 1935, 1; *La Vanguardia*, February 22, 1935, 2.

7. See, for example, Vials, *Haunted by Hitler*, 28; Lambe, *No Barrier Can Contain It*, 12.

8. Fanesi, *El exilio antifascista*, and "El antifascismo italiano"; Pasolini, "Anti-

fascismo italiano, antifascismo argentino"; Grillo, "El antifascismo italiano"; Newton, "*Ducini, Prominenti, Antifascisti,*" 54–57, passim; Huernos, "El Consejo Nacional Italiano," and "Italia Libre y sus relaciones." On Italian Fascist influence, see
Finchelstein, *Transatlantic Fascism*; and Prislei, *Los orígenes del fascismo argentino.*

9. *La Protesta*, December 1938, 2; *Vida Femenina*, June 15, 1936, 41; Fernández de Ullivarri, "Trabajadores, sindicatos y política," 210.

10. *La Protesta*, November 1937, 1.

11. *La Protesta*, February 1937, 1.

12. *La Obra*, April 1937, 1.

13. *La Protesta*, November 2, 1930, 1–2.

14. Deutsch, "New School Lecture," 100–103.

15. *La Vanguardia*, October 28, 1933, 10, February 23, 1934, 12; *El Litoral*,
April 30, 1935, 3; *El Alba*, January 1, 1935, 2, July 30, 1935, 1; Pasquali, "Sin voto
pero con voz," 3–6; Deutsch, *Crossing Borders*, 178–81. The comité may have been
connected to transnational efforts against antisemitism; see *El congreso de la solidaridad*. On the PSO's origins, see Ilana Martínez, "Trayectorias de una disidencia
partidaria."

16. Alvaro Guillot Muñoz, Secretary General, Comité Contra el Racismo y el
Antisemitismo de la Argentina, to Oliver, December 9, 1940, box 3, folder 6, María
Rosa Oliver Papers, C0829, Department of Rare Books and Special Collections,
Princeton University Library, Princeton, NJ (Oliver Papers).

17. *Vida Femenina*, June 15, 1936, 41; Filer, interview.

18. *Revista del Consejo Nacional de Mujeres de la República Argentina*, June
25, 1915, 9–15; June-December 1937, 19–20; July-September 1938, 7; October-
December 1938, 11–15. Argentine women's pacifism before 1945 received little attention until Manzoni's *Organizar la paz*, which I received too late to take into
account. Barrancos, *Mujeres en la sociedad*, 172, mentioned some efforts and called
for studies of them. On the CNM, see Vasallo, "Entre el conflicto"; Vignoli, "Cecilia Grierson" and "Intentos de adhesión." Ablard offered a gendered examination
of militarism and its opponents in "'The Barracks Receives Spoiled Children and
Returns Men.'"

19. Argentina Collective box, Folder Confederación Femenina de la Paz Americana, CDGB, Swarthmore College Peace Collection (SCPC), Swarthmore, PA;
Máxima Olmos de Giménez to Heloise Brainerd, August 1936, box 22, folder
1934–1936, and September 1, 1938, box 22, folder Correspondence of Brainerd
with . . . Argentina and Chile, 1937–1938, both in Women's International League
for Peace and Freedom Papers, United States, A,4: Pt. 1, DG043 (WILPF Records),
SCPC.

20. *La Vanguardia*, November 9, 1931, clipping, box 14, folder 46, Frances
R. Grant Papers, Special Collections and University Archives, Rutgers University
Libraries (Grant Papers), New Brunswick, NJ; *La Vanguardia*, June 6, 1931, 8;
Claridad, August 12, 1932, 9.

21. *Ahora*, September 30, 1932. On Samatán's life, see Pasquali, "Marta Samatán"; Coudannes, "Tradición y cambio social"; *Marta Samatán*; Escobar, "Marta Elena Samatán." See also Pasolini, *Los marxistas*, 36.

22. *La Vanguardia*, September 2 1934, 3; *Mujeres de América*, May-June 1934; January-February 1935; July-August 1935; *El Alba*, June 18, 1935, 1; Pasquali, "Sin voto pero con voz."

23. *El Ideal*, July 4, 1934, clipping, caja 1, Sección Nazi-Fascismo, no. 4, Subfondo P. Luisi, Fondo Centro Republicano Español, Facultad de Humanidades y Ciencias de la Educación, Universidad de la República, Montevideo; Congreso Internacional de Mujeres contra la Guerra y el Fascismo, Paris, 1934, caja 256, carpeta 5, no. 19, Archivo Paulina Luisi, Archivo General de la Nación, Montevideo. See also, among other sources, Carle, "Women, Anti-Fascism and Peace in Interwar France," 306–8; Coons, "Gabrielle Duchêne," 128–29, 131–32; Fisher, *Romain Rolland and the Politics of Intellectual Engagement*, 147–70; Blasco Lisa, "El Comité Mundial de Mujeres"; Ceplair, *Under the Shadow*, 78–93; H. Senado, *Represión del Comunismo*, esp. 99–100. This last source contains Communist Party documents.

24. *New York Times*, August 5, 1934, 5; Sandi E. Cooper, "Pacifism, Feminism, and Fascism in Inter-War France"; Coons, "Gabrielle Duchêne"; Carle, "Women, Anti-Fascism and Peace in Interwar France"; Reynolds, *France between the Wars*, 194–97; Bruley, "Women against War and Fascism."

25. On Luisi, see *A Plateia*, October 23, 1935, 1, carpeta 1935, Colección Paulina Luisi, Archivo Literario, Departamento de Investigaciones, Biblioteca Nacional (Colección Luisi), Montevideo; Ehrick, *Shield of the Weak*; Cuadro Cawen, *Feminismos y política*; Sapriza, *Memorias de rebeldía*, 79–107; Marino, *Feminism for the Americas*. On Lamarque, see *Juventud Antifascista*, December 15 1934, courtesy of Laura Pasquali; *L'Humanité: journal socialiste quotidien, partí communiste français*, August 1, 1934, Bibliothèque Nationale de France, https://gallica.bnf .fr/ark:/12148/bpt6k4050832/f4.item.r=Nydia%20Lamarque.zoom, courtesy of Lowry Martin; "Presentación," and *Boletín del Comité Organizador del Congreso Antiguerrero Latinoamericano*, no. 1 (December 15, 1932), 1–4, microfilm reel 6, Centro de Documentación e Investigación de la Cultura de Izquierdas (CeDinCI), Buenos Aires. *Claridad*, December 10, 1932, 27, mentioned an Argentine branch of this committee. See also *Claridad*, October 22, 1932, 33–35, and March 25, 1933, 56–57; Ryle, "International Red Aid."

26. *Unidad*, January 1936, 1, 19, April 1936, 20, August 1937, September 1937; *Nueva Gaceta*, November 1942, 6, January 1943, 4; *La Prensa*, July 15, 1940, 10. See also Pasolini, *Los marxistas liberales*, 35–44, passim; Cane, "'Unity for the Defense of Culture'"; Bisso and Celentano, "La lucha antifascista"; Celentano, "Ideas e intelectuales en la formación"; Oliveira, "Antifascismo e o ideal de 'defesa da cultura.'" Bertúa, "'Si me quieres escribir,'" described other antifascist cultural producers.

27. On Amsterdam-Pleyel's ramifications in Chile and Uruguay, see Marino, *Feminism for the Americas*, 128–30; Vergara, *Memorias de una mujer irreverente*, 130. On MEMCH and FUPDM, see chapter 2.

28. For this and the next two paragraphs, see Telma Reca to Heloise Brainerd, January 30, 1936, and attached Agrupación Femenina Antiguerrera manifesto, n.d., box 22, folder Correspondence of Brainerd with persons in Argentina and Chile, 1937–1938, WILPF Records; and *U.M.A. 1947–1967*, 9, Miscellaneous Peace Material file, both in SCPC. See also Agrupación Femenina Antiguerrera, *La mujer argentina y sus derechos*; H. Senado, *Represión del Comunismo*, 206, 210; Del Franco, *Mujeres, ese fuego, esas luchas*, 16–18; *¡Mujeres!*, May 1937; *Vida Femenina*, June 15, 1936, 44; Edelman, *Banderas, pasiones, camaradas*, 28; Manzoni, "Antimilitarismo y antifascismo"; *Flecha*, December 30, 1935, 5.

29. Roniger and Senkman, "Fuel for Conspiracy."

30. Oliver, for example, did not; see chapter 5.

31. *¡Mujeres!*, April? 1937, 5–6, May 1937; Del Franco, *Mujeres, ese fuego, esas luchas*, 18; Hilton, *Who's Who in Latin America*, 67.

32. Rojas to Dr. Gregorio Bermann, May 11, 1936, Registrador Predilecto Cartas, Correspondencia 1935–1936, Archivo Gregorio Bermann, Biblioteca del Centro de Estudios Avanzados, Universidad Nacional de Córdoba (Archivo Bermann); Deodoro Roca to Nicolás Repetto and Enrique Dickman, September 14, 1935, Fondo de Archivo Nicolás Repetto, carpeta 30.101, CeDinCI; *Claridad*, December 1935, 32.

33. *Flecha*, November 14, 1935, 4, December 30, 1935, 5 (quote); Bergel, "*Flecha*." On the University Reform campaign, the larger context, and Aricó, see *Orientación*, November 5, 1947, clipping, Archivo Bermann; Tcach, "El reformismo; Walter, *Student Politics in Argentina*.

34. Reports of the Committee of Latin American Contacts, and of the Inter-American Committee, January 1936, box 1A, folder 1, Committees, 1920–1949, WILPF Records, microfilm reel 130:23, SCPC. See also *Liga Internacional de Mujeres Pro Paz y Libertad, Comité de las Américas*, and Ellen Star Brinton, various letters to Latin American women, 1934, all in box 12, folder General, Committees and Conferences, 1920–1959, Committee on the Americas, WILPF Records, SCPC; as well as *Freeport Journal-Standard*, February 17, 1941, clipping (quote), box 1, folder Heloise Brainerd Biographical Information, Heloise Brainerd Papers, CDG-A, SCPC; Brainerd, "Activities of the Inter-American Committee." On WILPF, see Rupp, *Worlds of Women*, 35, 126, passim; Schott, *Reconstructing Women's Thoughts*; Bussey and Tims, *Pioneers for Peace*; Foster, *Women for All Seasons*.

35. Extract from Mabel Vernon speech, 1939, and "People's Mandate to Governments," box 2, folder Programmatic Materials 1939; *El Amigo del Pueblo*, February 1, 1936, box 4, folder Clippings from Latin American Papers, 1935–1940 (contin. 2), and various in box 5, folder Press Clippings 1935–1949 (cont. 3), figure in *La Prensa*, August 1, 1936, box 5, folder Press Clippings 1935–1949 (cont. 5),

PM, Series A: General, and "Women of Prominence in the American Republics," n.d., box 12, folder Latin America, PM, General Correspondence Series B: DG 109, SCPC; *Vida Femenina*, November 15, 1936, 35, 46.

36. Máxima Olmos de Giménez to Brainerd, September 1, 1938, box 22, folder Correspondence . . . 1937–1938, WILPF Records; WILPF Records Section, Committee on the Americas, Carta Circular 5, June 30, 1939, WILPF Noticias box, DG 043, all in SCPC.

37. *Vida Femenina*, September 15, 1936, 41.

38. *New York Herald Tribune*, December 5, 1936.

39. *Pueblo F* (place unknown), November 1936, box 4, folder Clippings from Latin American Papers, 1935–1950 (contin. 2), PM, Series A, General: DG 109, SCPC. See also Conferencia Resolutions, box 63, folder 2, and assorted documents in box 63, folder 3, IACW Subseries A, Doris Stevens Papers, MC 546, Arthur and Elizabeth Schlesinger Library on the History of Women in America, Radcliffe Institute for Advanced Study, Harvard University, Cambridge, MA (Stevens Papers). On the AFA's role, see *Frente Único*, May 1936.

40. Marino, *Feminism for the Americas*, 141–59, 168, 236n32. See also Marino, "Marta Vergara"; *Frente Único*, May 1936, 27; *Claridad*, May 1938, 59–60; *Noticias Gráficas*, July 21, 1939, clipping, box 259, carpeta 5, no. 71, Archivo Luisi; Argentina Collective box, folder Federación Argentina de Mujeres por la Paz, CDGB; letters between Lapacó and Brainerd, box 22, folder Correspondence of Brainerd . . . 1937–1938, WILPF Records; *Noticias*, no. 7 (March 1940): 2, box WILPF Noticias, all in SCPC. See also Helen Hayes to Josephine Schain, October 7, 1938, and June 12, 1939, box 6, folder 20, Josephine Schain Papers, Sophia Smith Collection, Smith College (Schain Papers), Northampton, MA, courtesy of Katherine Marino; Expediente 801–36, vs. 82, Ezras Noschim, INV 4349, Central Archive for the History of the Jewish People, Jerusalem. (This collection has since been recataloged.) Haas described the World Youth Congress in *Fighting Authoritarianism*, 175–79.

41. *Vida Femenina*, April 15, 1936, 25–26, June 15, 1936, 44, September 15, 1935, 41, December 15, 1936, 16–18, 35–37; Vergara, *Memorias de una mujer irreverente*, 140–42; *Claridad*, May 1936, 95–96; *Inter-American Commission of Women Bulletin* (*IACW Bulletin*), March 1, 1937. See also Argentina Collective box, folder Conferencia Popular por la Paz de América, SCPC; *New York Times*, November 22, 1936, box 5, folder Press Clippings 1935–1949 (cont. 3), PM, Series A, General: DG 109, SCPC.

42. *Acción Femenina*, n.d., 4 (quote), 5, 27, Argentina Collective box, folder Conferencia Popular por la Paz de América, SCPC; García-Bryce, *Haya de la Torre*.

43. *Vida Femenina*, December 15, 1936, 17–18, 35–37; Marino, *Feminism for the Americas*, 134–38.

44. On Argentine feminism before 1945, see, among other works, Barrancos, *Mujeres en la sociedad* and *Inclusión/Exclusión*; Lavrin, *Women, Feminism, and So-*

cial Change; Carlson, *¡Feminismo!*; Guy, *White Slavery and Mothers Alive and Dead*; Hammond, *Women's Suffrage Movement*; Valobra, *Del hogar a las urnas* ; Vignoli, "Intentos de adhesión"; Palermo, "El sufragio femenino" and "Sufragio femenino y ciudadanía."

45. Asociación Argentina del Sufragio Femenino (AASF), *Estatutos*, box 60, folder 17; Partido Argentino Feminista Independiente, "Bases," n.d., box 61, folder 2; *El Diario*, October 7, 1938, and Adelia Di Carlo, "Doña C. H. de Burmeister," *Caras y Caretas*, April 14, 1934, box 61, folder 3, all in Stevens Papers. See also *La Prensa*, July 24, 1940. AASF changed its name several times.

46. H. Senado, *Represión del Comunismo*, 207, 211 (quote); Oliver, *La vida cotidiana*, 348–57, and interview, Proyecto de Historia Oral del Instituto Torcuato di Tella, 1971, Universidad Torcuato di Tella, Buenos Aires, 50–51; *Claridad*, October 1937, 58; Hayes to Schain, October 7, 1938, attachment "Union of Argentine Women," box 6, folder 20, Schain Papers, courtesy of Katherine Marino. See also Halperín Donghi, *Son memorias*, 80, and *La república imposible*, 209–10; Valobra, ""Formación de cuadros," 138–42; Verónica Giordano, "Los derechos civiles" and *Ciudadanas incapaces*, 153–66; Queirolo, "La mujer en la sociedad"; Barrancos, *Mujeres en la sociedad*, 174–75; Lavrin, *Women, Feminism, and Social Change*, 94, 282–83, 316; Carlson, *¡Feminismo¡*, 177–79; Clementi, *María Rosa Oliver*, 110; Hammond, *Women's Suffrage Movement*, 135–36; Sitman, *Victoria Ocampo*. On Rawson and Oliver, see Deleis et al., *Mujeres de la política argentina*, 275–89, and 387–99, respectively.

47. Sociedad Unión Argentina de Mujeres (Filial Rosario), Expediente 5066, 17–19, Ministerio de Gobierno, Justicia y Culto, Mesa de Entradas y Salidas, Archivo General de la Provincia de Santa Fe, Santa Fe (AGPSF). The Santa Fe chapter issued a similar statement; see unidentified newspaper clipping, n.d., Carpeta Género, Archivo Marta Samatán, Universidad Nacional del Litoral, Santa Fe (AMHMS).

48. Morgan to Stevens, September 1938, box 61, folder 1, and UAM, *Boletín Informativo Año 1937*, 1–3, 5, box 61, folder 8, Stevens Papers; Anastasi, *Derechos civiles*; Ocampo, *La mujer*. See also Oliver, *La vida cotidiana*, 350; *El Litoral*, April 2, 1938, Carpeta Género, AMHMS; *Orientación*, December 5, 1940, 6; and Samatán in *Vida Femenina*, January 15, 1937, 38–39, and March 15, 1937, 18–19.

49. *El Litoral*, September 14, 2005, clipping, Carpeta Género, AMHMS.

50. Unidentified newspaper clipping, October 1938, box 61, folder 1; *El Mundo*, October 7, 1938, box 61, folder 4; Larguía to Stevens, May 6, 1938, box 61, folder 8, all in Stevens Papers. See also Valobra, "Formación de cuadros," 139; Oliver, interview, 51; Larguía to Brainerd, May 2, 1938, and attached flyer, Unión Argentina de Mujeres, "La mujer que trabaja demanda" (quotes), box 22, folder Correspondence of Brainerd . . . 1937–1938, WILPF Records, SCPC; *España Republicana*, July 4, 1942, 8; Norando, "Relaciones de género." On Piacenza, see *La Capital*, December 31, 1942, 4; *Flecha*, December 30, 1935, 5; Bordegaray, "Lu-

chas antifascistas y trayectorias generizadas"; *Argentina Libre*, July 4, 1940, 12. The Santa Fe chapter also distributed flyers against changing the civil code; see UAM, *Boletín Informativo Año 1937*, 3. On Madanes, see Di Corleto, "Las visitadoras," 136–38.

51. *La Prensa*, November 12, 1940, 11; *Nuestra Idea*, November 15, 1936, 4, September 11, 1937, 24, August 1939, 4, July 1942, 16; Travadelo, *Marta Samatán, maestra*, 38; *La Capital*, December 27, 1942, 4.

52. *Caja de Resonancia*, 50, 69, 114; *El Litoral*, April 2, 1938; *La Capital*, November 26, 1941, 15; *Claridad*, February-March 1939, 3–4; *New York Times*, March 23, 1939, clipping, courtesy of Margaret Power; Norando, "Relaciones de género y militancia política."

53. Elena Barreda Rojas, November 23, 1938, Correspondencia de la Secretaría General de MEMCH, Elena Caffarena, Memoria Chilena, Biblioteca Nacional, Santiago, Chile; Argentina Collective box, folder Federación Argentina de Mujeres por la Paz, SCPC; Larguía to Stevens, December 30, 1937, box 61, folder 8, Stevens Papers.

54. Membership estimate in Mary Cannon, "Description of UAM," n.d., box 1, folder Cannon, Mary 1941, November, Women's Bureau, International Division, General Records 1919–1952, Cannon, Mary (1932–1941), Entry A1/Entry 46, RG 86, National Archives and Records Administration, College Park, MD (NARA); *La Capital*, October 15, 1941, 15; *Argentina Libre*, October 2, 1941, 5; *Estampa Chaqueña* (Resistencia), November 29-December 6, 1941, 15–17; Larguía to Brainerd, April 22, 1944, box 23, folder Correspondence of Brainerd with Persons in Argentina, 1948–1950, WILPF, Pt. 3: U.S. Section, Series A4, Pt. 1, DG043, SCPC.

55. Oliver, *La vida cotidiana*, 352–54 (quote); Queirolo, "La mujer en la sociedad"; *El Aguijón*, March 28, 1942, courtesy of Laura Pasquali; Larguía to Stevens, December 30, 1937, box 61, folder 8, Stevens Papers.

56. Marino, *Feminism for the Americas*, 139–40, 142, 159, 168, 173; Sociedad Unión Argentina de Mujeres, 2–7, AGPSF; *Anuario El Litoral*, January 1, 1937, photo of Unión Argentina de Mujeres Comisión Directiva, courtesy of Mariela Rubinzal; dispersed information in AMHMS; Valobra,"Formación de cuadros," 138–42. Complete UAM membership lists are not available.

57. *History of the Inter-American Commission*; *Inter-American Commission of Women*; Marino, *Feminism for the Americas*; Miller, *Latin American Women*, 95–96, 105, 108. Feminists from other American countries had been in touch with their Argentine counterparts at least since 1910; see *Primer Congreso Femenino*.

58. Oscar Alberto Ibar to Stevens, April 30, 1937, and Stevens to Ibar, June 7, 1937, box 60, folder 18, Stevens Papers.

59. Carolina Horne de Burmeister to Carlos Saavedra Lamas, November 1936, box 62, folder 16, and Stevens to Dr. James Brown Scott, October 30, 1936, box 63, folder 4, Stevens Papers.

60. Stevens, Memorandum to Secretary of State, December 10, 1936, box 62,

folder 16, Stevens Papers; IACW to Tulio Cestero, December 15, 1936, box 11, folder Inter-American Commission of Women, PM, General Correspondence Series B, SCPC.

61. "Declaración de la Mujer Argentina," box 62, folder 16; Stevens, "Records of Main Events of Trip . . . November 7, 1936-January 13, 1937," 16–51, box 63, folder 6, Stevens Papers. On Stevens's and the People's Mandate visitors' disdain for antifascism, and Steven's insincere use of the issue, see *El Mercurio* (Santiago), November 17, 1937, box 4, folder "Flying Caravan," PM, Series A: General, SCPC; Helen A. Archdale to Stevens, February 6, 1939, box 85, folder 18, Stevens Papers; Marino, *Feminism for the Americas*, 149.

62. Marino, *Feminism for the Americas*.

63. Stevens to Ocampo, April 13, 1938, box 61, folder 1; correspondence between Stevens and Ana S. de Martínez Guerrero, and *El Mundo*, October 7, 1938, 22, box 61, folder 4; Oliver to Stevens, June 6, 1938, box 61, folder 8; Stevens to John White, November 16, 1938, box 74, folder 17, all in Stevens Papers.

64. Typed page on Schlieper, n.d., and *El Mundo*, October 7, 1938, 22 (quote), box 61, folder 4, Stevens Papers; *Quién es quién*, 1950, 383; AASF, *Estatutos*, 14; www.genealogiafamiliar.net and www.records.ancestry.com (link no longer valid); Municipalidad de General Madariaga, Schlieper de Martínez Guerrero.

65. *El Territorio* (Posadas), November 19, 1942, 1 (quote); *El Mundo*, October 7, 1938, 22, box 61, folder 4, Stevens Papers; Vergara, *Memorias*, 142, 189; Ubelaker, "Impossible Americas," 12.

66. Elise Musser to Sumner Welles, September 8, 1939, 710.F Inter-American Commission of Women/127, US Department of State; and *Washington Star*, October 28, 1942, clipping, box 119, folder 843, RG 84, Foreign Service Posts of the Department of State, Buenos Aires Embassy, General Records, NARA.

67. *UAM Boletín Informativo*, May 7, 1938 (transcript of broadcast), and Stevens to Martínez Guerrero, May 6, 1938, box 61, folder 8, Stevens Papers.

68. Martínez Guerrero, transcript of speech, box 76, folder 7, Stevens Papers.

69. On this and the next paragraph, see Stevens to Horne, April 25, 1939, box 61, folder 3, and press release, January 4, 1939, box 75, folder 9, Stevens Papers; Marino, *Feminism for the Americas*, 158–69; Hammond, *Women's Suffrage Movement*, 133; Towns, "Inter-American Commission of Women," 793, 799.

70. Brainerd, "Notes from . . . Lima," December 22, 1939, box 1a, folder Committee on the Americas 1938–1939, WILPF Records, SCPC microfilm reel 130:23.

71. Marino, *Feminism for the Americas*, 173.

72. Martínez Guerrero to Stevens, November 17, 1939, box 61, folder 1, and Gaeta Wold Boyer to John White, February 29, 1940, box 85, folder 18, Stevens Papers; Winslow memorandum, August 10, 1940, A-53, box 1, folder 2r, and unsigned letter [from Ana Berry] to Winslow, July 21, 1940, A-53, box 1, folder 3b, Mary N. Winslow Papers, Schlesinger Library (Winslow Papers), Cambridge, MA; Nelson Rockefeller to Mary Anderson, October 24, 1941, forwarded Martínez

Guerrero letter, n.d., Folder Mary Cannon 1941, October, RG 86, NARA. Sometimes the Office of Inter-American Affairs is referred to as the Coordinator of Inter-American Affairs.

73. Cannon to Mary Anderson, April 20, 1941, May 9, 1941, box 1, folders Mary Cannon 1941, April and May, RG 86, NARA. On Cannon, see Sealander, "In the Shadow of Good Neighbor Diplomacy," esp. 241–50.

74. Draft of speech, Twentieth Annual Convention of the National Council of Catholic Women, October 30, 1940, A-53, box 1, folder 3b, Winslow Papers. On Mooney, see chapter 4; Tentler, *Seasons of Grace*, chap. 11; *Orden Cristiano*, October 1, 1942.

75. Martínez Guerrero to Winslow, August 10, 1940, A-53, box 1, folder 3b, Winslow Papers; Deutsch, *Crossing Borders*, 185, 220.

76. *Claridad*, July 1939, 30–31; Mendoza, *Cárcel de Mujeres*; Ferreira, "Angélica Mendoza y su trayectoria americana"; Belucci, "Angélica Mendoza"; Becerra, "'Soy comunista y maestra.'"

77. Casas, "La guerra civil española"; Rein, "Trans-National Struggle"; Quijada, *Aires de república*; Schvartzstein, *Entre Franco y Perón*; Trifone and Svarzman, *La repercusión de la guerra civil*. Among works on its impact elsewhere in Latin America, see Lambe, *No Barrier Can Contain It*; Zubillaga, *Niños de la guerra*; Ojeda Revah, *Mexico and the Spanish Civil War*.

78. Edelman, *Banderas, pasiones, camaradas*, 34.

79. Oliver, "Queridas amigas, mujeres de España," n.d., 1–4, box 1, folder 44, Oliver Papers; Oliver, interview, 43.

80. Oliver, *Mi fe es el hombre*, 10–12, 35. Oliver did not mention joining a particular organization.

81. *España Republicana*, February 27, 1937, 15 (quotes), reprinted in Bisso, ed., *El antifascismo argentino*, 426–27. The Argentine Conference of Women for Peace had supported a similar measure; see *Pueblo F*, November 1936, box 4, folder Clippings from Latin American Papers, 1935–1950 (contin. 2), PM, Series A, General: DG 109, SCPC.

82. *¡Mujeres!*, May 1937; *U.M.A. 1947–1967*, 9, Miscellaneous Peace Material file, SCPC; *La Vanguardia*, April 19, 1942, 8; Edelman, *Banderas, pasiones, camaradas*, 45–53, passim.

83. Eleonora Ardanaz, communication, n.d., and "Maternalismo y política en el antifascismo argentino"; Edelman, *Banderas, pasiones, camaradas*, 46. Membership lists are not available.

84. *Contra-fascismo*, August-September 1936, 27–28 (quote). On the Argentine Popular Front, see Romero, *History of Argentina in the Twentieth Century*, 79–88.

85. *La Protesta*, November 1939, 3, June 1940, 1; *Orientación*, May 30, 1940, 1, October 24, 1940; Cane, "'Unity for the Defense of Culture,'" 466–75.

86. *Vida Femenina*, September-October 1940, 4–5, 12.

87. *Argentina Libre*, July 4, 1940, 5.

88. *Vida Femenina*, June 1940, 20 (quote); WILPF (International), August 13, 1940, WILPF, Fourth Accession, Records of the International, Series III: National Sections and Other Countries, 1914–1979, SCPC Microfilm Reel 133:54.

89. *Argentina Libre*, June 20, 1940, 2.

90. *Argentina Libre*, May 30, 1940, 1; Nállim, *Transformations and Crisis of Liberalism in Argentina*, 109.

91. *Argentina Libre*, May 30, 1940, 8; Bisso, *Acción Argentina*, 83, and *El antifascismo*, 152–55.

92. *Argentina Libre*, June 5, 1941, 2.

93. Bisso, *Acción Argentina*, 212, 215, 228–31, 255, 270, and *El antifascismo*, 155–57; *La Prensa*, November 4, 1940, 11. Precise membership figures are not available.

94. *Vida Femenina*, November-December 1940, (quote), August-September 1942, 6; *Argentina Libre*, June 5, 1941, 2; *La Prensa*, July 30, 1940, 12, October 7, 1940, 22, October 9, 1940, 11, October 15, 1940, 14, October 18, 1940, 12, October 23, 1940, 13, November 28, 1940, 15, November 30, 1940, 14, and April 2, 1941, 14, April 15, 1941, 11; April 24, 1941, 10, May 13, 1941, 12, May 31, 1941, 11; Bisso, *Acción Argentina*, 117, 120, 122, 324–25, 331, 341, 343–46.

95. *Standard: Standard Victory Supplement*, 103, 106, 116–19, 120, 133–34; *Standard*, November 3, 1941, 9, November 18, 1941, 17; *La Prensa*, April 26, 1941, 14, May 21, 1941, 15; *La Hora*, March 22, 1942, 5, April 26, 1942, 7; *El Hogar*, May 15, 1942, 14; Pelosi, *Vichy*, esp. 78, 81–82; Deutsch, *Crossing Borders*, 183–84.

96. *La Prensa*, April 24, 1941, 10, October 19, 1941, 19; *Standard*, November 20, 1941, 2, November 28, 1941, 4, May 8, 1942, 2, November 21, 1942, 2.

97. "Report of Exercises of May 1940–41 of the Organism for Direct Aid to the Jewish Victims of War" (English translation of original) and other documents in box 1071, file 1, American Jewish Joint Distribution Committee Archive, New York; Jenny O. Berliner, Report on the Popular Conference in Buenos Aires, 1936, box 63, folder 3, Stevens Papers.

98. *Claridad*, July 29, 1933, 52.

99. Valobra, "Elogio de la mujer que vota."

Chapter 2: Defining Women's Roles in the Era of Fascism

1. Simões, "Nem só mãe, esposa e professora," 13–14.

2. Badilla Urrutia in *Acción Chilena* 5, no. 1 (1936): 53.

3. Gottlieb, *Feminine Fascism*, 8.

4. Ullrich and Keller, "Comparing Discourse between Cultures," 113–39. Page numbers in this extract differ from the book; the extract's page numbers used are 10–12, 14 (quote).

5. This contrasts with the emphasis on strategies and intertwined fates in Ortiz de Zárate et al., *Su revolución contra nuestra revolución*.

6. Mayer, *Dynamics of Counterrevolution*. Here I discuss only fascist movements that originated in Latin America, largely leaving out strictly Catholic groups.

7. I do not include anarchists, who nevertheless deserve attention.

8. Valdivia Ortiz de Zárate, "Presentación," 9–10 (quotes), and "Izquierdas y derechas," 207.

9. Traverso, *Fire and Blood*, 236; Grandin, "Living in Revolutionary Time," 16.

10. For example, see Finchelstein, *From Fascism to Populism in History*, 70.

11. Hobsbawm, *Age of Extremes*, 144.

12. Oliver, "Queridas amigas," 3, box 1, folder 44, Oliver Papers.

13. Traverso, *Fire and Blood*, 254, 259.

14. Falcoff and Pike, eds., *Spanish Civil War*; Bertonha, "Los latinoamericanos de Franco."

15. *La Nación*, June 1, 1936, 1, June 2, 1936, 1.

16. Gálvez, *Este pueblo*, 102–103; Deutsch, *Las derechas*, esp. 141–42; Finchelstein, *Fascismo*, esp. 71–94; Klein, "Comparative Analysis." On fascists as revolutionaries or not, see Hobsbawm, *Age of Extremes*, 117; Paxton, *Anatomy of Fascism*, 98, 145–47. See also "Del otro lado."

17. Orozco, "Las mujeres sinarquistas."

18. *Anauê*, September 1937, 58.

19. *La Fronda*, June 12, 1931, 3, June 17, 1931, 6, July 24, 1931, 3; *La Prensa*, June 17, 1931, 6.

20. Finchelstein, *Fascismo, liturgia e imaginario*, 101–2; *La Fronda*, June 4, 1932, 1, June 21, 1932, 1, July 20, 1932, 1, July 18, 1933, 6.

21. World Committee of Women manifesto in *El Ideal*, July 4, 1934, clipping, Serie Italia, Sección Nazi-Fascismo, caja 1, no. 4, Subfondo P. Luisi, ACRE; Congreso Internacional de Mujeres contra la Guerra y el Fascismo, Paris, 1934, caja 256, carpeta 5, no. 19, Archivo Luisi.

22. Agrupación Femenina Antiguerrera, *La mujer argentina*, 4, 8–9; Agrupación Femenina Antiguerrera flyer, "A todas las mujeres contra la guerra," n.d., attached to Telma Reca to Brainerd, January 30, 1936, box 22, folder Correspondence of Brainerd with Persons in Argentina, 1934–1936, WILPF, Pt. 3: U.S. Section, A4, Pt. 1, DG 043, SCPC.

23. *La Fronda*, November 29, 1938, 3; Alianza de la Juventud Nacionalista, *Postulados de nuestra lucha*. See also Klein, "Argentine Nacionalismo before Perón," 106–10, 115; Besoky, "El nacionalismo populista."

24. Agrupación Femenina Antiguerrera, *La mujer argentina*, esp. 5–6.

25. Arzarello in *Uruguay*, April 20, 1936, carpeta 1936–1938, and Primer Congreso Nacional de Mujeres, April 17–22, 1936, programa, carpeta 1939, both in Colección Luisi, BN; Pastoriza in *El Día* (Montevideo), April 21, 1936, caja 259, carpeta 5, no. 8, Archivo Luisi; García Martínez, "Mujeres afrouruguayas."

26. H. Senado de la Nación, *Represión del Comunismo*, 211.

27. Sociedad Unión Argentina de Mujeres, Expediente 5066, 17–19, AGPSF; Oliver, *La vida cotidiana*, 350, 352–54.

28. Tuñón Pablos, *Mujeres que se organizan*, 71 (quote), and passim; Oikión Solano, "Mujeres en el Partido Comunista Mexicano," 154–63; Olcott, "Center Cannot Hold," 229 (statistic); Olcott, *Revolutionary Women in Postrevolutionary Mexico*; Pasquali, "El activismo antifascista."

29. For example, Passalaqua Eliçabe, *El movimiento fascista argentino*, 50.

30. *Acción Chilena* 5, no. 1 (1936): 51–56, esp. 51 and 53.

31. Orozco, "Las mujeres sinarquistas"; *A Offensiva*, October 16, 1936, 1. In 1938, when Nacistas shifted toward the left, their principal newspaper, *Trabajo*, began to mention women's names. Argentine Socialist women founded *Vida Femenina*, MEMCH published *La Mujer Nueva*, and the FUPDM periodical was *Mujer Nueva*. See also Deutsch, *Las derechas*, 257; Payne, *Fascism*, 7, 12–13.

32. *Monitor Integralista*, December 5, 1936, 6; *A Offensiva*, September 8, 1936, 1. See also Finchelstein, "Anti-Freudian Politics of Argentine Fascism."

33. *Anauê*, November 1937, 49.

34. Valobra, "Sufragismo y acción política femenina," 200.

35. *A Offensiva*, July 24, 1936, 3; Bertonha and Bohoslavsky, eds., *Circule por la derecha*, esp. Almeida, "Representaciones y relaciones entre la Legión Cívica Argentina"; Bohoslavsky and Broquetas, "Local and Global Connections." Morant i Ariño, however, described how Spanish Fascist women cultivated ties with their German and Italian peers in "Spanish Fascist Women's Transnational Relations." See also Finchelstein, *Transatlantic Fascism*; Bauerkämper and Rossoliński-Liebe, eds., *Fascism without Borders*; Ledeen, *Universal Fascism*; Roberts, *Fascist Interactions*.

36. *Vida Femenina*, May 15, 1936, 27–28.

37. *La Vanguardia*, August 16, 1932, 8, February 13, 1933, 10, February 27, 1933, 8, February 23, 1934, 12.

38. Marino, "Anti-Fascist *Feminismo*," 212.

39. Movimiento Pro-Emancipación de las Mujeres de Chile (MEMCH), "A las mujeres," flyer, May 28, 1935 (quotes), Correspondencia de la Secretaria General de MEMCH, Elena Caffarena, Memoria Chilena; *La Mujer Nueva*, November 8, 1935, 1, 3, February 1936, 1. See also Antezana Pernet, "Mobilizing Women in the Popular Front Era"; Gaviola Artigas et al., *Queremos votar en las próximas elecciones*; Rosemblatt, *Gendered Compromises*. On birth control and abortion, see Lavrin, *Women, Feminism, and Social Change*, 174–91; Mooney, *Politics of Motherhood*.

40. *Uruguay*, April 18, 1936, clipping, no. 5, and *El Día* (Montevideo), April 24, 1936, clipping, no. 16, both in box 259, folder 5, Archivo Luisi.

41. *A Offensiva*, June 15, 1935, 5 (photos), September 8, 1936, 1; Penna, "A mulher, a familia," 52; Geraldo, "Entre a raça e a nação."

42. *A Offensiva*, June 15, 1935, 5.

43. De Grazia, *How Fascism Ruled Women*, 65; Chalmers, "Maternity Care in

the Former Soviet Union," 497–98; Chernyaeva, "Childcare Manuals and Construction of Motherhood," 142–204.

44. *La Vanguardia*, October 30, 1938, clipping, carpeta 1936–1938, Colección Luisi.

45. *Vida Femenina*, December 15, 1936, 36–37.

46. Del Franco, *Mujeres, ese fuego, esas luchas*, 21, 23. See also Sarnoff, "Domesticating Fascism."

47. Ferreyra, "La conformación de un consenso," esp. 92–128; Quijada, *Aires de república*; Rein, "Another Front Line," esp. 26; Ardanaz, email communication, February 14, 2019. On women's pro-Franco statements, see Ferreyra, "La conformación de un consenso," 200–208; Valobra, "El particular ideario," 219–21; Zanca, "Eugenia en su laberinto." *Franquistas* and anti-*franquistas* included Spanish-born women. Fears of children being shipped to the Soviet Union foreshadowed right-wing Chilean concerns that Salvador Allende would send youngsters to Cuba; see Power, *Right-Wing Women in Chile*, 81, and passim.

48. On connections between the Spanish Falange, Nationalism, and Argentina, see González Calleja, "El hispanismo autoritario español"; Camaño Semprini, "Ecos de la Guerra Civil Española"; Lvovich, *El águila y el haz de flechas*, chap. 5. On Republican and Falangist Spanish women, see Cenarro, "Movilización femenina para la guerra total."

49. *Bandera Argentina*, September 2, 1938, 1; *A Offensiva*, June 15, 1935, 5; *Trabajo*, March 14, 1935, 5.

50. *Argentina Libre*, February 12, 1942, 10; Koonz, *Mothers in the Fatherland*, 198; Durham, *Women and Fascism*, 14, 23, 25–26; De Grazia, *How Fascism Ruled Women*, 180.

51. *A Offensiva*, February 9, 1936, 16; *Trabajo*, May 20, 1936. A MEMCH chapter endorsed the family salary—if it were handed to housewives; see Rosemblatt, *Gendered Compromises*, 75, but few leftists shared this view. According to Besse, *Restructuring Patriarchy*, 133, by this time Brazilians commonly accepted women's need to work.

52. *Monitor Integralista*, December 5, 1936, 6.

53. Rubinzal, "Women's Work in Argentina's Nationalist Lexicon," 236.

54. Rubinzal, "Women's Work in Argentina's Nationalist Lexicon," 236 (quote), 237; Jorge de Tella in Marino, *Feminism for the Americas*, 184.

55. Deutsch, "Catholic Church, Work, and Womanhood in Argentina," esp. 313–14.

56. *Vida Femenina*, April 15, 1935, 30–31.

57. *Enciclopédia do Integralismo* IX, 67–69.

58. *Brasil Feminino*, November 1937, 8.

59. *Brasil Feminino*, November 1937, 22–23. See also Simões, "Nem só mãe, esposa e professora," 11.

60. *Anauê*, July 1936, 8.

61. *Anauê*, October 1935, 29; *Brasil Feminino*, November 1937, 1. These ideas resembled the Catholic feminism discussed by Besse, *Restructuring Patriarchy*, 183–90. Robin, "You Say You Want a Counterrevolution," analyzed rightist appropriation of progressive ideas and practices.

62. Women had attained suffrage in Ecuador and Cuba, which apparently lacked important fascist movements.

63. Deutsch, "What Difference Does Gender Make?" After women attained the municipal vote in Chile in 1934, Nacistas allowed them to enter the MNS, which they claimed practiced "feminist politics"; see Deutsch, *Las derechas*, 173. In *Paradox of Paternalism*, Manley showed how women asserted their citizenship under the right-wing Trujillo and Balaguer governments, laying the groundwork for feminism.

64. Ferla, *Doctrina del Nacionalismo*, 49–50; Mosley in Gottlieb, *Feminine Fascism*, 1.

65. Carulla in *La Nueva República*, April 28, 1928, 1; *Bandera Argentina*, July 9, 1938, cited in Hammond, *Women's Suffrage Movement*, 136.

66. *A Offensiva*, May 1, 1937, 1–2, November 4, 1937, 2; *Monitor Integralista*, October 3, 1936, 13–14; *Anauê*, May 1937, 41; Marino, email communication, November 25, 2017, and *Feminism*, 165, 291n109. See also Cavalari, *Integralismo*, 62–68; Possas, "O integralismo e a mulher"; Simões, "Nem só mãe, esposa e professora, 1–11, 15, and "A educação do corpo," 159–60, 173; Bairros, "O integralismo de saia." Orozco's protagonists in "Las mujeres sinarquistas," 50–52, held their first national meeting in December 1944.

67. Simões, "Nem só mãe, esposa e professora," 13–14.

68. *Vida Femenina*, January 1935, 5–6, 16.

69. Carrera in *El Rayo* (Valdivia), April 3, 1935, 1; *Trabajo*, June 10, 1936, 6. Only after Nacismo turned to the left did it support (temporarily) equal political rights for men and women; see *Trabajo*, January 17, 1939, 1.

70. Giménez Bustamante in *La Fronda*, August 5, 1932, 6. On the AASF, see chapter 1; Lavrin, *Women, Feminism, and Social Change*, 279; Barrancos, *Inclusión/Exclusión*, 115–20; Carlson, *¡Feminismo!*, 173–74.

71. *Crisol*, August 20, 1933, 5.

72. *Bandera Argentina*, July 7, 1938, 1 (quote); *Bandera Argentina*, July 9, 1938, cited in Hammond, *Women's Suffrage Movement*, 136.

73. Possas, "O integralismo e a mulher."

74. Besse, "Pagu," 103–17, and *Restructuring Patriarchy*, 44, 180–83, passim.

75. Orozco, "Teresa Bustos, 'la mujer bandera.'"

76. *Bandera Argentina*, May 13, 1937.

77. Gottlieb, *Feminine Fascism*, 267.

78. Deutsch, *Counterrevolution in Argentina*, 212.

79. Maffei, *A batalha da Praça da Sé*.

80. Corbisier, interview, 1969–1970, 3.

81. *Anauê*, July 1936.

82. Simões, "Nem só mãe, esposa e professora," 13–14.

83. *Brasil Feminino*, November 1937, 33.

84. The Nacista newspaper *Trabajo* frequently mentioned the feminine brigades. Martial descriptions of leftist women seemed to become more common with their participation in the Spanish Civil War and World War II, although this deserves investigation.

85. *Trabajo*, December 14, 1935, 3.

86. *Trabajo*, April 27, 1933, 3.

87. Colley, *Gun, the Ship, and the Pen*, 7–8, 271–75, 410–11.

88. Suh, *Fascism and Anti-Fascism in Twentieth-Century British Fiction*, 11.

89. González and Kampwirth, "Introduction," 17–21.

90. González and Kampwirth, "Introduction," 20–22.

91. Mayer, *Dynamics of Counterrevolution*, 62–63, 66, 80; Deutsch, *Las derechas*.

92. Traverso, *Fire and Blood*, 233, 246–47. On Gucovsky, see *La Vanguardia*, August 29, 1932, 2, September 12, 1932, 1, September 13, 1932, 1, September 16, 1932, 2; *La Nación*, August 20, 1932, 5, August 21, 1932, 7.

93. Mayer, *Dynamics of Counterrevolution*, 65. Paxton, *Anatomy of Fascism*, 218, identified the desire for cleansing as a fascist characteristic.

Chapter 3: Knitting Together the Local, National, and Transnational

1. Oliver, *Mi fe es el hombre*, 41–42, and interview; "Homenaje a Winston Churchill."

2. "Homenaje a Winston Churchill," 69.

3. Finchelstein, *Transatlantic*, 59.

4. During the 1930s, a newspaper cost 20 cents, a movie ticket 20–50 cents, and a paperback book 1–1.5 pesos, according to Mariela Rubinzal, email communication, March 12, 2019. One peso was worth 25 cents in US currency in May 1941; see Mary Cannon to Mary Anderson, May 9, 1941, box 1, folder May 1941, Cannon, Mary; RG 86, NARA. See also *La Hora*, September 5, 1941, 4, September 8, 1941, 4, September 28, 1941, 9–10; Oliver, "A Porteña Reports," 21 (quote); Junta de la Victoria, *Estatutos*, 12, Caja de Mujeres, Archivo del Partido Comunista, Buenos Aires (Archivo Comunista). I found only two organizations that affiliated with the Victory Board: the Centro Argentino de Mujeres Israelitas and Centro de Damas Lituanas, both in Rosario; see Junta de la Victoria, *Primera convención nacional*, 60. However, many donated goods and money.

5. Oliver, *Mi fe es el hombre*, 43.

6. Oliver, *Mi fe es el hombre*, 42–43, 52–53, 95, 98.

7. Clementi, *Lautaro*, 46; Tarcus, ed., *Diccionario biográfico de la izquierda*, 553–54.

8. Unsigned (Ana Berry) to Mary Winslow, July 21, 1940, A-53, box 1, folder

3b, Winslow Papers. On Schlieper's involvement in Acción Argentina, see Bisso, *Acción Argentina*, 117, 176, 294, 341. Whether Schlieper was active in Acción Argentina after participating in its Primer Cabildo Abierto of May 1941 is unclear.

9. *Orientación*, April 23, 1942, 1, also in Bisso, ed., *El antifascismo argentino*, 162; *La Hora*, September 14, 1941, 5.

10. *La Hora*, September 13, 1941, 4, September 14, 1941, 5.

11. *El Día* (La Plata), January 26, 1946, 5 (Schlieper); Ratto in Junta de la Victoria, *Primera convención nacional*, 22.

12. Edelman, interview, 2009.

13. *La Hora*, July 15, 1942, 6.

14. *Crítica*, September 14, 1941, 4. The United States had not yet entered the war.

15. *La Hora*, September 27, 1941, 5; Junta de la Victoria, "Las mujeres argentinas a la señora del presidente," 1941, and Eleanor Roosevelt to Ana Rosa de Martínez Guerrero, undated telegram, Eleanor Roosevelt Papers, 1941, Franklin D. Roosevelt Presidential Library, Hyde Park, NY.

16. *La Voz del Interior*, October 1, 1941, 7.

17. Finchelstein, *Transatlantic Antifascisms*, 57, 167; Cane, *Fourth Enemy*, 86; Privitellio, "La política bajo el signo," 135; Caterina, "Los gobiernos de provincia," 18–29; Kelly, *Ruling Few*, 287–89; Sheinin, *Argentina and the United States*, 73–83.

18. *Chicago Tribune*, December 17, 1941, 15, http://archives.chicagotribune .com/ . . . /state-of-siege . . . /index.html; *Standard*, December 23, 1941, 2; *La Hora*, December 13, 1941, 5, December 17, 1941, 5, December 23, 1941, 1; Junta de la Victoria, "Fiesta por la Libertad"; *La Prensa*, March 21, 1943, 6.

19. Greenup, *Revolution before Breakfast*, 77–79; Newton, *'Nazi Menace' in Argentina*; Argentina, *Comisión Investigadora*; Rubinzal, "La circulación cultural."

20. Junta de la Victoria, *Primera convención nacional*, 25–26.

21. *La Hora*, August 28, 1941, 4.

22. *La Hora*, April 24, 1942, 7. On antifascist couples, see chapter 5.

23. As Jackson suggested in *British Women and the Spanish Civil War*, 57, 81.

24. See, for example, Junta de la Victoria, *Primera convención nacional*, 15; Ana Rosa Schlieper de Martínez Guerrero, president, Junta de la Victoria, to President Pedro P. Ramírez, June 30, 1943, 3, Junta de la Victoria file, Centro de Documentación e Investigación de la Cultura de las Izquierdas en la Argentina (CeDInCI), Buenos Aires.

25. Junta de la Victoria, *Primera convención nacional*, 23; see also Jackson, *British Women and the Spanish Civil War*, 45, 47.

26. Junta de la Victoria, *Primera convención nacional*, 34.

27. *Mujeres en la Ayuda* (1941–1942), 14–16, 24; *Boletín de la Comisión Interamericana de Mujeres* (*Boletín de la CIM*) 1, no. 1 (June 1943): 11.

28. Newspaper accounts alone are available for its second national convention in 1943 and the Buenos Aires provincial convention in 1942.

29. *Mujeres en la Ayuda*, 14; Junta de la Victoria, *Primera convención nacional*, 40–41; *La Hora*, September 13, 1941, 4, February 27, 1942, 5.

30. *Mujeres en la Ayuda*, 14; Junta de la Victoria, *Primera convención nacional*, 40–41; *La Hora*, October 17, 1941, 4 (quote), October 25, 1941, 7.

31. Junta de la Victoria, *Primera convención nacional*, 40–41.

32. *La Hora*, January 29, 1942, 4.

33. *La Voz del Interior*, September 15, 1941, 7.

34. *La Hora*, December 15, 1942, 5.

35. Junta de la Victoria, *Primera convención nacional*, 37, 41. On Jews in these industries, see, among other sources, Elkin, *Jews of Latin America*, 135–36. On Jews and the Victory Board, see chapter 4.

36. *Orientación*, November 19, 1942, 1; *La Hora*, September 28, 1941, 9, May 29, 1942, 5, November 25, 1942, 5, January 9, 1943, 5, February 28, 1943, 3; *Toledo Blade*, October 16, 1941. I found only one issue of *Mujeres en la Ayuda*, for 1941–42. Chapter 6 describes US and British collaboration.

37. *El Orden*, December 16, 1941, 8 (quote), September 9, 1942, 4.

38. *El Litoral*, October 25, 1942, 4, May 7, 1943, 3, May 30, 1943, 4; *El Hogar*, May 15, 1942, 14. The mixed-sex Comisión Sanitaria Argentina (see chapter 5) probably made the medical goods it remitted. Some men and women factory laborers remained on the premises after hours to make garments and supplies; see *La Hora*, November 2, 1941, 7, December 25, 1941, 5; May 12, 1942, 5; October 20, 1942, 5; November 29, 1942, 6.

39. Root, *Couture and Consensus*, 40, 47–48.

40. Oliver, interview; *La Hora*, August 22, 1941, 4, August 28, 1941, 4, December 17, 1941, 5; *La Voz del Interior*, September 15, 1941, 7. On the Victory Board and race, see chapter 4.

41. Junta de la Victoria, *Primera convención nacional*, 38; *La Hora*, January 10, 1942, 4, June 3, 1942, 5, August 18, 1942, 5, October 5, 1942, 3.

42. Chinese contact mentioned in *La Hora*, May 8, 1943, 6; Junta de la Victoria, receipt for twenty cent contribution to China, Campaña de Ayuda Sanitaria, Caja Mujer-Niñez, Archivo Comunista; *Inter-American Commission of Women Information Bulletin* (*IACW Information Bulletin*), September 1942, 2; *Boletín de la CIM* 1, no. 2 (July 1943): 17–18; *El Día* (La Plata), March 17, 1943, 8; *La Prensa*, October 23, 1941, 13, March 21, 1943, 6, April 17, 1943, 7, April 21, 1943, 9; *La Hora*, December 31, 1941, 8, January 16, 1942, 4, March 7, 1942, 5, July 14, 1942, 5, September 8, 1942, 5, April 21, 1943, 5; Junta de la Victoria, *Primera convención nacional*, 37–38.

43. *La Hora*, June 3, 1942, 5.

44. *La Hora*, October 5, 1942, 3, October 14, 1942, 1, November 29, 1942, 6; Junta de la Victoria, "¡Por los Héroes de Stalingrado!"

45. *La Hora*, August 9, 1942, 5.

46. Anonymous, interview, n.d.

47. Oliver, "A Porteña Reports," 21.

48. Roosevelt in *La Hora*, May 6, 1943, 3. See other confirmations of aid received in Junta de la Victoria, "A Ud. que ayuda a las democracias"; Oliver to María Rita de Romero, January 8, 1943, box 7, folder 25, Oliver Papers; *El Orden*, July 3, 1942, 4, July 6, 1942, 8; *El Día* (La Plata), April 23, 1943, 2; *La Hora*, July 14, 1942, 5, December 23, 1942, 1; *Standard*, July 30, 1942, 1.

49. Bisso, *Acción Argentina*, 274–91, 347–65 (number and locations of chapters); *La Gaceta de Acción Argentina*, September 1942, 30, November 1942, 18.

50. *La Hora*, September 14, 1941, 5 (Schlieper); *La Unión*, April 14, 1943, 7; *La Gaceta*, April 16, 1943, clipping, courtesy of María Ulivarri; Mosset Iturraspe, interview, 2013.

51. *El Territorio* (Resistencia), July 6, 1942, 3; Leoni de Rosciani, consultation, and *El Ateneo*, 6. People also joined Acción Argentina to share in its prestige; see Bisso, *Acción Argentina*, 276–77.

52. *Mujeres en la Ayuda*, 14; Junta de la Victoria, *Primera convención nacional*, 45, 47–8, 50–52, 55–56, 62.

53. See, for example, Junta de la Victoria, *Primera convención nacional*, 24; *La Hora*, October 15, 1941, 4, September 30, 1942, 5. Acción Argentina leaders conducted similar tours; see Bisso, *Acción Argentina*, 274–75.

54. Oliver, *Mi fe es el hombre*, 44.

55. Junta de la Victoria, *Primera convención nacional*, 5–9, 34, 37, 39–40. These proceedings alternately indicated that there were seventeen, eighteen, and nineteen secretariats, but the map on page 39 showed twenty, one of which was left out of the chart on page 40. Seventeen sent delegates to the convention. Page 39 mentioned forty-five chapters, but the list of *filiales* that sent delegates to the convention, plus those that adhered to it but were unable to send representatives, added up to forty-two.

56. Schlieper to Ramírez, 2.

57. See, for example, the Resistencia affiliate's experience in *El Territorio*, May 27, 1942, 3, June 15, 1942, 3, and April 2, 1943, 5. Yet some major cities had subsidiary or neighborhood chapters that newspapers did not always mention.

58. Dora Barrancos and Adriana Valobra, email communications, February 7, 2020. AASF numbers in Lavrin, *Women, Feminism, and Social Change*, 279; Hammond, *Women's Suffrage Movement*, 122–23; Carlson, *¡Feminismo!*, 172–73. See also Edelman, *Banderas, pasiones, camaradas*, 146.

59. República Argentina, *Tercer Censo Nacional*, 3–107; República Argentina, Presidencia, *Cuarto censo general*, lxiii.

60. On Rosario, see Quijada, *Aires de república*, 143. See also República Argentina, *Tercer Censo Nacional*, 42; Presidencia, *Cuarto censo general*, 41; Bonaudo and Bandieri, "La cuestión social agraria," 229–82; Palacios, "La antesala de lo peor"; Korol, "La economía."

61. Jefe de División de Investigaciones Miguel Yagas, Posadas, to Jefe de Policía

del Territorio D. Leandro A. Berón, May 9 and 20, 1942; Comisario Inspector de Policía Armando Caracciolo, Oberá to Berón, May 11, 1942, all in caja 5, No. 147, 1942, Gobernación de Misiones, Comisión de Ordenamiento de Archivos, Expedientes Secretos, Confidenciales y Reservados, 1939–1952, Archivo Intermedio, Fondo Ministerio del Interior, Archivo General de la Nación (AGN Intermedio). See also Secretario a Cargo de Gobernación, Angel H. Ruiz, Posadas, to Ministerio del Interior, March 16, 1936, caja Oberá 11, Copiador R, 21–11–33 al 19–11–42, Archivo General de Gobernación de Misiones, Posadas; Kaner and Herrera, ¡Abajo la guerra!; Nueva Época, October 23, 1942, 4; Martínez Chas, Marcos Kanner; Furtembach de Kanner and Kanner, interview, 2013; Abínzano, Weinstein, and Urquiza, consultations, all in 2013; Abínzano, "Política y etnicidad."

62. Gori, La Forestal; Bonaudo and Bandieri, "La cuestión social agraria," 250–57; Junta de la Victoria, Primera convención nacional, 63–66.

63. Crespo, "Una sensibilidad a flor," http://perio.unlp.edu.ar/ojs/index.php/cps/index, and email communications, July 16, 2014, and March 21, 2019; La Hora, September 22, 1941, 1, January 28, 1942, 8, February 1, 1942, 8, February 5, 1942, 8, June 7, 1942, 4; Junta de la Victoria, Primera convención nacional, 44–45; Ratto in Boletín de la CIM 1, no. 1 (June 1943): 12.

64. Comisario Gregorio Vicente Gómez, Jefatura de Policía, Gobierno del Chaco to Gobernador, October 3, 1942, and Extracto del Informe de la Gendarmería Nacional de Villa Ángela, August 24, 1942, caja 6, no. 306, Coordinación de Ordenamiento de Archivos, Expedientes Secretos, Confidenciales y Reservados, 1939–82, AGN Intermedio. See also Gobernador Dr. Gustavo R. Lagerheim, Resistencia, Memoria del Año 1940, and Gobernador Coronel Alberto M. Castro, Síntesis de la labor administrativa desarrollada por la gobernación del Chaco, desde el 4/6/43, both in Archivo Provincial del Chaco, Resistencia, courtesy of Oscar Nari. See also Iñigo Carrera and Podestá, Movimiento social y alianza de obreros; Girbal-Blacha, Vivir en los márgenes; El Territorio (Resistencia), June 6, 1942, 3; El Alba, January 7, 1936, 1; La Vanguardia, May–December 1936; La Capital, August 20, 1936, clipping, courtesy Laura Pasquali; Dellatorre and Iñigo Carrera, consultations; Barreto, El sindicalismo, 188.

65. El Territorio (Resistencia), June 8, 1942, 3, June 13, 1942, 3, July 6, 1942, 3; Orientación, June 25, 1942, 6.

66. Junta de la Victoria, Primera convención nacional, 58–59.

67. Junta de la Victoria, Primera convención nacional, 46 (quote). Anti-Personalist Radicals had split from the rest of the party and formed part of the Concordancia. As Radicals in Córdoba managed to win elections and take control, antifascist groups could function there relatively freely. On party politics and governance in the interior, see Macor, "Partidos, coaliciones y sistema de poder"; Privitellio, "La política bajo el singo"; and Caterina, "Los gobiernos de provincia," esp. 18–25. I disagree with Ferrero, "La guerra y el interior," 58, who concluded that fascist-antifascist conflicts were more "muffled" outside the federal capital.

On such conflicts in Tucumán, see Fernández de Ullivarri, "Trabajadores, sindicatos y política en Tucumán"; Jorrat, "Expresiones del antisemitismo."

68. Junta de la Victoria, *Primera convención nacional*, 46, 50, 53–54, 59; Reati, email communication, December 9, 2013, containing Inés Drallny's testimony. The press amply covered harassment and restrictions; for example, see *La Hora*, December 28, 1942, 5.

69. Junta de la Victoria, *Primera convención nacional*, 43. Some chapters did not describe such relations.

70. *El Orden*, May 28, 1942, 5.

71. Lang, interview, 2000; *La Hora*, April 24, 1942, 8, December 10, 1942, 6, December 27, 1942, 5, December 28, 1942, 6, December 31, 1942, 5, January 10, 1943, 7 (Centro), February 11, 1943, 5 (Villa Lugano).

72. Wind, interview, 2000.

73. Junta de la Victoria, *Primera convención nacional*, 48–49; *La Hora*, April 13, 1942, 8, May 7, 1943, 6, May 9, 1943, 6, May 14, 1943, 5.

74. *El Día* (La Plata), April 4, 1943, 6, April 21, 1943, 5; *El Territorio* (Resistencia), November 7, 1941, 3, January 3, 1942, 3; *La Hora*, October 22, 1942, 3, January 6, 1943, 5, January 9, 1943, 5, January 28, 1943, 5, May 9, 1943, 6; *Orientación*, October 22, 1942, 3.

75. Junta de la Victoria, *Primera convención nacional*, 41; *Mujeres en la Ayuda*, 14; *La Hora*, February 8, 1943, 5, February 23, 1943, 5; Junta de la Victoria, "A Ud. que ayuda a las democracias."

76. I thank Rebekah Pite for this term.

77. Quote in Walzer, "Pluralism and Democracy." See also Staudt, "Political Representation," esp. 21 and 65; Pamela Paxton, "Gendering Democracy," 48–51, 68–70; Waylen, "Women and Democratization," 331–32; Bachelet, "Chilean Path to Progressive Change," 6, 8, 9.

78. *La Hora*, September 14, 1941, 5.

79. See, for example, *La Hora*, September 28, 1941, 9.

80. Junta de la Victoria, *Estatutos*.

81. *La Hora*, May 10, 1943, 2–3, May 18, 1943, 5.

82. *Córdoba*, April 28, 1943, 3, described some of these activities.

83. *El Día* (La Plata), April 27, 1943, 5; *La Hora*, April 13, 1942, 8; April 14, 1942, 5; April 15, 1942, 5; Junta de la Victoria, *Primera convención nacional*, 2–5, 12–13, 16. Another important theme of the second convention was the Victory Board's relationship with its Uruguayan sister organization, discussed in chapter 6.

84. Rubinzal, "La circulación cultural."

85. Junta de la Victoria, *Primera convención nacional*, 15–16; *La Hora*, May 10, 1943, 2.

86. Bisso, *Acción Argentina*, 221–24. Whether this also characterized the women's branch is uncertain.

87. *Orientación*, May 13, 1943, 5.

88. *Mujeres en la Ayuda*, 11–12; *La Tribuna*, April 23, 1942, 8; *El Litoral*, May 13, 1943, 5.

89. Furtembach de Kanner and Kanner, interview, 2013. See also chapter 4.

90. Martínez Guerrero, February 3, 1943, and March 25, 1943, and Winslow, April 23, 1943, box 1, folder 3a, Winslow Papers.

91. Junta de la Victoria, *Primera convención nacional*, 5, and *Mujeres en la Ayuda*, 11–12; *La Hora*, May 18, 1943, 5, May 21, 1943, 5. Shortly after Mitre assumed this position, however, the new military regime closed the Victory Board.

92. Despite their regard for charity, Jewish members tended to see it differently, as supporting the anti-Nazi struggle.

93. Mauss, *Gift*, esp. 66 (quote) and 72; Surowitz-Israel, "Gifts from the Center"; Laura Leibman and Misha Klein, communications, 2019.

94. Junta de la Victoria, *Ayuda de las mujeres argentinas*, in caja 1070, Instituto Científico Judío (IWO), Buenos Aires. The IWO has since recatalogued its boxes. See also *Mujeres en la Ayuda*, 27.

95. *Vida Femenina*, November 15, 1938, 3–6.

96. On Europe fading as a model, see Navarro, "La 'nueva intelectualidad,'" 38; Lomnitz, *Nuestra América*, 264–66; Marino, *Feminism for the Americas*, 140, 147.

97. *La Hora*, December 10, 1942, 5.

98. Sameh, "Solidarity," 181–82. I explain solidarity at greater length in Deutsch, "New School Lecture."

99. Sameh, "Solidarity," 181–82.

100. Edward L. Reed to Secretary of State, May 11, 1942, no. 5039, box 21, folder 843–1942, RG 84, NARA.

101. Counihan, "Ethnography, Food Studies, and the Humanities" (quote); Pite, *Creating a Common Table*, 19–20, 219, 222, passim.

102. *La Hora*, April 13, 1942, 8, April 14, 1942, and April 15, 1942 (Schlieper), April 18, 1942, 5 (Bahía Blanca).

103. Stevenson, "Inside Highlander," 37.

104. Staudt and Coronado, *Fronteras No Más*, 23.

105. *Orientación*, November 6, 1941, 9.

106. *La Hora*, November 29, 1942, 4, December 11, 1942, 5 (quote).

107. Junta de la Victoria, *Primera convención nacional*, 48.

108. *El Día* (La Plata), October 28, 1942, 5. On this convention, see *La Libertad de Avellaneda*, October 23, 1942, 2, October 25, 1942, 1, October 26, 1942, 1.

109. Kurt Bayertz, "Four Uses of Solidarity," in *Solidarity*, ed. Kurt Bayertz (Dordrecht: Kluwer, 1999), 16, quoted in Scholtz, *Political Solidarity*, 10.

110. *La Hora*, May 7, 1943, 6.

111. Dellatorre, consultation; Power and Charlip, "Introduction," 3–4.

112. Junta de la Victoria, *Primera convención nacional*, 47.

113. Junta de la Victoria, *Primera convención nacional*, 52.

114. *El Día* (La Plata), April 23, 1943, 2.

115. Prize ceremony mentioned in Junta de la Victoria, *Ayuda de las mujeres argentinas*.

116. As Smarsh observed of a Catholic parish in *Heartland*, 58.

117. *La Voz del Interior*, August 23, 1942, 8.

118. Junta de la Victoria, *Primera convención nacional*, 23.

119. *La Gaceta*, April 11, 1943, 9.

120. Junta de la Victoria, *Ayuda de las mujeres argentinas*.

121. Svampa, *El dilema argentino*, explored the long-term deployment of Sarmiento's dictum.

122. Some Argentines considered Jews nonwhite; see Deutsch, "Insecure Whiteness." Chapter 8 shows that antifascists, including Victory Board members, tended to denigrate Perón's nonwhite supporters.

123. *El Territorio* (Resistencia), November 10, 1941, 3.

124. Iber, *Neither Peace nor Freedom*, 9.

125. On Forner, see López Anaya, *Historia del arte argentino*, 150–51; Malosetti and Burucúa, "Iconografía de la mujer." See also *Time*, February 18–25, 2019, 69; *La Hora*, September 13, 1941, 4, October 12, 1941, 4, November 24, 1941, 4, May 30, 1942, 5, June 3, 1942, 5.

126. *La Voz del Interior*, June 14, 1943, 7.

127. *El Día* (La Plata), October 24, 1942, 5, October 25, 1942, 2; *La Hora*, October 27, 1942, 5, October 28, 1942, 5.

128. Oliver, "A Porteña Reports," 46.

Chapter 4: Bridging Divides

1. Fernando Oscar Reati, email communications, December 4 and 9, 2013, and interview, 2014; Alejandro Drallny, email communication, December 10, 2013.

2. *La Voz del Interior*, May 15, 1942, 6.

3. *La Tribuna*, April 23, 1942, 8. I found insufficient data to address the age variable.

4. Pririzant, interview, 2007.

5. Oliver, *Mi fe es el hombre*, 44, as quoted in chapter 3.

6. Mathias, "Long-Distance Charisma."

7. Adamovsky, *Historia de la clase media argentina*; Hora and Losada, "Clases altas y medias."

8. Adamovsky, *Historia de la clase media argentina*; Milanesio, *Workers Go Shopping in Argentina*, 126–28. See chapter 8.

9. Elena, *Dignifying Argentina*, 25–27; Guy, *Women Build the Welfare State*.

10. Karush, *Culture of Class*.

11. Josephs, *Argentine Diary*, 115.

12. Chase, *Revolution within the Revolution*, 88, noted how the upper-class women's presence protected other Cuban activists.

13. *Argentina Libre*, September 18, 1941, 12.

14. Junta de la Victoria, *Primera convención nacional*, 41.

15. Edelman, interview, 2009; Scaliter de Monín, interview, 1997; Halperin, interview, 2000.

16. *La Hora*, September 28, 1941, 10; Eduardo Aunós, *Viaje a la Argentina* (Madrid: Ed. Nacional, 1943), 115, cited in Elena, *Dignifying Argentina*, 26; Guy, *Women Build the Welfare State*, 59–60. On poor young women, see Deutsch, *Crossing Borders*, 66.

17. To what extent servants joined the Victory Board is unclear. Later in this chapter I mention a cook.

18. *Standard*, May 6, 1942, 11.

19. *La Voz del Interior*, September 15, 1941, 7.

20. Burman, "Made at Home by Clever Fingers," 38, noted that poor women maintained respectability by making their clothes at home.

21. For example, see *La Hora*, June 3, 1942, 5.

22. Deutsch, *Las derechas*, 238. As did pupils in public schools.

23. *Orientación*, November 9, 1941, 9.

24. Information on members came from interviews with Victory Board members, their relatives, descendants, and friends; consultations with historians and longtime residents; newspapers and their social pages; and other printed sources. See the interviews, consultations, and biographical sections of the bibliography.

25. Cusien, interview, 2000; Rapaport, consultation, 1998.

26. For how I determined class affiliation, see table 2.

27. In Table 2, I considered commercial and office employees working-class; in Tables 3 and 4, I listed them separately from laborers.

28. Othar, Edelman, and Hernández, interviews, 2009; Pasquali, "Entrevista a Amor Hernández," 2016; Del Franco, *Mujeres, ese fuego, esas luchas*, 28–29 (quote on 29). Mariela Rubinzal, Laura Pasquali, and María Ulivarri, in numerous email communications, provided information on neighborhoods. I studied only full-fledged chapters. Tafí Viejo, however, was sometimes called a *sub-filial* rather than a *filial*.

29. Edelman, interview, 2009; *Orientación*, October 22, 1942, 3; Junta de la Victoria, *Primera convención nacional*, 15, 40–41; *La Hora*, August 16, 1942, 5.

30. *El Territorio* (Resistencia), April 15, 1943, 2; *El Orden*, March 26, 1942, 5.

31. *La Hora*, November 24, 1941, 4, May 10, 1943, 3.

32. *La Hora*, June 17, 1942, 5, August 19, 1942, 5.

33. Queirolo, *Mujeres en las oficinas*; "Dactilógrafas"; and email communication, June 9, 2019. Adamovsky, *Historia de la clase media argentina*, 51, noted the problems of categorizing such persons as middle-class. Porter, *From Angel to Office Worker*, found that Mexicans considered women office workers middle-class,

yet they engaged in union struggles, feminism, and the antifascist Frente Único Pro-Derechos de la Mujer.

34. Junta de la Victoria, *Primera convención nacional*, 48, 60; *La Gaceta*, May 29, 1943, 4; *La Capital*, September 6, 1942, 13, November 6, 1942, 7; *La Tribuna*, April 19, 1942, 3; *La Hora*, April 23, 1942, 7, May 6, 1942, 5.

35. *La Hora*, May 7, 1943, 6, May 14, 1943, 5.

36. *Orientación*, April 23, 1942, 1–2, also in Bisso, ed., *El antifascismo argentino*, 164.

37. *La Voz del Interior*, May 15, 1942, 6. On malnourishment, see Salvatore, "Net Nutritional Inequality."

38. *La Hora*, January 23, 1942, 8, January 24, 1942, 4.

39. *La Hora*, August 3, 1942, 6, February 2, 1943, 3; *Vosotras*, August 14, 1942, 74; Marino, *Feminism for the Americas*, 130–34.

40. I found only one issue of *Mujeres en la Ayuda* (1941–1942), 8; *La Capital*, June 7, 1942, 13.

41. *Mujeres en la Ayuda* (1941–1942), 50.

42. See, for example, *La Unión*, December 3, 1942, 4; *Córdoba*, May 16, 1943, 6; *El Hogar*, June 26, 1942, 3; *Diario Popular*, March 27, 1944, 2.

43. *Argentina Libre*, June 5, 1941, 2.

44. Seidman, *Transatlantic Fascisms*, 19–23. On Spanish women's attitudes in this regard, see Nash, *Defying Male Civilization*, 72–74, 81–82; Ackelsberg, "Women and the Politics of the Spanish Popular Front," 8; Alcalde, *La mujer en la guerra civil española*, 145.

45. Nállim, *Transformations and Crisis of Liberalism in Argentina*, 145.

46. *La Unión*, December 7, 1942, 5.

47. See chapter 7.

48. Junta de la Victoria, *Primera convención nacional*, 16; *La Hora*, May 10, 1943, 3.

49. Del Franco, *Mujeres, ese fuego, esas luchas*, 29. Pite, *Creating a Common Table*, 5, 122–23, 222–23, passim, emphasized women's leadership in food-related matters. Bisso, "'Abajo con la tiranía pueblera y totalitaria,'" noted that an Acción Argentina chapter helped fund a school dining hall and raised money for school cooperatives.

50. *El Territorio* (Resistencia), March 3, 1942, 4; *La Unión*, March 24, 1943, 5, April 4, 1943, 3 (quote).

51. *La Hora*, April 14, 1942, 5, April 7, 1943, 5.

52. *La Tribuna*, June 7, 1942, 7.

53. *El Hogar*, May 15, 1942, 14.

54. *La Gaceta de Acción Argentina*, August 1942, September 1942, 30, November 1942, 18; *La Prensa*, July, 30, 1942, 10, August 3, 1942, 8, August 29, 1942, 8, November 16, 1942, 8.

55. Sameh, "Solidarity," 181–82.

56. *Boletín de la CIM* 1, no. 1 (June 1943): 11. This training prepared many women for participation in the Unión de Mujeres de la Argentina; see chapter 8.

57. Moya, *Cousins and Strangers*, 180–88.

58. Schwarzstein, *Entre Franco y Perón*, 154; Del Franco, *Mujeres, ese fuego, esas luchas*, 27–28.

59. Maeder, consultation, 2013.

60. *El Territorio* (Resistencia), November 12, 1942, 3.

61. "Comités adheridos a la Fiesta por la Libertad." On Rosario, see *La Capital*, November 21, 1941, 5, May 17, 1942, 5, January 21, 1943, 4; Junta de la Victoria *Primera convención nacional*, 60; *La Hora*, January 26, 1942, 5. See also *La Hora*, October 13, 1941, 4, December 5, 1941, 5, October 18, 1942, 5; *Mujeres en la Ayuda* (1941–1942), 22; *La Voz del Interior*, December 7, 1942, 8.

62. One can regard Jews as a religious group, an ethnic group, or a set of groups of different ethnicities and cultures. See Deutsch, *Crossing Borders*, 2–3.

63. On Nationalism and race, see Deutsch, "Insecure Whiteness," 42–44. The Congreso de la Solidaridad de los Pueblos (see its proceedings), an international meeting on racism in which Argentines participated, was mostly devoted to antisemitism.

64. See, among other works, Alberto and Elena, eds., *Rethinking Race in Modern Argentina*, esp. Chamosa, "People as Landscape," 53–54, and Pite, "*La cocina criolla*," 101–2, 114–15; and Chamosa, "'Indigenous or Criollo.'"

65. *La Hora*, September 28, 1941, 9.

66. Quotes in *La Hora*, May 9, 6, May 14, 1943, 5.

67. Moya, *Cousins and Strangers*, 180–87.

68. Deutsch, "Insecure Whiteness," 29–33 (quote), 46; Yarfitz, *Impure Migration*, 10.

69. Feierstein, *Historia de los judíos argentinos*, 399.

70. Junta de la Victoria, *Primera convención nacional*, 39; *Mujeres en la Ayuda* (1941–1942), 14. Seventeen chapters appear in table 8, but one of them may have melded with another at a later point. The Victory Board was growing and later claimed to have more branches in the interior. Among many sources on Jewish colonies, see Elkin, *Jews of Latin America*, 101–13; Deutsch, *Crossing Borders*, 13–41, passim.

71. Argentines distinguish between Ashkenazim (of Yiddish-speaking descent) and Jews of German-speaking descent.

72. See, for example, *La Hora*, May 8, 1943, 6.

73. *Mujeres en la Ayuda* (1941–1942), 14, 16, 47–48, 62–64. The two agricultural hubs were Machagai and Presidente Roque Sáenz Peña (Chaco), and the six Jewish colony communities were Gilbert-Escriña, Villa Domínguez, and Las Palmeras (Entre Ríos), Moisés Ville and Palacios (Santa Fe), and Rivera (Buenos Aires). The rural chapters with Jewish vice presidents were Villa Domínguez, Presidente Roque Sáenz Peña, and Las Breñas (Chaco). See also Deutsch, "Antifascist Jewish Women."

74. In 1946 there were approximately 350,000 Jews in Argentina. For statistics, see *American Jewish Year Book* 48 (1946–1947): 603, https://www.ajcarchives.org/AJC_DATA/Files/1946_1947_13_Statistics.pdf.

75. Jewish Italians did not necessarily define themselves as Sephardim. On their participation in the Victory Board, see Smolensky and Vigevani Jarach, *Tantas voces, una historia*, 62, 280.

76. *Mujeres en la Ayuda* (1941–1942), 47; Junta de la Victoria, *Ayuda de las mujeres argentinas*; Junta de la Victoria, *Primera convención nacional*, 39. *La Hora*, November 27, 1941, 5, reported that Scheiner presided over the secretariat of Ciudadela, just outside Buenos Aires.

77. *La Hora*, February 17, 1943, 5; Visacovsky, *Argentinos, judíos y camaradas*.

78. *Mujeres en la Ayuda* (1941–1942), 42, 48, 62–63.

79. *Mujeres en la Ayuda* (1941–1942), 11–13; *La Hora*, May 10, 1943, 3; Junta de la Victoria, *Primera convención nacional*, 5.

80. *La Hora*, February 8, 1943, 5. Simón Romero, "Outpost in the Pampas Where Jews Once Found Refuge Wilts as They Leave," *New York Times*, June 10, 2013, estimated a population of five thousand; "Moises Ville Argentina. Jewish Gauchos," scatteredamongthenations.org/agentina, estimated 7,000.

81. Deutsch, *Crossing Borders*, 187.

82. *Orientación*, November 6, 1941, 9.

83. *La Hora*, April 15, 1942, 1, April 16, 1942, 5.

84. *Orientación*, April 23, 1942, 1.

85. *El Territorio* (Resistencia), February 1, 1943, 2.

86. *Mujeres en la Ayuda* (1941–1942), 20 (quote), 21, 32, 50.

87. *Boletín de la CIM* 1, no. 1 (June 1943): 13; *Córdoba*, April 13, 1943, 5; Deutsch, *Crossing Borders*, 220. Schlieper and Silveyra spoke at Jewish events in 1944, when the Victory Board operated clandestinely; see *Clarinada*, June 1944, 17, and September 1944, 20–21, respectively.

88. *La Hora*, February 26, 1942, 5.

89. Mónica Szurmuk, email communication, May 26, 2019, and *La vocación desmesurada*; Dujovne, "Impresiones del judaísmo"; Deutsch, *Crossing Borders*.

90. Lida, *Monseñor Miguel de Andrea*, 137 (quote); Deutsch, *Las derechas*, 240–44; Zanatta, *Del estado liberal*.

91. Finchelstein, *Transatlantic Fascism*.

92. *Orientación*, November 13, 1941, 5.

93. As did Acción Argentina; see *La Prensa*, November 7, 1940, 16, May 13, 1941, 12; Bisso, *Acción Argentina*, 199–204.

94. Parts of this pamphlet appeared in *Orientación*, April 9, 1942, 8. The OIAA sent a consignment of pamphlets titled *La guerra nacista contra la Iglesia Católica*, published by the National Catholic Welfare Council, to its representatives in Argentina. This pamphlet probably resembled the Victory Board's pronouncements discussed above. The Argentine customs and postal service categorized it as danger-

ous and recommended destroying the copies. See Robert C. Wells, memorandum 1643, July 28, 1943, box 1245, folder Communication to the U.S., 1601–1700, RG 229, OIAA, Records of the Dept. of Information, Regional Division, Coordination Committee for Argentina, General Records, Communication to and from the U.S., NARA.

95. *Orientación*, April 23, 1942, 1, May 13, 1943, 5; *La Gaceta*, December 2, 1942, 4; *La Hora*, October 27, 1942, 5, November 29, 1942, 7; *El Día* (La Plata), December 22, 1941, 3. On the ACA see, among other sources, Ivereigh, *Catholicism and Politics in Argentina*, 77–78, 88–91, passim.

96. *La Voz del Interior*, September 6, 1942, 9; *La Hora*, September 2, 1942, 5.

97. *Mujeres en la Ayuda* (1941–1942), 11, 35, 58; *La Hora*, February 4, 1942, 4, May 10, 1943, 2; Queirolo, *Mujeres en las oficinas*, 163–208.

98. FACE, *Anales*, no. 1 (1936); *Agremiación Femenina*, November-December 1942, 4, January-February 1942, 5; *La Prensa*, July 1, 1940, 11; *La Hora*, October 14, 1941, 6. Among other works, see Lida, *Monseñor Miguel de Andrea*, esp. 110–14, 135–76; Queirolo, "La Federación de Asociaciones Católicas"; Deutsch, "Catholic Church, Work, and Womanhood"; Caimari, *Perón y la iglesia católica*, 44–45, 86–90; Zanatta, *Del estado liberal*, 239, 341–42.

99. *La Hora*, October 27, 1942, 5. *La Prensa*, May 11, 1941, 24; Deutsch, *Counterrevolution in Argentina*, 156–58.

100. On Mooney and US Catholic reformers, see Tentler, *Seasons of Grace*; Abell, "Monsignor John A. Ryan"; Kennedy et al., eds., *Religion and Public Life*; *Los Andes*, February 8, 1943, 4. Mooney's support for segregated parishes marred his Social Catholicism; see Southern, *John La Farge and the Limits of Catholic Interracialism*, 255.

101. *Time*, September 7, 1942, 86 (quote). On OIAA support, see Walter T. Pendergast, CIAA Project Evaluation Report, April 13, 1944, box 364, folder SE-1249, OEMcr210, Conference on Social Problems in Hemispheric War Effort, RG 229, OIAA, General Records, Central Files, 3, Information, Science and Education, Catholic, NARA; Cramer and Prutsch, "Nelson A. Rockefeller's Office," 31.

102. *Time*, September 7, 1942, 86. On the seminar and Andrea's views, see his *Pensamiento cristiano*, 184; *Agremiación Femenina*, September-October 1941, 22; *La Prensa*, May 18, 1941, 12; Lida, *Monseñor Miguel de Andrea*, 180–84. Andrea's speeches in *Pensamiento cristiano* reveal the elitist limits of his democratic beliefs, which presaged his opposition to Perón.

103. See, for example, *La Gaceta*, September 3, 1942, 2.

104. November 25, 1942, Minutes of Executive Committee of American Organizations meeting October 30, 1942, box 1249, folder 103.9/000, Minutes of the Coordinating Committee (1942–3), OIAA, Records of the Department of Information, Regional Division, Coordinating Committee for Argentina, General Records (E-98), Minutes of Meetings, RB 229, NARA; Lida, *Monseñor Miguel de Andrea*, 184–86.

105. Espósito to Cannon, June 1, 1943, box 3, folder Cannon, Mary 1943, June, Women's Bureau, International Division, General Records 1919–1952, RG 86, NARA.

106. *Orden Cristiano*, October 1, 1942, 8–10, published Andrea's speech at the "The Americas and the Crisis of Civilization" seminar. See also Lida and González Warcalde, "El sinuoso camino," 260. Jorge Nállim, email communication, June 14, 2019, said that the military government (1943–1946) did not close *Orden Cristiano*, as it did other antifascist periodicals and groups, probably because the magazine supported religious education in the public schools.

107. Zanca, *Cristianos antifascistas*, 132–36; Valobra, "El particular ideario"; Finchelstein, *Ideological Origins of the Dirty War*, 45; Nállim, *Transformations and Crisis of Liberalism in Argentina*, 111, 115; *Argentina Libre*, January 8, 1942, 3, 10.

108. On this and the previous paragraph, see *Argentina Libre*, September 18, 1941, 9; *Antinazi* (the continuation of *Argentina Libre*), February 22, 1945, 5; *Orden Cristiano*, October 19, 1941, 9–10, June 1, 1942, 3–4, 15; August 15, 1942, 8–9; January 15, 1944, 161–63 (quotes on 161). Acción Argentina engaged in similar rhetoric to attract Catholics and had clerical members until the Catholic Church forbade it; see Bisso, *Acción Argentina*, 198–201.

109. *Argentina Libre*, December 10, 1942, 5; *Orden Cristiano*, July 15, 1944, 399–402. Among numerous sources on the church's record, see Phayer, *Catholic Church and the Holocaust*.

110. Lvovich and Finchelstein, "Nazismo y holocausto," esp. 316–17; Ben-Dror, *La iglesia*, 247–249.

111. Junta de la Victoria, *Primera convención nacional*, 18; *La Hora*, October 16, 1941, 4, April 15, 1942, 1. Silveyra also appeared at other Victory Board events; for example, see *La Acción*, June 7, 1942, 3.

112. *La Voz del Interior*, August 23, 1942, 8 (quote); *El País*, August 21, 1942, 9.

113. *La Voz del Interior*, August 24, 1942, 7.

114. *La Tribuna*, April 23, 1942, 8; *El Territorio* (Resistencia), June 15, 1942, 3.

115. *La Hora*, May 7, 1942, 5; *La Voz del Interior*, August 24, 1942, 7.

116. Ardanaz, "Con el puño en alto," 122n215, found Spiritist involvement in Bahía Blanca.

117. Edelman, interview, 2009.

118. Macor, "Partidos, coaliciones y sistema de poder"; Privitellio, "La política bajo"; Fernández de Ulivarri, "Trabajadores, sindicatos y política"; Persello, *el partido radical*; Camarero and Herrera, eds., *El Partido Socialista en Argentina*; Laura Pascuali, email communication, September 15, 2009.

119. Nicolás Iñigo Carrera, consultation, 2013.

120. Butiérrez de Báez, interview, 2009; *El Día* (La Plata), October 15, 1942, 5; Valobra, "'En bien de mis ideales,'" and "Acción y sociabilidad políticas"; Gallo, *Las mujeres en el radicalismo argentino*, 27, 32, 38, 44, 49, 52, 55.

121. *La Prensa*, October 11, 1941, 13; *Standard*, December 4, 1941, 2; *El Territorio* (Resistencia), June 15, 1942, 3; *Los Andes*, April 17, 1943, 4; *La Hora*, December 8, 1941, 6; May 19, 1942, 5; Bisso, *Acción Argentina*, 120; Marcela Vignoli, email communication, April 10, 2019.

122. *La Vanguardia*, February 1, 1942, 4; and *La Verdad*, August 29, 1942, (quote), courtesy of Elsa Dellatorre.

123. *Los Andes*, May 31, 1942, 13. Ávila was the sister-in-law of Franco Romero Day, an elected PDN provincial official and Acción Argentina member. Dr. Enrique Day, another PDN liberal, belonged to the CSA. Mariana Garzón Rogé, consultation, 2013, and "De nacionalismo a antifascistas"; Bisso, *Acción Argentina*, 340. The two PDN women's committees in Buenos Aires Province in the 1930s, however, aligned with rightist governor Manuel Fresco; see Valobra, "Sufragismo y acción política femenina," 204–10. On the PDN in Buenos Aires, see Walter, *Province of Buenos Aires*; Béjar, *El régimen fraudulento*.

124. *La Hora*, September 14, 1941, 5, April 15, 1942, 1 and 7, August 22, 1942, 5, August 25, 1942, 5, September 27, 1942, 5, October 4, 1942, 6, October 14, 1942, 1, October 27, 1942, 5, November 21, 1942, 5; *El Día* (La Plata), October 24, 1942, 5; *Los Andes*, April 18, 1943, 4; *La Vanguardia*, December 23, 1941, 3; Cora Ratto de Sadosky to Nicolás Repetto, December 18, 1942, carpeta 30.103, Fondo de Archivo Nicolás Repetto, CeDInCI.

125. See chapter 1. On Ocampo's regard for British literature, see *La Prensa*, October 4, 1940, 13. *La Hora*, January 8, 1942, 5, claimed that numerous pro-British women belonged to the Victory Board. According to Bisso, *Acción Argentina*, 84–90, Acción Argentina also used the mystiques of French culture and British resistance to appeal to potential recruits.

126. On this and the preceding paragraph, see Buchanan, "Antifascism and Democracy in the 1930s"; Pasquali, email communication, August 13, 2014; Nállim, email communication, July 17, 2014; Nállim, *Transformations and Crisis of Liberalism in Argentina*, chaps. 2 and 5, esp. 108, and "An Unbroken Loyalty in Turbulent Times"; Scheiner in *La Vanguardia*, February 13, 1933, 10, February 23, 1934, 12.

127. *La Capital*, September 26, 1941, 11; Junta de la Victoria, *Primera convención nacional*; *Orientación*, May 13, 1943, 5 (quote).

128. *La Hora*, September 28, 1941, 10.

129. Schneider, "Two Faces of Modernity." Ardanaz, "Con el puño en alto," 111n183, however, considered antifascism a possible means of absorbing ethnic communities, implying assimilation.

130. Lorde, *Sister Outsider*, 110–14, courtesy of Marion Rohrleitner.

131. *El Territorio* (Resistencia), April 7, 1943, 2, April 15, 1943, 2 (quotes). Musicians and dancers of foreign origin often performed at Victory Board functions. See, for example, *Estampa Chaqueña*, February 21–28, 1942, 13.

132. Furtembach de Kanner, interview, 2013.

133. Fernández, "Olga Cosettini y el Colegio Libre," 152–53.

134. Alejandra Pita González supplied insights into analyzing networks in her comments at the panel on "Networks in Latin American History: Theoretical and Empirical Approaches," Latin American Studies Association meeting, Boston, May 24–27, 2019.

135. Baaclini, Cutín, Kaufman, Serrano Pérez, interviews, 2013. See also Cutín, Polly Jánover de., n.d., Subfondo Archivo de Redacción de *Qué sucedió en 7 días*, Fondo Centro de Estudios Nacionales (Fondo CEN), Archivos y Colecciones Particulares, Biblioteca Nacional, Buenos Aires.

136. Wexler and Molinas, interview, 2009; Susana Molinas, interview, 2013.

137. Kaufman and Serrano Pérez, interviews, 2013; Leoni de Rosciano, *El Ateneo del Chaco*; "Recortes de periódicos referentes a la vida de la institución," El Fogón de los Arrieros, Resistencia; Tío Nicucho, "Rosa Diner," essay, 2005, Rosa Diner de Babini file, Archivo Samatán.

138. Juan Pablo Jaroslavsky, email communication, June 25, 2013; Maeder, consultation, 2013; Ardanaz, "Con el puño en also," 122; *La Voz del Interior*, May 15, 1942, 6. Mosset Iturraspe and Kedinger, interviews, 2013.

139. Cutín, Feigin, and Ternavasio, interviews, 2013; Garber (of Villa Ángela), and Peczak, consultations, 2013. Szurmuk, *La vocación desmesurada*, described how Gerchunoff, an autodidact, rose from extreme poverty through cultural attainment.

140. Pompert de Valenzuela, consultation, 2013.

141. Mosset Iturraspe and Susana Molinas, interviews, 2013; Gattegno and Weinstein, consultations, 2011.

142. Rein, *Populism and Ethnicity*.

143. Power, email communication, May 4, 2019.

144. Nadal, consultation, 2013.

145. I reviewed the *Revista del Consejo Nacional de Mujeres de la República Argentina*, whose name changed from *Revista* to *Boletín* in 1940, for 1915 and 1934–1946. On the Consejo's early years, see Vasallo, "Entre el conflicto"; Vignoli, "Cecilia Grierson y las damas de la Beneficencia" and "Intentos de adhesión a una agenda feminista." Vignoli suggested comparing the two groups.

146. Carolina L. de Argerich, president of the Consejo Nacional de Mujeres, to Elvira Rawson de Dellepiane, n.d., box 1, folder 44, Correspondence 1932, Elvira Rawson de Dellepiane Collection, MSH/LAT 0045, Department of Special Collections, Hesburgh Libraries of the University of Notre Dame, Notre Dame, IN; Hammond, *Women's Suffrage Movement*, 122, 127.

147. *Revista*, January-June 1938, 10–18; *Boletín*, July 1943, 7–8, July 1944, 7–8.

148. The French branch of the World Committee of Women Against War and Fascism faced similar problems; see Brown, "'Pour Aider Nos Frères D'Espagne,'" 34.

Chapter 5: Gendering Antifascism in a Patriarchal Society

1. *El Territorio* (Resistencia), October 20, 1941, 2, and July 6, 1942, 3.

2. Becerra, "Maternidad y ciudadanía en la Argentina"; Oliver, interview, 1971, *Mundo mi casa*, and *La vida cotidiana*, esp. 316–19. See also Rodolfo Aráoz Alfaro to Oliver, n.d., box 2, folder 21; Carmen Baeza to Oliver, n.d., box 2, folder 29; Waldo Frank to Oliver, August 3, 1937, box 3, folder 50, all in Oliver Papers.

3. Deutsch, "New School Lecture 'An Army of Women,'" 99.

4. *La Nación*, November 29, 1941, clipping, box 9, folder 19, Oliver papers. Chapter 3 mentions this celebration.

5. *La Hora*, April 15, 1942, 7.

6. Junta de la Victoria, "Colabore." For Ratto's statement, see chapter 3.

7. *La Hora*, January 29, 1942, 4.

8. *Mujeres en la Ayuda* (1941–1942), 7.

9. *La Voz del Interior*, September 23, 1941, 7, September 26, 1941, 9, October 3, 1941, 7, October 10, 1941, 7, October 24, 1941, 9, October 25, 1941, 7, October 27, 1941, 7; *Córdoba*, January 5, 1943, 5; *La Hora*, April 16, 1942, 5.

10. Junta de la Victoria, *Primera convención nacional*, 15; *IACW Information Bulletin*, September 1942, 1; *La Hora*, May 19, 1942, 5, October 10, 1942, 5, October 14, 1942, 1, November 21, 1942, 5, November 22, 1942, 5, November 29, 1942, 6.

11. *La Hora*, September 14, 1941, 5; *IACW Information Bulletin*, September 1942, 1 (Schlieper).

12. *History of the Inter-American Commission*, 213.

13. See, for example, *Argentina Libre*, February 27, 1941, 3, October 9, 1941, 3.

14. Bisso, *El antifascismo argentino*, 171, 173, and *Acción Argentina*, 121–23, 324–25.

15. Kaufman, 2013; Edelman, 2009; Braslavsky, 2000, interviews.

16. Camarero, consultation, 2013.

17. Kaufman, interview, 2013.

18. Regarding FUPDM, see chapter 2; on MEMCH, see Antezana-Pernet, "Mobilizing Women in the Popular Front Era," 335–42.

19. De Haan, "Eugénie Cotton" (quote on 179), "Continuing Cold War Paradigms," and "La Federación Democrática," 19; Mooney, "Fighting Fascism," 54; Gradskova, "Women's International Democratic Federation." Weigand, *Red Feminism*, 10, found that rank-and-file women took advantage of Soviet silences on certain issues and altered the US party's position on them.

20. On agency, see Bonfiglioli, "Red Girls' Revolutionary Tales"; Valobra and Yusta, eds., *Queridas camaradas*.

21. *Comisión Israelita de Ayuda a los Aliados. Solidaridad*, October 1942, 2, New York Public Library. CCFIS's name changed several times.

22. Comisión Femenina Israelita de Solidaridad, *Nuestros talleres*, 27–28 (quotes), box 1070, IWO (since recatalogued); *Mujeres en la Ayuda* (1941–1942), 22. On this organization's head, see Visacovsky, "Berta Blejman de Drucaroff."

23. Mónica Szurmuk, comment, Primer Coloquio sobre Género y Trayectorias Antifascistas, Universidad Nacional de La Plata, Argentina, June 24, 2013.

24. Weigand, *Red Feminism*; Boxer, "Rethinking the Socialist Construction"; Lynn, "Women on the March."

25. *La Voz del Interior*, October 1, 1941, 7 (Schlieper), October 27, 1941, 7; Junta de la Victoria, *Estatutos*; membership card quoted in Junta de la Victoria, *Ayuda de las mujeres*, n.p. The Victory Board's 1945 statutes declared that the Victory Board aimed to "defend the rights of the woman." See "Estatutos, Junta de la Victoria," in Bisso, ed., *El antifascismo argentino*, 148, 151.

26. *La Capital*, June 7, 1942, 13 (quote); *La Tribuna*, June 7, 1942, 7; *El Territorio* (Posadas), November 19, 1942, 6; *Vida Femenina*, August-September 1942, 7–9. On the Sociedad, see Guy, *Women Build the Welfare State*, and "La 'verdadera historia'"; Mead, "Beneficent Maternalism"; Pita, "¿La ciencia o la costura?"

27. *Vida Femenina*, August-September 1942, 7.

28. Sociedad Unión Argentina de Mujeres (Filial Rosario), Expediente 5066, 2–7, AGPSF.

29. Samatán in *Vida Femenina*, August-September 1942, 27. On Olivé, see De Bertero, *Quién es ella*, 411. Laura Pascuali, email communication, May 14, 2009, noted her ties to a women's literature group connected to the local pro-Franco Club Español.

30. Ardanaz, "Con el puño," 116, 118, 120–22; Juárez, interview, 2014. Future Victory Board members Anatilde Yuquerí Rojas and Sara Papier advocated feminism in *Claridad*, July 29, 1933, 52, and February 1937, 33–34, respectively.

31. Chase, *Revolution*, 104.

32. *La Tribuna*, April 4, 6 (quote), April 10, 1943, 6. On Borzone's participation in the Victory Board, see Hernández, *Con la marca*, 221–22.

33. Susana Molinas, interview, 2013. Porta Echagüe and Yofre were her grandmothers.

34. Martínez Chas, consultations, 2013; Furtembach and Kanner, interview, 2013.

35. *El Territorio* (Resistencia), December 5, 1941, 3.

36. Such concerns lingered. Milanesio, *Destape*, 212, discussed a magazine article in 1984 whose female author claimed that feminist discussions of sex and demands for sexual pleasure alienated ordinary women.

37. *Mujeres en la Ayuda* (1941–1942), 14; *La Hora*, May 21, 1943, 5.

38. Mercedes Micene, interview with Eleonora Ardanaz, 2006, cited in Ardanaz, "Con el puño," 122n217.

39. Elkin, interview, 2013.

40. *La Tribuna*, June 7, 1942, 7; Schlieper to Ramírez, 3 (quote).

41. Ratto in *Boletín de la CIM,* June 1943, 11. Unlike Radical and Socialist women's committees, the Victory Board did not offer courses to prepare members for the labor force. See Valobra, "Sufragismo y acción política femenina," 208.

42. *La Tribuna*, April 23, 1942, 8.

43. *La Hora*, April 15, 1942, 5.

44. *La Hora*, May 5, 1943, 5, May 8, 1943, 6, May 9, 1943, 6.

45. *La Hora*, May 25, 1942, 1; Juárez and Reati, interviews, both in 2014.

46. Miller, *Latin American Women*, 108; Marino, *Feminism for the Americas*, 172–82; *IACW Information Bulletin*, September 1942, 3, 6–7.

47. On citizenship, voting, and military service, see *Argentina Libre*, October 9, 1941, 3; Valobra, *Del hogar a las urnas*, 31; Hammond, *Women's Suffrage Movement*, 137; Olcott, *Revolutionary Women in Postrevolutionary Mexico*, 11, 20–21; and esp. Colley, *Gun, the Ship, and the Pen*, 7–8, 271–75, 410–11.

48. *El Día* (La Plata), March 31, 1943, 5.

49. *La Hora*, May 7, 1943, 6.

50. Scholars should analyze church references to devout Catholics as the "army of Christ."

51. *New York Times*, November 8, 1941, 9; *IACW Information Bulletin*, December 1941, 3; Cano, "El 'feminismo de estado,'" 65.

52. IACW Resolution, draft, 1941, in Eleanor Roosevelt Papers. See also Mary Winslow to Carl B. Spaeth, January 7, 1942, and attachment, and Lawrence Duggan to John C. McClintock, April 4, 1942, box 72, folder Civilian Defense Programs for the O.A.R.; Winslow to Harrison, March 12, 1942, and to Rockefeller, June 29, 1942, box 72, folder Civilian Defense Miscellaneous, OIAA, General Records, Central Files, 1. Basic Economy: Emergency Rehabilitation, Civilian Defense, Economic Relief, Natural and War Disasters, RG 229, NARA; *New York Times*, January 12, 1942, clipping, box 76, folder 8, Stevens Papers. On Eleanor Roosevelt and civilian defense, see Lash, *Eleanor and Franklin*, 637–42, 644–52; Goodwin, *No Ordinary Time*, 280–81, 323–26, 628.

53. *Vosotras*, June 19, 1942, 4–5; Schlieper de Martínez Guerrero to Cannon, June 17, 1942, box 2, folder Cannon, Mary—1942, July, RG 86, and Winslow to L. M. Mitchell, June 10, 1942, box 72, folder Civilian Defense Miscellaneous, RG 229, NARA.

54. *Washington Star*, October 28, 1942, clipping, box 119, folder 843, Foreign Service Posts of the Department of State, Buenos Aires Embassy, General Records, 1941: 800–811.4, RG 84, NARA; Junta de la Victoria, *Primera convención nacional*, 12; *La Hora*, April 14, 1942, 5, October 5, 1942, 3, October 27, 1942, 5; *La Voz del Interior*, September 5, 1942, 8, September 6, 1942, 9, October 26, 1942, 9; *El Día* (La Plata), November 10, 1942, 9, November 17, 1942, 6; *La Tribuna*, June 14, 1942, 5; *Orientación*, April 16, 1942, 3, also in Bisso, ed., *El antifascismo argentino*, 161; Ramacciotti, 2013, and Valobra, 2014, consultations.

55. *La Prensa*, July 3, 1940, 14.

56. Schlieper de Martínez Guerrero to Cannon, June 17, 1942, box 2, folder Cannon, Mary—1942, July, RG 86, NARA.

57. *Argentina Libre*, June 4, 1942, 8, February 4, 1943, 5. The other advisor was conservative pacifist Máxima Olmos de Jiménez. The Red Cross sent blood transfusion materials and plasma through Winslow to Schlieper, which the Victory Board president probably intended for the DCF. See Winslow to Mitchell, June 10, 1942, box 72, folder Civilian Defense Miscellaneous, RG 229, NARA.

58. *Argentina Libre*, June 4, 1942, 8, February 4, 1943, 5 (quotes), also found in Bisso, *El antifascismo argentino*, 168–69, 178–80; *La Capital*, February 13, 7, March 11, 1943, 4; *Vosotras*, June 19, 1942, 4–5, November 27, 1942, 74; *La Hora*, August 17, 1942, 3.

59. Pririzant, interview, 2007.

60. *PANAM* 5, no. 3 (1944): 49–51; Winslow to Dorothy Brown, January 5, 1943, and attachment, box 72, folder Civilian Defense Miscellaneous, August 1, 1942—, RG 229, NARA; *Boletín de Información de la Comisión Interamericana de Mujeres*, no. 3 (n.d.), 2–6.

61. *Argentina Libre*, February 4, 1943, 5.

62. Deutsch, *Crossing Borders*, 50–54, 209; Lavrin, *Women, Feminism, and Social Change*, 69–70, 72–74; Milanesio, *Workers Go Shopping in Argentina*, 203–5; Girbal-Blacha, "El hogar o la fábrica"; Guy, email communication, July 31, 2019. The following informed this and the next paragraph: Burman, "Introduction," 11, and "Made at Home by Clever Fingers," 35–38, 40; Buckley, "On the Margins," 57, 67; Wilson, "Commodified Craft," 146.

63. Milanesio, *Workers Go Shopping in Argentina*, 203; Scates, "Unknown Sock Knitter," 34, 38, 45; Ipsen, "Patricias, Patriarchy, and Popular Demobilization"; Dumenil, "Women's Reform Organizations," 220–21.

64. As Dumenil argued for groups in Los Angeles during World War I in "Women's Reform Organizations," 239 (quote).

65. Dumenil, "Women's Reform Organizations," 241; Scates, "Unknown Sock Knitter," 43; Chesterton, "Composing Gender and Class." One might argue that these "godmothers" created a cross-class space through their letters, but it was hierarchical.

66. Acree, *"Divisas y deberes,"* 214, 228; Colley, *Britons*, 260–61 (quote); Rohrleitner, "Who We Are," esp. 426.

67. See chapter 2; Blee and Deutsch, eds., *Women of the Right*, 117–207.

68. Filer, interview, 1999.

69. Valobra, "Formación de cuadros," 144–45. Valobra, "Las comunistas argentinas," 74–75, later judged that the Victory Board's appeal was not exclusively maternalistic. On Nationalist women, see chapter 7. I only found the first issue of the Victory Board's magazine, *Mujeres en la Ayuda* (1941–1942), and it did not contain articles on motherhood and domesticity. According to *El Litoral*, April 25, 1943, 4, however, issue 6 did.

70. *El Territorio* (Resistencia), June 15, 1942, 3; *La Hora*, December 1, 1942, 5 (quote).

71. *La Hora*, January 29, 1942, 4, June 3, 1942, 5; Junta de la Victoria, *Primera convención nacional*, 59, 63 (quote); *La Libertad de Avellaneda*, November 2, 1942, 1.

72. *Argentina Libre*, December 4, 1941, 10 (Saslavsky), *Orientación*, April 30, 1942, 6. On antifascist women's concerns for children, see Lambe, *No Barrier Can Contain It*, 101–30; Damousi, "Humanitarianism and Child Refugee Sponsorship"; Gottlieb, "Broken Friendships and Vanished Loyalties," 213.

73. My thoughts on maternalism and rhetoric draw upon Weinstein, "Inventing the 'Mulher Paulista'"; Marino, "Transnational Pan-American Feminism"; and esp. Chase, *Revolution within the Revolution*, 79–80, 85–87, 89, 91 (quote).

74. *La Nación*, November 29, 1941, clipping, box 9, folder 19, Oliver Papers; Oliver, *Mi fe es el hombre*, 42, 44 (quote).

75. Junta de la Victoria, *Primera convención nacional*, 23; Clementi, *Lautaro*, 47.

76. *La Hora*, March 18, 1942, 4 (quote); Junta de la Victoria, *Primera convención nacional*, 46, 53 (Mendoza quote).

77. *El Orden*, December 16, 1941, 3.

78. *Boletín de la CIM*, June 1943, 3–4.

79. Chase, *Revolution within the Revolution*, 86.

80. *La Hora*, October 16, 1941, 8.

81. *La Voz del Interior*, September 15, 1941, 7.

82. *El Orden*, April 1, 1942, 8.

83. *La Hora*, March 19, 1942, 5; Barrancos, *Mujeres en la sociedad argentina*, 77–87; Brewster, "Women and the Spanish American Wars"; Root, *Couture and Consensus*, 38–40.

84. See, for example, *La Voz del Interior*, September 6, 1942, 9.

85. *Diario Popular*, July 4, 1944, 2; Emilio Troise, historia biográfica, and caja 4, carpeta 5, documento 6, "Discurso pronunciado en acto oganizado por Acción Femenina por la Victoria," Uruguay, [1944], Fondo Emilio Troise, CeDInCI.

86. Junta de la Victoria, *Primera convención nacional*, 44.

87. For examples, see *La Hora*, March 17, 1942, 5, February 24, 1943, 2.

88. *La Nación*, June 3, 1943, clipping courtesy of Mónica Szurmuk; *La Hora*, September 6, 1942, 6.

89. *La Voz del Interior*, October 19, 1941, 9; Bisso, "Deodoro Roca y la polémica," xi–xxxviii.

90. *Orientación*, February 12, 1942, 3, and April 16, 1942, 3, excerpted in Bisso, ed., *El antifascismo argentino*, 157–61; OIAA, Records of the Department of Information, Regional Division, Coordinating Committee for Argentina, General Records (E-98), Minutes of Meetings, Minutes of the Executive Committee of America Organizations, May 7, 1943, box 1249, folder 103.9, RG 229, NARA; *Los Andes*, May 23, 1942, 4.

91. Bordagaray, "Luchas antifascistas y trayectorias generizadas."

92. For this and the next paragraph, see Vergara, *Memorias de una mujer ir-reverente*; Marino, "Marta Vergara"; "Marcos Chamudes Reitich (1907–1989)," MemoriaChilena, memoriachilena.gob.cl/602/w3-article-741.html; Chamudes, *El libro blanco*. On other Communist antifascist couples, see Morais, *Olga*; Gadea, *My Life with Che*; March, *Remembering Che*.

93. Regarding party interference, compare to Cosse, "Infidelities."

94. Lambe, *No Barrier Can Contain It*, esp. 32, 35 (quote), 79 (quote), 81, 87, 101, 129–30.

95. This and the previous paragraph draw upon Furtembach de Kanner and Kanner, interview, 2013; Martínez Chas, consultations, 2013. Jackson, *British Women and the Spanish Civil War*, 27–28, discussed antifascist women who admired and learned from their male partners.

96. Cutín, interview, 2013; Campi, consultations, 2013; file Cutín, Polly Jánover de, Subfondo Archivo de Redacción de *Qué sucedió en 7 días*, Fondo CEN; *La Gaceta*, April 24, 1945, 4.

97. Reati, email communication, December 9, 2013, containing Inés Drallny's testimony and Oscar Eugenio Reati's police record; Reati, interview, 2014; Drallny, email communication, December 10, 2013. Other Communist antifascist marriages include Fanny and Bernardo Edelman and Cora Ratto and Manuel Sadosky.

98. *Orientación*, September 25, 1941, 1; *El Litoral*, October 24, 1942, 4, April 4, 1943, 5, April 20, 1943, 5. Active in Rosario and Santa Fe, Frente members were married to Victory Board members in both cities. Sors of Paraná and UCR congressman Santander; Emilia G. de (president of the Centro secretariat) and Socialist congressman Julio González Iramaín; Minetti of Tucumán and Dr. Miguel Figueroa Román (UCR); Clara Craven of Santa Fe and PDP congressman Dr. Mario Mosset Iturraspe; Josefina Barbat of Tucumán and Dr. Risieri Frondizi (UCR), and Cremades of Córdoba and UCR senator Oddone were among the many non-Communist marriages.

99. Susana Molinas, interview, 2013; Wexler and Luis Molinas, interview, 2009.

100. Norman Armour to Secretary of State, October 24, 1939, No. 3024, U.S. State Dept., RG 710.F, Inter-American Commission of Women/139, NARA, courtesy of Katherine Marino; Luzuriaga, *Centinela de libertad*, 157–58, 276, 278, 291, 294–97, 301–8, photos on pages after 336 and 352; Walter, *Province of Buenos Aires*, 40.

101. Gasió, *El Jefe del Estado Mayor*, 169; unsam.edu.ar/escuelas/política/centro_historia_política/_materiales.asp.

102. I borrow this term from Boylan, "Gendering the Faith," 216.

103. *La Hora*, October 14, 1941, 4, May 7, 1943, 6, May 9, 1943, 3; Elkin and Cutín, interviews, 2013; Deutsch, *Crossing Borders*, 198–201. On ICUF, see Visacovsky, *Argentinos, judíos y camaradas*.

104. Faingold de Villagra, interview, 1997; Molodesky, interview, 2013; Elsa Dellatorre, email communication, August 25, 2013.

Chapter 6: The Cloth That Binds

1. Oliver, "A Porteña Reports," 46.

2. *Diario Popular*, October 1, 1945, 4.

3. *La Nación*, November 29, 1941, clipping, box 9, folder 19, Oliver Papers.

4. David Sheinin, email communication, June 19, 2019; for these and other examples, see *La Capital*, June 7, 1942, 13, July 19, 1942, 4, July 23, 1942, 4; *Standard*, July 22, 1942, 7; *La Voz del Interior*, December 1, 1942, 8, December 5, 1942, 7; *La Hora*, December 31, 1941, 4, March 15, 1942, 5, September 1, 1942, 5, November 21, 1942, 5.

5. Chapter 4 mentions Anglo-Argentine women in the San Fernando, Buenos Aires chapter. See also *El País*, August 3, 1942, 9; Feigin, interview, 2013; *El Litoral*, September 30, 1942, 8, October 14, 1942, 8, April 5, 1943, 8; *La Gaceta*, April 25, 1943, 5; *La Unión*, November 12, 1942, 8. J. N. Macintosh was the British vice-consul in Santa Fe.

6. *Standard Victory Supplement 1939–1945*, 103; Kelly to Foreign Office, telegram, July 26, 1943, 0078, 11/286/43, Great Britain, Foreign Office, Embassy and Consulates, Argentine Republic, General Correspondence, FO 118: 721; Junta de la Victoria, *Primera convención nacional*, 18; *La Hora*, September 14, 1941, 5, May 3, 1942, 7, April 21, 1943, 5, May 9, 1943, 6; *La Prensa*, September 26, 1941, 13.

7. Feigin, interview, 2013; *La Vanguardia*, February 5, 1942, 4. Regarding Hoover, see note 33.

8. S. R. Robertson to Foreign Office, Minute Sheet, August 21, 1942, 0010–0018, 69A/131/42, FO 118: 709; *New York Times*, July 16, 1943, 7. I found no such Victory Board statements.

9. I only found one press mention of such involvement, a Victory Board film festival sponsored by the embassy; see *La Prensa*, December 8, 1942, 6. See also Bisso, *Acción Argentina*, 176n47.

10. Illegible (perhaps Wells) to Sheldon Thomas, December 24, 1942, box 119, folder 843, Records of Foreign Service Posts of the Department of State, Argentina, U.S. Embassy, Buenos Aires, Classified General Records, 1936–1942, RG 84, NARA.

11. *La Hora*, October 25, 1941, 7; *El Territorio* (Resistencia), November 7, 1941, 3.

12. Cultural Sub-Committee minutes, April 7, 1942, box 1249, folder 103.9 Minutes Cultural Sub-Committee (1942–1943), OIAA Records of Dept. of Information, Regional Division, Coordinating Committee for Argentina, General Records (E-98), Minutes of Meetings, RG 229. See also Schlieper to Mr. and Mrs. Armour, invitation on IACW stationery, April 6, 1942; E. P. M., Memoranda,

April 8, 1942, and April 13, 1942; Hadow, British Embassy, to Armour, April 9, 1942, all in box 119, folder 843, Foreign Service Posts, Buenos Aires Embassy, General Records, RG 84.

13. Schlieper to Anderson, September 4, 1941, box 1, folder: Cannon, Mary, 1941, September, RG 84. The IACW secretary in Buenos Aires, Angélica Mendoza, who received a scholarship to Columbia, may have been one such woman.

14. Cramer and Prutsch, eds., ¡Américas unidas!.

15. *Independent Woman*, December 1941, 356–58, 376–77.

16. President [Marguerite Wells], League of Women Voters, to Rockefeller, COIAA, September 5, 1941, in Subject File Señora de Martínez Guerrero tour, II: 462, League of Women Voters (U.S.) Records, Manuscript Division, Library of Congress, Washington, DC. See also Cannon to Anderson, September 2, 1941, box 1, folder: Cannon, Mary 1941, September, RG 86; box 61, folder Women's Conferences and Folder L.A. Consultant for Women's Organizations—National League of Women Voters, OEMar-32 (Señora MG), OIAA, General Records, Central Files, O, Inter-American Activities in the U.S., Women, RG 229; *New York Times*, October 5, 1941, 37, October 11, 1941, 7, October 12, 1941, D5, January 4, 1942, 51; *Washington Post*, November 5, 1941, 16.

17. Marino, *Feminism for the Americas*, 174.

18. Marino, *Feminism for the Americas*, 180–82.

19. *IACW Information Bulletin*, December 1941, 3; *New York Times*, November 8, 1941, 9, January 12, 1942, 14; Organización de los Estados Americanos, *Resoluciones sobre derechos*, 3, 36–38, WASMI International, accessed February 10, 2012. See also Henry Wallace, "The Century of the Common Man," delivered May 8, 1932, New York, americanrhetoric.com/speeches/henrywallacefreeworldassoc .htm.

20. Larguía to Luisi, November 25, 1942, "L" folder, Colección Luisi, courtesy of Katherine Marino.

21. See, for example, Schlieper to Winslow, February 3, 1943, A-53, box 1:3a, folder Inter-American Commission of Women, 1943–44, Winslow Papers; *Boletín de la CIM*, June 1943, 10–12.

22. *La Hora*, May 6, 1943, 5.

23. C. R. Train to Winslow, April 27, 1942; Winslow to William N. Haskell, May 2, 1942; Haskell to Winslow, May 5, 1942, all in box 61, folder Women's Organizations, RG 229; Winslow to L. M. Mitchell, June 10, 1942, Winslow to Rockefeller, June 24, 1942, and attachment of June 23, 1942, box 72, folder Civilian Defense Miscellaneous, OIAA, General Records, Central Files, 1, Basic Economy: Emergency Rehabilitation, Civilian Defense, Economic Relief, Natural and War Disasters, RG 229.

24. Escudé, "U.S. Destabilization"; Rock, *Argentina*, 246.

25. Winslow to Welles, April 23, 1943, A-53, box 1:3a, folder Inter-American Commission of Women, 1943–1944, Winslow Papers; Marino, *Feminism for the*

Americas, 181; *New York Times,* November 13, 8, November 14, 1942, 6. See also DuBois and Derby, "Strange Case of Minerva Bernardino."

26. Ana M. Berry to Schlieper, November 24, 1942, with enclosed copy of letter to Leo Rowe, president of the Pan American Union, Office of Censorship, U.S., Record No. MI-160751, box 21, folder 843–1942, Foreign Service Posts, Buenos Aires Embassy, Classified General Records, RG 84. On Berry's political beliefs, see Oliver, *La vida cotidiana,* 322. Larguía to Luisi, November 25, 1942, Colección Luisi, verified that UAM asked Minister of Foreign Relations Enrique Ruiz Guiñazú to break ties with the Axis.

27. Winslow to Cannon, August 9, 1943, folder Cannon, Mary 1943, August 1943; Cannon to Schlieper, September 27, 1943, Folder Cannon, Mary 1943, September 1943; Schlieper to Cannon, November 29, 1943, Folder Cannon, Mary 1943, November, all in box 3, Women's Bureau, International Division, General Records 1919–1952, Cannon, Mary (1943), RG 86.

28. Cannon to Anderson, April 18, 1943, with attachment on Argentina, box 2, folder Cannon, Mary 1943, April, RG 86.

29. E. P. M. to Ambassador, Memorandum, April 10, 1942, box 21, folder 843–1942, Foreign Service Posts, Buenos Aires Embassy, Classified General Records, RG 84.

30. Edward L. Reed for the Ambassador, to Secretary of State, May 11, 1942, No. 5039, box 21, folder 843–1942, Foreign Service Posts, Buenos Aires Embassy, Classified General Records, RG 84.

31. Junta de la Victoria, *Primera convención nacional,* 17; *La Hora,* April 15, 1942, 1.

32. Illegible name, to Mr. Ambassador, December 24, 1942, box 119, folder 843, Foreign Service Posts, Buenos Aires Embassy, Classified General Records, RG 84.

33. Hoover to Adolf A. Berle, Jr., July 2, 1943, box 3079, folder 800.00 B—Covas, Guillermo/1, General Records of Dept. of State, Central Decimal File 1940–1944, RG 59; Hoover to Berle, June 15, 1943, Memorandum, "Junta de la Victoria: Communist Front Organization in Buenos Aires, Argentina," 835.00B/146, PS/TL, and September 1, 1943, Memo, Junta de la Victoria in La Plata, 835.00B/169, PS/VL, both in U.S. Dept. of State, General Records, Central Decimal File 1940–1944, M1322, roll 8. Regarding its financial records, see Junta de la Victoria, *Primera convención nacional,* 28–33; Josephs, *Argentine Diary,* 115 (quote).

34. Becker, *FBI in Latin America,* 70–85.

35. Excerpts from a letter dated May 19, 1942, from Señora Schlieper de Martínez Guerrero, box 375, folder: Lecture of Waldo Frank, OEMcr-149, OIAA, General Records, Central Files, 3, Information, Science and Education, Teachers, Libraries, Lectures, RG 229; Robert C. Wells to Rockefeller, Memorandum 615, October 15, 1942, box 1243, folder 601–700, and Memorandum 906, January 13,

1943, box 1244, folder 801–1000, both in OIAA, Records of Dept. of Information, Regional Division, Coordination Committee for Argentina, General Records (E-98), RG 229; Wells to Thomas, December 24, 1942, with attached Rockefeller note, December 14, 1942, and illegible name, to Ambassador, December 24, 1942, both in box 119, folder 843, Foreign Service Posts, Buenos Aires Embassy, RG 84.

36. Wells to Rockefeller, Memorandum 906, January 13, 1943, box 1244, folder 801–1000, OIAA, Dept. of Information, Regional Division, Coordination Committee for Argentina, General Records (E-98); Rockefeller to Wells, February 1, 1943, box 62, folder Women, OIAA, General Records, O., Inter-American Activities in the U.S., Country Files Argentina Brazil, RG 229.

37. J. R. Josephs to Coordinating Committee, Motion Picture Memorandum No. 172, July 30, 1942, folder 301–400, and Wells to Rockefeller, Memorandum 615, October 15, 1942, folder 601–700, both in box 1243, OIAA, Coordination Committee for Argentina; G. F. Granger to Rockefeller, November 7, 1942, box 222, folder Argentine Film Industry, OIAA, General Records, Central Files, 3. Information, Motion Pictures, Country Files, Argentina; Minutes, September 30, 1942, box 1250, folder 103.9/000, Minutes, Motion Picture Sub-Committee, OIAA, Dept. of Information, General Records (E-98), all in RG 229.

38. Wells to Rockefeller, Memorandum 615, October 15, 1942, box 1243, folder 601–700, and Minutes of Meetings, May 27, 1942, box 1249, folder 103.9/000, both in OIAA, Dept. of Information, General Records (E-98), RG 229.

39. Wells to Thomas, December 24, 1942, with attached Reed note, and illegible name to Ambassador, December 24, 1942, box 119, folder 843, Foreign Service Posts, Buenos Aires Embassy, RG 84.

40. J. R. Josephs to Francis Alstock, January 4, 1943, and attached clipping from *La Nación*, December 30, 1942, box 222, folder Argentine Film Industry, OIAA, General Records, Central Files, 3, RG 229. See also *La Hora*, December 31, 1942, 5. On OIAA-sponsored programs in Argentina, see Prutsch, *Creating Good Neighbors*, 333–440, and Cramer, "World War at the River Plate."

41. Minutes, April 8, June 10, August 6, and September 23, 1942, box 1250, folder 103.9/000, OIAA, Dept. of Information, General Records (E-98), RG 229; Prutsch, *Creating Good Neighbors*, 429–30. A Victory Board member in Oberá pilfered some of the chapter's funds, according to Furtembach and Kanner, interview, 2013.

42. *La Hora*, September 27, 1941, 5, December 17, 1941, 5; *La Capital*, December 17, 1941, 15. I found little evidence of US consuls' interaction with the Victory Board.

43. Schlieper to Armour and Señora, April 6, 1942, with attached E. P. M. response, April 13, 1942; Schlieper and Ratto to Armour, May 9, 1942, with attached Junta de la Victoria message and Armour to Secretary of State, Memorandum 5045, May 12, 1942; all in box 119, folder 843, Foreign Service Posts, Buenos Aires Embassy, General Records, RG 84; *La Capital*, June 7, 1942, 13.

44. Oliver, *Mi fe es el hombre*, 43.

45. Cannon to Bertha M. Nienburg, July 21, 1941, box 1, folder Cannon, Mary 1941, July, RG 86.

46. Oliver, *Mi fe es el hombre*, 43, 47–48, 91, 96–97; Becerra, "María Rosa Oliver," esp. 38, 41–43; Frank, *South American Journey*, 74, 165–166; Marino, *Feminism for the Americas*, 179.

47. Oliver, *Mi fe es el hombre*, 52–53, 95–6, 98, 116, 153, 155, 186.

48. For this and the preceding paragraph, see Oliver, *Mi fe es el hombre*, 98; clippings of Roland Hall Sharp, "The Wide Horizon. A Noble Argentine Woman," *Christian Science Monitor*, June 19 [1943?]; *El Tiempo*, September 2 and 7, 1944; *Pasadena Playhouse* 1944; *El Siglo*, September 7, 1944; *Quito*, September 12, 1944; *La Crónica* (Lima), September 15, 1944; *Connecticut Inter-American Monthly*, no. 9, all in box 8, folder 47, Oliver Papers. See also Oliver, remarks, "Inter-Racial Understanding—A Key to Inter-American Unity Conference, sponsored by Pan American Women's Association, American Museum of Natural History, May 3, 1943, box 18, folder 1, Grant Papers; Enrique S. de Lozada to Lawrence Duggan, January 15, 1943, box 62, folder Visitors from Argentina, OIAA, General Records, Central Files, O. Inter-American Activities in the U.S., Country Files Argentina Brazil, RG 229; Prutsch, *Creating Good Neighbors*, 430–35; Szurmuk, *La vocación desmesurada*, 356–59. In addition, see Oliver to Rockefeller, Memorandum, February 14, 1944, and Report, Latin American Trip, October 9, 1944, esp. 5, 11–12; Rockefeller to Larry Duggan, February 25, 1944; and Mary J. Escudero to Rockefeller, August 2, 1944, all in box 7, folder 45, Record Group 4, Rockefeller Archive Center (RAC).

49. Anderson to LaDame, April 20, 1943, box 2, folder Cannon, Mary 1943, April, RG 86.

50. Rockefeller to Edwin M. Watson, June 15, 1943, RAC.

51. Cannon speeches, "South Americans in Wartime," and "Women's Organizations in South America," box 3, folder Cannon, Mary, 1943, October, RG 86; Tuñón Pablos, "Tres momentos," 88; Towns, "Inter-American Commission," 799; Marino, *Feminism for the Americas*, 176–77; Miller, *Latin American Women*, 115. The Mexican Committee was known by several names.

52. I draw upon Power's methodology for analyzing transnational relationships, in "Latin American Solidarity." I discuss this approach and, at greater length, the Uruguayan context in "Hands across the Río de la Plata."

53. Broquetas, *La trama autoritaria*, 33–43; Nahum et al., *Crisis política y recuperación económica*, 9–71; Porrini, *Derechos humanos y dictadura terrista*; Jacob, *El Uruguay de Terra*; Camou, *Resonancia del nacional-socialismo*.

54. For comparisons, see Bohoslavsky and Broquetas, "Local and Global Connections"; Echeverría, "Las derechas de Argentina."

55. Hernández Méndez, "Religión, política y sociedad."

56. Luisi to Brainerd, June 1936, box 30, folder Correspondence of Brainerd with Persons in Uruguay, 1936–1941, WILPF, U.S., SCPC.

57. Ruiz and Paris, *El frente en los años '30.*

58. *El Día* (Montevideo), January 27, 1936, and March 3, 1937, carpeta 1936–1938; Primer Congreso Nacional de Mujeres, 17–22 abril 1936, programa, carpeta 1939, Colección Luisi. See also caja 256, carpeta 5, nos. 63, 69, 72, 83–90, and caja 257, carpeta 1, esp. nos. 88 (untitled undated flyer) and 127, "¡Por una gran jornada femenina antiguerrera el 1 de agosto!," Archivo Luisi; Paulina Luisi, "Pro-mitín 23 de Julio 1938," radio address, caja 3, Serie Derechos Políticos de la Mujer, no. 35, ACRE; Sapriza, *Memorias de rebeldía*, 168–70, passim; Gravina, *A los diez años*, 50–51, 53–54.

59. "Llamado Pro-Congreso de unidad contra el fascismo y la guerra," n.d., caja 257, carpeta 1, nos. 39–40, Archivo Luisi; Luisi, "La mujer en la democracia," conferencia en la UAM, 19 October 1938, caja 3, Serie Derechos Políticos de la Mujer, no. 36, ACRE.

60. *Argentina Libre*, May 14, 1942, 10.

61. Rilla et al., *Nosotros que nos queremos tanto.*

62. Miller, *Latin American Women*, 82; See also Lavrin, *Women, Feminism, and Social Change*; Ehrick, *Shield of the Weak.*

63. *Uruguay*, April 18 and 23, 1936, *El Día* (Montevideo), April 22, 1936, n.p., caja 259, carpeta 5, nos. 5, 15, and 12, respectively; *El Día* (Montevideo), January 3, 1942, caja 256, carpeta 7, no. 78; Comité de Acción Nacional en Defensa de la Soberanía y la Democracia, June 28, 1940, caja 252, carpeta 7, no. 2, all in Archivo Luisi. See also *La Vanguardia*, October 30, 1938, carpeta 1936–1938, Colección Luisi.

64. *New York Times*, March 23, 1939, courtesy of Margaret Power; *Claridad*, February-March 1939, 3–4.

65. *Diario Popular*, August 23, 1941, 4, August 29, 1941, 8, September 5, 1941, 8, September 15, 1941, 7, September 17, 1941, 7, October 24, 1941, 7, October 25, 1941, 7, October 27, 1941, 7, November 7, 1941, 7 (statistic).

66. *Diario Popular*, December 14, 1941, 7, December 22, 1941, 7, January 29, 1942, 7; Junta de la Victoria, *Primera convención nacional*, 9. Convention records listed the two women as officers of a Comité Femenino Uruguayo, which meant the Comisión.

67. *Justicia*, July 17, 1942, 4.

68. *Justicia*, July 3, 1942, 8; *Diario Popular*, July 3, 1942, 5, July 4, 1942, 16.

69. *Diario Popular*, September 2, 1942, 5, September 19, 1942, 6, October 3, 1942, 5, October 24, 1942, 5, September 30, 1944, 2 (statistics); Acción Femenina, "Empleadas y obreras trabajan," courtesy of Ana Laura de Giorgi.

70. Barrios Pintos, *Montevideo*; *Diario Popular*, April 9, 1944, 2.

71. *Diario Popular*, June 23, 1944, 2, July 24, 1944, 2.

72. On Cortinas, see *Argentina Libre*, May 14, 1942, 10; mujeresquehacenla historia.blogspot.com/2009/05/siglo–xix–laura–cortinas.html, and anaforas.fic.edu .uy/jspui/handle/123456789/44301.

73. I gleaned names of members from *Diario Popular* and Acción Femenina publications, and biographical information from the Uruguayan periodicals, interviews, consultations, and biographical sections in the bibliography. On Arévalo, see Gravina, *A los diez años*; Leibner, *Camaradas y compañeros*; Sapriza, *Memorias de rebeldía*. On Arce, see Cannon to Anderson, August 10, 1941, box 1, folder Cannon, Mary 1941 August, and Arce to Cannon, n.d., folder Cannon, Mary 1942, August, RG 86.

74. *Justicia*, July 3, 1942, 8; *Diario Popular*, August 26, 1942, 5, April 15, 1944, 2.

75. *Justicia*, July 24, 1942, 5; *Diario Popular*, May 20, 1944, 2.

76. See, for example, *Diario Popular*, August 29, 1941, 3, November 23, 1942, 3, December 4, 1942, 1, March 17, 1944, 2.

77. Acción Femenina, "Autoridades emanadas de la Primera"; Deutsch, "Antifascist Jewish Women."

78. On this speech, see *Diario Popular*, July 3, 1942, 5, July 21, 1942, 1, July 22, 1942, 8. Heloise Brainerd of WILPF initiated correspondence with Feminine Action, but at the war's end. See Laura Cortinas to Brainerd, May 23, 1945, box 30, folder Correspondence of Brainerd with Persons in Uruguay, 1942–1945, WILPF Papers.

79. On these visits, see *Diario Popular*, July 24, 1942, 6, September 20, 1942, 1, September 21, 1942, 1, September 25, 1942, 3, October 2, 1942, 5, October 5, 1942, 5. Antifascist men also communicated with their counterparts across the estuary; see, for example, *Diario Popular*, September 16, 1942, 5.

80. *Diario Popular*, October 27, 1942, 5, November 8, 1942, 3, November 12, 1942, 3, November 18, 1942, 2, December 10, 1942, 3.

81. *Diario Popular*, March 27, 1944, 2.

82. *Diario Popular*, December 25, 1943, 1, February 15, 1944, 2, March 11, 1944, 2 (quote); Acción Femenina, "Bolsa de Navidad," courtesy of Ana Laura de Giorgi.

83. *Diario Popular*, October 10, 1942, 5, November 16, 1942, 4, November 29, 1942, 4; May 3, 1943, 2; March 27, 1944, 2 (quote), April 9, 1944, 2, May 9, 1944, 2.

84. *Justicia*, July 30, 1943, 3; *Diario Popular*, March 16, 1943, 2.

85. *Diario Popular*, May 12, 1943, 2.

86. *La Hora*, May 8, 1943, 6, May 9, 1943, 6; *Orientación*, May 13, 1943, 5; *Diario Popular*, May 12, 1943, 2. On Álvarez Vignoli, see *Argentina Libre*, May 13, 1943, 2.

87. *La Hora*, May 10, 1943, 2.

88. Senkman, "El nacionalismo y el campo," 39–42; Sheinin, *Argentina and the United States*, 82–83.

89. Ana Rosa Schlieper to President Pedro Ramírez, June 30, 1943, CeDinCI; Bisso, *Acción Argentina*, 235–36.

90. Josephs, *Argentine Diary*, 84.

91. British Embassy to Ministro de Relaciones Exteriores, Urgent Note Verbale no. 114, n.d., 2/286/43, 0095, FO 118: 721.

92. Greenup, *Revolution before Breakfast*, 15; Kelly to Foreign Office, telegram, July 26, 1943, 0078, 11/286/43, FO 118: 721.

93. BCC Executive Committee Secretary to Hadow, August 10, 1943, 0012–13, 39/286/43, FO 118:721.

94. Embassy and consulate correspondence with the Foreign Office covered this problem extensively from July through September 1943. See, for example, Kelly to Foreign Office, telegram, September 8, 1943, 0086, 95/286/43, FO 118: 723. See also Kelly, *Ruling Few or the Human Background*, 298–99.

95. Armour to Secretary of State, telegrams, July 15, 1943, 835.00/1645, and July 19, 1943, 835.00/1652; Hoover to Berle, August 2, 1943, 835.00/1709, all in U.S. Department of State, Records of the Department of State Relating to the Internal Affairs of Argentina, 1940–1944, microfilm M1322, roll 3. See also Frank, *South American Journey*, 214–20; Sheinin, *Argentina and the United States*, 69–70.

96. Armour to Secretary of State, telegrams, July 22, 1943, 835.00/1665, and August 6, 1943, 835.00/1705; Hull to Armour, telegram, July 23, 1943, 835.00/1665, all in M1322, roll 2. See also J. M. Byrne, memo, August 4, 1943, box 37, folder 843, 1943, Foreign Service Posts, Buenos Aires Embassy, Classified General Records, RG 84.

97. Fuselli, speech, box 13, folder Luncheon for Inter-American Committee of Women, April 17, 1944, General Correspondence, Series B, DG 109, SCPC; Schlieper to Cannon, November 29, 1943, box 3, folder Cannon, Mary, 1943, November, RG 86.

98. Zanca, "Dios y libertad," 70, 73, 81.

99. Schlieper to Cannon, November 29, 1943, box 3, folder Cannon, Mary, 1943, November, RG 86; Guy, *Women Build the Welfare State,* and "La 'verdadera' historia," 321–41.

100. Greenup, *Revolution before Breakfast*, 15.

101. *El Patriota*, April 14, 1945, 4; *Unidad Nacional*, fourth week, November 1944, 8; *La Voz del Interior*, September 4, 1945, 5; Hernández, *Con la marca*, 221; Caffaratti, "Samatán y el batallar," 6–7.

102. Josephs, *Argentine Diary*, 115.

103. *Justicia*, July 30, 1943, 3 (quote); August 13, 1943, 2; *Diario Popular*, June 30, 1943, 1, March 30, 1944, 2 (figure); Bisso, *Acción Argentina*, 238. Hoover, September 11, 1943, confirmed the seizure of pro-Allied groups' assets, 835.00B/164, PS/VL, M1322, roll 8. Dollar amount in *New York Times*, June 6, 1945, 1.

104. D. C. M., 2011, and Edelman, 2013, interviews; *Diario Popular*, June 26, 1943, 1, June 27, 1943, 1, March 30, 1944, 2, April 27, 1944, 2; Del Franco, *Mujeres, ese fuego, esas luchas*, 30.

105. *Diario Popular*, July 25, 1944, 2, August 1, 1944, 2; Acción Femenina por la Victoria, *Campaña Argentino-Uruguaya*.

106. *Diario Popular*, April 27, 1944, 2, July 3, 1944, 2, July 4, 1944, 2, July 5, 1944, 2, July 6, 1944, 4; Dr. Emilio Troise, "Discurso pronunciado en acto organizado por Acción Femenina por la Victoria," 1944, caja 4, carpeta 5, documento 6, Fondo Emilio Troise, CeDInCI. The women's words did not appear in the press.

107. *Diario Popular*, May 28, 1944, 2.

108. On the importance of friendship among Latin American antifascist feminists, see Marino, "Transnational Pan-American Feminism."

Chapter 7: "V for Victory" or *Vendepatria*?

1. It was called the UNS branch of the Southern Zone (including Rosario). I saw only one mention of any other UNS branch, one in the Northern Zone. *Vendepatria* means one who sells out one's country.

2. *Crisol*, September 28, 1941, 3.

3. *Crisol*, December 16, 1941, 3.

4. On traditionalist notions of ideal and transgressive women, see Tossounian, *La Joven Moderna in Interwar Argentina*, esp. chaps. 2 and 3.

5. *El Fortín*, second half January 1941, 3.

6. Recall the disgruntled *Crisol* reader in chapter 2.

7. *Crisol*, January 29, 1942, 1 (quote), May 3, 1942, 5, August 30, 1942, 7, September 13, 1942, 3, November 24, 1942, 7; *Clarinada*, November 1942, 10. On *Crisol*, its successors *El Pampero* and *El Federal*, and their editor, see Klein, "Political Lives and Times." While sharing these ideas, rightist Spanish women adopted more radical roles; see Arce Pinedo, "De la mujer social."

8. *Crisol*, December 16, 1941, 3 (Méndez); *Clarinada*, September 1943, 5 (quote). On this rhetoric, see Payne, *Fascism*, 7, 13.

9. *Crisol*, January 29, 1942, 1; August 30, 1942, 7, February 18, 1943, 5 (quotes).

10. Rubinzal, "El nacionalismo frente," esp. 124–30; Klein, "Argentine Nacionalismo before Perón"; Besoky, "El nacionalismo populista."

11. *Bandera Argentina*, March 7, 1942, 1, June 22, 1943, 1; *Crisol*, July 8, 1941, 1.

12. *Criterio*, August 20, 1942, 405–6, April 15, 1943, 345–48, May 13, 1943, 30–31. On Franceschi, see Lida, "El enigma Franceschi"; Echeverría, "Virtudes de la doctrina."

13. *Criterio*, September 24, 1942, 83–85; Deutsch, "Catholic Church, Work, and Womanhood," 314–15.

14. *Crisol*, December 3, 1941, 3, December 27, 1941, 1.

15. *Crisol*, May 27, 1943, 3 (Dumrauf); *Bandera Argentina*, May 13, 1943, 1.

16. *La Hora*, September 14, 1941, 5, April 15, 1942, 1.

17. Junta de la Victoria, *Primera convención nacional*, 15; *New York Times*, January 25, 1942, 1, 16.

18. *La Razón*, February 28, 1942, clipping, 0120, 13/131/42, FO 118: 704; Civil Attaché to Foreign Office, September 17, 1946, 0032–0037, 223/131/46, FO 118: 748. See also *Crisol*, April 21, 1942, 3, September 6, 1942, 1 (statistic), September 13, 1942, 3; *Bandera Argentina*, February 28, 1942, 2; *El Orden*, April 9, 1942, 3; *Los Andes*, April 5, 1942, 22; Senkman, "El nacionalismo y el campo," 37.

19. *Clarinada*, January 31, 1942, 13; *Crisol*, January 10, 1942, 3; Zuleta Álvarez, *El nacionalismo argentino*, 1:404–14, esp. 408.

20. *Criterio*, October 22, 1942, 185–88.

21. *El Fortín*, second half January, 12, 1941, first half February 1941, 3.

22. *La Voz del Plata*, June 11, 1943, 1 (Irazusta); David Sheinin, email communication, June 18, 2020; Raanan Rein, email communication, June 22, 2020; Newton, *'Nazi Menace' in Argentina*, 62; Goñi, *Real Odessa*, 11, 19; article in *London Mail*, reprinted in *El Pueblo*, August 2, 1944, 1.

23. *Crisol*, January 8, 1942, 1; *Bandera Argentina*, January 31, 1943, 1; Tato, "El ejemplo alemán."

24. Catholics and Nationalists excluded private property from their definition of capitalism; see Deutsch, *Las derechas*, 224–25.

25. *Nueva Política*, August 1941, 16–18.

26. *Clarinada*, August 1942, 2–3.

27. *El Pueblo*, August 13, 1944, 9, August 20, 1944, 9.

28. *Crisol*, February 24, 1942, 1.

29. *Crisol*, October 21, 1941, 1.

30. *Clarinada*, March-April 1942, 5, and September 1944, 25; José Zanca, email communication, November 9, 2019.

31. Lvovich, *Nacionalismo y antisemitismo*.

32. *Crisol*, May 14, 1942, 1.

33. *Crisol*, January 6, 1942, 3.

34. *Crisol*, August 22, 1941, 1.

35. Quoted in *La Hora*, April 15, 1942, 1.

36. *Clarinada*, November 1942, 9–11, December 1942, 13.

37. *Clarinada*, May 1942, 24, December 1942, 13 (quote), September 1943, 17.

38. *Crisol*, September 6, 1941, 1, May 8, 1942, 2.

39. *Crisol*, January 5, 1943, 5.

40. *Crisol*, June 25, 1942, 5, July 24, 1942, 2, August 6, 1942, 2, June 2, 1943, 3; *Bandera Argentina*, July 14, 1943, 1 (quote).

41. *Clarinada*, November 42, 1942, 10; *Crisol*, November 24, 1942, 7.

42. *Crisol*, April 15, 1942, 3.

43. *La Hora*, May 8, 1943, 6.

44. *Clarinada*, June 1943, 18–19.

45. See table 7.

46. *Clarinada*, March-April 1942, 4, and September 1944, 20, 25.

47. Deutsch, *Las derechas*, 207; Campbell, "Political Extremes in South America," 528; Tato, "El ejemplo alemán," 15.

48. *Bandera Argentina*, December 12, 1941, 1.

49. See chapter 3.

50. *Bandera Argentina*, September 28, 1941, 1.

51. *Bandera Argentina*, December 16, 1941, 1 (quotes), December 18, 1941, 1.

52. Rock, *Authoritarian Argentina*, 115; Dolkart, "Right in the Década Infame," 84–86.

53. *Bandera Argentina*, January 10, 1943, 1–2; Valobra, "Sufragismo y acción política femenina," 196–203.

54. *Crisol*, January 1, 1942, 1. On the trope of the nationalist and "traditional" interior, see, among many works, Deutsch, *Counterrevolution in Argentina*, 39, 41–43; Rock, *Authoritarian Argentina*, 41–54. Healey, *Ruins of the New Argentina*, brought together the capital and provinces.

55. *Crisol*, September 11, 1942, 2, April 14, 1943, 1. On earlier anti-immigrant Nationalism, see Tato, "Del crisol de razas."

56. *Clarinada*, September 1944, 2–3.

57. *Crisol*, April 14, 1943, 1; *Clarinada*, July-August 1944, 7. On fascist "truths," see Finchelstein, *Brief History of Fascist Lies.*.

58. *Nueva Política*, November 1941, 30; *Crisol*, January 21, 1942, 1, May 10, 1942, 3 (quote), June 19, 1943, 5; *Clarinada*, March-April 1942, 6.

59. *El Aguijón*, March 28, 1942, June 1942 (quotes). For Schlieper's speech, see chapter 5; on Nationalist hatred of Rivadavia, see Goebel, *Argentina's Partisan Past*, 49.

60. *Bandera Argentina*, January 12, 1943, 1.

61. *El Pueblo*, January 11, 1942, 11, January 14, 1942, 9: Finchelstein, *Transatlantic Fascism*, 129–31.

62. *Crisol*, January 21, 1942, 1. On "charity begins at home," see, for example, *Crisol*, September 13, 1942, 3, *Criterio*, November 26, 1942, 300; *Bandera Argentina*, January 10, 1942, 1.

63. *Crisol*, May 14, 1942, 1.

64. *Crisol*, November 24, 1942, 7.

65. *Bandera Argentina*, January 10, 1942, 1, May 13, 1943, 1, May 15, 1943, 1; *Clarinada*, February 1943, 7–8.

66. *Bandera Argentina*, January 28, 1942, 1; *Crisol*, June 2, 1943, 3.

67. *Crisol*, June 17, 1943, 5.

68. *La Hora*, September 8, 1942, 5, November 23, 1942, 3; *Clarinada*, July 1943, 9.

69. Schlieper, letter to Ramírez, June 30, 1943; Bisso, *Acción Argentina*, 235–36.

70. *El Litoral*, October 16, 1942, 4,

71. *El Litoral*, October 24, 1942, 4.

72. Rebekah Pite, email communication, March 3, 2021.

73. *Crisol*, December 30, 1941, 5, January 18, 1942, 1, December 19, 1942, 4, January 5, 1943, 5, May 6, 1943, 4–5, July 16, 1943, 4; *El Federal*, August 5, 1944, 5 (quote).

74. *Crisol*, January 18, 1942, 1, May 7, 1943, 5 (quote).

75. *Crisol*, January 1, 1942, 1, 3.

76. *Alianza*, second half December 1943, 6–7.

77. *Crisol*, February 18, 1943, 5, June 6, 1943, 1.

78. *El Federal*, September 1, 1944, 5.

79. *El Federal*, September 8, 1944, 3.

80. *Criterio*, November 12, 1942, 258–259.

81. *La Hora*, April 15, 1942, 1.

82. *Crisol*, January 29, 1942, 1.

83. *La Hora*, February 15, 1942, 4, January 3, 1943, 5; *La Voz del Interior*, June 6, 1946, 4; Junta de la Victoria, *Primera convención nacional*, 50; Caffaratti, "Marta Samatán y el batallar," 6–7.

84. *Crisol*, May 11, 1943, 3.

85. As had their precursors; see Rubinzal, "La disputa en las plazas"; Deutsch, *Counterrevolution in Argentina*, 137–39.

86. *La Hora*, April 29, 1942, 5; *Crisol*, April 22, 1942, 1, May 3, 1942, 1, 3.

87. *El Federal*, August 5, 1944, 5, mentioned Méndez.

Chapter 8: Transnational Citizens

1. *El Patriota*, April 14, 1945, 4.

2. *La Nación*, January 1, 1944, clipping, 0177; telegram no. 30, January 12, 1944, 0150, 10/131/44; Kelly to Foreign Office, January 12, 1944, 0139–1040, 11/131/44; Chancery to Foreign Office, January 26, 1944, 0087–0089, 21/131/44, all in FO 118: 726; Bisso, *Acción Argentina*, 238.

3. Walter, "Right and the Peronists," 105. *Alianza (periódico clausurado)*; *Ante la patria en peligro*, March 7, 1944, carpeta 59, Colección de Volantes, 2.1., Volantes Partidos Políticos, Nacionalismos, 1944–2004, CeDInCI.

4. *La Gaceta*, November 17, 2019, courtesy of Daniel Campi; Unknown, Villa Nogués, Tucumán, January 30, 1944, to Isabel Giménez Bustamante (hereafter IGB), box 8, Beláustegui Bustamante Family Papers, University of Notre Dame Rare Books and Special Collections, Notre Dame, IN (BB Papers); Pavetti, "Una experiencia de gobierno," 185–86.

5. Historians have debated what the initials *GOU* stood for, as primary sources offer different names. Grupo Obra de Unificación appears in Potash's document collection, *Perón y el GOU*, 16, 48, passim.

6. Acting Secretary of State to Diplomatic Representatives, March 4, 1944, document 219, 835.00/2528, and Armour to Secretary of State, March 11, 1944,

document 222, 835.00/2618, *Foreign Relations (FRUS)*, consulted online October 28–29, 2019; Walter, "Right and the Peronists," 104–5.

7. Kelly, *Ruling Few*, esp. 299–301.

8. For this and the next two paragraphs, see Greenup, *Revolution before Breakfast*, 84–91 (quote on 84); *La Prensa*, August 21, 1944, 10, August 23, 1944, 9, August 24, 1944, 11–13, August 25, 1944, 9–10; Shuckburgh to Foreign Office, August 25, 1944, 0035, 307/131/44, FO 118: 730.

9. Edelman, *Banderas, pasiones, camaradas*, 89; Singerman, *Mis dos vidas*, 112–15; *Clarín*, July 7, 1985, 16; *La Prensa*, August 24, 1944, 11 (quotes); Halperin, interview, 2000; *El Patriota*, April 14, 1945, 4.

10. Greenup, *Revolution before Breakfast*, 91.

11. *La Unión*, August 25, 1944, 3.

12. On Tucumán, see Jorge Aranda, August 30 and September 5, 1944, and Silvano P. Larrosa, August 30, 1944, all to Ministro de Gobierno; *La Gaceta*, August 31, 1944, clipping, all in caja 20, no. 657, Archivo Intermedio. See also *La Gaceta*, August 25, 1944, 4, August 26, 1944, 3, Aug 27, 1944, 3, 7; *El Federal*, August 25, 1944, 4; *El Orden*, August 24, 1944, 12; and Almaráz, et al, *¡Aquí FUBA!*, 42. Bisso analyzed events in Buenos Aires province in "Festejos."

13. *El Territorio* (Resistencia), August 28, 1944, 2.

14. Shuckburgh to Foreign Office, September 20, 1944, 0150–0153, 319/131/44, FO 118: 731, and "Argentina in Isolation," December 18, 1944, 0114–0117, 45/131/45, FO 118: 736; Greenup, *Revolution before Breakfast*, 86.

15. Shuckburgh to Foreign Office, August 25, 1944, 0035, 307/131/4; *La Nación*, August 25, 1944, clipping, 0036; Mellow to Foreign Office, August 26, 1944, 0028–0029, 311/131/44, all in FO 118: 730. See also Greenup, *Revolution before Breakfast*, 36; *Bandera Argentina*, August 26, 1944, 1.

16. *El Federal*, August 28, 1944, 2; *El Pueblo*, August 26, 1944, 8.

17. *El Federal*, September 8, 1944, 3; *El Pueblo*, August 27, 1944, 8.

18. Teitelbaum, "Itinerarios," 109; *El Federal*, August 25, 1944, 1, September 7, 1944, 3 (quotes); *Bandera Argentina*, August 25, 1944, 1.

19. *El Pueblo*, August 27, 1944, 8.

20. Marino, *Feminism for the Americas*, 192–95; Miller, *Latin American Women*, 116. Among many works covering this context, see Halperín Donghi, *Argentina en el callejón*; Luna, *El 45*; Page, *Perón*; Almaráz et al., *¡Aquí FUBA!*.

21. *El Patriota*, April 7, 1945, 1, April 14, 1945, 4; *Los Andes*, May 5, 1945, 4, May 8, 1945, 5; *El Territorio* (Resistencia), April 7, 1945, 5.

22. For this and the next two paragraphs, see *El Patriota*, April 14, 1945, 3, 5, and April 21, 1945, 4.

23. Memorandum of the Argentine Political Situation for the Month of April, 1945, Political—Monthly Situation Reports (1945), 0058–0064, 5/134/45, FO 118: 742; *Antinazi*, April 12, 1945, 5, reprinted in Bisso, ed., *El antifascismo argentino*, 228–29.

24. *Diario Popular,* April 12, 1945, 2 (quote), May 7, 1945, 2, May 26, 1945, 4; Memorandum . . . April, 1945, FO 118: 742; *Los Andes,* May 7, 1945, 5; *La Gaceta,* June 8, 1945, 4.

25. Bisso, *Acción Argentina,* 246, 249.

26. *La Gaceta,* April 19, 1945, 5; *El Territorio* (Resistencia), April 27, 1945, 5; *La Voz del Interior,* April 8, 1945, 6, April 19, 1945, 6; *El Día* (La Plata), November 9, 1945, 2; *Los Andes,* May 8, 1945, 6, May 24, 1945, 5, May 31, 1945, 4, June 3, 1945, 7, June 26, 1945, 6; Garzón Rogé, "Antifascistas y política," 12n24.

27. No name, May 22, 1945, 0036–0037, 123/131/45, FO 118: 737; *Antinazi,* May 17, 1945, 3.

28. *La Gaceta,* May 3, 1945, 11, *El Territorio* (Posadas), May 9, 1945, 7; *El Día* (La Plata), May 14, 1945, 6, May 16, 1945, 6; *El Territorio* (Resistencia), May 26, 1945, 3; *La Voz del Interior,* May 29, 1945, 8; *El Litoral,* April 22, 1945, 4, May 6, 1945, 5.

29. *El Día* (La Plata), August 10, 1945, 6.

30. Kelly to Foreign Office, August 7, 1945, 0102, 203/131/45; August 17, 1945, 0077, 219/131/45, August 20, 1945, 0072, 223/131/45; September 21, 1945, 0019, AS4875/92/2, FO 118: 739. See also *El Día* (La Plata), August 17, 1945, 3; *La Voz del Interior,* August 17, 1945, 7; Tcach, "El reformismo," 138–39; Page, *Perón,* 104.

31. *El Territorio* (Resistencia), August 16, 1945, 3, August 17, 1945, 3, August 20, 1945, 6; Kedinger, interview, 2013.

32. *La Gaceta,* August 12, 1945, 9 (quote), August 13, 1945, 2, August 14, 1945, 5.

33. *La Gaceta,* August 6, 1945, 5.

34. *La Voz del Interior,* July 15, 1945, 7; *Los Andes,* July 16, 1945, 3.

35. Palermo, "Sufragio femenino y ciudadanía," 49, thought Perón explicitly mentioned a decree; Barry, "Una cruzada de Evita?," 116, suggested it vaguely surfaced. Valobra, *Del hogar a las urnas,* 38, found no documentary evidence to this effect. Hammond, *Women's Suffrage Movement,* 147, noted that Perón "prepared to remove all legal barriers to women's suffrage and officially allow women to participate in the elections scheduled for 1946."

36. *El Patriota,* July 6, 1945, 2. For similar views, see *Antinazi,* July 19, 1945, 4.

37. *Los Andes,* July 31, 1945, 7.

38. Fuselli, *A las mujeres,* esp. 18, 22.

39. *Criterio,* July 5, 1945, 5–9; Acha, "Género y política," esp. 73–80.

40. *Criterio,* July 26, 1945, 87–88 (quotes); survey reprinted in *Criterio,* August 9, 1945, 134–37, August 16, 1945, 161–62. On Forn and other Catholic women authors, see Zanca, "Dios y libertad"; Acha, "Género y política"; and Perrig, "Mujeres, antiperonismo y antifascismo." On the Centro, see Deutsch, "Catholic Church, Work, and Womanhood," 318–19.

41. *El Pueblo*, October 22–23, 1945, 5, 8, 13, 15.

42. *La Fronda*, July 16, 1945, 7.

43. Using similar language, the Cuban feminist antifascist Ofelia Domínguez Navarro prioritized institutional normality over women's suffrage in 1931, during the struggle against the dictator Machado. See Marino, *Feminism for the Americas*, 91–92.

44. Susana Molinas, interview, 2013.

45. *La Voz del Interior*, September 14, 1945, 7; Elisa Élida Canciani, email communication, December 4, 2019.

46. Fuselli, *A las mujeres*; Acha, "Género y política," 74–75; Zanca, "Dios y libertad," 82; Barrancos, "El Partido Socialista"; *Antinazi*, August 30, 1945, 7.

47. *Diario Popular*, October 7, 1944, 2.

48. *Diario Popular*, October 9, 1944, 4, October 25, 1944, 1, November 3, 1944, 4, November 18, 1944, 1, November 25, 1944, 1, November 29, 1944, 1, December 3, 1944, 1, December 20–31, 1944, 1. See also Unión Nacional Femenina, "Las mujeres nos unimos," flyer attached to Teolinda Daray Vera to Brainerd, November 1945, box 30, folder Correspondence of Brainerd with Persons in Uruguay, 1946–1947, WILPF, US, SCPC.

49. *El Plata*, April 14, 1945, clipping (quote), carpeta de recortes, 1941–1947, Colección Luisi; *Acción Femenina por la Victoria. Periódico de Ayuda*, March 1946, 7; Marino, *Feminism for the Americas*, 202–14.

50. *Orientación*, August 19, 1945, 1; *La Gaceta*, October 23, 1945, 5; *El Día* (La Plata), August 30, 1945, 4; *La Capital*, August 27, 1945, 4; *Los Andes*, August 11, 1945, 5, August 18, 1945, 6, August 21, 1945, 5; *El Patriota*, August 31, 1945, 2; Rein, "Melting the Pot?," 109.

51. *La Nación*, September 4, 1945 (statistic), clipping, Fanny Edelman Papers, Archivo Comunista; *El Patriota*, September 7, 1945, 2, 4; *Diario Popular*, September 8, 1945, 2, October 1, 1945, 4; Edelman, *Banderas, pasiones, camaradas*, 94–95.

52. For this and the next paragraph, see Rein, *Franco-Perón*, 150–52, 286n39; Edelman, *Banderas, pasiones, camaradas*, 95. On board activities, see *La Hora*, November 22, 1945, 1, December 3, 1945, 7; December 19, 1945, 3, February 14, 1946, 7, March 12, 1946, 3, May 13, 1946, 14; *El Día*, October 3, 1945, 7; *La Gaceta*, April 10, 1946, 6, May 1, 1946, 11; *El Territorio* (Resistencia), November 16, 1945, 5, December 22, 1945, 5, March 25, 1946, 5; *La Voz del Interior*, November 2, 1945, 6; *Junta de la Victoria, Boletín Informativo*, June 7, 1946, caja mujeres, Archivo Comunista.

53. Kelly to Foreign Office, October 8, 1945, 0177–0179, 254/131/45, FO 118: 740; *Antinazi*, September 27, 1945, 2 (quote); *Los Andes*, September 20, 1945, 1–2; *Orden Cristiano*, October 1, 1945, 27–29; *New York Times*, clipping, in unmarked brown folder, Archivo Bermann; Page, *Perón*, 107–10; García Sebastiani, *Los antiperonistas*, 53.

54. *La Fronda*, September 19, 1945, 5, 7, September 20, 1945, 4, 6, 7.

55. *New York Times*, September 24, 1945, 8. Neither *FRUS* (*Foreign Relations of the United States*) nor the Spruille Braden Papers, 1903–1977, Rare Book and Manuscript Library, Columbia University, New York, NY, contained evidence of such contact. NARA has been closed during the pandemic.

56. Kelly to Foreign Office, October 15, 1945, 0147, 264/131/45, FO 118: 740; *El Pueblo*, October 5–6, 1945, 1; women's flyers, November 1945, and "¡Por qué están en huelga los universitarios!," 1945, flyer, box 3, folder 4, Argentina Subject Collection, Subject File 1939–1944, Hoover Institution Archives, Stanford, CA (Hoover Archives); IGB, diary entries September 26 and October 8, 1945, box 9, folder Diario Pages 1945 September-October, BB Papers; García Sebastiani, *Los antiperonistas*, 54; Page, *Perón*, 107–8, 110–11; Almaráz et al., ¡Aquí FUBA!; Halperín Donghi, *Argentina en el callejón*.

57. Liga Argentina por los Derechos del Hombre, October 28, 1945, and President Julio González Iramain of the Liga Argentina por los Derechos del Hombre, October 13, 1945, carpeta Misión ante United Nations Organization 1946, Archivo Bermann; Kelly to Foreign Office, October 5, 1945, 0116, 271/131/45, and October 6, 1945, 0114, 273/131/1945, FO 118: 740.

58. *Diario Popular*, October 8, 1945, 1, October 10, 1945, 1, October 11, 1945, 1, October 15, 1945, 1, October 16, 1945, 1, October 17, 1945, 1, October 20, 1945, 1, October 21, 1945, 1; *Antinazi*, October 18, 1945, 1, 3; Kelly to Foreign Office, October 26, 1945, 0082–0085, AS5580/92/2, FO 118: 740.

59. Halperín-Donghi, *Argentina en el callejón*, 29–30, argued that the relationship between Peronism and fascism was ambiguous. Perón had regarded fascism as a model; his movement was not fascist but rather the "residue" of an attempt to alter Argentine politics along fascist lines. Finchelstein, *Ideological Origins of the Dirty War*, 67, claimed that the military dictatorship of 1943–1946 "was the closest the Argentine government would come to a classic fascist regime."

60. *La Fronda*, October 18, 1945, 6.

61. Romero, *History of Argentina*, 96.

62. James, "October 17th," esp. 454 (quote).

63. *Antinazi*, October 25, 1945, 5.

64. UFD flyers in box 3, folder 7, Argentina Subject Collection, Hoover Archives; Milanesio, *Workers Go Shopping in Argentina*, 126–28, 141–43. On behavior and race, see Deutsch, "Insecure Whiteness."

65. *Los Andes*, December 4, 1945, 7.

66. *Antinazi*, November 29, 1945, 6.

67. Drallny in untitled newspaper clipping, October 19, 1945, from Fernando Oscar Reati, email communication, December 11, 2013.

68. *El Pueblo*, October 25, 1945, cited in "Delfina Bunge De Galvez y el 17 de Octubre," *La Ciudad*, October 18, 2022, https://laciudadrevista.com/Delfina-bunge-de-galvez-y-el-17-de-octubre/.

69. *Alianza*, n.d., 1–6, and October 23, 1945, 1; Fiorucci, *Intelectuales y peronismo*, 93–101; Walter, "Right and the Peronists," 104–10.

70. *La Hora*, December 1, 1945, 1, December 20, 1945, 1; *El Territorio* (Posadas), November 21, 1945, 1.

71. Lvovich, *Nacionalismo y antisemitismo*, 539–44; Rein, *Populism and Ethnicity*, 40–43.

72. Comisión Coordinadora, *Declaración*, and Unión Democrática, *Un programa*, caja 1, Volantes Antiperonismo, 1945–1946, Fondo de Archivo José Pañal, CeDinCI; Nállim, *Transformations and Crisis of Liberalism in Argentina*, 151; García Sebastiani, *Los antiperonistas*, 66. Luna, *Perón y su tiempo*, 1:305–6, noted there was a broad consensus among most of the Peronist and Radical congressmen elected in 1946 on socioeconomic issues, and many laws passed unanimously.

73. *International League Monthly Bulletin*, December 1945, carpeta Misión, and Frances Grant, speech delivered at December 16, 1945 meeting, both in unmarked brown folder, Archivo Bermann.

74. Brainerd to Schlieper, September 24, 1945, box 23, folder Committee on the Americas, Correspondence of Brainerd with persons in Argentina, 1948–1950, and WILPF press release, February 6, 1946, (quote), box 12, folder General, Committee on the Americas, Committees and Conferences, 1920–1959, WILPF, U.S., SCPC.

75. Brainerd, March 17, 1947, clipping, WILPF, U.S., SCPC, courtesy of Katherine Marino.

76. "Manifiesto de la democracia argentina," and *New York Times*, January 19, 1946, clipping, unmarked brown folder, Archivo Bermann.

77. For this and the next paragraph, see Women's International Democratic Federation, "Original Resolutions of the Women's International Democratic Federation at the International Congress of Women Paris November December 1945," typed draft, Women and Social Movements, International: 1840 to the Present (WASMI), http://wasi.alexanderstreet.com/; *Orientación*, November 21, 1945, 2, January 4, 1946, 15; *La Hora*, November 15, 1945, 6 (quote), November 18, 1945, 6, November 21, 1945, 3, November 22, 1945, 3, November 24, 1945, 3, December 30, 1945, 3; *Diario Popular*, October 19, 1945, 4; Junta de la Victoria, "Informe de las delegadas de la Junta de la Victoria al Primer Congreso Mundial de Mujeres en París," flyer, 1945; De Haan, "La Federación Democrática," esp. 20–21, 28–29, as well as "Continuing Cold War Paradigms" and "Women's International Democratic Federation," both in WASMI, accessed August 5, 2015; Mooney, "Fighting Fascism," and "El antifascismo." The Victory Board delegates' remarks at the congress are unavailable.

78. *Orientación*, December 19, 1945, 2; *La Hora*, December 15, 1945, 3, December 17, 1945, 3. On President Perón's consumption policies, see Elena, *Dignifying Argentina*, 84–118.

79. John Phillimore to Powell, copy of letter, December 7, 1945, in Victor

Peroune to Kelly, December 27, 1945, 0071–0076, 19/131/46, FO 118: 744; A. N. Noble to Foreign Office, April 26, 1946, 0050–0054, 127A/131, 46, FO 118: 746; Smith, "Social Base of Peronism," 55 (statistic).

80. *El Pueblo*, August 13, 1944, 8.

81. *La Gaceta*, May 7, 1946, 5; Taylor, *Eva Perón*, 47, 49; *Orientación*, July 16, 1946, clipping, Junta de la Victoria file, Archivo de la Prensa, Archivos y Colecciones Particulares, Biblioteca Nacional (BN), Buenos Aires; Ratto in *Nosotras*, July 1946, 2.

82. *La Hora*, April 4, 1946, 6; *Orientación*, April 10, 1946, 1.

83. The old version probably appeared in 1941 (see chapter 3, note 4); the newer one, probably issued in 1946, is Junta de la Victoria, *Estatutos*, 1941 [*sic*], in Bisso, ed., *El antifascismo argentino*, 148–52.

84. Junta de la Victoria, *Boletín Informativo*; *La Hora*, March 23, 1946, 6, May 17, 1946, 12; *El Territorio* (Resistencia), December 21, 1946, 5, *La Voz del Interior*, March 13, 1946, 6; *La Gaceta*, April 10, 1946, 6; *El Día*, May 8, 1946, 7.

85. Junta de la Victoria, *Boletín Informativo*, 1; *La Hora*, June 6, 1946, 8, June 13, 1946, 11, June 15, 1946, 12, June 17, 1946, 1, 1946. See also *La Nación*, June 17, 1946; *La Prensa*, June 17, 1946, 10; *Orientación*, July 16, 1946, clippings, all in Junta de la Victoria file, Archivo de la Prensa, BN.

86. *La Hora*, June 17, 1946, 6–7; McPherson, ed., *Encyclopedia of U.S. Military Interventions*, 2:641.

87. For example, the San Luis chapter had a Peronist officer, according to Elisa Élida Canciani, email communication, October 9, 2019.

88. Comisión Femenina Nacional, *La mujer y sus derechos*, esp. 38, 40, 46; *Mujeres Argentinas*, April 1, 1947; *Los Andes*, January 25, 1946, 6 (quote); Edelman, *Banderas, pasiones, camaradas*, 99–100; Rubinzal, interview, 2013; and Braslavsky, interview, 2000.

89. De Haan, "La Federación Democrática," 30; Valobra, "Las comunistas argentinas," 77.

90. *La Prensa*, August 2, 1947, 9; Edelman, *Banderas, pasiones, camaradas*, 102.

91. Edelman, *Banderas, pasiones, camaradas*, 100, 102–3; *Mujeres Argentinas*, July 15, 1947, August 1, 1947; Del Franco, *Mujeres, ese fuego, esas luchas*, 30; Pasquali, "Entrevista a Amor Hernández," 37; Valobra, "La UMA en marcha," 167–68, Boschi, interview with Valobra, n.d.

92. Leibner, *Camaradas y compañeros*, 83, 87–88, 101–28.

93. *Diario Popular*, March 31, 1946, 2, May 13, 1946, 2,

94. De Haan, "La Federación Democrática," 30; De Giorgi, "Entre la lucha," 219–20; *Diario Popular*, February 6, 1945, 1, March 1, 1946, 1.

95. On this and the next paragraph, see *Nosotras*, April 1946, 1, July 1946, 2, August 1946, 2, 16; *Diario Popular*, August 23–27, 1946; *La Hora*, March 7, 1946, 3, August 23–September 12, 1946; *Mujeres Argentinas*, August 9, 1946, 2; Moorehead, *A Train*; *Auschwitz*.

96. Boschi, interview, n.d.

97. *Diario Popular*, August 23, 1946, 4.

98. De Haan, "La Federación Democrática," 30–31, 43; Mooney, "El antifascismo."

99. Adams, *"World We Live In"*; *New York Times*, October 11–25, 1946; Noyes, "International Assembly of Women," 86–91; Labarca, *Feminismo contemporáneo*, 67–97, courtesy of Katherine Marino; *Argentina Libre*, January 9, 1947, 6. See statistics in *New York Times*, October 11, 1946, 36; Adams, *"World We Live In,"* 121–22; Labarca, *Feminismo contemporáneo*, 73.

100. Labarca, *Feminismo contemporáneo*, 80–82; *New York Times*, October 20, 1946, 53, October 25, 1946, 5; "Pro-Member: UAW Women, "A History of Activism"; Cooper, *Raphael Lemkin*, 82, agreed this was the organizers' goal.

101. Adams, *"World We Live In,"* 33–35, 41; Labarca, *Feminismo contemporáneo*, 73–74; *New York Times*, October 16, 1946, 4, Noyes, "International Assembly of Women," 87; Rupp, *Worlds of Women*, 46–47.

102. Adams, *"World We Live In,"* 28, 46, 90 (quotes); Marino, *Feminism for the Americas*, 199, 204; Labarca, *Feminismo contemporáneo*, 84; *New York Times*, October 16, 1946, 4.

103. *New York Times*, October 15, 1946, 15, October 19, 1946, 8, October 20, 1946, 3; Noyes, "International Assembly of Women," 88; *Argentina Libre*, January 9, 1947, 6; Adams, *"World We Live In,"* 45 (quote), 52 (quote).

104. *New York Times*, October 25, 1946, 5 (quotes); Adams, *"World We Live In,"* 72, 75.

Conclusion

1. The first mentions I found in secondary sources were Carlson, ¡*Feminismo!*, 180, 184–86, in 1988; Clementi, *María Rosa Oliver*, 143, in 1992; and, in 1993, Rein, *Franco-Perón*, 150–52, 286n39. Other works followed, beginning in 2001.

2. Avni, *Argentina and the Jews*, 177–95; Rein, *Populism and Ethnicity*.

3. Luna, *Perón y su tiempo*, 1:276–79.

4. *New York Times*, April 20, 1958, 12, September 5, 1964, 19; Valobra, *Del hogar a las urnas*, 101–2, 111.

5. *New York Times*, April 20, 1958, 12 (quote); *New York Herald Tribune*, April 20, 1958, clipping, courtesy of Kathleen Banks Nutter, Sophia Smith Collection, Smith College, Northampton, MA.

6. Clementi, *Lautaro*, 45.

7. Kedinger, interview, 2013; Singerman, *Mis dos vidas*, 115–16.

8. Filer, interview, 1999.

9. Sanjurjo, "Rosa Ziperovich"; *El Litoral*, January 16, 1995.

10. Reati, interview, 2014; email communication, December 9, 2013, with testimony from Inés Drallny.

11. Mesa C, Referencia Especial Legajos 443, 1754, 3551, 7246, 13095, Archivo de la Dirección de Inteligencia de la Policía de la Provincia de Buenos Aires, Comisión Provincial por la Memoria, La Plata, Argentina. Similar archives exist in other provinces and at the national level.

12. Amaral, "Peronismo y marxismo"; Fiorucci, *Intelectuales y peronismo*, 101–2; Spinelli, *Los vencedores vencidos*, 242–44. Other militants questioned the Communist Party's stance on Peronism; see Jáuregui, "El peronismo en los debates."

13. Tarcus, ed., *Diccionario biográfico*, 553–54; Cora Ratto de Sadosky, Biographies of Women Mathematicians, https://mathwomen.agnesscott.org/wom en/sadosky.htm; Camarero, consultation, 2013; Weitz, "Del Tzitzit al Bit"; "Cora Ratto de Sadosky, científica," *La Voz*, January 21, 2014, https://www.lavoz.com.ar/ opinion/cora-ratto-de-sadosky-cientifica/; "Cora Susana Sadosky," MacTutor, May 2018, mathshistory.st-andrews.ac.uk/Biographies/Sadosky/, with link to *New York Times*, August 19, 1966.

14. Petra, "Cultura comunista y guerra fría"; Iber, *Neither Peace nor Freedom*, 50–52, 65–68.

15. Oliver to Cannon, November 4, 1952, box 2, folder 51, Oliver Papers.

16. Oliver to Brainerd, November 3, 1952, box 6, folder 56, Oliver Papers.

17. Their correspondence reveals their warm friendship: Rockefeller, September 22, 1945; Oliver, November 5, 1945; and succeeding letters, RAC; and Oliver, April 9, 1952, box 5, folder 57, Oliver Papers, the last letter between them that I found. Also see Iber, *Neither Peace nor Freedom*, 66, 68.

18. Box 5, folder 17, Oliver Papers; Iber, *Neither Peace nor Freedom*, 66–67.

19. Power, "Friends and Comrades."

20. Dellatorre and Martínez Chas, consultations, 2013. A member of the Junta de Estudios Históricos de Misiones concurred.

21. Wickstrom, interview, 2013.

22. Véliz, interview, 2013.

23. Dellatorre, consultation, 2013.

24. Fogeler and Urquiza, consultations, 2013.

25. Juárez, interview, 2014.

26. I borrow this phrasing from Falcoff's and Dolkart's coedited *Prologue to Perón*, covering 1930–1943, although it treated this time period as significant in itself.

27. Luna, *Perón y su tiempo*, 1:279; Torre, *La vieja guardia*, 171–74.

28. Kundera, *Book of Laughter and Forgetting*, 8–9, 23–24.

29. Lambe, *No Barrier Can Contain It*, 211–16.

30. Cernadas et al., "Para una historia."

31. Cernadas et al., "La historiografía," 31.

32. Hyde, *Primer for Forgetting*, 12. See also Friedman and Kenney, "Introduction," 10.

33. Barrancos, "Historia, historiografía y género," esp. 51–52, 58–60; Valobra, "Algunas consideraciones," esp. 2–4; Pite, "Engendering Argentine History."

34. "Raíces en el pueblo," 3–4, undated, unpublished manuscript, in the UMA office, Buenos Aires. It also cited Peronist and other women among its forerunners. The UMA's account contrasts with Fischer's tale of "mutual forgetting," in which Brazilian shantytown dwellers and the party elided Communist Party participation in slum inhabitants' resistance to removal. See Fischer, "Red Menace Reconsidered."

35. Some women's groups elsewhere exhibited several Victory Board traits, but not its unique ones. See, among other sources, Jackson, *British Women and the Spanish Civil War*; Patai, "Heroines of the Good Fight"; Louro, *Comrades against Imperialism*; Tannoury-Karam, "No Place for Neutrality."

36. Some activists and movements discussed below may not have called themselves feminist, but they supported women's rights. Edelman was among those who later described themselves as such; see *Feminismo y marxismo*, 13.

37. Barrancos, *Inclusión/Exclusion*, 152; Barrancos, *Mujeres, entre la casa*, 154–57; Gil Lozano, "Las experiencias de la segunda."

38. Feijoó, "Democratic Participation and Women in Argentina," 33, 35.

39. Hammond, *Women's Suffrage Movement*, 177, 182, 199–200; Valobra, *Del hogar a las urnas*, 75, 77, 79, 124, 143, 150; Barrancos, *Inclusión/Exclusion*, 122–25, 144; Barrancos, *Mujeres, entre la casa*, 177, 182; Feijoó, "Democratic Participation and Women in Argentina," 40–42.

40. Borland and Sutton, "Quotidian Disruption and Women's Activism."

41. Giordano, "La celebración del Año Internacional"; Nari, "Feminist Awakenings," 528–29, 533 (quote), 534; Barrancos, *Mujeres, entre la casa*, 155–56, 158.

42. Sutton and Borland, "Abortion and Human Rights," 37.

43. Encarnación, *Out in the Periphery*, 75; Barrancos, *Mujeres, entre la casa*, 158, 178–79.

44. Bouvard, *Revolutionizing Motherhood*; Borland and Sutton, "Quotidian Disruption and Women's Activism"; Branigan, "Feminists Fight Covid," 4; Tabbush and Friedman, "Feminist Activism Confronts COVID-19."

45. Borland and Sutton, "Quotidian Disruption and Women's Activism," 701, 712–13 (quote on 713).

46. Nari, "Feminist Awakenings," 535; Álvarez et al., "Encountering Latin American and Caribbean Feminisms"; Barrancos, *Mujeres, entre la casa*, 161 (quote); Edelman, *Feminismo y marxismo*, 44, 128–33.

47. Marino, "Anti-Fascist *Feminismo*."

48. Nari, "Feminist Awakenings," 529. On leftist and rightist women's struggles for autonomy, see González and Kampwirth, eds., *Radical Women in Latin America*, esp. 17–21.

49. Feijoó and Nari, "Women and Democracy in Argentina," 110.

50. Di Marco, "'Feminist People.'"

51. Gordon, "Scars of Democracy," courtesy of Kathleen Staudt.

52. On distinctions and overlaps between rightist populism and fascism, see Finchelstein, *From Fascism to Populism*; Finchelstein, *Brief History of Fascist Lies*.

53. See, for example, Blee, "Where Do We Go from Here?"; Lavin, *Cultural Warlords*; Stern, *Proud Boys and the White Ethnostate*.

54. Quoted by Bray, *Antifa*, 216.

55. Quoted in Bray, *Antifa*, 214.

56. Among other works, see Hochschild, *Strangers in Their Own Land*.

BIBLIOGRAPHY

Archives

Argentina

Archivo de la Dirección de Inteligencia de la Policía de la Provincia de Buenos Aires. Comisión Provincial por la Memoria. La Plata

Archivo de la Escuela Sarmiento. Tucumán

Archivo de la Palabra. Centro Marc Turkow, Asociación Mutual Israelita Argentina. Buenos Aires

Archivo del Partido Comunista. Buenos Aires

Archivo General de Gobernación de Misiones. Casa de Gobierno. Posadas

Archivo General de la Provincia de Santa Fe

Archivo Gregorio Bermann. Biblioteca del Centro de Estudios Avanzados. Universidad Nacional de Córdoba

Archivo Histórico de la Provincia de Tucumán

Archivo Histórico de la Provincia del Chaco "Mons. José Alumni." Resistencia

Archivo Intermedio. Fondo Ministerio del Interior, Archivo General de la Nación. Buenos Aires

Archivo y Museo Histórico Marta Samatán. Universidad Nacional del Litoral. Santa Fe

Biblioteca M. E. Valentié. Centro Cultural Alberto Rougés, Fundación Miguel Lillo. Tucumán

Biblioteca Nacional Mariano Moreno. Departamento de Archivos. Buenos Aires

Centro de Documentación e Investigación de la Cultura de Izquierdas (CeDinCI). Buenos Aires

El Fogón de los Arrieros. Resistencia

Instituto Judío de Investigación (IWO). Buenos Aires

Museo de la Casa Histórica. Tucumán

Chile

Memoria Chilena. Biblioteca Nacional. Santiago

France

Bibliothèque Nationale. Paris

Great Britain

Foreign Office, Embassy and Consulates, Argentine Republic. General Correspondence (FO). Center for Research Libraries. Chicago, IL

International

Women and Social Movements, International: 1840 to the Present. Online

Israel

Central Archive for the History of the Jewish People. Jerusalem

United States

American Jewish Joint Distribution Committee Archive. New York, NY
Arthur and Elizabeth Schlesinger Library on the History of Women in America. Radcliffe Institute for Advanced Study, Harvard University. Cambridge, MA
Department of Rare Books and Special Collections. Princeton University Library. Princeton, NJ
Franklin D. Roosevelt Presidential Library. Hyde Park, NY
Hoover Institution Archives. Stanford, CA
Library of Congress, Manuscript Division. Washington, DC
National Archives and Records Administration (NARA). College Park, MD
New York Public Library. New York, NY
Rare Book and Manuscript Library. Columbia University. New York, NY
Rockefeller Archive Center. Sleepy Hollow, NY
Rutgers University Libraries, Special Collections and University Archives. New Brunswick, NJ
Sophia Smith Collection. Smith College. Northhampton, MA
Swarthmore College Peace Collection. Swarthmore, PA
University of Notre Dame Rare Books and Special Collections, Hesburgh Library. Notre Dame, IN

Uruguay

Archivo General de la Nación. Montevideo
Archivo Literario. Departamento de Investigaciones, Biblioteca Nacional. Montevideo
Fondo Centro Republicano Español (ACRE). Facultad de Humanidades y Ciencias de la Educación, Universidad de la República. Montevideo

Interviews with Participants, Witnesses, Descendants, and Relatives (with the author, unless otherwise noted)

Anonymous. Interview with Nerina Visacovsky, n.d., Buenos Aires, Argentina

Ávalos, Ileana. Phone interview, 2013, Resistencia, Argentina

Baaclini, Esther. Phone interview, 2013, Tucumán, Argentina

Bohoslavsky, Carlos y Pablo. 2014, email

Bonazzola de Maciel, Sonia. Phone interview, Santa Fe, Argentina

Boschi, Delia. Interview with Adriana María Valobra, n.d., Buenos Aires, Argentina

Braslavsky, Berta P. 2000, Buenos Aires, Argentina

Browning, Gwendolyn. Phone interview, 2013, Santa Fe, Argentina

Butiérrez de Báez, Alcira. 2009, La Plata, Argentina

Corbisier, Margarida. Interview with Hélgio Trindade, 1969–1970. Porto Alegre, Brazil

Cusien, Rosa de. 2000, Buenos Aires, Argentina

Cutín, Lucho. 2013, Tucumán, Argentina

D.C.M. 2011, Buenos Aires, Argentina

D.D. 2015, Montevideo, Uruguay

Edelman, Fanny. 2009, Buenos Aires, Argentina

Elkin, Benjamín. 2013, Córdoba, Argentina

Faingold de Villagra, Rosa. 1997, Buenos Aires, Argentina

Feigin, Betty. 2013, Córdoba, Argentina

Feo, Ana María. 2013, email, Tucumán

Filer, Malva. 1999, New York, United States

Furtembach de Kanner, Elsa, and Libertad Kanner. 2013, Oberá, Argentina

Furtembach de Kanner, Elsa. 2013, Oberá, Argentina

Galina, Edith. 2013, Córdoba, Argentina

Halperín, Ida. 2000, phone interview, United States

Jaroslavsky, Juan Pablo. 2013, email, Barcelona, Spain

Juárez, Marcela. 2014, phone interview, United States

Kaufman, Samuel. 2013, Tucumán, Argentina

Kedinger, Ana María. 2013, Resistencia, Argentina

Lang, Anita. 2000, Buenos Aires, Argentina

Legorburu, Maita. 2013, Tucumán, Argentina

Massera, Ema. 2015, Montevideo, Uruguay

Molinas, Susana. 2013, Santa Fe, Argentina

Molodesky, Fito. 2013, Resistencia, Argentina

Mosset Iturraspe, Dr. Jorge. 2013, Santa Fe, Argentina

Oliver, María Rosa. Proyecto de Historia Oral del Instituto Torcuato di Tella. 1971, Buenos Aires, Argentina

Ostrorog, Francisco, 2013, phone interview, Oberá, Argentina

Othar, Irma. 2009, phone interview, Buenos Aires, Argentina

Penchansky, Juan. 2013, Resistencia, Argentina
Pririzant, Aida. 2007, Buenos Aires, Argentina
Reati, Fernando Oscar. 2014, phone interview, United States
Ritvo, Berta. 2013, Santa Fe, Argentina
Rubinzal, Susana de. 2013, Santa Fe, Argentina
Scaliter de Monín, Ana. 1997, Buenos Aires, Argentina
Serrano Pérez, Manuel. 2013, Tucumán, Argentina
Sorrentino, Pedro. 2013–2014, in person and email, Córdoba, Argentina
Ternavasio, Nilda. 2013, Tucumán, Argentina
Véliz, María Angélica. 2013, Tucumán, Argentina
Wexler, Berta, and Luis Molinas. 2009, Rosario, Argentina
Wickstrom, Jorge Lloyd. 2013, Posadas, Argentina
Wind, Peter. 2000, Buenos Aires, Argentina

Consultations with Scholars and Informed Observers about Victory Board and Feminine Action Members and the Context

Abínzano, Roberto Carlos. 2013, Posadas, Argentina
Alonso, Luciano. 2013, Santa Fe, Argentina
Barrancos, Dora. 2013, Buenos Aires, Argentina
Bisso, Andrés. 2011, La Plata, Argentina
Bravo, María Celia. 2013, Tucumán, Argentina
Broquetas, Magdalena. 2015, Montevideo, Uruguay
Camarero, Hernán. 2013, Buenos Aires, Argentina
Campi, Daniel. 2013, Tucumán, Argentina
Canciani, Elisa Élida. 2019, San Luis, Argentina
Coudannes, Mariela. 2013, Santa Fe, Argentina
Cuadro, Inés. 2015, Montevideo, Uruguay
Damiani, Salvador, and others. 2013, Club del Orden, Santa Fe
De Giorgi, Ana Laura. 2015, Montevideo, Uruguay
Dellatorre, Elsa. 2013, Resistencia, Argentina
Fernández de Ulivarri, María. 2011, 2013, in person and email, Tucumán, Argentina
Fernández, Sandra. 2009, Rosario, Argentina
Fogeler, María Rosa. 2013, Oberá, Argentina
Gajate, Clides. 2009, Rosario, Argentina
Galina, Esther, and other Asociación Cultural Israelita de Córdoba members. 2013, Córdoba, Argentina
Garber, Jacobo. 2013, email, Villa Ángela, Chaco, Argentina
Garzón Rogé, Mariana. 2013, Buenos Aires, Argentina
Gattegno, Andrés. 2011 2021, Buenos Aires, Argentina
Giordano, Mariana. 2013, Resistencia, Argentina
Girbal-Blacha, Noemí. 2019, Greater Buenos Aires, Argentina

González, Marcela. 2013, Córdoba, Argentina

Gordillo, Mónica. 2013, Córdoba, Argentina

Gutkowski, Hélène. 2013, Buenos Aires, Argentina

Guzmán, Daniel. 2013, email, Santiago del Estero, Argentina

Iñigo Carrera, Nicólas. 2013, Greater Buenos Aires, Argentina

Kessler, Anita, Catalina Kovensky de Kessler, Mario Jitrom, and Raquel Rejovitzky, of the Asociación Cultural Israelita Argentina "I.L. Peretz." 2013, Santa Fe, Argentina

Leibner, Gerardo. 2015, email, Tel Aviv, Israel

Leoni de Rosciani, María Silvia. 2013, Resistencia, Argentina

Lichtmajer, Leandro. 2011, 2013, in person and email, Tucumán, Argentina

López D'Alessandro, Fernando. 2015, Montevideo, Uruguay

Maeder, Ernesto. 2013, Resistencia, Argentina

Mari, Oscar. 2013, Resistencia, Argentina

Martínez Chas, Lida. 2013, Oberá, Argentina

Martínez, Ana Teresa. 2013, email, Santiago del Estero, Argentina

Mathias, Christine. 2013, Buenos Aires, Argentina

Morciadri de Morini, María Teresa. 2013, Córdoba, Argentina

Nadal, Pocha. 2013, Resistencia, Argentina

Pasquali, Laura. 2009, 2011, 2013, Rosario, Argentina

Peczak, Ana Rosa. 2013, Oberá, Argentina

Penna, Patricia. 2013, Tucumán, Argentina

Perilli, Carmen and Elena. 2013, Tucumán, Argentina

Peruchena, Lourdes. 2015, Montevideo, Uruguay

Piazzesi, Susana, and her research group. 2013, Santa Fe, Argentina

Piossek Prebisch, Lucía. 2013, Tucumán, Argentina

Pompert de Valenzuela, Cristina de. 2013, Resistencia, Argentina

Porrini, Rodolfo. 2015, Montevideo, Uruguay

Ramacciotti, Karina. 2013, Buenos Aires, Argentina

Rapaport, Rosa. 1998, Buenos Aires, Argentina

Requena, Pablo. 2013, Córdoba, Argentina

Rovelli, María Rosa. 2013, Córdoba, Argentina

Rubinzal, Mariela. 2013, Santa Fe, Argentina

Ruiz, Esther. 2015, Montevideo, Uruguay

Sapriza, Graciela. 2015, Montevideo, Uruguay

Silber, Daniel. 2013, Santa Fe, Argentina

Silva, Ariel. 2015, Montevideo, Uruguay

Staroselsky de Jaraz, Esther, and Mario Jaraz. 2013, Resistencia, Argentina

Suárez, Teresa. 2013, Santa Fe, Argentina

Szurmuk, Mónica. 2013, Buenos Aires, Argentina

Tasso, Alberto. 2013, email, Tucumán, Argentina

Tavares, Zulma Estela. 2013, Oberá, Argentina

Tcach, César. 2013, Córdoba, Argentina
Urquiza, Yolanda. 2013, Posadas, Argentina
Valobra, Adriana. 2013, La Plata, Argentina
Videla, Oscar. 2009, Rosario, Argentina
Vignoli, Marcela. 2013, Tucumán, Argentina
Vinocur, Rita. 2015, Montevideo, Uruguay
Weinstein, Ana de. 2011, 2013, Buenos Aires, Argentina

Periodicals

Argentina

Agremiación Femenina (Buenos Aires)
Ahora. Edición de la Unión de Escritores Proletarios (Santa Fe)
Alianza and *Alianza (periódico clausurado)* (Buenos Aires)
Antinazi (Buenos Aires)
Argentina Libre (Buenos Aires)
Bandera Argentina (Buenos Aires)
Boletín de la Comisión Interamericana de Mujeres (published in Buenos Aires in June and July 1943, then in Washington, DC)
Boletín del Comité Organizador del Congreso Antiguerrero Latinoamericano (Buenos Aires)
Boletín Informativo (Buenos Aires)
Caras y Caretas (Buenos Aires)
Claridad (Buenos Aires)
Clarinada (Buenos Aires)
Comisión Israelita de Ayuda a los Aliados. Solidaridad (Buenos Aires)
Contra-fascismo (Buenos Aires)
Córdoba (Córdoba)
Crisol (Buenos Aires)
Crítica (Buenos Aires)
El Aguijón (Rosario)
El Alba (Moisés Ville)
El Argentino (La Plata)
El Defensor (Villa Constitución, Santa Fe)
El Día (La Plata)
El Fogón de los Arrieros Boletín Mensual (Resistencia)
El Hogar (Buenos Aires)
El Litoral (Santa Fe)
El Orden (Santa Fe)
El País (Córdoba)
El Patriota (Buenos Aires)
El Pueblo (Buenos Aires)

El Territorio (Posadas)
El Territorio (Resistencia)
España Republicana (Buenos Aires)
Estampa Chaqueña (Resistencia)
FACE, *Anales* (Buenos Aires)
Flecha (Córdoba)
Frente Único. Órgano del Frente Único Popular Argentino y Federación Antiguerrera de Mujeres Argentinas (Córdoba)
Junta de la Victoria. Boletín Informativo (Buenos Aires)
Juventud Antifascista (Rosario)
La Acción (Rosario)
La Capital (Rosario)
La Fronda (Buenos Aires)
La Gaceta (Tucumán)
La Gaceta de Acción Argentina (Buenos Aires)
La Hora (Buenos Aires)
La Libertad de Avellaneda (Avellaneda)
La Nación (Buenos Aires)
La Nueva República (Buenos Aires)
La Obra (Buenos Aires)
La Prensa (Buenos Aires)
La Protesta (Buenos Aires)
La Tarde (Posadas)
La Tribuna (Rosario)
La Unión (Tucumán)
La Vanguardia (Buenos Aires)
La Verdad (Resistencia)
La Voz del Chaco (Resistencia)
La Voz del Interior (Córdoba)
Los Andes (Mendoza)
Los Principios (Córdoba)
Mujeres Argentinas (Buenos Aires)
Mujeres de América (Buenos Aires)
Mujeres en la Ayuda (Buenos Aires)
¡Mujeres! Órgano de la Agrupación Femenina Antiguerrera (Buenos Aires)
Norte Argentino (Tucumán)
Nuestra Idea (Santa Fe)
Nueva Época (Posadas)
Nueva Gaceta (Buenos Aires)
Nueva Política (Buenos Aires)
Orden Cristiano (Buenos Aires)
Orientación (Buenos Aires)

Revista del Consejo Nacional de Mujeres de la República Argentina (Buenos Aires)
(name changed from *Revista* to *Boletín* in 1940)
The Standard (Buenos Aires)
Unidad Nacional (Buenos Aires)
Unidad. Por la defensa de la cultura (Buenos Aires)
Vida Femenina (Buenos Aires)
Vosotras (Buenos Aires)

Brazil

A Offensiva (Rio de Janeiro)
A Plateia (São Paulo)
Anauê (Rio de Janeiro)
Brasil Feminino (Rio de Janeiro)
Monitor Integralista (São Paulo)

Chile

Acción Chilena (Santiago)
El Rayo (Valdivia)
La Mujer Nueva (Santiago)
Trabajo (Santiago)

United States

American Jewish Yearbook
Boletín de Información de la Comisión Interamericana de Mujeres
Bulletin of Information, Inter-American Commission of Women (note name changes below)
Chicago Tribune
Freeport
Independent Woman
Inter-American Commission of Women Bulletin
Inter-American Commission of Women Information Bulletin
International League Monthly Bulletin
New York Herald Tribune
New York Times
PANAM
TIME
Toledo (OH) Blade
Washington Post

Uruguay

Acción Femenina por la Victoria. Periódico de Ayuda a las Naciones Liberadas por los Fascismos (Montevideo)

Boletín. Federación del Magisterio Industrial (Montevideo)
Diario Popular (Montevideo)
El Día (Montevideo)
El Ideal (Montevideo)
El Plata (Montevideo)
El Sol (Montevideo)
Justicia (Montevideo)
Nosotras (Montevideo)
Revista AIAPE (Montevideo)
Uruguay (Montevideo)

Biographical Sources (also see interviews, consultations, and social pages of provincial periodicals)

Actas del Ateneo del Chaco. 1938–1941. Photocopy.
Alonso, Luciano M. *Haydee Guy de Vigo. La docente militante*. Santa Fe: Ediciones AMSAFE, 2000.
www.ancestry.com.
Anuario El Litoral. Santa Fe: El Litoral, 1937.
Aráoz de Isas, María Florencia. *La masonería en el ideario liberal de la Argentina del siglo xix. Su proyección en Tucumán*. Tucumán: Jardín de la República, 2011.
Ardanaz, Eleonora. "Con el puño en alto: Sara Fradkin y la lucha antifascista judía." In *Mujeres en espacios bonaerenses*, edited by Adriana Valobra, 111–24. La Plata: EDULP, 2009.
"Artículo muerte Laura Cortinas." Anáforas. https://anaforas.fic.edu.uy/jspui/handle/123456789/44340.
Bach, Caleb. "The Other Borges." *Américas* 59, no. 2 (March 2007): 36–43.
Barrancos, Dora. *Educación, cultura y trabajadores (1890–1930)*. Buenos Aires: CEAL, 1991.
Becerra, Marina. "María Rosa Oliver (1898–1977), de la historia a la autobiografía." *Arenal* 22, no. 1 (January-June 2015): 31–47.
Becerra, Marina. "Maternidad y ciudadanía en la Argentina de principios del siglo XX: un análisis de la autobiografía de María Rosa Oliver." *A Contracorriente* 10, no. 2 (Winter 2013): 202–18.
Belucci, Mabel. "Angélica Mendoza, la primera candidata a presidente de un partido político." *Todo Es Historia*, no. 215 (March 1985): 63–64.
Béssero, Antonio Pedro. *Tafí Viejo: 100 años de historia*. Municipalidad de la Ciudad de Tafí Viejo: n.p., n.d.
"Blanca Irurzun." ADN Santiago del Estero. Accessed January 15, 2023. http://Bibliotecajwa.com.ar/Santiago/doku.php/irurzun-blanca.
Caffaratti, Ana María. "Marta Samatán y el batallar sin fin por la cultura." In *Marta Samatán. Edición homenaje en el centenario de su nacimiento 1901–2001*,

5–10. Santa Fe: AMSAFE, La Capital, Instituto Sarmientino de Santa Fe, Universidad Nacional del Litoral, 2001.

Carpetas Género, Marta Samatán, and Rosa Diner de Babini. Archivo y Museo Histórico Marta Samatán. Universidad Nacional del Litoral, Santa Fe.

Cincuentenario de Las Breñas (Chaco). Gran Revista Bodas de Oro. 1921–11 de julio—1971. Las Breñas: n.p., 1971.

Clementi, Hebe. *Lautaro. Historia de una editorial.* Buenos Aires: Leviatán, 2004.

Clementi, Hebe. *María Rosa Oliver.* Buenos Aires: Planeta, 1992.

Consejo de la Ciudad de Santa Fe. *Mujeres en el puerto.* Santa Fe: n.p., n.d.

Cora Ratto de Sadosky, Biographies of Women Mathematicians, https://math women.agnesscott.org/women/corasadosky.htm.

Coudannes, Mariela. "Tradición y cambio social en dos regiones de América del Sur. Mujeres elquinas y santafesinas en la narrativa de Marta Samatán." *SudHistoria*, no. 3 (July-December 2011): 1–22.

De Bertero, Gloria. *Quién es ella en Santa Fe.* Buenos Aires: Palabra Gráfica, 1995.

De Diego, Bernardo M. *Club del Orden. Anales. Contribución a la historia de Santa Fe.* Santa Fe: Imprenta Macagno, 1990.

De Martina, Ángeles de Dios. *Mujeres inmigrantes. Historias de vida.* Buenos Aires: Dunken, 2001.

Deleis, Mónica, Richard de Titto, and Diego L. Arguindeguy. *Mujeres de la política argentina.* Buenos Aires: Aguilar, 2001.

Dip, Davíd. *Guía informativo y comercial de la ciudad de Tafí Viejo.* Tucumán: n.p., 1961.

Edelman, Fanny. *Banderas, pasiones, camaradas.* Buenos Aires: Dirple, 1996.

El Chaco de 1940. Buenos Aires: Guillermo Kraft, 1941.

El Chaco. Album gráfico descriptivo. Buenos Aires: Compañía Impresora Argentina, 1935.

Escobar, Luis A. "Marta Elena Samatán, una voz intelectual en el litoral argentino: gremialismo, antiimperialismo, antifascismo y feminismo (1920–1946)." *Cuadernos de Historia. Serie economía y sociedad*, no. 28 (2021): 87–118.

Ferreira, Florencia. "Angélica Mendoza y su trayectoria americana." https://unami radafilosofica.files.wordpress.com/2013/07/mendoza.pdf.

Fraire, Osvaldo. *Diccionario biográfico de la mujer en el Uruguay.* Montevideo: n.p., 1999.

Fraire, Osvaldo. *Quién es quién en el Uruguay.* Montevideo: Central de Publicaciones, 1978.

Garber, Jacobo. *Algunos relatos de Villa Ángela.* Buenos Aires: Dunken, 2006.

García Pulido, José. *Chaco Crisol de Razas. Homenaje a los inmigrantes y sus descendientes (pioneros del progreso).* Resistencia: Casa García, 1981.

Genealogía Familiar. www.genealogiafamiliar.net.

Guía del Chaco V (1935–1936). Resistencia: Juan Moro, 1936.

Guía Social Argentina "Régar." Buenos Aires: Régar, 1931.

Guía social del norte. Tucumán y Catamarca. Tucumán: La Velocidad, 1936.

Guía Social Fredriksson. Rosario: Fredriksson, 1939.

Guía Social Palma. Buenos Aires: Palma, 1945.

Guía social y biográfica de Santa Fe. Santa Fe: El Litoral, 1943.

Hilton, Ronald. *Who's Who in Latin America.* Part 5, *Argentina, Paraguay, Uruguay.* Stanford, CA: Stanford University Press, 1950.

Jeifets, Victor, and Lazar Jeifets. *América Latina en la Internacional Comunista, 1919–1943: diccionario biográfico.* Buenos Aires: Clacso, Ariadna Ediciones, 2017.

Jokmanovich de Derka, Mabel. "Inmigrantes eslavos en el corazón del Chaco." *Todo Es Historia*, no. 535 (February 2012): 44–58.

https://mathshistory.st-andrews.ac.uk/Biographies/Ratto_de_Sadosky/.

Libro de Oro. Buenos Aires: Guillermo Kraft, 1942.

https://www.madariaga.gob.ar/noticias/19865/ciclo-de-charlas-en-el-museo-disertarán-sobre-la-vida-de-ana-rosa-schlieper-de-martinez-guerrero.

Marta Samatán. Edición homenaje en el centenario de su nacimiento 1901–2001. Santa Fe: AMSAFE, La Capital, Instituto Sarmientino de Santa Fe, Universidad Nacional del Litoral, 2001.

Martínez Trucco, Amelia. *Acción gremial del magisterio de Santa Fe: su trayectoria y aporte a la construcción del sistema educativo.* Santa Fe: Universidad Nacional del Litoral, 2004.

Miranda, Guido. *Los orígenes de Las Breñas.* Resistencia: Imprenta Región, 1979.

Municipalidad de General Madariaga. "Ciclo de Charlas en el Museo: Disertarán sobre la vida de Ana Rosa Schlieper de Martínez Guerrero."

Nader, Raúl F. *Voces de la memoria.* San Miguel de Tucumán: Programa CIUNT-CONICET, Facultad de Filosofía y Letras, UNT, 1999.

Oliver, María Rosa. *La vida cotidiana.* Buenos Aires: Sudamericana, 1969.

Oliver, María Rosa. *Mi fe es el hombre.* Buenos Aires: Carlos Lohlé, 1981.

Oliver, María Rosa. *Mundo mi casa.* Buenos Aires: Ediciones de la Flor, 1995.

Palacios, Gerardo. *Recuerdos del atardecer.* San Miguel de Tucumán: Lucio Piérola Ediciones, 1997.

Pasquali, Laura. "Marta Samatán: Una loca margarita." In *Maestras argentinas. Entre mandatos y transgresiones*, edited by Eduardo Mancini and Mariana Caballero. Rosario: Centro Cultural La Toma/Asociación Civil Inconsciente Colectivo, 2000.

Quién es quién en la Argentina. Biografías contemporáneas. Buenos Aires: Guillermo Kraft, 1943, 1950.

Raíces, 1904–2004. Tucumán: Departamento Ciencias Humanas, Escuela y Liceo Vocacional Sarmiento-UNT, 2004.

Ramacciotti, Karina Inés. "Telma Reca en la gestion estatal de la sanidad Argentina (1930–1948)." *Asclepio* 70, no. 1 (January-June 2018): 1–13.

Recuerdos. Escuela Sarmiento. UNT. 1947–1957. Tucumán: Imprenta Campi, n.d.

Sanjurjo, Liliana Olga. *Rosa Ziperovich: Una lección de vida.* Rosario: Ediciones de Aquí a la Vuelta, 1990.

Scarone, Arturo. *Uruguayos contemporáneos. Nuevo diccionario de datos biográficos y bibliográficos.* Montevideo: Casa A. Bairreiro y Ramos, 1937.

sgodelest.blogspot.com/2011/08/el-trasiego-emocional-de-blanca-irurzun.html.

Sociedad de Beneficencia. *Memoria correspondiente al ejercicio de mayo de 1931 a mayo de 1932.* Córdoba: Imprenta de la Universidad, 1932.

Sociedad El Hogar y Ayuda Social. *Memoria correspondiente al ejercicio del período 1938 al 1 de octubre de 1939.* Córdoba: Imprenta Rossi Argentina, 1940.

Sosa de Newton, Lily. *Diccionario biográfico de mujeres argentinas.* 2nd. ed. Buenos Aires: Plus Ultra, 1980.

Tarcus, Horacio. *Diccionario biográfico de la izquierda argentina. De los anarquistas a la "nueva izquierda" (1870–1976).* Buenos Aires: Emecé, 2007.

Telma Reca. Premio Aníbal Ponce 1979. Buenos Aires: Ediciones "Amigos de Aníbal Ponce," 1979.

Todo en la provincia. Anuario y guía de la Provincia de Córdoba. Córdoba: El Diario Córdoba, 1937, 1942.

Travadelo, Delia A. *Marta Samatán, maestra.* Santa Fe: Universidad Nacional del Litoral, 2001.

Universidad Nacional del Litoral, Instituto Social, Sección Extensión Universitaria. "Conferencias. Zona norte provincia Santa Fe," 1937–1943.

UNT. Escuela y Liceo Vocacional Sarmiento. "Egresadas: 1916–1977." Unpublished list.

Valobra, Adriana María. "Acción y sociabilidad políticas de radicales feministas en La Plata de los '30." In *Historias políticas de la provincia de Buenos Aires en el siglo XX*, edited by Marcela Ferrari and Nicolás Quiroga, 57–83. La Plata: EDULP, 2009.

Valobra, Adriana María. "'En bien de mis ideales': María Luisa Coutouné y el radicalismo feminista platense." In *Mujeres en espacios bonaerenses*, edited by Adriana Valobra, 125–37. La Plata: EDULP, 2009.

Valobra, Adriana María. "El particular ideario de Eugenia Silveyra de Oyuela, 1936–1957." *Cuadernos del Sur—Historia*, no. 41 (2012): 215–52.

Weitz, Darío. "Del Tzitzit al Bit: Aportes Judíos en Computación e Informática: Manuel Sadosky." Diariojudio.com. June 27, 2019. https://diariojudio.com/ticker/del-tzitzit-al-bit-aportes-judios-en-computacion-e-informatica-manuel-sadosky/300555/.

Wickstrom, Lloyd Jorge. *Pioneros. Biografías.* Oberá Virtual, http://oberavirtual.blogspot.com/2014/02/pioneros-biografias-de-lloyd-jorge.html.

Wickstrom, Lloyd O. R. *Oberá. Anuario social y commercial 1939.* Oberá: n.p., 1939.

Margot Portela Parker. https://www.arte-online.net/Artistas/Portela_Parker_Mar got/(section)/Biografía.

Zanca, José. "Eugenia en su laberinto. Catolicismo y antifascismo en el itinerario de Eugenia Silveyra de Oyuela." Paper presented at the Latin American Studies Association meeting, New York, NY, May 30, 2016.

Primary and Secondary Sources

Abell, Aaron I. "Monsignor John A. Ryan: An Historical Appreciation." *Review of Politics* 8, no. 1 (January 1946): 128–34.

Abínzano, Roberto Carlos. "Política y etnicidad en un contexto rural de frontera: El Nacional Socialismo en las colonias alemanas de Sudamérica." *Estudios Regionales*, Serie Relaciones Interétnicas (Posadas), no. 2 (1991): 58–74.

Ablard, Jonathan. "'The Barracks Receives Spoiled Children and Returns Men': Debating Military Service, Masculinity and Nation-Building in Argentina, 1901–1930." *The Americas* 74, no. 3 (July 2017): 299–329.

Acción Antinazi de Ayuda a los Pueblos Libres. *Tercera Conferencia Nacional de Ayuda a los Aliados, 26–27–28 de enero 1945.* Montevideo: n.p., 1945.

Asociación Argentina del Sufragio Femenino. *Estatutos.* Buenos Aires: n.p., 1932.

Acción Femenina por la Victoria. "Autoridades emanadas de la Primera Convención Nacional, Agosto 27–29 de 1943." Montevideo, 1943. Flyer.

Acción Femenina por la Victoria. "Bolsa de Navidad para los Niños Aliados." Montevideo, 1944. Flyer.

Acción Femenina por la Victoria. *Campaña Argentino-Uruguaya Sanitaria y de Abrigo, 1943–1944.* Montevideo: n.p., 1944.

Acción Femenina por la Victoria. "Empleadas y obreras trabajan para la causa de la Victoria." In *Campaña Argentino-Uruguaya Sanitaria y de Abrigo, 1943–1944.* Montevideo: n.p., 1944.

Acción Femenina por la Victoria. *Entregas efectuadas por Acción Femenina por la Victoria.* Montevideo: n.p., n.d. [1944?]

Acción Femenina por la Victoria. *Estatutos.* Montevideo: n.p., 1945.

Acción Femenina por la Victoria. *Fines de Acción Femenina por la Victoria.* Montevideo: n.p., n.d. [1944?]

Acha, Omar. "Género y política ante el voto femenino en el catolicismo argentino, 1912–1955." In *Sufragio femenino: prácticas y debates políticos, religiosos y culturales en la Argentina y América*, edited by Carolina Barry, 63–90. Caseros, Buenos Aires: Universidad Nacional de Tres de Febrero, 2011.

Ackelsberg, Martha A. "Women and the Politics of the Spanish Popular Front: Political Mobilization or Social Revolution?" *International Labor and Working-Class History* 30 (1986): 1–12.

Acle-Kreysing, Andrea. "Antifascismo: Un espacio de encuentro entre el exilio y la política nacional. El caso de Vicente Lombardo Toledano en México (1936–1945)." *Revista de Indias* 76, no. 267 (2016): 573–609.

Acle-Kreysing, Andrea. "Shattered Dreams of Anti-Fascist Unity: German Speaking Exiles in Mexico, Argentina and Bolivia, 1937–1945." *Contemporary European History* 25, no. 4 (2016): 667–86.

Acree, Jr., William G. "*Divisas y deberes*: Women and the Symbolic Economy of War Rhetoric in the Río de la Plata, 1810–1910." *Journal of Latin American Cultural Studies: Travesía* 22, no. 2 (2013): 213–37.

Adamovsky, Ezequiel. *Historia de la clase media argentina. Apogeo y decadencia de una ilusión, 1919–2003.* Buenos Aires: Planeta, 2009.

Adams, Mildred. "*The World We Live In—The World We Want.*" *The Record of the International Assembly of Women Held at South Kortright New York, U.S.A. in October 1946.* Hartford, CT: Stone Book Press, 1946.

Agrupación Femenina Antiguerrera. "A todas las mujeres contra la guerra." Undated flyer.

Agrupación Femenina Antiguerrera. *La mujer argentina y sus derechos.* Buenos Aires: n.p., 1936.

Alberto, Paulina L., and Eduardo Elena, eds. *Rethinking Race in Modern Argentina.* New York: Cambridge University Press, 2016.

Alcalde, Carmen. *La mujer en la guerra civil española.* Madrid: Cambio 16, 1976.

Alianza de la Juventud Nacionalista. *Postulados de nuestra lucha.* Buenos Aires: n.p., n.d.

Almaráz, Roberto, Manuel Corchón, and Rómulo Zemborain. *¡Aquí FUBA! Las luchas estudiantiles en tiempos de Perón (1943–1955).* Buenos Aires: Planeta, 2001.

Almeida, Daniela Moraes de. "Representaciones y relaciones entre la Legión Cívica Argentina y el integralismo brasileño (década de 1930)." In *Circule por la derecha. Percepciones, redes y contactos entre las derechas sudamericanas, 1917–1973,* edited by Ernesto Bohoslavsky and João Fábio Bertonha, 129–47. Los Polvorines: Universidad Nacional de General Sarmiento, 2016.

Álvarez, Sonia E., et al. "Encountering Latin American and Caribbean Feminisms." *Signs* 28, no. 2 (Winter 2003): 537–79.

Amaral, Samuel. "Peronismo y marxismo en los años fríos. Rodolfo Puiggrós y el movimiento obrero comunista: 1947–55." *Investigaciones y ensayos* no. 50 (2000): 171–94.

Anastasi, Dr. Leonidas. *Derechos civiles de la mujer.* Buenos Aires: UAM, 1938.

Ante la patria en peligro, Junta Revolucionaria Nacionalista. Buenos Aires: n.p., 1944.

Antezana-Pernet, Corinne. *El MEMCH hizo historia.* Santiago: SEIT, 1997.

Antezana-Pernet, Corinne. "Mobilizing Women in the Popular Front Era: Feminism, Class, and Politics in the *Movimiento Pro-Emancipación de la Mujer Chilena* (MEMCh), 1935–1950." PhD diss., University of California Irvine, 1996.

Arce Pinedo, Rebeca. "De la mujer social a la mujer azul: La reconstrucción de la feminidad por las derechas españolas durante el primer tercio del siglo XX." *Ayer* 57 (2005): 247–72.

Ardanaz, Eleonora. "Maternalismo y política en el antifascismo argentino: el caso del Comité Argentino Pro Huérfanos Españoles." *Zona Franca*, no. 25 (2017): 7–35.

Ardanaz, Eleonora. "'Pelando papas se combate el fascismo': roles y funciones en las asociaciones antifascistas de Bahía Blanca durante la Guerra Civil Española." *Cuadernos de H Ideas* 7, no. 7 (December 2013). http://perio.unlp.edu.ar/ojs/index.php/cps.

Argentina, Congreso de la Nación, Cámara de Diputados. *Comisión Investigadora de Actividades Antiargentinas.* Buenos Aires: Congreso de la Nación, 1942.

Asociación Argentina del Sufragio Femenino. *Estatutos.* Buenos Aires: n.p., 1932.

Auschwitz: apéndice, Marie-Claude Vaillant Couturier en el Tribunal de Nuremberg. Buenos Aires: Junta de la Victoria, 1946.

Avni, Haim. *Argentina and the Jews: A History of Jewish Immigration.* Translated by Gila Brand. Tuscaloosa: University of Alabama Press, 1991.

Bachelet, Michelle. "The Chilean Path to Progressive Change." *Berkeley Review of Latin American Studies* (Spring-Summer 2010): 3–11.

Bairros, Lilian Tavares de. "O integralismo de saia: militancia feminina nas fileiras Integralistas em Santos." Seminário Internacional Fazendo Gênero 10: Desafios Actuais dos Feminismos (Anais Eletrônicos), Florianópolis, 2013.

Barrancos, Dora. "El Partido Socialista y el sufragio femenino, 1947–1951." In *Sufragio femenino: prácticas y debates políticos, religiosos y culturales en la Argentina y América*, edited by Carolina Barry, 175–98. Caseros, Buenos Aires: Universidad Nacional de Tres de Febrero, 2011.

Barrancos, Dora. "Historia, historiografía y género. Notas para la memoria de sus vínculos en la Argentina." *La Aljaba*, 2nda época, 9 (2004–2005): 49–72.

Barrancos, Dora. *Inclusión/Exclusion. Historia con mujeres.* Buenos Aires: Fondo de Cultura Económica, 2001.

Barrancos, Dora. "Maternalismo." In *Diccionario de estudios de género y feminismos*, edited by Susana B. Gamba, 205–6. Buenos Aires: Biblos, 2007.

Barrancos, Dora. *Mujeres en la sociedad argentina: una historia de cinco siglos.* Buenos Aires: Sudamericana, 2007.

Barrancos, Dora. *Mujeres, entre la casa y la plaza.* Buenos Aires: Sudamericana, 2008.

Barreto, Eduardo Atilio. *El sindicalismo del Chaco en el período territorial, 1887–1951.* Resistencia: Grafic Center, 2009.

Barrios Pintos, Aníbal. *Montevideo: Los barrios I.* Montevideo: Nuestra Tierra, 1971.

Barry, Carolina. "¿Una cruzada de Evita? El peronismo y la Ley de Sufragio Femenino." In *Sufragio femenino: prácticas y debates políticos, religiosos y culturales en la*

Argentina y América, edited by Carolina Barry, 113–43. Caseros, Buenos Aires: Universidad Nacional de Tres de Febrero, 2011.

Bauerkämper, Arnd, and Grzegorz Rossoliński-Liebe, eds. *Fascism without Borders: Transnational Connections and Cooperation between Movements and Regimes in Europe from 1918 to 1945*. New York: Berghahn Books, 2017.

Becerra, Marina. "'Soy comunista y maestra': resistencias a la maternalización de las mujeres a través de la obra de Angélica Mendoza en la Argentina de los años 20' y 30.'" *Revista Izquierdas*, no. 49 (April 2020): 385–411.

Beck, Hugo Humberto. *Inmigrantes europeos en el Chaco. Transición del pluralismo al crisol*. Resistencia: Instituto de Investigaciones Geohistóricas, 2001.

Becker, Marc. *The FBI in Latin America: The Ecuador Files*. Durham, NC: Duke University Press, 2017.

Béjar, María Dolores. *El régimen fraudulento. La política en la provincia de Buenos Aires, 1930–1943*. Buenos Aires: Siglo XXI, 2005.

Belastegui, Horacio M. *Los colonos de Misiones*. Posadas: Editorial Universitaria de Misiones, 2004.

Ben-Dror, Graciela. *La iglesia católica ante el holocausto: España y América Latina, 1933–1945*. Madrid: Alianza, 2003.

Bergel, Martín. "*Flecha*, o las animosas obsesiones de Deodoro Roca." Preface to *Deodoro Roca, Obra reunida, Vol. 4: Escritos políticos*, edited by Diego Tatián and Guillermo Vásquez, n.p. Córdoba: Universidad de Córdoba, 2012.

Bergin, Cathy. "African American Internationalists and Anti-Fascism." In *Anti-Fascism in a Global Perspective: Transnational Networks, Exile Communities, and Radical Internationalism*, edited by Kasper Braskén, Nigel Copsey, and David Featherstone, 254–72. Abingdon, UK: Routledge, 2021.

Bertonha, João Fábio. "Anarquistas italianos nas Américas: a luta contra o fascismo entre o Velho e o Novo Mundo." *Historia social* 22/23 (2012): 270–93.

Bertonha, João Fábio. "Los latinoamericanos de Franco. La 'Legión de la Falange Argentina' y otros voluntários hispanos en el bando sublevado durante la Guerra Civil Española." *Alcores* 14 (2012): 143–67.

Bertonha, João Fábio, and Ernesto Bohoslavsky, eds. *Circule por la derecha. Percepciones, redes y contactos entre las derechas sudamericanas, 1917–1973*. Los Polvorines: Universidad Nacional de General Sarmiento, 2016.

Bertúa, Paula. "'Si me quieres escribir . . . ' Mujeres en la prensa cultural antifascista (Argentina, 1930–1940)." *Arenal* 22, no. 1 (January–June 2015): 5–30.

Besoky, Juan Luis. "El nacionalismo populista de derecha en Argentina: la Alianza Libertadora Nacionalista, 1937–1975." *Mediações* 19, no. 1 (January–June 2014): 61–83.

Besse, Susan K. "Pagu: Patrícia Galvão—Rebel." In *The Human Tradition in Latin America: The Twentieth Century*, edited by William H. Beezley and Judith Ewell, 103–17. Wilmington, DE: Scholarly Resources, 1987.

Besse, Susan K. *Restructuring Patriarchy: The Modernization of Gender Inequality in Brazil, 1914–1940*. Chapel Hill: University of North Carolina Press, 1996.

Bisso, Andrés. "'Abajo con la tiranía pueblera y totalitaria.' *Mechita* o ciertas consideraciones en torno a un periódico pueblerino y ferroviario del antifascismo argentino." *Prismas*, no. 17 (2013): 221–25.

Bisso, Andrés. *Acción Argentina. Un antifascismo nacional en tiempos de guerra mundial*. Buenos Aires: Prometeo, 2005.

Bisso, Andrés. "Deodoro Roca y la polémica con la Comisión Directiva de la filial cordobesa de Acción Argentina." In *Deodoro Roca, Obra reunida*, Vol. 3: *Escritos jurídicos y de militancia*, edited by Guillermo Vásquez and Diego Tatián, xi–xxxviii. Córdoba: Universidad Nacional de Córdoba, 2009.

Bisso, Andrés, ed. *El antifascismo argentino. Selección documental y estudio preliminar*. Buenos Aires: Buenos Libros and CeDinCI editores, 2007.

Bisso, Andrés. "Festejos propios de victorias ajenas. La liberación de París y el fin de la Segunda Guerra Mundial con ojos bonaerenses." *Entrepasados* 17, no. 34 (2008): 13–31.

Bisso, Andrés, and Adrián Celentano. "La lucha antifascista de la Agrupación de Intelectuales, Artistas, Periodistas y Escritores (AIAPE) (1935–1943)." In *El pensamiento alternativo en la Argentina del siglo XX*, Vol. 2: *Obrerismo, vanguardia, justicia social (1930–1960)*, edited by Hugo E. Biagini and Arturo A. Roig, 225–65. Buenos Aires: Biblos, 2006.

Blasco Lisa, Sandra. "El Comité Mundial de Mujeres contra la Guerra y el Fascismo y sus Relaciones con España." Paper presented at the Seminario Permanente México-España, El Colegio de México, Mexico City, March 9, 2022.

Blee, Kathleen. "Where Do We Go from Here? Positioning Gender in Studies of White Supremacist and Far-Right Politics." *Politics, Religion and Ideology* 21, no. 4 (December 2020): 416–31.

Blee, Kathleen M., and Sandra McGee Deutsch, eds. *Women of the Right: Comparisons and Interplay across Borders*. University Park: Pennsylvania State University Press, 2012.

Blinkhorn, Martin, ed. *Fascists and Conservatives: The Radical Right and the Establishment in Twentieth-Century Europe*. London: Unwin Hyman, 1990.

Bohoslavsky, Ernesto, and Magdalena Broquetas. "Local and Global Connections of Argentinian, Uruguayan, and Chilean Fascists in the Thirties and Early Forties." In *Intellectuals in the Latin Space during the Era of Fascism*, edited by Valeria Galimi and Annarita Gori, 171–94. Abingdon, UK: Routledge, 2020.

Bonaudo, Marta, and Susana Bandieri. "La cuestión social agraria en los espacios regionales." In *Nueva Historia Argentina*, Vol. 6: *Democracia, conflicto social y renovación de ideas (1916–1930)*, edited by Ricardo Falcón, 229–82. Buenos Aires: Sudamericana, 2000.

Bonfiglioli, Chiara. "Red Girls' Revolutionary Tales: Antifascist Women's Autobiographies in Italy." *Feminist Review*, no. 106 (2014): 60–77.

Bordegaray, María Eugenia. "Antifascismo, género e historia de las mujeres en la Argentina: acerca de una historia "generizada" del antifascismo en nuestro país." *Cuadernos del Sur—Historia* 41 (2012): 127–32.

Bordegaray, María Eugenia. "Luchas antifascistas y trayectorias generizadas en el movimiento libertario argentino (1936–1955)." *Cuadernos de H Ideas* 7, no. 7 (December 2013). http://perio.unlp.edu.ar/ojs/index.php/cps.

Borland, Elizabeth, and Barbara Sutton. "Quotidian Disruption and Women's Activism in Times of Crisis. Argentina 2002–2003." *Gender & Society* 21, no. 5 (October 2007): 700–722.

Bouvard, Marguerite Guzmán. *Revolutionizing Motherhood: The Mothers of the Plaza de Mayo*. Wilmington, DE: Scholarly Resources, 1993.

Boxer, Marilyn. "Rethinking the Socialist Construction and International Career of the Concept of 'Bourgeois Feminism.'" *American Historical Review* 112, no. 1 (2007): 131–58.

Boylan, Kristina A. "Gendering the Faith and Altering the Nation: Mexican Catholic Women's Activism, 1917–1940." In *Sex in Revolution: Gender, Politics, and Power in Modern Mexico*, edited by Jocelyn Olcott, Mary Kay Vaughan, and Gabriela Cano, 199–222. Durham, NC: Duke University Press, 2006.

Brainerd, Heloise. "Activities of the Inter-American Committee." In *Report of the Ninth Congress of the Women's International League for Peace and Freedom, Luhacovice, Czechoslovakia. July 27th to 31st, 1937*, 101–2. Geneva, Switzerland: n.p., 1937.

Branigan, Claire. "Feminists Fight Covid on Buenos Aires' Urban Margins." *NACLA*, June 16, 2020. https://nacla.org/news/2020/06/16/feminists-covid-argentina.

Braskén, Kasper, Nigel Copsey, and David Featherstone. "Introduction." In *Anti-Fascism in a Global Perspective: Transnational Networks, Exile Communities, and Radical Internationalism*, edited by Kasper Braskén, Nigel Copsey, and David Featherstone, 1–20. Abingdon, UK: Routledge, 2021.

Braskén, Kasper, Nigel Copsey, and David Featherstone, eds. *Anti-Fascism in a Global Perspective: Transnational Networks, Exile Communities, and Radical Internationalism*. Abingdon, UK: Routledge, 2021.

Bray, Mark. *Antifa: The Antifascist Handbook*. Brooklyn: Melville House, 2017.

Brewster, Claire. "Women and the Spanish American Wars of Independence: An Overview." *Feminist Review*, no. 79 (2005): 20–35.

Broquetas, Magdalena. *La trama autoritaria. Derechas y violencia en Uruguay (1958–1966)*. Montevideo: Banda Oriental, 2014.

Brown, Laurence. "'Pour Aider Nos Frères D'Espagne': Humanitarian Aid, French Women, and Popular Mobilization during the Front Populaire." *French Politics, Culture & Society* 25, no. 1 (Spring 2007): 30–48.

Bruley, Sue. "Women against War and Fascism: Communism, Feminism and the People's Front." In *Fascism and the Popular Front*, edited by Jim Fyrth, 131–56. London: Lawrence and Wishart, 1985.

Buchanan, Tom. "Antifascism and Democracy in the 1930s." *European History Quarterly* 32, no. 1 (2002): 39–57.

Buchrucker, Cristián. *Nacionalismo y peronismo: la Argentina en la crisis ideológica mundial, 1927–1955*. Buenos Aires: Sudamericana, 1987.

Buckley, Cheryl. "On the Margins: Theorizing the History and Significance of Making and Designing Clothes at Home." In *The Culture of Sewing: Gender, Consumption and Home Dressmaking*, edited by Barbara Burman, 55–72. Oxford: Berg, 1999.

Burman, Barbara. "Introduction." In *The Culture of Sewing: Gender, Consumption and Home Dressmaking*, edited by Barbara Burman, 1–18. Oxford: Berg, 1999.

Burman, Barbara. "Made at Home by Clever Fingers: Home Dressmaking in Edwardian England." In *The Culture of Sewing: Gender, Consumption and Home Dressmaking*, edited by Barbara Burman, 33–53. Oxford: Berg, 1999.

Bussey, Gertrude, and Margaret Tims. *Pioneers for Peace: The Women's International League for Peace and Freedom, 1915–1965*. Oxford: Alden Press, 1965.

Caimari, Lila M. *Perón y la iglesia católica: religión, estado y sociedad en la Argentina (1943–1955)*. Buenos Aires: Ariel, 1994.

Caja de Resonancia. Colección Sociedad Cosmopolita. Santa Fe: Universidad Nacional del Litoral, 2013.

Camaño Semprini, Rebeca. "Ecos de la Guerra Civil Española. La derecha nacionalista y los frentes antifascistas en los espacios locales argentinos." *Diacronie*, no. 17 (2014).

Camarero, Hernán. *A la conquista de la clase obrera. Los comunistas y el mundo de trabajo en la Argentina, 1920–1935*. Buenos Aires: Siglo XXI, 2007.

Camarero, Hernán, and Carlos Miguel Herrera, eds. *El Partido Socialista en Argentina: Sociedad, política e ideas a través de un siglo*. Buenos Aires: Prometeo, 2005.

Cameselle-Pesce, Pedro M. "Italian-Uruguayans and Serafino Romaldi's Quest for Transnational Anti-Fascist Networks during World War II." *Americas* 77, no. 2 (2020): 247–73.

Camou, María M. *Resonancia del nacional-socialismo en el Uruguay*. Montevideo: Facultad de Humanidades y Ciencias, Universidad de la República, 1988.

Campbell, John C. "Political Extremes in South America." *Foreign Affairs* 20, no. 3 (1942): 517–34.

Cane, James. *The Fourth Enemy: Journalism and Power in the Making of Peronist Argentina*. University Park: Pennsylania State University Press, 2011.

Cane, James. "'Unity for the Defense of Culture': The AIAPE and the Cultural Politics of Argentine Antifascism, 1935–1943." *Hispanic American Historical Review*, 77, no. 3 (August 1997): 443–82.

Cano, Gabriela. "El 'feminismo de estado' de Amalia de Castillo Ledón durante los gobiernos de Emilio Portes Gil y Lázaro Cárdenas." *Relaciones* 38 (Winter 2017): 39–69.

Carle, Emmanuelle. "Women, Anti-Fascism and Peace in Interwar France: Gabrielle Duchêne's Itinerary." *French History* 18, no. 3 (2004): 306–8.

Carlson, Marifran. *¡Feminismo! The Woman's Movement in Argentina from its Beginnings to Eva Perón*. Chicago: Academy Chicago, 1988.

Casas, Saúl. "La guerra civil española y el antifascismo en la Argentina (1936–1941). Los baleares y la ayuda a la República." Master's thesis, Universidad Nacional de La Plata, 2006.

Caterina, Luis María. "Los gobiernos de provincia." In *Nueva historia de la nación Argentina*, vol. 8, part 4: *La Argentina del siglo XX, c. 1914–1983*, edited by Academia Nacional de la Historia, 13–42. Buenos Aires: Planeta, 1997.

Cavalari, Rosa Maria Feiteiro. *Integralismo: ideologia e organização de um partido de massa no Brasil (1932–1937)*. Bauru: EDUSC, 1999.

Celentano, Adrián. "Ideas e intelectuales en la formación de una red sudamericana antifascista." *Literatura y Lingüística*, no. 17 (2006): 195–218.

Cenarro, Angela. "Movilización femenina para la guerra total (1936–1939). Un ejercicio comparativo." *Historia y política*, no. 16 (2006): 159–82.

Ceplair, Larry. *Under the Shadow of War: Fascism, Antifascism, and Marxists, 1918–1939*. New York: Columbia University Press, 1987.

Cernadas, Jorge, Roberto Pittaluga, and Horacio Tarcus. "La historiografía sobre el Partido Comunista de la Argentina. Un estado de la cuestión." *El Rodaballo*, no. 8 (Fall/Winter 1998): 31–40.

Cernadas, Jorge, Roberto Pittaluga, and Horacio Tarcus. "Para una historia de la izquierda en la Argentina. Reflexiones preliminares." *El Rodaballo*, nos. 6/7 (Fall/Winter 1997): 28–35.

Chalmers, Beverley. "Maternity Care in the Former Soviet Union." *BJOG: An International Journal of Obstetrics and Gynaecology* 112, no. 4 (April 2005): 495–99.

Chamosa, Oscar. "'Indigenous or Criollo': The Myth of White Argentina in Tucumán's Calchaqui Valley." *Hispanic American Historical Review* 88, no. 1 (February 2008): 71–106.

Chamosa, Oscar. "People as Landscape: The Representation of the *Criollo* Interior in Early Tourist Literature in Argentina, 1920–1930." In *Rethinking Race in Modern Argentina*, edited by Paulina L. Alberto and Eduardo Elena, 53–72. New York: Cambridge University Press, 2016.

Chamudes, Marcos. *El libro blanco de mi leyenda negra*. Santiago: P.E.C., 1964.

Chase, Michelle. *Revolution within the Revolution: Women and Gender Politics in Cuba, 1952–1962*. Chapel Hill: University of North Carolina Press, 2015.

Chernyaeva, Natalia. "Childcare Manuals and Construction of Motherhood in Russia, 1890–1990." PhD diss., University of Iowa, 2009. http://ir.uiowa.edu/etd/344.

Chesterton, Bridget María. "Composing Gender and Class: Paraguayan Letter Writers during the Chaco War, 1932–1935." *Journal of Women's History* 26, no. 3 (Fall 2014): 59–80.

Cohen, Deborah, and Maura O'Connor, eds. *Comparison and History: Europe in Cross-National Perspective*. Abingdon, UK: Routledge, 2004.

Colley, Linda. *Britons: Forging the Nation, 1707–1837*. 2nd ed. London: Pimlico, 2003.

Colley, Linda. *The Gun, the Ship, and the Pen: Warfare, Constitutions, and the Making of the Modern World*. New York: Liveright, 2021.

Comisión Coordinadora de Asociaciones Femeninas Democráticas. *Declaración de principios*. Buenos Aires: n.p., n.d.

Comisión Femenina Israelita de Solidaridad. *Nuestros talleres en plena labor*. Buenos Aires: n.p, n.d.

Comisión Femenina Nacional del Partido Comunista. *La mujer en su lucha por su emancipación*. Buenos Aires: Anteo, 1946.

"Comités adheridos a la Fiesta por la Libertad." Buenos Aires, 1941. Flyer.

El congreso de la solidaridad de los pueblos (realizado en Paris—Setiembre de 1937). Buenos Aires: Alerta, 1937.

Coons, Lorraine. "Gabrielle Duchêne: Feminist, Pacifist, Reluctant Bourgeoise." *Peace & Change* 24, no. 2 (April 1999): 121–47.

Cooper, John. *Raphael Lemkin and the Struggle for the Genocide Convention*. Basingstroke, UK: Palgrave MacMillan, 2008.

Cooper, Sandi E. "Pacifism, Feminism, and Fascism in Inter-War France." *International History Review* 19, no. 1 (February 1997): 103–14.

Copsey, Nigel. "Preface: Towards a New Anti-Fascist 'Minimum'?" In *Varieties of Anti-Fascism: Britain in the Inter-War Period*, edited by Nigel Copsey and Andrzej Olechnowicz, xiv–xxi. London: Palgrave Macmillan, 2010.

Cosse, Isabella. "Infidelities: Morality, Revolution and Sexuality in Left-Wing Guerilla Organizations in 1960s and 1970s Argentina." *Journal of the History of Sexuality* 23, no. 3 (September 2014): 415–50.

Counihan, Carole. "Ethnography, Food Studies, and the Humanities: Crossing Borders between Places, People, and Disciplines." Presentation at the Rubin Center, University of Texas at El Paso, February 6, 2014.

Cramer, Gisela. "The World War at the River Plate: The Office of Inter-American Affairs and the Argentine Airwaves, 1940–46." In *¡Américas unidas! Nelson A. Rockefeller's Office of Inter-American Affairs (1940–46)*, edited by Gisela Cramer and Ursula Prutsch, 213–47. Madrid: Iberoamericana; Frankfurt: Vervuert, 2012.

Cramer, Gisela, and Ursula Prutsch. "Nelson A. Rockefeller's Office of Inter-American Affairs and the Quest for Pan-American Unity: An Introductory Essay." In *¡Américas unidas! Nelson A. Rockefeller's Office of Inter-American Affairs (1940–46)*, edited by Gisela Cramer and Ursula Prutsch, 15–52. Madrid: Iberoamericana; Frankfurt: Vervuert, 2012.

Crespo, Edda Lía. "Comunidades mineras. Prácticas asociativas y construcción de ciudadanías en la zona litoral del Golfo San Jorge. Comodoro Rivadavia y Caleta Olivia, 1901–1955." Master's thesis, Universidad Nacional de San Martín, 2011.

Crespo, Edda Lía. "Una sensibilidad a flor de la piel . . . Pilar Martínez de Moirón y el antifascismo en la zona litoral del Golfo San Jorge (Patagonia, Argentina)." *Cuadernos de H Ideas* 7, no. 7 (December 2013). http://perio.unlp.edu.ar/ojs/index.php/cps.

Cuadro Cawen, Inés. *Feminismos y política en el Uruguay del novecientos. Internacionalismo, culturas políticas e identidades de género (1906–1932)*. Montevideo: Asociación Uruguaya de Historiadores, Ediciones de la Banda Oriental, 2017.

Damousi, Joy. "Humanitarianism and Child Refugee Sponsorship: The Spanish Civil War and the Global Campaign of Esme Rodgers." *Journal of Women's History* 32, no. 1 (Spring 2020): 111–34.

De Andrea, Miguel. *Pensamiento cristiano y democrático de Monseñor de Andrea. Homenaje del Congreso Nacional*. 2nd ed. Buenos Aires: Imprenta del Congreso de la Nación, 1965.

De Giorgi, Ana Laura. "Entre la lucha contra la carestía y por los derechos de la mujer. Las comunistas uruguayas durante la segunda mitad del siglo XX (1942–1973)." In *Queridas camaradas. Historias iberoamericanas de mujeres comunistas, 1935–1975*, edited by Adriana Valobra and Mercedes Yusta, 215–34. Buenos Aires: Miño y Dávila, 2017.

De Grazia, Victoria. *How Fascism Ruled Women: Italy, 1922–1945*. Berkeley: University of California Press, 1992.

De Haan, Francisca. "Continuing Cold War Paradigms in Western Historiography of Transnational Women's Organisations: The Case of the Women's International Democratic Federation (WIDF)." *Women's History Review* 19, no. 4 (2010): 547–73.

De Haan, Francisca. "Eugénie Cotton, Pak Chong-Ae, and Claudia Jones: Rethinking Transnational Feminism and International Politics." *Journal of Women's History* 25, no. 4 (2013): 174–89.

De Haan, Francisca. "La Federación Democrática Internacional de Mujeres (FDIM) y América Latina, de 1945 a los años setenta." In *Queridas camaradas, historias iberoamericanas de mujeres comunistas*, edited by Adriana Valobra and Mercedes Yusta, 17–44. Buenos Aires: Miño y Dávila, 2017.

De Haan, Francisca. "The Women's International Democratic Federation (WIDF): History, Main Agenda, and Contributions, 1945–1991." Women and Social Movements, International—1840 to the Present. http://wasi.alexanderstreet.com/.

Del Franco, Clara. *Mujeres, ese fuego, esas luchas: 1930–1960*. Buenos Aires: Cuadernos Marxistas, 2011.

"Del otro lado del conflicto: las derechas frente a la clase obrera y las izquierdas

(1890–1970)." Special Issue, *Archivos de historia del movimiento obrero y la izquierda*, no. 13 (September 2018): 9–117.

Deutsch, Sandra McGee. "Antifascist Jewish Women in Argentina and Uruguay: Inclusion and Identities, 1941–1945." In *Jewish Experiences across the Americas: Local Histories through Global Lenses*, edited by Katalin F. Rac and Lenny A. Ureña Valerio, 249–76. Gainesville: University Press of Florida, 2022.

Deutsch, Sandra McGee. "Argentine Women against Fascism: The Junta de la Victoria, 1941–1947." *Politics, Religion, and Ideology* 13, no. 2 (2012): 221–36.

Deutsch, Sandra McGee. "The Catholic Church, Work, and Womanhood in Argentina, 1890–1930." *Gender and History* 3, no. 3 (Autumn 1991): 304–25.

Deutsch, Sandra McGee. *Counterrevolution in Argentina, 1900–1932: The Argentine Patriotic League.* Lincoln: University of Nebraska Press, 1984.

Deutsch, Sandra McGee. *Crossing Borders, Claiming a Nation: A History of Argentine Jewish Women, 1880–1955.* Durham, NC: Duke University Press, 2010.

Deutsch, Sandra McGee. "Hands across the Río de la Plata: Argentine and Uruguayan Antifascist Women, 1941–1945." *Revista Contemporánea* 8 (2017): 29–54.

Deutsch, Sandra McGee. "Insecure Whiteness: Jews between Civilization and Barbarism, 1880s–1940s." In *Rethinking Race in Modern Argentina*, edited by Paulina L. Alberto and Eduardo Elena, 25–52. New York: Cambridge University Press, 2016.

Deutsch, Sandra McGee. "A Labor Filled with Love: The Communist Party, Solidarity, and Women in Argentina, 1930–1947." In *The Global Impacts of Russia's Great War and Revolution*, book 2: *The Wider Arc of Revolution*, part 2, edited by Choi Chatterjee, Steven G. Marks, Mary Neuburger, and Steven Sabol. Bloomington, IN: Slavica Press, 2019.

Deutsch, Sandra McGee. "La liberación de la mujer. Conflictos, (des)encuentros y paralelismos entre mujeres derechistas y progresistas en América Latina durante las décadas de 1920 y 1930." In *Las derechas iberoamericanas. Desde el final de la Primera Guerra hasta la Gran Depresión*, edited by Ernesto Bohoslavsky, David Jorge, and Clara E. Lida, 319–50. Ciudad de México: El Colegio de México, 2019.

Deutsch, Sandra McGee. *Las derechas: The Extreme Right in Argentina, Brazil, and Chile, 1890–1939.* Stanford, CA: Stanford University Press, 1999.

Deutsch, Sandra McGee. "The New School Lecture 'An Army of Women': Communist-Linked Solidarity Movements, Maternalism, and Political Consciousness in Argentina, 1930s–1940s." *Americas* 75, no. 1 (2018): 1–31.

Deutsch, Sandra McGee. "What Difference Does Gender Make? The Extreme Right in the ABC Countries in the Era of Fascism." *Estudios Interdisciplinarios de América Latina y el Caribe* 8, no. 2 (July-December 1997): 5–21.

Di Corleto, Julieta. "Las visitadoras de las presas: el Patronato de Recluidas y Liberadas de la Capital Federal (1933–1950)." *Derecho Penal* 1, no. 2 (2016): 132–53. www.pensamientopenal.com.ar.

Di Marco, Graciela. "The 'Feminist People' and Its Contradictory Relationships with Democracy." Paper presented at the virtual Latin American Studies Association meeting, May 26–29, 2021.

Di Marco, Graciela. "Maternidad social." In *Diccionario de estudios de género y feminismos*, edited by Susana B. Gamba, 211–13. Buenos Aires: Biblos, 2007.

Dolkart, Ronald H. "The Right in the Década Infame, 1930–1945." In *The Argentine Right: Its History and Intellectual Origins, 1910 to the Present*, edited by Sandra McGee Deutsch and Ronald H. Dolkart, 65–98. Wilmington, DE: Scholarly Resources, 1993.

Domínguez Prats, Pilar. "La actividad de las mujeres republicanas en México." *Arbor* 185, no. 735 (2009): 75–85.

DuBois, Ellen, and Robin Derby. "The Strange Case of Minerva Bernardino." *Women's Studies International Forum* 32, no. 1 (2009): 43–50.

Dujovne, Alejandro. "Impresiones del judaísmo: Una sociología histórica de la producción y circulación transnacional del libro en el colectivo social judío de Buenos Aires, 1919–1979." PhD diss., Universidad Nacional de General Sarmiento, Instituto de Desarrollo Económico y Social, 2010.

Dumenil, Lynn. "Women's Reform Organizations and Wartime Mobilization in World War I–Era Los Angeles." *Journal of the Gilded Age and Progressive Era* 10, no. 2 (April 2011): 213–45.

Durham, Martin. *Women and Fascism*. Abingdon, UK: Routledge, 1998.

Echeverría, Olga. "Las derechas de Argentina y Uruguay en tiempos de nazi fascismos: radicalización, redefiniciones e influencias." *Oficina do Historiador* 9, no. 1 (January-June 2016): 151–70.

Echeverría, Olga. "Virtudes de la doctrina y errores de la política. Monseñor Gustavo Franceschi ante los 'totalitarismos' soviético, fascista y nacionalsocialista." *Quinto Sol* 21, no. 1 (January-April 2017): 1–24.

Edelman, Fanny. *Feminismo y marxismo. Conversación con Claudia Korol*. Buenos Aires: Carlos A. Firpo, 2001.

Ehrick, Christine. *The Shield of the Weak: Feminism and the State in Uruguay, 1903–1933*. Albuquerque: University of New Mexico Press, 2005.

Elena, Eduardo. *Dignifying Argentina: Peronism, Citizenship, and Mass Consumption*. Pittsburgh: University of Pittsburgh Press, 2011.

Elkin, Judith Laikin. *The Jews of Latin America*. 3rd ed. Boulder, CO: Lynn Rienner, 2014.

Encarnación, Omar G. *Out in the Periphery: Latin America's Gay Rights Revolution*. New York: Oxford University Press, 2016.

Escudé, Carlos. "The U.S. Destabilization and Economic Boycott of Argentina of the 1940s, Revisited." Universidad del CEMA, Serie de Documentos de Trabajo no. 323, July 2006. https://www.econstor.eu/bitstream/10419/84408/1/516371762.pdf.

Falcoff, Mark, and Frederick B. Pike, eds. *The Spanish Civil War, 1936–1939: American Hemispheric Perspectives*. Lincoln: University of Nebraska Press, 1982.

Falcoff, Mark, and Ronald H. Dolkart, eds. *Prologue to Perón: Argentina in Depression and War, 1930–1943*. Berkeley: University of California Press, 1976.

Fanesi, Pietro Rinaldo. "El antifascismo italiano en la Argentina (1922–1945)." *Estudios Migratorios Latinoamericanos* 4 (1989): 319–52.

Fanesi, Pietro Rinaldo. *El exilio antifascista en la Argentina*. 2 vols. Buenos Aires: CEAL, 1994.

Fanesi, Pietro Rinaldo. "Italian Antifascism and the Garibaldine Tradition in Latin America." In *Italian Workers of the World: Labor Migration and the Formation of Multiethnic States*, edited by Donna R. Gabaccia and Fraser M. Ottanelli, 170–77. Urbana: University of Illinois Press, 2001.

Fazzio de Bejas, Rosa. "Tafí Viejo, Ayer y Hoy." *El Taficeño*, November 11, 1990.

Feierstein, Ricardo. *Historia de los judíos argentinos*. Buenos Aires: Ameghino, 1999.

Feijoó, María del Carmen. "Democratic Participation and Women in Argentina." In *Women and Democracy: Latin America and Central and Eastern Europe*, edited by Jane S. Jaquette and Sharon L. Wolchik, 29–46. Baltimore: Johns Hopkins University Press, 1998.

Feijoó, María del Carmen, with Marcela María Alejandra Nari. "Women and Democracy in Argentina." In *The Women's Movement in Latin America: Participation and Democracy*, 2nd ed., edited by Jane Jaquette, 109–29. Boulder, CO: Westview Press, 1994.

Ferla, Salvador. *Doctrina del Nacionalismo*. Buenos Aires: Talleres Gráficos Rafael, 1947.

Fernández Aceves, María Teresa. "Belén Sárraga Hernández y las mujeres españolas en México, 1939–1950." *Anuario IEHS* 28 (2013): 177–206.

Fernández de Ullivarri, María. "Trabajadores, sindicatos y política en Tucumán, 1930–1943." PhD diss., Universidad de Buenos Aires, 2010.

Fernández, Sandra. "Olga Cosettini y el Colegio Libre de Estudios Superiories en Rosario (Argentina), 1939–1940." *Historia y Sociedad* 36 (January-June 2019): 133–59.

Ferrero, Roberto A. "La guerra y el interior." *Todo Es Historia*, no. 148 (September 1979): 58–69.

Ferrero, Roberto A. *Sabattini y la decadencia del yrigoyenismo*. 2 vols. Buenos Aires: CEAL, 1984.

Ferreyra, Alejandra Noemí. "La conformación de un consenso pro-franquista en la comunidad española de Buenos Aires: solidaridad material y propaganda política-cultural (1936–1945)." PhD diss., Universidad de Buenos Aires, 2018.

Finchelstein, Federico. "The Anti-Freudian Politics of Argentine Fascism: Anti-

Semitism, Catholicism, and the Internal Enemy, 1932–1945." *Hispanic American Historical Review* 87, no. 1 (February 2007): 77–110.

Finchelstein, Federico. *A Brief History of Fascist Lies*. Berkeley: University of California Press, 2020.

Finchelstein, Federico. *Fascismo, liturgia e imaginario. El mito del general Uriburu y la Argentina nacionalista*. Buenos Aires: Fondo de Cultura Económica, 2002.

Finchelstein, Federico. *From Fascism to Populism in History*. Berkeley: University of California Press, 2017.

Finchelstein, Federico. *The Ideological Origins of the Dirty War: Fascism, Populism, and Dictatorship in Twentieth Century Argentina*. New York: Oxford University Press, 2014.

Finchelstein, Federico. *Transatlantic Fascism: Ideology, Violence, and the Sacred in Argentina and Italy, 1919–1945*. Durham, NC: Duke University Press, 2010.

Fiorucci, Flavia. *Intelectuales y peronismo, 1945–1955*. Buenos Aires: Biblos, 2011.

Fischer, Brodwyn. "The Red Menace Reconsidered: A Forgotten History of Communist Mobilization in Rio de Janeiro's Favelas, 1945–1964." *Hispanic American Historical Review* 94, no. 1 (February 2014): 1–33.

Fisher, David James. *Romain Rolland and the Politics of Intellectual Engagement*. Berkeley: University of California Press, 1988.

Flores, John H. *The Mexican Revolution in Chicago: Immigrant Politics from the Early 20th Century to the Cold War*. Urbana: University of Illinois Press, 2018.

Foreign Relations of the United States: Diplomatic Papers 1944, The American Republics. Vol. 7. Washington DC: Government Printing Office, 1967.

Foster, Catherine. *Women for All Seasons: The Story of the Women's International League for Peace and Freedom*. Athens: University of Georgia Press, 1989.

Framke, Maria. "Political Humanitarianism in the 1930s: Indian Aid for Republican Spain." *European Review of History* 23, nos. 1–2 (2016): 63–81.

Frank, Waldo. *South American Journey*. New York: Duell, Sloan, and Pearce, 1943.

Friedman, Max Paul, and Padraic Kenney. "Introduction: History in Politics." In *Partisan Histories: The Past in Contemporary Global Politics*, edited by Max Paul Friedman and Padraic Kenney, 1–14. New York: Palgrave Macmillan, 2005.

Fronczak, Joseph. "Local People's Global Politics: A Transnational History of the Hands Off Ethiopia Movement of 1935." *Diplomatic History* 30, no. 2 (2015): 245–74.

Fuselli, Angélica. *A las mujeres de mi país*. Buenos Aires: Comisión Interamericana de Mujeres, Representación Argentina, 1945.

Gadea, Hilda. *My Life with Che: The Making of a Revolutionary*. New York: St. Martin's Press, 2008.

Gallo, Edit Rosalía. *Las mujeres en el radicalismo argentino, 1890–1991*. Buenos Aires: Eudeba, 2001.

Gálvez, Manuel. *Este pueblo necesita*. Buenos Aires: A. García Santos, 1934.

García Martínez, Mónica. "Mujeres afrouruguayas en el contexto del Primer Congreso Nacional de Mujeres del Uruguay (1936)." *Corpus* 8, no. 2 (July-December 2018): 1–20.

García Sebastiani, Marcela, ed. *Fascismo y antifascismo. Peronismo y antifascismo. Conflictos políticos e ideológicos en la Argentina (1930–1955)*. Madrid: Iberoamericana; Frankfurt: Vervuert, 2006.

García Sebastiani, Marcela. *Los antiperonistas en la Argentina peronista. Radicales y socialistas en la política argentina entre 1943 y 1951*. Buenos Aires: Prometeo, 2005.

García, Hugo. "Transnational History: A New Paradigm for Anti-Fascist Studies?" *Contemporary European History* 25, no. 4 (2016): 563–72.

García, Hugo, Mercedes Yusta, Xavier Tabet, and Cristina Climaco, eds. "Beyond Revisionism: Rethinking Antifascism in the Twenty-First Century." In *Rethinking Antifascism: History, Memory and Politics, 1922 to the Present*, edited by Hugo García, Mercedes Yusta, Xavier Tabet, and Cristina Climaco, 1–19. New York: Berghahn, 2016.

García, Hugo, Mercedes Yusta, Xavier Tabet, and Cristina Climaco, eds. *Rethinking Antifascism: History, Memory and Politics, 1922 to the Present*. New York: Berghahn Books, 2016.

García-Bryce, Iñigo. *Haya de la Torre and the Pursuit of Power*. Chapel Hill: University of North Carolina Press, 2018.

Garzón Rogé, Mariana. "Antifascistas y política en la dimensión local. Mendoza, 1943–1945." Conference paper, 2013.

Garzón Rogé, Mariana. "De nacionalismo a antifascistas: los conservadores mendocinos ante la irrupción militar de 1943." Unpublished manuscript, 2010.

Gasió, Guillermo. *El Jefe del Estado Mayor de la Revolución. El coronel Juan Perón en el gobierno de la revolución del 4 de junio de 1943*. Buenos Aires: Teseo, 2013.

Gaviola Artigas, Edda, Ximena Jiles, Lorella Lopresti, and Chaudia Rojas. *Queremos votar en las próximas elecciones: historia del movimiento femenino chileno, 1913–1952*. 2nd ed. Santiago: LOM, 2007.

Geraldo, Endrica. "Entre a raça e a nação: A familia como alvo dos projetos eugenista e integralista de nação brasileira nas décadas de 1920 e 1930." Master's thesis, Universidade Estadual de Campinas, Brazil, 2001.

Gil Lozano, Fernanda. "Las experiencias de la segunda ola del feminismo en Argentina y Uruguay." In *Historia de las mujeres en España y América Latina*, vol. 4: *Del siglo XX a los umbrales del XXI*, edited by Isabel Morant, 881–902. Madrid: Cátedra, 2006.

Giordano, Verónica. *Ciudadanas incapaces. La construcción de los derechos civiles de las mujeres en Argentina, Brasil, Chile y Uruguay en el siglo XX*. Buenos Aires: Teseo, 2012.

Giordano, Verónica. "La celebración del Año Internacional de la Mujer en Argentina (1975): acciones y conflictos." *Estudios Feministas* 20, no. 1 (January-April 2021): 75–94.

Giordano, Verónica. "Los derechos civiles de las mujeres y el proyecto de reforma del Código Civil de 1936: el acontecimiento, la estructura, la coyuntura." III Jornadas de Jóvenes Investigadores del Instituto de Investigaciones Gino Germani, Facultad de Ciencias Sociales, September 29–30, 2005.

Girbal-Blacha, Noemí M. "El hogar o la fábrica: De costureras y tejedoras en la Argentina Peronista (1946–1955)." *Revista de Ciencias Sociales*, no. 6 (September 1997): 217–30.

Girbal-Blacha, Noemí M. *Vivir en los márgenes. Estado, políticas públicas y conflictos sociales. El Gran Chaco Argentino en la primera mitad del siglo XX.* Rosario: Prohistoria, 2011.

Goebel, Michael. *Argentina's Partisan Past: Nationalism and the Politics of History.* Liverpool: Liverpool University Press, 2011.

Goñi, Uki. *The Real Odessa: Smuggling the Nazis to Perón's Argentina.* London: Granta, 2002.

González Calleja, Eduardo. "El hispanismo autoritario español y el movimiento nacionalista argentina: balance de medio siglo de relaciones políticas e intelectuales (1898–1946)." *Hispania*, no. 226 (May-August 2007): 599–642.

González, Victoria, and Karen Kampwirth. "Introduction." In *Radical Women in Latin America: Left and Right*, edited by Victoria González and Karen Kampwirth, 1–28. University Park: Pennsylvania State University Press, 2001.

Goodwin, Doris Kearns. *No Ordinary Time: Franklin & Eleanor Roosevelt: The Home Front in World War II.* New York: Simon & Schuster, 1994.

Gordon, Peter E. "The Scars of Democracy: Theodore Adorno and the Crisis of Liberalism." *The Nation*, December 15, 2020. https://www.thenation.com/article/politics/adorno-aspects-new-right-wing-extremism/.

Gori, Gaston. *La Forestal (La tragedia del quebracho Colorado).* Buenos Aires: Editoriales Platina/Stilcograf, 1965.

Gottlieb, Julie. "'Broken Friendships and Vanished Loyalties': Gender, Collective (In)Security and Anti-Fascism in Britain in the 1930s." *Politics, Religion & Ideology* 13, no. 2 (June 2012): 197–219.

Gottlieb, Julie. *Feminine Fascism: Women in Britain's Fascist Movement.* London: I. B. Tauris, 2003.

Gradskova, Yulia. "Women's International Democratic Federation, the 'Third World' and the Global Cold War from the Late-1950s to the Mid-1960s." *Women's History Review* 29, no. 2 (2020): 270–88.

Gramajo de Seligman, María Teresa. "El proceso de configuración de las 'Humanidades' en la década del cuarenta en la Facultad de Filosofía y Letras de la UNT." In *El Viejo Tucumán en la memoria*, vol. 4, edited by Marta Omil, 7–14. Tucumán: Universidad Nacional de Tucumán, 1999.

Grandin, Greg. "Living in Revolutionary Time: Coming to Terms with the Violence of Latin America's Long Cold War." In *A Century of Revolution: Insurgent and Counterinsurgent Violence during Latin America's Long Cold War*, edited by Greg Grandin and Gilbert M. Joseph, 1–42. Durham, NC: Duke University Press, 2010.

Gravina, Alfredo. *A los diez años proletaria. Imagen de Julia Arévalo*. Montevideo: Mundo Nuevo, 1970.

Greenup, Ruth, and Leonard Greenup. *Revolution before Breakfast: Argentina, 1941–1946*. Chapel Hill: University of North Carolina Press, 1947.

Grillo, María Victoria. "El antifascismo italiano en Francia y Argentina: reorganización política y prensa." In *Fascismo y antifascismo en Europa y Argentina en el siglo XX*, edited by Judith Casali de Babot and María Victoria Grillo, 87–98. Tucumán: Instituto de Investigaciones Históricas, Facultad de Filosofía y Letras, Universidad Nacional de Tucumán, 2002.

Guy, Donna J. "La 'verdadera historia' de la Sociedad de Beneficencia." In *La política social antes de la política social (Caridad, beneficencia y política social en Buenos Aires, siglos XVII a XX)*, edited by José Luis Moreno, 321–41. Buenos Aires: Trama/Prometeo, 2000.

Guy, Donna J. *White Slavery and Mothers Alive and Dead: The Troubled Meeting of Sex, Gender, Public Health, and Progress in Latin America*. Lincoln: University of Nebraska Press, 2000.

Guy, Donna J. *Women Build the Welfare State: Performing Charity and Creating Rights in Argentina, 1880–1955*. Durham, NC: Duke University Press, 2009.

H. Senado de la Nación, *Represión del Comunismo. Proyecto de ley, informe y antecedentes por el senador Matías Sánchez Sorondo*. Vol. 2: *Antecedentes*. Buenos Aires: H. Senado de la Nación, 1940.

Haas, Britt. *Fighting Authoritarianism: American Youth Activism in the 1930s*. New York: Fordham University Press, 2017.

Halperín Donghi, Tulio. *Argentina en el callejón*. Buenos Aires: Espasa Calpe/Ariel, 1995.

Halperín Donghi, Tulio. *La república imposible: 1930–1945*. Buenos Aires: Ariel, 2004.

Halperín Donghi, Tulio. *Son memorias*. Buenos Aires: Siglo Veintiuno, 2008.

Hammond, Gregory. *The Women's Suffrage Movement and Feminism in Argentina from Roca to Perón*. Albuquerque: University of New Mexico Press, 2011.

Hatsky, Christine, and Jessica Stites Mor. "Latin American Transnational Solidarities: Contexts and Critical Research Paradigms." *Journal of Iberian and Latin American Research* 20, no. 2 (2014): 127–40.

Healey, Mark A. *The Ruins of the New Argentina: Peronism and the Remaking of San Juan after the 1944 Earthquake*. Durham, NC: Duke University Press, 2011.

Hernández Méndez, Sebastián. "Religión, política y sociedad de masas en el Uruguay de los años treinta. La Iglesia uruguaya y el XXXII Congreso Eucarístico Internacional de Buenos Aires (1934)." Paper presented at the IV Jornadas Catolicismo y Sociedad de Masas en la Argentina del Siglo XX, Mar del Plata, May 21–22, 2015.

Hernández, Amor Alba. *Con la marca en el orillo. La memoria de los héroes que no tienen monumento.* Rosario: self-published, 2015.

History of the Inter-American Commission of Women (CIM), 1928–1997. Washington, DC: CIM/OEA, 1999.

Hobsbawm, Eric. *The Age of Extremes: A History of the World, 1914–1991.* New York: Vintage Books, 1996.

Hochschild, Arlie Russell. *Strangers in Their Own Land: Anger and Mourning on the American Right.* New York: New Press, 2018.

"Homenaje a Winston Churchill." *Sur,* December 1941, 67–69.

Hora, Roy, and Leandro Losada. "Clases altas y medias en la Argentina, 1880–1930. Notas para una agenda de investigación." *Desarrollo Económico* 50 (January-March 2011): 611–30.

Huernos, Marcelo Carlos. "El Consejo Nacional Italiano. Un proyecto del antifascismo en las Américas. Italia Libre y la Mazzini Society (1940–1942)." Unpublished manuscript, n.d.

Huernos, Marcelo Carlos. "Italia Libre y sus relaciones con el partido comunista." Unpublished manuscript, n.d.

Huernos, Marcelo Carlos. "Las redes americanas del antifascismo italiano. Italia Libre y la Mazzini Society (1940–1942)." Paper presented at the XVI Jornadas Interescuelas/Departamentos de Historia, Universidad Nacional del Mar del Plata, 2017.

Hyde, Lewis. *A Primer for Forgetting: Getting Past the Past.* New York: Farrar, Straus and Giroux, 2019.

Iber, Patrick. *Neither Peace nor Freedom: The Cultural Cold War in Latin America.* Cambridge, MA: Harvard University Press, 2015.

Iñigo Carrera, Nicólas. *Estrategias de la clase obrera en los orígenes del peronismo.* Buenos Aires: Grupo Editor Universitario, 2019.

Iñigo Carrera, Nicólas, and Jorge Podestá. *Movimiento social y alianza de obreros y campesinos. Chaco (1934–1936).* Buenos Aires: CEAL, 1991.

Instituto de Investigaciones Geohistóricas. *Décimo Octavo Encuentro de Geohistoria Regional. Resistencia, 1–2 septiembre 1998.* Resistencia: IIGHI, 1999.

The Inter-American Commission of Women. Documents Considering Its Creation and Organization. Washington, DC: Pan American Union, n.d.

Ipsen, Wiebe. "Patrícias, Patriarchy, and Popular Demobilization: Gender and Elite Hegemony in Brazil at the End of the Paraguayan War." *Hispanic American Historical Review* 92, no. 2 (May 2012): 303–30.

Ivereigh, Austen. *Catholicism and Politics in Argentina, 1810–1960.* New York: St. Martin's Press, 1995.

Jackson, Angela. *British Women and the Spanish Civil War*. Abingdon, UK: Routledge, 2002.

Jacob, Raúl. *El Uruguay de Terra, 1931–1938: Una crónica del terrismo*. Montevideo: Banda Oriental, 1983.

James, Daniel. "October 17th and 18th, 1945: Mass Protest, Peronism and the Working Class." *Journal of Social History* 21, no. 3 (Spring 1988): 441–61.

Jáuregui, Aníbal. "El peronismo en los debates del Partido Comunista Argentino: 1945–1953." *A Contracorriente* 9, no. 3 (Spring 2012): 22–40.

Jorrat, Marcela. "Expresiones del antisemitismo. Recepción de la política racial nazi y cultura política en Tucumán." Master's thesis, Universidad Nacional de Tucumán, 2006.

Josephs, Ray. *Argentine Diary: The Inside Story of the Coming of Fascism*. New York: Random House, 1944.

Junta de la Victoria. "A Ud. que ayuda a las democracias en la Junta de la Victoria le interesa conocer." Flyer, 1942.

Junta de la Victoria. *Ayuda de las mujeres argentinas a los países que luchan contra el nazismo. 13 septiembre 1941—13 enero 1942*. Buenos Aires: n.p., 1942.

Junta de la Victoria. "Colabore." Flyer, n.d.

Junta de la Victoria. *Estatutos*. Buenos Aires: n.p., n.d. [1941?]

Junta de la Victoria. "Fiesta por la Libertad organizada por la Junta de la Victoria." Flyer, 1941.

Junta de la Victoria. "Informe de las delegadas de la Junta de la Victoria al primer Congreso Mundial de Mujeres en París, 27 dic. 1945." Flyer, 1945.

Junta de la Victoria. "¡Por los Héroes de Stalingrado!" Flyer, 1942.

Junta de la Victoria. *Primera convención nacional*. Buenos Aires: n.p., 1942.

Kaner, Marcos, and Mario O. Herrera. *¡Abajo la guerra imperialista! ¡Por la paz y la fraternización de los pueblos!* Posadas: Ediciones Misioneras Unidad, 1939.

Karush, Matthew B. *Culture of Class: Radio and Cinema in the Making of a Divided Argentina, 1920–1946*. Durham, NC: Duke University Press, 2012.

Kelly, Sir David. *The Ruling Few or the Human Background to Diplomacy*. London: Hollis & Center, 1952.

Kennedy, Robert G., Mary Christine Athans, Bernard V. Brady, William C. McDonough, and Michael J. Naughton, eds. *Religion and Public Life: The Legacy of Monsignor John A. Ryan*. Lanham, NJ: University Press of America, 2001.

Kirk, Tim, and Anthony McElligott. "Introduction: Community, Authority and Resistance to Fascism." In *Opposing Fascism: Community, Authority and Resistance in Europe*, edited by Tim Kirk and Anthony McElligott, 1–11. Cambridge: Cambridge University Press, 1999.

Klapper, Melissa R. "Those by Whose Side We Have Labored: American Jewish Women and the Peace Movement between the Wars." *Journal of American History* 97, no. 3 (December 2010): 636–58.

Klein, Marcus. "Argentine Nacionalismo before Perón: The Case of the Alianza de la Juventud Nacionalista, 1937-c. 1943." *Bulletin of Latin American Research* 20, no. 1 (January 2001): 102–21.

Klein, Marcus. "A Comparative Analysis of Fascist Movements in Argentina, Brazil, and Chile between the Great Depression and the Second World War." PhD diss., University of London, Institute of Latin American Studies, 2000.

Klein, Marcus. "The Political Lives and Times of Enrique P. Osés (1928–1944)." In *Fascismo y antifascismo, peronismo y antiperonismo. Conflictos políticos e ideológicos en la Argentina (1930–1955)*, edited by Marcela García Sebastiani, 13–41. Madrid: Iberoamericana; Frankfurt: Vervuert, 2006.

Koonz, Claudia. *Mothers in the Fatherland: Women, the Family, and Nazi Politics.* New York: St. Martin's Press, 1987.

Korol, Juan Carlos. "La economía." In *Nueva Historia Argentina*, vol. 7: *Crisis económica, avance del estado e incertidumbre política (1930–1943)*, edited by Alejandro Cattaruzza, 17–48. Buenos Aires: Sudamericana, 2001.

Kundera, Milan. *The Book of Laughter and Forgetting.* Translated by Michael Henry Heim. New York: Alfred A. Knopf, 1980.

Labarca H., Amanda. *Feminismo contemporáneo.* Santiago: Zig-Zag, 1947. https://laciudadrevista.com/delfina-bunge-de-galvez-y-el-17-de-octubre.

Lambe, Ariel Mae. *No Barrier Can Contain It: Cuban Antifascism and the Spanish Civil War.* Chapel Hill: University of North Carolina Press, 2019.

Lash, Joseph P. *Eleanor and Franklin: The Story of Their Relationship, Based on Eleanor Roosevelt's Private Papers.* New York: W. W. Norton, 1971.

Lavin, Talia. *Cultural Warlords: My Journey into the Dark Web of White Supremacy.* New York: Hachette, 2020.

Lavrin, Asunción. *Women, Feminism, and Social Change in Argentina, Chile, and Uruguay, 1890–1940.* Lincoln: University of Nebraska Press, 1995.

Ledeen, Michael A. *Universal Fascism: The Theory and Practice of the Fascist International, 1928–1936.* New York: Howard Fertig, 1972.

Leibner, Gerardo. *Camaradas y compañeros. Una historia política y social de los comunistas de Uruguay.* Montevideo: Ediciones Trilce, 2011.

Leoni de Rosciani, María Silvia. *El Ateneo del Chaco.* Resistencia: Chaco, Ministerio de Educación, Cultura, Ciencia y Tecnología, Subsecretaría de Cultura, Dirección de Difusión Cultural, 1999.

Lida, Miranda. "El enigma Franceschi. Su lento e irreversible *aggiornamento* en la década de 1940." In *La revista Criterio y el siglo XX argentino. Religión, cultura y política*, edited by Miranda Lida and Mariano Fabris, 79–96. Rosario: Prohistoria, 2019.

Lida, Miranda. *Monseñor Miguel de Andrea. Obispo y hombre del mundo (1877–1960).* Buenos Aires: Edhasa, 2013.

Lida, Miranda. "Redes atlánticas de solidaridad con la resistencia francesa. La Revista de los intelectuales europeos en América en los debates del exilio francés

(Buenos Aires, 1942–1946)." Paper presented at the virtual Latin American Studies Association meeting, May 26–29, 2021.

Lida, Miranda, and María González Warcalde. "El sinuoso camino de Monseñor De Andrea al catolicismo antifascista en la década de 1940." *Anuario IEHS*, nos. 29–30 (2014–2015): 251–66.

Liga Internacional de Mujeres Pro Paz y Libertad, Comité de las Américas. n.p.: n.p., 1945.

Lomnitz, Claudio. *Nuestra América: My Family in the Vertigo of Translation*. New York: Other Press, 2021.

López Anaya, Jorge. *Historia del arte argentino*. 2nd ed. Buenos Aires: Emecé, 1997.

López Cantera, Mercedes. "Criminalizar al rojo. La represión al movimiento obrero en los informes de la Sección Especial de 1934." *Archivos de historia del movimiento obrero y la izquierda* 2, no. 4 (2014): 101–22.

Lorde, Audre. *Sister Outsider: Essays and Speeches*. Berkeley, CA: Crossing Press, 1984.

Louro, Michele L. *Comrades against Imperialism: Nehru, India, and Interwar Internationalism*. Cambridge: Cambridge University Press, 2018.

Luna, Félix. *El 45*. Buenos Aires: Hyspamerica, 1984.

Luna, Félix. *Perón y su tiempo. La Argentina era una fiesta, 1946–1949*. Vol. 1. Buenos Aires: Sudamericana, 1984.

Lusardi, Doralice. "Aguirre Cámara, el conservador cordobés." *Todo Es Historia*, no. 349 (August 1996): 80–92.

Luzuriaga, Raúl G. *Centinela de libertad (historia documental de una época). 1914–1940. Radicalismo—Dictadura—Exilio—Cárcel—Ideas*. Buenos Aires: Talleres Gráficos de Aniceto López, 1940.

Lvovich, Daniel. *El águila y el haz de flechas: El espionaje de Estados Unidos al falangismo en el Río de la Plata, 1941–1944*. Santander: Universidad de Cantabria, 2022.

Lvovich, Daniel. *Nacionalismo y antisemitismo en la Argentina*. Buenos Aires: Javier Vergara, 2003.

Lvovich, Daniel, and Federico Finchelstein. "Nazismo y holocausto en las percepciones del catolicismo argentino (1933–1945)." *Anuario IEHS*, nos. 29/30 (2014–2015): 303–25.

Lynn, Denise. "Antifascism and the Fear of Pronatalism in the American Popular Front." *Radical Americas* 1, no. 1 (2016): 25–43.

Lynn, Denise. "Fascism and the Family: American Communist Women's Antifascism during the Ethiopian Invasion and Spanish Civil War." *American Communist History* 15 (August 2016): 177–90.

Lynn, Denise. "Socialist Feminism and Triple Oppression: Claudia Jones and African American Women in American Communism." *Journal for the Study of Radicalism* 8, no. 2 (2014): 1–20.

Lynn, Denise. "Women on the March: Gender and Anti-Fascism in American

Communism, 1935–1939." PhD diss., Binghamton University, State University of New York, 2006.

Macor, Darío. "Partidos, coaliciones y sistema de poder." In *Nueva Historia Argentina*, vol. 7: *Crisis económica, avance del estado e incertidumbre política (1930–1943)*, edited by Alejandro Cattaruzza, 49–95. Buenos Aires: Sudamericana, 2001.

Maffei, Eduardo. *A batalha da Praça da Sé*. Rio de Janeiro: Philobiblion, 1984.

Malosetti, Laura, and José Emilio Burucúa. "Iconografía de la mujer y lo femenino en la obra de Raquel Forner." *Cuadernos de Historia del Arte* 2, no. 27 (2016): 53–65.

Manley, Elizabeth S. *The Paradox of Paternalism: Women and the Politics of Authoritarianism in the Dominican Republic*. Gainesville: University Press of Florida, 2017.

Manzoni, Gisela. "Antimilitarismo y antifascismo: particularidades de la intervención pública de las anarquistas argentinas." *Cuadernos del Sur* 41 (2012): 189–213.

Manzoni, Gisela. *Organizar la paz: Las mujeres y las luchas contra la Guerra en América Latina (1910–1936)*. Buenos Aires: Grupo Editor Universitario, 2021.

March, Aleida. *Remembering Che: My Life with Che Guevara*. North Melbourne, Australia: Ocean Press, 2012.

"Marcos Chamudes Reitich (1907–1989)." Memoriachilena, Biblioteca Nacional de Chile, n.d. memoriachilena.gob.cl/602/w3-article-741.html.

Mari, Oscar Ernesto. *El territorio nacional del Chaco durante la época conservadora (1930- 1943)*. Resistencia: IIGHI-CONICET, 1999.

Marino, Katherine M. "Anti-Fascist *Feminismo*: Suffrage, Sovereignty, and Popular-Front Pan- American Feminism in Panama." In *Engendering Transnational Transgressions: From the Intimate to the Global*, edited by Eileen Boris, Sandra Trudgen Dawson, and Barbara Molony, 204–20. Abingdon, UK: Routledge, 2021.

Marino, Katherine M. *Feminism for the Americas: The Making of an International Human Rights Movement*. Chapel Hill: University of North Carolina Press, 2018.

Marino, Katherine M. "Marta Vergara, Popular-Front Pan-American Feminism and the Transnational Struggles for Working Women's Rights in the 1930s." *Gender & History* 26, no. 3 (November 2014): 642–60.

Marino, Katherine M. "Transnational Pan-American Feminism: The Friendship of Bertha Lutz and Mary Wilhelmine Williams, 1926–1944." *Journal of Women's History* 26, no. 2 (2014): 63–87.

Martínez Chas, María Lida. *Marcos Kanner: militancia, símbolo y leyenda*. Posadas: Editorial Universitaria, 2011.

Martínez, Ilana. "Trayectorias de una disidencia partidaria: el grupo de izquierda del socialismo argentino de los años treinta." *A Contracorriente* 14, no. 3 (Spring 2017): 23–48.

Massera, José Luis. *40 años de la derrota del fascismo*. Montevideo: Centrograf, 1985.

Mathias, Christine. "Long-Distance Charisma: Peronist Identities in the Argentine Interior after 1955." Paper presented at the Latin American Studies Association meeting, Boston, MA, May 2019.

Mauss, Marcel. *The Gift: Forms and Functions of Exchange in Archaic Societies*. Translated by Ian Cunnison. New York: W. W. Norton, 1967.

Mayer, Arno. *Dynamics of Counterrevolution, 1870–1956: An Analytic Framework*. New York: Harper & Row, 1971.

McDuffie, Erik S. *Sojourning for Freedom: Black Women, American Communism, and the Making of Black Left Feminism*. Durham, NC: Duke University Press, 2011.

McPherson, Alan L., ed. *Encyclopedia of U.S. Military Interventions in Latin America*. Vol. 2. Santa Barbara, CA: ABC-CLIO, 2013.

Mead, Karen. "Beneficent Maternalism: Argentine Motherhood in Comparative Perspective, 1880–1920." *Journal of Women's History* 12, no. 3 (Autumn 2000): 120–45.

Mendoza, Angélica. *Cárcel de Mujeres. Impresiones recogidas en el Asilo del Buen Pastor*. Buenos Aires: Claridad, 1933.

Merithew, Caroline Waldron. "'O Mother Race': Race, Italian Colonialism, and the Fight to Keep Ethiopia Independent." *Zapruder World: An International Journal for the History of Social Conflict* 4 (2017). https://zapruderworld.org/journal/past-volumes/volume-4/o-mother-race-race-italian-colonialism-and-the-fight-to-keep-ethiopia-independent/.

Milanesio, Natalia. *Destape: Sex, Democracy and Freedom in Postdictatorial Argentina*. Pittsburgh: University of Pittsburgh Press, 2019.

Milanesio, Natalia. *Workers Go Shopping in Argentina: The Rise of Popular Consumer Culture*. Albuquerque: University of New Mexico Press, 2013.

Miller, Francesca. *Latin American Women and the Search for Social Justice*. Hanover, NH: University Press of New England, 1991.

"Moises Ville Argentina. Jewish Gauchos." Accessed April 18, 2017. https://www.scatteredamongthenations.org/agentina.

Montero Miranda, Claudia, and Graciela Rubio Soto. "El Movimiento pro-Emancipación de las Mujeres de Chile (MEMCH). Desarrollo de una política integral y formas de educación popular para el reconocimiento de los derechos de las mujeres, 1935–1941." *Trashumante*, no. 17 (2021): 174–97.

Mooney, Jadwiga E. Pieper. "El antifascismo como fuerza mobilizadora: Fanny Edelman y la Federación Democrática Internacional de Mujeres (FDIM)." *Anuario IEHS* 28 (2013): 207–26.

Mooney, Jadwiga E. Pieper. "Fighting Fascism and Forging New Political Activism: The Women's International Democratic Federation (WIDF) in the Cold

War." In *De-Centering Cold War History: Local and Global Change*, edited by Jadwiga E. Pieper Mooney and Fabio Lanza, 52–72. Abingdon, UK: Routledge, 2013.

Mooney, Jadwiga E. Pieper. *The Politics of Motherhood: Maternity and Women's Rights in Twentieth-Century Chile*. Pittsburgh: University of Pittsburgh Press, 2009.

Moorehead, Caroline. *A Train in Winter: An Extraordinary Story of Women, Friendship, and Resistance in Occupied France*. New York: HarperCollins, 2011.

Morais, Fernando. *Olga*. São Paulo: Companhia das Letras, 1994.

Morant i Ariño, Toni. "Spanish Fascist Women's Transnational Relations during the Second World War: Between Ideology and Realpolitik." *Journal of Contemporary History* 54, no. 4 (2019): 834–57.

Movimiento Pro-Emancipación de las Mujeres de Chile (MEMCh). "A las mujeres." Flyer, May 28, 1935.

Moya, José C. *Cousins and Strangers: Spanish Immigrants in Buenos Aires, 1850–1930*. Berkeley: University of California Press, 1998.

Nahum, Benjamín, Angel Cocchi, Ana Grega Novales, and Yvette Trochon. *Crisis política y recuperación económica, 1930–1958*. Montevideo: Banda Oriental, 1998.

Nállim, Jorge A. "Del antifascismo al antiperonismo: *Argentina Libre . . . Antinazi*, y el surgimiento del antiperonismo politico e intellectual." In *Fascismo y antifascismo, peronismo y antiperonismo: conflictos politicos e ideológicos en la Argentina, 1930–1955*, edited by Marcela García Sebastiani, 77–106. Madrid: Iberoamericana; Frankfurt: Vervuert, 2006.

Nállim, Jorge A. "An Unbroken Loyalty in Turbulent Times: *La Prensa* and Liberalism in Argentina, 1930–1946." *Estudios Interdisciplinarios de América Latina y el Caribe* 20, no. 2 (2009): 35–62.

Nállim, Jorge A. *Transformations and Crisis of Liberalism in Argentina, 1930–1955*. Pittsburgh: University of Pittsburgh Press, 2012.

Nari, Marcela. "Feminist Awakenings." In *The Argentina Reader: History, Culture, Politics*, edited by Gabriela Nouzeilles and Graciela Montaldo, 528–36. Durham, NC: Duke University Press, 2002.

Nari, Marcela. "Maternidad política y feminismo." In *Historia de las mujeres en la Argentina*, Vol. 2: *Siglo XX*, edited by Fernanda Gil Lozano, Valeria Silvina Pita, and Maria Gabriela Ini, 197–221. Buenos Aires: Taurus, 2000.

Nari, Marcela. *Políticas de maternidad y maternalismo político: Buenos Aires (1890–1940)*. Buenos Aires: Biblos, 2005.

Nash, Mary. *Defying Male Civilization: Women in the Spanish Civil War*. Denver: Arden Press, 1995.

Navarro Gerassi, Marysa. *Los nacionalistas*. Translated by Alberto Ciria. Buenos Aires: Jorge Álvarez, 1968.

Navarro, Mina Alejandra. "La 'nueva intelectualidad cordobesa' y la Reforma Universitaria de 1918." In *Universidad Nacional de Córdoba: Cuatrocientos años de historia*, vol. 2, edited by Daniel Saur y Alicia Servetto, 27–42. Córdoba: Universidad Nacional de Córdoba, 2013.

Newton, Ronald C. *"Ducini, Prominenti, Antifascisti*: Italian Fascism and the Italo-Argentine Collectivity, 1922–1945." *Americas* 52, no. 1 (July 1994): 41–66.

Newton, Ronald C. "Indifferent Sanctuary: German-Speaking Refugees and Exiles in Argentina, 1933–1945." *Journal of Interamerican Studies and World Affairs* 24, no. 4 (November 1982): 395–420.

Newton, Ronald C. *The 'Nazi Menace' in Argentina, 1931–1947.* Stanford, CA: Stanford University Press, 1992.

Norando, Verónica. "Relaciones de género y militancia política: Las obreras textiles y el comunismo entre 1936 y 1946." *Trabajos y Comunicaciones*, 2nda época, no. 39 (2013).

Noyes, Henrietta. "International Assembly of Women." *Pi Lambda Theta Journal* 25, no. 3 (1946): 86–91.

Ocampo, Victoria. *La mujer y sus derechos y sus responsabilidades.* Buenos Aires: UAM, n.d.

Oikión Solano, Verónica. "Mujeres en el Partido Comunista Mexicano. Desigualdad social y lucha política, 1935–1955." In *Queridas camaradas. Historias iberoamericanas de mujeres comunistas, 1935–1975*, edited by Adriana Valobra and Mercedes Yusta, 153–72. Buenos Aires: Miño y Dávila, 2017.

Ojeda Revah, Mario. *Mexico and the Spanish Civil War: Political Repercussions for the Republican Cause.* Eastbourne, UK: Sussex Academic Press, 2015.

Olcott, Jocelyn. "The Center Cannot Hold: Women on Mexico's Popular Front." In *Sex and Revolution: Gender, Politics, and Power in Modern Mexico*, edited by Jocelyn Olcott, Mary Kay Vaughan, and Gabriela Cano, 223–40. Durham, NC: Duke University Press, 2006.

Olcott, Jocelyn. *Revolutionary Women in Postrevolutionary Mexico.* Durham, NC: Duke University Press, 2005.

Oliveira, Ângela Meirelles de. "Antifascismo e o ideal de 'defesa da cultura' nos Boletins AIAPE (Uruguai) e Unidad (Argentina). *Anais Eletrônicos do X Encontro Internacional da ANPHLAC*, São Paulo, 2012. antigo.anphlac.org/sites/default/files/angela_oliveira2012.pdf.

Oliver, María Rosa. "A Porteña Reports." *Inter-American Monthly* 1, no. 2 (June 1942): 20–21, 46.

Organización de los Estados Americanos, Comisión Interamericana de Mujeres. *Resoluciones sobre derechos civiles y políticos de la mujer, aprobadas en asambleas de la Comisión Interamericana de Mujeres (1940–1957) y en conferencias interamericanas.* Washington, DC: Unión Panamericana, 1959.

Orozco, Eva Nohemí. "Las mujeres sinarquistas (1937–1962): Las manos ocultas en la construcción del sentimiento nacionalista mexicano." PhD diss., University of Texas at El Paso, 2019.

Orozco, Eva Nohemí. "Teresa Bustos, 'la mujer bandera': los caídos sinarquistas, su simbología religiosa y la mártir que traspasó las barreras de género." *Estudios Interdisciplinarios de América Latina y el Caribe*, 31, no. 1 (2020): 79–103. http://www3.tau.ac.il/ojs/index.php/eial/article/view/1653.

Ortiz, Michael P. "Spain! Why? Jawaharlal Nehru, Non-Intervention, and the Spanish Civil War." *European History Quarterly* 49, no. 3 (2019): 445–66.

Páez de la Torre (hijo), Carlos. *Tucumán y La Gaceta: 80 años de historia 1912–1992.* San Miguel de Tucumán: La Gaceta, 1992.

Page, Joseph. *Perón: A Biography.* New York: Random House, 1983.

Palacios, Juan Manuel. "La antesala de lo peor: la economía argentina entre 1914 y 1930." In *Nueva Historia Argentina*, vol. 6: *Democracia, conflicto social y renovación de ideas (1916–1930)*, edited by Ricardo Falcón, 101–50. Buenos Aires: Sudamericana, 2000.

Palermo, Silvana. "El sufragio femenino en el Congreso Nacional: ideologías de género y ciudadanía en la Argentina 1916–1966." *Boletín del Instituto de Historia Argentina y Americana Dr. Emilio Ravignani*, Tercera Serie, nos. 16–17 (June 1998): 151–78.

Palermo, Silvana. "Sufragio femenino y ciudadanía política en la Argentina, 1912–1947." In *Sufragio femenino: prácticas y debates políticos, religiosos y culturales en la Argentina y América*, edited by Carolina Barry, 29–62. Caseros, Buenos Aires: Universidad Nacional de Tres de Febrero, 2011.

Pasolini, Ricardo. "Antifascismo italiano, antifascismo argentino." *Archivio Storico dell' Emigrazione Italiana* no. 13/07 (September 4, 2007).

Pasolini, Ricardo. "The Antifascist Climate and the Italian Intellectual Exile in Interwar Argentina." *Journal of Modern Italian Studies* 15, no. 5 (2010): 693–714.

Pasolini, Ricardo. *Los marxistas liberales. Antifascismo y cultura comunista en la Argentina. Antifascismo y cultura comunista en la Argentina del siglo XX.* Buenos Aires: Sudamericana, 2013.

Pasquali, Laura. "El activismo antifascista femenino en México y Argentina en los años 30." Unpublished manuscript, n.d.

Pasquali, Laura. "Entrevista a Amor Hernández." In *Mujeres y política en escenarios de conflicto del siglo XX*, edited by Laura Pasquali, 21–54. Rosario: Ishir, 2016.

Pasquali, Laura. "Sin voto pero con voz: la militancia de las mujeres en los frentes antifascistas del sur santafesino en la primera mitad del siglo XX." Paper presented at the XXX Encuentro de Geohistoria Regional, Instituto de Investigaciones Geohistóricas/Conicet, Resistencia, Argentina, August 19–21, 2010.

Passalaqua Eliçabe, H. V. *El movimiento fascista argentino.* Buenos Aires: La Argentina, 1935.

Patai, Frances. "Heroines of the Good Fight: Testimonies of U.S. Volunteer Nurses in the Spanish Civil War, 1936–1939." *Nursing History Review* 3 (1995): 79–104.

Pavetti, Oscar A. "Una experiencia de gobierno del nacionalismo católico en Tucumán." *Anuario IEHS* 26 (2011): 167–86.

Paxton, Pamela. "Gendering Democracy." In *Politics, Gender and Concepts: Theory and Methodology*, edited by Gary Goertz and Amy G. Mazur, 47–70. New York: Cambridge University Press, 2008.

Paxton, Robert O. *The Anatomy of Fascism*. New York: Vintage Books, 2004.

Payne, Stanley G. *Fascism: Comparison and Definition*. Madison: University of Wisconsin Press, 1980.

Pelosi, Hebe Carmen. *Vichy no fue Francia. Las relaciones franco-argentinas (1939–1946)*. Buenos Aires: Grupo Editor Latinoamericano, 2003.

Penna, Belisário. "A mulher, a familia, o lar, e a escola." In *Enciclopédia do Integralismo* IX: *O integralismo e a educação*, edited by Everardo Backeuser et al., 41–59. Rio de Janeiro: Livraria Clássica Brasileira, 1960.

Perrig, Sara. "Mujeres, antiperonismo y antifascismo en Argentina (1943–1955)." *Aposta: Revista de Ciencias Sociales*, no. 73 (April–May 2017): 139–67.

Persello, Ana Virginia. *El Partido Radical. Gobierno y oposición, 1916–1943*. Buenos Aires: Siglo XXI, 2004.

Petra, Adriana. "Cultura comunista y guerra fría: los intelectuales y el Movimiento por la Paz en la Argentina." *Cuadernos de Historia* 38 (June 2013): 99–130.

Phayer, Michael. *The Catholic Church and the Holocaust, 1930–1965*. Bloomington: Indiana University Press, 2000.

Pita, Valeria. "¿La ciencia o la costura? Pujas entre médicos y matronas por el dominio institucional. Buenos Aires, 1880–1900." In *Historia de enfermedades, salud y medicina en la Argentina del siglo XIX y XX*, edited by Adriana Álvarez, Irene Molinari, and Daniel Reynoso, 81–109. Mar del Plata: Universidad Nacional de Mar del Plata, 2004.

Pite, Rebekah E. *Creating a Common Table in Twentieth-Century Argentina: Doña Petrona, Women, and Food*. Chapel Hill: University of North Carolina Press, 2013.

Pite, Rebekah E. "Engendering Argentine History: A Historiographical Review of Recent Gender-Based Histories of Women during the National Period." *Estudios Interdisciplinarios de América Latina y el Caribe* 25, no. 1 (2014): 41–62.

Pite, Rebekah E. "*La cocina criolla*: A History of Food and Race in Twentieth-Century Argentina." In *Rethinking Race in Modern Argentina*, edited by Paulina L. Alberto and Eduardo Elena, 99–125. New York: Cambridge University Press, 2016.

"¡Por qué están en huelga los universitarios!" Flyer, 1945.

"¡Por una gran jornada femenina antiguerrera el 1 de agosto!" Montevideo, n.d. Flyer.

Porrini, Rodolfo. *Derechos humanos y dictadura terrista*. Montevideo: Vintén, 1994.

Porter, Susie. *From Angel to Office Worker: Middle-Class Identity and Female Consciousness in Mexico*. Lincoln: University of Nebraska Press, 2018.

Possas, Lídia Maria Vianna. "O integralismo e a mulher." In *Integralismo: novos estudos e reinterpretações*, edited by Renato Alencar Dota and Rosa Maria

Feiteiro Cavalari, n.p. Rio Claro: Arquivo Público do Município de Rio Claro, 2004.

Potash, Robert A. *The Army and Politics in Argentina, 1928–1945: Yrigoyen to Perón.* Stanford, CA: Stanford University Press, 1969.

Potash, Robert A., ed. *Perón y el GOU: Los documentos de una logia secreta.* Buenos Aires: Sudamericana, 1984.

Power, Margaret. "Friends and Comrades: Political and Personal Relationships between Members of the Communist Party USA and the Puerto Rican Nationalist Party, 1930s– 1940s." In *Making the Revolution: Histories of the Latin American Left,* edited by Kevin A. Young, 105–28. Cambridge: Cambridge University Press, 2019.

Power, Margaret. "Latin American Solidarity with Puerto Rican Nationalism: A Transnational Expression of Anti-Imperialism, 1920s-1950s." Paper presented at the Research Cluster on Power and Resistance in Latin America, University of Manitoba, Winnipeg, February 25, 2016.

Power, Margaret. *Right-Wing Women in Chile: Feminine Power and the Struggle against Allende, 1964–1973.* University Park: Pennsylvania State University Press, 2002.

Power, Margaret, and Julie A. Charlip. "Introduction: On Solidarity." *Latin American Perspectives* 36, no. 6 (November 2009): 3–9.

"Presentación." *Boletín del Comité Organizador del Congreso Antiguerrero Latinoamericano,* no. 1 (December 15, 1932): Microfilm Roll 6, CeDinCI.

Primer Congreso Femenino Internacional de la República Argentina. Buenos Aires: Alfa y Omega, 1910.

Prislei, Leticia. *Los orígenes del fascismo argentino.* Buenos Aires: Edhasa, 2008.

Privitellio, Luciano de. "La política bajo el signo de la crisis." In *Nueva Historia Argentina,* vol. 7: *Crisis económica, avance del estado e incertidumbre política (1930- 1943),* edited by Alejandro Cattaruzza, 97–142. Buenos Aires: Sudamericana, 2001.

"Pro-Member: UAW Women—A History of Activism." UAW, April 6, 2017. uaw .org/solidarity_magazine/pro-member-uaw-women-history-activism/.

Prutsch, Ursula. *Creating Good Neighbors? Die Kultur- und Wirtschaftspolitik der USA in Lateinamerika, 1940–1946.* Stuttgart: Franz Steiner Verlag, 2008.

Queirolo, Graciela. "Dactilógrafas y secretarias perfectas: el proceso de feminización de los empleos administrativos (Buenos Aires, 1910–1950)." *Historia Crítica,* no. 57 (July-September 2015): 117–37.

Queirolo, Graciela. "La Federación de Asociaciones Católicas de Empleadas frente al trabajo femenino (Argentina, 1922–1954)." *Trabajos y Comunicaciones,* 2nda. época, no. 43 (2016): 1–14.

Queirolo, Graciela. "La mujer en la sociedad moderna a través de los escritos de Victoria Ocampo (1935–1951)." *Zona Franca,* no. 14 (May 2005): 144–54.

Queirolo, Graciela. *Mujeres en las oficinas. Trabajo, género y clase en el sector administrativo (Buenos Aires, 1910–1950)*. Buenos Aires: Biblos, 2018.

Quijada, Mónica. *Aires de república, aires de cruzada: La guerra civil española en Argentina*. Barcelona: Sendai, 1991.

"Raíces en el pueblo y unión para la lucha. El nacimiento y los primeros pasos de la Unión de Mujeres de la Argentina." Unpublished manuscript, n.d.

Rein, Raanan. "Another Front Line: Francoists and anti-Francoists in Argentina, 1936–1949." *Patterns of Prejudice* 31, no. 3 (1997): 17–33.

Rein, Raanan. *The Franco-Perón Alliance: Relations between Spain and Argentina, 1946–1955*. Translated by Martha Grenzeback. Pittsburgh: University of Pittsburgh Press, 1993.

Rein, Raanan. "Melting the Pot? Peronism, Jewish Argentines, and the Struggle for Diversity." In *Making Citizens in Argentina*, edited by Benjamin Bryce and David M. K. Sheinin, 110–26. Pittsburgh: University of Pittsburgh Press, 2017.

Rein, Raanan. *Populism and Ethnicity: Peronism and the Jews of Argentina*. Translated by Isis Sadek. Montreal: McGill-Queens University Press, 2020.

Rein, Raanan. "A Trans-National Struggle with National and Ethnic Goals: Jewish-Argentines and Solidarity with the Republicans during the Spanish Civil War." *Journal of Iberian and Latin American Research* 20, no. 2 (2014): 171–82.

República Argentina, Presidencia de la Nación, Ministerio de Asuntos Técnicos. *Cuarto censo general de la nación*, vol. 1: *Censo de población*. Buenos Aires: Dirección Nacional del Servicio Estadístico, 1952.

República Argentina. *Tercer censo nacional levantado el 1 de junio de 1914*, vol. 2: *Población*. Buenos Aires: L. J. Rosso, 1916.

Reynolds, Siân. *France between the Wars: Gender and Politics*. Abingdon, UK: Routledge, 1996.

Rilla, José, Gabriel Quirici, and Oscar Brando. *Nosotros que nos queremos tanto. Uruguayos y argentinos, voces de una hermandad accidentada*. Montevideo: Debate, 2013.

Roberts, David D. *Fascist Interactions: Proposals for a New Approach to Fascism and Its Era, 1919–1945*. New York: Berghahn Books, 2016.

Robin, Corey. "You Say You Want a Counterrevolution: Well, You Know, We All Want to Change the World." In *A Century of Revolution: Insurgent and Counterinsurgent Violence during Latin America's Long Cold War*, edited by Greg Grandin and Gilbert M. Joseph, 371–80. Durham, NC: Duke University Press, 2010.

Robinson, Cedric J. *On Racial Capital, Black Internationalism, and Cultures of Resistance*. Edited by H. L. T. Quan. London: Pluto Press, 2019.

Rock, David. *Argentina, 1516–1987: From Spanish Colonization to Alfonsín*. Berkeley: University of California Press, 1987.

Rock, David. *Authoritarian Argentina: The Nationalist Movement, Its History and Its Impact*. Berkeley: University of California Press, 1993.

Rohrleitner, Marion. "Who We Are: Migration, Gender, and New Forms of Citizenship." *American Quarterly* 63, no. 2 (June 2011): 419–29.

Rojas Mira, Claudia Fedora, and Ximena Jiles Moreno. *Epistolario emancipador del MEMCH: Catálogo histórico comentado (1935–1949)*. Santiago: Archivo Nacional de Chile, 2017.

Rojas Mira, Claudia Fedora, and Ximena Jiles Moreno. "La extraordinaria acción política protagonizada por el Movimiento pro-Emancipación de las Mujeres de Chile (MEMCH): 1935–1949." *Revista Izquierdas*, no. 49 (May 2020): 3352–72.

Romero, Luis Alberto. *A History of Argentina in the Twentieth Century: Updated and Revised*. Translated by James P. Brennan. University Park: Pennsylvania State University Press, 2013.

Romero, Simón. "Outpost in the Pampas Where Jews Once Found Refuge Wilts as They Leave." *New York Times*, June 10, 2013.

Roniger, Luis, and Leonardo Senkman. "Fuel for Conspiracy: Suspected Imperialist Plots and the Chaco War." *Journal of Politics in Latin America* 11, no. 1 (2019): 3–22.

Root, Regina A. *Couture and Consensus: Fashion and Politics in Postcolonial Argentina*. Minneapolis: University of Minnesota Press, 2010.

Rosemblatt, Karin Alejandra. *Gendered Compromises: Political Cultures & the State in Chile, 1920–1950*. Chapel Hill: University of North Carolina Press, 2000.

Rubinzal, Mariela. "El caso del cinematógrafo escolar en entreguerras: tensiones entre estado, mercado y política en Santa Fe." In *Política y cultura de masas en la Argentina en la primera mitad del siglo XX*, edited by Sandra Gayol and Silvana A. Palermo, 73–97. Buenos Aires: Universidad Nacional de General Sarmiento, 2018.

Rubinzal, Mariela. "El nacionalismo frente a la cuestión social en Argentina (1930–1943): discursos, representaciones y prácticas de las derechas sobre el mundo del trabajo." PhD diss., Universidad Nacional de La Plata, 2011.

Rubinzal, Mariela. "La circulación cultural de las derechas en la Argentina: el caso del nacionalsocialismo y la Comisión Especial Investigadora de Actividades Antiargentinas (1941–1943)." Second prize winner, Congreso de la Nación Argentina, Concurso Ensayo Histórico, 2019.

Rubinzal, Mariela. "La disputa en las plazas. Estrategias, símbolos y rituales del primero de mayo nacionalista (Buenos Aires, 1930–1943)." *Historia y política. Ideas, procesos y movimientos sociales*, no. 19 (January-June 2008): 255–85.

Rubinzal, Mariela. "Women's Work in Argentina's Nationalist Lexicon, 1930–1943." In *Women of the Right: Comparisons and Interplay across Borders*, edited by Kathleen M. Blee and Sandra McGee Deutsch, 226–41. University Park: Pennsylvania State University Press, 2012.

Ruiz, Esther, and Juana Paris. *El frente en los años '30.* Montevideo: Proyección, 1987.

Rupp, Leila J. *Worlds of Women: The Making of an International Women's Movement.* Princeton, NJ: Princeton University Press, 1997.

Ryle, J. Martin. "International Red Aid and Comintern Strategy, 1922–1926." *International Review of Social History* 15, no. 1 (April 1970): 43–68.

Salvatore, Ricardo D. "Net Nutritional Inequality in Argentina, 1875–1950: New Evidence and Some Conjectures." *Revista de Historia Económica-Journal of Iberian and Latin American Economic History* 37, no. 2 (2019): 339–76.

Sameh, Catherine. "Solidarity." In *Gender: Love,* edited by Jennifer C. Nash, 181–95. Farmington Hills, MI: MacMillan Reference USA, 2016.

Sapriza, Gabriela. "Historia reciente de un sujeto con historia." *Revista Encuentros* 7 (July 2001): 87–105.

Sapriza, Gabriela. *Memorias de rebeldía. Siete historias de vida.* Montevideo: Puntosur, 1988.

Sarnoff, Daniella. "Domesticating Fascism: Family and Gender in French Fascist Leagues." In *Women of the Right: Comparisons and Interplay across Borders,* edited by Kathleen M. Blee and Sandra McGee Deutsch, 163–76. University Park: Pennsylvania State University Press, 2012.

Scates, Bruce. "The Unknown Sock Knitter: Voluntary Work, Emotional Labour, Bereavement and the Great War." *Labour History,* no. 81 (November 2001): 29–49.

Schneider, Arnd. "The Two Faces of Modernity: Concepts of the Melting Pot in Argentina." *Critique of Anthropology* 16, no. 2 (1996): 178–98.

Scholtz, Sally J. *Political Solidarity.* University Park: Pennsylvania State University Press, 2008.

Schott, Linda K. *Reconstructing Women's Thoughts: The Women's International League for Peace and Freedom before World War II.* Stanford, CA: Stanford University Press, 1997.

Schvartzstein, Dora. *Entre Franco y Perón: Memoria e identidad del exilio republicano español en Argentina.* Barcelona: Crítica, 2001.

Scobie, James R. *Argentina: A City and a Nation.* 2nd ed. New York: Oxford University Press, 1971.

Sealander, Judith. "In the Shadow of Good Neighbor Diplomacy: The Women's Bureau and Latin America." *Prologue* 11, no. 4 (Winter 1979): 236–50.

Segal, Silvia. "Universidad: peronismo y antiperonismo." In *Universidad Nacional de Córdoba: Cuatrocientos años de historia,* vol. 2, edited by Daniel Saur and Alicia Servetto, 145–61. Córdoba: Universidad de Córdoba, 2013.

Seidman, Michael. *Transatlantic Antifascisms: From the Spanish Civil War to the End of World War II.* Cambridge: Cambridge University Press, 2018.

Seigel, Micol. "Beyond Compare: Comparative Method After the Transnational Turn." *Radical History Review* 91 (2005): 62–90.

Senkman, Leonardo. "El nacionalismo y el campo liberal argentinos ante el neutralismo: 1939– 1943." *Estudios Interdisciplinarios de América Latina y el Caribe* 6, no. 1 (1995): 23–49.

Sheinin, David M. K. *Argentina and the United States: An Alliance Contained*. Athens: University of Georgia Press, 2006.

Simões, Renata Duarte. "A educação do corpo no jornal *A Offensiva* (1932–1938)." PhD diss., Universidade de São Paulo, 2009.

Simões, Renata Duarte. "Nem só mãe, esposa e professora: os múltiplos campos de atuação da mulher militante Integralista." *Anais do XXVI Simpósio Nacional de História—ANPUH,* São Paulo, July 2011.

Singerman, Berta. *Mis dos vidas*. Buenos Aires: Ediciones Tres Tiempos, 1981.

Sitman, Rosalie. *Victoria Ocampo y Sur: Entre Europa y América*. Buenos Aires: Lumiere, 2003.

Smarsh, Sarah. *Heartland: A Memoir of Working Hard and Being Broke in the Richest Country on Earth*. New York: Scribner, 2018.

Smith, Peter H. "The Social Base of Peronism." *Hispanic American Historical Review* 52, no. 1 (1972): 55–73.

Smolensky, Eleonora María, and Vera Vigevani Jarach. *Tantas voces, una historia. Italianos judíos en la Argentina, 1938–1948*. Buenos Aires: Temas, 1999.

Southern, David. *John La Farge and the Limits of Catholic Interracialism, 1911–1963*. Baton Rouge: Louisiana State University Press, 1996.

Spektorowski, Alberto. *The Origins of Argentina's Revolution of the Right*. Notre Dame, IN: University of Notre Dame Press, 2003.

Spinelli, María Estela. *Los vencedores vencidos: el antiperonismo y la "revolución libertadora."* Buenos Aires: Biblos, 2005.

The Standard: Standard Victory Supplement, 1939–1945. Buenos Aires: *The Standard*, 1945.

Staudt, Kathleen, and Irasema Coronado. *Fronteras No Más: Toward Social Justice at the U.S.- Mexico Border*. New York: Palgrave Macmillan, 2002.

Staudt, Kathleen. "Political Representation: Engendering Politics." In *Background Papers, UN Human Development Report 1995*, 21–70. New York: United Nations Development Programme, 1996.

Stern, Alexandra Minna. *Proud Boys and the White Ethnostate: How the Alt-Right Is Warping the American Imagination*. Boston: Beacon, 2019.

Stevenson, Gary. "Inside Highlander." *In These Times*, June 2019, 34–37.

Suh, Judy. *Fascism and Anti-Fascism in Twentieth-Century British Fiction*. New York: Palgrave Macmillan, 2009.

Surowitz-Israel, Hilit. "Gifts from the Center: Gifting and Religious Authority in Colonial Curaçao." In *Jewish Experiences across the Americas: Local Histories through Global Lenses*, edited by Katalin Franciska Rac and Lenny A. Ureña Valerio, 83–107. Gainesville: University Press of Florida, 2022.

Sutton, Barbara, and Elizabeth Borland. "Abortion and Human Rights for Women in Argentina." *Frontiers: A Journal of Women's Studies* 40, no. 2 (2019): 27–61.

Svampa, Maristela. *El dilema argentino: Civilización o barbarie. De Sarmiento al revisionismo peronista.* Buenos Aires: El Cielo por Asalto, 1994.

Szurmuk, Mónica. *La vocación desmesurada. Una biografía de Alberto Gerchunoff.* Buenos Aires: Sudamericana, 2018.

Tabbush, Constanza, and Elizabeth Jay Friedman. "Feminist Activism Confronts COVID-19." *Feminist Studies* 46, no. 3 (2020): 629–38.

Tannoury-Karam, Sana. "No Place for Neutrality: The Case for Democracy and the League against Nazism and Fascism in Syria and Lebanon." In *Anti-Fascism in a Global Perspective: Transnational Networks, Exile Communities, and Radical Internationalism*, edited by Kasper Braskén, Nigel Copsey, and David Featherstone, 133–51. Abingdon, UK: Routledge, 2021.

Tato, María Inés. "Del crisol de razas a la Argentina desintegrada: un itinerario de la idea de nación, 1911–1932." *Historia y política*, no. 17 (January-June 2007): 153–73.

Tato, María Inés. "El ejemplo alemán. La prensa nacionalista y el Tercer Reich." *Escuela de Historia*, no. 6 (2007): 34–60.

Tato, María Inés. "La contienda europea en las calles porteñas. Manifestaciones cívicas y pasiones nacionales en torno de la Primera Guerra Mundial." In *Del centenario al peronismo. Dimensiones de la vida política argentina*, edited by María Inés Tato and Martín O. Castro, 33–63. Buenos Aires: Imago Mundi, 2010.

Tato, María Inés. "La movilización de la sociedad argentina frente a la Primera Guerra Mundial." In *Miradas sobre la historia social en la Argentina en los comienzos del siglo XXI*, edited by Silvia C. Mallo and Beatriz I. Moreyra, 725–41. Córdoba: Centro de Estudios Históricos "Prof. Carlos S. A. Segreti"; La Plata: Centro de Estudios de Historia Americana Colonial, 2008.

Taylor, Julie. *Eva Perón: The Myths of a Woman.* Chicago: University of Chicago Press, 1979.

Tcach, César. "El reformismo: ¿movimiento social o movimiento estudiantil? (1918–1946)." In *Universidad Nacional de Córdoba: Cuatrocientos años de historia*, vol. 2, edited by Daniel Saur and Alicia Servetto, 121–43. Córdoba: Universidad de Córdoba, 2013.

Tcach, César. "Sabattinismo: Identidad radical y oposición disruptiva." *Desarrollo Económico* 28 (July–September 1988): 183–208.

Teitelbaum, Vanesa. "Itinerarios de inmigración y construcción de identidades en mujeres judías en Argentina durante la época de la Segunda Guerra Mundial." *Estudios Interdisciplinarios de América Latina y el Caribe* 32, no. 1 (2021): 98–120. http://eial.tau.ac.il/index.php/eial/article/view/1702.

Tentler, Leslie Woodcock. *Seasons of Grace: A History of the Catholic Archdiocese of Detroit.* Detroit: Wayne State University Press, 1990.

Torre, Juan Carlos. *La vieja guardia sindical y Perón. Sobre los orígenes del peronismo.* Buenos Aires: Sudamericana, 1990.

Tossounian, Cecilia. *La Joven Moderna in Interwar Argentina: Gender, Nation, and Popular Culture.* Gainesville: University Press of Florida, 2020.

Towns, Ann. "The Inter-American Commission of Women and Women's Suffrage, 1920–1945." *Journal of Latin American Studies,* 42, no. 4 (November 2010): 779–807.

Traverso, Enzo. *Fire and Blood: The European Civil War, 1914–1945.* Translated by David Fernbach. London: Verso, 2016.

Trifone, Víctor, and Gustavo Svarzman. *La repercusión de la guerra civil española en la Argentina (1936–1939).* Buenos Aires: CEAL, 1993.

Tuñón Pablos, Enriqueta. "Tres momentos claves del movimiento sufragista." In *La revolución de las mujeres en México,* edited by Patricia Galeana et al., 81–98. México, DF: Instituto Nacional de Estudios Históricos de las Revoluciones en México, 2014.

Tuñón Pablos, Esperanza. *Mujeres que se organizan: El Frente Único Pro Derechos de la Mujer, 1935–1938.* México, DF: UNAM, Miguel Ángel Porrúa, 1992.

U.M.A. 1947–1967. Buenos Aires: n.p., 1967.

US Department of State. Records of the Department of State Relating to the Internal Affairs of Argentina, 1940–1944, microfilm M1322, rolls 2 and 8.

Ubelaker, Lisa A. "The Impossible Americas: Argentina, Ecuador, and the Geography of U.S. Mass Media, 1938–1948." PhD diss., Yale University, 2013.

Ullrich, Peter, and Reiner Keller. "Comparing Discourse between Cultures: A Discursive Approach to Movement Knowledge." In *Conceptualizing Culture in Social Movement Research,* edited by B. Baumgarten, P. Daphi, and P. Ullrich, 113–39. Basingstoke, UK: Palgrave Macmillan, 2014.

Unión Argentina de Mujeres. "La mujer que trabaja demanda." Flyer, 1938.

Unión Democrática. *Un programa constructiva para toda la nación.* Buenos Aires: n.p. n.d.

Unión Nacional Femenina. "Las mujeres nos unimos para el bien de la Patria." Flyer, 1945. http://www.unsam.edu.ar/escuelas/politica/centro_historia_po litica/_materiales.asp.

Valdivia Ortiz de Zárate, Verónica. "Izquierdas y derechas en los años setenta: La reversión de la historia." In *Su revolución contra nuestra revolución. Izquierdas y derechas en el Chile de Pinochet (1973–1981),* by Verónica Valdivia Ortiz de Zárate, Rolando Álvarez Vallejos, and Julio Pinto Vallejos, 207–25. Santiago: LOM, 2006.

Valdivia Ortiz de Zárate, Verónica. "Presentación." In *Su revolución contra nuestra revolución. Izquierdas y derechas en el Chile de Pinochet (1973–1981),* by Verónica Valdivia Ortiz de Zárate, Rolando Álvarez Vallejos, and Julio Pinto Vallejos, 9–13. Santiago: LOM, 2006.

Valobra, Adriana María. "Algunas consideraciones acerca de la historia de las mujeres y género en Argentina." *Nuevo Topo,* no. 1 (2005): 101–22.

Valobra, Adriana María. *Del hogar a las urnas. Recorridos de la ciudadanía política femenina argentina, 1946–1955*. Rosario: Prohistoria, 2010.

Valobra, Adriana María. "Elogio de la mujer que vota. El voto municipal femenino en Santa Fe, Argentina." *Meridional. Revista Chilena de Estudios Latinoamericanos* 17 (2021): 125–55.

Valobra, Adriana María. "Formación de cuadros y frentes populares: relaciones de clase y género en el Partido Comunista de Argentina, 1935–1951." *Revista Izquierdas*, no. 23 (April 2015): 127–56.

Valobra, Adriana María. "Las comunistas argentinas durante la política de frentes y la guerra fría, 1935–1967." In *Queridas camaradas. Historias iberoamericanas de mujeres comunistas, 1935–1975*, edited by Adriana Valobra and Mercedes Yusta, 71–90. Buenos Aires: Miño y Dávila, 2017.

Valobra, Adriana María. "La UMA en marcha. Tradiciones y estrategias de movilización social en los partidos opositores durante el peronismo. El caso del Partido Comunista y la Unión de Mujeres de la Argentina." *Canadian Journal of Latin American and Caribbean Studies* 30 (2005): 155–82.

Valobra, Adriana María. "Partidos, tradiciones y estrategias de movilización social: de la Junta de la Victoria a la Unión de Mujeres de la Argentina." *Prohistoria* 9 (2005): 67–82.

Valobra, Adriana María. "Sufragismo y acción política femenina en un contexto conservador, Buenos Aires 1935–1940." In *El gobierno de Manuel Fresco*, edited by Emir Reitano, 181–214. La Plata: Archivo Histórico de la Provincia de Buenos Aires, 2010.

Valobra, Adriana, and Mercedes Yusta, eds. *Queridas camaradas. Historias iberoamericanas de mujeres comunistas, 1935–1975*. Buenos Aires: Miño y Dávila, 2017.

Vasallo, Alejandra. "Entre el conflicto y la negación. Los feminismos argentinos en los inicios del Consejo Nacional de Mujeres, 1900–1910." In *Historia de las mujeres en la Argentina*, vol. 2: *Siglo XX*, edited by Fernanda Gil Lozano, Valeria Silvina Pita, and Maria Gabriela Ini, 177–95. Buenos Aires: Taurus, 2000.

Vergara, Marta. *Memorias de una mujer irreverente*. Santiago: Zig-Zag, 1961.

Vials, Christopher. "Red Feminists and Methodist Missionaries: Dorothy McConnell and the Other Afterlife of the Popular Front." In *Lineages of the Literary Left: Essays in Honor of Alan M. Wald*, edited by Howard Brick, Robbie Lieberman, and Paula Rabinowitz. Ann Arbor, MI: Maize Books, 2015. http://dx.doi.org/10.3998/maize.13545968.0001.001.

Vials, Christopher. *Haunted by Hitler: Liberals, the Left, and the Fight against Fascism in the United States*. Amherst: University of Massachusetts Press, 2014.

Vignoli, Marcela. "Cecilia Grierson y las damas de la Beneficencia oficial en los orígenes del Consejo Nacional de Mujeres de Argentina (1887–1906)." *Boletín del Instituto de Historia Argentina y Americana "Dr. Emilio Ravignani"* 55 (July–December 2021): 1–26.

Vignoli, Marcela. "Intentos de adhesión a una agenda feminista internacional en los orígenes del Consejo Nacional de la Mujer en Argentina, 1901–1910." In *Género, cultura y sociabilidad en el espacio rioplatense, 1860–1930*, edited by Marcela Vignoli and Lucía Reyes de Deu, 67–82. Rosario: Prohistoria, 2018.

Vigo, Juan M. "Luciano Molinas: El gobernador que cumplió." *Todo Es Historia*, no. 54 (October 1971): 8–27.

Visacovsky, Nerina. *Argentinos, judíos y camaradas. Tras la utopía socialista*. Buenos Aires: Biblos, 2015.

Visacovsky, Nerina. "Berta Blejman de Drucaroff (1903–1991)." *Shalvi-Hyman Encyclopedia of Jewish Women*, June 23, 2021. https:/jwa.org/encyclopedia/article/drucaroff-berta-blejman.

Von Mentz, Brígida, and Verena Radkau. *"Notas en torno al exilio político alemán en México (1939–1946)." In Fascismo y antifascismo en América Latina y México (apuntes históricos)*, edited by Brígida Von Mentz, Richardo Pérez Montfort, and Verena Radkau, 43–59. México, DF: Centro de Investigaciones y Estudios Superiores en Antropología Social, Cuadernos de la Casa Chata, 1984.

Wallace, Henry. "The Century of the Common Man." Delivered at the Free World Association Dinner, New York, May 8, 1942. https://www.americanrhetoric.com/speeches/henrywallacefreeworldassoc.htm?trk=public_post_comment_text.

Walter, Richard J. *The Province of Buenos Aires and Argentine Politics, 1912–1943*. New York: Cambridge University Press, 1985.

Walter, Richard J. "The Right and the Peronists, 1943–1945." In *The Argentine Right: Its History and Intellectual Origins, 1910 to the Present*, edited by Sandra McGee Deutsch and Ronald H. Dolkart, 99–118. Wilmington, DE: Scholarly Resources, 1993.

Walter, Richard J. *Student Politics in Argentina: The University Reform and Its Effects, 1918– 1964*. New York: Basic Books, 1968.

Walzer, Michael. "Pluralism and Democracy." *Atlantic*, November 2007. https://www.theatlantic.com/magazine/archive/2007/11/pluralism-and-democracy/306321/.

Waylen, Georgina. "Women and Democratization: Conceptualizing Gender Relations in Transition Politics." *World Politics* 46, no. 3 (1994): 254–327.

Weigand, Kate. *Red Feminism: American Communism and the Making of Women's Liberation*. Baltimore: Johns Hopkins University Press, 2001.

Weinstein, Barbara. "Inventing the 'Mulher Paulista': Politics, Rebellion, and the Gendering of Brazilian Regional Identities." *Journal of Women's History* 18, no. 1 (2006): 22–49.

Wilson, Kathryn E. "Commodified Craft, Creative Community: Women's Vernacular Dress in Nineteenth-Century Philadelphia." In *The Culture of Sewing: Gender, Consumption and Home Dressmaking*, edited by Barbara Burman, 141–56. Oxford: Berg, 1999.

Women's International Democratic Federation. "Original Resolutions of the Women's International Democratic Federation at the International Congress of Women Paris November December 1945." Typed draft. Women and Social Movements, International: 1840 to the Present. http://wasi.alexanderstreet .com/.

Yarfitz, Mir. *Impure Migration: Jews and Sex Work in Golden Age Argentina*. New Brunswick, NJ: Rutgers University Press, 2019.

Zanatta, Loris. *Del estado liberal, a la nación católica. Iglesia y ejército en los orígenes del peronismo, 1930–1943*. Bernal: Universidad Nacional de Quilmes, 1996.

Zanca, José. *Cristianos antifascistas: conflictos en la cultura católica argentina*. Buenos Aires: Siglo Veintiuno, 2013.

Zanca, José. "Dios y libertad: católicas antifascistas en la Argentina de entreguerras." *Arenal* 22, no. 1 (January-June 2015): 67–87.

Zubillaga, Carlos. *Niños de la guerra. Solidaridad uruguaya con la República Española, 1936– 1939*. Montevideo: Linardi y Risso, 2013.

Zuleta Álvarez, Enrique. *El nacionalismo argentino*. Vol. 1. Buenos Aires: Ediciones La Bastilla, 1975.

INDEX